D0884394

1|07

THE WISDOM OF PRACTICE

Essays on Teaching, Learning, and Learning to Teach

Lee S. Shulman

○

Edited by Suzanne M. Wilson

Foreword by Pat Hutchings

JOSSEY-BASS
A Wiley Imprint
www.josseybass.com

Published by Jossey-Bass

A Wiley Imprint

989 Market Street, San Francisco, CA 94103-1741 www.josseybass.com

Jossey-Bass books and products are available through most bookstores. To contact Jossey-Bass directly call our Customer Care Department within the U.S. at 800-956-7739, outside the U.S. at 317-572-3986 or fax 317-572-4002.

Jossey-Bass also publishes its books in a variety of electronic formats. Some content that appears in print may not be available in electronic books.

Library of Congress Cataloging-in-Publication Data

Shulman, Lee S.
The wisdom of practice : essays on teaching, learning, and learning to teach / Lee S. Shulman ; edited by Suzanne M. Wilson ; foreword by Pat Hutchings.— 1st ed.
p. cm. — (The Jossey-Bass higher and adult education series)
Includes bibliographical references and index.
ISBN 0-7879-7200-2 (alk. paper)
1. Teaching. 2. Learning. 3. Teachers—Rating of. I. Wilson, Suzanne M., 1955- II. Title. III. Series.
LB1027.S475 2004
371.102—dc22

2003025429

Printed in the United States of America

FIRST EDITION

HB Printing 10 9 8 7 6 5 4 3 2 1

This volume is dedicated to Judy Shulman.

CONTENTS

SOURCES

CHAPTER ONE

"Reconstruction of Educational Research." *Review of Educational Research,* 1970, *40.* Copyright © 1970, the American Educational Research Association. Reprinted by permission of the publisher.

CHAPTER TWO

"Psychology and Mathematics Education." *Mathematics Education: The Sixty-Ninth Yearbook of the National Society for the Study of Education* (Edward G. Begle, Ed.). Chicago: National Society for the Study of Education, 1970, pp. 23–71.

CHAPTER THREE

"The Psychology of School Subjects: A Premature Obituary?" *Journal of Research in Science Teaching,* 1974, *11*(4), 319–339.

CHAPTER FOUR

"Autonomy and Obligation: The Remote Control of Teaching." *Handbook of Teaching and Policy* (Lee S. Shulman and Gary Sykes, Eds.). Boston: Allyn and Bacon, 1983, pp. 484–504. Copyright © 1983 by Pearson Education. Reprinted by permission of the publisher.

CHAPTER FIVE

"The Practical and the Eclectic: A Deliberation on Teaching and Educational Research." *Curriculum Inquiry,* 1984, *14*(2).

CHAPTER SIX

"Those Who Understand: Knowledge Growth in Teaching." *Educational Researcher,* 1986, *15*(2), 4-14. Copyright 1986, the American Educational Research Association. Reprinted by permission of the publisher.

CHAPTER SEVEN

"Knowledge and Teaching: Foundations of the New Reform." *Harvard Educational Review,* 1987, *57*(1), pp. 1–22. Copyright © 1987 by the President and Fellows of Harvard College. All rights reserved.

CHAPTER EIGHT

"The Wisdom of Practice: Managing Complexity in Medicine and Teaching." *Talks to Teachers: A Festschrift for N. L. Gage* (David C. Berliner and Barak V. Rosenshine, Eds.). New York: Random House, 1987, pp. 369–387.

CHAPTER NINE

"Disciplines of Inquiry in Education: A New Overview." *Complementary Methods for Research in Education* (Richard M. Jaeger, Ed.). Washington D.C.: American Educational Research Association, 1997. Copyrights 1997, the American Educational Research Association. Reprinted by permission of the publisher.

CHAPTER TEN

"Teaching Alone, Learning Together: Needed Agendas for the New Reforms." *Schooling for Tomorrow: Directing Reforms to Issues That Count* (Thomas J. Sergiovanni and John H. Moore, Eds.). Boston: Allyn and Bacon, 1988, pp. 166–187. Copyright © 1988 by Pearson Education. Reprinted by permission of the publisher.

CHAPTER ELEVEN

"The Paradox of Teacher Assessment." *New Directions for Teacher Assessment: Proceedings of the 1988 ETS Invitational Conference.* Princeton, N.J.: Educational Testing Service, 1988.

CHAPTER TWELVE

"A Union of Insufficiencies: Strategies for Teacher Assessment in a Period of Educational Reform." *Educational Leadership,* November 1988, pp. 36–39. Copyrighted 1988 by the Association for Supervision and Curriculum Development. Reprinted with permission from ASCD.

CHAPTER THIRTEEN

"Research on Teaching: A Historical and Personal Perspective." *Effective and Responsible Teaching: The New Synthesis* (Fritz K. Oser, Andreas Dick, and Jean-Luc Patry, Eds.). San Francisco: Jossey-Bass, 1992, pp. 14–29.

CHAPTER FOURTEEN

"Teacher Portfolios: A Theoretical Activity." *With Portfolio in Hand: Validating the New Teacher Professionalism* (Nona Lyons, Ed.). New York: Teachers College Press, 1998.

CHAPTER FIFTEEN

"Aristotle Had It Right: On Knowledge and Pedagogy." East Lansing, Mich.: The Holmes Group, 1990.

CHAPTER SIXTEEN

"Joseph Jackson Schwab (1909–1988)." *Remembering the University of Chicago: Teachers, Scientists, and Scholars* (Edward Shils, Ed.). Chicago: The University of Chicago Press, 1991.

CHAPTER SEVENTEEN

"Calm Seas, Auspicious Gales". Conclusion to *Detachment and Concern: Conversations in the Philosophy of Teaching and Teacher Education* (Margaret Buchmann and Robert E. Floden, Eds.). New York: Teachers College Press, 1993.

CHAPTER EIGHTEEN

"Teaching as Community Property: Putting an End to Pedagogical Solitude." *Change Magazine,* November/December 1993, 6–7. Reprinted by permission of the Helen Dwight Reid Educational Foundation. Published by Heldref Publications, 1319 18th Street, NW, Washington, DC, 20036-1802. www.heldref.org. Copyright © 1993.

CHAPTER NINETEEN

"Just in Case: Reflections on Learning from Experience." *The Case for Education: Contemporary Approaches for Using Case Methods* (Joel A. Colbert, Peter Desherg, and Kimberly Trimble, Eds.). Boston: Allyn and Bacon, 1996, pp. 197–217. Copyright © 1996 by Pearson Education. Reprinted by permission of the publisher.

CHAPTER TWENTY

"Communities of Learners and Communities of Teachers." *Monographs from the Mandel Foundation #3*. Jerusalem: The Mandel Foundation, 1997.

CHAPTER TWENTY-ONE

"Professional Development: Learning from Experience." *Common Schools, Uncommon Futures: A Working Consensus for School Renewal* (Barry S. Kogan, Ed.). New York: Teachers College Press, 1997.

CHAPTER TWENTY-TWO

"Theory, Practice, and the Education of Professionals." *The Elementary School Journal,* 1998, *98*(5), 511–526.

CHAPTER TWENTY-THREE

"Professing the Liberal Arts." *Education and Democracy: Re-imagining Liberal Learning in America* (Robert Orrill, Ed.). New York: College Entrance Examination Board, 1997. Copyright © 1997 by the College Entrance Examination Board. Reproduced with permission. All rights reserved. www.collegeboard.com.

ABOUT THE AUTHOR

LEE S. SHULMAN is a Chicagoan, despite his years at Michigan State University, Stanford University, and his current tenure as president of The Carnegie Foundation for the Advancement of Teaching. It was in the city of his birth that he received not only his elementary and secondary education but also all of his academic degrees. The reverence for classic texts, the familiarity with dissecting original sources, and the generalist and collegial philosophy of learning in the Chicago education institutions where Lee studied and learned were the perfect foundation for his lifelong scholarly inquiry and work.

Shulman's family owned a small delicatessen in the Logan Square neighborhood, and many of his perspectives on life were formed through interactions with customers and vendors. His formal education began at an Orthodox Jewish day school, where he studied Talmud in the morning and secular subjects in the afternoon. He went on to learn at the Hutchins College of the University of Chicago, where the generalist curriculum revered the Great Books, encouraged student engagement, and echoed the respect for classic texts that marked his Talmudic studies. The small seminar classes encouraged a collegial way of working that continues to shape his views on scholarship and teaching to this day.

Shulman entered the university's doctoral program in educational psychology because of a full-tuition fellowship, which included enough of a stipend to give him the courage to propose marriage to the young Judy Horwitz, who has been his partner in the joys of family, community, and scholarship ever since. From 1963 to 1982, Shulman was professor of educational psychology and medical education at Michigan State University, where with Judith Lanier he founded and codirected the Institute for Research on Teaching. From 1982 through 2000, he was on the faculty at Stanford University, first as a professor of educational psychology and then as the Charles E. Ducommun Professor of Education. He investigated and promulgated a way of studying teaching, and in his efforts to make teaching a profession, he helped found the National Board for Professional Teaching Standards.

Shulman's research and writings have dealt with the study of teaching and teacher education; the growth of knowledge among those learning to teach; the assessment of teaching; medical education; the psychology of instruction in science, mathematics, and medicine; the logic of educational research; and the quality of teaching in higher education. His most recent studies emphasize the importance of "teaching as community property" and the central role of a "scholarship of teaching" in supporting needed changes in the cultures of higher education.

In 1997, he was selected as the eighth president of The Carnegie Foundation for the Advancement of Teaching, a research and education policy center in Stanford, California, created by Andrew Carnegie in 1905. He continues to work to elevate teachers and the profession of teaching, as well as to deepen understanding of preparation for service in other professions such as medicine. Under his leadership, the Carnegie Foundation supports the study of moral and civic education; professions that include law, the clergy, and engineering; liberal and doctoral education; and the preparation of teachers. Shulman continues to expand the notion of a scholarship of teaching and learning through the Carnegie Academy for the Scholarship of Teaching and Learning.

Shulman is past president of the American Educational Research Association (AERA) and received its highest honor, the career award for Distinguished Contributions to Educational Research. He is a member of the National Academy of Education, having served as both vice president and president. He is the recipient of the American Psychological Association's 1995 E. L. Thorndike Award for Distinguished Psychological Contributions to Education. Shulman has also been a Guggenheim Fellow and a Fellow of the Center for Advanced Study in the Behavioral Sciences. He was named an American Association for the Advancement of Science (AAAS) Fellow in 2002 for his "fundamental contributions that have deeply impacted educational research, policy, institutional practices, and teacher education in science and mathematics worldwide." He is a Fellow of the American Academy of Arts and Sciences.

In a profile written for his inclusion in the *Fifty Modern Thinkers on Education,* the authors wrote:

> Shulman has had enormous impact on the field of education, in large part because of the grand ideas and visions that have marked his work.
>
> His visions now permeate everyday discourse about teaching, in talk about teaching portfolios, pedagogical content knowledge, and the scholarship of teaching. Shulman's genius lies in his ability to unite the worlds of thought and action, to turn his creative energies not only to research but into building institutions and structures that transport his visions of the possible into the world of practice.

ACKNOWLEDGMENTS

THERE IS A LOVELY PUN implicit in the very word *acknowledgment.* This is the page where an author lists those without whom the knowledge contained in the pages that follow could never have been acquired, understood, or communicated. To *ack-knowledge* is to direct the reader to the author's sources of knowledge. It is certainly the case here.

Without Suzanne Wilson, this volume would not exist. In editing and writing the introduction to this volume and its individual selections, Suzanne has performed an act of uncommon generosity and friendship. She volunteered for the task, persisted in the face of its growing size and demands, and showed both patience and warm understanding whenever I expressed ambivalence over an omission or asked for "just one more" after all the decisions had mercifully been made. Suzanne understands my work and its flaws far better than I do. She was my doctoral advisee at Stanford during the 1980s, and, like so many of her colleagues, she instructed her teacher far more than he was able to mentor her. We have had the great pleasure of continuing to work together during her superb career at Michigan State, and I am delighted that she now spends part of her time as a Senior Scholar at the Carnegie Foundation. There is no way to express adequately the depth of my appreciation for her role in making this volume a reality. And in thanking Suzanne, I thank the many students over the years who have insisted on continuing my education, both while they studied with me and after they left to continue their own careers.

At the Carnegie Foundation, Pat Hutchings and Stephanie Waldmann have worked with Suzanne to move the collection forward. While in the process of editing a companion volume of my essays on higher education, Pat read every draft of the general introduction and the essay introductions of this volume and made many suggestions for their improvement. Stephanie reviewed the entire manuscript and then took on the onerous task of preparing it for submission to the publisher. At Jossey-Bass, our editor David Brightman has been relentlessly helpful and supportive.

I have learned from all my teachers. The University of Chicago was a remarkable crucible of undergraduate liberal and graduate education.

Joseph Schwab was my teacher and colleague from 1957, when I first sat in his class in the College, until he died in 1988. Benjamin Bloom, Bruno Bettelheim, Philip Jackson, and Fred Lighthall continued that arduous task in graduate school. I continue to draw on the investment in learning at the University of Chicago and continue to mourn the tragic and needless demise of its distinguished Department of Education. My colleagues at Michigan State University, Stanford University, and The Carnegie Foundation for the Advancement of Teaching have continued with that mentorship.

The essays in this volume grew out of many years of research, nearly all of which was supported by grants from both public and private sources. The National Institute of Education, the National Institutes of Health, the Spencer Foundation, the Carnegie Corporation of New York, the Mellon Foundation, and The Carnegie Foundation for the Advancement of Teaching have all supported this work, for which they have my gratitude, but which they need not endorse. Although rarely acknowledged, the funds that supported this work produced far more than the work itself. They typically supported the education of dozens of graduate students whose current and future contributions will certainly eclipse those gathered together in this volume. Research grants support the creation of both intellectual capital and human capital.

Before any of the work printed in this volume began, I was blessed with a relationship that has served as the bedrock of my life and my scholarship. Judy Horwitz Shulman has been my partner, my colleague, my collaborator, my critic, and my love for more than forty years. When she would read a manuscript and remark, "I hope this passage works for you; I doubt that anyone else will have a clue," I usually got the message and attempted to repair the damage. Our children and grandchildren are the "collected works" that we value beyond all others. She has been the silent partner in all this work. This book is dedicated to Judy Shulman.

Lee S. Shulman

FOREWORD

SEVERAL YEARS AGO AT A CONFERENCE session where Lee Shulman was speaking, a woman sitting behind me, apparently having noticed my Carnegie Foundation name tag when I sat down, tapped me on the shoulder. "I have an idea," she whispered. "Why doesn't someone pull together Shulman's writing over the past couple of decades and publish a collection? I've read *some* of the important pieces," she continued, "but I'd love to see what I *haven't* read and to find it all in one place."

That suggestion stayed with me long after the conference, and I heard it affirmed by comments from others as well. Now, some three years later, this volume and its companion collection respond to my fellow conference-goer's excellent idea. *The Wisdom of Practice: Essays on Teaching, Learning, and Learning to Teach* is a collection of most of Lee Shulman's work on educational research, teacher education, and K–12 teaching. *Teaching as Community Property* provides a selection of his writing on higher education. Some of what you'll find in both volumes has been previously published, but a number of pieces are newly available, offering readers a chance to see the trajectory and significance of Shulman's work in ways that would otherwise not be possible.

It's important to say that this collection is not meant to stand for the work of the organization that Shulman now leads. Many of the pieces were written before he was appointed president of The Carnegie Foundation for the Advancement of Teaching in 1997, and, as he himself would insist on saying, the programs he directs in that role are shaped by the thinking of many colleagues on the staff and beyond, including our very thoughtful Board of Trustees. On the other hand, the ideas represented here are clearly evident in the Foundation's current efforts, and they are notable, as well, for their continuity with two features that have defined the organization's work since it was founded by Andrew Carnegie almost a century ago in 1905.

First, the Carnegie Foundation's animating interest and sustained commitment has always been the quality of the educational experience. For 100 years, and in many different ways, the Foundation has been in the business of asking hard questions about good teaching: What knowledge, skills, and values are required? How are those best developed, and how can they be assured? How can teaching excellence be recognized, rewarded, and built upon?

A second hallmark of the Foundation's work has been a faith in the power of good ideas. As an advanced study center, Carnegie is committed, of course, to inquiry and to evidence, and it routinely puts its ideas to the test. But its most important products, I would argue, are fresh, vivid ideas about education and how to improve it. Carnegie is a think tank, an idea factory; ideas are the eggs we put in our baskets, the horses we place our bets on.

Shulman's work is completely in keeping with these two Carnegie hallmarks. What the essays collected here propose, and what they leave us with, are vivid, transformative ideas about educational quality. Central to these ideas is a view of teaching as intellectual work—not simply as a set of techniques for delivering content, that is, but as a set of practices that requires preparation, documentation, inquiry, and improvement according to ambitious, professional standards. Moreover, it is a vision that implicates us all. The quality of teaching, as Shulman sees it, requires commitment and collaboration across the educational spectrum, not only in formal teacher education classrooms or professional development settings for K–12 teachers. Just as important are undergraduate classrooms where, for better or worse, many of us develop our ideas about what it means to teach, and in graduate education programs where the formation of future teachers and teachers of teachers—at all levels—succeeds or fails.

It is fitting, in light of this vision of a continuum, that the editor of this volume, Suzanne Wilson, was once one of Lee Shulman's students. Now teaching teachers, teacher educators, and researchers at Michigan State University, she is also working with the Carnegie Foundation to strengthen teacher education nationally. Her thoughtful introduction and notes on each essay will provide invaluable guidance to readers of this collection, be they longtime followers of Shulman's work or newcomers to it.

Pat Hutchings
Vice President
The Carnegie Foundation for the
Advancement of Teaching
Fall 2003

THE WISDOM OF PRACTICE

INTRODUCTION

Foxes (the great ones, not the shallow or showy grazers) owe their reputations to a light (but truly enlightening) spread of real genius across many fields of study, applying their varied skills to introduce a key and novel fruit for other scholars to gather and seed in a thoroughly different kind of field. Hedgehogs (the great ones, not the pedants) locate one vitally important mine, where their particular and truly special gifts cannot be matched. They then stay at the site all their lives, digging deeper (because no one else can) into richer and richer stores from a mother lode whose full generosity has never been so well recognized or exploited.

—Stephen Jay Gould (2003, p. 5)

STEPHEN JAY GOULD is extending a contrast between the hedgehog and the fox made by Isaiah Berlin, who, in turn, perhaps borrowed it from Erasmus. Single-minded hedgehogs go deep; cunning foxes range. At first blush, the career of Lee S. Shulman most certainly seems like that of an intellectual fox. The titles of the essays included in this volume touch on educational psychology, medical problem solving, teacher knowledge, performance assessment, higher education, the scholarship of teaching and learning, the characteristics and pedagogies of the professions, and the liberal arts.

His interests have been as far-ranging as his collaborations: the Institute for Research on Teaching (a federally funded research center that explored teaching and teacher thinking) at Michigan State University, followed by the Knowledge Growth in a Profession Project (funded by the Spencer Foundation and focused on tracking how the subject matter knowledge of prospective secondary school teachers shaped and was shaped by their learning to teach), the Teacher Assessment Project (a project funded by the Carnegie Corporation of New York, which explored various forms of performance assessment for teachers, laying the foundations for the National Board for Professional Teaching Standards), and the Communities of Learners Project (funded by the Mellon Foundation) while at Stanford University. And now, as president of The Carnegie Foundation for the Advancement of Teaching, his projects include—among other things—investigations of the pedagogies of the professions, the scholarship of teaching and learning, and cultivating civic responsibility. A fox, no doubt, spreading real genius across many fields.

But we live in a postmodern world, where one particularly popular sport is deconstructing our own categories. So I begin this introduction by making an argument that will become obvious to readers as they peruse, chronologically, the full range of essays in this volume (and its companion, *Teaching as Community Property*): over the course of his career, Shulman has been burrowing while ranging, a powerful combination. Indeed, Gould argues for integrating the best qualities of the fox and the hedgehog: "What can be more powerful than combining the virtue of a clear goal pursued relentlessly and without compromise (the way of the hedgehog), and the flexibility of a wide range of clever and distinct strategies for getting to the appointed place . . . (the way of the fox)" (Gould, 2003, p. 262).

Hedgehogs are persistent; they know what interests them, and they stay the course. If Shulman has been burrowing, into what mine has he been persistently digging? The answer is simple: teaching. Long fascinated with medical practice, Shulman has consistently argued that teaching is a profession more complex than medicine. The regular classroom teacher

> is confronted, not with a single patient, but with a classroom filled with 25 to 35 youngsters. The teacher's goals are multiple; the school's obligations far from unitary. Even in the ubiquitous primary reading group, the teacher must simultaneously be concerned with the learning of decoding skills as well as comprehension, with motivation and love of reading as well as word-attack, and must both monitor the performance of the six or eight students in front of her while not losing

> touch with the other two dozen in the room. . . . The only time a physician could possibly encounter a situation of comparable complexity would be in the emergency room of a hospital during or after a natural disaster ["The Wisdom of Practice"].

Moreover, Shulman believes that teachers are critical to the education enterprise—irreplaceable, in fact. "We will sooner de-school society than de-teacher it" ("The Psychology of School Subjects"). "No microcomputer will replace them, no television system will clone and distribute them, no scripted lessons will direct and control them, no voucher system will bypass them" ("Autonomy and Obligation").

Shulman's interests in teaching of all sorts—in K–12 schools, in teacher education, in graduate programs for educational researchers, in liberal education—are diverse. Four focal interests are clear, each of which has entailed extensive hedgehog-like explorations: teachers' professional knowledge and judgment; the pedagogies of the professions (most centrally, the pedagogy of teacher education); the assessment of teaching; and the content and character of education research. These ideas have not sprung fully formed in Shulman's writing; rather, they have evolved gradually over time. (That evolution is seen in the brief introductions that precede each essay.) As a preface to the collection that follows, I consider each of these themes briefly.

Shulman's interest in professional knowledge began with inquiries into professional reasoning. In his work with Arthur Elstein, he investigated the nature of medical problem solving and documented and described how diagnosticians reasoned through the symptoms presented by patients (Shulman and Elstein, 1979; Elstein, Shulman, and Sprafka, 1978). In this work, the researchers found that problem formulation and hypothesis generation were critical to effective diagnoses and that a physician's substantive knowledge and prior experience played an important role in reasoning.

Simultaneously, Shulman, in his collaborations with a broad array of colleagues at Michigan State University, began studying the nature of reasoning required in teaching. In fact, the Institute for Research on Teaching (which he codirected with Judith Lanier)—anticipating the cognitive revolution in psychology—held as a central principle that it was critical for researchers to understand teachers' thinking (as well as teachers' behaviors and characteristics). Burrowing away, Shulman's excursions into professional thinking in medicine and teaching led him deeper into the area of professional reasoning and knowledge. After moving to Stanford, a new question emerged: What kinds of knowledge do teachers use as they reason? Asking this question about teaching, Shulman and his colleagues began with some obvious candidates—subject matter knowledge, knowledge of students, knowledge of teaching techniques, among them—and then hypothesized that teaching perhaps also involved a specialized kind of knowledge, pedagogical content knowledge (dubbed "PCK" by some). Pedagogical content knowledge was a "particular form of content knowledge that embodies the aspects of content most germane to its teachability . . . the most useful forms of representation . . . the most powerful analogies, illustrations, examples, explanations, and demonstrations—in a word, the ways of formulating the subject that make it comprehensible to others" ("Those Who Understand"). This knowledge, critical to teaching, represents the most profound understanding of subject matter, Shulman claimed: "Aristotle had it right, the deepest understanding one can have of any field is an understanding of its pedagogy, because pedagogy is predicated on the kind of multiple readings, the kind of contingent understandings that reflect the deep objectives of a liberal education" ("Aristotle Had It Right").

Like Gould's hedgehog, Shulman continued tunneling in the area of teacher reasoning and knowledge as he inquired into the forms in which professional knowledge is held. His work with physicians suggested that diagnosticians drew both on substantive knowledge from research and on case knowledge from personal experience. Shulman proposed that teachers might also draw on multiple forms of knowledge: using strategies, applying principles, and reasoning from cases. In particular, Shulman was taken with the idea of cases—"the children born of a liaison between design and chance" ("Just in Case"). "An educative case," he claims, "is a form of communication that places intention and chance into the context of a lived and reflected experience. A case doesn't just happen; it creates conditions that demand of its narrator (or protagonist) that she both render judgments among alternative tacks and act on those judgments" ("Just in Case"). His work on cases highlighted for Shulman the centrality of judgment under uncertainty in teaching. This emphasis on judgment led him to additional questions about how such judgment might be characteristic of all professions.

In short, Shulman's contributions in the realm of teachers' professional knowledge and reasoning have been considerable. He delineated a knowledge base of teaching (including the introduction of key terms such as pedagogical content knowledge) and described teacher reasoning first as a process of managing complexity, shifting later in his career to thinking of teacher reasoning as entailing judgment under uncertainty. Finally, he argued for the creation of a knowledge base of teaching that included both principles or strategies generated through research and cases generated through experience and reflection.

Shulman's interest in cases is intimately tied to the second domain in which he has done considerable tunneling: the pedagogies for preparing professionals. If professional work is uncertain, he wondered, and requires both drawing on deep knowledge and making judgments, how do we prepare new generations of professionals? How do we teach both the knowledge necessary to teach well, while also creating opportunities for new teachers/professionals to learn how to make sound judgments? His work in this area began as a modest enterprise. Based on the studies he conducted about medical problem solving, he and his colleagues wondered how to prepare medical students to generate hypotheses quickly and effectively. At the same time, he wondered about the pedagogy of teacher education. In "The Practical and the Eclectic," his commentary on an essay by his teacher and friend, Joseph Schwab, Shulman proposed that teaching requires various kinds of knowledge, including knowledge of rules, knowledge of particular cases, and knowledge of how to apply those rules to cases. "Where," Shulman asks, in teacher education is "the opportunity to learn of particular cases and ways of applying rules to cases?"

As he further developed his ideas about the professional knowledge base of teaching, in essays like "Those Who Understand" and "Knowledge and Teaching," Shulman dug deeper into the implications of case knowledge for the pedagogy of teacher education. He argued that the "case method," well established in the teaching of law, was particularly valuable in teaching teachers about theory, for "to call something a case is to make a theoretical claim" ("Those Who Understand"). He continues, "I envision the use of case method in teacher education, whether in our classrooms or in special laboratories with simulations, videodisks and annotated scripts, as a means for developing strategic understanding, for extending capacities toward professional judgment and decision-making. These methods of instruction would involve the careful confrontation of principles with cases, of general rules with concrete documented events—a dialectic of the general with the particular in which the limits of the former and the boundaries of the latter are explored" ("Those Who Understand").

Shulman both wrote about such case teaching while also experimenting with it in his own teacher education classes. He read, interpreted, and deliberated about cases with his teacher education students, and he asked them to write their own cases, comment on each other's cases, and participate in case conferences. Simultaneously, he inspired and conspired with numerous colleagues (including, perhaps most notably, his wife, Judith Shulman) interested in creating such a case-based pedagogy of teacher education and professional development. In his current work, Shulman continues to play with ideas of cases as pedagogy, developing the argument that liberal education needs to tie itself to practice in order to make it more meaningful and more liberal. Cases and a case pedagogy might serve this end:

> If we were to actively connect learning with service, with practice, with application, and were further to capture that practice in a kind of pedagogy that uses cases and case methods in ways analogous to some of the ways we use them for professional preparation, we would not only achieve the moral ends of service, we would very likely do better at overcoming the challenges to liberal learning. Through service, through application, through rendering their learning far more active, reflective, and collaborative, students would actually learn more liberally, understand what they have learned more deeply, and develop the capacity to use what they have learned in the service of their communities ["Professing the Liberal Arts"].

Shulman's most recent work as hedgehog in this second domain of the pedagogies of the professions resonates with his early cross-professional investigations comparing teaching and medicine. Since all professions face the same intractable problem—"How do we prepare people for uncertain work?"—Shulman and his colleagues are inquiring into the pedagogies of multiple professions: the clergy, engineering, the law, teacher education, medicine, and nursing.

Shulman's work is dialectical: explorations of pedagogies circle back to conceptions of professional knowledge and judgment. In returning to his interest in professional knowledge, he continues to tunnel further, proposing core characteristics of professional work (obligation and moral vision, substantive knowledge, a practice, judgment under uncertainty, learning from experience, and community membership) that include his earlier work on professional knowledge and judgment but subsume them under a more expansive theoretical umbrella.

A third interest that Shulman has mined is the assessment of professional knowledge. One critical characteristic of professions is that members both monitor their own ranks and take responsibility for preparing and assessing the quality of all members of the profession. Another critical characteristic, as already noted, is that professional work requires judgment. Shulman became intrigued with how might we create assessments—to be used by professionals themselves—that get to the core of professional work: judgment under uncertainty. Shulman's initial foray into this arena involved the Teacher Assessment Project, a project that explored the potential for performance assessments for K–12 teachers. Initially conceptualized in a white paper he wrote with his colleague Gary Sykes (Shulman and Sykes, 1986), Shulman's work—both in the theoretical domain of teacher knowledge and the technical domain of performance assessments—played an important role in laying the foundations for both the standards and the assessments of the National Board for Professional Teaching Standards (NBPTS). The Teacher Assessment Project staff developed a normative framework for teacher knowledge that influenced the NBPTS's later work of "What Teachers Need to Know and Be Able to Do." They developed performance assessments for high school history teaching and elementary mathematics teaching, and administered them in an assessment center in the summer of 1987. They then went on to explore the potential for portfolios in teacher assessment in elementary literacy and secondary science teaching. In a world in which most teacher tests took the form of standardized, multiple choice, generic questions, this work on teacher assessment was groundbreaking, exciting, and threatening. Eventually, that work led to a reconceptualization of what it meant to be an accomplished teacher, with subject matter at the core.

But teaching is not the sole purview of K–12 schools, and Shulman's empirical and theoretical work in teacher assessment began to influence his work as a faculty member in higher education as well. As a member of Stanford University's Advisory Board, which reviewed every appointment or promotion to tenure in the university, Shulman began to wonder about how those of us in higher education document and assess an individual's capacity to teach. At the same time, Shulman's ideas about professional teaching knowledge began to capture the interest of leaders in higher education. He dug further still, collaborating with colleagues on the Peer Review of Teaching Project sponsored by the American Association for Higher Education, which supported faculty across the country as they created course portfolios, offered pedagogical colloquia, and wrote analyses of their students' learning. This project evolved into his current work, which extends and elaborates on Ernest Boyer's (1997) conception of a "scholarship of teaching" through the Carnegie Academy for the Scholarship of Teaching and Learning (CASTL). The CASTL program works with educators at all levels—K–12 teachers, teacher educators, and professors from a range of fields (chemistry, mathematics, pharmacology, literature, among them)—and aims to make the intellectual work of teaching a recognized, respected aspect of the profession. As Shulman notes: "Colleges and universities have always taken justifiable pride in their commitment to inquiry and criticism in all fields, even those where dogma and habit make real scrutiny uncomfortable. Now we must turn this tough scrutiny on our own practices, traditions, and culture. Only by doing so will we make teaching truly central to higher education" (Shulman, 1993, p. 7).

While Shulman, the hedgehog, has burrowed into these three interests concerning teaching—professional knowledge and reasoning, the pedagogies of the professions, and the assessment of teaching knowledge—he has also consistently dug into the question, What forms should educational research take? Early on in his career, he argued that educational research needed to be reconstructed, to develop more sophisticated and nuanced measures of the environments in which students learn and teachers teach. This work anticipated the later shift in psychology and other fields to an emphasis on the situated and social nature of knowledge and action. He argued, too, against a narrow range of methodologies, and for a "methodological mosaic" ("Disciplines of Inquiry in Education") and encouraged education researchers to use multiple methods that drew upon the work of myriad disciplines—anthropology, sociology, history, linguistics, psychology, and the like. Long before the explosion of method the field of education witnessed in the 1980s, Shulman imagined new methodologies: "epidemiological" research strategies inspired by research in public health, "grammar of behavior" strategies based on work done by linguists:

> We must be prepared to broaden the range of methods we employ in our research, as we reformulate the questions we propose to raise. Although good experimental and correlational investigations will continue to be useful, we need add more varied kinds of studies—longitudinal case studies, anthropological analyses of classrooms and teachers, information-processing modelings of the thought processes of teachers and learners using methods of controlled introspection and retrospection, investigations of basic phenomena, such as transfer, under conditions varying subject matter, to name but a few ["The Psychology of School Subjects"].

He also urged education researchers to heed both—equally important—meanings of "discipline," namely discipline as "the management of impulse and the control of intellectual caprice" ("The Practical and the Eclectic") and discipline as a community of scholars with shared knowledge, questions, substantive interests, and methods for constructing, testing, and verifying knowledge. I return to this second meaning of discipline momentarily.

While writing about this disciplined eclectic in research, Shulman also enacted it in his own work as researcher and teacher. He co-taught a research course with two Stanford colleagues—Milbrey McLaughlin (a policy analyst) and Shirley Brice Heath (an anthropologist)—whose epistemological, methodological, and pedagogical perspectives were quite different from his own. On his research projects, he consistently invites both graduate students and faculty with different disciplinary perspectives—ranging from measurement to philosophy—to deliberate with him, challenge his ideas, and extend the work.

In sum, Shulman and his colleagues have delved persistently into these four lines of work—professional knowledge and reasoning, the pedagogies of the professions, the assessment of professional knowledge and skill, and the nature of educational research—for close to thirty years now. Clearly, these lines of work are far from distinct, as I have already noted. His first fully elaborated thesis on teacher knowledge—"Those Who Understand"—uses teacher tests as a site for exploring those issues. The portfolios developed by hundreds of teachers who have applied for National Board of Professional Teaching Standards Certification (an assessment what was heavily influenced by Shulman's empirical and theoretical work) now constitute a case knowledge of teaching. Similarly, the products of the K–12 CASTL fellows' scholarship of teaching and learning projects at The Carnegie Foundation for the Advancement of Teaching are now being used by teacher educators to support a case-based pedagogy in teacher education.

Yet naming these foci alone does not explain Shulman's career, for equally important have been the fox-like strategies he has employed along the way. A critical strategy of Shulman's has entailed looking across contrasting cases. As he tried to understand professional reasoning, Shulman began in medicine and teaching, using both their similarities and differences to understand professional reasoning in a generic sense, as well as those aspects that are specific to particular professions. In his current work at the Carnegie Foundation, he has expanded that pool of professions and has projects looking across fields as diverse as nursing, teaching, and the clergy. In a similar fashion, when his attention turned to the subject-specific aspects of teaching, Shulman collaborated with colleagues who examined this issue across school subjects—mathematics, English, history and the social studies, science. Current Foundation projects continue this tradition: the Carnegie Initiative on the Doctorate includes collaborations with departments of mathematics, English, education, chemistry, history, and neuroscience.

And so we return to the central role that discipline has played in Shulman's career, for this focus on cross-field comparisons is not simply a methodological strategy. It is also a substantive belief that knowledge varies in important ways across fields and that we ought to attend to those differences in our research and teaching. For many educational scholars, Shulman's most important contribution to the field has been his insistence that subject matter matters. Well into the 1980s, educational research was still dominated by educational psychologists who presumed a generic approach to teaching and learning—teaching and learning mathematics was comparable to teaching and learning history or English or biology. Their generic conception of teaching led to generic research questions and methods, which, in turn, led to generic conclusions. Shulman (1986) argued against that trend, calling for a reconsideration of the role that subject matter played in teaching and learning (what he called the "missing paradigm" in educational research):

> Where the teacher cognition program has clearly fallen short is in the elucidation of teachers' cognitive understanding of subject matter and the relationships between such understanding and the instruction that teachers provide for students. . . . The general public and those who set educational policy are in general agreement that teachers' competence in the subjects they teach is a central criterion of teacher quality. They remain remarkably vague, however, in defining what sort of subject-matter knowledge they have in mind—basic skills, broad factual knowledge, scholarly depth—and the research-on-teaching community has been of little help with this matter [pp. 25–26].

This attention to subject-specific aspects of knowing was at the core of his early work on medical problem solving, and appeared and reappeared in his work on the knowledge growth of new teachers, the wisdom of practice of experienced teachers, teacher assessment, and continues in his CASTL work. More than anyone else, Shulman has bridged the content-free tradition of educational research with the discipline-specific nature of higher education and disciplinary work. For many, this is his sine qua non.

Yet another strategy Shulman has used involves working between theory, research, and practice. Consider the idea of cases. Shulman developed the theoretical notion of teaching involving a case knowledge in his presidential address to the American Educational Research Association in 1985. At the same time, doctoral students working with him were busily using cases as a research method to document new teachers' learning and the role of their subject matter knowledge in that learning, as well as cases to document experienced teachers' wisdom of practice in the Teacher Assessment Project. Gradually, he also began using cases as a pedagogical tool, by asking that the prospective teachers in his teacher education classes write and share cases of their own teaching. By constantly moving back and forth between theory (Shulman has always had a predilection toward Robert Merton's theories of the middle range), research, and practice, Shulman's work has produced both practical tools (prototypes for the assessments used by the NBPTS, for example) and inspiring theoretical constructs (pedagogical content knowledge, for another).

A third strategy has been his own disciplined eclecticism, the legacy of his work with Joseph Schwab, and resonating with his hedgehog interests in the qualities and character of educational research. As I have already noted, Shulman has long argued for eclecticism in education research, both in terms of the approaches that we use and the theories that we build or borrow to explain our results. (Here, again, he was heavily influenced by Robert Merton, as well as by Lee J. Cronbach.) In his writing on educational research, he makes a case for eclecticism of methods—and the need to educate future educational researchers in multiple methods (see, for example, "Reconstruction of Educational Research," "The Psychology of School Subjects," and "Disciplines of Inquiry in Education"). One sees this disciplined eclecticism emerge again in his work on assessment. In both the Teacher Assessment Project and the Peer Review of Teaching Project, Shulman argued persuasively that no single form of assessment would do, and we would be wise to aim for a "union of insufficiencies," rather than rely on a necessarily narrow measure of teaching knowledge and skill: "What we need, therefore, is a union of insufficiencies, a marriage of complements, in which the flaws of individual approaches to assessment are offset by the virtues of their fellows" ("A Union of Insufficiencies").

A final strategy may be obscured by the fact that, in this volume, Shulman is the sole author of each essay. For while he often writes alone, Shulman learns together, first, as a student of his teachers—Joseph Schwab (and by association due to his significant influence on Schwab, John Dewey) and Benjamin Bloom, as well as others at the University of Chicago. In particular, he was significantly influenced by his experiences as a student both in Schwab's seminars ("his directness to the point of insult, his commitment to doubt as a source of wisdom, and his devotion to the 'other view' as the key to the growth of understanding" (["Joseph Jackson Schwab"] and in his classes in the Hutchins' College, founded on a commitment to all students learning the Great Books. He went on to learn with and from his colleagues both at Michigan State and Stanford University, including Arthur Elstein, Judy Lanier, Bob Floden, Susan Florio Ruane, Lee Cronbach, Milbrey McLaughlin, Shirley Brice Heath, Joan Talbert, Ed Haertel, and Denis Phillips. He also learned alongside a long line of students, on whose work he draws extensively and generously in his essays. His learning continues in collaboration with colleagues who work at the Carnegie Foundation.

Throughout his writing, both on teacher learning and on the character of educational research, Shulman has argued for the importance of community, a value he learned as a student at the University of Chicago and an important forum for taking advantage of eclectic views: "Collegiality is needed to overcome the limitations of individual rationality. If any individual actor's capacity to learn is bounded, if human reasoning of all kinds—theoretical, practical, or moral—remains restricted when pursued alone or without access to a competing point of view, then the collegium is indispensable" ("Teaching Alone, Learning Together"). Shulman has consistently created collegiums throughout his career. He invited Joseph Schwab to lead a faculty seminar in the Institute for Research on Teaching, where faculty and students read and deliberated collectively. He invited colleagues at Stanford—including Lee Cronbach, Denis Phillips, and Ed Haertel—to collaborate on the Knowledge Growth in a Profession Project and the Teacher Assessment Project. He co-taught with a number of colleagues at Stanford, including Denis Phillips, Larry Cuban, John Baugh, Nate Gage, Milbrey McLaughlin, Shirley Brice Heath, Teresa Laframboise, and Linda Darling-Hammond. The entire staff of the Carnegie Foundation meets regularly to listen to speakers and to discuss work in progress.

Gould's point in arguing for the power of the combination of hedgehog and fox was not to persuade us all to become hedgehog-foxes, for we need to hold on to our differences in order to stimulate the best possible work. In some important ways, Shulman has remained a fox. Gould writes that foxes apply "their varied skills to introduce a key and novel fruit for other scholars to gather and improve in a particular orchard" (Gould, 2003, p. 5). Indeed, Shulman has consistently demonstrated a gift for sparking new lines of work with imagination and intelligence, often accompanied by a felicitous use of language. Without introducing unnecessary jargon, he has a gift for coining phrases that are at once lyrical and intellectually provocative.[1]

His argument in that subject matter was that the "missing paradigm" in research on teaching led to major initiatives in research on the subject-specific aspects of teaching, including the work of Sam Wineberg in high school history, Pamela Grossman in high school English, and Deborah Ball in elementary mathematics. The concept of "pedagogical content knowledge" became an inspiration for research on teaching, the redesign of teacher education programs, and the design of teacher assessment systems. University faculty were also taken with the idea, and it has found its way into numerous discussions concerning the knowledge base for teaching in higher education. Higher education has long presumed that teaching comes naturally to scholars; that Shulman's notion of pedagogical con-

---

1. The exception here is "pedagogical content knowledge," which may lack lyricism but has more than made up for that with its conceptual power.

tent knowledge has captured the attention of those in higher education is no small feat.

Other ideas he has borrowed from others and extended in important ways. His work on the "wisdom of practice" was launched by an idea of David Hawkins (1966). His substantial contributions to the scholarship of teaching and learning—by writing about such a scholarship, by working with myriad institutions of higher education to create centers or programs for the scholarship of teaching, and by supporting the work of generations of CASTL fellows through The Carnegie Foundation for the Advancement of Teaching—picked up an idea introduced by Ernest Boyer (1997) and remodeled it for new use.

In sum, across all of this work, Shulman has been the consummate fox, introducing interesting ideas, offering those ideas generously to the people of like and different mind and disposition, and learning—with interest and genuine pleasure—from the inquiries of his colleagues. He has also been a hedgehog, for his passion for teaching is clear. His belief that some aspects of teaching as subject-specific is equally clear. For all the twists and turns in his career, his driving commitment has been to understand teaching, specifically the teaching of subject matter.

I close this introduction on a more personal note, for I have been Lee's student and collaborator. More than any interest or strategy, I have always been most taken with Lee's humanity. Lee has explored this medley of ideas about teaching and learning, disciplines and eclecticism, knowledge and assessment, professionalism and higher education, and educational research with passion and warmth, offering them to the rest of us with an intellectual generosity that has enriched both his writing and ourselves. Our field is richer for his ideas. Our lives are richer for his grace.

Suzanne M. Wilson
Michigan State University
October 2003

REFERENCES

Boyer, E. L. *Scholarship Reconsidered: Priorities of the Professoriate.* San Francisco: Jossey-Bass, 1997.

Elstein, A. S., Shulman, L. S., and Sprafka, S. A. *Medical Problem Solving: An Analysis of Clinical Reasoning.* Chicago: University of Chicago Press, 1978.

Gould, S. J. *The Hedgehog, the Fox, and the Magister's Pox: Ending the False War Between Science and the Humanities.* New York: Harmony, 2003.

Hawkins, D. "Learning the Unteachable." In L. S. Shulman and E. R. Keislar (eds.), *Learning by Discovery: A Critical Appraisal.* Chicago: Rand McNally, 1966.

Shulman, L. S. "Paradigms and Research Programs for the Study of Teaching." In M. C. Wittrock (ed.), *Handbook of Research on Teaching* (3rd ed.). New York: Macmillan, 1986.

Shulman, L. S. "Teaching as Community Property: Putting an End to Pedagogical Solitude." *Change,* 1993, November/December, 6–7.

Shulman, L. S., and Elstein, A. S. "Studies of Problem Solving, Judgment, and Decision Making: Implications for Educational Research." In F. N. Kerlinger (ed.), *Review of Research in Education,* Vol. 3. Itasca, Ill.: Peacock, 1979.

Shulman, L. S., and Sykes, G. *A National Board for Teaching? In Search of a Bold Standard.* Paper commissioned by Task Force on Teaching as a Profession, Carnegie Forum on Education and the Economy, 1986.

INTRODUCTION

RECONSTRUCTION OF EDUCATIONAL RESEARCH (1970)

IN 1970, Shulman had just finished two research programs that came immediately after his dissertation, which was a study of teacher thinking, more specifically of problem finding or problem sensitivity, using a simulated classroom environment as its research setting. Shulman continued that work in a three-year study of problem-solving strategies among prospective teachers at Michigan State. The second study was an experimental, longitudinal study of the impact of a vocational simulation of a factory setting (a "sheltered workshop" in the vernacular of that field) on the vocational development of handicapped adolescents.

Shulman was invited to give a speech at a conference of the Southern Christian Leadership Conference (SCLC) led by Martin Luther King, Jr.—who also spoke on the same program—in Atlanta. The invitation came from a colleague, Bob Green, who had started as an assistant professor with Shulman at MSU in 1963. As one of the few African American education researchers around, Bob was invited to help lead the empirical study of the impact of non-schooling on the black children of Prince Edward County, Virginia, where the schools had closed for four years to avoid desegregation. Shulman was part of the team that conducted the study, and two of the first dissertations he directed at MSU grew out of that work: Egon Mermelstein studied the impact of non-schooling on the emergence of the Piagetian concept of conservation among young children, and Milton Hillery studied the impact of non-schooling on the development of creativity. Bob eventually left MSU to become Director of Research for the SCLC, and he wanted Shulman to speak to the focus of the conference, "The Role of Social Scientists in Social Reform."

Eventually, Shulman expanded that talk into this paper, which was published in the *Review of Educational Research.* In the essay, Shulman takes educational researchers to task and suggests several ways in which the field must improve if it is to make a difference in the lives of all children. He begins the essay by echoing the words of Arthur Jensen, who had published a long and controversial essay in the *Harvard Education Review,* arguing that compensatory education was fated to fail because the differences between blacks and whites were not attributable to environment but to heredity. Appearing within the same year as *The Coleman Report* and Jencks's *Inequality*—both of which acknowledged powerful individual and probably innate sources of variance for intelligence and achievement—the attack on the essentially environmental policies of compensatory education was quite powerful. Jensen's opening line in his essay became quite famous: "Compensatory education has been tried, and apparently it has failed." Shulman opens with "Educational research has been tried and apparently it has failed" and then devotes the essay to a critique of educational research, an enterprise that did not understand how to measure environments nor to conduct socially significant research in education.

Written in the late 1960s, before the fields of psychology and education began to recognize the importance of context, this essay foreshadows the later prominence of theories of situated cognition. Shulman begins by tracing the roots of research on education, noting that there was a growing awareness that studying individual differences was insufficient, for environmental forces exercised considerable influence on what, when, and whether students learned. However, at the time this essay was written—the late 1960s—the field of educational research was much more sophisticated about measures of individual differences than it was in the arena of measures of environment or treatment. For example, educators at that time would label the environments of many minority children as "disadvantaged," a phrase that did little to describe the features or characteristics of their home environments. Shulman argues that the field of educational research needed to become more sophisticated in both research and a language for describing the educationally relevant aspects of the settings in which students learn.

Shulman's second suggestion is that educational researchers would also have to become much more sophisticated in their knowledge and use of experimental settings in research meant to inform classroom learning. While experiments increase the internal validity of a study, researchers need to also attend to the external validity of their work. Shulman argues that researchers needed to create deeper understandings of the features of both classrooms and experiments in order to deal with the discontinuities that existed between the research settings (at that time, laboratories) and school settings.

In addition, Shulman argues, the field needs to embrace a broader array of research methodologies if it is to conduct research with more external validity. He describes five candidate methods, including (1) epidemiological strategies, which would involve identifying the variables that distinguish between effective and ineffective performances (in reading or teaching, for example); (2) "grammars of behaviors" strategies, which would entail describing in detail the grammar of the behaviors of good teachers; (3) simulations; (4) multivariate experimental-longitudinal strategies; and (5) replications. He concludes by suggesting that, in addition to these new methods, the field would benefit from an organizational shift away from the individual researcher to interdisciplinary teams of researchers whose combined expertise could produce a new, improved educational research that had a greater potential for improving educational practice.

I

RECONSTRUCTION OF EDUCATIONAL RESEARCH

If there are some subjects on which the results obtained have finally received the unanimous assent of all who have attended to the proof, and others which . . . have never succeeded in establishing any considerable body of truths, so as to be beyond denial or doubt; it is by generalizing the methods successfully followed in the former enquiries, and adapting them to the latter, that we may hope to remove this blot on the face of science.

—John Stuart Mill

Some of the major disasters of mankind have been produced by the narrowness of men with a good methodology. . . . To set limits to speculation is treason to the future.

—Alfred North Whitehead

EDUCATIONAL RESEARCH HAS BEEN TRIED and apparently it has failed. Or has it?

If the object of such research is the development of coherent and workable theories, researchers are nearly as far from that goal today as they are from controlling the weather. If the goal of educational research is significant improvement in the daily functioning of educational programs, I know of little evidence that researchers have made discernible strides in that direction. Which way then do they turn? To more of the same? Or to a pragmatic attack on highly specific educational problems, eschewing theory development as a goal? Or do they reexamine the basic paradigms and parameters of both education and research in order to seek new directions? In this paper, I argue that neither a slavish continuation of current practices nor a monolithic rejection of them is likely to solve the problems of educational research. Researchers must step back, regain perspective, and then identify clearly the most fruitful routes toward development of an empirically based discipline of education.

I begin this paper with a brief examination of the nature of education and the history of its relations with the behavioral sciences, especially psychology. Then I discuss certain characteristics of the instructional process and problems involved in its study. I conclude this paper with a review of potentially useful strategies of educational research and the institutional prerequisites for their successful implementation.

Retrospect: Education and Psychology

Moving up the phylogenetic scale, one finds that the period of childhood characteristic of the different species increases in length. Moving from the less complex to the more complex organisms, the relative proportions of instinct to learning as forces influencing behavior rapidly change, until, with man, the role of learning is so central that the concept of instinct becomes nearly irrelevant. Even in the highly nativistic theory of language acquisition proposed by Chomsky (1965) and his followers (see Lenneberg, 1967), learning plays a central role in the development of specific linguistic performance. Thus, the major discontinuity between the human species and all others lies in what McNeil (1963) has called "systematic developmental retardation."

> Indeed, the helplessness of human young must at first have been an extraordinary hazard to survival. But this handicap had compensations, which in the long run, redounded in truly extraordinary fashion to the advantage of mankind. For it opened wide the gates to the possibility of cultural as against merely biological evolution. . . . Biologically considered, the interesting mark of humanity was systematic developmental retardation, making the human child infantile in comparison to the normal protohuman. But developmental retardation, of course, meant prolonged plasticity, so that learning could be lengthened. Thereby, the range of cultural as against mere biological evolution

> widened enormously; and humanity launched itself upon a biologically as well as historically extraordinary career. . . . By permitting, indeed compelling, men to instruct their children in the arts of life, the prolonged period of infancy and childhood made it possible for human communities to eventually raise themselves above the animal level from which they began. (McNeil, 1963, pp. 20, 21)

Thus, the absence of instinct, the absence of prefabricated behavior patterns which program the organism at a very early stage in his development, provides man with his most human characteristic—his educability. This malleability acts as a two-edged sword, for with plasticity comes not only the potential for limitless growth, but also the danger of inestimable damage.

Recognizing that man's education and the scope of his educability are the most human things about him, it seems only appropriate that those disciplines which purport to study man and his nature should concentrate rather heavily upon studies of his schooling. American psychology at the beginning of this century did precisely that. The great men of that period of American psychology—William James, E. L. Thorndike, G. Stanley Hall, Robert Woodworth, John Dewey, and others—were vitally interested in studies of the educational process. Such investigations lay at the heart of American psychological thinking during that time. However, influenced by Lloyd Morgan's (1894) Canon which effectively placed unobservable mental processes out of bounds for psychological study, the discipline of scientific psychology in America was slowly transformed from James's (1890) "Science of Mental Life" to Watson's (1913) "Science of Behavior." In that generally fruitful antimentalistic revolution was discarded not only the bath water of Titchenerian introspectionism but also, tragically, the baby of experimental educational research. Despite Thorndike's continuing admonitions that the proper laboratory for the psychologist was the classroom and its proper subject was the pupil, the study of infrahuman species and their behavior came to dominate psychology. In many ways the efforts of the rat- or primate-oriented psychologists contributed significantly to man's understanding of the natural world. It would be an overstatement to assert that the study of school learning disappeared completely from psychology. It would be even more misleading to deny that such studies were now peripheral to the developing tradition of American experimental psychology.

Ironically, Soviet psychology, though greatly influenced by the Pavlovian tradition, never abandoned studies of school learning as a major component of psychological research (Menchinskaya, 1969). Because of the political and social importance of education in the Marxist-Leninist tradition, Soviet psychological studies focused frequently on instruction as a variable of interest. Kilpatrick and Wirszup (1969) report that in a recent year 37.5% of all materials published in Soviet psychology was devoted to educational and child psychology.

The only area of educational psychological research in America which remained unscathed by this post-Watsonian revolution was that of the then still infant investigations of mental measurement. This tradition, growing out of the work of Galton, Spearman, Binet and Simon, J. M. Cattell, Terman, and others, continued to flourish and received its greatest impetus from the success of mental testing during World War I. The emphasis of this movement was quantitative and descriptive. The objectives were the careful measurement and prediction of individual differences in human abilities. The schism between the respective *Weltauschauungen* of experimental psychology and mental measurement grew progressively wider, and it was not totally inappropriate that for many years educational psychology was identified with educational measurement.[1] It is only in the most recent period that these trends began to reverse. The two traditions with their respective and almost nonoverlapping methodologies are beginning to coalesce.

A good sign that a new field is becoming popular is the creation and proliferation of shorthand ways of exchanging fundamental concepts. *ATI* is already recognized by many educational researchers as the acronym for "aptitude-treatment interaction" (Cronbach and Snow, 1969), a research strategy characterized by the marriage of experimental and differential approaches. One of the major problems attendant on this marriage is the prosperity gap between the two principals. Whereas differential psychologists possess a wealth of methods for characterizing individual differences, the classification of environments, settings, or treatments remains relatively primitive (Mitchell, 1969). "Aptitude-treatment interaction" will likely remain an empty phrase as long as aptitudes are measured by micrometer and environments are measured by divining rod.

In the next section I examine several aspects of environment as a factor in educational research: the problems of investigating the effects of environments, the kinds of variables that can be used to characterize environments, and the relevance of environmental analysis to the methodology of educational experimentation.

1. For fuller discussion of the meaning and implication of this distinction, see Cronbach (1957, 1967), see also Cattell (1966b).

The Study of Environments

Social scientists are dramatically impotent in their ability to characterize environments. Generally, they do not even try. It should by now be a truism to point out that neither individuals nor groups can be adequately described without reference to some setting. Thus, for Dewey, the starting point of his discussions was always "some organism in some environment" (Dewey, 1938). Murray (1938) posited two equally important categories for his studies of personality: *needs* and *press*, i.e., person variables and environment variables. The language of education and the behavioral sciences is in great need of a set of terms for describing environments that is as articulated, specific, and functional as those already possessed for characterizing individuals.

An example that is familiar to all educators is the continued use of such gross terms as "deprived" or "disadvantaged" to characterize the environments of many minority-group children. Labeling the setting as "disadvantaged," of course, communicates little that is meaningful about the characteristics of that environment. Educators seem unable to progress beyond such a simple dichotomy as "advantaged-disadvantaged." Reviewers and critics of research have long realized that even those few categories which attempt to describe environments, such as *social class,* have been remarkably ineffectual in pinpointing the educationally relevant differences in the backgrounds of individuals (Bloom, 1964; Karp and Sigel, 1965).

Imagine if the nutritionist, in his attempts to characterize the nutritional status of the diets of individuals, were to be limited to a distinction between "well-nourished" and "malnourished" individuals. One would be quite skeptical of the value of generalizations such as "malnourished individuals have a higher incidence of respiratory ailments than well-nourished," or "well-nourished subjects were observed to run significantly faster than malnourished subjects." Are educators' pronouncements about all the differences between culturally-disadvantaged and culturally-advantaged children any more fruitful? And are the myriadic studies contrasting lower-class and middle-class youngsters of any greater value? Such descriptive studies do not begin to suggest the necessary ingredients of experimental programs to change the conditions. Should one simply elevate all lower-class people to the middle-class? What could that possibly mean?

The nutritionist can describe the nutritional environment of individuals in terms of caloric content, relative proportions of carbohydrates, fats and protein, the presence or absence of quantities of vitamins and minerals, etc. (Eichenwald and Fry, 1969). Possessing such precise terms allows him to plan systematic tactics of modifying the nutritional status of individuals in terms of highly complex, yet manageable patterns. Attaining such a level of facility in characterizing the *educationally-relevant* facets of environments should be one of the major goals of educational research. Without such an understanding, researchers are clearly handicapped in any attempt to make intelligent comparisons among proposed educational programs (such as Headstart models), for these programs are themselves planned environments.

A number of behavioral scientists have begun to study the characteristics of environments in a systematic fashion. Bloom's work (1964) is of special interest. Bloom reported many instances of great improvement in the effectiveness of academic prediction when measures of the intervening environments were taken into account in the prediction equations. He emphasized that researchers must replace the older, static terms for describing environments (e.g., social class) with dynamic, process variables (e.g., achievement press). As evidence for this assertion, he cited the research of Dave (1963) and Wolf (1964). Such process variables could well prove to have causal influences on the characteristics of interest. This would have to be demonstrated through techniques of cross-validation. The goal of all such predictive research should be, Bloom maintained, not the inexorable stamping of fates on helpless children, but the identification of the critical processes contributing to those fates. An understanding of the process variables most responsible for the ultimate status of individuals in some growth area can provide valuable guidance as researchers attempt to develop effective methods for modifying those processes and, hence, for destroying the accuracy of their predictions.

The work of Barker and his colleagues (1968) reflects a totally different set of strategies—those of ecological psychology—for studying the environment. Pace and Stern (1958) applied the tools of psychological measurement to the task of characterizing the essential differences among college environments. Henry (1963) used the methods of anthropological investigations to study the home and school as elements of culture. From his work came the compelling concept of the "hidden curriculum" in the middle-class home. Workers in the field of sociology have long been involved in studies of the environment. In a recent review, Cartwright (1968) examined the sociologists' approaches to the problems of "ecological variables." Mitchell (1969) discussed the characterization of environments for studies of person-environment interactions in educational research. It is only through such environment-centered research that behavioral scientists can develop adequate terms to describe the educationally relevant attributes of the settings within which human learning occurs.

The Experimental Setting: Environment for Research

In addition to the need for increased activity in the characterization and measurement of general environments, educational researchers must devote attention to one particular kind of environment with which they work most frequently—the experimental setting, with special reference to the tasks they create for the study of human behavior.

Most formal education currently involves groups of children studying standard school subjects. It seems clear that the classical psychological theories of learning and motivation are not capable of explaining or guiding those school activities. The reason for this incapacity can be expressed in terms analogous to those used to explain the limitations of transfer-of-training. To the extent that research is conducted in a setting similar in its characteristics to the school situation, to that extent one will get reasonable extrapolations from it to the classroom milieu.

It should be no surprise that the history of behavioral science research in education is not particularly glorious. The differences between the human learning laboratory and the typical classroom are numerous. The differences between the animal learning laboratory and the classroom are far greater. Researchers have been all too quick to generalize even from the latter setting to classroom behavior. In discussing the inadequacy of psychoanalysis as a general personality theory, Bettelheim (1960) cited quite parallel conditions. He pointed out that psychoanalysis was doomed to failure as a general personality theory because all of its generalizations were extrapolations from that most restricted of experimental settings, the psychoanalytic couch. In the same manner, does it not seem presumptuous to expect that a learning theory based upon evidence from the T-maze, the pigeon's press-bar, or the memory drum can effectively be used to guide the planning of that most complex of human endeavors, the typical classroom? This is not to deny the future relevance of "conclusion-oriented" inquiry (Cronbach and Suppes, 1969) to the conduct of schooling. The present gap between such studies and needed educational applications is simply too great. An intermediate level of investigation is needed to bridge that gap and create the basis for educational theory.

There is a danger in the overextension of this principle of judging the relevance of research settings by their congruence with actual school settings. One must not be trapped into always viewing the contemporary configuration in which pupils, teachers, and schools are found as the necessary setting to which experimental results must always transfer. There is no *ipso facto* reason to judge that the current status of schooling is the only possible or necessary way to organize education. The educational researcher must be prepared to introduce change, not only into the experimental treatment, but into his conception of the accepted forms of instruction as well.

Researchers are caught in a bind. To maximize the *internal validity* of experiments, they develop carefully monitored settings within which they can govern their research. This has long been recognized as a necessity, but it is likely that the experimental tradition in America overemphasized the importance of reliability and precision at the expense of the characteristics affecting that other factor of equal importance in the development of experimental settings, *external validity* (Campbell and Stanley, 1963; Wiggins, 1968). It is not sufficient that the individuals studied as a sample are truly representative of that human population to which the results of a particular experiment will be inferred. Researchers must also ascertain that the experimental conditions can serve as a sample from which to make inferences to a population of external conditions of interest. That is, researchers must also attempt to *maximize the similarity* between the conditions in which they study behavior and those other conditions, whatever they may be, to which researchers may ultimately wish to make inferences. The similarity should hold between psychologically meaningful features of the settings, not merely between the manifest aspects of the two situations.

Brunswick (1956, p. 39) wrote that "proper sampling of situations and problems may in the end be more important than proper sampling of subjects, considering the fact that individuals are probably on the whole much more alike than are situations among one another." Bracht and Glass (1968) analyzed in detail some of the problems of external validity in educational research, distinguishing *population validity* from *ecological validity.* Their emphasis in the latter category, however, is typically on the features associated with the research context, rather than on the specific features of the experimental tasks themselves. There is no doubt that such factors as Hawthorne Effect, Experimenter Effect, Pretest or Posttest Sensitization are important sources of ecological invalidity. I would focus, however, on the problem of *task validity.* Are the actual mental operations or behaviors the subject is called upon to perform in the course of the experiment reasonably congruent with what takes place in the external domain of interest?

Psychological investigation of verbal learning, concept learning, and problem solving—which ought to be most useful to educators—is most culpable on these grounds. Within these three areas lie most of the objectives of formal education. An excellent example of lack of external validity comes from verbal learning research which is shackled to the ubiquitous memory drum or to its apparent heir, the tachistoscope-linked Carousel slide projector. If by external validity is meant the ability to infer the results of studies using a Lafayette memory drum to others using a drum by MTA, then little criticism can be leveled against verbal learning investigators. But if one sees the goals of such research more broadly, as Ebbinghaus, James, and others among its earliest practitioners did, then the fruits of this scholarship must appear quite disappointing.

If there is a single unit of analysis which distinguishes this domain of research (as well as most of the concept learning and problem solving literature), it is the *trial* (Melton, 1963). By any means of analysis, the *trial* must stand as an experimentally created artifact, devoid of the barest semblance of external validity. It is remarkably convenient to organize and arrange sequentially the material for learning experiments in the form of trials, timed or untimed. Such arrangements yield nicely manageable data in the form of "trials to criterion," "average errors per trial," and the like. Even a large field of "metatrialosophy" can develop, which deals with the alternative ways of computing or plotting trial data and the complexities of trials by subjects designs. But where, in the actual world of human beings attempting to learn new material, attain novel concepts, or solve unfamiliar problems does one find the external analogue of a trial? For example, those learning the vocabulary of a second language in a natural setting rarely seem to present themselves with a list of new words, limiting their practice to timed exposures in unchanging sequence. Most often they learn new words in the context of ongoing discourse, either explicitly asking for a definition or making a shrewd guess from contextual clues.

To deal with the discontinuity between the settings of research and of educational application, a common language or set of terms for characterizing both experimental educational settings and curricula is needed. Researchers must seriously strive to develop a means of analyzing the characteristics of both experimental and school settings into a complex of *distinctive features,* so the task validity of any particular experiment can be estimated in terms of the particular criterion setting to which inferences are being made. The distinctive features approach was originally developed by Jakobson and Halle (1956) in a study of phonetic systems in language and was initially applied to educational problems by Gibson (1968) in her studies of reading. Gibson and her associates developed a distinctive features analysis for the characteristics of letters or graphemes and demonstrated that they could use such an analysis to generate many fruitful hypotheses concerning problems in learning to discriminate among letters.

A distinctive features approach uses a minimum of categories in combinations to characterize sets of phenomena. Thus, by using only twelve facets, such as grave-acute, lax-diffuse, or vocalic-non-vocalic in a variety of "bundles," Jakobson and Halle differentiated among all the phonemes of all languages. Hunt (1962) discussed a similar strategy for identifying the minimum necessary set of features for specifying a particular concept. Barton (1955) described the sociologists' attempts to define the characteristics of social "property space," an analogous problem.

I envisage ultimately a situation in which use of such a distinctive features approach would allow one to characterize the instructional settings to which a particular body of experimental research would most effectively be applicable. Conversely, one could begin with a curriculum of interest and use such an approach to identify critical experiments that might be conducted to examine particular features of the complex curricular *Gestalt*. By specifying the precise degree of overlap between the settings under investigation, the relevance of particular studies to particular applications could be judged more accurately.

Such research might also stimulate progress in related areas. Currently there exists a great deal of argument about the validity of aptitude and achievement tests for disadvantaged populations. These debates usually focus on whether schools in the inner-city ought to rid themselves of all forms of standardized testing. Similarly, the question of using standard entrance examinations for disadvantaged college applicants is of major contemporary importance (Kendrick and Thomas, 1970).

There is no uniform response to such concerns. Clearly, a monolithic judgment cannot be made on the validity of educational tests. Like experiments, tests have internal and external validity. When one assesses a test's *reliability*, one is measuring its internal validity. When he examines what the test maker calls *validity*, he is looking at what the experimenter calls external validity. And like the experiment, the external validity of a test must be judged on at least two bases: population and task validity.

It is possible for members of two subgroups to receive the same average score on a standardized test but for this score to be predictive of very different consequences for each group. Thus, the similarity of scores may mask more fundamental underlying differences. The validity of a test score is not only contingent upon the correlation which scores on that test bear with some criterion in the general population. A generally valid test may be differentially valid for different subgroups within the general population. Thus, when questioning the validity of a particular test, one must always ask, "valid *for whom?*" (population validity) as well as "valid *for what?*" (task validity).

In some cases, cross-validation for new populations and settings will confirm the validity of measures that had been held suspect. Thus, Stanley and Porter (1967) demonstrated that the Scholastic Aptitude Test

(SAT) was as valid a predictor of academic performance for black students in Southern Negro colleges as it was for white students. Conversely, Shulman (1968a) reported that among adolescents classified as mentally handicapped, the Stanford-Binet is valid as a predictor of vocational competence only for a white middle-class group but not for a black lower-class sample.

By combining both concepts of external test validity, one can generate a "validity matrix" for any test of interest. Such a matrix would cross populations and criteria, reporting the empirically demonstrated validity coefficients for the joint occurrence of a population with a particular set of distinctive features and categories of criterion tasks with their own sets of distinctive features. Whenever a new test is standardized or an old one is restandardized, educators should insist on a standardization design which will yield a validity matrix for that test, rather than a single, generally uninterpretable, validity coefficient. Such an approach would also be consistent with the orientation of the growing body of research on aptitude-treatment interactions in learning (Cronbach and Snow, 1969).

It should be apparent that effectively studying the distinctive features of any settings—experimental treatments, curricula, or tests—requires a carefully developed body of research on the nature of environments *per se*.

The educational significance of environment has become a focus of scholarly attention in the light of the most recent reformulations of the nature-nurture issue (Jensen, 1969). Before I examine the problems of weaving the data on environments into the fabric of externally valid educational investigations, a brief analysis of the implications of the nature-nurture issue for the study of environments may be in order.

Environment and Heredity

Stimulated by recent controversies, too many educators have assumed extreme positions with regard to the nature and sources of the environment's impact on the educability of the child. Some lean in the direction of treating young pupils as examples of the classical *tabula rasa,* the clean slate of epistemology, upon which anything they write with the stylus of instruction should cut deeply and without interference. Others insist that educators view most of variability among students in terms of inherited individual differences.

The clear and erroneous implication of the above polarity is that declaring a developing characteristic (such as intelligence) "environmental" testifies to its infinite plasticity while labeling it "inherited" stains it eternally as fixed and immutable.

The recent period has seen the emergence of a new body of literature dealing with such matters, punctuated by Jensen's (1969) provocative assertion that "compensatory education has been tried, and apparently it has failed." (For responses to Jensen's paper see especially Cronbach, 1969; Hunt, 1969; Light and Smith, 1969; and the issues of the *Harvard Educational Review* in which they appear.) Once the unfortunate, if inevitable, polemics and recriminations are eliminated, a number of fundamental misunderstandings remain which contribute greatly to the confusion on this issue. My argument in this section grows from the following propositions:

(a) There are no grounds for asserting that when the variance in the development of a characteristic is attributable mainly to heredity, that it is therefore *not* amenable to change via environmental intervention.

(b) There are no grounds for asserting that when the variance in the development of a characteristic is attributable mainly to environment, that it is therefore a relatively straightforward and simple task, given enough time and resources, to modify that characteristic via environmental intervention.

When an investigator has wished to demonstrate the effects of heredity on the development of a trait such as intelligence, he has generally looked to the data on heritability. Such demonstrations are many. The correlation between the IQs of monozygotic twins is much higher than between dizygotic twins, who are essentially not distinguishable from siblings. The correlation between the IQs of foster children and their natural mothers is always higher than it is with their foster mothers. Roberts (1952) demonstrated the strong effect of genetic factors in the analysis of data on the contrasting IQs of the siblings of the severely and mildly retarded. Such observations say nothing about the *changes* possible in measured intelligence. They assert only that a substantial portion of the *variability* of intelligence scores can be attributed to heredity.

Often the same studies are approached by those supporting a strong environmental hypothesis, and what appears to be an utterly contradictory conclusion is reached. They choose to ignore the correlational findings which the first group finds so seductive. Instead, they compare the mean IQs of twins raised in different environments, emphasizing how *different* the scores are from each other. They also take pains to show that correlations not withstanding, the actual IQs of foster children are generally more similar to those of the foster parents than they are to the natural mothers.

What is important here is that *both* conclusions are drawn reasonably from the data and both are tenable. High correlations can hold between two sets of scores while the mean values of the two sets are highly disparate. Although heredity appears to make a major contribution to the relative rank-ordering of intelligence scores with environment held constant, it is the degree of abundance or deprivation of the environment that seems to contribute most to the attained IQ *status* of individuals.

Much of the heat in the nature-nurture controversy is a function of the assumption that a nurtured characteristic is easily changed, while a "natured" one is stubbornly resistant to modifications. This is simply not the case.

Research in psychotherapy has found emotional disorders, most likely environmental in etiology, remarkably difficult to ameliorate. The cure-rate for infantile autism, which at least some theorists (Bettelheim, 1967) insist is learned, is depressingly low. Conversely, the effects of phenylketoneuria (PKU), an inherited disorder, can be ameliorated by careful control of diet. Certain inherited hemalitic anemias, such as spherocytosis, are brought under control through chemotherapeutic or surgical procedures. No facile generalizations can be made concerning the relationship between the sources of variability underlying a trait and the changes that can be brought about in its attained status.

Finally, we must keep in mind the important differences between the data on IQ, a variable of primarily theoretical interest, and school achievement, a variable of great practical significance. All studies show school achievement with a significantly lower heritability than IQ (Jensen, 1969). School achievement also stabilizes later than IQ, thus remaining sensitive to environmental change for a longer period (Bloom, 1964).

Thus, an understanding of the ways environment influences human growth and functioning remains a critical domain of inquiry for the educator, whatever his position on nature, nurture, and intelligence. Until the gene is as manipulable as the printed word, the educator's only tool will be the modifiable environment. It is the environment which he must manipulate in his studies and from which he fashions the settings of formal instruction.

The study of environments is only one aspect of the needed reconstruction of educational research. In the next section, I discuss a broader conception of desirable general directions for educational research strategy.

Reconstruction of Research Strategy

Research in education will have to venture forth from the safe and sterile surrounding of the traditional laboratory and address itself to that most threatening of settings for the educational researcher, the classroom or its carefully created equivalent. Instead of viewing experimental treatments in terms of single variables, such as "phonetic" versus "whole-word" or "discovery" versus "rote," researchers must begin to contrast total educational approaches, e.g., curricula or their parts, whose components have been carefully selected and combined.

Cronbach (1966) advocated that an educational tactic be studied in its proper context. This context includes its place in a sequence of other tactics which have been combined because they are particularly suited to each other. In this sense, the concept of a set of experimental groups which are equivalent to each other in all matters *save one dimension* whose effect is being studied, all of which are in turn compared to some "control group," is probably an anachronism.

> A particular educational tactic is part of an instrumental system; a proper educational design calls upon that tactic at a certain point in the sequence, for a certain period of time, following and preceding certain other tactics. No conclusion can be drawn about the tactic considered by itself. . . .
>
> An educational procedure is a system in which the materials chosen and the rules governing what the teacher does should be in harmony with each other and with the pupil's qualities. If we want to compare the camel with the horse, we compare a good horse and a good camel; we don't take two camels and saw the hump off one of them. (Cronbach, 1966, pp. 77, 84)

Because educational programs are far more complex than the present psychological theories which purport to explain the teaching-learning process, it might be in the long-range interest of both psychological theory and education to ignore those theories for the moment and proceed along a relatively atheoretical path in the study of education. If educators but look around, they will see that in contrast to their theoretical impotence, they do not lack for ideas and even numerous successes in the teaching of many things to a wide variety of children. In fact, were there not a fairly large proportion of successful teaching experiences with working-class children, a strikingly large proportion of those currently active in educational research would not be there.

It is not my intent to collapse the distinction between research and evaluation, or between "conclusion-oriented" and "decision-oriented" inquiries (Cronbach and Suppes, 1969). I am advocating the pursuit of different types of conclusion-oriented inquiry aimed at creating theoretical formulations that can be useful in guiding educational thought.

In the following section I review a number of research strategies for education. I have not invented them for this paper, nor do I claim that they are totally unique or novel. Other workers in related domains (e.g., Thoresen, 1969) have independently arrived at a partially overlapping list of such recommendations. The strategies I recommend are generally not independent alternative approaches but can be seen to fit into a larger overall strategy of research which I would call, after Schwab (1960), a "grand strategy" (Keislar and Shulman, 1966, p. 197).

Epidemiological Strategies

The epidemiological strategy derives from the kinds of research often conducted in the public health field (Rogers, 1965; Sartwell, 1965). Often an epidemic will spread rapidly through an area, affecting some parts of the population and leaving others unscathed. An important question raised in such a situation is what distinguished those who were susceptible to infection from those who were left unharmed. Similarly, in studies of such social phenomena as delinquency (Glueck and Glueck, 1968), it appears that individuals may come from what is ostensibly a common environment, with some turning to crime and others turning to more socially acceptable activities.

Researchers are warranted in inferring that while, in either case, the two groups in question may appear to come from the same setting, there must be some significant differences between them. Although these two groups were not created experimentally, questions can be raised by identifying representative members of each of the two contrasting groups and by attempting to analyze back and discover all of the differences between them. From such analysis, hopefully, would come working hypotheses about kinds of purposeful differences in treatments one might develop either to raise the probability of immunity or the development of socially acceptable behavior patterns in future individuals. These hypotheses could in turn be tested in long-range experimental programs.

It is apparent that similar kinds of epidemiological strategy can and do work in areas such as the study of effective and ineffective teachers, successful and unsuccessful readers, and many others. The important thing to recognize is that researchers do not confirm hypotheses in such a manner, but rather they generate them. Educators have for too long used only armchair or laboratory-based theories for generating hypotheses, or the residue of many years of intuitive experience, rather than systematically gathering careful descriptive data to generate working hypotheses. Such epidemiological strategies could be extremely useful as the early stages of a complex program of educational research. The critical attribute of such a strategy is examining in detail the background variables which distinguish effective from ineffective performers in a particular domain for the purpose of using such discriminators as the basis for creating experimental treatment or training programs.

"Grammars of Behavior" Strategies

A second strategy for using descriptive research to develop a testable set of models for education comes from the work done by field linguists as they confront previously unexplored aspects of linguistic systems and attempt to write adequate grammars for them. When a linguist confronts the problem of writing a new grammar, he generally begins by collecting a large corpus of speech from selected informants who are designated *a priori* as "native speakers" of that language. It is then asserted that their capacity to *perform* the operations of speaking and hearing that language rest upon an underlying system of rules, of which they are generally not conscious, which constitute the grammatical *competence* of the speaker. The linguist's task, once he has collected his corpus of speech, is to subject the data to a series of careful analyses in order to discover and make explicit that underlying rule system, which is known as the *grammar* of the language (Chomsky, 1965). As in my earlier examples, such formulations must subsequently be confirmed through cross-validation.

Analogous processes have been used in psychology for generating rule systems for proving mathematical theorems (Newell, Shaw, and Simon, 1958) and for interpreting protocols of the Minnesota Multiphasic Personality Inventory (Kleinmuntz, 1968). It appears that similar approaches could be developed for studying the processes of education. The strategy would involve initially identifying *criterial educators,* who, like the native speaker of the language in linguistic studies, are taken to represent some standard of excellence as practitioner of the educational arts. Careful descriptive protocols of the criterial educators' *verbal and non-verbal* behavior would then be gathered and, using behavioral equivalents of the linguistic rule discovery tactics, educational researchers would attempt to write a grammar of their teaching behaviors. This grammar would be a set of rules adequate to account for their functioning. I would hypothesize that once made explicit and cross-validated, such rules could be used to develop instructional procedures to help new students attain the criterial performer's level of competence. Jenkins (1969) reported that he and his co-workers are attempting similar grammatical analyses of the behavior of children attempting to perform certain of the Piagetian tasks. My colleagues and I

(Shulman, 1968b) are also working with such a model for the study of criterial performance among medical diagnosticians.

An important lesson to be learned from experience with this kind of strategy as used by psychologists is that one does not limit himself to observation of the overt physical behavior of the subject alone. The evidence from the studies of general mathematical problem solving by Newell, Shaw, and Simon, of interpretation of the MMPI by Kleinmuntz, and of chess playing by De Groot (1965, 1966) has made it abundantly clear that psychology's long dormant interest in introspective data must be reawakened. The most effective protocols gathered by these investigators included reports of not only what the subjects did, but also what they said about what they were doing, while doing it. Although I recognize the admonitions concerning introspection raised recently by Hebb (1969), I must insist that the evil reputation which introspection has received is more a function of its misuse by such distinguished figures as Titchener, than it is a function of some intrinsic insufficiency of the approach itself.

Simulation in Research

I indicated above the need to increase the task validity of experiments by maximizing the similarity between the features of the experimental tasks and those of the ultimate transfer settings to which the research findings were to be inferred. Techniques of *simulation* can be extremely useful in creating such research settings. Here simulation does not refer to the use of games in teaching (Boocock and Schild, 1968) nor to the use of computers to mimic men or systems (Kleinmuntz, 1968). An investigator using simulation attempts to create an artificial environment that resembles the actual environment of interest as closely as possible. However, careful control over every input into the simulation is maintained, and elements of the situation can be experimentally manipulated as needed. Thus, the experimental simulation can serve as the ideal middle ground between the artificiality of the typical experimental laboratory and the totally uncontrolled research environment of the behavioral ecologist studying organisms in their natural habitats.

Simulation can be used to create settings for studying widely diverse phenomena in education (Twelker, 1969) as well as specific cognitive functions in realistic situations (Shulman, Loupe, and Piper, 1968). Simulation approaches afford a means of taking the working hypotheses generated from the descriptive tactics of epidemiological or behavioral grammar studies and testing them at an intermediate level between the laboratory and the field.

Multivariate Experimental-Longitudinal Strategies

Most conceivable schooling situations will possess certain common characteristics: (1) They involve the attempt to modify or manipulate a setting (with or without teacher) to bring about desired changes in a learner; (2) They take place over relatively extended periods of time; (3) They involve the simultaneous input of multiple influences and the likely output of multiple consequences—some predicated, others not; and (4) They are characterized by variability of reaction to ostensibly common stimuli, that is, not all learners learn equally or react similarly to specific acts of teaching.

What is described above is a highly complex and variegated activity, involving students, subject-matter, and sources of instruction in an educational setting. Any research which purports to deal systematically with phenomena at this level of complexity must itself reflect an appropriate level of complexity. The ideal research setting, to be congruent with the description of the educational setting offered above, must be (1) *experimental;* (2) *longitudinal;* (3) *multivariate* at the level of both independent and dependent variables, and consistent with that, (4) *differential,* in that the interactions of the experimental programs with the students' entering individual differences are treated not as error variance, but as data of major interest in the research.

In experimental-longitudinal studies the long-term effects of continuing educational programs are examined (Carroll, 1965). As he does with experiments in general, the researcher attempts to equate the groups of subjects at the beginning of the study either through simple or stratified randomization. These are unlike the typical experiment because the researcher looks at the cumulative effects of ongoing programs rather than at the one-shot effects of a single exposure to instruction. Hence, the educational program is something that continues for a duration of months or years. The evaluation of these programs also is continuous during the full course of the investigation, rather than limited to the program's termination. The criterion variables are chosen to cover as wide a range of relevant behaviors as possible. This longitudinal quality characterizes current studies of computer-managed instruction (Cooley and Glaser, 1969) and computer-assisted instruction (Atkinson, 1968). For this reason alone, these studies are likely to prove educationally relevant, whether or not computer hardware is ever seriously used in schools.

A number of tactics are possible within the general experimental-longitudinal framework. Instead of beginning the entire study at a single point in time, the researcher can stagger the onset of the program over a period of months or years, with different experimental groups entering the treatment phase at different stages. In a situation in which the entire population must receive a program for political or social reasons, but justification can be made for a gradual implementation, the groups beginning the program later can serve as functional controls until their turn comes (Campbell, 1969). Also, a staggered longitudinal design has a built-in replication mechanism in the groups who begin later. These groups can also serve as controls for the possible effect of historical variables on the research results. Finally, a staggered design provides the opportunity for systematic tinkering with programs in midstream without washing out the entire study. In this sense, the problems dealt with in this research strategy become similar to those encountered when evaluating ongoing school programs (Provus, 1969; Brickell, 1969).

In general, such research can and should use the techniques of experimental studies whenever possible. For example, while randomization is often a major problem in dealing with the assignment of individual students to program components, it can often be more easily achieved if the unit of analysis is classrooms or schools. That is, it is sometimes easier to randomly assign classrooms or schools than it is to assign pupils (Campbell, 1969).

Testing the hypotheses in experimental-longitudinal designs need not, however, stand or fall on the availability of random assignment and formal control or comparison groups. Approaches to the employment of correlation or regression-based techniques for the assessment of change in non- or quasi-experimental settings are increasing in usefulness and availability (Campbell, 1963, 1967; Campbell, Ross, and Glass, in press; Yee and Gage, 1968; Land, 1968).

Designs of the proposed experimental-longitudinal genre will be multivariate in their independent and dependent variables. Cronbach (1966) pointed out the need for a broad spectrum of outcome measures in research on learning by discovery. His recommendations hold equally well for research in other learning areas. Campbell (1969) made a similar point for quasi-experimental studies in the public policy domain.

Cattell (1966b) argued that behavioral science research, previously moribund and sterile, will make visible progress only when it shakes off the constraints of bivariate studies and begins to deal with a multivariate universe in a multivariate way. Naturally, Cattell believes that the multivariate experimental techniques reviewed in his imposing handbook (Cattell, 1966a) hold the methodological keys to conducting such investigations. It is a bit ironic that I recommend this family of techniques to my colleagues in education, since Cattell observes that many of these, such as factor analysis and multivariate analysis of variance, were initially employed for solving educational or psychometric research problems.

When conducting such studies, researchers must not ignore the teacher as an independent variable. Stephens (1967), in a compelling and disturbing review of research, argued that no systematic effects for curriculum or program are observable in fifty years of educational research. He concluded that what determines the effectiveness of a program is that variable generally ignored or ostensibly randomized away—the teacher. Instead of pretending that teachers are merely sources of error variance, researchers must use multivariate experimental designs which include teachers' educationally significant characteristics as factors. At the present time, unfortunately, researchers have no idea what those characteristics are. Epidemiological or behavioral grammar studies may be useful in identifying those features.

In summary, researchers have fallen into the habit of conducting educational research in the classical two-group experimental mode or in the simple correlation descriptive mode. Examination of the true state of educational problems reveals that such approaches are extremely short on educationally relevant external validity. The tools and settings exist, however, for significantly improving such research through use of multivariate experimental-longitudinal designs of many kinds.

Replication

The time has arrived for educational researchers to divest themselves of the yoke of statical hypothesis testing and to assign the test of significance to its proper role. Tukey (1969, p. 85) observed that the use of statistical significance testing was never meant to serve as a substitute for replication:

> The modern test of significance, before which so many editors of psychological journals are reported to bow down, owes more to R. A. Fisher than to any other man. Yet Sir Ronald's standard of firm knowledge was not one very extremely significant result, but rather the ability to repeatedly get results significant at 5%.
>
> Repetition is the basis for judging variability and significance and confidence. Repetition of results, each significant, is the basis, according to Fisher, of scientific truth.

I would recommend the following general strategy for establishing the educational significance of an experiment: (1) Identify the *magnitude* of the treatment effect that will be considered significant in a particular study ("To be meaningful, this tactic should lead to an increase of at least two reading levels within six months"). (2) Establish the *proportion* of subjects who must achieve the desired magnitude of change for the results to be considered significant ("At least 60% of the pupils should achieve the meaningful level of change"). (3) Report the findings in terms of the proportion of subjects who actually do achieve the desired magnitude of change, as well as in terms of the usual measures of mean difference. Apply techniques analogous to statistical significance testing at this stage to answer questions of inferential stability. In such studies, these "tests" will resemble estimation procedures such as confidence intervals, much more than classical significance testing. (4) Employ a wide range of entering individual difference measures to provide a basis for generating subsequently verifiable hypotheses about the characteristics of those subjects who profit especially from the treatment, and those who do not. (5) Employ a broader range of criterion variables than would be suggested directly by the independent variable alone. The greatest value of a program could turn out to be in its effect on categories of change never considered in its initial development (Campbell, 1969; Schwab, in press). (6) Whatever the findings, *replicate* them. Make replication as integral a part of the research designs as posttesting or data analysis. Researchers are so unused to conducting replications that many of their current conceptions of replication turn out, after critical scrutiny, to be disturbingly naïve and simplistic. Cronbach's (1968) discussion of the problems of replicating findings on creativity and intelligence at different age levels illustrates these problems well.

Closing the Method Gap

Cattell (1966a) observed that progress in science is almost always presaged by methodological innovations or breakthroughs. He cites as examples the telescope, microscope, and factor analysis, among others. Although Kuhn (1962) would doubtless remind us of the frequency with which new paradigms are created through empirically stimulated *theoretical* rather than methodological reorientations, Cattell's point remains a compelling one. It also raises an important question.

The present era is one of significant methodological progress in the behavioral sciences and education. The development of new techniques, especially in the multivariate domain, proceeds at a rate which dazzles the non-specialist, even though in the eyes of the educational statistician most of the "new developments" are merely variations on a few major themes. Why then do researchers not observe the application of such techniques in the conduct of substantive research? If anything, the gap between the methodologist and substantive researcher in education has grown wider in the past decade. Why has not this undeniable progress in research techniques given birth to the badly needed end of educational research's Dark Age?

The microscope, telescope, and factor analysis were not created by men who considered themselves primarily to be methodologists. They were scholars confronted by compelling research problems for which their extant methods could provide no solutions. Hence, from substantive puzzlement grew methodological innovation. For all practical purposes, there were not two groups—the methodologists and the substantive researchers. There were only researchers, striving to develop methods appropriate to solve the key problems confronting their disciplines.

In the present era this has changed. Educationists currently train "research design specialists" almost independently of "learning and development men." The disaffection is two-way. Not only do the methodologists tend to disdain the necessity of gaining understanding in the substantive domains; the substantive researchers react defensively by denying the importance of methodological advances and by leading a generalized retreat to Chi Square.

It is rather ironic that most medical schools require at least one year of college mathematics for their entering medical students, although the typical medical curriculum makes woefully little use of any mathematical expertise. Yet, those in educational research, a domain which is becoming increasingly mathematics-involved, generally require no mathematics prerequisites for graduate students in areas like educational psychology.

Educational research training programs and many institutional organizations perpetuate this method gap. Unless it is breached, educational researchers are not likely to become capable of conducting the kinds of externally valid experiments discussed earlier in this paper.

The Organization of Research

The need for conducting educational research on a multivariate and longitudinal scale has been recognized by a number of scholars in education. These men suggested many specific strategies for dealing with the problems created by such research (Carroll, 1965; Thoresen, 1969; Baker, 1967). Studies of this magnitude are in vivid contrast to the type most often reinforced in academic circles. These latter studies are usually short, quick, and speedily analyzed. The experimental treatments can be administered in a matter of minutes or hours and the results are assessed immediately thereafter. They are as unlike the form of experiment I have been discussing as they are unlike anything that happens to children in real classrooms. Yet, on the grounds that the greater complexity of classroom activities constitutes no more than a concatenation of these more simple operations sequentially linked together to form a curriculum, the argument is made that such strategies of research are justified for educational investigations.

Researchers must recognize, however, that there is also a network of institutions which work to reinforce this approach to research. As long as the academic setting is one where the patterns of reinforcement are contingent upon the number of articles published by an investigator, rather than the relevance and quality of his investigations; as long as the educational researcher is encouraged to operate as an individual entrepreneur, rather than as part of a research team; as long as the overwhelming proportion of studies conducted in education are one-shot doctoral dissertations designed to collect the most data in the shortest time, educational researchers will continue to produce research which is of little value to developing educational theory. What is needed is more than a change in the way in which the next generation of researchers is trained. A revolution is needed both in the structure of the research enterprise and in the kinds of criteria utilized by administrators who judge the quality of academic performance and parcel out the subsequent monetary and status rewards.

Tukey (1969) made the observation that research in psychology continues to operate as if the individual Ph.D. thesis served as the prototype for scholarly efforts in the field. Education suffers from the same malady. Tukey commented, "Other sciences have faced the transition from the Ph.D. thesis that stood on its own feet to the Ph.D. thesis that is part of a bigger entity. No Ph.D. builds his own cyclotron as part of his thesis. No Ph.D. orbits his own satellite to get his data" (Tukey, 1969, p. 88). He recommended increased cooperative efforts in psychological research, with Ph.D. theses planned as part of broader general programs of research engaged in collectively by their thesis supervisors.

Education must echo Tukey's call for reorganization of the structure of the educational research enterprise, leaving behind the model of the individual entrepreneur and replacing it with the coordinated, institutionally supported research team. (Are we now to hear cries against "socialized educational research"?) My experience with several R & D Centers suggests that too often these ostensibly team operations are merely fiscal umbrellas facilitating the same kinds of individual and independent investigation conducted unprofitably for years. Perhaps it should be no surprise that the research "rockets" launched individually so often abort.

Summing Up

Has educational research been tried? Has it failed? Surely a kind of educational research has been attempted without notable success. But from its often clumsy gropings (or its ever-so-precise figure eights, carefully retracing well-worn patterns) have emerged general strategies and approaches that could show promise for the future.

Educators need not feel uniquely culpable because of the necessity to make dramatic shifts in their most basic tactics of investigation. Even the hitherto impregnable fortress of experimental psychology is currently being shaken by that most devastating of saboteurs—the critic from within. Such eminent experimentalists as James Jenkins (1968) and James Deese (1969) are challenging not only the usefulness of classical S-R behavior theory, but the very behavioral emphasis of psychology itself and the future fruitfulness to psychology of the traditional methods of experimentation. That both Deese and Jenkins were nominated in 1969 for the presidency of the Division of Experimental Psychology of the American Psychological Association makes the situation doubly ironic. In all of the behavioral sciences, well-worn paradigms are being called into question as accomplishment falls far short of promise (Cattell, 1966a). Educational researchers are simply sharing in the long overdue discomfort of their parent and sister disciplines.

The solutions to these difficulties will not arise from a mere reshuffling of the "in" research designs. The approaches employed for training the next generation of educational researchers must change radically. Even more important, the structure of the educational research establishment must be significantly modified to create the necessary conditions for research in education.

REFERENCES

Atkinson, R. C. Computerized instruction and the learning process. *American Psychologist,* 1968, 23, 225–239.

Baker, F. B. Experimental design considerations associated with large-scale research projects. In J. C. Stanley (Ed.), *Improving experimental design and statistical analysis.* Chicago: Rand McNally, 1967.

Barker, R. L. *Ecological psychology.* Stanford, Calif.: Stanford University Press, 1968.

Barton, A. H. The concept of property-space in social research. In P. F. Lazarsfeld & M. Rosenberg (Eds.), *The language of social research.* New York: Free Press, 1955.

Bettelheim, B. *The informed heart.* Glencoe, Ill.: Free Press, 1960.

Bettelheim, B. *The empty fortress.* New York: Free Press, 1967.

Bloom, B. S. *Stability and change in human characteristics.* New York: John Wiley, 1964.

Boocock, S. S., & Schild, E. O. (Eds.). *Simulation games in learning.* Beverly Hills, Calif.: Sage Publications, 1968.

Bracht, G. H., & Glass, G. V. The external validity of experiments. *American Educational Research Journal,* 1968, 5, 437–474.

Brickell, H. M. Appraising the effects of innovations in local schools. In R. W. Tyler (Ed.), *Educational evaluation: New roles, new means.* Sixty-eighth Yearbook, National Society for the Study of Education. Chicago: University of Chicago Press, 1969.

Brunswick, E. *Perception and the representative design of psychological experiments.* Berkeley, Calif.: University of California Press, 1956.

Campbell, D. T. From description to experimentation: Interpreting trends as quasi-experiments. In C. W. Harris (Ed.), *Problems in measuring change.* Madison, Wis.: University of Wisconsin Press, 1963.

Campbell, D. T. Administrative experimentation, institutional records, and nonreactive measures. In J. C. Stanley (Ed.), *Improving experimental design and statistical analysis.* Chicago: Rand McNally, 1967.

Campbell, D. T. Reforms as experiments. *American Psychologist,* 1969, 24, 409–429.

Campbell, D. T., & Stanley, J. C. Experimental and quasi-experimental designs for research on teaching. In N. L. Gage (Ed.), *Handbook of research on teaching.* Chicago: Rand McNally, 1963.

Campbell, D. T., Ross, H. L., & Glass, G. V. British crackdown on drinking and driving: A successful legal reform. *American Behavioral Scientist,* in press.

Carroll, J. B. School learning over the long haul. In J. D. Krumboltz (Ed.), *Learning and the educational process.* Chicago: Rand McNally, 1965.

Cartwright, D. S. Ecological variables. In E. F. Borgatta & G. W. Bohrnstedt (Eds.), *Sociological methodology 1969.* San Francisco: Jossey-Bass, 1968.

Cattell, R. B. (Ed.). *Handbook of multivariate experimental psychology.* Chicago: Rand McNally, 1966a.

Cattell, R. B. Psychological theory and scientific method. In R. B. Cattell (Ed.), *Handbook of multivariate experimental psychology.* Chicago: Rand McNally, 1966b.

Chomsky, N. *Aspects of a theory of syntax.* Cambridge, Mass.: MIT Press, 1965.

Cooley, W. W., & Glaser, R. The computer and individualized instruction. *Science,* 1969, 166, 574–582.

Cronbach, L. J. The two disciplines of scientific psychology. *American Psychologist,* 1957, 21, 11.

Cronbach, L. J. The logic of experiments on discovery. In L. S. Shulman & E. R. Keislar (Eds.), *Learning by discovery: A critical appraisal.* Chicago: Rand McNally, 1966.

Cronbach, L. J. How can instruction be adapted to individual differences? In R. M. Gagné (Ed.), *Learning and individual differences.* Columbus, Ohio: Charles E. Merrill, 1967.

Cronbach, L. J. Intelligence? Creativity? A parsimonious reinterpretation of the Wallach-Kogan data. *American Educational Research Journal,* 1968, 5, 491–512.

Cronbach, L. J. Heredity, environment, and educational policy. *Harvard Educational Review,* 1969, 39, 338–347.

Cronbach, L. J., & Snow, R. E. *Individual differences in learning ability as a function of instructional variables.* U.S. Department of Health, Education and Welfare, Office of Education, Contract No. OEC 4–6–061269–1217. Stanford, Calif.: Stanford University, March 1969.

Cronbach, L. J., & Suppes, P. (Eds.). *Research for tomorrow's schools: Disciplined inquiry for education.* London: Macmillan, 1969.

Dave, R. H. *The identification and measurement of environmental process variables that are related to educational achievement.* Unpublished doctoral dissertation, University of Chicago, 1963.

Deese, J. Behavior and fact. *American Psychologist,* 1969, 24, 515–522.

DeGroot, A. D. *Thought and choice in chess.* The Hague: Mouton, 1965.

DeGroot, A. D. Perception and memory versus thought: Some old ideas and recent findings. In B. Kleinmuntz (Ed.), *Problem solving: Research, method and theory.* New York: John Wiley, 1966.

Dewey, J. *Logic: The theory of inquiry.* New York: Henry Holt, 1938.

Eichenwald, H. F., & Fry, P. C. Nutrition and learning. *Science,* 1969, 163, 644–648.

Gibson, E. J. Perceptual learning in educational situations. In R. M. Gagné & W. J. Gephart (Eds.), *Learning research and school subjects.* Itasca, Ill.: F. E. Peacock, 1968.

Glueck, S., & Glueck, E. *Delinquents and non-delinquents in perspective.* Cambridge, Mass.: Harvard University Press, 1968.

Hebb, D. O. The mind's eye. *Psychology Today,* 1969, 2(12), 54–57, 67–68.

Henry, J. *Culture against man.* New York: Random House, 1963.

Hunt, E. B. *Concept learning, an information processing problem.* New York: John Wiley, 1962. (Ch. 2, analysis of the problem.)

Hunt, J. McV. Has compensatory educational failed? Has it been attempted? *Harvard Educational Review,* 1969, 39(2), 278–300.

Jakobson, R., & Halle, M. *Fundamentals of language.* The Hague: Mouton, 1956.

James, W. *The principles of psychology.* Vol. I. New York: Henry Holt, 1890.

Jenkins, J. J. The challenge to psychological theorists. In T. R. Dixon & D. L. Morton (Eds.), *Verbal behavior and general behavior theory.* Englewood Cliffs, N.J.: Prentice-Hall, 1968.

Jenkins, J. Language and thought. In J. Voss (Ed.), *Approaches to thought.* Columbus, Ohio: Merrill, 1969.

Jensen, A. R. How much can we boost IQ and scholastic achievement? *Harvard Educational Review,* 1969, 39, 1–23.

Karp, J. M., & Sigel, I. Psychoeducational appraisal of disadvantaged children. *Review of Educational Research,* 1965, 35, 401–412.

Keislar, E. R., & Shulman, L. S. The problem of discovery: Conference in retrospect. In L. S. Shulman & E. R. Keislar (Eds.), *Learning by discovery: A critical appraisal.* Chicago: Rand McNally, 1966.

Kendrick, S. A., & Thomas, C. L. Transition from school to college. *Review of Educational Research,* 1970, 40, 151–179.

Kilpatrick, J., & Wirszup, I. *The learning of mathematical concepts: Soviet studies in the psychology of learning and teaching mathematics.* Chicago: University of Chicago Press, 1969.

Kleinmuntz, B. The processing of clinical information by man and machine. In B. Kleinmuntz (Ed.), *Formal representation of human judgment.* New York: John Wiley, 1968.

Kuhn, T. S. *The structure of scientific revolutions.* Chicago: University of Chicago, 1962.

Land, K. C. Principles of pathanalysis. In E. F. Borgatta & G. W. Bohrnstedt (Eds.), *Sociological methodology 1969.* San Francisco: Jossey-Bass, 1968.

Lenneberg, E. H. *Biological foundations of language.* New York: John Wiley, 1967.

Light, R. J., & Smith, P. V. Social allocation models of intelligence: A methodological inquiry. *Harvard Educational Review,* 1969, 39, 484–510.

McNeil, W. *Rise of the west.* Chicago: University of Chicago Press, 1963.

Melton, A. W. Implications of short-term memory for a general theory of memory. *Journal of Verbal Learning and Verbal Behavior,* 1963, 2, 1–21.

Menchinskaya, N. A. Fifty years of Soviet instructional psychology. In J. Kilpatrick & I. Wirszup (Eds.), *The learning of mathematical concepts: Soviet studies in the psychology of learning and teaching mathematics.* Vol. 1. Chicago: University of Chicago Press, 1969.

Mitchell, J. V. Education's challenge to psychology: The prediction of behavior from person-environment interactions. *Review of Educational Research,* 1969, 39, 695–722.

Morgan, C. L. *Psychology for teachers.* London: Edward Arnold, 1894.

Murray, H. A. *Explorations in personality.* New York: Oxford University Press, 1938.

Newell, A., Shaw, J. C., & Simon, H. A. Elements of a theory of human problem solving. *Psychological Review,* 1958, 65, 151–166.

Pace, C. R., & Stern, G. G. An approach to the measurement of psychological characteristics of college environments. *Journal of Educational Psychology,* 1958, 49, 269–277.

Provus, M. Evaluation of ongoing programs in the public school system. In R. W. Tyler (Ed.), *Educational evaluation: New roles, new means.* Sixty-eighth Yearbook, National Society for the Study of Education. Chicago: University of Chicago Press, 1969.

Roberts, J.A.F. The genetics of mental deficiency. *Eugenics Review,* 1952, 44, 71–83.

Rogers, F. (Ed.). *Studies in epidemiology: Selected papers of Morris Greenberg, M.D.* New York: C. P. Putnam's Sons, 1965.

Sartwell, P. In K. F. Maxey & M. Rosenau (Eds.), *Preventive medicine and public health* (9th ed.). New York: Appleton-Century-Crofts, 1965.

Schwab, J. J. What do scientists do? *Behavioral Science,* 1960, 5, 1–27.

Schwab, J. J. Curriculum and the practical. *School Review,* in press.

Shulman, L. S. Negro-white differences in employability, self-concept, and related measures among adolescents classified as mentally handicapped. *Journal of Negro Education,* 1968a, 37, 227–240.

Shulman, L. S. Inquiry, computers and medical education. *Proceedings of the conference on the use of computers in medical education.* Oklahoma City, Okla.: University of Oklahoma Medical Center, 1968b, 48–52.

Shulman, L. S., Loupe, M. J., & Piper, R. M. *Studies of the inquiry process.* Department of Health, Education and Welfare, Office of Education, Project No. 5–0597. East Lansing, Mich.: Michigan State University, July 1968.

Stanley, J. C., & Porter, A. C. Correlation of scholastic aptitude test score with college grades for negroes versus whites. *Journal of Educational Measurement,* 1967, 4, 199–218.

Stephens, J. M. *The process of schooling, a psychological examination.* New York: Holt, Rinehart and Winston, 1967.

Thoresen, C. E. Relevance and research in counseling. *Review of Educational Research,* 1969, 39, 263–281.

Tukey, J. W. Analyzing data: Sanctification or detective work? *American Psychologist,* 1969, 24, 83–91.

Twelker, P. A. (Ed.). *Instructional simulation systems: An annotated bibliography.* Corvallis, Ore.: Continuing Education Publications, Oregon State University, 1969.

Watson, J. B. Psychology as the behaviorist views it. *Psychological Review,* 1913, 20, 158–177.

Wiggins, J. A. Hypothesis validity and experimental laboratory methods. In H. M. Blalock, Jr. & A. B. Blalock (Eds.), *Methodology in social research*. New York: McGraw-Hill, 1968.

Wolf, R. W. *The identification and measurement of environmental process variables related to intelligence*. Unpublished doctoral dissertation, University of Chicago, 1964.

Yee, A. H., & Gage, N. L. Techniques for estimating the source and direction of causal influence in panel data. *Psychological Bulletin*, 1968, 70, 115–126.

ACKNOWLEDGMENTS

Dr. Joe L. Byers and Dr. Andrew C. Porter, Michigan State University, are to be thanked for their comments on an early draft of this paper. Mr. Stevan Bauman assisted in collecting the bibliographic materials.

INTRODUCTION

PSYCHOLOGY AND MATHEMATICS EDUCATION (1970)

IN 1965, Shulman was invited to serve as rapporteur for the Social Science Research Council's invitational conference on the learning-by-discovery controversy. His job was to observe and to take notes. The conference was small and filled with the giants of the field—Jerome Bruner, Lee Cronbach, David Hawkins, Robert Gagné, Robert Glaser, and others of that eminence. At the end of the conference, Evan Keislar of UCLA, who had chaired the meeting, invited Shulman to serve as coeditor. The book, based on the conference, was popular and gave Shulman quite a bit of visibility.

Focusing on the psychology of learning and instruction, the volume dealt especially with the relationship between the type and amount of guidance a teacher provides and how well students learn. Bruner epitomized less-guided, discovery approaches; Gagné was associated with the more guided approaches. After editing the book and co-authoring the summarizing essay, Shulman was invited to give a talk at the American Association for the Advancement of Science on the topic, and the talk later became an article on conceptions of learning in *Science Teacher.* Ed Begle of Stanford, one of the leaders with New Math, read the *Science Teacher* essay and commissioned Shulman to write the opening essay in the National Society for the Study of Education (NSSE) Yearbook on mathematics education, intended to deal with the psychology of mathematics education. Since so much of educational psychology had been conducted using mathematics learning as its focus (ever since Thorndike), Shulman began the essay with a reference to the two fields—psychology and mathematics education—having been strange yet persistent bedfellows for many years.

One thing led to another. When Robert Travers, editor of the *Handbook for Research on Teaching* (second edition), read the NSSE chapter, he immediately asked Shulman to write a chapter on the topic of research on teaching in the natural sciences. When Shulman protested that he did not know anything about the field, Travers observed that this had not hampered Shulman's mathematics education chapter and suggested that Shulman find a co-author. On his way to a sabbatical in Israel, Shulman found Israel's one researcher on science education, Pinchas Tamir, with whom he later wrote that chapter (not included in this volume).

In this essay, Shulman explores the relevance of some contemporary theoretical issues in psychology for mathematics education. He grounds the analysis in an example borrowed from Jerome Bruner that concerns the representation of quadratic equations and illustrates the "discovery method" (then popular among educational psychologists). Shulman then explores the contemporary antitheses of this method, by examining the work of David Ausubel and Robert M. Gagné. While Gagné was a behaviorist, Ausubel was a cognitivist who advocated highly structured instruction using advance organizers. He was thus a fascinating hybrid of Bruner's cognitivism and Gagné's direct instruction. Shulman goes on to assert that the learning-by-discovery controversy is a mixture of many issues that, while bound together indiscriminately, deserve to be considered separately. One such issue concerns our educational objectives, for, as it turns out, different learning theorists have different ideas about what we want children to learn. We differ also in our assumptions about the entering characteristics of students, both in terms of their readiness to learn and their aptitudes. A third matter on which theorists differ concerned their instructional tactics and assumptions about the appropriate sequence of instruction. Underlying these significant differences, however, is a deeper epistemological one, Shulman notes, for learning theorists differ dramatically in their assumptions about the manner in which anything becomes known. Shulman concludes the piece by proposing a process by which teachers can navigate through this confusing set of controversies and shape a pedagogy of mathematics education that is responsible and effective.

2

PSYCHOLOGY AND MATHEMATICS EDUCATION

PSYCHOLOGY AND MATHEMATICS EDUCATION are neither strange nor merely transient bedfellows. Their affair has a long and occasionally torrid past, during which mathematics instruction has been quite sensitive to shifts in psychological theories. However, much like the advice given to new mothers in successive editions of Doctor Spock, the psychological "word" has frequently changed each decade. For this reason, earlier yearbook chapters paralleling this one, by Knight,[1] Wheeler,[2] McConnell,[3] and Buswell,[4] can almost be read as a history of controversies, cease-fires, and temporary truces among educational learning theorists over the last forty years. It would surely be an error to suggest that innovations in mathematics education have been caused wholly by developments in psychology. On many occasions the two disciplines may have responded commonly to a more general change in the *Zeitgeist* of education and the sciences. Most often, mathematics educators have shown themselves especially adept at taking hold of conveniently available psychological theories to buttress previously held instructional proclivities.

The curriculum revolution which laymen and professionals alike have called the "new math" has been supported by a "new psychology." What are the characteristics of this ostensibly new approach to the psychological analysis of the educational process? Just as the mathematician recognizes that, in point of age, there is nothing particularly new about the new mathematics, the psychologist must observe that many aspects of the "new psychology" are practically candidates for "intellectual medicare."

Scott[5] has attempted to state the basic principles of this new psychology in the following series of ten statements.

1. The structure of mathematics should be stressed at all levels. Topics and relationships of endurance should be given concentrated attention.
2. Children are capable of learning more abstract and more complex concepts when the relationship between concepts is stressed.
3. Existing elementary arithmetic programs may be severely condensed because children are capable of learning concepts at much earlier ages than formerly thought.
4. Any concept may be taught a child of any age in some intellectually honest manner, if one is able to find the proper language for expressing the concept.
5. The inductive approach or the discovery method is logically productive and should enhance learning and retention.
6. The major objective of a program is the development of independent and creative thinking processes.
7. Human learning seems to pass through the stages of preoperations, concrete operations, and formal operations.
8. Growth of understanding is dependent upon concept exploration through challenging apparatus and concrete materials and cannot be restricted to mere symbolic manipulations.
9. Teaching mathematical skills is regarded as a tidying-up of concepts developed through discovery rather than as a step-by-step process for memorization.
10. Practical application of isolated concepts or systems of concepts, particularly those applications drawn from the natural sciences, are valuable to reinforcement and retention.[6]

It must be recognized that the theoretical and empirical foundations for many of these assertions reach back to the truly excellent work of an earlier generation of investigators in the psychology of mathematics learning. Such outstanding contributors as Brownell[7] anticipated many current developments both in the studies they conducted and in the pedagogical techniques they advocated.

The extent to which Scott's ten principles accurately reflect the general psychological foundation of many of the new approaches to mathematics instruction bespeaks the pervasive influence of a small book, *The Process of Education,*[8] and its author, Jerome S. Bruner. No single work embodied the letter and spirit of that psychology which undergirds the new curricula as did Bruner's short distillation of the deliberations of a conference of scientists and educators. Each of Scott's ten points can be found highlighted in the barely one hundred pages of that volume. Although we have come to associate with Bruner such ideas as *discovery, structure, early readiness,* and *intuitive thinking,* his writings did not initially stimulate those early renovative efforts in mathematics education. Yet, at the end of the 1950s, he managed to capture their spirit, provide them with a framework of cognitive theory, and stimulate the development of their late forms and eventual successors.

The phrase around which much of the new psychology of learning developed was "learning by discovery." It was far from a new idea.[9] Bruner's version of learning by discovery involved a theoretical mélange of Piaget and Plato—an environmentally dynamic version of contemporary developmental theory in conjunction with a twentieth-century form of classical rationalism.

Our discussion of the psychological issues surrounding the teaching of mathematics will begin as do so many of the new curricula—concretely. We shall begin our examination of these issues by citing in some detail an example of what Bruner considers learning by discovery. We will then analyze that example in order to relate it to the principles stated by Scott as well as to derive any further insights or clarifications. After characterizing what is meant by discovery learning, we will examine two additional theories which will serve as useful counterpoints to the discovery approach.

We will then attempt to disentangle the many complexities of this instructional question from the vantage point of the educational psychologist. We will use that analysis as a jumping-off point for a systematic analysis of a number of critical contemporary issues in the psychology of education.

This chapter will *not* attempt a comprehensive review of literature in the psychology of mathematics learning. It will instead examine some of the current theoretical issues in psychology that have relevance to education in mathematics, citing empirical literature only for illustrative purposes.

An Example of Discovery Learning

In a number of his papers, Bruner uses an instructional example from mathematics that derives from his collaboration with the mathematics educator, Z. P. Dienes.[10]

The class is composed of eight-year-old children who are to learn some mathematics. As one of the instructional units, children are first introduced to three kinds of flat pieces of wood or "flats." The first one, they are told, is to be called either the "unknown square" or "x square." The second flat, which is rectangular, is called "1 x" or just x, since it is x long on one side and 1 long on the other. The third flat is a small square which is 1 by 1, and is called 1.

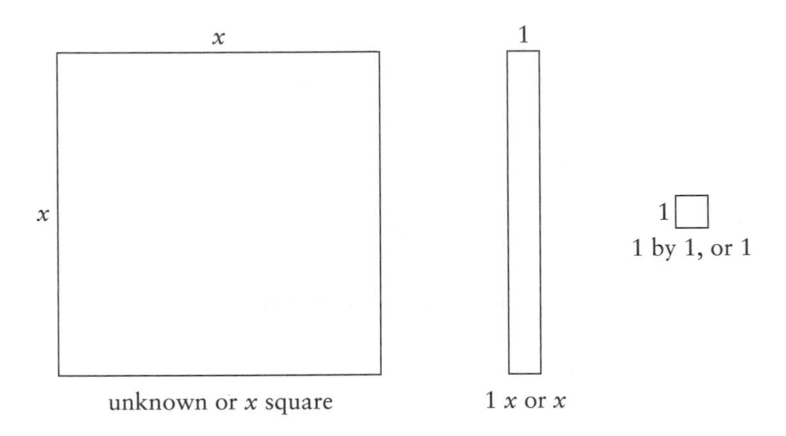

After allowing the children many opportunities simply to play with these materials, to do things with them, and to get a feel for them, he presents them with a problem. The problem is "Can you make larger squares than this x square by using as many of these flats as you want?" This is not a difficult task for most children, and they readily make another square such as the one illustrated below.

Bruner then asks them if they can describe what they have done. They might reply, "We have one $x^{\square}$, with two x's and a 1." He then asks them to keep a record of what they have done. He may even suggest a notational system to use. The symbol $x^{\square}$ can represent the square x, and a + for "and." Thus, the pieces used can be described as $x^{\square} + 2x + 1$.

Another way to describe their new square, he points out, is simply to describe each side. With an x and a 1 on each side, the side can be described as $x + 1$ and the square as $(x + 1)(x + 1)$ after some work with parentheses. Since these are two basic ways of describing the same square, they can be written in this way: $x^{\square} + 2x + 1 = (x + 1)(x + 1)$. This description, of course, far oversimplifies the procedures used.

The children continue making squares and generating the notation for them.

Bruner hypothesizes that at some point they will begin to discern a pattern. While the x's are progressing at the rate of 2, 4, 6, 8, the ones are going 1, 4, 9, 16; on the right side of the equation, the pattern is 1, 2, 3, 4. Provocative or leading questions are often used Socratically to elicit this discovery. Even if they are initially unable to break the code, Bruner maintains, they will sense that there is a pattern and try to discover it. Bruner then illustrates how the pupils transfer what they have learned to working with a balance beam. The youngsters are ostensibly learning not only something about quadratic equations but, more important, something about the discovery of mathematical regularities (see figure on page 54).

The general learning process described by Bruner occurs in the following manner. First, the child finds in his manipulation of the materials regularities that correspond with intuitive regularities he has already come to understand. Notice that what the child does for Bruner is to find some sort of match between what he is doing in the outside world and some models or templates that he has already grasped intellectually. For Bruner, it is rarely something *outside* the learner that is discovered. Instead, the discovery involves an internal reorganization of previously known ideas in order to establish a better fit between those ideas and the regularities of an encounter to which the learner has had to accommodate.

This is precisely the philosophy of education we associate with Socrates. Remember the lovely dialogue of the *Meno* by Plato, in which the young slave boy is brought to an understanding of what is involved in doubling the area of a square. Socrates maintains throughout this dialogue that he is not teaching the boy anything new; he is simply helping the boy reorganize and bring to the fore what he has always known.

Bruner almost always begins with a focus on the production and manipulation of materials. He describes the child as moving through three levels of representation as he learns.[11] The first level is the *enactive level*, where the child manipulates materials directly. He then progresses to the *ikonic level*, where he deals with mental images of objects but does not manipulate them directly. Finally he moves to the *symbolic level*, where

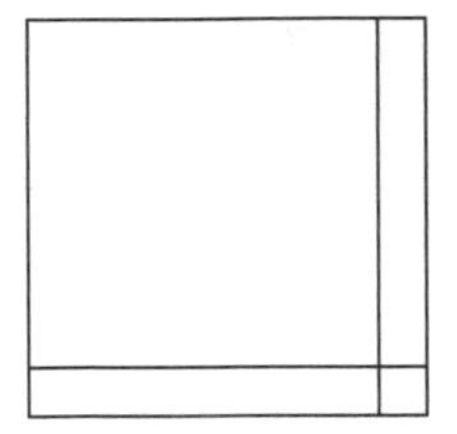

$x^{\square} + 2x + 1 = (x + 1)\ (x + 1)$

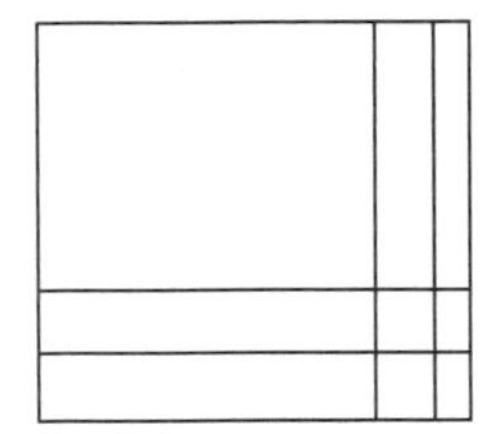

$x^{\square} + 4x + 4 = (x + 2)\ (x + 2)$

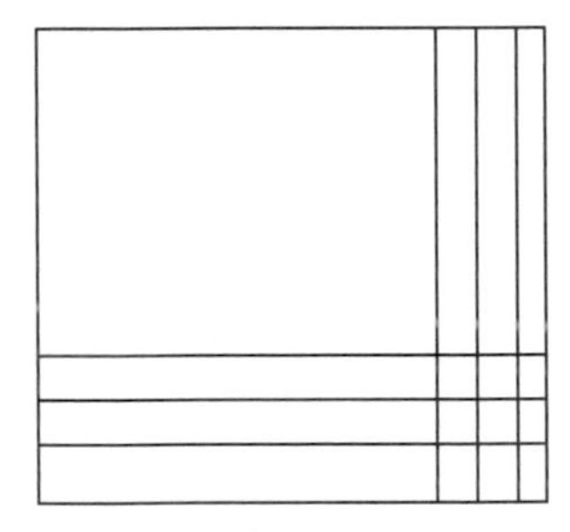

$x^{\square} + 6x + 9 = (x + 3)\ (x + 3)$

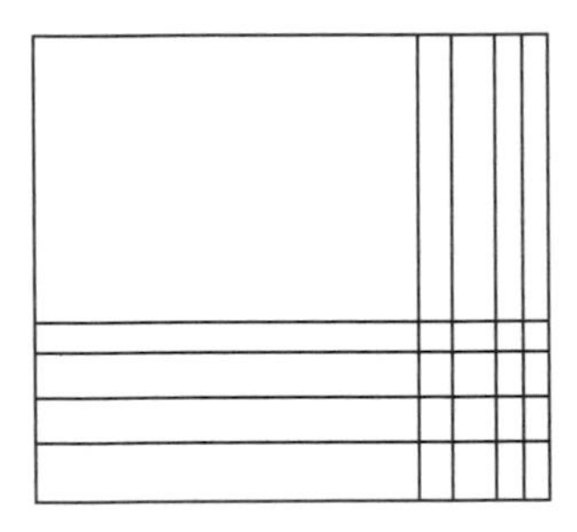

$x^{\square} + 8x + 16 = (x + 4)\ (x + 4)$

he is strictly manipulating symbols and no longer mental images of objects. This sequence is based on Bruner's interpretation of the developmental theory of Jean Piaget. The combination of these concepts of manipulation of actual materials as part of a developmental model and the Socratic notion of learning as internal reorganization into a learning-by-discovery approach is the unique contribution of Bruner.

The Process of Education was written in 1959, after most mathematics innovations that use discovery as a core had already begun. It is an error to say that Bruner initiated the learning-by-discovery approach. It is far more accurate to say that, more than any one man, he managed to capture its spirit, provide it with a theoretical foundation, and disseminate it. Bruner is not the discoverer of discovery; he is its prophet.

Counterpoints to Discovery

As Hegel recognized nearly two centuries ago, there is a dialectical quality to history. Every successfully advanced thesis seems to generate its own antithesis. In the present instance, the success of the discovery position (as expounded by Bruner and as reflected in a multitude of curricular innovations in mathematics, the sciences, and the social studies) inevitably resulted in the calling forth of antagonistic positions. These positions were by no means created solely to oppose learning by discovery. Since the days of William James, psychology has always harbored opposing camps on the battleground of learning theory.[12] The respective banners might read "behaviorists and mentalists," "connectionists and gestalt psychologists," "neobehaviorists and cognitive psychologists"—the fundamental epistemological stances which stand opposed to each other have been only moderately changed from the early confrontation of Hume and Kant or, for that matter, from that of Plato and Aristotle. We shall examine these epistemological assumptions in detail at a later point in this chapter.

Although it is often B. F. Skinner who is identified as Bruner's primary antagonist, for purposes of the present chapter the work of two other learning theorists, Robert M. Gagné and David Ausubel, each of whom has taken a position in marked opposition to Bruner, will be examined. Each of these men is an advocate of approaches to instruction that may be interpreted as the antithesis of discovery. Such an approach may be called "guided learning," "expository learning," or "reception learning." Each has written at least one major volume elucidating his position.[13] They are by no means wholly in agreement with each other on all matters. Both, however, represent a theoretical position which raises serious questions concerning the fruitfulness of encouraging students to discover answers for themselves as a major vehicle for general instruction. We shall first examine the work of Gagné.

Instructional Example: Guided Learning

Gagné begins with a task analysis of the instructional objectives. He always asks the question, "What is it you want the learner to be able to do?" This *capability,* he insists, must be stated *specifically* and *behaviorally.*

By "capability," he means the ability to perform certain specific functions under specified conditions. A capability could be the ability to solve a number series. It might be the ability to solve some problems in nonmetric geometry.

This capability can be conceived of as a terminal behavior and placed at the top of what will eventually be a complex pyramid. After analyzing the task, Gagné asks, "What would you need to know in order to do that?" Let us say that one could not complete the task unless he could first perform prerequisite tasks *a* and *b.* So a pyramid begins.

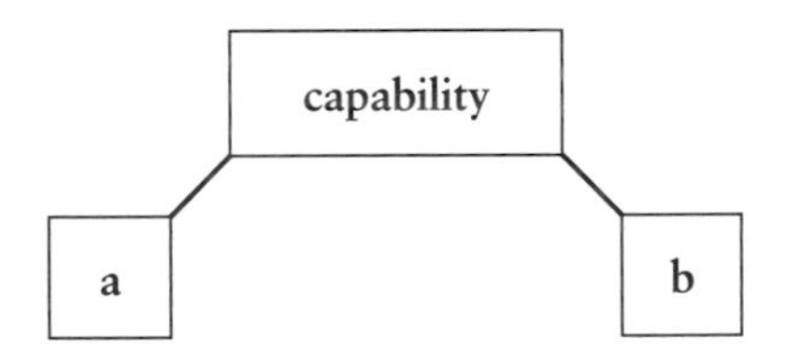

But in order to perform task *a,* one must be able to perform tasks *c* and *d* and for task *b,* one must know *e, f,* and *g.*

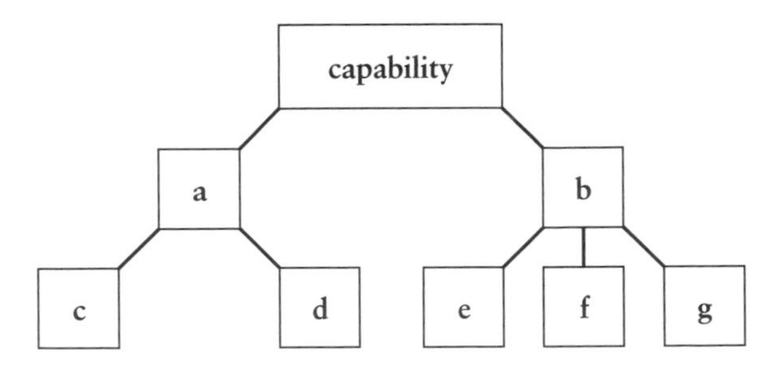

So one builds a very complex pyramid of prerequisites to prerequisites to the objective which is the desired capability.

Gagné has developed a model for discussing the different levels of such a hierarchy. If the final capability desired is a *problem-solving* capability, the learner first must know certain *principles.* But to understand those principles, he must know specific *concepts.* But prerequisite to these are particular *simple associations* or *facts* discriminated from each other in a distinctive manner. He continues the analysis until he ends up with the fundamental building blocks of learning—classically or operantly conditioned responses.

Gagné, upon completing the whole map of prerequisites, administers pretests to determine which have already been mastered. The pattern of responses to these diagnostic tests identifies precisely what must be taught. This model is particularly conducive to subsequent programming of material and programmed instruction. When prerequisites are established, a very tight teaching program or package can develop. Figure 1 illustrates such a task hierarchy for the terminal objectives identified by the boxes labeled Task 1 and Task 2.[14]

The work of Ausubel also stands in dramatic counterpoint to the body of theory and research which advocates discovery over exposition in teaching. Ausubel has long argued against the "mystique" of discovery. He argues that much of the apparent superiority of discovery approaches in empirical studies derives from the use of a straw man, *rote learning,* as the basis for comparison. The opposite of discovery learning need not be rote learning, insists Ausubel. It ought to be *meaningful verbal learning.*

Ausubel, like Gagné, emphasizes the great importance of systematically guided exposition in the process of education. The key is the careful sequencing of instructional experiences so that any unit taught is clearly related to those that precede it. It is this continuity between the learner's existing cognitive structure and the new material to be learned that makes the new material meaningful. There is certainly no basis for asserting that anything learned through reception has been learned rotely.

Ausubel discusses this problem of the confounding of discovery and meaningfulness in the following manner.

> In reception learning (rote or meaningful) the entire content of what is to be learned is presented to the learner in final form. The learning task does not involve any independent discovery on his part. He is required only to internalize or incorporate the material . . . that is presented to him so that it is available or reproducible at some future date. In the case of meaningful reception learning, the potentially meaningful task

Figure 1. A Task Hierarchy for Objectives of Assigned Tasks.

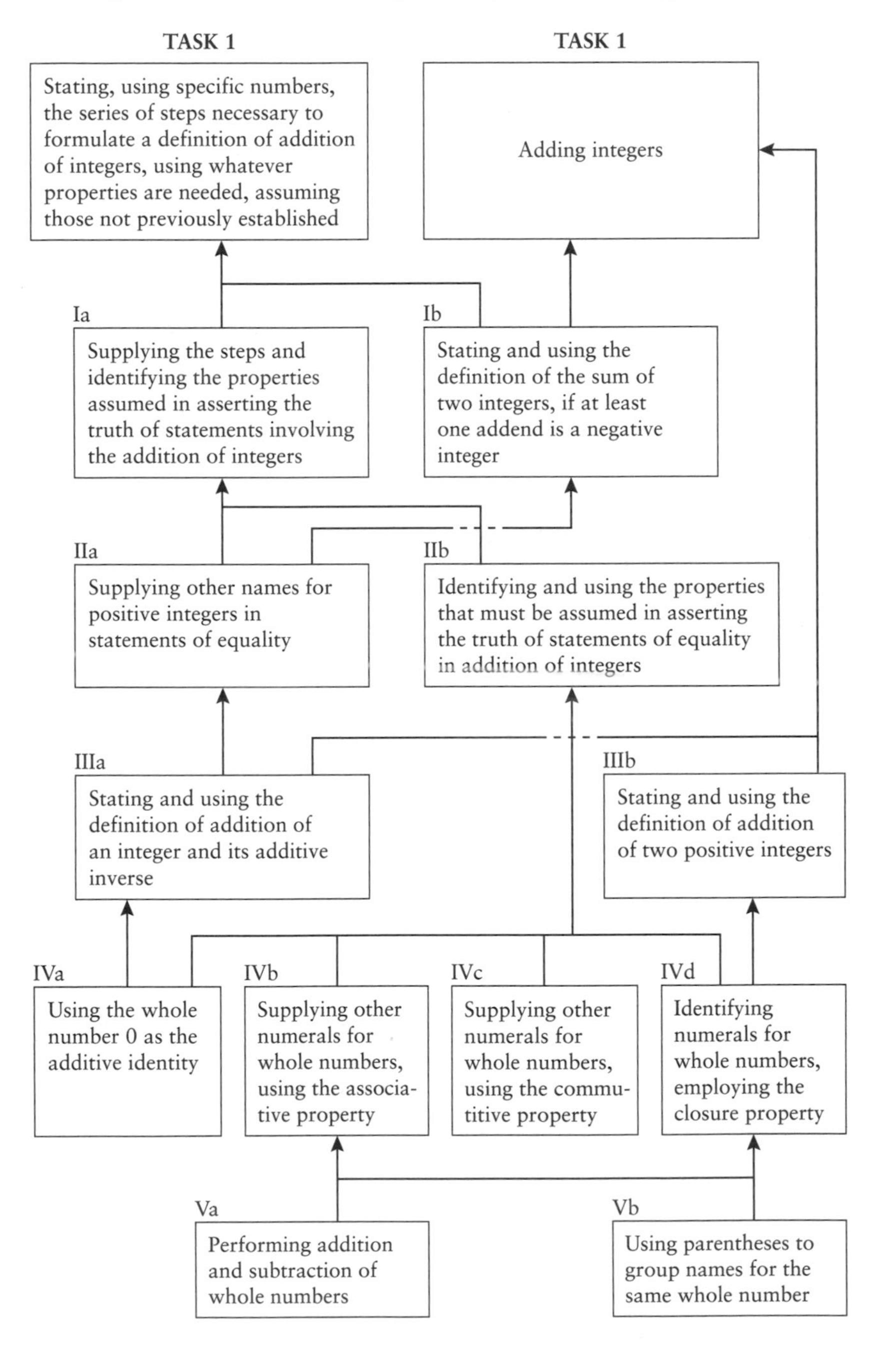

From Robert M. Gagné, "Learning Hierarchies," Educational Psychologist, *VI (November, 1968), 1.*

> or material is comprehended or made meaningful in the process of internalization. In the case of rote reception learning, the learning task either is not potentially meaningful or is not made meaningful in the process of internalization.
>
> The essential feature of discovery learning . . . is that the principal content of what is to be learned is not given but must be discovered by the learner *before* he can incorporate it meaningfully into his cognitive structure. The distinctive and *prior* learning task, in other words, is to discover something. . . . The first phase of discovery learning involves a process quite different from that of reception learning. The learner must rearrange information, integrate it with existing cognitive structure, and reorganize or transform the integrated combination in such a way as to generate a desired end-product or discover a missing means-end relationship. *After* discovery learning itself is completed, the discovered content is made meaningful in much the same way that presented content is made meaningful in reception learning.
>
> It is evident, therefore, that reception and discovery learning are two quite different kinds of processes, and . . . that most classroom instruction is organized along the lines of reception learning. In the next section it will be pointed out that verbal reception learning is not necessarily rote in character, that much ideational material (concepts, generalizations) can be internalized and retained meaningfully without prior problem-solving experience, and that at no stage of development does the learner have to discover principles independently in order to be able to understand and use them meaningfully.[15]

In contrast to Bruner, Ausubel sees no reason why problem-solving activity must precede the internalization of new facts, concepts, or principles. If the material can be meaningfully organized by the instructor, the need for student discovery is removed and the process of learning rendered far more efficient.

Although often approached simplistically, the learning-by-discovery controversy is in fact a vast psychoeducational collage—a heterogeneous mixture of many issues bound together indiscriminately. In the following pages, we shall attempt to disentangle the separate issues and discuss them individually. We will then return to instructional problems and attempt to assess these in the light of our discussion.

Any discussion of a psychology of instruction must deal with the three basic components of that process: (*a*) the entering characteristics of the students, (*b*) the teaching-learning activities and processes, and (*c*) the instructional objectives. We shall discuss each of these in turn, beginning with the ends of education—the objectives of instruction.

Objectives

What are the ends of education? What objectives should we seek? Although such questions may appear, at first blush, better suited to a discussion of philosophy than of psychology, they in fact form the very crux of the issues being examined.

For Bruner, the emphasis is upon the kinds of *processes* learned by the student, in contrast to the specific subject-matter *products* he may acquire. One paragraph from *Toward a Theory of Instruction*[16] communicates the essence of educational objectives for Bruner. After discussing the mathematics example previously mentioned, he concludes:

> Finally a theory of instruction seeks to take account of the fact that a curriculum reflects not only the nature of knowledge itself [the specific capabilities] but also the nature of the knower and of the knowledge-getting process. It is the enterprise *par excellence* where the line between the subject matter and the method grows necessarily indistinct. A body of knowledge, enshrined in a university faculty and embodied in a series of authoritative volumes, is the *result* of much prior intellectual activity. To instruct someone in these disciplines is not a matter of getting him to commit results to mind. Rather, it is to teach him to participate in the process that makes possible the establishment of knowledge. We teach a subject not to produce little living libraries on that subject, but rather to get a student to think mathematically for himself, to consider matters as a historian does, *to take part in the process of knowledge-getting. Knowing is a process, not a product.* [italics mine][17]

Gagné has come out in substantial agreement with Bruner on the priority of processes over products as the objectives of instruction. His emphasis, however, is not on teaching general strategies or heuristics of discovery; he is much more concerned with the teaching of the rules or intellectual skills that are relevant to particular instructional domains. The following paragraph could well be read as a clear, if gentle, demurrer to Bruner's approach to the issue of objectives.

> Obviously, strategies are important for problem-solving, regardless of the content of the problem. The suggestion from some writings is that they are of overriding importance as a goal of education. After all, should not formal instruction in the school have the aim of teaching the student "how to think"? If strategies were deliberately taught, would not this produce people who could then bring to bear superior problem-solving capabilities to any new situation? Although no one

would disagree with the aims expressed, it is exceedingly doubtful that they can be brought about solely by teaching students "strategies" or "styles" of thinking. Even if these can be taught (and it is likely that they can), they do not provide the individual with the basic firmament of thought, which is a set of externally-oriented intellectual skills. Strategies, after all, are rules which govern the individual's *approach* to listening, reading, storing information, retrieving information, or solving problems. If it is a mathematical problem the individual is engaged in solving, he may have acquired a strategy of applying relevant subordinate rules in a certain order—but he must also have available the mathematical rules themselves. If it is a problem in genetic inheritance, he may have learned a way of guessing at probabilities before actually working them out—but he must also bring to bear the substantive rules pertaining to dominant and recessive characteristics. Knowing strategies, then, is not all that is required for thinking; it is not even a substantial part of what is needed. *To be an effective problem-solver, the individual must somehow have acquired masses of organized intellectual skills.* [italics mine][18]

For Gagné, the objectives of instruction are intellectual skills or capabilities that can be specified in operational terms, can be task-analyzed, and then can be taught. Gagné would subscribe to the position that psychology has been successful in suggesting ways of teaching only when objectives have been made operationally clear. When objectives are not clearly stated, the psychologist can be of little assistance. Objectives clearly stated in behavioral terms are the cornerstones of Gagné's position.[19]

Ausubel strongly rejects the notion that any kind of process, be it strategy or skill, should hold priority among the objectives of education. He remains a militant advocate of the importance of mastering well-organized bodies of subject-matter knowledge as the most important goal of education.

. . . As far as the formal education of the individual is concerned, the educational agency largely transmits ready-made concepts, classifications, and propositions. In any case, discovery methods of teaching hardly constitute an efficient *primary* means of transmitting the *content* of an academic discipline.

It may be argued with much justification, of course, that the school is also concerned with developing the student's ability to use acquired knowledge in solving particular problems, that is, with his ability to think systematically, independently, and critically in various fields of inquiry. *But this function of the school, although constituting a legitimate*

> *objective of education in its own right, is less central than its related transmission-of-knowledge function* [italics mine] in terms of the amount of time that can be reasonably allotted to it, in terms of the objectives of education in a democratic society, and in terms of what can be reasonably expected from most students . . .[20]

We may thus observe that, while Gagné and Ausubel tend to agree that exposition is a more generally useful form of instruction than discovery, they disagree regarding the appropriate objectives of instruction. More generally, we may see that a theorist's preferred mode of instruction can be, and often is, independent of the objectives he holds most important. Decisions about objectives reflect more than the psychologist's preferred theory of learning. They also reflect his judgments concerning the nature of knowledge and the social utility of the different kinds of intellectual accomplishment.

Differences among competing theorists with respect to the objectives of education contribute to the difficulty of assessing the relative potencies of the theories they espouse. One can argue endlessly over the relative merits of a jeep and a Cadillac because the purposes to which each is put are generally so disparate; the criteria of success are thus different. One can also dispute over the respective qualities of the White Sox and the Bears, but no meaningful resolution is likely to emerge. Thus, though most learning theorists espouse the acquisition of knowledge as the major objective of education, their respective definitions of *knowledge* and *knowing* are often so incongruent that they scarcely overlap.

The psychological and philosophical bases for these differences will be discussed later in this chapter. For the moment, we may note that when conflicting approaches seek such contrasting objectives, the conduct of comparative educational experiments becomes extremely difficult. How can one investigate the conflicting claims of two points of view when each aims at distinctly different goals?

One solution that deserves attention is that of planning educational experiments with multiple criterion measures.[21] For example, evaluate the extent to which both processes and product objectives are reached through employment of a particular approach. One might further assess such additionally important outcomes as attitudes, motivation, and self-esteem. In this way we can generate a sufficiently broad range of criteria to compare meaningfully across instructional approaches which begin with radically disparate assumptions.

We may, at this point, pause to reflect on the analyses we have completed. Ausubel has made the important observation that the rote-meaningful and reception-discovery continua are not coextensive. They are logically independent.

For Ausubel, something has been learned meaningfully:

> . . . if the learning task can be related in nonarbitrary, substantive (nonverbatim) fashion to what the learner already knows, and if the learner adopts a corresponding learning set to do so. Rote learning, on the other hand, occurs if the learning task consists of purely arbitrary associations; . . . if the learner lacks the relevant prior knowledge necessary for making the learning task potentially meaningful; and also, . . . if the learner adopts a set merely to internalize it in an arbitrary, verbatim fashion (that is, as an arbitrary series of words).[22]

Thus, the reception-discovery dimension reflects what the learner is doing in the course of instruction—the cognitive processes in which he is engaged as he learns. The rote-meaningful dimension represents the degree to which what is learned articulates with the learner's prior knowledge and cognitive structure, with no reference to how he learns it.

Table 1 reflects the orthogonality of these two dimensions and provides examples of the kinds of activities that can be classified in each of the four cells.

Hence, all that is discovered is not meaningful; all that is received is not rote.

Our discussion of objectives has introduced yet another dimension into our analysis—the product-process distinction. In Table 2 we can observe that another typical plaint, that products are learned by rote while processes are mastered meaningfully, is also a *non sequitur.*

Table 1.

	Rote	**Meaningful**
Reception	Memorize multiplication tables	Learn to solve problems of adding number series
Discovery	Use trial-and-error procedures to calculate square roots	Work from a set of specific examples to induce a mathematical rule

Note: *Any of these examples could shift between the rote and meaningful categories as a function of how, when, and why they are taught.*

Table 2.

	Rote	Meaningful
Product	2 + 2 = 4	Multiplication tables
Process	"Invert and multiply"	Application of heuristics in estimation problems

Learning to parrot the words "two plus two equal four" would be an example of the student learning a rote product. The student who, when confronted with a problem of dividing one fraction by another, knows that he must "invert and multiply" but has not the faintest idea why, has mastered a process rotely. The student who has mastered his multiplication tables and understands the conceptual relationships among the various orders of multiplication has mastered a product or set of products meaningfully. Finally, the student who has learned to apply a heuristic or set of heuristics when confronted with the problem of estimating a particular solution in an arithmetic problem and who understands why the heuristic works has come to master a process meaningfully.

By the end of the 1960s, it appears that the rote-meaningful argument has been mercifully put to rest. In contrast to the 1920s and 1930s, general advocates of drill without understanding either have retired or are in hiding. This is not to imply that rote learning has ceased to occur in our classrooms. Far from it. It now occurs, however, through inadvertence rather than through careful planning.

We have now observed that a number of dimensions that are usually confounded in discussions of discovery learning can and must be distinguished. These include matters of student learning (reception-discovery), educational objectives (product-process), and instructional articulation with past learning (rote-meaningful). There are yet other aspects of the psychology of instruction that have become inextricably bound up in the polemics over discovery. We shall now turn to one of the most critical of these, the concept of readiness for learning.

Entering Characteristics

What does the student bring with him to the instructional situation? In what manner do the characteristics of the students at the inception of instruction affect the subsequent teaching-learning process? We shall examine this topic under two traditional educational headings: (a) readiness for learning, and (b) aptitude for learning.

Readiness

One indication of the rapidity of change in the psychological theories underlying mathematics instruction is reflected in the role assigned to Piaget.[23] Twenty years ago the work of this eminent Swiss psychologist received not a single mention in the yearbook on mathematics education.[24] Today it is literally impossible to discuss the psychology of instruction in mathematics without placing his contributions at center stage. His influence is not limited to the psychology of instruction. Many psychologists are seriously suggesting that his stature will eventually equal that of Freud as a pioneering giant in the behavioral sciences.

Piaget is a man of multiple talents and widespread contributions. He is an epistemologist, logician, biologist, and developmental psychologist. It is only in the latter capacity that we will consider his work in the present chapter. We will examine the implications of Piaget's view of cognitive development as it relates to readiness to learn.

Piaget first became fascinated with problems of cognitive growth while translating and standardizing into French a series of English intelligence tests. He was struck by the observation that the character of the *errors* made by children held as much interest as the nature of their correct answers. In fact, there were systematic internal consistencies in the kinds of errors made by children of different ages. It was as if they were operating with their own forms of logic which, though unlike adult logical forms, were regular and amenable to formal analysis. These observations of the character of children's errors stimulated a half-century of research into the problems of cognitive development.

We shall not in this chapter reiterate the Piagetian stages of cognitive development. This task has been ably performed in many other volumes.[25] Instead, we shall focus on the characteristics of Piaget's view of the growth of intelligence as they may relate to the process of instruction.

Piaget views the development of intelligence as part of the more general process of biological development. Gallagher[26] has suggested five major themes running through Piaget's work.

1. Continuous and progressive changes take place in the structures of behavior and thought in the developing child.
2. Successive structures make their appearance in a fixed order.
3. The nature of accommodation (adaptive change to outer circumstances) suggests that the rate of development is, to a considerable degree, a function of the child's encounters with his environment.

4. Thought processes are conceived to originate through a process of internalizing actions. Intelligence increases as thought processes are loosened from their basis in perception and action and thereby become reversible, transitive, associative, and so on.
5. A close relationship exists between thought processes and properties of formal logic.[27]

For Piaget the child is a developing organism passing through biologically determined cognitive stages. These stages are more or less age-related, although wide variations in cultures or environments will yield differences in individual rates of development. One might view the process of cognitive growth as a drama. The script or scenario describing the drama's plot and characters is given by the biological component. The role of the director—that of determining the onset and pace of the episodes—is a function of the environment.

Although development is a continuous process of structural change, it is still possible to characterize certain growth periods by the formal logical structures most useful for describing the child's cognitive functioning during that time span. These growth periods, when a temporary stability of cognitive functioning is achieved, define for Piaget the major stages of intellectual growth.

There is one other principle which is extremely important for an understanding of Piaget's system and its impact on education. This is the principle of *autoregulation* or *equilibration.* Piaget sees the development of intelligence as a sequence of successive disequilibria followed by adaptations leading to new states of equilibrium. The imbalance can occur because of an ontogenetic change occurring naturally as the organism matures. It can also occur in reaction to an input from the environment. Since disequilibrium is uncomfortable, the child must accommodate to new situations through active modification of his present cognitive structure.

Piaget observes that only in man can intelligence develop to the point where the domain of ideas and symbols can serve as the "environmental" sources of disequilibrium. That is, we can construct intellectual universes, for example, transintuitive spaces, which can stimulate our own cognitive growth as surely as the confrontation by a baby with the problem of reaching his pacifier can lead to new insights or equilibria on his part.

Piaget has written little specifically directed at problems of education. He has repeatedly disavowed any expertise in the pedagogical domain. Yet, either directly or through such interpreters as Bruner, his influence has been strongly felt.

Piaget's emphasis upon action as a prerequisite to the internalization of cognitive operations has stimulated the focus upon direct manipulation of mathematically relevant materials in the early grades. His description of cognitive development occurring through autoregulation has reinforced tendencies to emphasize pupil-initiated, problem-solving activities as a major vehicle of mathematics instruction. His characterization of the number-related concepts understood by children of different ages (e.g., one-to-one correspondence, reversibility, conservation, and the like) has influenced our grasp of what children at different stages can be expected to learn meaningfully.

The latter point reflects Piaget's influence on some current conceptions of readiness. To determine whether a child is ready to learn a particular concept or principle, one analyzes the structure of that to be taught and compares it with what is already known about the cognitive structure of the child of that age. If the two structures are consonant, the new concept or principle can be taught; if they are dissonant, it cannot. One must then, if the dissonance is substantial, wait for further maturation to take place. If the degree of dissonance is minimal, there is nothing in Piaget's general theory to preclude the introduction of training procedures to achieve the desired state of readiness. However, Piaget seems to prefer the "waiting" to the "training" strategy under such conditions. Though his theory admits of both external and internal sources of developmental change, he seems to favor the internal ontogenetic mechanisms.

The chapter in *The Process of Education* entitled "Readiness for Learning" was ostensibly based on the work of Piaget. The largest single segment of that chapter was written by Piaget's chief collaborator, Barbel Inhelder. Imagine then the shock of that chapter's opening assertion: "We begin with the hypothesis that any subject can be taught effectively in some intellectually honest form to any child at any stage of development."[28] Considering the earlier description of Piaget's position, it seems hardly consistent.

Many are puzzled by this stand, including Piaget. In a paper delivered in the United States, he admitted that he (in the light of his own experiments) did not understand how Bruner could make such a statement. If Bruner meant the statement literally (i.e., *any* child can learn *any*thing), then it just is not true! There are always things a child cannot learn, especially not in an intellectually honest way. If he meant it homiletically (i.e., we can take almost anything and somehow resay it, reconstruct it, restructure it so that it now has a parallel at the child's level of cognitive functioning), then it may be a truism.

What Bruner is saying, however (and it is neither trivial nor absurd), is that our older conceptions of readiness have tended to apply Piagetian theory in the same way as some have for generations applied Rousseau's. There has been the belief that neither the nature of the child nor that of the subject matter can tolerate systematic tampering. We take the subject matter as our starting point, carefully observe as the child develops, and feed in the content as "readiness" is reached.

Bruner is suggesting that we must modify our conception of readiness so as to include not only the child, but the subject matter as well. Subject matter, too, can be passed through stages of readiness. We view the child as evolving through stages in which his preferred modes of representation are (serially) enactive, ikonic, and symbolic. Similarly, the basic principles or structures of a discipline can be represented manipulatively, as visual representations or as formal symbolic expressions.

We may look to the example of discovery presented earlier in this chapter to illustrate the principles of alternative modes of representation. When the pupil is working solely with the flat pieces of wood, he is contending with problems presented in the enactive mode. When we help the child conceive of the problem in terms of manipulating the placement of any number of "flats," we have shifted to an ikonic mode, wherein visual images of objects are manipulated. When the learner can finally begin to manipulate the abstract symbols by themselves, thinking of x^2, $2x$, and 1 without invoking their imaginal or concrete manifestations, he has managed to deal with the problem at a symbolic level. The problem itself has remained the same. Only the modality in which it is being represented has been changed. Bruner would assert that similar transformations through modes of representation could be achieved for any fundamental concept or principle in mathematics.

How is it that Bruner, though beginning from a Piagetian starting point, reaches such a contrasting conclusion? It appears that they do not use the same criteria for determining whether a stage has been reached. Piaget employs far more stringent criteria for establishing whether a child has achieved, for example, the stage of concrete operations, including the expectation that the child should be able to provide a coherent verbal rationale for his assertions about phenomena. Bruner, viewing cognitive growth in terms of progressive changes in modes of representation, is prepared to accept non-verbal, behavioral evidence for the onset of a given stage. Thus, a child may appear "ready" to Bruner substantially earlier than he will to Piaget.

Bruner's position also appears to rest on an assertion about the nature of knowledge itself. The spiral curriculum, wherein the structures of disciplines are represented *seriatim* enactively, ikonically, and symbolically, may represent Bruner's conception of how any idea becomes known. The assertion is double-barreled. First, it is asserted that the fundamental principles or structures of disciplines are essentially simple; second and consequently, these simple structures can be taught and learned in an intellectually honest form through any mode of representation.

This conception of the simplicity of fundamental principles is neither unique to Bruner nor attributable only to Plato. The Nobel laureate Szent-Györgyi has written:

> Science tends to generalize, and generalization means simplification. My own science, biology, is today not only very much richer than it was in my student days, but is simpler, too. Then it was horribly complex, being fragmented into a great number of isolated principles. Today these are all fused into one single complex, with the atomic model in its center. Cosmology, quantum mechanics, DNA and genetics, are all, more or less, parts of one and the same story—a most wondrous simplification. And generalizations are also more satisfying to the mind than details. We, in our teaching, should place more emphasis on generalizations than on details.[29]

We may thus observe and understand how, through the interpretation of Bruner, Piaget's essentially conservative position regarding readiness becomes a major impetus for the trend toward earlier introduction of subject matter to elementary school children.

Piaget himself remains quite dubious over the attempts to accelerate cognitive development that are reflected in many modern mathematics and science curricula. On a recent trip to the United States, Piaget commented:

> . . . we know that it takes nine to twelve months before babies develop the notion that an object is still there even when a screen is placed in front of it. Now kittens go through the same stages as children, all the same substages, but they do it in three months—so they're six months ahead of babies. Is this an advantage or isn't it? We can certainly see our answer in one sense. The kitten is not going to go much further. The child has taken longer, but he is capable of going further, so it seems to be that the nine months probably were not for nothing.
>
> It's probably possible to accelerate, but maximal acceleration is not desirable. There seems to be an optimal time. What this optimal time is will surely depend upon each individual and on the subject matter. We still need a great deal of research to know what the optimal time would be.[30]

The question that has not been answered, and which Piaget whimsically calls the "American question," is the empirical experimental question—to what extent is it possible through instruction to accelerate what Piaget maintains is the invariant clockwork of the order? Studies conducted by Smedslund,[31] Sigel,[32] Mermelstein,[33] and others are attempting to identify the degree to which these processes can be accelerated. At this point the results remain equivocal. Successful acceleration is usually not achieved. When it is achieved, the success is relatively modest. However, we are far from having exhausted the full range of creative approaches to the problem. Much more work is needed. Even if successful, is there a long-term danger in such acceleration, as Piaget suggests? Or is early introduction to the basic principles of disciplines the key to educating a generation of citizens who, rather than patronizingly tolerating the sciences and mathematics, truly understand and appreciate them? (This is not to mention its value to those who will devote their lives to such pursuits.) These are questions to which future inquiries need be directed, for at the moment we have access only to opinions and personal prejudices.

For those theorists who advocate the systematic guidance of learning, the problem of readiness is free of ontogenetic and epistemological encumbrances. Gagné maintains that readiness is essentially a function of the presence or absence of prerequisite learning. When the child is capable of tasks *d* and *e,* he is by definition ready to learn *b.*

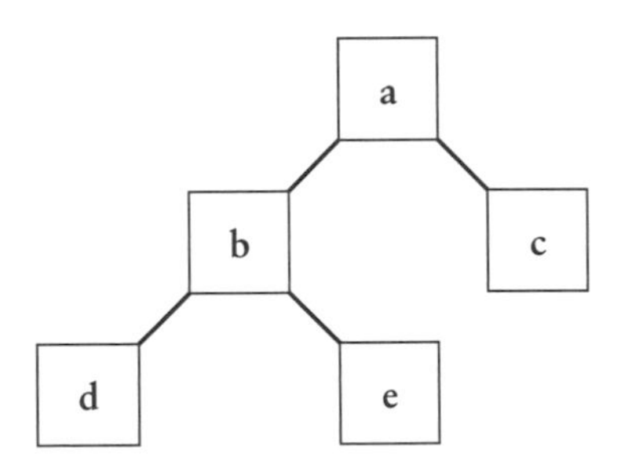

Until then, he is not ready. Gagné is not concerned with genetically developmental considerations except of the most gross variety. If the child at age five does not have the concept of the conservation of liquid volume, it is not because a natural mental unfolding has failed to take place; he has not had the necessary prior experiences. Ensure that he has acquired the prerequisite capabilities and he will be able to conserve.[34]

The key for understanding readiness is *prerequisite* knowledge or capabilities. Ausubel, who is in fundamental agreement with Gagné on this issue, has stated the point eloquently in the following aphorism.

> If I had to reduce all of educational psychology to one principle, I would say this: The most important single factor influencing learning is what the learner already knows. Ascertain this and teach him acordingly.[35]

Ausubel felt that this point was so central to his general theoretical position as an educational psychologist that he placed it in the frontispiece of his textbook on educational psychology.

Problems of readiness, early learning, and acceleration are, thus, far less complex for the proponents of expository teaching than for their discovery-oriented counterparts. It is a matter of identifying prerequisite knowledge or capabilities and teaching these. Ironically, one might contend that Bruner's "shocking" proposition regarding readiness is as consistent (if not much more so) with the theories of Gagné and Ausubel as with that of Piaget. Surely, they (Gagné and Ausubel) might find the assertion less shocking to their conceptions of intellectual development. Their doubts, and they are major ones, would grow out of the unlikely probability of providing sufficient prerequisite understanding in a given time period to prepare "any child" to learn "any subject."

The psychological stance of those advocating guided expository learning has had interesting and potentially revolutionary consequences for our perspective on a concept that falls somewhat beyond the pale of considerations of discovery learning. This is the question of *aptitude for learning*. Working within the guided-learning tradition, theorists such as Carroll[36] and Bloom[37] have challenged educators to recast their ancient conceptions of mental ability. The next section is devoted to that challenge.

Aptitude

When we discuss the entering characteristics of students, we are generally referring either to their readiness or to their aptitudes. Typically these two topics have been handled separately. Discussions of aptitude have usually centered about such issues as: What are the respective contributions of nature and nurture to individual intelligence? Is intelligence general or subject-specific? How stable or unchanging is aptitude?

Problems of planning for particular instructional units or curricula have usually treated student aptitude as a given. A student's aptitude was perceived as setting a theoretical limit on the level of complexity or abstraction he could be expected to attain in his attempts to master a given capability or substantive domain. It has always seemed a quite reasonable proposition, and few educators have bothered to question it.

Not so Carroll and, more recently, Bloom. Carroll[38] has challenged us with the view that *aptitude is the amount of time required by the learner to attain mastery of a learning task*. As Bloom has observed:

> Implicit in this formulation is the assumption that, given enough time, all students can conceivably attain mastery of a learning task. If Carroll is right, then learning mastery is theoretically available to all, if we can find the means for helping each student. It is this writer's belief that this formulation of Carroll's has the most fundamental implications for education.[39]

Carroll's formulation bridges the gap between aptitude and readiness. If aptitude is seen as a measure of the *rate* at which a given student can master an instructional objective, clearly the prerequisite capabilities he brings to the learning task achieve major importance. Gagné[40] has demonstrated that once a carefully sequenced learning unit has begun, it is not the student's general aptitude that predicts best how well he will achieve any particular step. It is the extent to which he has attained the prerequisites to that step that predicts best. Thus, his readiness and aptitude come to coincide. Aptitude becomes a matter of *how long* it takes to achieve readiness, rather than *whether* a student is or can ever become ready.

Our traditional conceptions of readiness happen to fit nicely with the institutionalized tempo of our school systems. In education we characteristically treat *time* as a constant while allowing *achievement* to act as a variable. That is, we provide a predetermined span of time for the mastery of a given body of subject matter and then measure the varying degrees of learning mastery attained by the students at the end of that time. We not only expect variability in achievement; we welcome it, for it serves as the basis for our grading systems. We then attribute the variability (wherein, as Bloom observed, hardly one-third of our students ever truly attain the objectives of instruction under the best of conditions) to those mystically immutable student characteristics—aptitude and motivation.

Let us use the analogy of a track meet.[41] Imagine the mile run if it began with the firing of a gun and ended at the end of four minutes when another gun went off and everyone had to stop wherever they were. It would be even more startling if about five minutes later another gun went off for the next race and everyone began that race from the same point at which they had ended the previous one.

By repeating such a process, we would guarantee the development of cumulative deficits for some runners as they fell progressively further behind after each successive race. As long as time were held constant and no source of external assistance or remediation were provided, such a consequence would be inevitable. We would find such a practice ludicrous in track, yet we run our educational programs in precisely this manner. Our purposes in education are to see to it that a certain minimal level of competence is achieved by each learner. To do so, we should logically set *levels of achievement* as constants and let *time* act as a variable.

Such a study has already been carried out in mathematics education. Herriot[42] reports that "slow-learning" students achieve as well in SMSG math as average students when they are allowed substantially more time than is usually allotted to the mathematics curriculum. In this case, they spent two years studying material originally designed for a one-year program. We are not arguing here whether certain topics in mathematics are really worth such extra time expenditures. It is merely our purpose to demonstrate that one's aptitude does not determine the amount that can be learned, but merely the amount of time necessary for that learning.

Such a modification in our view of aptitude for learning would have multiple consequences. It would quickly broaden the range of instruments used to measure aptitude, probably leading to the use of many more differential aptitude measures in place of general aptitude tests. In addition, tests of prerequisite knowledge would also be used. We would find ourselves blending testing and teaching into a more integrated general process of instruction. Student-entering characteristics would be used diagnostically, rather than prophetically—that is, to plan for differentiated programs of instruction, rather than to anticipate "inevitable" instructional disasters. It is such an approach to the question of aptitude that has developed from the analyses of learning exemplified by the work of Gagné and carried forward by Carroll, Bloom, and others.

Having examined the objectives of instruction and the entering characteristics of students, we turn in the next section to the tactics of instruction and the problem of transfer of training.

Tactics and Sequence of Instruction

The theoretical issues we have been examining are educationally relevant because they are related to what people actually do in classrooms. Those who march under the learning-by-discovery banner behave quite differently as instructors from those whose pulses quicken at the thought of guided learning. Though we have already described some instructional examples and briefly characterized them, it would now seem appropriate to treat in greater detail certain of these specific pedagogical contrasts. For purposes of clarity, the major distinction will be between the guided-learning approach of Gagné and the discovery-learning strategy of Bruner.

The task analysis of subordinate capabilities that are prerequisite to attainment of a given objective generates, for Gagné, a hierarchical structure of learning. Gagné[43] is quick to point out that this resultant structure by no means describes a universally necessary single pathway to the terminal objective. Specific individuals may vary from the derived learning hierarchy in the absence of specified stages, the interpolation of other stages not specified in the particular hierarchy, or in the reordering of the sequence. However, the structure and sequence suggested by the analysis of subordinate capabilities will generally describe a teaching program that will effectively accomplish the desired objective. That is, although it is possible to achieve the terminal capability via alternate routes, the pathway identified in the learning hierarchy will be preferable in general.

The model of teaching most closely following Gagné's expository or guided approach would be some form of programmed instruction. Here the specific steps undertaken by the learner are carefully specified and sequenced. The medium may be a machine, a book, or a programmed teacher closely following a predetermined instructional sequence. The achievement of each prerequisite step is firmly established before instruction on its successor is begun. Hence, learning is highly guided, errors are minimized, and meaningfulness—in the sense of articulation of new material with what the learner already knows or can do—is thereby assured.

In contrast, Bruner would emphasize much less system or order in his approach, although he would not, in principle, preclude such structure. He prefers to have the learner begin with manipulation of materials or tasks that present problems. These problems may take the form of (a) goals to be achieved in the absence of readily discernible means for reaching those goals, (b) contradictions between sources of information of apparently equal credibility, or (c) the quest for structure or symmetry in situations where such order is not readily apparent.

For Bruner the first step of discovery is a sensed incongruity or contrast.[44] He is always attempting to build potential or emergent incongruities into the materials of instruction. An example of such teaching is the use of "torpedoing" by Davis[45] in the Madison Project. Davis will teach something to a child (or have the child derive a rule inductively for himself) until the learner is confident of his mastery of the principle and its application. He then provides the child with a "whopper" of a counterexample. Such contradictions are used to engage the child, because of the resulting intellectual discomfort, in an attempt to resolve this disequilibrium by making some new discovery in the form of a reorganization of his understanding—what the Gestalt psychologists would have called "cognitive restructuring."

This discovery may require forming a new distinction, thus creating a new category of experience which will account for the now-recognized complexity of the situation. Or the discovery may involve a higher-order synthesis, whereby the two apparently discrepant events—the previous understanding and the unexpected counterexample—are now seen jointly accounted for through some more abstract rule. As indicated earlier, the essence of the discovery for Bruner is something which takes place inside the learner, through the education of new relations and the creation of new structures.

The use of a technique like "torpedoing" reflects the dual roots of Bruner's approach both in the Piagetian model of cognitive development and in the Socratic model of teaching. Piaget maintains that the growth of intelligence follows the path of successive disequilibria and equilibria. The child, confronted by a new situation which is not directly assimilable, gets out of balance and must accommodate to achieve a new balance by modifying his existent cognitive structure. This modification will usually take one or both of the forms described earlier: increased differentiation of cognitive structure and/or enhanced generalizability and integration of structure.

The Socratic method is simply a pedagogical approach in which it is not nature which supplies the source of contrast or contradiction, but a community gadfly—the teacher. Through dialogue, Socrates manages to help his friends make their principles explicit. Through further questioning, he leads them to recognize that they inevitably practice or value certain other behaviors which, in principle, must contradict their earlier stated belief. Clearly something has got to give. Usually the principle as stated must be modified, and a higher, more abstract, yet better differentiated understanding must take its place.

It can also be argued that the dialectical quality of Socratic learning sequences simulates most accurately the manner in which new knowledge is actually discovered in a scientific community. Such a model for the creation of new theoretical paradigms would be quite consistent with Kuhn's characterization of the dynamics of theoretical changes in science.[46]

Even Davis' term "torpedoing" refers to the Socratic approach from which it derives. Meno refers to Socrates as a "torpedo fish, who torpifies whose who come near him and touch him," thus shocking them into recognition of their own ignorance and self-contradiction.

We may thus characterize the difference between the instructional approaches of expository and discovery teaching in the following manner: For

Gagné, instruction is a smoothly guided tour up a carefully constructed hierarchy of learning tasks; for Bruner, instruction is a roller-coaster ride of successive disequilibria and equilibria terminating in the attainment or discovery of a desired cognitive state.

The implications for the sequence of the curriculum growing from these two positions are quite different. For Gagné, the highest level of learning is problem-solving; lower levels involve facts, concepts, principles, and so on. Clearly, for Gagné, the appropriate sequence in learning is, in terms of the diagram below, from the bottom up. One begins with simple prerequisites and works up, pyramid fashion, to the complex capability sought.

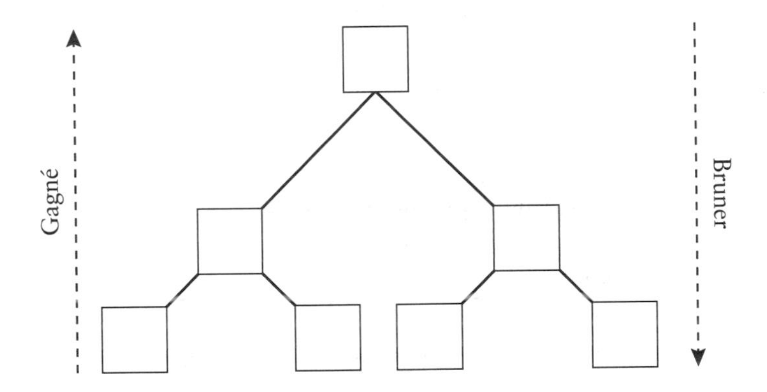

For Bruner the same diagram may be appropriate, but the direction of the arrow would be changed. He has the learner begin with *problem-solving*. Once confronted with a problem, whether embedded in the materials of instruction or directly presented by the teacher, the learner will be led to move back through the hierarchy to form the needed associations, attain the necessary concepts, and, finally, derive the appropriate rules for solving the problem.

This strategy appears to have two rationales. First, it is thought to be, in contrast to the guided-learning sequence, a more motivating approach to learning. That is, children may be more motivated when confronted with an enticing problem they cannot solve than they are when given some specific objectives to master on the promise that, if they learn them well, at some indeterminate future point they may be able to solve an exciting problem.

The second rationale for this strategy is based on the ostensibly greater transferability of knowledge discovered in a problem-solving context over that learned in a didactic mode. We may note that two separable issues are confounded in this question: (a) the organization of the material to be learned—by problem or by logical learning structure—and (b) the optimal sequence of the learning process—inductively from problems to rules or deductively from rules to problems. Suffice it to observe that the fundamental argument here is over which of these approaches will optimize transfer of training most effectively. As usual, current statements of the problem manage to confound more aspects of the issue than they usefully clarify.

Ausubel's concept of instructional sequence once again reflects certain positions of both the other theorists. Like Gagné, he advocates a carefully guided, expository sequencing. However, like Bruner, he would advocate initiating the sequence at a higher point on the hierarchy. This is Ausubel's principle of the *advance organizer.*[47]

Ausubel begins the instructional sequence with a set of organizing statements at a level of abstraction *higher* than what must be learned subsequently. He uses it to establish an "ideational scaffolding" which both links what is to be learned with what the learner already knows and creates an organization or structure within which the new learning will be embedded. These organizers are expositorily taught to the learners as the first step in a unit of instruction. They are not to be discovered, as would be the initial stage of a Bruner program of instruction.

All these positions have but one major objective—that of optimizing subsequent retention and transfer of learning. It is to a consideration of transfer that we now turn.

Transfer of Training

Transfer of training is the most important single concept in any educationally relevant theory of learning. Without transfer, our students could be expected only to practice what we teach. The span of their learning could never exceed the range of situations or problems actually encountered in the course of instruction. The phenomenon of transfer makes it possible to collect many educational dividends from a relatively modest initial learning investment. In Bruner's apt phrase, it allows us "to go beyond the information given."[49]

There are none who would deny the reality of transfer. The disagreements revolve around such questions as the breadth of transfer—whether the concept applies only to acquisition of specific products and narrow processes or can account equally well for the generalizable learning of broad principles, general strategies of inquiry, motivations to learn in certain domains, and attitudes about learning and about oneself as a learner. The contrasts of the preceding section on tactics of instruction reflect yet another dimension of the transfer question, i.e., identification of the optimal instructional conditions for the facilitation of transfer.

It may be useful here to invoke a distinction suggested by Gagné between *lateral* and *vertical* transfer. *Lateral transfer* refers to the manner in which the learning of a capability in one domain can facilitate the mastery of some parallel capability in another domain. These parallel capabilities would be at the same levels of their respective learning hierarchies. *Vertical transfer* refers to the manner in which the learning of a subordinate capability serves to facilitate the mastery of some subsequent learning at a higher level of the same hierarchy.

An example of lateral transfer would be learning certain elements of logical inference in the proof of geometric theorems subsequent to initially learning similar logical principles while deriving and proving theorems relating to numbers and arithmetic operations. We would expect that there would be positive lateral transfer across the two parallel kinds of problems.

We would expect to observe vertical transfer in the manner in which previous mastery of multiplication would transfer to subsequent learning of the more complex task of long division.

As we examine the topic of transfer, we will ask (a) what is transferred, (b) how broadly does the transfer occur, and (c) what are the optimal instructional conditions for transfer? Finally, some recent research on transfer in mathematics learning will be reviewed and evaluated.

The major theorists differ in their respective emphases upon *what* is transferred in learning. Bruner stresses the lateral transfer of broad principles and strategies from one domain or topic to another. Bruner believes that we can have massive transfer from one learning situation to another. He recognizes that some may find his position reminiscent of *faculty psychology*—the theory that a person can study geometry and become a better logical thinker, or study Latin and come to know more English vocabulary. This theory and its concept of broad massive transfer was thought to have been put permanently to rest by William James and Edward Lee Thorndike at the turn of this century.

Bruner adheres to an analogous concept of transfer. His theory is not faculty psychology in the sense that the mind is perceived as a muscle made stronger through exercise. Broad transfer of training occurs when one can identify in the structures of subject matters basic, fundamentally simple concepts—principles or strategies which, if learned well, can be transferred both to other topics within that discipline and to other disciplines as well. He gives examples such as the concept of conservation or balance. Is it not possible to teach balance of trade in economics so that, when ecological balance is considered, pupils see the parallel? This could then be extended to balance of power in political science, or to balancing equations. Of equal, if not greater, importance for Bruner is the broad transferability of the knowledge-getting processes—strategies, heuristics, investigatory methods, and the like. In his view, learning by discovery leads to the ability *to* discover, that is, to the development of broad inquiry competencies in students.

Bruner does not ignore vertical transfer in his theorizing. His conception of learning moving from enactive through ikonic and symbolic modes of representation is a theory of vertical transfer. Bruner would use such learning sequences wherein learners make the necessary discoveries themselves for the teaching of the most broadly transferable principles and processes.

Gagné considers himself a conservative on matters of transfer. He states that "transfer occurs because of the occurrence of specific identical (or highly similar) elements within developmental sequences."[49] To the extent that an element which has been learned (be it association, concept, or principle) can be directly employed in a new situation, transfer will occur. If the new context requires a behavior substantially different from the specific capability mastered earlier, there will be no transfer. He thus clearly identifies himself with the "identical elements" position of Thorndike, a point of view in clear contrast to Bruner.

Gagné is concerned primarily with the conditions for *vertical* transfer. His theory of learning hierarchies is clearly a theory of positive vertical transfer. Though not denying the possibility of lateral transfer—he goes so far as to describe the theoretical conditions for such transfer, such as practicing the capability to be transferred in as wide a variety of contexts as is feasible—his massive body of theoretical and empirical work is directed at the vertical transfer problem.

Gagné distinguishes between the learning of "verbalizable knowledges" and "intellectual skills or strategies,"[50] which are parallel to what we earlier referred to as products and processes. He asserts that his hierarchical model of learning is only appropriate to the acquisition of intellectual skills. Furthermore, like Bruner, he finds the acquisition of such processes far more important for learners than the acquisition of verbalizable knowledge.

Ausubel asserts that *what* is transferred is subject matter knowledge. This places him in clear contrast to the positions of Bruner and Gagné. With respect to the breadth of transfer, he maintains an intermediate position between Bruner and Gagné—less conservative than Gagné's insistence on identical elements, yet more moderate than Bruner's claims of the most far-reaching process transfer. He compares his position to that of Judd, who spoke of transfer by generalization. Finally, like Gagné, he prescribes guided learning as providing the optimal conditions for transfer but differs with Gagné on the optimal sequence. While Gagné recommends an instructional sequence in which learning proceeds from less abstract to more abstract materials, Ausubel advocates *progressive differentiation,* where material is initially presented in the more abstract form of an *advance organizer.* This is then followed by the less abstract material to be mastered.

In summary, Bruner argues that the kinds of approaches to which the rubric *discovery* has been applied establish the optimal conditions for transfer, and that the most important things to be transferred are the broadest kinds of processes and principles. Gagné and Ausubel both argue for the general superiority of the guided or expository approaches to learning in optimizing transfer, though they would differ both in the specific type of expository sequence advocated and in the form of knowledge—product or process—which is transferred.

What does the evidence from empirical studies of this issue seem to demonstrate? The findings are not all that consistent. Most often guided or expository sequences seem to be superior methods for the *acquisition* of immediate learning. With regard to long-term *retention,* the results seem equivocal, with neither approach consistently better. Discovery-learning approaches appear to be superior when the criterion of *transfer* of principles to new situations is employed. Notably absent are long-term studies which deal with the question of whether general techniques, strategies, heuristics of discovery can be learned—by discovery or in any other manner—which will transfer across grossly different kinds of tasks. Also absent are studies which assess whether long-term use of particular instructional approaches results in fairly stable attitudinal or motivational changes. The latter achievement is frequently claimed by advocates of "the discovery method."

Craig[51] has reviewed the results of a number of studies of transfer in discovery learning by Gagné and Brown,[52] Guthrie,[53] Roughead and Scandura,[54] and Worthen.[55] He concludes that "the discovery treatment has been inadequately tested; but, when differences among treatment groups in later ability to infer and use new principles have been found, they favor discovery techniques over the giving of guidance."[56]

Although Worthen's study contains certain inconsistencies that raise some serious questions concerning its generalizability,[57] his investigation possesses a number of characteristics which could well serve as a model for future research in this area. He conducts the research in the classroom rather than in the laboratory, thus reducing the inevitable credibility gap encountered whenever generalizing from the psychologist's hothouse to the educator's garden. The duration of the experimental treatments is six weeks instead of the all-too-frequent sixty minutes. An attempt is made to specify carefully the particular experimental variables manipulated—in this case, example-rule and rule-example sequences. Tests of retention cover a reasonably long term, in contrast to the ludicrous habit among experimental psychologists of referring to a posttest twenty-four hours after initial learning as the measure of "long-term retention." Finally, attitude measures as well as intellectual measures are employed as criterion variables.

The superiority of transfer for the discovery treatment in the cited studies is impressive, but no swift generalizations can be made. For example, in the Worthen research, the discovery treatment had only one characteristic of discovery approaches, the withholding of rules until presentation of examples had been completed. There is every indication that the discovery treatment was highly guided. The students were by no means engaging in long periods of relatively undirected "messing around" with materials or problems as in some of Bruner's favorite examples. Furthermore, there is no indication that the expository treatment in any way reflected an attempt to apply systematically the tenets of either Gagné's or Ausubel's models. Hence, though in some ways exemplary in its research design, the Worthen investigation or any of the others cannot be said to have resolved the theoretical issue. No single study is capable of doing so. Only a carefully planned *program* of research is likely to clarify this issue in some ultimate sense.

Epistemology

When theorists differ so systematically over principles of learning and teaching, it is not surprising to find that their differences are rooted deeply in far more fundamental issues. Although the field of psychology ostensibly achieved emancipation from philosophy some eighty years ago, contemporary psychologists continue to fight the same battles that bloodied their philosophical forebears. Thus, the clamor over the relative merits of expository and discovery teaching is much more than a mere disagreement concerning pedagogical policy. It can best be understood in terms of certain basic controversies relating to the manner in which *anything* becomes known. These issues of the nature of knowledge and the knowing process are the domain of epistemology.

The Gagné position grows directly out of the epistemology that began with Aristotle, bore fruit with the British associationists (Hume, Berkeley, Locke), and took root in psychology with the American associationists (Thorndike, Watson, Hull, Skinner, and Osgood). The essence of this epistemology is simple. The child begins as a blank slate, a *tabula rasa*. Human development can be described as the cumulative effects of experience; what is learned is strictly a function of the imprint that experience makes upon this blank slate. Therefore, learning can be thought of additively and connectively; what is learned is something that is added and connected to what was learned before.

Bruner's thinking traces back to Plato, through Hegel and Dewey. Psychologically, it is influenced by the Gestalt psychologists in the thirties, and, most recently, by Piaget. If we can call the Gagné tradition one of neobehaviorism, the position of Bruner is a particularly Platonic branch of cognitive psychology, or genetic-cognitive psychology. In general, there is a bit of Plato in any man who advocates teaching by discovery because of the way in which the approach attempts to elicit from the learner things that he has always known, but in a reconstructed structural form. There is an emphasis upon structure, upon meaning, upon relationships, upon organization, which is reminiscent of Gestalt psychology. If we draw a diagram of what is to be learned, Gagné would be more interested in what is inside the boxes and Bruner, in the arrows between the boxes. For Gagné the fundamental question is, "What is to be learned?" For Bruner, it is, "How do you get there and to similar places?" These are quite consonant with their contrasting epistemologies. The nature of knowledge is different for Bruner and for Gagné. In contrast to Gagné's additive and cumulative notion, Bruner would maintain that the whole is greater than the sum of its parts and that the process cannot be taught didactically but must be undergone *in toto*.

To understand the Bruner position on learning by discovery, one must surely understand the pervasiveness of his Platonic idealism—a characteristic that sets Bruner apart from almost all other cognitive psychologists. We observed earlier that Bruner views the most fundamental and abstract ideas as inherently simple. Ultimate knowledge of these ideas consists of freeing oneself from the encumbering effects of their enactive and imaginal aspects and dealing with them in their purely symbolic, most efficiently transferable form. Most individuals have the "basic stuff" of which these ideas are made, but must confront suitable problems or contrasts in order to clarify and restructure them. Hence, some variation of Socratic teaching suggests itself.

For the empiricist, such as Gagné, the ultimate source of all knowledge is *experience*. Hence, one learns best through having experience organized optimally and presented expositorily. For the rationalist, such as Bruner, it is not experience but *reason* which is the ultimate source of understanding. Therefore, that mode of instruction is best which aids the learner to reflect on his own thinking and to reorganize his own understanding to grasp the world of experience more effectively.

A distinction originally made by Aristotle may be usefully invoked at this point. Aristotle distinguished between two different structures of knowledge: *ordo essendi,* the order of being, and *ordo cognoscenti,* the order of knowing. There is an important difference between the way things *are* and the manner in which they *become known.* Aristotle's implication is that we must distinguish between the structure of some knowledge in its fully developed form as grasped by the mature intellect and the structure of that same idea as it is presented for most effective and expeditious acquisition. Both Bruner and Gagné use the term *structure* in their writings; Bruner speaks of the centrality of the "structure of the subject matter," while Gagné calls his hierarchies "learning structures."

In referring to the structure of the subject matter, Bruner collapses the distinction between the structure of being and the structure of knowing. The activities of the child and those of the mature scholar are to be quite parallel for Bruner, and will differ mainly in the mode of representation used to cope with the fundamental ideas or structures. In contrast, Gagné clearly distinguishes between the two kinds of structures. The order of knowing is reflected in the optimal sequence of a learning hierarchy. The order of being is a more abstract set of relationships that can only be comprehended when learning is complete.

The epistemological roots of Ausubel's position do not flow as directly from the traditions of rationalism and empiricism as do those of Bruner and Gagné, respectively. He assumes a somewhat more eclectic epistemological stance which reflects some elements of both approaches.

There is another aspect of an educator's theory of knowledge which is relevant to our discussions, and which has been mentioned somewhat obliquely earlier in this chapter. This is the question of which kind of knowledge is of most value or worth. Bruner and Gagné are both of the persuasion that *processes* of knowledge-getting and knowledge-using are the most valuable forms of knowledge and are, therefore, the most important objectives of education. Ausubel asserts that it is the organized bodies of subject matter understanding themselves, the *products* of knowledge, which are most important as educational objectives.

We may thus see that the implicit theories of knowledge or epistemologies underlying the positions we have been discussing go a long way toward accounting for many specific characteristics of the positions themselves.

Prerequisites for a Psychology of Mathematics Education

Where is the practitioner to turn when confronted by such a confusing array of positions, theories, and prescriptions? How can he sort out the strengths, weaknesses, and implications of these positions in order to assist in his own curriculum-planning and instructional decision-making?

In this concluding section, we shall present a model for examining those variables which must be considered in formulating any propositions about the best forms of instruction. We shall then discuss the characteristics of those positions examined in the preceding sections and evaluate their claims and implications.

In a paper concerning "the logic of experiments on discovery," Cronbach[58] suggests that any theoretical generalization about the nature of instruction must necessarily take the form of the following five-fold interaction:

> With subject matter of this nature,
> inductive experience of this type,
> in this amount,
> produces this pattern of responses,
> in pupils at this level of development.[59]

Figure 2 presents our paraphrase and generalization of Cronbach's admonition, along with examples of each of the five kinds of variables.

This chapter began with the perennial pedagogical question: Which mode of instruction is best—discovery or exposition? We may now observe that any such question involves a number of issues which must be considered jointly. Previous sections have already established that both

Figure 2. Theoretical Generalization About the Nature of Instruction.

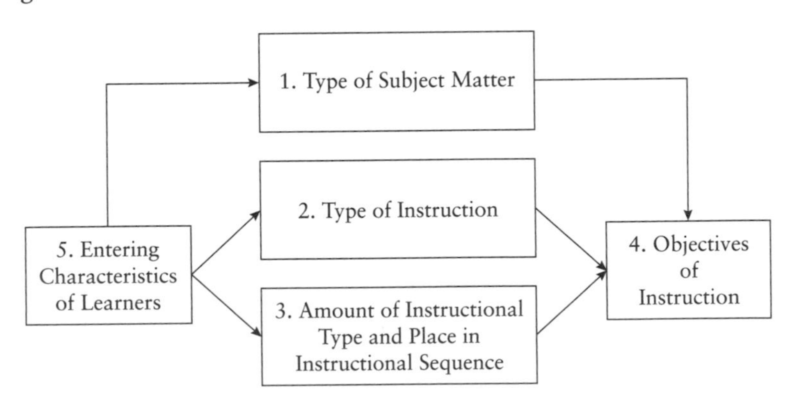

Example of each kind of variable

1. Mathematics, foreign languages, social studies (subject matter defined in task terms)
2. Expository-discovery (degree of guidance); inductive-deductive
3. Number of minutes or hours of instruction; position in sequence of instructional types
4. Products; processes; attitudes; self-perception
5. Prior knowledge; aptitude; cognitive style; values

the preferred objectives of instruction and the entering characteristics of learners will affect one's choice of instructional mode. Moreover, the particular subject matter to be learned will also influence the selection of approach. A teaching method deemed suitable for instruction in mathematical reasoning may be wholly inappropriate for the teaching of Latin noun declensions. Furthermore, the type of instruction itself cannot be judged *in vacuo*. As Cronbach observes, ". . . A particular educational tactic is part of an instrumental system; a proper educational design calls upon that tactic at a certain point in the sequence, for a certain period of time, following and preceding certain other tactics. No conclusion can be drawn about the tactic considered by itself."[60]

Entering Characteristics

A whole host of student-entering characteristics can be considered in any discussion of instruction. Although many theorists, most notably Cronbach,[61] have argued persuasively for the importance of individual differences in learning, the research literature in this area is remarkably underrepresented with studies demonstrating the differential effectiveness of contrasting instructional tactics for different types of individuals. Nevertheless, there may be a number of such kinds of characteristics worth considering in our discussions.

The student's *knowledge* of the area in which instruction must proceed will be an important factor. Successful inductive or Socratic teaching is clearly contingent upon some previously attained knowledge base. This would suggest that certain minimal prerequisites of understanding may be necessary before effective instruction leading to cognitive reorganization can be successful.

The learner's *developmental level* may also be significant. Ausubel[62] describes discovery learning as much more characteristic of the intellectual activities of the preadolescent child than of the more mature individual. He maintains that the trial-and-error concrete coping of discovery learning is useful in first establishing those conceptual foundations necessary for future understanding. However, once this initial underpinning has been established through discovery learning, most subsequent instruction can proceed both more effectively and more efficiently through meaningful expository learning. Hence, Ausubel would view the child's level of cognitive development, however attained, as a major criterion in selecting among instructional tactics.

An additional variable to consider, if only we knew more about it, would be the learner's *cognitive style*. Here again we confront a type of variable that combines intuitive feast with empirical famine. The convincing data on learning-relevant individual differences in cognitive style are rare indeed. One promising stylistic variable is Kagan's *conceptual tempo*[63] dimension. Others include *achievement motivation,*[64] *extraversion-introversion,*[65] *creativity,*[66] and *anxiety.*[67] Though it is intuitively obvious that such aspects of entering characteristics *ought* to interact significantly with mode of instruction, there is as yet no convincing empirical evidence that supports our intuitions. To assert that such is likely to be the case, as the writer would, is to utter a wish rather than a demonstrated reality.

Type and Amount of Instruction

The discovery issue has revolved almost totally around the question of instruction. However, it has been demonstrated repeatedly that the very term *discovery* is itself instructionally ambiguous. We earlier attempted to clarify the multiple meanings of discovery when used to describe an intervening process within the learner, distinguishing reception learning from discovery learning, and rote learning from meaningful learning. We shall now attempt to do the same for discovery as a description of a method of teaching.

Once again, at least two somewhat independent dimensions must be distinguished. The first is the *degree of guidance.* In the act of teaching anything, a teacher may exercise nearly total guidance over the learner's behavior or practically none. In the former case, we generally speak of expository or didactic teaching. In the latter instance, we would be likely to call the teaching method discovery. However, these two characterizations merely highlight the extreme ends of a continuum. Much instruction occupies intermediate points between them.

Wittrock[68] has suggested that we characterize the degree of guidance in terms of whether the rule and the solution to the problem being taught are given. Table 3 depicts the four possibilities.

Table 3.

Rule	Solution	Type of Guidance
Given	Given	Exposition
Given	Not Given	Guided Discovery (deductive)
Not Given	Given	Guided Discovery (inductive)
Not Given	Not Given	"Pure" Discovery

When both the rule and solution are given, the teaching method is thoroughly expository. When neither rule nor solution is given, we are engaging in "pure" discovery teaching. When one of the two is given, we are in an intermediate instructional situation that may best be characterized as *guided discovery.* However, it is usually the case that situations where the rule is given get labeled "exposition," irrespective of the tactics regarding the solution. Furthermore, situations where the rule must be generated to fit the given examples are almost inevitably dubbed with the title "discovery."

The reason for this apparent anomaly is that a second dimension, somewhat independent of degree of guidance, is also used to discuss teaching. This dimension is *sequence of instruction.* Inductive sequences, in which learners must invent the rule underlying a series of examples, are considered expository sequences. As can be seen in Table 4, the two dimensions can be considered separately.

Thus, for example, in the Worthen[69] study cited earlier, what distinguishes expository from discovery treatments is strictly instructional sequence, since both forms of instruction occupy roughly the same position on the degree of guidance dimension.

A further wrinkle may be introduced when one observes that the breakdown provided in Table 3, wherein either or both rule and solution are given, assumes that a *problem* is already formulated for the learner. Clearly one can conceive of many situations that are considerably less guided by an order of magnitude, because not even the formulated problem is given. Rather, the learner is simply placed in a potentially problematic instructional situation. Shulman[70] has referred to this latter type of situation as requiring the process of *inquiry,* in contrast to situations where the formulated problem is given, which require *problem solving.* Since much of significant human endeavor involves situations in which the critical problems must first be sensed and formulated before they can be solved, the relevance of inquiry as a process to be taught and investigated should be clear.

Table 4.

	Guided	Unguided
Inductive	Discovery Treatment (Worthen)	Bruner Mathematics Example
Deductive	Expository Treatment (Worthen)	Hypothetical Example: Provide learner with rule, must discover relevant examples

A similar model, involving the interplay of problem, rule, and solution, is discussed in an earlier yearbook by Getzels.[71]

Although we are far from exhausting the possible dimensions along which instructional types can be classified, only one more will be discussed. It, too, is partially independent of the dimensions discussed above. This is the *didactic-Socratic* dimension. Didactic instruction is most similar to maximally guided, deductive teaching. Socratic instruction refers to teaching in which the dialectic of the "torpedoing" process, as discussed earlier, is paramount. Socratic teaching may range along a large portion of the continuum of guidance, including situations so highly guided that the learner merely answers "yes" or "no" to the teacher's questions.

An interesting corollary to Socratic teaching is the inverse of that process, as reflected in Suchman's [72] inquiry-training approach. In this approach, the learner is visually confronted by an apparently anomalous physical event and must remove the anomaly by directing questions to the teacher, who answers "yes" or "no." Hence, once the initiating problem has been presented, guidance by the teacher is essentially absent.

Cronbach[73] cites briefly a number of other dimensions along which instruction can be classified—e.g., hints given or not given, individual versus group instruction, and verbalized or unverbalized rules. We will not be able to deal with such examples in the present chapter, but the possibility of generating many more examples should be recognized.

It should now be clear why the simple descriptor *discovery* can in no way characterize adequately a type of instruction. The term may be associated with any number or combination of approaches. The range of tactics excluded by the term is even more vast. One obvious prerequisite to further progress in this area is the replacement of such general terms as *discovery* and *exposition* with far more precise descriptors, except in the most informal discourses on education. The growing body of research being produced by Scandura[74] and his co-workers is exemplary of the fruitfulness of orienting research in mathematical learning toward the experimental study of psychologically meaningful variables rather than ambiguously labeled techniques.

Subject Matter

The characteristics of the subject matter to be taught are a major determinant of the suitability of inductive and/or minimally guided forms of instruction. Cronbach[75] has suggested that methods in which learners are called upon to discover rules and solutions are likely to be most fruitful with tasks in which the system or discipline of which they are a part is logical or rational. One may here contrast the task of finding the sum of a number series with that of finding which nouns take *le* and which *la*. The solution to the first problem is rational and is thus amenable to an inductive approach. The latter task is apparently arbitrary, hence would make less sense as the subject of inductive instruction.

If the logic or rationality of a subject matter is of prime importance in assessing its teachability via inductive methods, the signal popularity of such "discovery" tactics in mathematics instruction may be more easily understood. If it can also be asserted that mathematics is the discipline which has the most easily discernible structure, then the powerful impact of Bruner's theorizing becomes easier to explain. Which among the disciplines could be better fitted than mathematics to a neo-Platonic epistemology wherein true understanding is reached when ideas can be represented as formal symbols, free from the shackles of actions and images? Such concepts as number, point, and line are parts of a discipline far more "discoverable" in Bruner's terms than one whose concepts might be epoch, *Zeitgeist,* and king. In recognizing the relationship between subject matter and teaching mode, we may also be seeing the reason for the long romance of mathematics education and Brunerian discovery.

Educational Outcomes

Even within a single discipline, the objectives of instruction may vary. We earlier examined an important distinction between products and processes as objectives of instruction. Both these terms refer to clearly specifiable cognitive or intellectual consequences of education. There are other outcomes as well, which include broad cognitive strategies and expectancies, motives, values, and self-perceptions. For example, in addition to mastery of a particular set of principles and/or capabilities, we could seek as objectives of instruction: (a) the desire to learn more mathematics, (b) the judgment of mathematical knowledge as worthwhile, and (c) self-confidence in oneself as a mathematical reasoner and problem-solver. Under what instructional conditions can such objectives be achieved? Advocates of discovery approaches claim such benefits for their methods. We currently have no evidence either to confirm or to disconfirm these claims. Furthermore, the necessary evidence is likely to be forthcoming only if we begin to perform more of the systematic long-term studies such as the SMSG longitudinal research of Begle.[76]

If the writer had to identify a single dimension most critical as a determinant of the choice of an instructional strategy, it would be the objectives sought. Since an entire earlier section of this paper was devoted to that topic, we will not belabor the point here.

Summing Up

Dewey observed that a problem well put is half solved.[77] Those who might have anticipated that this chapter would report a great number of psychologically rooted solutions to the problems of mathematics instruction must remain disappointed. Though psychology can provide numerous answers, they fall short of the myriad questions mathematics educators can raise. The major contribution that psychology can presently make, the examination of which was the major objective of this chapter, is to ensure that the questions formulated are "well put." The primary prerequisite of any developing theory of mathematics education is the most fruitful formulation of its questions.

We must see that decisions concerning such theories cannot rest upon comparisons of positions, in principle. One must also invoke an understanding of the structure of knowledge and inquiry within the particular subject matter discipline whose mastery is sought. For example, if one perceives "mathematics" as basically a body of strategies, heuristics, or methods of inquiry, then clearly an approach to instruction calculated to optimize process learning is most advisable. If mathematics is seen as a compendium of subject matter understandings (e.g., arithmetic facts, computational algorithms, specific postulates or theorems), an approach which optimizes subject matter mastery would be preferred.

It is when one's conception of the structure and contents of an entire discipline is put in such starkly contrastive terms that the absurdity of a parallel forced choice between learning theories becomes evident. The mathematician will surely respond that mathematics is both an organized body of knowledge *and* a set of methods for critiquing and extending that knowledge. Both aspects are equally important to the mathematician, though the problem at hand may dictate that one or another aspect holds transient attention. Similarly, the individual careers of mathematicians may focus primarily upon a single aspect for scholarly purposes.

The mathematics curriculum designer cannot, therefore, select a particular psychologically based strategy of instruction because it is, in principle, most consonant with the nature of man, the knowing process, or the essential nature of mathematics. He must first identify (a) the precise characteristics of the subject matter to be mastered as objectives, and (b) the distinctive qualities of the learners who will be engaged; only then can an intelligent choice of teaching strategy be made. As learning continues, both the learner's characteristics and the objectives sought are likely to change. We need to think of instruction in terms of the selection of teaching modules chosen to fit optimally with specific objectives and student characteristics. Our problem then ceases to be "which method?" and becomes one of identifying the most effective sequences and combinations of methods for achievement of a wide range of instructional goals.

The solutions to such problems are likely to grow neither out of intuition nor out of common sense. These are empirical questions demanding empirical answers. Once well put in terms of psychologically meaningful variables rather than in terms of stirring slogans, these issues are amenable to systematic scientific investigation.[78] It is hoped that the present chapter and the volume in which it is contained will assist in the effective formulation of these questions. If so, our problems in mathematics education may soon be half solved.

NOTES

1. F. B. Knight, "Some Considerations of Method," *Report of the Society's Committee on Arithmetic* (Twenty-ninth Yearbook of the National Society for the Study of Education [Chicago: University of Chicago Press, 1930]), pp. 145–267.
2. R. H. Wheeler, "The New Psychology of Learning," *The Teaching of Arithmetic* (Tenth Yearbook of the National Council of Teachers of Mathematics [New York: Teachers College, Columbia University, 1935]).
3. T. R. McConnell, "Recent Trends in Learning Theory: Their Application to the Psychology of Arithmetic," *Arithmetic in General Education* (Sixteenth Yearbook of the National Council of Teachers of Mathematics [New York: Teachers College, Columbia University, 1941]), pp. 268–89.
4. Guy T. Buswell, "The Psychology of Learning in Relation to the Teaching of Arithmetic," *The Teaching of Arithmetic* (Fiftieth Yearbook of the National Society for the Study of Education, Part II [Chicago: University of Chicago Press, 1951]), pp. 143–54.
5. Lloyd Scott, *Trends in Elementary School Mathematics* (Chicago: Rand McNally & Co., 1966), pp. 15–16.
6. *Ibid.*, pp. 15–16.
7. The psychology of school subjects has long been an area of active research. No other school subject has even approached the level and frequency of studies conducted in the area of arithmetic. See especially William A. Brownell, *Learning as Reorganization: An Experimental Study*

in Third Grade Arithmetic (Durham, N.C.: Duke University Press, 1939); William A. Brownell and Gordon Hendrickson, "How Children Learn Information, Concepts, and Generalizations," *Learning and Instruction* (Forty-ninth Yearbook of the National Society for the Study of Education, Part I [Chicago: University of Chicago Press, 1950], pp. 92–128). Excellent reviews of this body of research can be found in McConnell, *op. cit.*, and Buswell, *op. cit.*

8. Jerome S. Bruner, *The Process of Education* (Cambridge, Mass.: Harvard University Press, 1960).
9. Cf. M. C. Wittrock, "The Learning by Discovery Hypothesis," in Lee S. Shulman and Evan R. Keislar (eds.), *Learning by Discovery: A Critical Appraisal* (Chicago: Rand McNally & Co., 1966), pp. 33–75.
10. Jerome S. Bruner, *Toward a Theory of Instruction* (Cambridge, Mass.: Belknap Press, 1966), pp. 59–68.
11. Jerome S. Bruner, Rose R. Olver, and Patricia M. Greenfield, et al., *Studies in Cognitive Growth* (New York: John Wiley & Sons, 1966), pp. 12 ff.
12. Cf. E. G. Boring, "Human Nature and Sensation: William James and the Psychology of the Present," in Robert I. Watson and Donald T. Campbell (eds.), *History, Psychology and Science* (New York: John Wiley & Sons, 1963), pp. 92–108.
13. Robert M. Gagné, *The Conditions of Learning* (New York: Holt, Rinehart & Winston, 1965); David P. Ausubel, *Educational Psychology: A Cognitive View* (New York: Holt, Rinehart & Winston, 1968).
14. Robert M. Gagné, "Contributions of Learning to Human Development," *Psychological Review,* LXXV (May, 1968), 177–91.
15. Ausubel, *op. cit.,* p. 22.
16. Bruner, *Toward a Theory of Instruction, op. cit.*
17. *Ibid.,* p. 72.
18. Gagné, *Conditions of Learning,* 2nd ed. This second edition of Gagné's book is in preparation and contains several major departures from the first edition. This passage is quoted from the manuscript.
19. See the 1965 edition, footnote 13.
20. Ausubel, *op. cit.,* p. 23.
21. Cf. Lee J. Cronbach, "The Logic of Experiments on Discovery," in Shulman and Keislar (eds.), *op. cit.,* pp. 88–90.
22. Ausubel, *op. cit.,* p. 24.

23. Jean Piaget has produced an enormous body of work. See especially Jean Piaget, *The Child's Conception of Number* (New York: Humanities Press, 1952); Jean Piaget, *Logic and Psychology* (New York: Basic Books, 1957); Barbel Inhelder and Jean Piaget, *The Growth of Logical Thinking from Childhood to Adolescence* (New York: Basic Books, 1958). The best overviews of Piaget's work are through his interpreters. See note 25.

24. *The Teaching of Arithmetic,* ed. Guy T. Buswell (Fiftieth Yearbook of the National Society for the Study of Education, Part I [Chicago: University of Chicago Press, 1951]).

25. See especially John Flavell, *The Developmental Psychology of Jean Piaget* (Princeton, N.J.: Van Nostrand Co., 1963); J. McV. Hunt, *Intelligence and Experience* (New York: Ronald Press, 1961); Hans G. Furth, *Piaget and Knowledge* (Englewood Cliffs, N.J.: Prentice-Hall, 1969); Irving E. Sigel and Frank H. Hooper (eds.), *Logical Thinking in Children* (New York: Holt, Rinehart & Winston, 1968).

26. James J. Gallagher, "Productive Thinking," in Martin L. Hoffman and Lois W. Hoffman (eds.), *Review of Child Development Research* (2 vols.; New York: Russell Sage Foundation, 1964), I, 349–81.

27. *Ibid.,* p. 355. This listing is itself taken from Hunt, *op. cit.*

28. Bruner, *Process of Education, op. cit.*

29. Albert Szent-Györgyi, "Teaching and the Expanding Knowledge," *Science,* CXLVI (December 4, 1964), 1278–79.

30. Quoted in Frank G. Jennings, "Jean Piaget: Notes on Learning," *Saturday Review* (May 20, 1967), 82.

31. Four of Jan Smedslund's studies are reprinted in Sigel and Hooper, *op. cit.,* pp. 265–94.

32. Irving E. Sigel, Anna Marie Roeper, and Frank H. Hooper, "A Training Procedure for Acquisition of Piaget's Conservation of Quantity: A Pilot Study and Its Replication," in Sigel and Hooper, *op. cit.,* pp. 295–307. The entire Sigel and Hooper volume is extremely relevant to mathematics education research.

33. Egon Mermelstein et al., *The Effects of Various Training Techniques on the Acquisition of the Concept on Conservation of Substance* (U.S. Office of Education Project No. 6–8300, Hofstra University, February, 1967).

34. Gagné, "Contributions of Learning to Human Development," *op. cit.*

35. Ausubel, *op. cit.,* frontispiece.

36. John Carroll, "A Model of School Learning," *Teachers College Record,* LXIV (1963), 723–33.
37. Benjamin S. Bloom, "Learning for Mastery," in *Evaluation Comment* (Bulletin of the U.C.L.A. Center for the Study of Evaluation of Instructional Programs), May, 1968.
38. Carroll, *op. cit.*
39. Bloom, *op. cit.,* p. 3.
40. Robert M. Gagné, "The Acquisition of Knowledge," *Psychological Review,* LXIX (1962), 355–65.
41. I am grateful to Professor Joe L. Byers for suggesting this analogy, as well as for much advice and helpful criticism concerning this chapter.
42. Sarah T. Herriot, "The Slow Learner Project: The Secondary School 'Slow Learner' in Mathematics," *SMSG Reports,* No. 5 (Stanford University, 1967).
43. Robert M. Gagné, "Learning Hierarchies," *Educational Psychologists,* VI (November, 1968).
44. Jerome S. Bruner, "Some Elements of Discovery," in Shulman and Keislar (eds.), *op. cit.,* pp. 101–13.
45. Robert B. Davis, "Discovery in the Teaching of Mathematics," in Shulman and Keislar (eds.), *op. cit.,* pp. 118–19.
46. Thomas F. Kuhn, *The Structure of Scientific Revolutions* (Chicago: University of Chicago Press, 1962).
47. Ausubel, *op. cit.,* pp. 148–49.
48. Jerome S. Bruner, "Going Beyond the Information Given," in Jerome S. Bruner et al., *Contemporary Approaches to Cognition* (Cambridge, Mass.: Harvard University Press, 1957), pp. 41–70.
49. Gagné, "Contributions of Learning to Human Development," *op. cit.,* p. 186.
50. Gagné, "Learning Hierarchies," *op. cit.*
51. Robert C. Craig, "Recent Research on Discovery," *Educational Leadership,* XXVI (February, 1969), 501–8.
52. Robert M. Gagné and Larry T. Brown, "Some Factors in the Programming of Conceptual Learning," *Journal of Experimental Psychology,* LXII (1962), 12–18.
53. John T. Guthrie, "Expository Instruction Versus a Discovery Method," *Journal of Educational Psychology,* LXIII (1967), 45–59.
54. W. G. Roughead and Joseph M. Scandura, "'What Is Learned' in Mathematical Discovery," *Journal of Educational Psychology,* LIX (1968), 283–89.

55. Blaine R. Worthen, "Discovery and Expository Task Presentation in Elementary Mathematics," *Journal of Educational Psychology Monograph Supplement,* Part II, LIX (February, 1968).

56. Craig, *op. cit.,* p. 503. Craig also points out that when the criterion has been application of the specific rules taught, expository forms of presentation are superior.

57. Vernon Hall and Harold Cook, "Discovery vs. Expository 'Instruction': A Comment" (Unpublished Manuscript, Syracuse University, 1968).

58. Cronbach, *op. cit.,* pp. 76–92.

59. *Ibid.,* p. 77.

60. *Ibid.,* p. 77.

61. Lee J. Cronbach, "How Can Instruction Be Adapted to Individual Differences?" in Robert M. Gagné (ed.), *Learning and Individual Differences* (Columbus, Ohio: Charles E. Merrill Books, 1967), pp. 23–39.

62. Ausubel, *op. cit.,* pp. 23–24.

63. Jerome Kagan, "Impulsive and Reflective Children: The Significance of Conceptual Tempo," in John D. Krumboltz (ed.), *Learning and the Educational Process* (Chicago: Rand McNally & Co., 1965), pp. 133–61.

64. John W. Atkinson, "The Mainsprings of Achievement-Oriented Activity," in Krumboltz, *op. cit.*

65. Hans J. Eysenck, *The Structure of Human Personality* (2nd ed.; New York: John Wiley & Sons, 1960).

66. Michael A. Wallach and Nathan Kogan, *Modes of Thinking in Young Children* (New York: Holt, Rinehart & Winston, 1965). See also Lee J. Cronbach, "Intelligence, Creativity: A Parsimonious Reinterpretation of the Wallach-Kogan Data," *American Educational Research Journal,* V (November, 1968), 491–512.

67. Wallach and Kogan, *op. cit.*

68. M. C. Wittrock, "Verbal Stimuli in Concept Formation: Learning by Discovery," *Journal of Educational Psychology,* LIV (1963), 183–90.

69. Worthen, *op. cit.* See note 55.

70. Lee S. Shulman, "Seeking Styles and Individual Differences in Patterns of Inquiry," *School Review,* LXXIII (1965), pp. 258–66. See also Lee S. Shulman, Michael J. Loupe, and Richard M. Piper, *Studies of the Inquiry Process* (Cooperative Research Project No. 5–0597, Michigan State University, 1968).

71. Jacob W. Getzels, "Creative Thinking, Problem-Solving, and Instruction," in Ernest R. Hilgard (ed.), *Theories of Learning and Instruction* (Sixty-third Yearbook of the National Society for the Study of Education, Part I [Chicago: University of Chicago Press, 1964]), pp. 240–67.
72. J. Richard Suchman, "Inquiry Training: Building Skills for Autonomous Discovery," *Merrill-Palmer Quarterly of Behavior Development,* VII (1961), 147–69.
73. Cronbach, "The Logic of Experiments on Discovery," *op. cit.,* pp. 85–86.
74. Joseph M. Scandura, "An Analysis of Exposition and Discovery Modes of Problem Solving Instruction," *Journal of Experimental Education,* XXXIII (1964), 149–59. See also Roughead and Scandura, *op. cit.*
75. Cronbach, "The Logic of Experiments on Discovery," *op. cit.,* p. 79.
76. Edward G. Begle and James W. Wilson. "Chapter 10: Evaluation of Mathematics Programs," in Edward G. Begle (ed.), *Mathematics Education* (Sixty-ninth Yearbook of the National Society for the Study of Education, Part I [Chicago: University of Chicago Press, 1970]).
77. John Dewey, *Logic: The Theory of Inquiry* (New York: Henry Holt & Co., 1938), p. 108.
78. Readers interested in the large body of empirical research in the psychology of mathematics instruction, both past and present, have a number of sources from which to choose. These include periodic issues of the *Review of Educational Research* dealing with mathematics education; the *Arithmetic Teacher* and *Mathematics Teacher,* journals; and occasional papers in the *Journal of Educational Psychology, American Educational Research Journal, Journal of Research in Science Teaching,* and *Child Development,* among many others. Reviews of earlier research can be found in past issues of this yearbook (Notes 1 and 4) as well as periodic issues of the *Yearbook of the National Council of Teachers of Mathematics.*

INTRODUCTION

THE PSYCHOLOGY OF SCHOOL SUBJECTS: A PREMATURE OBITUARY? (1974)

THE YEAR 1973–1974 was a pivotal year for Shulman. Beginning in 1968 (and both interrupted and enriched by a sabbatical year at the Hebrew University of Jerusalem, where he split his time between the medical school and the school of education), Shulman had devoted most of his research energies to the research with Arthur Elstein on medical problem solving, which eventually became the 1978 book *Medical Problem Solving*. This work grew methodologically out of the simulation studies Shulman had used in his earlier research on teachers. It also epitomized in its design the "wisdom of practice" research method that he would later use with experienced teachers. In 1974, after studying the wisdom of practice in medicine and exploring the complex cognitive processes of internists for several years, Shulman was ready to return to his earlier interest in teachers.

Shulman had a Guggenheim Fellowship that year and was spending it at Stanford as a visiting scholar hosted by Lee Cronbach. Three significant events punctuated the year. His good friend Yehuda Elkana introduced him to Clifford Geertz's newly published essay "Thick Description," telling him that his notions of medical diagnosis and Geertz's concept of ethnographic investigation were remarkably resonant. Second, Elkana introduced Shulman to his good friend Robert

Merton, who was spending that year at the Center for Advanced Study in the Behavioral Sciences (with Elkana and others), and Shulman began both reading and talking with Merton, a connection that was to influence his thinking from that time forward. Third, Shulman was invited to chair a research planning panel on research on teaching titled "Teaching as Clinical Information Processing." Chairing this panel, whose members included Philip Jackson, Sarah Lawrence Lightfoot, Tom Good, and Greta Morine Dershimer, among others, afforded him the opportunity to fashion a conception of strategies for the study of teaching that integrated his approaches to the study of medical problem solving, Geertz's conceptions of thick description, Merton's notions of theories of the middle range, and Shulman's critique of extant approaches to the study of teaching, which he considered unremittingly behavioristic and reductionist.

The report of the panel on the study of teaching was selected to serve as the template for the federal competition for a new national center for the study of teaching, which had been located at Stanford University for ten years. The Michigan State University team succeeded in winning the Institute for Research on Teaching away from Stanford, and the creation of that institution and its program would dominate most of Shulman's energies until 1982. The "Psychology of School Subjects" paper thus represents a bridge between the intensive work on medical education and medical problem solving of 1968–1973 and the subsequent investment in the study of teaching that was to follow. It also foreshadows both the later work on pedagogical content knowledge and a chapter on the comparative psychology of school subjects written (with Katherine Quinlan) for the *Handbook of Educational Psychology.*

This essay began as an invited address at the 1974 annual meeting of the National Association for Research in Science Teaching. Having been deeply immersed in both research on teaching and research on medical problem solving, Shulman was beginning to articulate the connections between these two—apparently disparate—lines of work. He reports on some of the salient findings from his work on medical problem solving, as well as the implications for medical education. For example, in their research, Shulman and his colleagues had discovered that it was critical for doctors to be able to early on generate hypotheses concerning a patient's ailments. This then led them to wonder how this capacity could be effectively taught to medical students.

Based on his experiences investigating medical problem solving, Shulman proposes a prospectus for educational research. Drawing on the work of both Ulric Neisser and Jerome Bruner, Shulman suggests that educational research would benefit from a renaissance in the study of the psychology of school subjects, research that took seriously the subject-specific nature of teaching and learning. Such work would require collaborations between psychologists—whose perspectives are much more generic—and subject matter experts—whose deep knowledge of specific content would be critical to the work.

Drawing heavily on the work of Clifford Geertz, Robert Merton, and Joseph Schwab, Shulman also argues for the importance of theory in educational research, especially, using Merton's term, "theories of the middle range." Theory both guides empirical research—leading us into interesting questions and helping us frame sound research designs that can test our theories—and is a product of our research; that is, we generate new middle-range theories as a result of our investigations. This emphasis on building theory would be a signature characteristic of Shulman's work, most notably in his work on the knowledge base of teaching and the nature of professions.

Shulman concludes by arguing for a line of research that would study the reasoning of teachers, much like his colleagues documented physicians' reasoning, as well as for a more eclectic portfolio of research methods, including longitudinal case studies, anthropological analyses of classrooms and teachers, and information-processing modeling of teacher and student thinking.

3

THE PSYCHOLOGY OF SCHOOL SUBJECTS

A PREMATURE OBITUARY?

ALTHOUGH THE EXPERIENCE OF Lot's wife should have forewarned me, I continue to have the irritating habit of looking back. Not only am I the sort of driver who accords inordinate attention to his rearview mirror, I am the sort of educator and psychologist who has a compulsion to review the history of his subject. Alas, Ecclesiastes' observation that "there is nothing new under the sun" is repeatedly confirmed, as I recurrently discover that some earlier writer has long since captured my newest insight, engaging remorselessly in what Merton[35] has dubbed "anticipatory plagiary." Or, as Alfred North Whitehead put it with characteristic succinctness, "Everything of importance has been said before by somebody who did not discover it."

Yet, despite the negative reinforcement which typically accompanies my retrospective gazings, the compulsion to repeat (as Freud long ago recognized) is not easily extinguished. The invitation to prepare this paper elicited immediately the expected retro-ocular reflex. I looked back once again.

In this case, I looked back at three kinds of events: previous invited addresses to this association, especially those of Ralph Tyler,[54] Gene Glass,[2] and most recently, Joseph Schwab;[43] my own research activities during the past ten years on the inquiry processes of teachers and physicians; and scattered sources in the history of educational research, in general, and in the teaching of science, in particular. The latter topic had been the subject of a review I had completed in collaboration with Pinchas Tamir.[47] In this paper, I should like to invite you to join me in these three reminiscences, to share in the concerns that have both stimulated and vexed me in the course of those mental wanderings, and to examine the ways in which the three strands begin to intertwine. Finally, I should like to broach the tentative conclusions I now feel warranted to draw from these experiences.

The Critics and Their Criticisms

For reasons doubtless deeply rooted in human nature, the opportunity to speak before such forums as this elicits remarkably sadomasochistic impulses from the protagonists. It is the rare address whose import is not hortatory, reprimanding, and self-righteously soul-saving. (As partial proof of that assertion, this paper will be guilty of all three of those transgressions.) The message is usually in three parts—a characterization of the errors being perpetrated, suggestions regarding the manner in which business ought to be conducted, and admonitions concerning the likely consequences of continued misbehavior.

Tyler's[54] diagnosis of the ills besetting research in science education focused on a shortage of adequate *theory* and the attendant basic research programs needed to make research on science teaching more firmly grounded in theory. He outlined a program of research priorities for science education, aimed at developing "an adequate map of the factors and process in science education." Tyler's contribution reflected accurately the mainstream view regarding basic research in education. This view was more fully developed in a publication of the National Academy of Education, of which Tyler was first president.[8]

Only a few years later, Glass[21] argued for a position "diametrically opposed to Tyler's." His paper, which should be read in conjunction with an earlier essay[20] to capture the full thrust of his arguments, asserted that:

> . . . we should not strive to make research on science education or education generally more scientific. Indeed, we who call ourselves educational researchers should turn away from elucidatory inquiry in all areas of education. This type of inquiry, directed toward the construction of theories or models for the understanding and explanation of phenomena, should be left to the social and natural sciences because it is currently unproductive in education and is a profligate expenditure of precious resources of time, money, and talent.[21]

He maintained that educational researchers should devote their energies to "evaluative inquiry" rather than "elucidatory inquiry," eschewing the quest for laws, explanations, and generalizations in favor of systematic programs of educational development and evaluation. His arguments and examples are cogently presently and—more's the misery—convincingly stated.

Confronted simultaneously with the rhetorical power of both the Tyler and Glass positions, I found myself in the quandary of the famous Rabbi of Chelm, the town of fools. It is told that two men appeared before the rabbi, each holding tightly to a leg of a certain worse-for-wear chicken and each claiming ownership. Each recited the basis for his claim in turn. After the first man completed his argument, the rabbi nodded sagely and stated, "You are right. The chicken is yours." No sooner had the second claimant finished his testimony when the rabbi again averred, "You are correct. The chicken must be yours." While the contestants stood silently pondering this decision, the rabbi's wife, who had witnessed the entire transaction, gently tapped her spouse on the shoulder, "My dear, it is impossible for this one to be right, and that one too." Without a moment's reflection, the rabbi swiftly replied, "That's correct. You're also absolutely right!" Somehow, despite its Hegelian overtones, I found the rabbi's solution less than satisfying for my current dilemma.

A second image suggested itself. You will recall the famous story of how Boswell informed his good friend Johnson of Bishop Berkeley's proof that the external world did not exist. As they were walking along the country lane, Johnson proceeded to approach a large stone lying at the roadside, and sent it flying with a resounding kick and the unforgettable retort, "I refute him thus!" In a similar fashion, I somehow felt that my own work, if I were not thoroughly deceiving myself, stood as an exemplification of at least a partial counterargument to Glass. That is, our research in medical inquiry was elucidatory, sought explanations and general characterizations rather than the evaluation of particular developments, yet had led to both successful program changes and, we felt, a fruitful improvement in our understanding of certain educational processes. At the same time, however, our work also confirmed the wisdom of several of Glass' observations.

This then defines the agenda for the rest of my paper—a vigorous albeit gentle kicking of the stone. I shall describe in some detail the research my colleagues and I have conducted in the processes of inquiry in physicians. I will summarize its findings and conclusions regarding medical inquiry, and the implications we have been able to draw therefrom for the conduct of medical education in general. Finally, using those events as a case study, I shall attempt to draw some conclusions for research in education and the teaching of science.

Studies of Medical Inquiry

An active program of research on medical inquiry has been conducted at Michigan State University since late in 1968. We* have attempted to understand how excellent, experienced physicians conduct a typical medical work-up, from their initial encounter with a new patient to the reaching of a final diagnostic judgment.[18] Participating physicians were peer-nominated internists, selected for their reputed diagnostic acumen. In order to study their cognitive processes under conditions that were as natural as possible, yet were not subject to the uncontrolled "noise" of the office, clinic, or hospital ward, the roles of patients were played by actors and actresses, carefully trained to portray actual patients whose full records were already in hand. The setting was a realistically stimulated doctor's office, and laboratory data were supplied on carefully contrived lab report slips or real x-rays. When possible, an actual physical examination was performed on the simulated patient. Otherwise, physical findings were provided through the report of an "intern" or "resident." The raw data consisted of videotapes of the encounters made via remote-controlled TV cameras; transcriptions of audiotapes were made of the physicians' thinking aloud during the course of the work-up; periodic retrospective summings-up at junctures between major sections of the work-up, such as just before ordering tests from the laboratory; and final review using "stimulated recall"[5,27] in which the physician viewed a videotape of his work-up immediately after having completed it, in order to attempt to reconstruct in as much detail as possible his intellectual processes while gathering information necessary to render a diagnostic judgment.

What results from such data is a complex tri-level protocol which includes descriptions of what the physician is observed (and recorded) to say and do, his immediate introspections while doing it, and his stimulated retrospective recall. This complex protocol can be subjected to a variety of scoring procedures, the details of which cannot be elaborated here. Indeed a major problem of this research has been to reduce the data to manageable size and still construct an explanation of medical thinking that makes

---

* "We" is employed in neither its editorial nor pontificial form. The research has been guided throughout by the wisdom of my collaborator and friend, Professor Arthur Elstein, upon whose shoulders the full weight of this project has typically been borne. Drs. Sarah Sprafka, Michael Loupe, Linda Allal, and Michael Gordon contributed immeasurably to its development.

sense both to physicians and psychologists. Since precisely the same simulations are employed with the entire sample of physicians, the major features of the task environment become well understood, and the significance of subtle differences between the approaches of different physicians is more easily detected. Moreover, the multi-level quality of the data enables us to "triangulate" our observations and interpretations from the perspectives of each of the three data sources. We can check interpretations for intra-protocol consistency, thus protecting ourselves from some of the problems of introspective data, such as retrospective distortion.

In addition to the large-scale descriptive study just described, a series of experimental investigations were conducted. Space does not permit description of their methods, but their findings will be included in the next section.

Findings for Medical Inquiry

We began our treatment of the data under the assumption that we could develop a systematic model based on the actual behavior of the criterial physician—the transcribed record of what he said and did. Unfortunately, though perhaps, in retrospect, not surprisingly, that attempt failed. It seemed impossible to discern what a physician was *really* doing, that is, what *motivated* the asking of a question or the elicitation of a physical finding; and what meaning was attached to a datum which was gathered that appeared to direct subsequent inquiry. We thus found, to borrow an analogy from linguistics, that the "surface structure" itself was uninterpretable, because the sentences, i.e., the "strings" of behavior, were too ambiguous—they could mean too many different things. It was only by getting at a cognitive "deep structure" level that clearly understandable patterns emerged.

Perhaps the most important single unit of analysis for understanding the physicians' cognitive processes was the diagnostic *hypothesis* and its formulation in the guidance of medical inquiry. Within the first few moments of an encounter with a patient, physicians almost universally began generating diagnostic hypotheses regarding the likely causes of a patient's complaints. These hypotheses serve as the elements of a conceptual framework in terms of which the balance of the inquiry is conducted. This conceptual scaffolding becomes the superstructure on which the physician hangs the subsequently collected facts, whose identity and order are determined by those hypotheses.

In addition to hypotheses, the basic units of analysis are *cues,* the items of information volunteered by the patient or elicited by the physician, and a way of representing the evidential weights of each cue vis-à-vis each potential hypothesis. The resulting scoring grid is a two-way matrix of cues and hypotheses. Cues are listed along the vertical axis in the order in which they are acquired. Hypotheses are arranged horizontally as column heads, both those hypotheses actually generated by a given physician and those often put forward, though not necessarily in the work-up being analyzed. This allows us to assess the weight of accumulating evidence both for hypotheses that have been produced by the inquirer, and others that may be warranted but were not actively considered.

As each cue is acquired, its weight is entered with regard to each hypothesis: +1, if it supports the hypothesis; –1, if it is inconsistent with the hypothesis; and 0, if it is irrelevant to confirmation or disconfirmation of the hypothesis. Fancier weighting systems have been attempted, but manifest no superiority over unit weights (see also, Dawes and Corrigan[12]). It is thus possible to characterize the cumulative weight of evidence for or against any given hypothesis at any stage of the work-up. Finally, the points at which each hypothesis was generated and, when appropriate, was terminated, are indexed. Although description of this basic scoring scheme may appear simple and straightforward, developing the scoring rules, debugging their application, and achieving reliability in their employment constituted a complex and frustrating task.

What have we learned about the processes of medical inquiry from this and related studies carried out in our research program? First, medical inquiry is not an inductive reasoning process and the physician bears no resemblance to a Baconian logic machine. If anything, he is faintly reminiscent of a Bayesian decision maker, in that the hypotheses generated are usually capable of rank ordering with regard to likelihood, and those likelihoods can be said to change as new data are processed. However, our investigations have indicated that the physicians use probabilities, if at all, only in a most imprecise, intuitive fashion, and their subsequent revisions of hypotheses in the light of new data do not conform to Bayes' Theorem. The hypothetico-deductive character of medical thinking is in marked contrast to its depiction in standard treatises on internal medicine. These works typically admonish the physician to keep an open mind while collecting all the necessary data only thereafter drawing diagnostic conclusions.

Unfortunately, these same texts neglect to advise the reader how one can assess when all necessary data have been gathered, except in light of the information's adequacy for testing particular hypotheses. Apropos of this observation, Herbert Simon[48] has argued that human problem solving is basically a form of means-end analysis, in which the solver initially generates a *state description* of a desired or expected goal, then explores alternative sequences of processes for attaining that goal. As we have noted elsewhere, a parallel view is advanced by F. C. Bartlett[2] in his discussions of open-ended searching and echoed by Miller, Galanter, and Pribram[37] in their description of the TOTE as the basic psychological unit of analysis.

Ironically, the characteristic of medical students' work-ups about which their teachers most frequently complain is their interminable length. The students are purported to gather an enormous amount of data from their patients, only to become inundated by its weight and lack of organization. It turns out that Dewey[15] was quite correct. A "fact" has no status *per se;* hence Dewey's insistence upon the awkward term "fact-meaning" to describe a fact as interpreted, a "fact-of-the-case." And thus it is that in our studies we distinguish carefully between *cue acquisition* and *cue interpretation.*

A specific anecdote comes to mind that dramatically exemplifies that distinction. During our pilot studies, two experienced physicians conducted work-ups on the same simulated patient several days apart. The patient was paralyzed from the waist down, onset of the paralysis had been acute and as the physician enters the examination room, he finds the patient lying on an examining table weeping "hysterically." Both physicians rapidly generated *Hysteria* as one working diagnostic hypothesis, and then proceeded to explore the possibility of a neurological basis for the observed sensory and motor deficit. In the course of a routine review of systems, each physician asked the following questions:

> "Any trouble with your hearing?"
>
> "No."
>
> "Any difficulties with vision?"
>
> "Not lately." (!)

One of the physicians interpreted that response as a *cue,* pursued the matter to a description of transient visual disturbance several weeks earlier, and eventually was able to conclude correctly that the patient had experienced the acute onset of multiple sclerosis. The second physician, though having acquired the same "fact," failed to detect its meaning and ultimately diagnosed the case as hysterical paralysis. So much for letting the facts speak for themselves.

Here our work merely reaffirms for medicine what is well-known to science educators through reading contemporary philosophy and history of science.[17,29,33,40] It is not the accumulation of facts which constitutes progress in science; it is the organization and reorganization of those facts into a coherent conceptual scheme that characterizes the growth of knowledge.

In addition to giving lie to the image of medicine as inductive inquiry, we also identified that the cause of diagnostic errors in medical work is rarely an insufficient amount of data. Indeed, accuracy of diagnosis is uncorrelated with thoroughness of data collection. Thoroughness correlates significantly, however, with cost,[22] a not insignificant dependent variable in modern medicine. The insignificance of thoroughness alone is at least partly explained by the intrinsic redundancy of the human organism—*qua* psyche and soma—as an information source. The organism is a system of systems, and the consequences of a local malfunction will be detectable as a symptom at multiple sites and via many behavioral signs.

What does determine diagnostic accuracy is the set of working hypotheses which define the "problem space" within which the inquiry is conducted. These hypotheses can be characterized in terms of their relationships with one another.[1] The most frequently encountered relationship is that of *multiple competing hypotheses,* a pair (or more) of hypotheses formulated in such a manner that confirmation of one implies rejection of the other(s). We have come to understand the value of competing hypotheses in terms of the well-documented inabilities of human information processors to make proper use of *negative* information.[55] By erecting truly competing hypotheses, it was possible for the physician to transform evidence negative for one hypothesis into a corresponding positive weight for its competitor, thus permitting much more efficient use of his limited information-processing capabilities.

The number of hypotheses that could be held in working memory at any one time was clearly limited. Our estimate was 4 ± 1, which errs on the high side, if anything. This limitation, substantially lower than Miller's[36] magic number 7, is in accord with Simon's[49] more recent estimate of a five-chunk capacity. Our more modest estimate may be due to the fact that our research participants are not being asked merely to hold the items in memory, but to use them actively as conceptual tools for directing questions and interpreting evidence. Not only is the number of working hypotheses predictable, so is their very necessity. When warned against generating hypotheses early in the work-up, even inexperienced medical students appear unable to resist the hypothesis-generating impulse.[50]

Finally, and most surprisingly, it was impossible to generalize regarding the accuracy, thoroughness, or other indices of diagnostic quality of a physician as he moved from case to case. It appeared as if diagnostic competence were domain-specific. This was troublesome for two reasons. First, we had begun this research thinking we were investigating the operation of a single underlying set of intellectual processes—medical inquiry strategies or skills. Second, the finding flew in the face of our preconceptions regarding the broad transferability of cognitive skills, especially of the "higher cognitive processes."

Having summarized some of the salient findings of the medical inquiry research, let us now turn briefly to the impact this research has had for the practice of medical education.

Implications for Medical Education

The findings and conclusions of these studies have made a discernable impression on some of the practices of medical education and on our general conceptions of the total enterprise. We have been brought, first of all, to a modified conception of the intellectual functioning of the physician and, hence, of the proper goals of medical education. Recognizing the ubiquitous importance of the quality of early-generated hypotheses for the successful practice of medical inquiry leads necessarily to consideration of how that capability might be taught more effectively. We currently spend more time instructing medical students in thorough data gathering than in early problem formulation and cue interpretation. Our revised conception has led to reassessment of how the clinical skills of medicine should be taught and, equally important, on what basis the diagnostic skill of the medical student or physician should be evaluated, i.e., with emphasis upon the quality, scope, and interrelationships of his diagnostic formulations.

This, in turn, has also led to reexamination of one of the hottest political issues in contemporary medical care, physician accountability. Not only do we now recognize which aspects of medical inquiry competence should be assessed, we also recognize the stringent limitations on our warrant for generalizing from level of competence on one case to competence with some other domain of problems. This finding has been independently confirmed by Hoffman's[24] studies of the American Board of Internal Medicine, McGuire's and Page's[31] research in Patient Management Problems, and Maatsch's[30] analyses of performance patterns on the Canadian Family Medicine Boards Examinations. The particular combination of knowledge and skills on which solution of a class of problems rests is apparently very important. It appears necessary to possess domain-specific knowledge to solve most problems. While the knowledge alone may not be sufficient in the absence of appropriate information-processing skills and a proper set of problem formulations, it is abundantly clear that no amount of general intellectual skill or mastery over cognitive strategies will overcome lacks in content knowledge. It seems reasonable to assume that a fairly complex set of knowledge by process interactions are involved in the construct we call clinical competence.

A still open question remains the optimal blend of knowledge-in-the-head and skill in information retrieval from texts, references, or other memory storage units. Clearly, knowledge is needed to develop that initial problem formulation which guides the inquirer toward recognizing what additional information he is going to need. Nonetheless, there is no reason for him to be totally self-sufficient as a source of information. Far from it—but we as yet don't know how far.

Better understanding of the processes of medical inquiry also yields a clearer conception of where technological decision aids may be of greatest service to the practicing physician. Such aids, which are typically computerized, must meet at least two standards. They should assist the physician where he needs help, not in an area where he already performs adequately without prosthesis. Moreover, the introduction of the aids should, whenever possible, be consistent with the physician's already developed habits of thought and practice, not in conflict with them. Our findings suggest that Einhorn's[16] concept of "expert measurement and mechanical combination" is an eminently wise approach. That is, use the human being to collect data and (with possible stimulation of reminders from decision aids) to formulate the problem space of diagnostic hypotheses. Then employ the computer to exercise the typically straightforward decision rule that will work to evaluate the data, given the hypotheses. Thus, for our cases in the medical inquiry project, the diagnoses of the physicians were either predicted or improved by a decision rule which stated that the diagnosis selected should be that hypothesis with the greatest positive remainder after subtracting the sum of negative weights from the sum of positive weights. (In fact, merely adding positive weights may be sufficient in most cases.) The combination rule was a simple linear function, provided the hypotheses being assessed were at the same level of specificity.[51]

There is much ferment in the medical world today regarding the proper form for medical records. As trends grow toward medical auditing procedures for evaluating the quality of care and the justifiability of costs, many are insisting that the medical record reflect how the physician actually pursued the case, rather than serve as a neat summary of findings. Clearly, our research has suggested some particular emphases which must be reflected in any revised system of medical records which purports to be a veridical representation of physicians' thought processes.

In summary, our research has led to a richer general understanding of medical work, which serves to inform our efforts in curriculum planning, instructional development, teaching practices, and evaluation strategies. The research was not explicitly developmental, nor was it evaluative. It was directed toward the formation of generalizations of modest scope with implications for both understanding and for practice.

This recitation of the purposes, procedure, findings, and implications of our work in medical inquiry was meant to symbolize my kicking of the stone—to exemplify research in education that was neither evaluative nor fruitless. I am now led to a series of observations regarding the proper objects and methods of research in education.

Prospectus for Research in Education

I shall have six points to make: First, that the time has come for a renascence of a modern form of the psychology of school subjects, and that the parameters of that domain of inquiry are already definable; second, that an orientation toward the development of middle-range theories is highly desirable in educational research, and our problems are unlikely to be solved by a retreat to solely evaluative inquiries, any more than they were by an earlier retreat to utterly irrelevant theorizing and empirical work on basic processes; third, that the recent work of Schwab on the practical as both language and thought for curriculum is of great significance and may yield important insights regarding the proper roles of educational theory and research; fourth, that research on teaching must be pursued with an eye to understanding the teacher as clinician; fifth, that traditional behaviorism is nearly dead in psychology because of its theoretical and methodological limitations, and educational researchers might well pull the plug on its respirator in our own field; and sixth, that our conceptions of proper methods for research in education must be recast in light of these considerations.

Psychology of School Subjects

Our research in medical inquiry is clearly an example of an investigation in the psychology of a particular school subject—medicine, or more specifically, diagnostic thinking in internal medicine. Not only is it undertaken in a particular task environment, thus not necessarily generalizable outside of medicine, it is unlikely that basic social or behavioral scientists would have conducted it. Similarly, there are basic theoretical studies relevant to the teaching and learning of science that are properly of interest to this field, and not to the general educational researcher or behavioral scientist.

Examples of such studies in science education abound.

> Such science-relevant basic research would be on a topic like the cognitive development of science-relevant concepts in young children, e.g., cause and effect, space, time, mass, momentum. This sort of research is

> clearly in the tradition of Piaget. The purpose would be to identify some general normal expectancies for the evolution of particular concepts around which curriculum developers and program writers could plan their creative endeavors. It would not really matter whether such conceptual developments were the products of ontogenetic cognitive development or of learning. The importance would be to provide general maps that would be useful for the activities of the curriculum developers.
>
> [Another] kind of research which would be extremely useful would involve direct studies of criterial members of the scientific community to serve as operational models on the basis of which objectives for science teaching could be established. That is, if the working scientist is to serve as a useful model for the development of certain aspects of the science curriculum, much better empirical data are needed about how the working scientist actually conducts his inquiries, what his characteristics are and how they developed. These sorts of descriptive studies would be very useful for those who would plan and evaluate science programs.
>
> The work of Arthur Koestler[28] on thought among creative scientists, Hadamard on the analyses of mathematical discovery, and [our studies of] medical reasoning of expert physicians can serve as models for such work (Shulman and Tamir,[47] p. 1139).

Those investigators who would be put off by the complexity of investigating the cognitive processes of practitioners in their natural habitats, or reasonable simulations thereof, might gain courage (or at least adaptive resignation) from a recent paper by one of our leading cognitive psychologists, Ulric Neisser.[39] He notes that psychologists originally chose to study basic processes like serial learning or signal detection in highly artificial experimental settings because it was assumed that the simplicity of both the processes and the settings would render them more amenable to investigation. What we have learned after many years of studying such phenomena is that even the ostensibly simple processes are terribly complex—subject to individual strategies and under the influence of a host of other variables. The lesson Neisser derives from this experience is remarkably close to the position espoused here. He recommends that researchers forego the laboratory-based study of basic processes, since their ostensive simplicity has not offset their unarguable irrelevance. Instead, he urges that we turn to socially important phenomena (reading is his example) and study them in the contexts within which they typically occur. At best, we will learn something that can be generalized both to neighboring phenomena of social value or even back down to fundamental psychological processes. At worst, we learn only to understand the particular domain under investigation more clearly, no mean accomplishment in itself.[46]

Generalizations from basic process research conducted in artificial settings can also be extremely deceptive. An experience from our medical inquiry research may be illustrative. When we encountered the ceaselessly hypothetico-deductive character of medical work in our earliest studies, we were skeptical regarding the accuracy of our observations. The incredulity stemmed not only from the finding's apparent violation of the standard admonitions of medical lore; it also ran counter to a conclusion from *A Study of Thinking* by Bruner et al.[7] which had been embedded deeply into the belief system of cognitive psychology. Hypothesis-testing strategies, whether simultaneous and multiple, or serial, could not be maintained by problem solvers because they engendered too high a level of cognitive strain. If Bruner et al. were correct, how could our physicians be standing up under that cognitive strain, blithely continuing with the generation and simultaneous testing of multiple hypotheses?

The answer lay in the nongeneralizability of Bruner's work on thinking to the world of *real* people using *real* knowledge to solve *real* problems. Consistent with the traditions of experimental psychology, Bruner had created a task environment for which individual differences in knowledge brought to the task by subjects would be irrelevant. It was a pure process task. Under those conditions, when a problem solver attacks a concept attainment problem, he has no choice but do so in a conservative, hypothesis-free manner. It is as if there were no structure on which to hang a hypothesis once it has been generated (and in a knowledge-free task, that is precisely the case), so any hypotheses have to be juggled in the air to keep them alive and working.

In a word, hypothesis-guided inquiry is only strainful in task environments where the inquirer has no organized bodies of knowledge on which to draw. In the far more typical case, when the inquirer has a good deal of prior relevant knowledge, organized sets of intellectual skills, and experience in using the knowledge and skills jointly in problem solving, the finding is reversed, and it is hypothesis-guided inquiry which brings about the least cognitive strain. Such then is the danger of assuming the automatic validity of an experimental task for a real one.

Yet, it was the presumed scientific superiority of investigations of the general, the basic, and the abstract over the particular and subject matter specific, which contributed, in part, to the demise of the psychology of school subjects as a locus of scholarly interest. Whatever did happen to the psychology of school subjects?

In the introduction to the third volume of his series of digests of *Investigations in the Teaching of Science,* Francis Curtis[11] attempts to characterize the differences between the contents of that third volume, which summarized studies in science teaching between 1931 and 1937, and the earlier two volumes, which presented digests of studies beginning as early as 1910. He observed that, since the first volume, there was a striking trend toward more *learning* studies, greater *statistical sophistication,* and *more generality* in the targets of the investigators. Although still concerned with the teaching of science, the studies attempted to be relevant to "the entire field of science teaching," rather than to a particular course of instruction.

Ten years later, in his presidential address to the Division of Educational Psychology of the American Psychological Association, William Brownell was to bemoan the neglect of research on the psychology of school subjects by educational researchers.

> It is true that the various subjects call, in greater or less degree, for the same general types of learning; arbitrary associations have to be established, skills acquired, concepts understood, and so on. On this account research on the subjects separately might seem to be wasteful; why not, for example, investigate the acquisition of skill for all subjects at one and the same time? Yet, from subject to subject, and within the same subject, arbitrary associations differ; skills differ; concepts differ; and, withal, pupil behavior differs. The differences reside, in part, in the intrinsic relations involved; they reside in the opportunities afforded for the use of previous experience; they reside in varying amounts of complexity, they reside in sheer difficulty with respect to mastery. All these differences need to be explored (Brownell,[6] 1948, p. 496).

Brownell's recommendations place him squarely in the educational research tradition of Charles Judd, and in conflict with the E. L. Thorndike position that has come to dominate educational psychological thought. Although Thorndike also wrote on the psychology of school subjects (his *Psychology of Arithmetic* is deservedly a classic), his general inclination was to derive the methods for teaching any particular subject from the general laws of learning which he was developing. Judd, in contrast, placed much greater importance on the particular attributes of each subject matter field. Thus, their continuing debate covered not only issues regarding the basic units of transfer-of-training, but also the proper methods for applying psychology to education. (Joncich,[25] in her biography of Thorndike, notes the old rumor that the career-long disagreements between Judd and Thorndike may have stemmed from their competition for the favor of a young lady while both were students at Wesleyan University—a contest won by upperclassman Judd. Having piqued our interest, Joncich proceeds to dismiss the speculation as far-fetched and unsupported.)

Whereas the general trend away from school subjects studies continues to this day, there are a few hopeful signs worth noting. One of the most influential works on education of the past twenty years has been the Bloom taxonomy of educational objectives.[3] In that small volume, a general taxonomic system was put forward for all cognitive school learning. More recently, Bloom, Hastings and Madaus[4] published a handbook on evaluation which brought the work on taxonomies in line with more recent developments. In contrast to the original taxonomies, which attempted to employ a single set of categories to encompass the objectives of all subject matter areas, in the new handbook each discipline modifies (often radically) the cognitive and affective taxonomy categories to reflect more accurately the characteristics of its particular area. This is surely a step in the direction of recognizing the importance of distinguishing among the school subjects.

The quest for a process-based generality of educational theory reflects, in large measure, the way in which a single discipline—psychology—has provided the dominant paradigms for educational research. How glibly I speak of the *psychology* of school subjects, as if that phrase were synonymous with all studies of the teaching and learning of school subjects. Indeed, some problems masquerade as exclusively psychological questions when they are not.

A striking example is the concept of *transfer.* What are the limits of transfer of training? What units are transferred? What are the relationships between retention and transfer? Psychologists *(mea culpa)* have succeeded in convincing most educators that those are purely psychological questions, requiring research elucidating the cognitive functioning of human learners. In fact, such questions are not usefully answered in the general case, but must be addressed for the different subject matters separately. The following statement of Szent-Gyorgyi[52] suggests why this is the case.

> Science tends to generalize, and generalization means simplification. My own science, biology, is today not only very much richer than it was in my student days, but is simpler, too. Then it was horribly complex, being fragmented into a great number of isolated principles. Today these are all fused into one single complex, with the atomic

model in its center. Cosmology, quantum mechanics, DNA and genetics, are all, more or less, parts of one and the same story—a most wondrous simplification.

Thus, a study of broad transfer of learning in biology carried out in 1910 would likely result in dramatically lower estimates of degree of transfer than a parallel study in 1970. This would not be attributable to evolutionary changes in the information-processing characteristics of the human organism, but rather to evolution (or revolution) in the structure of scientific knowledge itself. Similarly, our findings on the absence of transfer in medical problem-solving may undergo change in coming years as more comprehensive theories of disease and therapy develop. This observation is parallel to the recognition that "learning-by-discovery" studies are subject-specific, since some subjects have a structure whose regularities are intrinsically more discoverable than others.[9,45] The observation is also consistent with recent work on human judgment and decision making[13] which argues that it is not the nature of the cognitive processing which is captured when a psychologist studies acts of judgment. Rather, it is the structure of the task itself, to which the human organism fits its cognitive functioning.

The enthusiasm for aptitude-treatment interaction studies has been high in recent years, and, though initially disappointing, results of such studies are beginning to encourage.[10] These studies might be called the psychology of "school learners," rather than school subjects. But the critical missing element may well be the character of the task, subject matter, or problem to be mastered. It seems eminently reasonable to argue that learning to fit instruction to the subject matter is at least as significant a challenge as learning to match instruction to learner characteristics.

All these assertions lead to the conclusion that, whereas the psychology of school subjects is undoubtedly deserving of immediate disinterment, its future vitality will be predicated on its no longer remaining the exclusive province of psychologists. It must become the joint focus of subject matter experts and psychologists, if its study is to be fruitfully pursued, and if useful theoretical statements are to emerge from that research.

The Role of Theory

What constitutes useful theory in education? Much of the criticism of elucidatory research in education is that it does not yield powerful enough bodies of theory. Part of the problem with that charge lies in the ambiguity surrounding the meaning of theoretical power. It is typically observed that theories in education lack sufficient scope; and that they do not provide for prediction and control of educational phenomena. I should like to argue that the proper scope for educational theory lies in what Merton[34] has called "theories of the middle range." I shall then propose that a proper function of theory is to help us understand or render meaningful the phenomena of education we observe. In that discussion, I shall draw heavily on the work of the anthropologist Clifford Geertz.[19] Finally, I shall suggest that an important role of research and theory is defined in Schwab's[43] conception of the practical.

Our work in medical inquiry was theory-based and theory producing. The theoretical propositions generated, however, did not lead directly to prediction and control, except in a few instances. The level of theorizing at which these theoretical formulations lay is best approximated by Merton's[34] concept of "theories of the middle range." These theories "lie between the minor but necessary working hypotheses that evolve in abundance during day-to-day research and the all-inclusive systematic efforts to develop a unified theory that will explain all the observed uniformities . . ." (ibid., p. 39).

These theories are principally used to guide empirical inquiry. As such, they assume the function of theory which Glass labeled "heuristic." Such theories take many forms, from extended metaphors to limited formal models. These formulations are abstractions from and about observed phenomena. They typically begin "with a concept and its associated imagery and generate an array of theoretical problems" (ibid., p. 45). These in turn lead to propositions that permit empirical testing. The theories are not expected to act as "laws of nature." They will likely be as limited in longevity as in scope, disappearing as they either wear out their usefulness, or are subsumed under more general conceptual schemes. As Merton observed, citing Tennyson,

> Our little systems have their day;
> They have their day and cease to be.

I would assert that the heuristic function of middle-range theory is as indispensable to the investigator engaged in evaluative inquiry as it is to the elucidatory inquirer. In the absence of such theories, intelligent instructional development and evaluative research become difficult, if not impossible. A set of theoretical concepts is needed to answer such questions as: How many dependent measures should we assess in the evaluation? What are likely to be the relevant outcomes, intended or not, of a program such as this? If we wish to measure intervening transactions during the course of this program, which events are worth monitoring? These are but a few examples of applied, evaluative, decision-oriented questions which are unanswerable without the help of middle-range theoretical understanding. And that understanding ought to represent a marriage of the theorist's armchair and systematic empirical reality testing.

The very act of describing a set of events, so important in curriculum planning and all evaluation, is deeply involved in theory. In fact, Clifford Geertz has argued that for his field, anthropology, the primary role of theory is to make meaningful descriptions and interpretations of events possible.

> Believing, with Max Weber, that man is an animal suspended in webs of significance he himself has spun, I take culture to be those webs, and the analysis of it to be therefore not an experimental science in search of law but an interpretive one in search of meaning (Geertz,[19] 1973, p. 5).

Geertz introduces the concept of "thick description," borrowed from the philosopher, Gilbert Ryle. Thick description refers to the process of describing complex social and cultural events, where any report is necessarily embedded in a network of implicit concepts and theoretical models. I have found his characterization of the function of theory for making thick description possible extremely suggestive for thinking about the potential uses of theory in educational research.

> . . . the essential task of theory building here is not to codify abstract regularities but to make thick description possible, not to generalize across cases but to generalize within them.
>
> To generalize within cases is usually called, at least in medicine and depth psychology, clinical inference. Rather than beginning with a set of observations and attempting to subsume them under a governing law, such inference begins with a set of (presumptive) signifiers and attempts to place them within an intelligible frame. Measures are matched to theoretical predictions, but symptoms (even when they are measured) are scanned for theoretical peculiarities—that is, they are diagnosed.
>
> Theory is not, at least in the strict meaning of the term, predictive. The diagnostician doesn't predict measles; he decides that someone has them, or at the very most *anticipates* that someone is rather likely shortly to get them. But this limitation, which is real enough, has commonly been both misunderstood and exaggerated, because it has been taken to mean that cultural interpretation is merely post facto: that, like the peasant in the old story, we first shoot the holes in the fence and then

> paint the bull's-eyes around them. It is hardly to be denied that there is a good deal of that sort of thing around, some of it in prominent places. It is to be denied, however, that it is the inevitable outcome of a clinical approach to the use of theory (ibid., p. 26).

I suggested earlier that our middle-range theoretical formulations must be empirically testable. Geertz now describes the manner in which theories whose purpose is not prediction are evaluated empirically.

> . . . the theoretical framework . . . must be capable of continuing to yield defensible interpretations as new social phenomena swim into view. Although one starts any effort at thick description, beyond the obvious and superficial, from a state of general bewilderment as to what the devil is going on—trying to find one's feet—one does not start (or ought not) intellectually empty-handed. Theoretical ideas are not created wholly anew in each study; as I have said, they are adopted from other, related studies, and, refined in the process, applied to new interpretive problems. If they cease being useful with respect to such problems, they tend to stop being used and are more or less abandoned. If they continue being useful, throwing up new understandings, they are further elaborated and go on being used.
>
> Studies do build on other studies, not in the sense that they take up where the others leave off, but in the sense that, better informed and better conceptualized, they plunge more deeply into the same things. Every serious cultural analysis starts from a sheer beginning and ends where it manages to get before exhausting its intellectual impulse. Previously discovered facts are mobilized, previously developed concepts used, previously formulated hypotheses tried out; but the movement is not from already proven theorems to newly proven ones, it is from an awkward fumbling for the most elementary understanding to a supported claim that one has achieved that and surpassed it. A study is an advance if it is more incisive—whatever that may mean—than those that preceded it; but it less stands on their shoulders than, challenged and challenging, runs by their side (ibid., pp. 27, 25).

Geertz's notions of theory as a means of rendering our perceptions of the world more coherent, meaningful, and sensible is consistent with conceptions of contemporary philosophers of science regarding the efficacy of theory. Stephen Toulmin[53] has argued convincingly in his *Foresight and Understanding* that the ultimate test of scientific theories is the quality of their explanations of phenomena, rather than the precision of their predictions.

It is instructive that E. G. Boring, the distinguished historian of experimental psychology, named Sigmund Freud as the most important psychologist of the first half of the twentieth century. To the spokesman for American psychology's most hard-nosed wing, a system of psychological thought yielding no predictions and less control, psychoanalysis, was deserving of that accolade. It has made thick description possible for so many—from the novelist to the teacher, from the clinical psychologist to the family physician, from the anthropologist to the man-on-the-street.

Research, Theory, and the Practical

Schwab's[43] conception of curriculum development as practical deliberation has stimulated much recent effort in the curriculum field. Schwab's position is frequently misinterpreted as taking a nihilist stance regarding the usefulness of educational research and theory. On the contrary, the very opposite is true. Ever since he began eloquently warning against "the corruption of education by psychology" some fifteen years ago, Schwab's admonitions have not been rooted in the indictment of theory, *per se*. Rather, he criticized confusing the partial truth of any theoretical formulation with some hoped-for whole truth; and, in turn, failing to employ theories appropriately in the solution of practical problems, such as designing a curriculum or instructional program.

There is no question that many kinds of theoretical formulations and research findings are indispensable inputs into a process of practical deliberation. Without such material for deliberation, the resulting eclectic would be of limited richness. What sorts of psychological theory and research would serve as the most useful inputs for deliberation? My estimate is that the middle-range theories of a psychology of school subjects with the empirical research they would stimulate are at the appropriate level for most fruitful practical deliberations.

Apropos of Schwab's continuing reminders of the limitations of theory, I note Merton's observation that "the middle-range orientation involves the specification of ignorance. Rather than to pretend to knowledge where it is in fact absent, it expressly recognizes what still must be learned. . . . *It does not assume itself to be equal to the task of providing theoretical solutions to all the urgent practical problems of the day* . . . [my italics]" (Merton,[34] pp. 68–69). Continued theory development and research are not only compatible with Schwab's conception of the practical; practical deliberation cannot work effectively without them. Theory thus becomes, not less important, but important in new ways.

Schwab has also repeatedly emphasized the importance of studies dealing with current educational practice as a necessary component of the practical in curriculum work. This recommendation contains at least two themes. First, there is a need to understand what is really going on in schools. Second, there is need to understand how practitioners really do their work—not only *what* they do, but *how* they deliberate, judge, make decisions, and assess consequences. Studies of the first kind have begun to emerge, though not in sufficient number. Studies of schooling in the anthropological mode are represented by Jackson[26] or Rist.[42] Applications of computer technology to the maintaining of ongoing "course histories" are under development and investigation by Rothkopf[41] and his colleagues.

Research of the second kind calls for studying teachers in much the same manner we have approached physicians—that is, studying teachers as gifted practitioners capable of performances which our best theories are not yet capable of explaining, much less predicting or generating. We could then use those investigations as important contributions to development of theories of teaching. It is to this topic that I now turn.

Research on Teaching as Clinical Work

We can look at the teacher in much the same fashion as we have looked at the physician. We must view the teacher as a clinician, not only in the sense of someone diagnosing specific forms of learning dysfunction or pathology and prescribing particular remedies, but more broadly as an individual responsible for aggregating and making sense out of an incredible diversity of information sources about individual students and the class collectively; bringing to bear a growing body of empirical and theoretical work constituting the research literature of education; somehow combining all that information with the teacher's own expectations, attitudes, beliefs, purposes . . . and having to respond, make judgments, render decisions, reflect, and regroup to begin again. The actual ratio of reflection to reflex in teaching is itself an important subject for study, both in terms of how teaching currently occurs and in terms of the potential limits of change.

In this context, we treat the teacher *as agent,* rather than as a passive employer of teaching skills and techniques, a marginal operator in a complex system of technology, or a set of personality traits and aptitude measures. From such studies we would hope to understand the ways in which teachers cope with the demands of classroom life, the circumstances under which those copings lead to successful teaching and learning, and the conditions under which they become maladaptive.

It is unfortunate how teachers have been studied in educational research. When possible, their effects are muted through random assignments of teachers to treatments, while prayers are offered that their unique contributions will be buried in a tiny residual sum of squares. Alternatively, they become scores on a personality scale, verbal fluency scores, years of education or experience, and thus entered as independent variables in multiple regression equations, there to pick up the few (if any) crumbs of variance remaining after the effects of student social class and IQ have been partialled out.

Many of our recent educational reforms attempt to bypass the thought and judgment of the teacher via instructional systems that are ostensibly teacher-proof. These developments are based on mistaken beliefs about the self-sufficiency of those "laws of learning" on which many of these systems are based; and a misplaced disdain for the competence and flexibility of the human teacher.

McKeachie,[32] in a paper aptly titled "The Decline and Fall of the Laws of Learning," makes a case for the insufficiency of psychological principles of learning for the conduct of educational practice. Our current learning principles are too simple, while meaningful educational learning is quite complex.

> This complexity, so frustrating to those who wish to prescribe education methods, is a reminder of the fascinating uniqueness of the learner. Fortunately most educational situations are interactive situations in which a developing, learning human being engages with a situation in ways designed to meet his learning needs. Part of that situation is *another human being who has some resources for instruction and some capacity to adapt it to the learner*" [my italics] (ibid., p. 11).

Thus, McKeachie too sees the gap between the limits of theory and the demands of practice bridged by the capabilities of the teacher. The teacher is seen as drawing upon "some resources for instruction" and "some capacity to adapt to the learner." Resources for instruction include the books, materials, programs, films, architecture, etc., that Glass[20] would have "carry knowledge into the school." But Glass goes on to argue, "The behavior of schoolmen can be subtly shaped by rationally designed instruments of education. Educational knowledge must be embodied in the media of teaching, not in the minds or prevailing views of schoolmen" (ibid., p. 28). In contrast, I am insisting that it will be necessary for any innovations in the context, practices, materials, or technology of education to be mediated through the minds and motives of teachers. This will entail serious studies of the cognitive processes of teachers, their capacities and limitations, in order to develop training programs, decision aids, record-keeping technologies, and the like, to further hone the teacher's skills in adapting to learners.

We are no more likely to remove the teacher from education than we are to delete the physician from medicine. Surely the distribution of roles in both those fields of practice will change, as will the organization of institutions for providing their respective basic services. Yet, even if Illich, Bereiter, and their followers are correct about the eventual (and perhaps welcome) demise of the school, the teacher will not go down with the ship. He will reappear in whatever form those new institutions may take.

We will sooner de-school society than de-teacher it.

The Mental Life of Teachers

The research I have described and am proposing is clearly cognitive in orientation, even mentalistic. There are revolutionary changes taking place in the field of psychology, as many of our most respected experimental psychologists have come to recognize the limitations of behaviorism. So it is that Donald Hebb[23] answers his own question, What is psychology about? with the straightforward proposition, "Psychology is about the mind" (ibid., p. 74). Leading behaviorists, such as James Deese[14] and James Jenkins, have come to recognize the insufficiency of the psychological stances that would have us treat the human as a black box.

It would be a tragedy if researchers in science education remained chained to an outmoded, outgrown, limited behavioristic psychology, just when their brethren in the behavioral sciences are rediscovering that psychology is truly William James' "science of mental life," not merely John Watson's "science of behavior." This entails more than a shift in slogans, however. It requires a changed image of the methods and emphases of research in education.

Aspects of Method

Given these notions of the aims of educational research, its appropriate objects of inquiry and relations of theory and practice, I am brought finally to a consideration of research *methods*. This discussion assumes its proper position at the end of a discourse on research, rather than as the starting point.

We must be prepared to broaden the range of methods we employ in our research, as we reformulate the questions we propose to raise. Although good experimental and correlational investigations will continue to be useful, we need add more varied kinds of studies—longitudinal case studies, anthropological analyses of classrooms and teachers, information-processing modellings of the thought processes of teachers and learners using methods of controlled introspection and retrospection, investigations of basic phenomena, such as transfer, under conditions of varying subject matter, to name but a few. We should be prepared to treat our subject more clinically, both in terms of the teacher and the investigator as clinicians.

True to Whitehead's warning, these words of mine are but echoes of William Brownell's exhortation to his educational psychological peers. That leader among psychologists of the school subjects, whose brilliant experimental work on the teaching of arithmetic reads as well today as it did forty years ago, affirmed that

> . . . it is a mistake to assume, as some do, that all research which deserves the name must follow this [classic experimental] pattern and that investigations which do not are, *ipso facto,* untrustworthy and valueless. To take this extreme position would be to deny to botany and to astronomy (to cite but two examples) any validity as fields for research. In these fields, as in many others, systematic observation, competent analysis, and rigorous classification of data largely take the place of research in accordance with the "Law of the Single Variable" (Brownell,[6] p. 495).

(In these days of multivariate analysis, I should perhaps amend Brownell's "Law" to read "and its multivariate equivalent, the Canon of the Canonical Correlate.")

Research employing these techniques of systematic observation, competent interpretation and analysis, rigorous classification, and theory construction may frequently bear more resemblance to anthropology or clinical medicine than to what we have learned to expect from educational research—and what of it. Nevertheless, changes in research method do not reduce the necessity to conduct our studies in as careful and disciplined a manner as is appropriate to the subject. Clifford Geertz expressed it well.

> I have never been impressed by the argument that, as complete objectivity is impossible in these matters (as, of course, it is) one might as well let one's sentiments run loose. As Robert Solow has remarked, that is like saying that as a perfectly aseptic environment is impossible, one might as well conduct surgery in a sewer (Geertz,[19] p. 30).

Thus Geertz warns against both the sloppiness of the unbridled romantic who would revolutionize education through the power of his intentions and the purity of his moral character, as well as against the "scientist" who would replace relevance and descriptive adequacy with super-precision and formality of models.

On Realistic Expectations

In this paper I have attempted to describe some ways in which currently neglected approaches to educational research might be pursued. Through a variation on "Show and Tell," I attempted to use our research on medical inquiry as a case in point, deriving some general principles from the scope, methods, findings, and practical consequences of that program of investigations. Those general principles dealt with the formulation of researchable questions for a psychology of school subjects; the level of theorizing appropriate to such research; the manner in which the resulting research findings and middle-range theories could be fruitfully treated in practical deliberation; the image of the teacher as clinician that emerges from such analysis, and the necessity, in principle, for someone to play that role in any system of instruction; and some guidelines for conducting research on teaching so conceived.

I would like to conclude with a few observations on the setting of appropriate expectations regarding what will emerge from these endeavors. Following his recent address to this group, Joseph Schwab[44] was asked about a set of activities he had directed in connection with the Biological Science Curriculum Study (BSCS) which seemed inconsistent with some recommendations he had offered in his talk. Schwab's response reminded the questioner that it was now fifteen years later, and what was appropriate policy for the late 1950s need not be so for the mid-1970s. This exchange reflected an important characteristic of education—indeed, of any practical art and its attendant policy sciences. As social, political, or personal circumstances change, the warrant of earlier generalizations must be re-evaluated. There is reason to believe that this will ever be the case, that in education we are never likely to reach theoretical bedrock.

This is one reason why educational innovations are so frequently needed and so often unsuccessful. Mosteller (1972)[38] has reported that roughly one out of seven systematically evaluated educational reforms are adjudged significantly superior to the program they are meant to replace. Apparently, however, this same "success ratio" holds for programs of social reform and—innovations in surgical technique! When one is dealing in a problem area requiring translation of theory into practice, and both components are constantly undergoing change, there is apparently a realistic level of expectation to be maintained for the likelihood of successful reform. The first satellite-bearing rockets aborted; the economy is more often a shambles than a well-oiled machine; heart transplants are now rarely performed, because they usually don't work. Yet physics, economics, anatomy, and immunology are much more advanced than are the behavioral sciences upon which education rests. So it is not merely the state of our science which limits our successes, it is apparently also the built-in error rate for any practical or policy field.

Geertz tells a story which captures the appropriate image quite well.

> There is an Indian story—at least I heard it as an Indian story—about an Englishman who, having been told that the world rested on a platform which rested on the back of an elephant which rested in turn on the back of a turtle, asked (perhaps he was an ethnographer; it is the way they behave), what did the turtle rest on? Another turtle. And that turtle? "Ah, Sahib, after that it is turtles all the way down" (Geertz,[19] pp. 28–29).

So it is with our research in education. As scientists (or, at least, teachers of science), we may stand on the shoulders of giants.[35] But as scholars and practitioners of education, we must learn to be comfortable as we teeter on the backs of an ever growing tower of turtles.

REFERENCES

1. Allal, L. K., "Training of Medical Students in a Problem-Solving Skill: The Generation of Diagnostic Problem Formulations," Unpublished doctoral dissertation, Michigan State University, 1973.
2. Bartlett, F. C., *Thinking: An Experimental and Social Study,* New York, Basic Books, 1958.
3. Bloom, B. S. (Ed.), *Taxonomy of Educational Objectives. Handbook 1: Cognitive Domain,* New York, McKay, 1956.
4. Bloom, B. S., J. T. Hastings, and G. Madaus, *Handbook on Formative and Summative Evaluation of Student Learning,* New York, McGraw-Hill, 1971.
5. Bloom, B. S., "The Thought Processes of Students in Discussion," In S. J. French (Ed.), *Accent on Teaching: Experiments in General Education,* New York, Harper, 1954.
6. Brownell, W. A., "Learning Theory and Educational Practice," *Journal of Educational Research, 41,* 7, 481–497 (1948).
7. Bruner, J. S., J. J. Goodnow, and G. A. Austin, *A Study of Thinking,* New York, John Wiley, 1956.
8. Cronbach, L. J., and P. Suppes, *Research for Tomorrow's Schools: Disciplined Inquiry for Education,* New York, Macmillan, 1969.

9. Cronbach, L. J., "The Logic of Experiments on Discovery," In Lee S. Shulman and Evan R. Keislar (Eds.), *Learning by Discovery: A Critical Appraisal,* Chicago, Rand-McNally, 1966, 77–92.
10. Cronbach, L. J., and R. E. Snow, *Aptitudes and Instructional Methods,* New York, Irvington, in press.
11. Curtis, F., *Third Digest of Investigations in the Teaching of Science,* Philadelphia, Blakiston, 1939.
12. Dawes, R. M., and B. Corrigan, "Linear Models in Decision Making," *Psychological Bulletin, 81,* 95–106 (1974).
13. Dawes, R. M., "The Mind, the Model and the Task," *Proceedings of the Seventh Annual Indiana Theoretical and Cognitive Psychology Conference,* Bloomington, Indiana, April, 1974.
14. Deese, J., *Psychology as Science and Art,* New York, Harcourt Brace Jovanovich, 1972.
15. Dewey, J., *Logic: The Theory of Inquiry,* New York, Holt, 1938.
16. Einhorn, H. J., "Expert Measurement and Mechanical Combination," *Organizational Behavior and Human Performance, 7,* 86–106 (1972).
17. Elkana, Y., "Science, Philosophy of Science, and Science Teaching," *Educational Philosophy and Theory, 2,* 15–35 (1970).
18. Elstein, A. S., N. Kagan, L. S. Shulman, H. Jason, and M. J. Loupe, "Methods and Theory in the Study of Medical Inquiry," *Journal of Medical Education, 47,* 2, 85–92 (1972).
19. Geertz, C., *The Interpretation of Cultures,* New York, Basic Books, 1973.
20. Glass, G. V., "Educational Knowledge Use," *Educational Forum,* 21–29, November, 1971.
21. Glass, G. V., "The Wisdom of Scientific Inquiry in Education," *Journal of Research in Science Teaching, 9,* 1, 3–18 (1972).
22. Gordon, M. J., "Heuristic Training for Diagnostic Problem Solving among Advanced Medical Students," Unpublished doctoral dissertation, Michigan State University, 1973.
23. Hebb, D. O., "What Psychology Is About," *American Psychologist, 29,* 2, 71–79 (1974).
24. Hoffman, P. J., Physicians Appraise Other Physicians: Improving the Decisions of a Medical Specialty Board, *Conference on Research in Medical Judgment,* Office of Medical Education Research and Development, 1974.
25. Joncich, G. M., *The Sane Positivist: A Biography of Edward L. Thorndike,* Middletown, Connecticut, Wesleyan University Press, 1968.

26. Jackson, P. W., *Life in Classrooms,* New York, Holt, Rinehart and Winston, 1968.

27. Kagan, N., D. Krathwohl, et al., *Studies in Human Interaction,* Bureau of Educational Research, College of Education, Michigan State University, 1967.

28. Koestler, A., *The Act of Creation,* New York: Macmillan, 1964.

29. Kuhn, T. S., *The Structure of Scientific Revolutions,* Chicago, University of Chicago Press, 1962.

30. Maatsch, J., Personal communication, 1973.

31. McGuire, C., and G. Page, "An Overview of Physicians' Performances on Simulated Clinical Encounters Presented in Patient Management Problem Format," Paper read at the annual meeting of the American Educational Research Association, New Orleans, February, 1973.

32. McKeachie, W. J., "The Decline and Fall of the Laws of Learning," *Educational Researcher,* 7–11, March, 1974.

33. Medawar, P. B., *Induction and Intuition in Scientific Thought,* London, Methuen, 1969.

34. Merton, R. K., *On Theoretical Sociology,* New York, The Free Press, 1967.

35. Merton, R. K., *On the Shoulders of Giants: A Shandean Postscript,* New York, Harcourt, Brace and World, 1965.

36. Miller, G. A., "The Magic Number Seven Plus or Minus Two," *Psychological Review, 63,* 81 (1956).

37. Miller, G. A., E. Galanter, and K. Pribram, *Plans and the Structure of Behavior,* New York, Holt, Rinehart and Winston, 1960.

38. Mosteller, F., Address, College of Education, Michigan State University, May, 1972.

39. Neisser, U., "Strategies for Cognitive Psychology," Unpublished manuscript, Cornell University, March, 1973.

40. Popper, K. R., *The Logic of Scientific Discovery,* New York, Wiley, 1961.

41. Rothkopf, E. R., "Course Content and Supportive Environments for Learning," *Educational Psychologist, 10,* 3, 123–128 (1973).

42. Rist, R., "Student Social Class and Teacher Expectations: The Self-Fulfilling Prophecy in Ghetto Education," *Harvard Educational Review, 40,* 411–451 (1970).

43. Schwab, J. J., "The Practical: A Language for Curriculum," *School Review, 78,* 1–23 (1969).

44. Schwab, J. J., "Decision and Choice: The Coming Duty of Science Teaching," *Journal of Research in Science Teaching, 11,* 4, 309–317 (1974).

45. Shulman, L. S., "Psychology and Mathematics Education," In Edward G. Begle (Ed.), *Mathematics Education.* The 69th Yearbook of the National Society for the Study of Education, Part I. Chicago: University of Chicago Press, 1970, 23–71.

46. Shulman, L. S., "Reconstruction of Educational Research," *Review of Educational Research, 40,* 371–396 (1970).

47. Shulman, L. S., and P. Tamir, "Research on Teaching in the Natural Sciences," In Robert M. W. Travers (Ed.), *Second Handbook of Research on Teaching,* Chicago, Rand-McNally, 1973, 1098–1148.

48. Simon, H. A., *The Sciences of the Artificial,* Cambridge, Massachusetts, M.I.T. Press, 1969.

49. Simon, H., "How Big Is a Chunk?" *Science, 183,* 482–488 (1974).

50. Sprafka, S. A., "The Effect of Hypothesis Generation and Verbalization on Certain Aspects of Medical Problem Solving," Unpublished doctoral dissertation, Michigan State University, 1973.

51. Sprafka, S., and A. S. Elstein, "What Do Physicians Do? An Analysis of Diagnostic-Reasoning," Conference on Research in Medical Judgment, Office of Medical Education Research and Development, Michigan State University, East Lansing, Michigan, 1974.

52. Szent-Gyorgyi, A., "Teaching and the Expanding Knowledge," *Science, 146,* 1278–79 (1964).

53. Toulmin, S., *Foresight and Understanding,* New York, Harper, 1961.

54. Tyler, R. W., "Resources, Models and Theory in the Improvement of Research in Science Education," *Journal of Research in Science Teaching, 5,* 43–51 (1967–1968).

55. Wason, P. C., and P. N. Johnson-Laird, *Psychology of Reasoning: Structure and Content,* Cambridge, Massachusetts, Harvard University Press, 1972.

ACKNOWLEDGMENTS

This paper was prepared while the author was on leave as Visiting Scholar, School of Education, Stanford University, and was presented in plenary session at the 1974 Annual Meeting of the National Association for Research in Science Teaching at Chicago, Illinois.

This publication was prepared pursuant to a contract with the National Institute of Education, United States Department of Health, Education, and Welfare. Contractors undertaking such projects under Government sponsorship are encouraged to express freely their judgment in professional and technical matters. Points of view or opinions do not, therefore, necessarily represent National Institute of Education position or policy.

The preparation of this paper was made possible, in part, by a fellowship from the John Simon Guggenheim Memorial Foundation. In the course of preparing this paper, the stimulation and advice of Lee Cronbach, Paul Hurd, Robert Merton, Richard Snow, Decker Walker, and Harriet Zuckerman proved indispensable. They are naturally to be absolved of blame for any of the paper's errors of judgment or fact.

INTRODUCTION

AUTONOMY AND OBLIGATION: THE REMOTE CONTROL OF TEACHING (1983)

BY 1979, Shulman had completed the first three and a half years of leading the Institute for Research on Teaching (IRT) with Judy Lanier. Shulman, Lanier, and their collaborators had created, with substantial federal research dollars, an unusual research center at Michigan State University. It was highly interdisciplinary and wildly eclectic methodologically. Further, the IRT hired eight public school teachers to devote half their time (the other half remaining in their classrooms) as teacher-collaborators associated with every research program in the Institute. It had become increasingly clear as they conducted this research that their conception of teachers as problem solvers, decision makers, thinkers, planners, in addition to actors or people who exhibited certain behaviors, had implications for policy, as well as for practice.

Shulman spent 1979–1980 as a Fellow at the Center for Advanced Study in the Behavioral Sciences at Stanford. In the spring of that year, Gary Sykes contacted Shulman. He was in the policy division of the National Institute for Education (directed by Marc Tucker), and they were exploring the radical notion that they should commission a series of papers on the connections between policy and teaching (another division which was directed by Virginia Richardson). Shulman thought it was an odd idea (indeed, the juxtaposition of teaching and policy in the same title shocked many colleagues), but eventually Shulman was lured into the enterprise and co-edited (with Sykes) a volume called the *Handbook of Teaching and Policy*.

As he read across chapters, Shulman was struck with the tension between professional autonomy and social obligation that lies at the heart of teaching. In this essay, he asks the question, "If the responsible and effective teacher must be both free and obligated, how shall we define the proper mix of those typically incompatible virtues?"

Shulman begins the essay by examining a concrete instance of school policy that was grounded in research on effective schools, and he uses that example to illustrate the tensions between teaching—which is individualistic and adaptive—and policy—which is remote and often unresponsive. Shulman then explores five reasons why policy-based solutions encounter problems when attempting to solve problems of teaching and learning: inconsistencies among mandates; limits on resources, time, and energy; limits on teacher expertise; limitations of working conditions; and the self-defeating mandate.

But there might be other problems as well, Shulman hypothesizes, problems rooted in the basic assumption that one can move from research directly to changing practice. First, policies cannot simply follow the incontrovertible data of research; policies have to assuage human concerns, and policymakers often face moral dilemmas that no research results can resolve. Second, we need a broad array of different kinds of research to inform the deliberations of policymakers: experiments and field studies, as well as theoretical and conceptual inventions like Robert Merton's concept of the self-fulfilling prophecy or John Carroll's model of school learning.

If teaching is impossible work, how are we to help teachers succeed? Autonomy, Shulman claims, is both the resolution and the problem, for it allows teachers to adapt their instruction, and it also allows them to withhold instruction. Loose-coupling can help, for properly understood, it can help us negotiate the conflict between policy and professional practice. Policies need to be designed to use loose-coupling as a solution, and this entails creating policies that are shells within which professional judgments can operate. We cannot escape the tension between the teacher's autonomy and obligation; it is fundamental to and inherent in the work. But Shulman asks that we continue to strive for ways that make teaching and educational systems both responsible and free.

4

AUTONOMY AND OBLIGATION

THE REMOTE CONTROL OF TEACHING

" . . . And above all is this matter of freedom. A German cannot think of freedom without rules. For us, all freedom is no freedom. We may dispute over the rules, but not that they must be there. . . . It depends, you see, on how you define the contrary of freedom. For us, it is chaos, for you . . . "

"Authority?"

He nodded. "We sacrifice some of our freedom to have order—our leaders would claim social justice, equality, all the rest. While you sacrifice some of your order to have freedom. What you call natural justice, the individual rights of man."

—John Fowles, *Daniel Martin,* pp. 557–558

The Nightmares

As the characters in John Fowles's powerful novel discuss images of contrasting political systems, they conclude that the ideals one seeks do not direct the shaping of a society's values and practices. Rather it is the darker image of one's worst fears and anxieties. We act not to achieve our ideals but to fend off our nightmares. Thus, to understand why people behave as they do, ask not what they value most, but what they fear most.

The participants in the struggles over teaching and public policy have their collective nightmares as well. For many of the policymakers, the vision is of teachers who do not teach, or teach only what they please to those who please them; who prefer the transient kicks of frills and fads to the tougher, less rewarding regimen of achieving tangible results in the basic skills; who close their schoolhouse doors and hide their incompetence behind union-sheltered resistance to accountability and merit increases; whose low expectations for the intellectual prowess of poor children leads them to neglect their pedagogical duties toward the very groups who need instruction most desperately; or whose limited knowledge of the sciences, mathematics, and language arts results in their misteaching the most able. The nightmares are remarkably parallel for liberals and conservatives among the policymakers. Each envisions an unwilling or inept teacher resisting the implementation of policies designed thoughtfully to help children, and through the young, to benefit the greater society.

Not surprisingly, teachers harbor their own nightmares. These portray a besieged and beleaguered group of dedicated professionals, inadequately appreciated or compensated, attempting to instruct responsibly and flexibly under impossible conditions. They are subject to endless mandates and directives emanating from faceless bureaucrats pursuing patently political agendas. These policies not only dictate frequently absurd practices, they typically conflict with the policies transmitted from other agencies, from the courts, or from other levels of government. Each new policy further erodes the teacher's control over the classroom for which she is responsible: pupils are yanked out of the room willy-nilly for special instruction, disrupting the continuity of their classroom experience while repeatedly upsetting the normal flow of classroom life for everyone else; a larger number of children, or bused children, or handicapped children, or inexperienced teacher aides must be accommodated in her classroom while she also, by the way, must take on an extra hour per day of reading, a new writing initiative, more rigorous mathematics and science, sex education, bicultural education, and carefully maintain the detailed individual records needed to create the bureaucrat's required audit trail.

The educational scholars have their own version of the nightmare. In it they see both policymakers and practitioners pursuing their respective chores mindlessly, or at least without benefit of the carefully collected, sifted, analyzed, and interpreted bodies of knowledge that constitute the stuff of educational scholarship. This body of work includes both the most esoteric products of basic social science research and the concrete results of systematic program evaluations and reviews; the quantitative results of large-scale surveys or teaching experiments or the rich descriptive portraits of educational ethnographers. The scholar's nightmare is of an educational system at all levels uninformed by the wisdom of research, unguided by the lessons of scholarship. Much of this scholarship is directed at understanding not only the enterprises of teaching and of policy per se but also the circumstances arising when these domains of practice collide. The present volume has been designed to examine the war of these worlds and to explore ways of thinking about the dilemmas they pose.

These portraits are certainly overdrawn. Yet nightmares are caricatures of fears. They feed on the anxieties produced by daily frustrations over failed attempts to do one's job. The policymaker sees well-crafted programs fall with an impotent thud at the threshold of a classroom door. Teachers see politicians and ideologues interfering with their responsibility to judge and implement what is best for their students, like a septic malpractice lawyer leaning over the physician's shoulder during surgery. And scholars see their work falling stillborn from the press, ignored equally by both parties or, even more likely, employed when convenient in support of positions already taken rather than being used to inform and guide emerging choices.

The plan of this volume has been to draw together the perspectives of the various parties to this enterprise. We have presented the results of research on the effectiveness of schools and of teachers, attempting to examine that research in the context of the inquiries which produced it. Here the question has been: What is the knowledge base which scholars claim ought to inform the decisions of both policymakers and practitioners? How adequate is the base for the guidance of policy?

Another set of papers discusses the character of teaching practice and of the profession. What do we know of the lives of teachers? How do they learn to teach, both from formal and informal sources? What effects have recent developments had on the performance and morale of teachers, as well as on the ability of the profession to attract and hold talented practitioners? What roles are played by the unions, state agencies, and other sources of influence on the minds, motives, and teaching performances of teachers?

Yet another set of contributions examines the policy process itself. What form have legislative policies on teaching taken? How have judicial decisions affected classroom practice? In what ways do the policy conflicts around teaching reflect far more fundamental controversies over values?

In confronting these questions we will return once more to the topic of conversation between the characters in *Daniel Martin*. If the responsible and effective teacher must be both free and obligated, how shall we define the proper mix of those typically incompatible virtues? Do we risk tyranny from above to achieve needed order and equity? Or do we foster liberty and autonomy while thereby risking anarchy and chaos?

The problems of teaching and policy defined in this volume are not ones that can be addressed lightly, much less solved readily. Nevertheless, both the problems formulated and the solutions suggested must be taken seriously by policymakers. The problems will not disappear; they will only fester. Their habitual neglect has long since ceased being benign. To evade them is no longer possible.

In this chapter we shall address several questions that bear upon the fundamental relationships among research, pedagogical practice, and educational policy. We shall begin by discussing a concrete case of policy which flows from bodies of research discussed in this volume—the school and teacher effectiveness literatures. We shall review in some detail the maxims for practice and policy emanating from this literature and the emerging experiences in implementing the policies. We will then examine the implicit model of school change and improvement which appears to underlie most discussions of teaching and policy. We shall attempt to understand the assumptions of the model and the reasons why it so rarely seems to succeed. We will then turn to the types of knowledge, both scientific and practical, which appear to provide the rationale for changes in educational policy. Finally, we will confront the central dilemmas of this volume. Can principles and practices be mandated through policy without thereby eroding the teacher's capacity to instruct flexibly and responsively? Can the rights of powerless groups to receive an equal and excellent education be protected without placing clear limits on the discretion of individual teachers? Can we devise a system in which teachers are both responsible and free?

The Plans

The dilemma should be examined concretely. A good example emerges from the literature on more effective schools. Drawing from a number of sources—studies by Rutter, Brookover, Edmonds, and others—a characterization has emerged of the features of unusually effective schools for economically disadvantaged youth. The characterizations are remarkably consistent with one another, as well as with the current interpretations of much of the teaching effectiveness literature.

Effective Schools

Early in the 1970s, in spite of the waves of despair regarding the value of schooling precipitated by the Coleman Report and its re-analyses, Jencks' *Inequality,* the apparent failure of Project Headstart, and other discouraging reports, the beginnings of a new research tradition emerged. Instead of asking whether schools or teachers made any difference, scholars modified the syntax of their inquiries. They asked instead what distinguished those teachers or schools that consistently produced high achievement in their pupils from those that consistently failed to do so. Moreover, they pursued their investigations through gathering data from within the walls of school buildings and individual classrooms. Instead of following resources to the schoolhouse door and then attempting to estimate their yield in schoolwide general achievement, they made direct observations of life in classrooms. They assumed that the important features of classrooms that made a difference for student achievement were not adequately represented by the levels of resources present in a school. Their assertion was that resources had to be transformed at the school and classroom level into teacher behavior and pupil responses to render a meaningful account of school effectiveness.

Edmonds (1982) has formulated five principles of effective schooling on the basis of these studies.

> The correlates of effective schools are (1) the leadership of the principal characterized by substantial attention to the quality of instruction, (2) a pervasive and broadly understood instructional focus, (3) an orderly, safe climate conducive to teaching and learning, (4) teacher behaviors that convey the expectation that all students are to obtain at least minimum mastery and (5) the use of measures of pupil achievement as the basis for program evaluation (Edmonds, 1982).

Edmonds is one of a number of educators who have attempted to draw prescriptions for the improvement of practice from the empirical research on effective schooling. He is careful to point out that these characteristics of effective schools have not been derived from studies of intervention programs in which schools experiencing difficulties undergo planned change. Nevertheless, in many parts of the country, districts are implementing plans based on principles similar to Edmonds' or their equivalents in an effort to improve the quality of urban public education. When leading public school officials testify to the success of these school improvement programs, they ascribe the design of the interventions to the results of educational research. The mandated changes are thus justified by their ostensible association with scientific research. Further, they claim to be validated by changes in average achievement test scores earned by pupils in the system.

Effective-schools programs are established in school systems in a number of ways. They typically employ total schools as their units of implementation, and the decision to become involved is usually an administrative one. Because of the key role assigned to the building principal, she must become actively involved early. The approach is highly rationalized, with the schoolwide use of record-keeping systems tied to objectives, frequent use of both locally and nationally developed achievement tests, and a broad-based commitment to academic performance and strong classroom discipline with backing from the principal's office. Efforts are directed at the achievement of tangible results—changes in the academic achievement of pupils.

It is not surprising that such programs rapidly become controversial. Opponents argue that the research base of such programs is inadequate because too small a sample of schools was studied or that programs involving planned change cannot be based on studies in which only static systems were examined without purposeful attempts to reform a system. They further point out how limited and limiting is the criterion employed in the school-effects enterprise—changes in scores on standardized achievement tests in basic skills. There is much more to school, they argue, than is reflected in students' rushed answers to multiple-choice tests. Finally, the opponents claim that such changes in practice mandated from above are rarely successful over the long haul. Teachers understandably and justifiably resist the remote control of teaching by distant bureaucrats.

There exist equally strong arguments in support of systematic mandates for teachers. Education is a public service and a public trust. It is not sufficient to engage in all the right processes of teacher involvement in policymaking and bottom-up planning if the desired academic results are not forthcoming. The bottom line that counts is results. The consequences of poor education not only harm the immediate recipients but ultimately deprive all members of the society through rendering some citizens less capable of caring for themselves, of contributing to the economic and social well-being of the nation, of exercising their political mandate wisely, and of increasing their general well-being. We all partake in the common good. Whatever diminishes the common good diminishes each of us.

An analogy can be drawn to the policies for general inoculation against communicable diseases. It is normally mandated that all members of a population receive such inoculations, not only for their own sakes but because their refusal or ignorance endangers others as well. Therefore, physicians are mandated to provide such inoculations and schools refuse to enroll youngsters who have not received the requisite immunizations. Do physicians feel that their professionalism is compromised by the mandate to vaccinate? Does not the obligation to take responsibility for the most general public good override concerns regarding the professional's need for autonomy?

The arguments that swirl about the effective-schools implementations are representative of the controversy surrounding the tension between teaching and policy. Why is the juxtaposition of "teaching" and "policy" the statement of a problem? We are wont to think of teaching as a highly clinical, artful, individual act. Since instruction is interactive, with teachers' actions predicated on pupil responses or difficulties, it appears ludicrous in principle to issue directives regarding how teachers are to perform. William James compared teaching to a war in which the pupil was the enemy. Although we make heroes of the occasional combat commander whose "Damn the torpedoes; full speed ahead!" leads to victory, we more typically remember the charge of the Light Brigade or Gettysburg to acknowledge the importance of sensitively adapting tactics to the realities of a situation. Teaching is the very prototype of the idiographic, individual, clinical enterprise. Policy connotes the remote, nomothetic, and unresponsive. Teaching is intended to promote excellence and repair difficulties. Policy is intended to ensure fairness and prevent selective oppression.

Indeed, most federally mandated policies are initiated in the interests of some pupil population—the poor, the educationally disadvantaged, the handicapped, the gifted, women—whom advocates wish to protect from miseducation. In the case of effective-schools innovations, the interests of children of the poor are most frequently represented. These programs are intended to ensure that these children receive the full benefits of active teaching by committed professionals enthusiastically employing methods with a high probability of producing satisfactory academic achievement. There is a clear explanation for why these mandates so typically emanate from the federal level. The relatively powerless groups whose interests they reflect are generally unable to marshal sufficient influence at the local level to effect policy changes. It is only as they aggregate their numbers and, hence, power, that they can wield the needed political muscle. The insistence that teachers at the local level maintain the autonomy to determine policy sounds disturbingly like a return to the status quo that made the new programs necessary in the first place—a situation composed of equal portions of good intentions and poor results.

The case of effective schools is but an instance of the larger issue to which this chapter is addressed. Having described the nightmares motivating the interested parties and a specific instance of a program which arouses such anxieties, we shall now turn to a more general question. What is the conception of policy, teaching, and research which governs our current approaches to designing and implementing policies for the improvement of teaching and learning?

The Myths

There exists a generally shared perception among many school administrators and laypersons regarding the improvement of public education. Its credibility is so unquestioned that few observers of contemporary schooling even think to challenge its assumptions. The following paragraph expresses its essential message.

> From a combination of recent experience and carefully conducted research, we have now come to understand the best ways to teach and the conditions for effective schooling. These understandings can be classified under such headings as "effective schools," "direct instruction," "time on task," "teacher expectations," "teaching effectiveness" and the like. Despite this knowledge, much elementary and secondary teaching is unsatisfactory. The solution is to establish and administer general educational policies designed to ensure that teachers practice those methods of teaching likely to achieve the desired results. To monitor compliance, employ a readily acceptable common metric to indicate the degree of success; standardized achievement tests are an obvious choice. Through a combination of policy and oversight, the schools can be improved.

Whenever a solution appears so simple and straightforward, the cynical among us can expect it to fail. It has achieved the status of a self-evident truth, yet it may only be a collectively held myth. Indeed, the common wisdom is that the simple solutions have thus far not borne the anticipated fruit. While most observers would consider schools better now than they were before Title I/ESEA, Headstart, Follow Through, and many of the other programs of the Great Society, the benefits are surely not unblemished. The revolution did not occur. The millennium has not arrived.

The astute reader will now raise an important question. How can the common wisdom so blithely contradict itself, by both claiming the simplicity of the solution and explaining the impossibility of the accomplishment? How can we both know that the key to educational improvement is straightforward and also know that it is doomed to the most modest of success?

One is reminded of the story of the Rabbi of Chelm, the legendary town of fools. When confronted by two men each claiming ownership of the same benighted chicken, the rabbi heard each party out in turn. When the first had finished stating his case, the rabbi nodded sagely and muttered: "You are right, absolutely right. The chicken is certainly yours." No sooner had the second congregant presented his claim when the rabbi acclaimed with equal sagacity: "No doubt about it, you are right. That chicken belongs to you." The rabbi's wife, who had been observing the litigation from a corner of the room, could contain herself no longer. "My dear husband, it is impossible that the chicken should belong to the first one and to the second as well." The rabbi turned to his perceptive spouse and responded firmly, "You are right, too, absolutely right." So it is with conventional wisdom. Its individual propositions may be absolutely right albeit mutually incompatible. As we have seen in this volume, this dilemma defines the essential character of policy questions.

Impediments to the Simple Solution

Why does the simple become so complex? What are the possible reasons for encountering difficulties when attempting to implement policy-based solutions to general problems of teaching and learning? We shall entertain five possibilities. The list is certainly not exhaustive, but the explanations entertained will illustrate the complexities of breeding practice from policy.

1. INCONSISTENCIES AMONG MANDATES. A policy becomes a plan of action when translated into specific mandates. But the specific mandates may themselves be functionally incompatible. This can occur for two reasons. The policies themselves may be designed for conflicting purposes. Thus Green argues that the teacher cannot simultaneously pursue mandates to achieve both excellence and equity. Another reason for incompatibility is the inconsistency between the mandate and its intent. That is, the manner in which a policy is implemented may carry unintended consequences that dilute the very results the mandate was designed to achieve. For example, the mandate to pull Title I pupils out of regular classrooms is clearly intended to ensure the quality and intensity of the instruction they receive. The "pull-out" itself is in large measure a tactic designed to

produce a readily examined audit trail. Serious questions are now being raised over the disruption in the flow of instruction, both to the target children and their colleagues, of the continuing pattern of exodus and return to classroom work.

Even in the absence of pull-out, the mandated procedures can have unintended deleterious outcomes. In a particular Title I program, funds were made available to hire teacher aides for assisting in the classrooms of high-need youngsters. Documentation was required that the aides were employed to help the Title I children. The aides indeed devoted all their energies to that specific subgroup of pupils, but unfortunately, the regular classroom teacher then devoted most of her energies to the other youngsters in the class. Thus, in the interest of responding to a particular procedural requirement of the policy, those pupils with the greatest need for skilled instruction received much of their assistance from the adult with the lowest level of preparation.

2. LIMITS ON RESOURCES, TIME, OR ENERGY. Another possible impediment occurs even where the policies are compatible. In this case, compatible mandates require an aggregate of time, energy, or other resources that are simply unavailable to the teacher or school. It has been said that the curriculum can only change in one direction—it grows. We improve schooling by adding responsibilities to the school's list, never by removing them. In recent years the additions have included mainstreaming of handicapped youth, sex education, new math and science curricula, teacher aides, among many others, often with shortened school days and larger class sizes. The state and federally funded programs typically carry the shadow of record-keeping, an audit-inspired array of forms whose completion is intended to assure the proper delivery of the desired services. Each of the prescribed program changes or augmentations is well-conceived and well-intended. Nevertheless, they are like individually benign sources of radiation or pollution which only become dangerous when they accumulate at a common locus. The teacher-in-the-classroom is ground zero, and these individually justified mandates land simultaneously on shoulders already burdened with the weight of teaching many subjects to diverse youngsters.

Although this image of overwhelming multiple burdens is certainly accurate, it is also undeniable that many skilled practitioners find ways to cope. They transform the zero-sum game into a productive synergy. Instead of feeling they must trade off teaching time among too many subjects or too diverse a range of students, they use inventive approaches to subject-matter integration (e.g., combining the teaching of reading skills with the study of science, literature, or social studies content) or nontraditional teaching techniques (employing peer tutoring or cooperative learning strategies that take advantage of classroom diversity for the benefit of all pupils) to exploit the opportunities presented by the complexity. But such resolutions are by no means commonplace. They require exceptional expertise—both in teaching skills and subject-matter knowledge; adequate time and support services to do the extensive extra planning and development necessary; a supportive context provided by both the work environment and the professional peer group which encourages such special efforts; and an educational system which affords professionals so skilled and committed the self-esteem and sense of efficacy needed to sustain them in the face of frequent frustration and failure. Absence of these conditions constitutes a further impediment to school improvement.

3. LIMITS OF TEACHER EXPERTISE. A third impediment may rest with the intellectual, emotional, or pedagogical demands made on teachers by some new programs. Many teachers may simply be incapable of implementing certain mandates. The demise of the "new math" in the sixties and early seventies may be attributed in large measure to the failures of both teachers and parents adequately to understand its rationale and principles. The current implementation of PL 94-142 may be hampered by the absence of sufficient training for ordinary classroom teachers to know how to teach handicapped youngsters. Or they may be paralyzed by attitudes toward handicapped pupils that neither training nor supervised experience has addressed adequately.

It must be remembered that our nation's teachers, though the most highly trained in the world, enter the teaching profession with far less preparation than is afforded almost any other profession. Compared to the typical eleven years of preparation afforded the contemporary family practitioner (four years undergraduate, four years medical school, and three years supervised internship/residency), the typical teacher's four years including only a single semester of supervised internship seems limited indeed. When we consider that only about one-sixth of the typical four-year undergraduate program in teacher education is devoted to pedagogical subjects per se, with the rest appropriately assigned to liberal arts plus major and cognate education in the subjects to be taught, the expectations we hold for our teacher work force should not be too great. What is truly amazing is the frequency with which outstanding instruction is accomplished by teachers who have been provided so little training and supervised practice before being thrust into responsibilities of a mature professional.

4. LIMITATIONS OF WORKING CONDITIONS. A teacher with adequate competence who is confronted with compatible mandates may remain unable to respond because of the working conditions of the schools. Teachers are a strange sort of professional. They lack the independence of prototypical professionals—physicians, lawyers, architects—because they function within complex, hierarchically organized bureaucracies. They are responsible to building principals (occasionally to department chairs), who report to superintendents, who are themselves answerable to local school boards. The teacher's choices are severely constrained by decisions made outside the individual classroom, e.g., the assignment of pupils to schools and of pupils-within-schools to classrooms, the selection of textbook series, the selection of criteria for assessing pupil growth, and the particular tests to measure those criteria. The increased emphasis on controls from above, on the remote control of teaching via policies promulgated at vast distances from the squeak of the chalk and the grinding of the pencil sharpener, attempts to create a different environment from that traditionally associated with the world of professionals in general, and the life of classrooms in particular.

5. THE SELF-DEFEATING MANDATE. The mandating process itself may be self-defeating, may be carried out in a manner that increases the likelihood that it will not be implemented as intended. There are many examples of that kind. These involve situations where the manner in which a desired end is communicated carries with it the seeds of its own failure.

During the time when this chapter was being written, the Argentine armed forces had occupied the Falkland Islands. They had informed the British that they had reclaimed the islands after a century and a half of imperialism and they would not negotiate regarding sovereignty over those islands. Ironically, the British had been trying to figure out how to divest themselves of the Falklands for years, considering them as an unnecessary burden with few benefits lying some 8000 miles from British soil. Yet the manner in which the Argentine government chose to communicate its intent to the British guaranteed a violently negative response from them—despite the consonance between the action's purposes and long-term British intentions.

Murnane (1981) has observed that the important question to ask regarding how to respond to the evidence on school effectiveness is not merely what to mandate for school policies. He asks how such policies can be mandated in a manner likely to enlist the willing decision making of the teachers as collaborating allies rather than as unwilling subordinates grudgingly conceding to their lack of power.

Assumptions of the Model

All the above discussions have emerged from the assumption that we indeed know how to improve schools and that the problems lie in the translation and implementation. However, the putative knowledge may be far less complete or adequate than is claimed. Translation from research to practical action may be more problematic than is generally considered. Thus we must examine two features of the "research-to-practice" model—its assumptions regarding the current state of knowledge and its conception of the processes of transferring research knowledge to practice.

When policymakers ask after the "lessons of research," whether to seek guidance regarding a decision over alternative policies or to lend support to a choice already made, what do they typically believe they are seeking? What image of research do they have in mind?

Certainly one type of investigation—perhaps the commonly shared prototype—is the critical experiment, unambiguous in its design, unquestionable in its implications. The examples that leap most readily to mind come from medicine—clinical trials of the Salk and Sabin vaccines, experimental field studies of fluoridation for prevention of dental caries, investigations demonstrating the effectiveness of antiseptic procedures in preventing postoperative infection, or research demonstrating the effectiveness of birth-control pills in preventing pregnancy. Other examples come from agriculture, where careful experiments can be used to demonstrate unequivocally the superiority of particular types of hybrid seed, the quality of varieties of fertilizer, or the power of specific kinds of herbicide. In cases like these the desired ends are relatively unambiguous. No polio or smallpox is surely better than annual epidemics. Few tooth caries are preferred to many. Higher yields are more desirable than famines or shortages. Moreover, the manner of measuring these outcomes is generally straightforward. There are few debates over how to measure postoperative infection rates, incidence of polio or tooth decay, or crop yields.

When we consider unintended side effects, or moral dilemmas associated with mandating the means for achieving desired ends, problems reminiscent of educational inquiries begin to emerge. An example can be drawn from the controversy that once surrounded policies regarding the fluoridation of public water supplies. The experimental evidence is unassailable. The presence of fluoride in public water supplies reduces incidence of tooth decay in the population, especially among children. Direct applications by dentists also work, but are more expensive and less certain to reach all who can benefit. How could there be any controversy over a general fluoridation policy with data so compelling?

Attacks on the policy took two forms. From the scientific perspective, opponents argued that data on side effects, usually involving the mottling of healthy teeth, had been suppressed. Fluoride was a potentially toxic material which could cause widespread harm if even slight errors in quantities of dose occurred. Moreover, the truly long-term effects of use were not yet fully understood.

From a moral/political perspective, opponents claimed that, experimental data aside, no government had the right to impose a form of medical treatment on all citizens. If fluorides could be added to a public water supply without the consent of all the affected citizens, what would prevent another government from administering birth-control drugs when it decided that the population was too large? If a population was deemed too restive, would some government prescribe tranquilizers for the public water supply? Where might it end?

Although fluoridation of water supplies is no longer controversial, this brief example should help us see that the acceptability of a policy rooted in research findings is not necessarily a function of the incontrovertibility of the data supporting the intervention. Policies must not only meet the tests of social science. They must also avoid undesired side effects and jibe with generally accepted political and moral standards. In the case of educational policies, it will not be sufficient merely to argue that well-conducted studies have demonstrated the efficacy of particular forms of instruction or school organization. We will have to examine what other policies may conflict with that in question, what bathwater of unintended outcomes may accompany the baby of this remedy, and what undesirable effects may develop because of the manner in which the innovation, desirable though it may be in principle, has been imposed unilaterally on members of a profession.

On the other hand, there may be good reasons why the fluoridation battles have essentially died. How long can one pursue debates over the proper forms of process when the desired positive results are achieved so unequivocally? Those who oppose the uses of educational policy to bring about changes in classroom teaching and learning must confront their responsibility to produce the educational results justifiably demanded by those who are disenfranchised by the status quo.

Discourse on Method

At this point in our argument, we will stop and take a closer look at the kinds of research that inform educational policy. Two aspects of research will be discussed. Having observed that the stereotype of medical or agricultural research does not ordinarily fit educational inquiries, we will review some of the other kinds of investigation that frequently help policymakers understand the educational enterprise they are attempting to influence. We will also briefly consider the ways in which research activity itself, far from occurring in isolation from policy disputes, is often informed by them. That is, not only does research influence policy; the conflicts of public policy also influence research.

The kinds of experiment that produce incontrovertible data rarely exist in the social science research on which educational policy rests. For example, disagreement over the "best" methods for teaching reading, arithmetic, or writing abound among both scholars and practitioners. Particular studies can clarify (or usefully obfuscate) specific issues, but rarely is the basis for a clear general policy laid by a program of research, much less a single investigation. However, bodies of educational research will frequently cumulate over time and interact with more general ideological shifts regarding the proper goals and methods of education to form prevailing views that significantly influence educational policy and practice. Neither the research nor the ideology can be viewed as the ultimate cause of the changes. They blend together to form the grounds for change. This is reminiscent of Lindblom and Cohen's (1979) description of how social science knowledge and ordinary knowledge interact to constitute usable knowledge for policymakers.

Given that the results of research interact with ordinary knowledge and broad moral/political commitments to yield policy initiatives, it is not surprising that many types of scholarship can inform policy. These not only include the relatively rare experimental contrasts, both in the laboratory and in the field. They also include the large-scale statistical studies in which natural variations are examined rather than those induced under the experimenter's control. Most of the research is of this type, since schools discovered to be more or less effective per se were typically contrasted. This follows the pattern of such well-known policy-relevant studies as the Surgeon General's reports on the links between smoking and cancer or the long-term Framingham studies of the correlates of heart disease.

Another increasingly influential type of research is the case study, persuasively drawn portraits of teachers, pupils, schools, or programs. They lack the hard statistical data of the more traditional policy study, but richness of portrayal or drama of human detail often sway the beliefs of decision makers far more effectively than do tables of means and frequencies. One major virtue of a case study is its ability to evoke images of the possible. One description of a successful Headstart program in Watts can persuade a policymaker to continue funding as readily as a statistical table summarizing objective data from one thousand programs. It is often the goal of policy to pursue the possible, not only to support the probable or frequent. The well-crafted case instantiates the possible, not only documenting that it can be done but also laying out at least one detailed example of how it was organized, developed, and pursued. For the practitioner concerned with process, the operational detail of case studies can be more helpful than the more confidently generalizable virtue of a quantitative analysis of many cases.

Other types of scholarship that frequently influence policy have no necessarily direct connection with the results of empirical social science research. One of these consists of conceptual or theoretical inventions, clarifications, or criticisms. Perhaps the best example of this generation was Robert Merton's conception of the self-fulfilling prophecy. This extended metaphor helped both social scientists and policymakers understand how labels and stereotypes applied to entire groups could lead to actions that would guarantee the negative outcomes predicted for them. Thus, if certain minority groups were labeled as stupid and treated accordingly, that very treatment would ensure fulfillment of the prophecy, although it would typically be interpreted as demonstration of the validity of the prediction. Merton's work stimulated the development of research on teacher expectations in classrooms, a body of work that continues to flourish today. Moreover, it forced educators to confront the consequences of their expectations and to become much more sensitive to the often deleterious effects of those expectancies.

Another significant conceptual invention was John Carroll's (1963) model of school learning. In this theoretical model, originally developed to explain second-language learning, Carroll posited that aptitude could best be understood as a function of the amount of time an individual required to achieve mastery of a given instructional task. He then elaborated on this proposition, showing how units of time could be used to define student motivation and aptitude, as well as the opportunity provided students to learn.

The Carroll model became the basis for a number of significant developments in educational research and practice. Benjamin Bloom based mastery learning in large measure on the model. The studies in which "engaged time" and "time-on-task" became bywords were motivated by the Carroll model. A whole host of technologies and policies, additional conceptual inventions, as well as subsequently fruitful applied research studies, have emerged from the Carroll model of school learning.

It is not only empirical propositions ("facts" about how pupils learn or the most productive ways to teach) and conceptual innovations that result from educational research. Another important product of educational research and development is instructional technology in the form of a system, or protocol. Such systems are exemplified by Mastery Learning (Bloom, 1976) as well as by more general procedural protocols such as "active teaching." In essence, these forms of technology combine the results of studies of school learning, important conceptual inventions, the intuitions of master developers (Rosenshine, 1981), and ordinary knowledge (Lindblom and Cohen, 1979) to produce systematic approaches to classroom instruction. At times these are formalized into computer-controlled objectives-based materials and methods. At other times, they are directed by detailed teachers' guides or manuals. When field tested, they are evaluated as total packages, and teachers are expected to implement them precisely as designed. At times, designers of such programs have striven to make them "teacher proof," immune to the modifications teachers might make in their workings. Of late, developers have more often come to understand that teachers must be free to use their judgment to adapt such programs to prevailing classroom conditions if they are to succeed.

As we review the types of research that exist to inform the policymakers, we should be reminded that the research enterprise does not roll along in serene isolation, unaffected by the *sturm und drang* of private passions and public policy. Educational researchers have always been quite sensitive to the prevailing ideological and political issues of their day. This is especially the case because the school and classroom have long been conceived as representing in microcosm the ideals of the democratic society into which the young are inducted. It is no surprise therefore when the trends and emphases of the research enterprise follow the ebb and flow of ideas in the marketplace of public opinion. This responsiveness of research has both positive and negative consequences. It certainly helps to ensure that educational research remains relevant to current concerns. On the other hand, such responsiveness can damage the continuity of the research enterprise, as the virtues of slow, cumulative growth of knowledge are sacrificed to the quest for political and social relevance.

However the research was conducted and whatever the social issues that motivated the inquiries, questions of translation and dissemination from research to practice remain. It will be recalled that the myth has two parts. The first is the existence of clear, objective bodies of research which can be readily translated into policy. We have seen that much knowledge exists, but it is certainly not packaged in the form of readily applicable sets of propositions. The second is a straightforward process of translation/dissemination, modelled after the common image of dissemination in medicine or agriculture.

The lack of correspondence between dissemination in agriculture and in education has been recognized by many. In a recent paper, Murnane (1981) observed how farmers were convinced to replace their time-honored rules of thumb with a pattern of resource allocation consistent with research findings and how these changes had brought about significant increases in productivity. He then asked why education was so different. Murnane argued that in agriculture the key inputs—seed, water, fertilizer—are inanimate and hence unaffected by the farmer's state of mind or motivation. In contract, an instructional method simply cannot be conceived in isolation from the teacher who employs it, the learning climate of the classroom and school in which it is deployed, and other factors that extend beyond the disseminated product. In education, it is rarely products we disseminate; it is principles and practices. These depend critically for their efficacy on the minds and motives of the teachers and students who jointly produce the events of classroom life.

It may seem obvious to the school reformer that any intervention is desirable that raises the standardized test scores of children. How could any teacher resist such a procedure? But what if those aspects of classroom life that enliven and enrich it are the day-to-day relationships among students and teacher, the excitement of learning new ideas and their applications, and the exchanges of insights between youngsters learning new things together? And what if the methods prescribed for raising test scores reduce the opportunities for teachers and pupils to pursue such activities? While the suppression of such learning certainly is not the objective of contemporary "back-to-basics" school reform (and we are raising the possibility only hypothetically), if it were found to be a side effect, would we not expect teachers to resist the reform efforts?

When public health officials in India attempted to employ agricultural dissemination models to bring birth-control principles and practices to the rural poor, they encountered frustrating failures. They found it difficult to understand, because it seemed so obvious that large families were economically and medically harmful. However, it was much more clear to farmers that it was good to produce more than it was to parents that it was preferable to reproduce less. The birth-control reformers had failed to appreciate the range of outcomes associated with large families in the Indian tradition, which brought satisfactions to parents far offsetting the disadvantages stressed by the public health officials and national planners.

At this point in our discussion we have examined the nightmares that concern teachers, policymakers, and researchers as they contemplate the problems of policy for the improvement of schools. We then described a concrete example of a current plan for school improvement and the arguments advanced both in its support and against its use. We then analyzed the underlying model of research-based change implicitly used by many policymakers. In discussing this model as myth, we looked in some detail at its assumptions and at the varieties of scholarship that are found useful to inform policy deliberations. We then briefly reviewed the concepts of dissemination implied in most approaches to educational change. In the concluding section we will confront the conceptions of teaching, teacher education, and the organization of the educational enterprise needed to forge the desired connections between policy and teaching.

The Dream

Teaching is impossible. If we simply add together all that is expected of a typical teacher and take note of the circumstances under which those activities are to be carried out, the sum makes greater demands than any individual can possibly fulfill. Yet, teachers teach. Moreover, despite oft-cited failures to achieve results with many types of pupils, teachers frequently elicit praise and recognition from all about them. We therefore confront two questions. What makes teaching impossible in principle? How is the impossible rendered possible in practice?

Our thesis is that precisely those characteristics that render teaching impossible also present it with the potential to transcend the apparent limitations of the job and make it professionally creative and autonomous. That is, the autonomy intrinsic to teaching is achieved as a function of its multiple competing and conflicting obligations, not in spite of them. This autonomy becomes both resolution and problem, however, if the freedom to teach is also the freedom to withhold teaching from the educationally disadvantaged and others who lack the power to exert influence at the local level. Thus our question remains, How can the impossible task of teaching be both responsible and free?

What makes teaching impossible? Within the classroom, the teacher is constantly torn among competing and incompatible pedagogical demands. Imagine a situation in which a fourth-grade teacher instructs a reading group of seven children while the remaining twenty-five pupils in the class are working individually on "seatwork" in arithmetic. Pupils are taking turns reading aloud from their basal readers. Dolores makes a reading error, and it is not immediately clear to the teacher whether the error stems primarily from ignorance of a basic phonic rule, from failure to apply a phonic rule that Dolores already knows, or from a fundamental misunderstanding of the meaning of the story being read. Each of these diagnoses would entail a somewhat different tactic of feedback and correction.

However, adequately pursuing this simple error to its proper resolution would demand that time be expended immediately with Dolores while the rest of the group sits and listens. Most of the others are unlikely to have the particular reading difficulty that Dolores has just displayed. Moreover, even were Dolores her only pupil, the teacher must choose between simple correction of the child's error, careful remediation of the underlying misconception likely to have caused the error, or ignoring the error entirely if paragraph meaning has not been disturbed seriously.

We thus already find the teacher trading off among competing educational demands. Some of these occur because instruction in even a single subject area—e.g., reading—entails a coordination among several frequently inconsistent purposes. Others occur because the pupil is only one of a classroom group of individuals, all of whom have a call upon the attention and care of the same teacher simultaneously. Adequately to respond to any one child's needs can frequently require that responsiveness to the just demands of other pupils be, at least temporarily, suspended.

We can conceive of the classroom as an economic system in which a scarce resource—the teacher's attention and the pupils' opportunities to perform—must be distributed on some equitable basis (e.g., Brown and Saks, 1981). The potential for each individual's personal development must be maximized, yet not at the expense of fellow members of the class, at least not over the long haul. Because some groups come to the classroom with more power than others, it cannot be claimed that perfect competition exists. For this reason, educational policies are established that attempt to equalize opportunities thus allowing the classroom marketplace to function fairly. These externally mandated equalizers are not always viewed as benign and facilitative by the teachers even though their necessity may be understood.

Another analogy can be drawn to the medical concept of "triage," whether on the battlefield or in the emergency room. Proper attention must be distributed among a group of patients in need of medical care. All cannot receive full treatment all of the time. Care must somehow be allocated to reduce involvement with those who can profit least from it while focusing on those who, for the present time, will benefit most from the therapy. Yet every patient, in principle, deserves the chance to survive.

As if the intraindividual competition among alternative educational purposes and the interindividual competition for instructional opportunities did not pose sufficient dilemmas for teachers, we must keep in mind a parallel concept of curricular competition as well. That is, as our teacher is pondering the proper way to respond to Dolores' reading error, she must also be mindful of the other curricular obligations she must meet. She must teach not only reading but all the other mandated subjects as well. Even if an approach to reading instruction can be devised that will adequately accomplish both the individual and collective needs of the full class of pupils, it must not encroach on the time allocated to the other subjects of the curriculum. If reading is taught well at the cost of teaching science not at all, or if adequate coverage of the basic computational skills is achieved through the reduction of time available for instruction in writing, our teacher is once again caught in an "impossible" bind. The notion of a good general education implies breadth of coverage in the several curriculum areas, not only depth in a few. A semblance of equity must be achieved not only among pupils and goals but also among topics and subjects.

Finally, the classroom teacher performs her functions in the larger context of a total school and school system. That aspect of the system reflected in the sequence of grade levels demands that certain topics within subjects be covered during certain years so that teachers of subsequent grades can properly fulfill their obligations. Those functions of the school involving management and discipline oblige each individual teacher to behave consistently with the more general patterns of school rules and standards. Research on the characteristics of unusually effective schools typically calls attention to the ways in which all the teachers in a building come to share similar goals, expectations, standards, and even teaching procedures.

The impossibility of teaching in the best of times results from the confluence of multiple competing role demands on the teacher. She must be individual tutor, distributor of scarce resources among many pupils, curriculum completer, and school team member. She is also a publicly employed representative of a society obligated to be mindful of its own unequal distribution of power and opportunity. Therefore, from outside the school itself descend policy mandates that further exacerbate the routinely devilish complexity of pedagogical life. Such policies as school integration or mainstreaming increase the variability among pupils and thereby make the allocation of teaching resources even more problematic. Minimum competence standards are established to ensure that all children receive a decent education, or new school topics are added to make the program more relevant to the technological or social concerns of the day. As this occurs, the teacher's responsibility for covering the mandated curriculum becomes an even heavier burden. Schoolwide disciplinary procedures or homework schedules are adopted to aid in the creation of a consistent academic learning climate, but the classroom management flexibility of the individual teacher is thereby reduced. Underlying the crossfire of policies, mandates, expectations, standards, and interactive demands are fundamental tensions between values as priorities for public education (See Green, 1983; Fenstermacher and Amarel, 1983; Greenstone and Peterson, 1983).

How can we think about the ways in which individuals cope with complex and contradictory expectations? From the perspectives of individual teachers, how can these multiple demands be tolerated? What makes teaching possible? Sociologists refer to the condition accompanying such multiple competing expectations as "role complexity." Although we have focused on teachers in this analysis, similar examples of such role complexity can be found in many occupational and personal situations. Moreover, it can be argued that role complexity, far from being a debilitating source of decisional paralysis, constitutes instead the seedbed of individual autonomy. Rose Coser expresses this position eloquently:

> The multiplicity of expectations faced by the modern individual, incompatible or contradictory as they are, makes role articulation possible in a more self-conscious manner than if there were no such multiplicity. Rather than automatically engaging in behavior that is expected, the modern individual has choices and makes choices consciously and rationally. By this it is not meant that everybody always makes conscious and rational choices, but that there is a greater possibility for doing so than there would be in the absence of such multiple expectations (Coser, 1975, p. 239).

How does this conception of teacher autonomy fit with broader notions of policy formation and implementation? Theorists who write about the character of large organizations such as business firms or governments have grown fond in recent years of referring to them as "loosely coupled systems" (e.g., Weick, 1976). Loose coupling describes the relationships between levels of an organization through which policy directives ostensibly flow. Rational models of such organizations predict that mandates should move vertically from level to adjoining level. With proper communication, training, and oversight, a directive emanating from the highest administrative level of the bureaucracy ought to be implemented as intended "where the rubber meets the road." But both general experience and disciplined empiricism have taught that such rational models of bureaucratic decision making and action function only in theory. In practice, policy is transformed as it moves through the system, receiving its final stamp at the hands of the "street-level bureaucrat" with ultimate responsibility for taking the actions mandated by the directive.

Therein lies the problem. When powerless groups must depend on the efforts of federal governmental policy to protect their interests, talk of professional autonomy and street-level bureaucracy brings precious little solace. The street-level bureaucrat can use that autonomy to preserve the inequities of the status quo, frustrating the intents of legislation or court orders. Loose coupling therefore buffers uncaring practitioners from the moral or legal consequences of their actions.

The language of loose coupling conjures up images of a somewhat random process of recombination and distortion, much like the old party game of Telephone, where a message is transmitted seriatim through a dozen celebrants until its thoroughly reconstituted form emerges for begiggled appreciation. Another image is that of a communication line with poor connections, so that pieces of messages are lost or muddled at random. In most of these views, the loosely coupled system is problematic, a defect in the system as it ideally should work. Our earlier analysis of the impossibility of teaching, however, and the autonomy fostered by the multiplicity and complexity of the role demands of teaching, demands a quite different interpretation of loose coupling. The loosely coupled system is adaptive, not defective. It is a response to the requirement for a system that can set policy, yet mandate autonomy. Loose coupling is not a problem for policymakers to overcome. Properly understood, it is the solution to the otherwise irresolvable conflict between policy and professional practice. Yet its critics are also correct. The freedom it creates is a two-edged sword. It can be used in the interests of the greater society and its goals. Or it can merely serve to shield the practitioner's expedient exercise of providing privilege to the powerful.

In a loosely coupled bureaucracy the local-level practitioner can act autonomously without facing inevitable sanctions for insubordination. The autonomous practitioner, confronted with a welter of individually well-grounded and justified directives can behave in response to some at one time, to others in other circumstances. While the goals of any particular policy will never be pursued unilaterally at all times, the goals of policy writ large can be addressed. A set of goals will have been set out that represent significant ideals in a pluralistic democratic society. Like any set of ideals—even the Ten Commandments—they will frequently be incompatible in practice. (If my father, whom I am to honor, asks me to violate the Sabbath . . .) The mandated regulations and auditing requirements that accompany each policy are intended to ensure that it is taken seriously. In a tightly structured "rational" system, in which no variability of response could be tolerated, the impossibility of coping with contradictory policies would lead to paralysis or an endless series of policy changes. The only solution would be to suspend the quest for representative pluralism and to replace it with an attempt to design monolithic values and their attendant policies. In a loosely coupled system, these contradictory role demands become the seedbed of individual autonomy. Without the autonomous actor, policymaking in a democratic society becomes impossible.

Without multiple competing policy demands, autonomy at the street level would be far too dangerous. The system does not result in mere anarchy because the total set of policies represents a particular subset of the universe of possible policies. The autonomy of the teacher is thus constrained and rendered responsible by the particular configuration of policies operating during a given period. Loose coupling permits the ostensibly incompatible elements of policy and autonomy to blend smoothly into the wisdom of practice.

This view of the virtues of loose coupling and teacher autonomy is certainly optimistic, perhaps even Pollyanna-ish. Little evidence can be marshaled to support the claim that the system in fact is working in this manner currently. Our argument is that the system ought to operate this way, given a proper combination of well-prepared professional educators and well-crafted, intelligently administered policies.

What forms should policymaking and implementation take if we come to view loose coupling as a matter of design rather than chance? How do we construe policy when judiciously managed variation of local response is understood as the necessary rule rather than as an anomaly? Coordinately, we must learn to think of the educational enterprise and of educators themselves in new ways. If professionals are to exploit the opportunities offered by autonomy in the interests of youngsters, how must they be educated, selected, supported, and supervised? What is needed on the part of educators if they are to render intelligent and proper judgments regarding choices among competing policies, trade-offs between alternative goals, or decisions regarding fruitful methods? Writers of many chapters in this volume have addressed themselves to those dual questions: how properly to reformulate the nature of educational policy and how to ensure that the talented and principled individuals needed in our teaching force are attracted, held, and nurtured in their roles.

Educational policies must be designed as a shell within which the kernel of professional judgment and decision making can function comfortably. The policymaker can no longer think of any given mandate as a directive which bears continuing correspondence to teacher actions at all times. Instead, policies represent moral and political imperatives designed with the knowledge that they must coexist and compete with other policies whose roots lie in yet other imperatives. Federal and state policies profess a prevailing view, orienting individuals and institutions toward collectively valued goals without necessarily mandating specific sets of procedures to which teachers must be accountable. The role of the teacher in such a situation is similar to that of a judge in a court of law. Laws and regulations are written to direct and control human action consistent with conceptions of individual and collective rights and obligations. But these rights and obligations often, even typically, come into conflict with one another. The rights of the accused conflict with those protecting person and property. The legitimate interests of landlords conflict with the just rights of renters. We do not expect that laws, regulations, or clear precedents cover each and every decision a judge must render. Indeed, the justification for courts and judges lies in the clear understanding that it is in the nature of any system of law that such controversies are inevitable.

In this sense, policies are very much like laws and teachers like judges. Educational systems are organized to permit the design of policies and their interaction in the court of the classroom. Teachers must understand the grounds for the competing demands on their time, energy, and commitment. They must be free to make choices that will cumulate justly in the interests of their students, the society, and humanity. Moreover, they need the opportunities to influence policy as well as respond, to initiate as well as broker.

The image of the teacher we have just drawn certainly does not correspond to the way teaching is. Papers by Lightfoot, Freedman et al., and Weinshank et al. have painted poignant portraits of the lives of teachers and their attempts to influence the system in which they work. Sykes, Kerr, and Feiman-Nemser have examined the problems of recruiting teachers, preparing them adequately before and after initial matriculation, and holding them for the duration of a professional career. These papers should be read together, for the conditions of teaching set severe limits on the potential for reform. The descriptions of teaching have helped us to appreciate the strains of the working teacher, the frustrations of the profession that foster burnout and the even more insidious charring that slowly eats away at a teacher in the performance of her duties. Without an improvement of those conditions, or a massive shift in the expectations that make them commonplace, talk of improvements in the teacher education process or of dramatic changes in the quality of those who opt for teaching seems pointless.

There is an agricultural analogy that may be helpful in thinking about the need for the educational system continuously to reinvest in the growth and instructional vitality of teachers. The learning teacher is as much a proper object of the system's concern as is the learning pupil. Much like the farmer's need to work with the soil so that it produces its crops yet does not lose its capacity to produce, the school must exploit the teacher's many skills yet nourish the continued fertility of the teacher as a medium for education. The society that mindlessly burns out its teachers will no more profit from their continued effectiveness than will the agricultural community that selfishly rapes its precious topsoil.

The solution requires a combination of improved human resources for the teaching profession and considerable improvement in the conditions of teaching. If the teacher's role is, in principle, that of a broker under siege, then the kind of person who becomes a teacher must be examined in relation to the kind of person a teacher becomes. It certainly cannot be the docile rule follower putatively sought by the regulatory policymaker. It is only the intelligent, moral, well-educated, and continually developing autonomous decision maker who can broker effectively among those legitimate, albeit competing demands. To attract and hold such people, we will have to make teaching a more satisfying, stimulating, and rewarding career, a profession rather than a form of technically sophisticated labor.

Mitchell and Kerchner provide a particularly illuminating analysis of four contrasting ways to formulate a conception of teaching: as profession, as art, as craft, and as labor. The four conceptions emerge from consideration of two aspects of work—its degree of rationalization, i.e., how precisely the activities of the practitioner are defined a priori and the mode of oversight, i.e., how meticulously the work is supervised and monitored. The only justification for minimal job specification and little direct oversight is when the nature of the job, the very structure of the setting and the character of its problems, requires the exercise of highly flexible decision making. Even here, the particular areas over which autonomy is to be exercised must be carefully defined. This is consistent with our notion of loose coupling by design, not exclusively by chance. Should the teacher be the final arbiter of means (methods of teaching), but not of ends (objectives of instruction)? Of proximal goals (today we shall concentrate on initial consonants) but not distal purposes (motivation to read will take precedence over technical skill)? Of immediate tactical means (calling on students in order rather than randomly) but not long-term procedural protocols (we shall employ mastery learning as a system for all math teaching)? Of strategy (discovery learning) but not content (whether or not to teach a geometry unit in fourth-grade mathematics)?

The issue of degree of autonomy will not be answerable easily. We must somehow find a way to make teaching and systems of education simultaneously both responsible and free. Schwille and his co-workers distinguish between authority over content and control of strategy. It can be inferred from their analysis that it is important for the control of content to lie beyond the individual teacher, thus ensuring the continuity and consistency needed to sustain an educational system. But teachers must maintain control over instructional strategies to be used in the teaching of that content. Through a combination of expert strategies for the teaching of consensual content, instruction will become both responsible and free.

A question which must be raised is whether this combination is consistent with the admonitions of Rutter and other school-effects scholars. Can the teacher follow the dictates of the effectiveness literature yet retain control over strategies of instruction? Or would Edmonds, Brookover, Rutter, and others mandate in the area of strategies as well? For example, mastery learning, a policy certainly within the realm of mandatable innovations, specifically limits itself to the definition of strategy, not content. It purports to be content neutral. Yet we must be prepared to raise serious questions about the usefulness of the convenient distinction between content and strategy. In many subject areas the two aspects of curriculum appear to interpenetrate inseparably.

Fenstermacher and Amarel argue strongly that the teacher must, above all, be responsible for setting the goals of instruction as she brokers between the powerful interests of the State and of the child. They argue that she must attempt to set these goals from the perspective of the interests of humanity, a perspective which has no other representative in the classroom except the teacher. Their view may appear highly idealistic at first blush. But their sense is that teachers must be imbued with a set of values that transcends those of particular policies or particular children. They cannot be merely value-free brokers, trading off among competing goods without any deep commitments of their own. Indeed, they must have commitments to a vision of educational excellence in fair and just societies, a vision that motivates their choices and lends wisdom to their exercise of professional autonomy.

Operationally, we will have to ask what is the size of the irreducible kernel of professional judgment without which teachers will not be able to respond adequately to the unpredictable complexities of life in classrooms? And what is the irreducible contour of the shell of policy if the State's obligation to ensure comprehensive and equitable education for all youngsters is to be fulfilled? These are questions that cannot be well answered abstractly and will probably have to be determined in particular contexts. In large measure, teachers will be collectively responsible for negotiating the role definition they acquire as they deliberate with school boards, administrators, and governmental policymakers regarding their future responsibilities and conditions of employment.

Finally, more intelligent use must be made of the research reported by Rutter, Good, and Dreeben and Barr, as well as others concerned with synthesizing the pedagogical and organizational techniques that lead to more effective teaching and learning of basic skills. We must go even further with such research. We have come to understand enough about teaching and learning to press on with the invention and deployment of systems of educational technology. These include approaches employing the hardware of computers to instruct as well as manage records. More important, this conception of technology calls for the formal deployment of systems of procedure that resemble the complex therapeutic protocols used in medicine to manage the treatment of many diseases. Examples of such protocols include Good and Grouws' approaches to mathematics teaching and Mastery Learning (Bloom, 1976). Rather than such forms of technology threatening to deprofessionalize teaching, properly deployed they become the prerequisites for professionalization. In the hands of gifted teachers empowered to use these methods rather than obligated to run alongside them, they help the teacher become a professional with powerful tools and a growing scientific base.

But the teacher must remain the key. The literature on effective schools is meaningless, debates over educational policy are moot, if the primary agents of instruction are incapable of performing their functions well. No microcomputer will replace them, no television system will clone and distribute them, no scripted lessons will direct and control them, no voucher system will bypass them. It seems unlikely that increasing the financial rewards of teaching alone will suffice, though it is certainly necessary. The character of the work itself will have to change in order to attract and hold the more highly trained, talented, and committed teacher required for the 1980s and beyond.

REFERENCES

Block, J. H. (ed.). *Schools, society, and mastery learning.* New York: Holt, Rinehart and Winston, 1974.

Bloom, B. S. *Human characteristics and school learning.* New York: McGraw-Hill, 1976.

Brown, B. and Saks, D. "The microeconomics of schooling." In D. Berliner (ed.) *Review of research in education,* 1981.

Carroll, J. A model of school learning. *Teachers College Record,* 1963, *64,* 723–733.

Coser, R. The complexity of roles as the seedbed of individual autonomy. In R. Coser (ed.), *The idea of social structure.* New York: Harcourt Brace Jovanovich, 1975, 237–264.

Dreeben, R., and Barr, R. "Educational policy and the working of schools." In L. S. Shulman and G. Sykes (eds.), *Handbook of teaching and policy.* New York: Longman, 1983, 81–94.

Edmonds, R. Working paper. Center for School Improvement, Michigan State University, 1982.

Feiman-Nemser, S. "Learning to teach." In L. S. Shulman and G. Sykes (eds.), *Handbook of teaching and policy.* New York: Longman, 1983, 150–170.

Fenstermacher, G. D., and Amarel, M. "The interests of the student, the state, and humanity in education." In L. S. Shulman and G. Sykes (eds.), *Handbook of teaching and policy.* New York: Longman, 1983, 392–408.

Freedman, S. Jackson, J., and Boles, K. "Teaching: An imperiled 'profession.'" In L. S. Shulman and G. Sykes (eds.), *Handbook of teaching and policy.* New York: Longman, 1983, 261–299.

Good, T. "Research on classroom teaching." In L. S. Shulman and G. Sykes (eds.), *Handbook of teaching and policy.* New York: Longman, 1983, 42–80.

Green, T. F. "Excellence, equity, and equality: Educational policy and the working of schools." In L. S. Shulman and G. Sykes (eds.), *Handbook of teaching and policy.* New York: Longman, 1983, 318–341.

Greenstone, J. D., and Peterson. P. E. "Inquiry and social function: Two views of educational practice and policy." In L. S. Shulman and G. Sykes (eds.), *Handbook of teaching and policy.* New York, Longman: 1983, 408–425.

Kerr, D. H. "Teaching competence and teacher education in the United States." In L. S. Shulman and G. Sykes (eds.), *Handbook of teaching and policy.* New York, Longman: 1983, 126–149.

Lightfoot, S. L. "The lives of teachers." In L. S. Shulman and G. Sykes (eds.), *Handbook of teaching and policy.* New York: Longman, 1983, 241–260.

Lindblom, C. K. and Cohen, D. K. *Usable knowledge.* New Haven: Yale University Press, 1979.

Mitchell, D. E., and Kerchner, C. T. "Labor relations and teaching policy." In L. S. Shulman and G. Sykes (eds.), *Handbook of teaching and policy.* New York: Longman, 1983, 214–238.

Murnane, R. J. Interpreting the evidence of school effectiveness. *Teachers College Record,* Fall 1981, *83*(1), 19–35.

Rosenshine, B. Master teacher or master developer. Colloquium address. Institute for Research on Teaching, 1981.

Rutter, M. "School effects on pupil progress: Research findings and policy implications." In L. S. Shulman and G. Sykes (eds.), *Handbook of teaching and policy.* New York: Longman, 1983, 3–41.

Sykes, G. "Public policy and the problem of teacher quality: The need for screens *and* magnets." In L. S. Shulman and G. Sykes (eds.), *Handbook of teaching and policy.* New York: Longman, 1983, 97–125.

Weick, J. Educational organizations as loosely coupled systems. *Administrative Science Quarterly,* March 1976, *21,* 1–19.

Weinshank, A. B., Trumbull, E., and Daly, P. L. "The role of the teacher in school change." In L. S. Shulman and G. Sykes (eds.), *Handbook of teaching and policy.* New York: Longman, 1983, 300–314.

ACKNOWLEDGMENTS

The careful reading and helpful suggestions of Jack Schwille and Chris Wheeler are gratefully acknowledged. Since my ability to respond to their thoughtful recommendations was limited both by understanding and ideology, they are naturally to be absolved of any responsibility for the errors remaining herein.

INTRODUCTION

THE PRACTICAL AND THE ECLECTIC: A DELIBERATION ON TEACHING AND EDUCATIONAL RESEARCH (1984)

AFTER ABOUT A DOZEN YEARS OF SILENCE, Joseph Schwab had finally finished the fourth in the series on "The Practical" in 1983. While working on the series, Schwab had spent considerable time at Michigan State University, where (among other things) he led a faculty seminar in the Institute for Research on Teaching. During that time, Schwab and Shulman became even closer friends and colleagues, and Shulman had begun to wonder about how Schwab's work was consistent with, and sometimes foreshadowed, work of other methodological critics like Robert Merton and Lee J. Cronbach. When "The Practical 4" was published in *Curriculum Inquiry,* and the editor invited a number of people to write responses, Shulman took the invitation as an opportunity to consider how Schwab's argument for a disciplined eclecticism in curriculum might also hold for education research, building on and extending the arguments that he had laid out in both the "Reconstruction of Educational Research" (1970) and in "The Psychology of School Subjects" (1974). Prepared during his transition from Michigan State to Stanford University, the essay foreshadows the methodological perspective of his essay on "Paradigms and Research Programs" in the *Handbook of Research on Teaching* (third edition).

Shulman begins the essay by considering the ways in which Dewey influenced Schwab, as well as some of their differences. In particular, he considers Schwab's interest in the role of group discussions and deliberations in liberal education. He then discusses the resonance between Schwab's work and that of Merton and Cronbach, both of whom argued for a range of research methods and questions, asserting the "superiority of a set of competing paradigms over the hegemony of a single overarching scheme." As Schwab argues for such eclecticism in curriculum deliberation, so Shulman argues that Schwab's argument can reasonably be extended to the nature of educational research and to the education of future researchers.

Shulman then describes Schwab's conception of teaching as a "complex and demanding art," one that requires various kinds of knowledge, including knowledge of rules, knowledge of particular cases, and knowledge of how to apply those rules to cases. "Where," Shulman asks, in teacher education is "the opportunity to learn of particular cases and ways of applying rules to cases?" Beyond field experience, prospective teachers have, in fact, very little opportunity to explore particular cases and learn to apply principles and rules to them. If teaching were to become much more like law, we would need a case knowledge to inform the work of new and practicing teachers. This interest in cases would emerge gradually as a central piece of Shulman's work, especially with regards both to how teaching knowledge is held and how one might develop a pedagogy of teacher education.

Shulman concludes the piece by imagining the education of future educational researchers, inspired by the disciplined eclecticism of Schwab, Merton, and Cronbach. Researchers would need to be familiar with more than one disciplinary perspective. They would need to learn about experimental, correlational, aptitude-treatment interactional, ethnographic, microethnographic, and sociolinguistic research traditions. They would need to explore how problems are formulated and how questions lead to choices in method.

5

THE PRACTICAL AND THE ECLECTIC

A DELIBERATION ON TEACHING AND EDUCATIONAL RESEARCH

WHEN READING THE WORKS of John Dewey, I am struck by the consistency with which the same fundamental model of biological and intellectual adaptation is employed to elucidate such different processes as art, political practice, logic, science, and school learning. Similarly, for Joseph Schwab, a consistent conception pervades his writings, whether of classroom discussions, curriculum deliberations, or scientific activity. Although *The Practical 4* is a practical treatise on the practice of school-based curriculum work, it stimulates my thinking anew regarding the ways in which Schwab's conceptions can guide our thinking in quite different areas.

I shall therefore write of Schwab and the practical from a perspective other than that of curriculum and its construction. My concern is with "something for research professors to do," with proper notions to guide the teaching of educational and social science research, and—since proper pedagogy models, in microcosm, the idealized image of the taught activity—with canons of method for educational enquiry *per se*.

This article, more properly construed as a set of variations on a theme by Schwab, will treat four topics, somewhat episodically. I will begin by considering the Deweyan tradition within which Schwab works, and will also examine the ways he has differed from Dewey. In this context, the continuing tension between individual learning and inquiry *and* group discussion and deliberation is examined.

I will next examine the conception of educational and social science research implicit in Schwab's conceptions of the practical. I say "conceptions" because they are examined in light of earlier positions he has taken in such essays as "Eros and Education" (Schwab, 1954), "On the Corruption of

Education by Psychology" (Schwab, 1958), and "What Do Scientists Do?" (Schwab, 1960). In this analysis, I will be especially interested in the ways his conceptions of social enquiry are consistent with and foreshadow the writings of such methodological critics as Robert K. Merton and Lee J. Cronbach.

I will then examine the conceptions of teaching and the knowledge base of teaching reflected in *The Practical 4*. His image of the school, the interacting roles of teachers, principal, and curriculum leader, and the nature of the curriculum deliberations carries with it a powerful image of teachers, their proper roles, and, by implication, the kinds of knowledge and skills they require and the conditions likely to be needed to educate teachers possessing those qualities. This section will contain several themes: (1) the role of the teacher as seen by Schwab; (2) the concept of knowledge for teaching implied by his definition of an art; (3) relationships between such conceptions of knower and knowledge and those appropriate to two other professions, medicine and law; and (4) conceptions of teacher education that flow from such analyses.

Finally, I will conclude with a consideration of the types of enquiry needed to support the designs for the teaching profession and the teacher education enterprise proposed. These types of enquiry and the institutional settings in which they can take place will be discussed in relation to Schwab's conceptions of educational and social science enquiry, with special attention to the kind of graduate education needed to prepare scholars to engage in such enquiry.

Dewey and Schwab

Schwab's writings on the practical are not only about curriculum and its making; they also enunciate a theory of educational research and, more broadly, a philosophy of social science. More specifically, Schwab's article (and its forbearers) focus our attention on the enduring problems of relating theory to practice and practice to theory. This places Schwab firmly in the tradition of John Dewey, a philosopher whose work Schwab has found influential for many years. In the preface to his *Experience and Education*, Dewey (1938) presents his perspective on the relationship between practice and theory in education, and the role of a philosophy of education in making clear those relationships.[1]

> All social movements involve conflicts which are reflected intellectually in controversies. It would not be a sign of health if such an important social interest as education were not also an arena of struggles,

> practical and theoretical. But for theory, at least for the theory that forms a philosophy of education, the practical conflicts and the controversies that are conducted upon the level of these conflicts, only set a problem. It is the business of an intelligent theory of education to ascertain the causes for the conflicts that exist and then, instead of taking one side or the other, to indicate a plan of operations proceeding from a level deeper and more inclusive than is represented by the practices and ideas of the contending parties. [Dewey, p. v]

In this passage, Dewey asserts that the worlds of theory and of practice, of conflict and of controversy, of idea and action, of principle and policy, are ineluctably related to one another. Moreover, each of these worlds gains richness and clarity from the incursion of the other. The full implications of principles can only be appreciated as they are translated into policies and their unintended consequences observed and accounted. Choices among actions take on clarity and meaning as the ideas represented by the actions can be formulated and discussed. The dialectic between the theoretical and the practical in their many manifestations requires a forum, a setting within which the abstract and the concrete, the general and the particular, the intended and the observed, can be laid bare and scrutinized. A danger intrinsic to such examinations is dogmatic dominance of the examination by a single principle or point of view. The rules of the forum must be established to ensure, as far as is prudent, that a full range of perspectives is brought to bear on the subjects of discussion.

Schwab's writings have frequently examined and explicated the necessary character of such forums. His continuing emphasis has been on the indispensable role of the well-led interacting group for such endeavors. For the college classroom, "Eros and Education" (Schwab, 1954) presents an image of the impassioned group discussion. For the school, we have the lessons of the "Learning Community" (Schwab, 1975, 1976). For curriculum development, we learn in great detail about the character of the deliberating group. In each case, the social setting is necessary to provide the broad range of perspectives required for an adequate understanding of the problem and its potential solutions. The virtues of heterogeneity of group membership, of the diverse contributions and perspectives uniquely brought to bear by members of a collaborating group, are forcefully drawn.

Equally important, the group introduces strong feelings and commitments to the otherwise unemotional quality of individual rumination. We can see cognition more closely linked to emotion, perspective to passion, idea to action. The dialogue among fully engaged participants not only achieves understanding, it elicits commitment and resolve. Participants in such a forum may not only be ready to think more clearly, but also to act more wisely, and, perhaps, even more justly.

Amidst these discussions of the special advantages of group activity for learning and deliberation, there is a rare reference to the possibilities of individuals pursuing such deliberations alone, albeit with little encouragement from the author. Schwab (1983) thus discusses "deliberative exchange and consideration among several persons or differing selves . . ." (p. 239). This reference to "differing selves" is the first indication we find in his writings that deliberation can occur productively within a single individual, without benefit of a group. Indeed, several pages later he seems to reconsider that matter when he observes that ". . . though inner deliberation on an extensive matter is possible, it is extremely difficult, especially because it requires a state of nonbias with respect to emphasis on one commonplace or another" (p. 244). The adequacy of individual or group for the collective enterprise of deliberation is an interesting problem for Schwab in much of his earlier writings. Whether in "Eros and Education," where he examines the virtues (and limitations) of group discussion for liberal education, or in his essay on the "Learning Community," Schwab displays a lifelong interest in the ways individual capacities are amplified and augmented when aggregated with the capacities of others. In the earlier discussions, the role of the group is seen as providing a vehicle for both the exploration of alternative interpretations and the elicitation of the strong emotions and commitments necessary to make liberal education a truly liberalizing emotional experience for participants.

One way of understanding (and perhaps extending) Schwab's position on this matter is to invoke Vygotsky's (1978) concept of the "zone of proximal development" and the manner in which (group) learning precedes and fosters (individual) development. Schwab appears to view the experience of working with others as an activity that permits the individual to accomplish far more than he or she could hope to achieve alone. Moreover, the group activity provides a setting within which important individual growth is fostered.

If the group discussion holds promise as a vehicle for the liberalization of learning in the individual, then why cannot individuals learn to replace the group as the proper context for deliberation? Why cannot individuals become eclectics? The answer, I believe, is that they can. Schwab is self-exemplifying in this regard, since the deliberations that produced *The Practical 4* were predominantly internal. The reason why the deliberating group is essential for the improvement of schooling has to do with its functions in enlisting general commitment to changes agreed upon, and in its role as a continuing source of staff development for both the veteran and novice members of the faculty. Similarly, the individual scholar can learn to think and act eclectically through a proper education. In subsequent sections of this article I shall treat both topics—how individual scholars can learn to think eclectically and the role of deliberation in staff development—in some detail. First, however, I shall turn to the contemporary line of social science research criticism with which I find Schwab resonant.

Theory and Method

Merton

The past decade has been a period of significant ferment in the social sciences. While many voices have contributed to the rethinking of traditional approaches to theory and method, I will let the positions of Robert Merton and Lee Cronbach represent the more general perspective.

While still considering himself a student of Talcott Parsons, Merton began quite early to eschew the search for a grand, integrative theory of social systems. In its place he advocated the development of "theories of the middle range" whose purpose would be the explanation of some particular social phenomenon—e.g., self-fulfilling prophecy or social deviance—rather than the entire universe of social interactions and institutions. While certain key concepts might well cut across a number of theories, such as the distinction between manifest and latent functions, the Holy Grail of a single superordinate theory was left by Merton for some future century's social scientists. He therefore viewed the coexistence of many middle range theories as a sign of vigor and relevance in his profession.

Yet what for Merton was a sign of health, for many of his fellow sociologists constituted a continuing crisis, a sign of conceptual confusion. Merton's response was to assert:

> . . . that the chronic crisis of sociology, with its diversity, competition and clash of doctrine, seems preferable to the . . . prescription of a single theoretical perspective that promises to provide full and exclusive access to the sociological truth. . . . No one paradigm has even begun to demonstrate its unique cogency for investigating the entire range of sociologically interesting questions. And given the variety of these questions, the past prefigures the future. [Merton, 1975, p. 28]

Merton proceeds to argue for the superiority of a set of competing paradigms over the hegemony of a single overarching scheme. He asserts that theoretical pluralism encourages the development of a variety of research problems rather than premature closure of enquiry to the problematics of a single paradigm. Different paradigms alert research workers to different phenomena of interest, different conceptions of problems, and different potential research strategies. In language reminiscent of Schwab's treatment of deliberation and eclecticism in *The Practical 1,* Merton proposes that:

> . . . the cognitive problems of coexisting paradigms call for discovering the capabilities and limitations of each. This involves identifying the kinds and range of problems each is good for (and noting those for which it is incompetent or irrelevant), thus providing for potential awareness of the respects in which they are complementary or contradictory. . . . Many ideas in structural analysis and symbolic interactionism, for example, are opposed to one another in about the same sense as ham is opposed to eggs: they are perceptibly different but mutually enriching. [Merton, 1975, p. 50, p. 31]

Merton refers to his position as "advocating a plurality of theoretical orientations in sociology in the form of a 'disciplined eclecticism'" (1975, p. 51). While Schwab's argument in the four essays on the practical is for eclecticism in the service of practical deliberation, concrete choice, and decision rather than theory development, Merton claims that such pluralism is both unavoidable and useful (necessary and virtuous) in the interests of theoretical understanding as well.

There is another sense in which Merton and Schwab have traveled parallel tracks for many years. In one of Merton's earliest published papers, he discusses "The Unanticipated Consequences of Purposive Social Action" (Merton, 1936). In this brief essay he discusses the inevitability that planned social action, whether by an individual or in the form of social policy, will have consequences that have not been anticipated by the actors. The inevitability is a consequence of several factors. First, the general image of the world on which the action was premised never quite corresponds to that particular portion of the world in which the action is played out. Second, once ideas are put into practice they are destined to produce outcomes that extend beyond the more limited scope of interest to the planners. It is only through following an idea into practice, therefore, that one begins to appreciate the greater richness or potential of the idea. (The parallel to Dewey is striking.) Moreover, as we examine the unanticipated consequences, we begin to learn much more about how the social system is organized than we knew before we began, an understanding that can be of great assistance in future attempts at planning and purposive social action. In this analysis we can begin to see the shape of what Merton will later develop into the central concepts in his approach to structural analysis in sociology, manifest and latent functions. These are concepts that also serve to enrich our grasp of Schwab's arguments for the necessity of practical deliberation in curriculum development, and, in fact, in educational enquiry more generally.

Cronbach

More recently, and in a remarkably similar vein, Cronbach has been calling for a reformulation of the character of social science research. In papers titled "Beyond the Two Disciplines of Scientific Psychology" (Cronbach, 1975), and "Prudent Aspirations for Social Research" (Cronbach, 1982), he seriously questions the traditions that separate social sciences from one another as well as from other sources of knowledge, such as the humanities. He calls for reduction in concern over methodological orthodoxies and urges that the most important criterion for effective social research be the clarity with which it illuminates specific problems in particular contexts of place and time. Much more than Merton, Cronbach treats the quest for theoretical knowledge as a typically hopeless one in the social sciences. What passes for such knowledge nearly always requires bounding and qualification in light of local conditions, particular circumstances, and a limited time span. The distinction between "research" and "evaluation" thus becomes a fuzzy one, since the purported generalizability of the former and particularity of the latter no longer serves as an adequate discriminator. Like both Merton and Schwab, he calls for mechanisms that would bring together scholars from diverse disciplinary backgrounds—e.g., psychology, history, literary criticism—to review jointly articles and proposals as well as work together in the study of specific research problems. He is certainly not alone in his critique of the traditional models of social science enquiry, citing Gergen (1982), Manicas and Secord (1983), and Meehl (1978), among like-minded writers both within the social sciences and among philosophical critics.

Cronbach (1982) not only raises questions regarding the adequacy of individual disciplines, he critically examines the claims that enquiries disciplined by the experimental and quantitative procedures of the social sciences can achieve the levels of generalization they claim.

> . . . What research styles and objectives follow from the intent to advance understanding? A mixed strategy is called for: censuses and laboratory

> experiments, managerial monitoring and anthropological Einfuhlung, mathematical modeling and unstructured observation. A few observations can be offered even for eclectic social science.
>
> Social inquiry reports on events in one or more sites during one slice of time. It can be viewed best as quantitatively assisted history. The more the observer learns of detail and process, the better; observation from afar is impoverished. The impersonal, predesigned research study is of precious little use in gaining a new idea (Glaser and Strauss, 1967), however useful it may be in confirmatory research or in routine monitoring. Though one may "lose objectivity" by appearing on the scene and attending to variables not specified in advance, the benefit outweighs the loss.
>
> Let me put it differently. All social scientists are engaged in case studies. The 1980 census is no less a case study than is Erikson's *Young Man Luther* (1958). The observations take meaning from their time and place, and from the conceptions held by those who pose the questions and decide how to tabulate . . . [Cronbach, 1982, pp. 73–75]

I have cited the work of Merton and of Cronbach to remind my readers that Schwab's perspectives on the limitations of theory and the need for eclectic combining of disciplinary perspectives are not unique among contemporary social theorists. Indeed, the movement in curriculum work which has developed around Schwab's conceptions has been paralleled by remarkably similar critiques and reappraisals of traditional approaches in all the social sciences. His thinking is therefore consistent with a much more general Zeitgeist regarding enquiry, theory, and practice. If there is an irony to be found here, it is in the observation that, among himself, Merton, and Cronbach, Schwab seems to maintain the strongest faith in the usefulness of research and theory to produce "theoretical generalizations." He has never been a critic of theory *qua* generalization, but of generalization as an adequate basis for practical choice. Merton, on the other hand, is critical about grand theory, but urges the prudence of focusing the energies of enquiry on the quest for theories of the middle range. Cronbach is the most skeptical of the three, viewing the opportunities for theory development as extremely limited, and probably only to a quite restricted genre of phenomenon, which he calls "capacities."

In his vivid portrayal of the process of curriculum deliberation and construction in schools, Schwab presents us with far more than an image of curriculum making. Before moving on to the question of how we might use Schwab's conceptions of deliberation and eclecticism to educate a generation of scholars for the conduct of educational research, an examination of his ideas regarding teaching and teacher education, two central topics for any useful body of educational research, will be examined.

Teaching and Teacher Education

Although *The Practical 4* is an essay on curriculum professors, curriculum deliberation, and the education of curriculum leaders or chairmen, it carries an implicit conception of teaching as art and profession. The first members of the deliberation group are to be teachers. They are first-named because they know most about the particularities of pupils and classrooms in the school and also because "(t)eachers will not and cannot be merely told what to do" (p. 245). As I read Schwab, the "will not and cannot" entails far more than a mere matter of frustrating fact, as in "children will not do what you ask of them." Schwab is arguing that they ought not and may not, that the responsible practice of the art of teaching requires that teachers reserve to themselves the obligation to make decisions and choices regarding "what to do, how to do it, with whom and at what pace" because the options "arise hundreds of times a school day, and arise differently every day and with every group of students" (see Shulman, 1983). He concludes with a statement about the professional autonomy of teachers relative to externally set policies that predicates their role on the necessary conditions for effective instruction.

> Therefore, teachers must be involved in debate, deliberation and decision about what and how to teach. Such involvement constitutes the only language in which knowledge adequate to an art can arise. Without such a language, teachers not only feel decisions as impositions, they find that intelligence cannot traverse the gap between the generalities of merely expounded instructions and the particularities of teaching moments. Participation in debate-deliberation-choice is required for learning what is needed as well as for willingness to do it. There is an obvious moral here for teacher-training. Persons involved in teacher-training might well puzzle over it. [pp. 245–246]

Several ideas are worth considering. Schwab's image of the teacher is of a practitioner of a complex and demanding art. While they will profit from the collective activities of joint deliberation and reflection, they must retain a fair measure of professional autonomy. The portrayal of both the process of deliberation and of the role of the chair are intriguing. The deliberative process resembles closely an ideal version of school-based staff development. Teachers are working together on a real problem of shared interest. Participants in the process are from outside the school as well as inside. The group leader is not someone with a day-to-day supervisory or evaluative responsibility for the teachers. The emphasis of activity is on individual reflection and group deliberation in the interests of short-term decisions and actions and long-term teacher development.

One of the fascinating uses of deliberation already underway among members of the teaching profession is that employed in the American Federation of Teachers (AFT) research dissemination project (American Federation of Teachers, 1983). The ostensible impetus for group discussion is the presentation of summaries, restatements, or reformulations of educational research literature. This literature can relate to classroom management, to teaching effectiveness or the like. The group leader is a fellow classroom teacher who has received special training in the interpretation and criticism of educational research, and in techniques for directing discussions on the uses of that research. The leader introduces the topic, and asks participants to think critically about the applicability of the research findings to their own classrooms. What are the ways in which the research results appear to fit with the practical experiences of the participating teachers and in what ways are they inappropriate?

What we frequently find in the AFT experience is that the presentation of the research results serves as a legitimizing context to permit teachers to exchange reports of their own experiences. They then discuss both the research results and their own professional experiences, subjecting both to critical scrutiny. They pay special heed to the limits of the generalizability of both empirical research and professional experience, of both the findings of "science" and the wisdom of practice. The research results themselves are of real value in this exchange, but the key contributions are made by the participants themselves. More accurately, the research results are treated as theoretical generalizations that must be deliberated upon in light of local conditions and the practical experiences of individual teachers before their applicability can be discerned. I view this example of teacher deliberation in groups using research findings a particularly compelling instance of deliberation as a form of teacher staff development.

While Schwab spends much of his essay in discussing the unique role of the curriculum chair in the school, and the special training he or she would require, it is interesting to speculate on the possibility that the role might be played by another kind of individual. Recent writings on school reform have advocated the creation of career ladders for teachers, with the role of "master teacher" at the top. Without going into great detail, it is provocative to speculate about Schwab's curriculum chair as a job description for a master teacher. The responsibilities of curriculum monitoring and modification, ongoing staff development and, by implication, guidance of neophyte teachers, seem quite consistent with both those positions. Since even the most ardent advocates of master teacher plans remain vague regarding their proper responsibilities, Schwab's characterization of the curriculum chair may be a useful starting point.

An even more important problem than defining the roles of master teachers remains that of understanding what one needs to know and do in order to function as a teacher *per se*. One of the most important paragraphs in the entire essay develops Schwab's conception of an art.

> . . . (E)very art, whether it be teaching, stone carving or judicial control of a court of law. Every art has rules but knowledge of the rules does not make one an artist. Art arises as the knower of the rules learns to apply them appropriately to the particular case. Application, in turn, requires acute awareness of the particularities of that case and ways in which the rule can be modified to fit the case without complete abrogation of the rule. In art, the form must be adapted to the matter. Hence the form must be communicated in ways which illuminate its possibilities for modification. [Note 2, p. 265]

Thus, to the extent that teaching is an art, its practice requires at least three forms of knowledge: knowledge of rules, knowledge of particular cases, and knowledge of ways to apply rules to cases. As we think about the education of teachers, we can see how most of the courses in our programs emphasize the teaching of rules *per se*. These include rules for planning instruction, for designing tests, for managing classrooms, for analyzing textbooks, for conducting lectures and discussions. We are often urged to derive such rules or maxims from the results of empirical research on teaching and learning. The propositions that capture the major findings of such research are to serve as the bases for pedagogical maxims to be practiced by teachers (e.g., Gage, 1978).

The example of medicine is often advanced as a proper model for educational knowledge. The results of basic and clinical research are seen as providing general principles that direct clinical choices made in particular circumstances. Pre-medical and pre-clinical education are organized to instruct medical students in those bodies of scientific knowledge. Clinical and graduate (residency) education is intended to provide knowledge of cases and of ways to apply rules to cases.[2]

Where in the education of teachers is the opportunity to learn of particular cases and ways of applying rules to cases? The facile response is that such opportunities are found in practice teaching, or in its quasi-medical alternative, the teaching internship. But the internship is typically defective in two ways. First, the selection and range of cases is restricted to the particular classroom in which the internship occurs and the particular youngsters and subjects taught. Not even a modestly systematic attempt is made to provide the novice teacher with a representative array of prototypic cases designed epidemiologically to correspond with the character of the broader "field." Nor are cases presented systematically to exemplify the application of designated rules or maxims of procedure. Despite their unarguable importance in shaping the art of teaching, cases and case knowledge play a very small role in the professional education of teachers.[3] With the exception of rare programs where a carefully selected diversity of clinical experiences is planned for candidates, the field experience is not augmented by an array of examples richly and thickly described to provide them with opportunities to reflect on the distinctive feature of those contexts.

An alternative to the medicine-like view of the knowledge base of teaching should be considered. We have considered the view that educational research produces findings that then become the propositions from which teaching choices are derived. In this view those general propositions which gain their power from a scientific process of observation, generalization, experiment, and interpretation come to act almost as major premises from which pedagogical practice is then deduced, as mediated by observations of particular circumstances serving as minor premises. But what if teaching is more like law than it is like this particular image of medicine?[4] In law, there is no significant body of empirically demonstrated generalizations that form the knowledge base of the field. Instead we find a set of general normative principles dealing with such generic concepts as justice, property, individual rights, and collective obligations. These are typically represented in the form of statutes and regulations. Legal education is a process of learning to find one's way through the thickets of documented cases in order to identify proper precedents for the problem at hand. Instead of reasoning deductively from general principles to particular cases, the attorney or judge more typically reasons analogically from other cases *qua* precedents to the particularities of the case-in-hand. Alternative proposals for precedents are weighed against the current case and in light of normative principles until a justifiable choice, a judgment, can be rendered. This judgment is then entered into the cumulative record that aggregates into the body of case law. Novice attorneys are given abundant opportunity to practice this combining of rules, cases, and analogical applications. The legal curriculum is designed to provide students with such practice.

A teacher education curriculum based on similar principles would look quite different from the kind we have come to expect in our schools of education. Two kinds of general rules would receive explicit treatment:

those derived from empirical research on teaching and learning and those broad normative rules derived from moral principles of education. Then systematic presentation, analysis, and deliberation on "cases" would ensue, both through vicarious reading of a currently unavailable case literature and through direct field experiences of the sort we now call practice teaching or internships. A good deal of work is needed from those of us engaged in teacher education to explicate such a conception of teaching and its knowledge base. Moreover, our conceptions of needed research will require the enrichment of a new conception of case literature, not all of which will look much like most contemporary school ethnography, given the tendency of that literature to focus on social interactions to the exclusion of considerations of specific subject matters and learning tasks. There are very few stories of learning, much less of the manifest curriculum, in ethnographic accounts of classrooms and schools. As Schwab has suggested, we might do well to expend considerable energy puzzling over teacher education and its knowledge base in this manner.

Finally, I find this inferred Schwabean image of teacher education provocatively parallel to that of Fenstermacher (1979). Following Green (1971), Fenstermacher argued that educating a teacher was not a matter of inculcating through training a set of teaching skills or competencies. To educate a teacher is to influence the premises of the practical argument in the teacher's mind. These premises are made up, in part, of generalizations derived from disciplined empirical enquiries and from normative principles. Practical arguments, as against theoretical ones, are engaged when one seeks to make particular judgments, choices, or decisions in particular circumstances. The premises serve to ground these decisions, they do not directly determine them. Teacher education therefore requires substantial instruction in the sources of such premises combined with the experiences needed to learn how to apply them well to particular cases.

Having treated, albeit superficially, the conception of teaching and teacher education implicit in *The Practical 4*, I shall now turn to my final topic, Schwab's challenge to those who train educational researchers. Given the preceding conceptions of educational research methodology and of both teaching and teacher education, what is there for educational research professors to do?

The Education of Educational Scholars

The dilemma of the graduate educator of educational researchers is quite similar to that of the curriculum professor. There is certainly a responsibility to provide education and training for the future scholar in some depth, which usually means an education in some particular disciplinary and/or methodological perspective. However, while any particular discipline can enlighten and empower an investigator, it also, in principle, shackles and limits his purview. This becomes particularly problematic since education as a field of study presents its topics, problems, and issues to the investigator in ways that do not readily fold into any one neat disciplinary package.

Nevertheless, the great virtue of disciplines is that they indeed discipline the investigator via rules for asking questions, canons of evidence, tests of precision and error, starting points for enquiry, and criteria for terminating enquiry. There are thus at least two senses in which we speak of "disciplines." First, they are traditional fields of scholarship (e.g., psychology, sociology, anthropology, history) that have both substantive and syntactic structures (Schwab, 1964). Substantive structures are those systems of concepts and principles that define and organize what shall constitute the facts and meanings of the domain. Syntactic structures are the procedures for initiating, conducting, and terminating enquiry and for determining the warrant of assertions offered. They comprise the procedural principles of discovery, invention, and verification.

Secondly, discipline refers to the management of impulse and the control of intellectual caprice. While flexibility and creativity are certainly to be valued in the attack on educational problems, scholarship must somehow be disciplined by some principles.

Schwab's solution to the dilemma is the creation of cross-disciplinary deliberation groups, collections of scholars representing a cross-section of disciplinary perspectives selected because of their bearing upon the topic or problem at hand. The selection of the participating disciplines and their representatives would be in the hands of the research equivalent of a curriculum leader—a chairman of the research team. But we remain with the question of how to educate such a chairman. Moreover, might there not be some virtue in educating many future scholars to possess the attributes of the chair, since they might either have to play that role themselves, or they might participate as team members far more successfully if they can understand the dilemmas of the chair more clearly, or because the convening of interdisciplinary groups is, in fact, a luxury of unusual and unlikely character. More likely, the skilled scholar may have to perform within his or her individual mind as if a deliberative group were present, in Schwab's words, engage in "deliberative exchange or consideration among . . . differing selves." An individual capable of such internal deliberation must be educated for disciplinary transactions.[5]

What might such an education entail? Certainly, the educational scholar must be conversant with more than a single disciplinary perspective. As he or she learns each, there should develop an emphasis both on the power of the approach, the techniques and theoretical models, their uses and abuses. There should be a continuing discussion of the limitations and distortions attending each approach, rendering the potential user acutely aware of the significant canalizations of thought characteristic of the enquiry form. Instruction would be often analogous to the strategies of psychoanalytic training, wherein the novice analyst must learn to be sensitive to precisely those personal sources of distortion, anxiety, and potential exploitation likely to interfere with psychotherapy. This emphasis on the need for scholars to be at least bi-disciplinary fits nicely with the thinking of Aristotle, whose words often seem to have a contemporary ring.

> It might be supposed that there was some single method of inquiry applicable to all objects whose essential nature we are endeavoring to ascertain . . . in that case what we would seek for would be this unique method. But if there is no such single and general method . . . our task becomes still more difficult; in the case of each different subject we shall have to determine the appropriate process of investigation. [De Anima 1:1]

In the midst of this theoretical essay on the implications for research of Schwab's conceptions of the practical, I feel compelled to follow his model in *The Practical 4*, i.e., to provide some concrete examples of how such research training might take place, by using specific descriptions of programs. How might our program for preparing future chairs for multidisciplinary research teams (or solitary polymaths) proceed? To be candid, I propose this as a means for preparing all education scholars, because of the peculiar character, so well described by Schwab, of Education as a field of study (see Shulman, 1981).

I will describe two forms of instructional program. The first focuses on teaching the techniques typically dubbed quantitative and qualitative. While the terms are gross and more is obscured by the distinction than is thereby illuminated, I shall write as if by quantitative I denote the now typical preparation in descriptive and inferential statistics, including the measurement of location, the major forms of least-squares analysis—analysis of variance and covariance, correlation and regression, and the families of bivariate and multivariate, parametric, and non-parametric statistical procedures normally associated with this topic, including strategies of experimental and quasi-experimental design.

By qualitative, I denote the increasingly frequent programs of preparation in ethnography, field study, participant observation, case study, and the like now finding their way into the previously impervious quantitative halls of educational investigation. I would require each student to pursue each program of study for at least a year. In the best of all possible worlds, the instruction would include the expectation that a *bona fide* piece of research would be designed, conducted, analyzed, and written as part of the course.

Within each course I would emphasize the differences among particular strategies within the same research family; for example, the experimental, correlational, and aptitude-treatment interactional among quantitative approaches and the traditional (flat-footed) ethnographic, microethnographic, and ethnomethodological, as well as connoisseurship and sociolinguistic approaches among the qualitative. In each we would examine how starting points, problem formulations, and conceptions of key questions are shaped by method-of-choice, not merely techniques of data gathering and analysis. The student of quantitative approaches would come to see how the goal of research is the comprehensive "outsider's" description of the patterns of correlation and causation that explain why things occur as they do in the setting under investigation. That same student in qualitative training will have the goal of understanding the phenomenology of those studied, i.e., the sets of rules, perceptions, and the like one needs to function smoothly in the setting (or as the individual) of interest.

These sequences would then be capped by a critical course or two on the nature of enquiry and the design of research, writ large. There the limitations of each family of approaches would be carefully discussed, using careful reading of original research reports as exemplars and placing special emphasis on the peculiar richness of research programs in which more than one approach is combined. When possible, team research in which several "ways of seeing" the same problem are simultaneously deployed would be initiated. Members of the group would report back to one another, and with the help of the research professor begin to see that problems are not the same when viewed through the eyes of different methods.

Any reader who claims to see in this description some influence of the Organizations, Methods, and Principles of Knowledge sequence taught in the College of the University of Chicago—a sequence in whose design the hand of Schwab could be clearly discerned—will certainly not be hallucinating. What is unusual is to find such a proposal advanced for graduate study. It is normally only at the undergraduate level that we call for "liberal" education or general study. The graduate school is seen as the place for specialization and intensity. Schwab's lesson is that the overspecialized graduate education is not only inadequate, it is a menace. In this matter he agrees with the economist Hayek, as quoted by Schultz (see Kruskal, 1982), "Nobody can be a great economist who is only an economist. . . .

(A)n economist who is only an economist is likely to become a nuisance if not a positive danger."

I shall add an even more concrete example, a design for an exercise to be practiced by novice educational scholars as part of their formal preparation. I shall preface it with the notion that all social research is a form of storytelling, the creation of a narrative to help us "make sense" of puzzling circumstances, or to make new sense out of situations we have come to take for granted. Thus, the methods of research and the disciplinary roots from which they sprout are strategies for spinning tales that are simultaneously persuasive to one's audience and grounded in a disciplined way of knowing about the world. The scholar educated in the spirit of Schwab will be capable of telling stories that reflect many perspectives. He will author his own Rashomons, alternating deftly among the potential points-of-view of several disciplinary participants. For example, we can present the group with a model of multidisciplinary social thought like that developed by Getzels and Thelen (1960). In this model, they present a five-level analysis of the determinants of a social system. Each level corresponds to a disciplinary perspective—biology, psychology, social psychology or group dynamics, sociology, and anthropology. The exercise exemplifying the multiple-narrative approach would require that each participant invent a life history of a particular individual whom they know, perhaps themselves, and write it from each of the disciplinary perspectives of the Getzels-Thelen model.

With just a little bit of practice, the participants will learn to create each kind of biography. The psychological narrative will emphasize individual motives and capacities, anxieties, and fears. The sociological tale will describe the protagonists as creatures inhabiting roles and responding to institutional norms or expectations. The anthropological tale will portray the protagonists as reflections of a larger culture, an ethos whose values and rituals give meaning to their daily existence, while the biological rendering will place individual drives and instinctive propensities at the center of the causal/explanatory stage. In this manner students will learn that *The Organization Man* (Whyte, 1956), *Street Corner Society* (Whyte, 1943), *Crime and Punishment* (Dostoyevsky, 1937), or *Growing Up in New Guinea* (Mead, 1962) are the result of choices, selections of starting points and principles of enquiry, of disciplinary perspectives and ways of seeing that are open to them as well.

I would hope they would not learn to view such storytelling as a glibly facile enterprise requiring merely imagination, verbal ability, and gall (though the three are certainly useful). Indeed, the message is that you must first determine what kind of story you wish to tell, and to understand the range of possibilities. You must recognize how useful it is to tell more than one tale to illuminate the phenomena under investigation, whether your goal is the clear description of a particular local setting for purposes of policy or the enrichment of theoretical constructs through analysis of social processes and contexts.

Finally, the student must come to understand how the disciplined narrator (in contrast to the "mere" storyteller) must master a set of conceptual and methodological tools that define the substantive and syntactic arsenal for the disciplined (in both senses) account to be drawn. He will also need to understand the special role of evidence (as against ungrounded impressions) in such a narrative. The student will also practice both "bottom-up" and "top-down" narration. In the former, the character of larger systems, such as groups, institutions, societies, cultures, are explained by reference to the more elemental components which comprise them: group character by individual personalities, cultural ethoi by institutional struggles. In the latter, the behavior of individuals is seen as a function of the larger aggregates in which they are embedded; institutional norms are interpreted as a function of broader cultural values; individual behavior is seen as determined by roles and role conflicts.

The danger of such an education is the learning of an utter relativism, the sense that one story is pretty much as good as any other, "let a thousand flowers bloom." The challenge is to communicate a sense of purpose and the need to generate criteria of relevance. It is not enough merely to "blur the genres" though the obscuring of these disciplinary lines will frequently be fruitful. Only if participants continue to return to the question of why they wish to tell these stories in the first place, what goals or purposes motivate their efforts, in whose interests the enquiry is pursued, can questions of which combination of approaches will fit a particular research program be adjudicated.[6]

Closing Observations

Whether in an elementary school, a secondary school, or a university research center, the formation of interdisciplinary groups for deliberation and collaboration is a difficult challenge. Whether the goal is curriculum development and correlated faculty enrichment or more powerful approaches to the conduct of social science research, the devising of methods to overcome the parochialism of narrowed views and the inertia of old intellectual habits resists easy solutions. The kinds of organizational change Schwab describes in *The Practical 4* will not come easily, in the schools or in the research centers. But if they are to have any chance of success, they will need to be grounded in programs of teacher education and research preparation directed at the purposes we have been describing. Otherwise, the familiar furniture of the mind will remain in its place, and we will be able to do little to replace it.

NOTES

1. In this, as in so many of the analyses to follow, I write as a student of Schwab. His mentorship began for me in 1958 when I was a student in the College of the University of Chicago. It continued through graduate work in education at that institution, though I was formally studying educational psychology, not Schwab's special field of educational philosophy. I feel the mentorship has continued to this day, though I surely cannot hold him responsible for the positions taken in this essay. Nevertheless, the discussion that follows of Dewey's preface to *Experience and Education* doubtless derives from discussions nearly a quarter century ago in Schwab's graduate seminar on the work of Dewey.
2. In *The Practical 1* Schwab uses medicine as his exemplar of successful employment of eclectic methods.

   Let it suffice for the moment that witness of the high effectiveness of eclectic methods and of their accessibility is borne by at least one field familiar to us all—Western medicine. It has been enormously effective, and the growth of its competence dates from its disavowal of a single doctrine and its turn to eclecticism (Schwab, 1969; p. 10).
3. The ambiguity of the term "case" will be obvious to the reader. I intend it to represent types of individual children, types of classrooms and schools, and types of subject matter to be taught in their various conjunctions. I use "types of" purposely since I do not view cases as unique events, but as instances of a broader class. To call something a case is to make the claim that it is a "case of something." Even in what may be argued is an idiographic enterprise, both cases and constructs must have some generalizability or the potential for professional education seems terribly limited.
4. The characterization of medicine is certainly more caricature than accurate portrayal. There is strong reason to assert that the ratio of case knowledge to scientific knowledge in medicine is far higher than the rubric "medical science" would have us believe.
5. That such an individual is possible can be concluded by the manner in which Schwab himself functions. While his teaching was almost exclusively conducted in a group setting, employing the tools of Socratic dialogue and group deliberation, his writing was exclusively solitary. It is both ironic and

instructive that this extraordinary spokesman for the power of group deliberation and learning communities authored all but four of his publications alone.

6. I am reminded of a conversation with Schwab in the Judd Hall Commons Room after a session of our seminar on Dewey. He commented that, if he could add one topic to the primary school curriculum, he would choose to teach young children to pun. I see the disciplinary and methodological eclecticism described above as a kind of very serious punning.

   This approach of multiple narratives is also consistent with that implicit in David Tyack's (1976) essay "Ways of Seeing," in which he demonstrates how the very same "hard facts," in his example the data describing increased rates of compulsory schooling in America during the 18th and 19th centuries, can be explained using very different narrative accounts.

REFERENCES

American Federation of Teachers. *Final report: Research Dissemination Project.* National Institute of Education, 1983.

Aristotle. De Anima (On the Soul). In *Introduction to Aristotle,* edited by R. McKeon. New York: Modern Library, 1947.

Cronbach, L. J. Beyond the two disciplines of scientific psychology. *American Psychologist,* 30, (1975): 116–127.

Cronbach, L. J. Prudent aspirations for social research. In *The future of the social sciences,* edited by L. Kruskal. Chicago: University of Chicago Press, 1982.

Cronbach, L. J. *Fields without fences.* (In preparation).

Dewey, J. *Experience and education.* New York: Macmillan, 1938.

Dostoyevsky, F. *Crime and punishment.* New York: Macmillan, 1937.

Erikson, E. *Young man Luther: A study in psychoanalysis and history.* New York: Norton, 1958.

Fenstermacher, G. A. philosophical consideration of recent research on teacher effectiveness. In *Review of Research in Education: VI,* edited by L. S. Shulman. Itasca, Ill.: F. E. Peacock, 1979.

Gage, N. L. *The scientific basis of the art of teaching.* New York: Teachers College Press, 1978.

Gergen, K. J. *Toward transformation in social knowledge.* New York: Springer-Verlag, 1982.

Getzels, J. W., and Thelen, H. A. The classroom group as a unique social system. In *The dynamics of instructional groups,* edited by G. E. Jensen.

Fifty-ninth Yearbook of the National Society for the Study of Education. Chicago: University of Chicago Press, 1960, pp. 53–82.

Glaser, B. G., and Strauss, A. L. *The discovery of grounded theory: Strategies for qualitative research.* Chicago: Aldine, 1967.

Green, T. F. *The activities of teaching.* New York: McGraw-Hill, 1971.

Kruskal, W. K., Ed. *The future of the social sciences.* Chicago: University of Chicago Press, 1982.

Manicas, P. T., and Secord, P. F. Implications for psychology of the new philosophy of science. *American Psychologist,* 38, (1983): 399–413.

Mead, M. *Growing up in New Guinea.* New York: Morrow, 1962.

Meehl, P. E. Theoretical risks and tabular asterisks: Sir Karl, Sir Ronald, and the slow progress of soft psychology. *Journal of Consulting and Clinical Psychology,* 46, (1978): 806–834.

Merton, R. K. The unanticipated consequences of purposive social action. *American Sociological Review,* 1, (1936): 894–904.

Merton, R. K. Structural analysis in sociology. In *Approaches to the study of social structure,* edited by P. Blau. New York: The Free Press, 1975.

Schwab, J. J. Eros and education. *Journal of General Education,* 8, (1954): 54–71.

Schwab, J. J. On the corruption of education by psychology. *School Review,* 66, (1958): 169–184.

Schwab, J. J. What do scientists do? *Behavioral Science,* 5, (1960): 1–27.

Schwab, J. J. The structure of the disciplines: Meanings and significances. In *The structure of knowledge and the curriculum,* edited by G. W. Ford and L. Pugno. Chicago: Rand McNally, 1964.

Schwab, J. J. The practical: A language for curriculum. *School Review,* 78, (1969): 1–23.

Schwab, J. J. Learning community. *The Center Magazine,* 8, 3 (May–June 1975): 30–44.

Schwab, J. J. Education and the state: Learning community. *The great ideas today, 1976.* Chicago: Encyclopedia Brittanica, 1976, pp. 234–271.

Schwab, J. J. The practical 4: Something for curriculum professors to do. *Curriculum Inquiry,* 13, (1983): 239–265.

Shulman, L. S. Disciplines of inquiry in education. *Educational Researcher,* 10, (1981): 5–12, 23.

Shulman, L. S. Autonomy and obligation: The remote control of teaching. In *The handbook of teaching and policy,* edited by L. S. Shulman and G. Sykes. New York: Longman, 1983.

Tyack, D. Ways of seeing: An essay on the history of compulsory schooling. *Harvard Educational Review,* 46, (1976): 355–389.

Vygotsky, L. S. *Mind in society: The development of higher psychological processes,* edited by M. Cole, V. John-Steiner, S. Scribner, and E. Souberman. Cambridge, Mass.: Harvard University Press, 1978.

Whyte, W. F. *Street corner society.* Chicago: University of Chicago Press, 1943.

Whyte, W. H. *The organization man.* New York: Simon and Schuster, 1956.

INTRODUCTION

THOSE WHO UNDERSTAND: KNOWLEDGE GROWTH IN TEACHING (1986)

ALONG WITH ITS "SEQUEL," "Knowledge and Teaching: Foundations of the New Reform," this essay is undeniably the best known of Shulman's work. It is based on his presidential address to the American Educational Research Association in 1985 and draws both from Shulman's earlier work at Michigan State University with colleagues in the Institute for Research on Teaching, like Sharon Feiman-Nemser, and on the Knowledge Growth in a Profession Project at Stanford University.

In the essay, Shulman interrogates historical and contemporary tests of teacher knowledge and skill as he attempts to answer the questions, What do teachers need to know? and What are the sources of teacher knowledge? He argues that research on teaching has tended to ignore the "missing paradigm": researchers have investigated generic questions about teaching but have failed to understand how teachers teach content. Shulman goes on to propose that teachers need to have many different kinds of knowledge, including content knowledge, pedagogical content knowledge, and curricular knowledge. This knowledge is held in myriad ways, as propositions, cases, and strategies. He concludes by considering the implications of this conception of teacher knowledge both for teacher examinations and for research on and pedagogy of teacher education.

Shulman's hypothesis that teachers might have a specialized content knowledge—"pedagogical content knowledge"—had a tremendous impact on the field. Researchers, nationally and internationally, began to conduct research on "PCK."

6

THOSE WHO UNDERSTAND

KNOWLEDGE GROWTH IN TEACHING

He who can, does.
He who cannot, teaches.

I DON'T KNOW IN WHAT fit of pique George Bernard Shaw wrote that infamous aphorism, words that have plagued members of the teaching profession for nearly a century. They are found in "Maxims for Revolutionists," an appendix to his play *Man and Superman.* "He who can, does. He who cannot, teaches" is a calamitous insult to our profession, yet one readily repeated even by teachers. More worrisome, its philosophy often appears to underlie the policies concerning the occupation and activities of teaching.

Where did such a demeaning image of the teacher's capacities originate? How long have we been burdened by assumptions of ignorance and ineptitude within the teaching corps? Is Shaw to be treated as the last word on what teachers know and don't know, or do and can't do?

Yesterday's Examinations

We begin our inquiry into conceptions of teacher knowledge with the tests for teachers that were used in this country during the last century at state and county levels. Some people may believe that the idea of testing teacher competence in subject matter and pedagogical skill is a new idea, an innovation spawned in the excitement of this era of educational reform, and encouraged by such committed and motivated national leaders as Albert Shanker, President, American Federation of Teachers; Bill Honig, State Superintendent of Schools, California; and Bill Clinton, Governor of Arkansas. Like most good ideas, however, its roots are much older.

Among the most fascinating archives in which to delve are the annual reports of state superintendents of education from over a century ago, in which we find copies of tests for teachers used in licensing candidates at the county level. These tests show us how teacher knowledge was defined. Moreover, we can compare those conceptions with their analogues today. I have examined tests from Massachusetts, Michigan, Nebraska, Colorado, and California. Let us take as a representative sample the California State Board examination for elementary school teachers from March 1875 and first look at the categories the examination covered:

1. Written Arithmetic
2. Mental Arithmetic
3. Written Grammar
4. Oral Grammar
5. Geography
6. History of the United States
7. Theory and Practice of Teaching
8. Algebra
9. Physiology
10. Natural Philosophy (Physics)
11. Constitution of the United States and California
12. School Law of California
13. Penmanship
14. Natural History (Biology)
15. Composition
16. Reading
17. Orthography
18. Defining (Word Analysis and Vocabulary)
19. Vocal Music
20. Industrial Drawing

The total number of points possible on this day-long essay examination was 1,000. The examiners were instructed to score for the correctness of responses and to deduct points for errors of composition, grammar, or spelling. What kinds of questions were asked on the examination? We shall review some from several of the categories.

- Find the cost of a draft on New York for $1,400 payable sixty days after sight, exchange being worth 102 1/2 percent and interest being reckoned at a rate of 7 percent per annum. (Written Arithmetic, one of ten items)
- Divide 88 into two such parts that shall be to each other as 2/3 is to 4/5. (Mental Arithmetic, one of ten items)
- When should the reciprocal pronouns *one another* and *each other* be used? the correlative conjunctions *so as* and *as as*?
- Name and illustrate five forms of conjugation. Name and give four ways in which the nominative case may be used. (Grammar, two of ten items)
- Define *specific gravity*. Why may heavy stones be lifted in water when on land they can scarcely be moved?
- What is adhesion? What is capillary attraction? Illustrate each. (two of ten items from Natural Philosophy)
- Name five powers vested in Congress.

Lest you think that all of the items on the 1875 California Teachers Examination deal with subject matter alone, rest assured that there is a category for pedagogical practice. However, only 50 out of the total 1,000 possible points are given over to the ten-item subtest on Theory and Practice of Teaching. Examples of those items are:

- What course would you pursue to keep up with the progress in teaching?
- How do you succeed in teaching children to spell correctly the words commonly misspelled?
- How do you interest lazy and careless pupils? Answer in full(!).

All the tests I have found from that period follow the same pattern. Ninety to ninety-five percent of the test is on the content, the subject matter to be taught, or at least on the knowledge base assumed to be needed by teachers, whether or not it is taught directly. Thus, aspects of physiology are apparently deemed necessary because of the expectation that teachers understand the biological functioning of their pupils.

How closely did the actual tests administered resemble these I have read? What was it like to take one of these examinations? A useful source for addressing such questions is the autobiographical literature by teachers, one of the most useful compendia of which is *Women's "True" Profession,* a collection of excerpts from the diaries or memoirs of women teachers. Among these, we find the following reminiscence of Lucia Downing (cited in Hoffman, 1981). She reported on the taking of her initial county examination in 1881, as administered by her family physician, who also served one day per month as county superintendent.

> When my sister, already a teacher, went to take another examination, the spring I was thirteen, I went along too, and said to the doctor, who was only a superintendent that day, that, if he had enough papers, I should like to see how many questions I could answer. The doctor smiled at me, and gave me an arithmetic paper for a starter. It proved to be easy, for it brought in some favorite problems in percentage, which would be an advantage to a merchant, as they showed how to mark goods in such a way that one could sell below the marked price, and still make a profit. I guess all merchants must have studied Greenleaf's *Arithmetic!* There was another problem under the old Vermont Annual Interest Rule . . . and then proudly started on Grammar. I knew I could do something with that, for I loved to parse and analyze and "diagram," according to Reed and Kellogg. In fact, my first knowledge, and for many years my only knowledge of "Paradise Lost" was gleaned from a little blue parsing book . . .
>
> Next came Geography. Though I had never traveled farther than Burlington, I knew, thanks to Mr. Guyot and his green geography, that Senegambia was "rich in gold, iron ore and gum-producing trees." . . . History and Civil Government were pretty hard for me, but next came Physiology, and I made the most of my bones and circulatory system, hoping to impress the physician. But it was in Theory and School Management that I did myself proud. I discoursed at length on ventilation and temperature, and knowing that "good government" is a most desirable and necessary qualification for a teacher, I advocated a firm, but kind and gentle method, with dignity of bearing. In giving my views of corporal punishment, I related a story I had read of the Yankee teacher who was asked his views on the subject. He said, "Wal, moral suasion's my theory, but lickin's my practice!" . . .
>
> Finally, one morning, there was an envelope addressed in Dr. Butler's scholarly hand . . . (and) out fluttered two yellow slips—two cer-

> tificates, entitling the recipients to teach in Vermont for one year. And one was in my name! I cannot recall any subsequent joy equal to what I felt at that moment—even a college diploma and a Phi Beta Kappa key, in later years, brought less of a thrill. (pp. 29–30)

The assumptions underlying those tests are clear. The person who presumes to teach subject matter to children must demonstrate knowledge of that subject matter as a prerequisite to teaching. Although knowledge of the theories and methods of teaching is important, it plays a decidedly secondary role in the qualifications of a teacher.

Today's Standards

The emphasis on the subject matter to be taught stands in sharp contrast to the emerging policies of the 1980s with respect to the evaluation or testing of teachers. Nearly every state is reexamining its approaches to defining what teachers must know to be licensed and subsequently tenured. Many states have introduced mandatory examinations, but these do not typically map onto the content of the curriculum. They are tests of basic abilities to read, write, spell, calculate, and solve arithmetic problems. Often they are treated as prerequisites for entry into a teacher education program rather than as standards for defining eligibility to practice.

In most states, however, the evaluation of teachers emphasizes the assessment of capacity to teach. Such assessment is usually claimed to rest on a "research-based" conception of teacher effectiveness. I shall take as my example a list of such competencies prepared by a state that I briefly advised during its planning for a state-wide system of teacher evaluation. The following categories for teacher review and evaluation were proposed:

1. Organization in preparing and presenting instructional plans
2. Evaluation
3. Recognition of individual differences
4. Cultural awareness
5. Understanding youth
6. Management
7. Educational policies and procedures

As we compare these categories (which are quite similar to those emerging in other states) to those of 1875, the contrast is striking. Where did the subject matter go? What happened to the content? Perhaps Shaw was correct. He accurately anticipated the standards for teaching in 1985. He who knows, does. He who cannot, but knows some teaching procedures, teaches.

Yet policymakers justify the heavy emphasis on procedures by referring to the emergent research base on teaching and teaching effectiveness. They regularly define and justify these categories by the extremely powerful phrase "research-based teacher competencies." In what sense can it be claimed that such a conception of teaching competence is research-based?

The designers of recent approaches to teacher evaluation cite the impressive volume of research on teaching effectiveness as the basis for their selection of domains and standards, and in fact, this basis is valid. They base their categories and standards on a growing body of research on teaching, research classified under the rubrics of "teaching effectiveness," "process-product studies," or "teacher behavior" research. These studies were designed to identify those patterns of teacher behavior that accounted for improved academic performance among pupils.

Whether by contrasting more effective with less effective teachers, or by conducting experiments in which teachers were trained to employ specific sets of teaching behaviors and monitoring the results for pupil achievement, this research program has yielded findings on the forms of teacher behavior that most effectively promote student learning. The work has been criticized from several perspectives, both technical and theoretical, but for our purposes I would consider the research program a thriving and successful one (Shulman, 1986).

Nevertheless, policymakers' decision to base their approaches to teacher evaluation standards on this work is simultaneously the source of their greatest strength and their most significant weakness. What policymakers fail to understand is that there is an unavoidable constraint on any piece of research in any discipline (Shulman, 1981). To conduct a piece of research, scholars must necessarily narrow their scope, focus their view, and formulate a question far less complex than the form in which the world presents itself in practice. This holds for any piece of research; there are no exceptions. It is certainly true of the corpus of research on teaching effectiveness that serves as the basis for these contemporary approaches to teacher evaluation. In their necessary simplification of the complexities of classroom teaching, investigators ignored one central aspect of classroom life: the subject matter.

This omission also characterized most other research paradigms in the study of teaching. Occasionally subject matter entered into the research as a context variable—a control characteristic for subdividing data sets by content categories (e.g., "When teaching 5th grade mathematics, the following teacher behaviors were correlated with outcomes. When teaching 5th grade reading, . . ."). But no one focused on the subject matter content itself. No one asked how subject matter was transformed from the knowledge of the teacher into the content of instruction. Nor did they ask how particular formulations of that content related to what students came to know or misconstrue (even though that question had become the central query of cognitive research on *learning*).

My colleagues and I refer to the absence of focus on subject matter among the various research paradigms for the study of teaching as the "missing paradigm" problem. The consequences of this missing paradigm are serious, both for policy and for research.

Policymakers read the research on teaching literature and find it replete with references to direct instruction, time on task, wait time, ordered turns, lower-order questions, and the like. They find little or no references to subject matter, so the resulting standards or mandates lack any reference to content dimensions of teaching. Similarly, even in the research community, the importance of content has been forgotten. Research programs that arose in response to the dominance of process-product work accepted its definition of the problem and continued to treat teaching more or less generically, or at least as if the content of instruction were relatively unimportant. Even those who studied teacher cognition, a decidedly non-process/product perspective, investigated teacher planning or interactive decision making with little concern for the organization of content knowledge in the minds of teachers. I shall have more to say about the missing paradigm and its investigation a bit later. Let us now return to the question with which we began.

Content and Pedagogy in thc History of the Academy

Why this sharp distinction between content and pedagogical process? Whether in the spirit of the 1870s, when pedagogy was essentially ignored, or in the 1980s, when content is conspicuously absent, has there always been a cleavage between the two? Has it always been asserted that one either knows content and pedagogy is secondary and unimportant, or that one knows pedagogy and is not held accountable for content?

I propose that we look back even further than those 1875 tests for teachers and examine the history of the university as an institution to discern the sources for this distinction between content knowledge and pedagogical method.

In *Ramus, Method and the Decay of Dialogue,* Father Walter Ong (1958) presents an account of teaching in the medieval university in a chapter with the captivating title "The Pedagogical Juggernaut." He describes a world of teaching and learning in those universities, where instead of separating content and pedagogy (what is known from how to teach it), no such distinction was made at all. Content and pedagogy were part of one indistinguishable body of understanding.

To this day, the names we give our university degrees and the rituals we attach to them reflect those fundamental connections between knowing and teaching. For example, the highest degrees awarded in any university are those of "master" or "doctor," which were traditionally interchangeable. Both words have the same definition; they mean "teacher." "Doctor" or "dottore" means teacher; it has the same root as "doctrine," or teaching. Master, as in school master, also means teacher. Thus, the highest university degree enabled its recipient to be called a teacher.

Ong's (1958) account of these matters is enlightening:

> The universities were, in principle, normal schools, not institutions of general education. This was true of all faculties: arts, medicine, law, and theology; and it was most true at Paris and at universities modeled on Paris (rather than on Bologna), such as Oxford and Cambridge and, later, the German universities. Such universities were in brief, medieval guilds, or were composed of four teachers' guilds or faculties with their associated pupils. The degree of master or doctor (the terms were equivalents, varying from university to university or from faculty to faculty) was the formal admission to the guild, just as the bachelorship which preceded it was admission to the body of apprentice teachers.
>
> . . . Officially, the bachelor of arts was an apprentice teacher on the arts faculty; bachelors of theology were apprentice teachers of theology, condemned to a long round of "practice" teaching; and bachelor butchers were apprentice butchers—for all these people were members of their respective trade guilds.
>
> . . . A physician whom a university faculty certifies as a practitioner of medicine is called a "doctor" of medicine, as though he were going to teach medicine, just as in some countries, one trained to practice the law is also called "master" or its equivalent. Graduation, too, is still a "commencement" or *inceptio*—in theory, the beginning of a teaching career. (pp. 153–154)

The *inceptio* of which Ong writes was the ceremony of doctoral examination—the final stage of demonstration that one possessed the necessary capacities for the highest university degree. The basic structure of the examination has remained constant to this day in the final oral examination for the doctorate. The purpose of the examination is to demonstrate that the candidate possesses the highest levels of subject matter competence in the domain for which the degree is awarded. How did one demonstrate such understanding in medieval times? By demonstrating the ability to *teach* the subject (Ong, 1958):

> Arrived at the cathedral, the licentiate delivered a speech and read a thesis on some point of law, which he defended against opponents who were selected from among the students, the candidates thus playing for the first time the part of a doctor in a university disputation. (pp. 227–228)

Consider the full current form of the oral exam. First, the candidate presents a brief oral exposition of the thesis. He then defends the thesis in dialogue with the examiners. These parallel the two modes of teaching: the lecture and the disputation. The oral examination is the ultimate test of subject matter expertise; it examines the candidate's ability to teach the subject by employing the dual method of lecture and discussion.[1]

The universities were, therefore, much like normal schools: institutions for preparing that most prestigious of professionals, the highest level of scholar, the teacher. The tradition of treating teaching as the highest demonstration of scholarship was derived from the writings of a far greater authority than George Bernard Shaw on the nature of knowledge. Aristotle, whose works formed the heart of the medieval curriculum, made these observations in *Metaphysics* (cited in Wheelwright, 1951).

> We regard master-craftsmen as superior not merely because they have a grasp of theory and *know* the reasons for acting as they do. Broadly speaking, what distinguishes the man who knows from the ignorant man is an ability to teach, and this is why we hold that art and not experience has the character of genuine knowledge (episteme)—namely, that artists can teach and others (i.e., those who have not acquired an art by study but have merely picked up some skill empirically) cannot. (p. 69)

We thus find in Aristotle a very different view of the relationship between knowing and teaching than we find in either Shaw or in the criteria for certification and licensure in some of our sovereign states.

Lest my readers conclude that the medieval university was a pedagogical utopia, to whose practices we need only return to redress the imbalances that plague contemporary teaching policies, permit me to provide a couple of counterexamples. From the classic treatise on the medieval university, Rashdall's (1895/1936) *The Universities of Europe in the Middle Ages* relates how problems of accountability were handled.

> Punctuality is enforced with extreme rigour. The professor was obliged to begin his lecture when the bells of St. Peter's began to ring for mass,

> under a penalty of 20 solidi for each offence, though he has the privilege of beginning at an earlier hour if he pleases; while he is forbidden to continue his lecture one minute after the bell has begun to ring for tierce. To secure the observance of the statute a more effectual means is adopted even than that of fining the doctor: his pupils are required under a penalty of 10 solidi to leave the lecture-room as soon as the bell begins.
>
> Even in the actual conduct of his lectures the doctor is regulated with the precision of a soldier on parade or a reader in a French public library. He is fined if he skips a chapter or decretal: he is forbidden to postpone a difficulty to the end of the lecture lest such a liberty should be abused as a pretext for evading it altogether. In medieval as in modern times lecturers had a tendency to spend a disproportionate time over the earlier portions of a book, and so leave none for the rest. With a view to checking this practice, an expedient was adopted at Bologna which became universal in the law-universities of Southern Europe. The law-texts were divided into portions known as *puncta;* and the doctor was required to have reached each *punctum* by a specified date. At the beginning of the academical year he was bound to deposit the sum of 10 Bologna pounds with a banker [the stakeholder was known as the *Depositarius*], who promised to deliver it up at the demand of the rectors: for every day that the doctor was behind time, a certain sum was deducted from his deposit by order of these officials . . . (pp. 196–197)

The medieval university was therefore hardly a paradise for its teachers, especially in Bologna, where the university was a guild of students that hired teachers (in contrast to the Paris model of a guild of teachers selling services to students). Moreover, it was also deeply flawed by an ultimate liability; it was open only to men and boys. This deficiency may account more than most others for the inability of the medieval university to accomplish as much as one would have hoped.

The Missing Paradigm

We have thus seen that the sharp distinction between knowledge and pedagogy does not represent a tradition dating back centuries, but rather, a more recent development. Moreover, identification of teaching competence with pedagogy alone was not even commonplace during Shaw's time. A century ago the defining characteristic of pedagogical accomplishment was knowledge of content.

The pendulum has now swung, both in research and in policy circles. The missing paradigm refers to a blind spot with respect to content that now characterizes most research on teaching and, as a consequence, most of our state-level programs of teacher evaluation and teacher certification.

In reading the literature of research on teaching, it is clear that central questions are unasked. The emphasis is on how teachers manage their classrooms, organize activities, allocate time and turns, structure assignments, ascribe praise and blame, formulate the levels of their questions, plan lessons, and judge general student understanding.

What we miss are questions about the *content* of the lessons taught, the questions asked, and the explanations offered. From the perspectives of teacher development and teacher education, a host of questions arise. Where do teacher explanations come from? How do teachers decide what to teach, how to represent it, how to question students about it, and how to deal with problems of misunderstanding? The cognitive psychology of *learning* has focused almost exclusively on such questions in recent years, but strictly from the perspective of learners. Research on teaching has tended to ignore those issues with respect to teachers. My colleagues and I are attempting to redress this imbalance through our research program, "Knowledge Growth in Teaching."

What are the sources of teacher knowledge? What does a teacher know and when did he or she come to know it? How is new knowledge acquired, old knowledge retrieved, and both combined to form a new knowledge base?

We assume that most teachers begin with some expertise in the content they teach. (This may be an unfounded assumption, and the consequences of varying degrees of subject matter competence and incompetence have become a serious topic of our research as well.) Secondary teaching candidates, in particular, have typically completed a major in their subject specialty.

Our central question concerns the transition from expert student to novice teacher. How does the successful college student transform his or her expertise in the subject matter into a form that high school students can comprehend? When this novice teacher confronts flawed or muddled textbook chapters or befuddled students, how does he or she employ content expertise to generate new explanations, representations, or clarifications? What are the sources of analogies, metaphors, examples, demonstrations, and rephrasings? How does the novice teacher (or even the seasoned veteran) draw on expertise in the subject matter in the process of teaching? What pedagogical prices are paid when the teacher's subject matter competence is itself compromised by deficiencies of prior education or ability?

Our work does not intend to denigrate the importance of pedagogical understanding or skill in the development of a teacher or in enhancing the effectiveness of instruction. Mere content knowledge is likely to be as useless pedagogically as content-free skill. But to blend properly the two aspects of a teacher's capacities requires that we pay as much attention to the content aspects of teaching as we have recently devoted to the elements of teaching process.

In our research, we have focused on the development of secondary teachers in English, biology, mathematics, and social studies. Our participants are all in California, thus each has already completed a bachelor's degree in the subject to be taught or has earned a waiver by examination. We are devoting at least one year, and often two, to the study of each novice teacher. We begin with their year of teacher preparation (which is nearly three-quarters completed as this paper is written) and, whenever possible, we will follow them into their first year of full-time teaching.

Our initial goal has been to trace their intellectual biography—that set of understandings, conceptions, and orientations that constitutes the source of their comprehension of the subjects they teach. This approach to assessing their content knowledge is quite different from the methods typically used to measure teacher content knowledge in the research literature; namely, administering an achievement test and employing a total test score as the index of teacher knowledge.

We follow them closely during this teacher-education year, conducting regular interviews, asking them to read and comment on materials related to the subjects they teach, and observing their instruction after having engaged them in a planning interview. We also gather data on the teacher education program in which they are prepared and the impact of both formal and informal preparation experiences on their pedagogy. Most of these references emerge naturally in the course of frequent conversations during the year.

A number of strategic research sites and key events are particularly illuminating for our understanding of how knowledge grows in teaching. Often a young teacher will be expected to teach a topic that he or she has never previously learned. For example, the biology major encounters a unit on levers and simple machines in a general science course. The English major must teach a novel or play never previously encountered. The political science major with strong preparation in Central America confronts a unit on India or the Middle East. Even the math major encounters such occasions, as when teaching introductory topics in algebra or geometry, topics he or she has not encountered since high school or even earlier. How does the teacher prepare to teach something never previously learned? How does learning *for* teaching occur?

Another strategic site occurs in conjunction with sections of textbooks that the teacher finds problematic, flawed in their conception of the topic, incomplete in their treatment, or inadequate in explanation or use of examples. How are these deficiencies in curriculum materials (which appear to be commonplace) apprehended and dealt with by teachers? How do teachers take a piece of text and transform their understanding of it into instruction that their students can comprehend?

We are not alone in our interest. Prominent among other investigators who are pursuing such questions are Gaea Leinhardt at the Learning Research and Development Center, University of Pittsburgh, and Charles Anderson and Edward Smith of Michigan State's Institute for Research on Teaching.

A Perspective on Teacher Knowledge

As we have begun to probe the complexities of teacher understanding and transmission of content knowledge, the need for a more coherent theoretical framework has become rapidly apparent. What are the domains and categories of content knowledge in the minds of teachers? How, for example, are content knowledge and general pedagogical knowledge related? In which forms are the domains and categories of knowledge represented in the minds of teachers? What are promising ways of enhancing acquisition and development of such knowledge? Because I see these as among the central questions for disciplined inquiry into teacher education, I will now turn to a discussion of some ways of thinking about one particular domain—content knowledge in teaching—and some of the categories within it.

How might we think about the knowledge that grows in the minds of teachers, with special emphasis on content? I suggest we distinguish among three categories of content knowledge: (a) subject matter content knowledge, (b) pedagogical content knowledge, and (c) curricular knowledge.

Content Knowledge

This refers to the amount and organization of knowledge per se in the mind of the teacher. We already have a number of ways to represent content knowledge; Bloom's cognitive taxonomy, Gagné's varieties of learning, Schwab's distinction between substantive and syntactic structures of knowledge, and Peters' notions that parallel Schwab's.

In the different subject matter areas, the ways of discussing the content structure of knowledge differ. To think properly about content knowledge requires going beyond knowledge of the facts or concepts of a domain. It requires understanding the structures of the subject matter in the manner defined by such scholars as Joseph Schwab. (See his collected essays, 1978.)

For Schwab, the structures of a subject include both the substantive and the syntactic structures. The substantive structures are the variety of ways in which the basic concepts and principles of the discipline are organized to incorporate its facts. The syntactic structure of a discipline is the set of ways in which truth or falsehood, validity or invalidity, are established. When there exist competing claims regarding a given phenomenon, the syntax of a discipline provides the rules for determining which claim has greater warrant. A syntax is like a grammar. It is the set of rules for determining what is legitimate to say in a disciplinary domain and what "breaks" the rules.

Teachers must not only be capable of defining for students the accepted truths in a domain. They must also be able to explain why a particular proposition is deemed warranted, why it is worth knowing, and how it relates to other propositions, both within the discipline and without, both in theory and in practice.

Thus, the biology teacher must understand that there are a variety of ways of organizing the discipline. Depending on the preferred color of one's BSCS text, biology may be formulated as (a) a science of molecules from which one aggregates up to the rest of the field, explaining living phenomena in terms of the principles of their constituent parts; (b) a science of ecological systems from which one disaggregates down to the smaller units, explaining the activities of individual units by virtue of the larger systems of which they are a part; or (c) a science of biological organisms, those most familiar of analytic units, from whose familiar structures, functions, and interactions one weaves a theory of adaptation. The well-prepared biology teacher will recognize these and alternative forms of organization and the pedagogical grounds for selecting one under some circumstances and others under different circumstances.

The same teacher will also understand the syntax of biology. When competing claims are offered regarding the same biological phenomenon, how has the controversy been adjudicated? How might similar controversies be adjudicated in our own day?

We expect that the subject matter content understanding of the teacher be at least equal to that of his or her lay colleague, the mere subject matter major. The teacher need not only understand *that* something is so; the teacher must further understand *why* it is so, on what grounds its warrant can be asserted, and under what circumstances our belief in its justification can be weakened and even denied. Moreover, we expect the teacher to understand why a given topic is particularly central to a discipline whereas another may be somewhat peripheral. This will be important in subsequent pedagogical judgments regarding relative curricular emphasis.

Pedagogical Content Knowledge

A second kind of content knowledge is pedagogical knowledge, which goes beyond knowledge of subject matter per se to the dimension of subject matter knowledge *for teaching*. I still speak of content knowledge here, but of the particular form of content knowledge that embodies the aspects of content most germane to its teachability.[2]

Within the category of pedagogical content knowledge I include, for the most regularly taught topics in one's subject area, the most useful forms of representation of those ideas, the most powerful analogies, illustrations, examples, explanations, and demonstrations—in a word, the ways of representing and formulating the subject that make it comprehensible to others. Since there are no single most powerful forms of representation, the teacher must have at hand a veritable armamentarium of alternative forms of representation, some of which derive from research whereas others originate in the wisdom of practice.

Pedagogical content knowledge also includes an understanding of what makes the learning of specific topics easy or difficult: the conceptions and preconceptions that students of different ages and backgrounds bring with them to the learning of those most frequently taught topics and lessons. If those preconceptions are misconceptions, which they so often are, teachers need knowledge of the strategies most likely to be fruitful in reorganizing the understanding of learners, because those learners are unlikely to appear before them as blank slates.

Here, research on teaching and on learning coincide most closely. The study of student misconceptions and their influence on subsequent learning has been among the most fertile topics for cognitive research. We are gathering an ever-growing body of knowledge about the misconceptions of students and about the instructional conditions necessary to overcome and transform those initial conceptions. Such research-based knowledge, an important component of the pedagogical understanding of subject matter, should be included at the heart of our definition of needed pedagogical knowledge.

Curricular Knowledge

If we are regularly remiss in not teaching pedagogical knowledge to our students in teacher education programs, we are even more delinquent with respect to the third category of content knowledge, *curricular knowledge*. The curriculum is represented by the full range of programs designed for the teaching of particular subjects and topics at a given level, the variety of instructional materials available in relation to those programs, and the set of characteristics that serve as both the indications and contraindications for the use of particular curriculum or program materials in particular circumstances.

The curriculum and its associated materials are the *materia medica* of pedagogy, the pharmacopeia from which the teacher draws those tools of teaching that present or exemplify particular content and remediate or evaluate the adequacy of student accomplishments. We expect the mature physician to understand the full range of treatments available to ameliorate a given disorder, as well as the range of alternatives for particular circumstances of sensitivity, cost, interaction with other interventions, convenience, safety, or comfort. Similarly, we ought to expect that the mature teacher possesses such understandings about the curricular alternatives available for instruction.

How many individuals whom we prepare for teaching biology, for example, understand well the materials for that instruction, the alternative texts, software, programs, visual materials, single-concept films, laboratory demonstrations, or "invitations to inquiry"? Would we trust a physician who did not really understand the alternative ways of dealing with categories of infectious disease, but who knew only one way?

In addition to the knowledge of alternative curriculum materials for a given subject or topic within a grade, there are two additional aspects of curricular knowledge. I would expect a professional teacher to be familiar with the curriculum materials under study by his or her students in other subjects they are studying at the same time.

This lateral curriculum knowledge (appropriate in particular to the work of junior and senior high school teachers) underlies the teacher's ability to relate the content of a given course or lesson to topics or issues being discussed simultaneously in other classes. The vertical equivalent of that curriculum knowledge is familiarity with the topics and issues that have been and will be taught in the same subject area during the preceding and later years in school, and the materials that embody them.

Content Examinations

What might the expectation that our teachers possess these varieties of content knowledge entail for the assessment of teacher competence? If such a conception of teacher knowledge were to serve as the basis for a subject matter content examination for teachers, that examination would measure deep knowledge of the content and structures of a subject matter, the subject and topic-specific pedagogical knowledge associated with the subject matter, and the curricular knowledge of the subject. We would have a form of examination that would be appropriate for assessing the capacities of a *professional.* It would not be a mere subject matter examination. It would ask questions about the most likely misunderstandings of photosynthesis among preadolescents, for example, and the strategies most likely to be useful in overcoming those difficulties. As such, it could distinguish between a biology major and a biology teacher, and in a pedagogically relevant and important way, it would be much tougher than any current examination for teachers.[3]

Forms of Knowledge

A conceptual analysis of knowledge for teachers would necessarily be based on a framework for classifying both the domains and categories of teacher knowledge, on the one hand, and the forms for representing that knowledge, on the other. I would like to suggest three forms of teacher knowledge: *propositional knowledge, case knowledge,* and *strategic knowledge.*

Recall that these are "forms" in which each of the general domains or particular categories of knowledge previously discussed—content, pedagogy, and curriculum—may be organized. (There are clearly other important domains of knowledge as well, for example, of individual differences among students, of generic methods of classroom organization and management, of the history and philosophy of education, and of school finance and administration, to name but a few. Each of these domains is subdivided into categories and will be expressible in the forms of knowledge to be discussed here.)

Much of what is taught to teachers is in the form of propositions. When we examine the research on teaching and learning and explore its implications for practice, we are typically (and properly) examining propositions. When we ask about the wisdom of practice, the accumulated lore of teaching experience, we tend to find such knowledge stored in the form of propositions as well.

The research-based principles of active teaching, reading for comprehension, and effective schools are stated as lists of propositions. The experience-based recommendations of planning five-step lesson plans, never smiling until Christmas, and organizing three reading groups are posed as sets of propositions. In fact, although we often present propositions one at a time, we recognize that they are better understood if they are organized in some coherent form, lodged in a conceptual or theoretical framework that is generative or regenerative. Otherwise they become terribly difficult to recall or retrieve. (The experimental studies of teaching effectiveness have been guilty of presenting lengthy lists of research-based behaviors for teachers to practice, without always providing a rationale or conceptual framework for the set.)

I will argue that there are fundamentally three types of propositional knowledge in teaching, corresponding to the three major sources of knowledge about teaching: disciplined empirical or philosophical inquiry, practical experience, and moral or ethical reasoning. I will refer to these three types of propositions as *principles, maxims,* and *norms.*

A principle typically derives from empirical research. One of my favorites is "Ordered turns are associated with higher achievement gains than are random turns in first grade reading groups" (Anderson, Evertson, & Brophy, 1979). The teaching and school effectiveness literatures contain many examples of useful principles for teaching.

The second kind of proposition makes not a theoretical claim, but a practical one. In every field of practice there are ideas that have never been confirmed by research and would, in principle, be difficult to demonstrate. Nevertheless, these maxims represent the accumulated wisdom of practice, and in many cases are as important a source of guidance for practice as the theory or empirical principles. "Never smile until Christmas" would qualify as such a maxim, as would "Break a large piece of chalk before you use it for the first time, to prevent squeaking against the board."

The third kind of proposition reflects the norms, values, ideological, or philosophical commitments of justice, fairness, equity, and the like, that we wish teachers and those learning to teach to incorporate and employ. They are neither theoretical nor practical, but normative. They occupy the very heart of what we mean by teacher knowledge. These are propositions that guide the work of a teacher, not because they are true in scientific terms, or because they work in practical terms, but because they are morally or ethically right. The admonitions to provide each student with equal opportunity for turn-taking, or not to embarrass a child in front of peers, are examples of normative knowledge.

The representation of knowledge in the form of propositions has both a distinct advantage and a significant liability. Propositions are remarkably economical in form, containing and simplifying a great deal of complexity. The weakness of propositions is two-fold. First, they become very hard to remember, especially as they aggregate into long lists. This is where theoretical frameworks as intellectual scaffoldings become indispensable. Second, they gain their economy precisely because they are decontextualized, stripped down to their essentials, devoid of detail, emotion, or ambience. Yet, to be remembered and then wisely used, it is precisely the detail and the context that may be needed.

Although principles are powerful, they are not particularly memorable, rendering them a problem to apply in particular circumstances. *How* does a teacher apply, for example, the principle "check for understanding," certainly among the most important in the direct instruction and the active teaching research bases? For these reasons, I am proposing that we look seriously at the usefulness of a second type of knowledge, a necessary complement to knowledge of propositions, *case knowledge*.

The roots of the "case method" in the teaching of law in this country, certainly the best known approach to employing cases as vehicles for professional education, lie in their value for teaching theory, not practice. Christopher Columbus Langdell, who became Dean of the Harvard University Law School in 1870, was responsible for advancing the case method of legal education. His rationale for employing this method was not its value as a way of teaching methods or approaches to practice. He believed that if practice were the essence of law, it had no place in a university. Instead, he advocated the case method of legal education because of its effectiveness in teaching law as science—in teaching legal *theory* through cases.

A case, properly understood, is not simply the report of an event or incident. To call something a case is to make a theoretical claim—to argue that it is a "case of something," or to argue that it is an instance of a larger class. A red rash on the face is not a case of something until the observer has invoked theoretical knowledge of disease. A case of direct instruction or of higher-order questioning is similarly a theoretical assertion. I am therefore not arguing that the preparation of teachers be reduced to the most practical and concrete; rather, using the power of a case literature to illuminate both the practical and the theoretical, I argue for development of a case literature whose organization and use will be profoundly and self-consciously theoretical.

Case knowledge is knowledge of specific, well-documented, and richly described events. Whereas cases themselves are reports of events or sequences of events, the knowledge they represent is what makes them cases. The cases may be examples of specific instances of practice—detailed descriptions of how an instructional event occurred—complete with particulars of contexts, thoughts, and feelings. On the other hand, they may be exemplars of principles, exemplifying in their detail a more abstract proposition or theoretical claim.

Parallel to my argument that there are three types of propositional knowledge of teaching—principles, maxims, and norms—I shall propose three types of cases. *Prototypes* exemplify theoretical principles. *Precedents* capture and communicate principles of practice or maxims. *Parables* convey norms or values. Naturally, a given case can accomplish more than a single function; it can, for example, serve as both prototype and precedent.

We are probably most accustomed to thinking of cases as precedents. Knowledge of how a particular teacher taught a particular lesson, or the way a teacher brought a classroom of misbehaving youngsters under control sticks in our minds. These remembrances of teachings past are valuable in guiding the work of a teacher, both as a source for specific ideas and as a heuristic to stimulate new thinking. But other kinds of cases exemplify, illustrate, and bring alive the theoretical propositions that are potentially the most powerful tools teachers can have. These are the prototypes within case knowledge. For example, when pharmacology is taught, specific drugs are often used as illustrations. The drugs selected for that purpose are not necessarily the most frequently used in practice. Instead, prototypes are selected that exemplify in their performance the mechanisms of action most characteristic of the *class* of drugs they represent. They are thus theoretically interesting cases for teaching purposes.

As part of an extensive interview study with teachers reputed to be excellent managers of classroom behavior problems, J. Brophy (personal communication, 1981) has reported the following case: A teacher was confronted with repeated incidents of students coming to class without pencils. Rather than either supplying them with replacements (thus making it possible for them to keep up with their work, although running the risk of reinforcing their poor habits) or forcing them to sit through the lesson without benefit of participation, the following strategy was reported. The teacher kept a box of very short pencil stubs in his desk. Whenever a student approached who had forgotten to bring a pencil, the teacher produced the shortest stub available and lent it to the student, who was then expected to use it in completing all of that day's work. In addition to serving as a fine classroom management precedent, this case can also serve as a memorable prototype for the principle of avoiding the inadvertent reinforcement of maladaptive behavior.

Parallel to the theoretical use of prototype cases and the practical use of precedents, we also encounter the moral or normative value of parables. A parable is a case whose value lies in the communication of values and norms, propositions that occupy the very heart of teaching as profession and as craft. Moreover, if we look at the recent literature on effective organizations and what keeps them working well and their members collaborating enthusiastically, we discover the importance of myths in organizations—tales about heroic figures or memorable events that somehow capture the values of those organizations and communicate them to everyone working within them. Those myths, I would argue, or their case equivalents—pedagogical parables—would be equally important in the socialization of teachers into their general professional obligations as well as into the special ethos of particular schools or districts as organizations.

The identification of case knowledge, a case literature, and case-based teacher education as central elements in our discussions and inquiries produces a rich and vital agenda for research. What is involved in the elevation of an event into a case? How are cases aggregated into case knowledge, or alternatively, how does knowledge of cases become case knowledge? How does one learn from and use cases in teaching? If the conception of propositional knowledge is deductive, where applications are deduced from general propositions, how is the analogical reasoning from cases learned, practiced, and tuned? Can we learn from other disciplines or professions such as law or architecture, where analogical reasoning from cases is much more typical, how to conceive of and use case knowledge in education? Why are cases memorable? Is it because they are organized as stories, reflecting the grammar of narrative forms of discourse, that makes them more readily stored, ordered, and retrieved than their expository or propositional analogues?[4]

Another reason that these conceptions of case knowledge may be timely is the shift of research paradigms currently underway in our field. We are developing well-reasoned, methodologically sophisticated, and logically argued approaches to the use of qualitative methods and case studies to parallel our already developed approaches of correlational and experimental inquiry. These newer approaches introduce both a new kind of data about which to reason and new modes of reasoning themselves. As Geertz (1983) has observed, "Inquiry is directed at cases or sets of cases, and toward the particular features that mark them off . . ." (p. 22). As these approaches grow in their educational applications, we will begin to develop a more extensive case literature, as well as a pool of scholars and reflective practitioners capable of preparing and interpreting cases.

Cases are documented (or portrayed) occasions or sets of occasions with their boundaries marked off, their borders drawn. What a given occasion is "a case of" is not immediately apparent from the account itself. Generalizability does not inhere in the case, but in the conceptual apparatus of the explicator. An event can be described; a case must be explicated, interpreted, argued, dissected, and reassembled. A case of Budweiser is marked off from other cases (or non-cases) by physical attributes that are immediately visible. But a case of direct instruction, or of teacher expectations, or of student misconception, is a theoretical construction. Hence, there is no real case knowledge without theoretical understanding. What passes for atheoretical case knowledge is mere anecdote, a parable without a moral.

I am not offering herein an argument against the conception of teaching as skill. I am instead arguing for its insufficiency—its incompleteness as an account of teaching ability and performance. We are only half way toward understanding the knowledge base of teaching when characterizing a research-based conception of the *skills* of teaching. This account must be complemented by a conception of teaching in which the principled skills and the well-studied cases are brought together in the development and formation of *strategic* pedagogical knowledge.

I have referred to *strategic knowledge* as the third "form" of teacher knowledge. Both propositions and cases share the burden of unilaterality, the deficiency of turning the reader or user toward a single, particular rule or practical way of seeing. Strategic knowledge comes into play as the teacher confronts particular situations or problems, whether theoretical, practical, or moral, where principles collide and no simple solution is possible. Strategic knowledge is developed when the lessons of single principles contradict one another, or the precedents of particular cases are incompatible. From Rowe's (1974) research on wait-time, for example, we learn the principle that longer wait-times produce higher levels of cognitive processing. Yet Kounin's (1970) research on classroom management warns the teacher against slowing the pace of the classroom too severely lest the frequency of discipline problems increase. How can the principle of longer wait-times and that of quicker pacing both be correct?

It is in the very nature of the practical or policy fields that individual principles are fated to clash on particular occasions. Knowledge of the relevant propositions and cases is needed to form the underlying knowledge base. Strategic knowledge must be generated to extend understanding beyond principle to the wisdom of practice. We generally attribute wisdom to those who can transcend the limitations of particular principles or specific experiences when confronted by situations in which each of the alternative choices appears equally "principled." Novice bridge players rapidly learn the principles of the game, embodied in such maxims as "Lead fourth highest from your longest and strongest suit," and "Never lead away from a king." But when you must lead away from a king to lead fourth highest, then propositional knowledge alone becomes limited in value. Strategic knowledge (or judgment) is then invoked.[5]

I envision the use of case method in teacher education, whether in our classrooms or in special laboratories with simulations, videodisks, and annotated scripts, as a means for developing strategic understanding, for extending capacities toward professional judgment and decision making. These methods of instruction would involve the careful confrontation of principles with cases, of general rules with concrete documented events—

a dialectic of the general with the particular in which the limits of the former and the boundaries of the latter are explored (Shulman, 1984). What happens when cases are applied to principles or principles to cases? What happens when two principles are in conflict, or when two cases yield contradictory interpretations?

When strategic understanding is brought to bear in the examination of rules and cases, professional judgment, the hallmark of any learned profession, is called into play. What distinguishes mere craft from profession is the indeterminacy of rules when applied to particular cases. The professional holds knowledge, not only of how—the capacity for skilled performance—but of what and why. The teacher is not only a master of procedure but also of content and rationale, and capable of explaining why something is done. The teacher is capable of reflection leading to self-knowledge, the metacognitive awareness that distinguishes draftsman from architect, bookkeeper from auditor. A professional is capable not only of practicing and understanding his or her craft, but of communicating the reasons for professional decisions and actions to others (see Shulman, 1983).

This sort of reflective awareness of how and why one performs complicates rather than simplifies action and renders it less predictable and regular. During the eight years that I attended the University of Chicago, I often took classes near Swift Hall, the theology building. On the side of that hall, facing me as I left my classroom building, a saying was carved in the stone: "You shall know the truth and the truth shall make you free." I suppose I never really understood those lines until I realized the implications of knowledge, of deep understanding, for the predictability and uniformity of behavior.

Reinforcement and conditioning guarantee behavior, and training produces predictable outcomes; knowledge guarantees only freedom, only the flexibility to judge, to weigh alternatives, to reason about both ends and means, and then to act while reflecting upon one's actions. Knowledge guarantees only grounded unpredictability, the exercise of reasoned judgment rather than the display of correct behavior. If this vision constitutes a serious challenge to those who would evaluate teaching using fixed behavioral criteria (e.g., the five-step lesson plan), so much the worse for those evaluators. The vision I hold of teaching and teacher education is a vision of professionals who are capable not only of acting, but of enacting—of acting in a manner that is self-conscious with respect to what their act is a case of, or to what their act entails.

The implications of our discussion are several. First, we can begin to conceive differently of how professional examinations for teachers might be organized and constructed. I firmly believe that we must develop professional examinations for teachers, though their existence will constitute no panacea. They must be defined and controlled by members of the profession, not by legislators or laypersons. They must reflect an understanding that both content and process are needed by teaching professionals, and within the content we must include knowledge of the structures of one's subject, pedagogical knowledge of the general and specific topics of the domain, and specialized curricular knowledge. Ultimately, that knowledge must be informed by a well-organized and codified case literature. Those tests will be useful when only those who have been professionally prepared as teachers are likely to pass them because they tap the unique knowledge bases of teaching. We are already well on our way to defining such a knowledge base.

I envision the design of research-based programs of teacher education that grow to accommodate our conceptions of both process and content. These programs will articulate with and build upon instruction in the liberal arts and sciences as well as the specialty content areas of each candidate. Instructions in the liberal arts and content areas will have to improve dramatically to meet the standards of understanding required for teaching. If these are special sections of such courses for teachers, they will entail evaluation of subject-matter treatment, not watering down. Such programs will draw upon the growing research on the pedagogical structure of student conceptions and misconceptions, on those features that make particular topics easy or difficult to learn. They will extensively employ a growing body of case literature, both to represent a far wider and more diverse range of teaching contexts than can possibly be experienced within any one teacher education program, and to provide teachers with a rich body of prototypes, precedents, and parables from which to reason.

The fact that we do not possess such a case literature at this time suggests new agendas for research in teacher education. In addition to the obvious tack of encouraging the continued growth of disciplined case studies of teaching by scholars, another alternative suggests itself. Fred Erickson has noted that one of the exciting features of case studies is that you don't necessarily have to be a Ph.D. social scientist or educator to learn to prepare useful case materials. Given proper preparation and support, teachers and teacher educators can contribute to the case literature themselves. As they do so, they will begin to feel even more membership in the broader academic guild of professional teachers.

We reject Mr. Shaw and his calumny. With Aristotle we declare that the ultimate test of understanding rests on the ability to transform one's knowledge into teaching.

Those who can, do. Those who understand, teach.

NOTES

1. There is, in fact, a delightful ambiguity surrounding use of the word *methodology* in educational circles. It can refer to methods of teaching as well as methods of research. A person introduced as a specialist in methodology might these days be claiming competence in either. But before the days of Descartes, the concept of methodology was far more unitary. Methods of inquiry did not typically involve elaborate empirical procedures and concomitant statistical analysis. Indeed, scholars did something far more revolutionary as the heart of method. They thought about their problem and organized a coherent, logical analysis of its structure. This analysis not only served as the structure of inquiry, it also constituted the structure of pedagogy. The scholar's expositions and disputations reflected the applications of the same method.
2. There is also pedagogical knowledge of teaching—as distinct from subject matter—which is also terribly important, but not the object of discussion in this paper. This is the knowledge of generic principles of classroom organization and management and the like that has quite appropriately been the focus of study in most recent research on teaching. I have no desire to diminish its importance. I am simply attempting to place needed emphasis on the hitherto ignored facets of content knowledge.
3. Although in this paper I discuss aspects of content knowledge (including content-specific pedagogical knowledge and curricular knowledge) exclusively, a proper professional board examination would include other equally important sections as well. These would assess knowledge of general pedagogy, knowledge of learners and their backgrounds, principles of school organization, finance and management, and the historical, social, and cultural foundations of education among many more. Exams would also tap teaching performance and other capabilities unlikely to be adequately assessed using conventional paper-and-pencil instruments. Discussion of the character of a professional board for teachers and its desirability, however, is appropriate for another paper.
4. I must also acknowledge some potential disadvantages of cases as sources of teacher knowledge. Kahneman, Slovic, and Tversky (1982) have pointed out the potentially misleading character of cases. They refer to the memorable quality of vivid cases as significant sources of bias in reasoning. Both availability and representativeness are characteristics of cases that make them readily retrieved from memory; they also bias the decision maker's estimates of the frequency of their occurrence. The important test of a case is its contrast with other cases and its examination in the light of principles. Such disciplined evaluation of cases can temper the

inappropriate inferences that might be drawn from cases without diminishing their other virtues.

5. It may well be that what I am calling strategic *knowledge* in this paper is not knowledge in the same sense of propositional and case knowledge. Strategic "knowing" or judgment may simply be a process of analysis, of comparing and contrasting principles, cases, and their implications for practice. Once such strategic processing has been employed, the results are either stored in terms of a new proposition (e.g., "Smiling before Christmas may be permissible when . . .") or a new case. These then enter the repertoire of cases and principles to be used like any others. In that sense, it is possible that strategic analysis occurs in the presence of the other forms of knowledge and is the primary means for testing, extending, and amending them.

REFERENCES

Anderson, L., Evertson, C., & Brophy, J. (1979). An experimental study of effective teaching in first-grade reading groups. *Elementary School Journal, 79*(4), 343–356.

Geertz, C. (1983). Blurred genres: The refiguration of social thought. In C. Geertz (Ed.), *Local knowledge*. New York: Basic Books.

Hoffman, N. (1981). *Women's "true" profession*. Old Westbury, NY: Feminist Press.

Kahneman, D., Slovic, P., & Tversky, A. (1982). *Judgment under uncertainty: Heuristics and biases*. New York: Cambridge University Press.

Kounin, J. (1970). *Discipline and group management in classrooms*. New York: Holt, Rinehart & Winston.

Ong, W. J. (1958). *Ramus, method and the decay of dialogue*. Cambridge, MA: Harvard University Press.

Rashdall, H. (1936). *The universities of Europe in the middle ages*. London: Oxford University Press. (Original work published 1895).

Rowe, M. B. (1974). Relation of wait-time and rewards to the development of language, logic, and fate control: Part II—Rewards. *Journal of Research in Science Teaching, 11*(4), 291–308.

Schwab, J. J. (1978). *Science, curriculum and liberal education*. Chicago: University of Chicago Press.

Shulman, L. S. (1981). Disciplines of inquiry in education: An overview. *Educational Researcher, 10*(6), 5–12, 23.

Shulman, L. S. (1983). Autonomy and obligation: The remote control of teaching. In L. S. Shulman & G. Sykes (Eds.), *Handbook of teaching and policy*. New York: Longman.

Shulman, L. S. (1984). The practical and the eclectic: A deliberation on teaching and educational research. *Curriculum Inquiry, 14*(2), 183–200.

Shulman, L. S. (1986). Paradigms and research programs for the study of teaching. In M. C. Wittrock (Ed.), *Handbook of research on teaching* (3rd ed.). New York: Macmillan.

Wheelwright, P. (Ed.). (1951). *Aristotle.* New York: Odyssey.

ACKNOWLEDGMENTS

This paper was a Presidential Address at the 1985 annual meeting of the American Educational Association, Chicago. Preparation of this address and of the research program "Knowledge Growth in Teaching" was supported in part by a grant from the Spencer Foundation.

INTRODUCTION

KNOWLEDGE AND TEACHING: FOUNDATIONS OF THE NEW REFORM (1987)

AT THE TIME HE WROTE THIS ESSAY, Shulman and his colleagues had been working on the Knowledge Growth in a Profession Project for several years and had just begun the Teacher Assessment Project, which laid the foundations for the National Board for Professional Teaching Standards (NBPTS).

An earlier version of this essay was written as a policy analysis for the Carnegie Commission for the Teaching Profession, and when *Harvard Educational Review* invited Shulman to contribute a piece for a special issue on teaching, teachers, and teacher education, Shulman took advantage of the opportunity to expand his vision of professional knowledge. In one way, it can be seen as the sequel to "Those Who Understand," for that essay focused on the content and character of teacher tests used in the past, and this essay lays the groundwork for the NBPTS.

The essay provoked quite a bit of controversy, for many colleagues saw Shulman's vision as too behavioristic and interpreted his focus on the knowledge aspects of teaching as obscuring teaching's moral dimensions. Shulman begins with a description of how an experienced high school English teacher flexibly adapts her instruction, depending on the material she is teaching, her educational purposes, as well as her students' interests and backgrounds. He goes on to claim that such teaching requires a knowledge base that includes content knowledge, pedagogical knowledge, pedagogical content knowledge, curricular knowledge, knowledge of learners, knowledge of educational contexts, and knowledge of educational goals. This knowledge base draws on resources as diverse as educational research, scholarship in the disciplines, educational materials, and experienced teachers' wisdom of practice. But teaching requires reasoning as well as knowledge, and Shulman goes on to elaborate a framework for pedagogical reasoning, proposing an iterative cycle that includes comprehension, transformation, instruction, evaluation, reflection, and new comprehension.

7

KNOWLEDGE AND TEACHING

FOUNDATIONS OF THE NEW REFORM

Prologue: A Portrait of Expertise

Richly developed portrayals of expertise in teaching are rare. While many characterizations of effective teachers exist, most of these dwell on the teacher's management of the classroom. We find few descriptions or analyses of teachers that give careful attention not only to the management of students in classrooms, but also to the management of *ideas* within classroom discourse. Both kinds of emphasis will be needed if our portrayals of good practice are to serve as sufficient guides to the design of better education. Let us examine one brief account.

○

A twenty-five-year veteran English teacher, Nancy, was the subject of a continuing study of experienced teachers that we had been conducting. The class was nearing the end of the second week of a unit on *Moby Dick*. The observer had been well impressed with the depth of Nancy's understanding of that novel and her skill as a pedagogue, as she documented how Nancy helped a group of California high school juniors grasp the many faces of that masterpiece. Nancy was a highly active teacher, whose classroom style employed substantial interaction with her students, both through recitations and more open-ended discussion. She was like a symphony conductor, posing questions, probing for alternative views, drawing out the shy while tempering the boisterous. Not much happened in the classroom that did not pass through Nancy, whose pacing and ordering, structuring and expanding, controlled the rhythm of classroom life.

Nancy characterized her treatment of literature in terms of a general theoretical model that she employed.

> Basically, I break reading skills into four levels:
>
> *Level 1* is simply translation. . . . It is understanding the literal meaning, denotative, and frequently for students that means getting a dictionary.
>
> *Level 2* is connotative meaning and again you are still looking at the words. . . . What does that mean, what does that tell us about the character? . . . We looked at *The Scarlet Letter.* Hawthorne described a rose bush in the first chapter. Literal level is: What is a rose bush? More important, what does a rose bush suggest, what is it that comes to mind, what did you picture?
>
> *Level 3* is the level of interpretation. . . . It is the implication of Levels 1 and 2. If the author is using a symbol, what does that say about his view of life? In *Moby Dick,* the example I used in class was the boots. The boots would be the literal level. What does it mean when he gets under the bed? And the students would say, he is trying to hide something. Level 3 would be what does Melville say about human nature? What is the implication of this? What does this tell us about this character?
>
> *Level 4* is what I call application and evaluation and I try, as I teach literature, to get the students to Level 4, and that is where they take the literature and see how it has meaning for their own lives. Where would we see that event occur in our own society? How would people that we know be behaving if they are doing what these characters are doing? How is this piece of literature similar to our common experiences as human beings? . . . So my view of reading is basically to take them from the literal on the page to making it mean something in their lives. In teaching literature I am always working in and out of those levels. (Gudmundsdottir, in preparation)

Nancy employed this conceptual framework in her teaching, using it to guide her own sequencing of material and formulation of questions. She taught the framework explicitly to her students over the semester, helping them employ it like a scaffolding to organize their own study of the texts, to monitor their own thinking. Although as a teacher she maintained tight control of the classroom discourse, her teaching goals were to liberate her students' minds through literacy, eventually to use great works of literature to illuminate their own lives.

Whichever work she was teaching, she understood how to organize it, frame it for teaching, divide it appropriately for assignments and activities. She seemed to possess a mental index for these books she had taught so often—*The Red Badge of Courage, Moby Dick, The Scarlet Letter, The Adventures of Huckleberry Finn*—with key episodes organized in her mind for different pedagogical purposes, different levels of difficulty, different kinds of pupils, different themes or emphases. Her combination of subject-matter understanding and pedagogical skill was quite dazzling.

When the observer arrived at the classroom one morning, she found Nancy sitting at her desk as usual. But her morning greeting elicited no response from Nancy other than a grimace and motion toward the pad of paper on her desktop. "I have laryngitis this morning and will not be able to speak aloud," said the note. What's more, she appeared to be fighting the flu, for she had little energy. For a teacher who managed her classroom through the power of her voice and her manner, this was certainly a disabling condition. Or was it?

Using a combination of handwritten notes and whispers, she divided the class into small groups by rows, a tactic she had used twice before during this unit. Each group was given a different character who has a prominent role in the first chapters of the novel, and each group was expected to answer a series of questions about that character. Ample time was used at the end of the period for representatives of each group to report to the whole class. Once again the class had run smoothly, and the subject matter had been treated with care. But the style had changed radically, an utterly different teaching technology was employed, and still the students were engaged, and learning appeared to occur.

Subsequently, we were to see many more examples of Nancy's flexible style, adapted to the characteristics of learners, the complexities of subject matter, and her own physical condition. When learners experienced serious problems with a particular text, she self-consciously stayed at the lower levels of the reading ladder, helping the students with denotative and connotative meanings, while emphasizing literary interpretations somewhat less. When teaching *Huck Finn,* a novel she saw as less difficult than *Moby Dick,* her style changed once again. She gave much more autonomy to the students and did not directly run the classroom as much.

> For *Huck Finn,* she abandoned the stage early on and let the students teach each other. She had the students working

> independently in eight multi-ability groups, each group tracing one of eight themes: hypocrisy; luck and superstition; greed and materialism; romantic ideas and fantasy; religion and the Bible; social class and customs; family, racism, and prejudice; freedom and conscience. There were only two reading checks at the beginning and only two rounds of reporting. Once the groups were underway, Nancy took a seat at the back of the class and only interacted with students when she was called upon, and during group presentations. (Gudmundsdottir, in preparation)

Thus Nancy's pattern of instruction, her style of teaching, is not uniform or predictable in some simple sense. She flexibly responds to the difficulty and character of the subject matter, the capacities of the students (which can change even over the span of a single course), and her educational purposes. She can not only conduct her orchestra from the podium, she can sit back and watch it play with virtuosity by itself.

What does Nancy believe, understand, and know how to do that permits her to teach as she does? Can other teachers be prepared to teach with such skill? The hope that teaching like Nancy's can become typical instead of unusual motivates much of the effort in the newly proposed reforms of teaching.

The New Reforms

During the past year the U.S. public and its professional educators have been presented with several reports on how to improve teaching as both an activity and a profession. One of the recurring themes of these reports has been the professionalization of teaching—the elevation of teaching to a more respected, more responsible, more rewarding and better rewarded occupation. The claim that teaching deserves professional status, however, is based on a more fundamental premise: that the standards by which the education and performance of teachers must be judged can be raised and more clearly articulated. The advocates of professional reform base their arguments on the belief that there exists a "knowledge base for teaching"—a codified or codifiable aggregation of knowledge, skill, understanding, and technology, of ethics and disposition, of collective responsibility—as well as a means for representing and communicating it. The reports of the Holmes Group (1986) and the Carnegie Task Force (1986) rest on this belief and, furthermore, claim that the knowledge base is growing. They argue that it should frame teacher education and directly inform teaching practice.

The rhetoric regarding the knowledge base, however, rarely specifies the character of such knowledge. It does not say what teachers should know, do, understand, or profess that will render teaching more than a form of individual labor, let alone be considered among the learned professions.

In this paper, I present an argument regarding the content, character, and sources for a knowledge base of teaching that suggests an answer to the question of the intellectual, practical, and normative basis for the professionalization of teaching. The questions that focus the argument are: What are the sources of the knowledge base for teaching? In what terms can these sources be conceptualized? What are the implications for teaching policy and educational reform?[1]

In addressing these questions I am following the footsteps of many eminent scholars, including Dewey (1904), Scheffler (1965), Green (1971), Fenstermacher (1978), Smith (1980), and Schwab (1983), among others. Their discussions of what qualities and understandings, skills and abilities, and what traits and sensibilities render someone a competent teacher have continued to echo in the conference rooms of educators for generations. My approach has been conditioned, as well, by two current projects: a study of how new teachers learn to teach and an attempt to develop a national board for teaching.

First, for the past three years, my colleagues and I have been watching knowledge of pedagogy and content grow in the minds of young men and women. They have generously permitted us to observe and follow their eventful journeys from being teacher education students to becoming neophyte teachers. In this research, we are taking advantage of the kinds of insights Piaget provided from his investigations of knowledge growth. He discovered that he could learn a great deal about knowledge and its development from careful observation of the very young—those who were just beginning to develop and organize their intelligence. We are following this lead by studying those just learning to teach. Their development from students to teachers, from a state of expertise as learners through a novitiate as teachers, exposes and highlights the complex bodies of knowledge and skill needed to function effectively as a teacher. The result is that error, success, and refinement—in a word, teacher-knowledge growth—are seen in high profile and in slow motion. The neophyte's stumble becomes the scholar's window.

Concurrently, we have found and explored cases of veteran teachers such as Nancy (Baxter, in preparation; Gudmundsdottir, in preparation; Hashweh, 1985) to compare with those of the novices. What these studies show is that the knowledge, understanding, and skill we see displayed haltingly, and occasionally masterfully, among beginners are often demonstrated with ease by the expert. But, as we have wrestled with our cases, we have repeatedly asked what teachers knew (or failed to know) that permitted them to teach in a particular manner.

Second, for much of the past year, I have engaged in quite a different project on the role of knowledge in teaching. In conjunction with the recent Carnegie initiative for the reform of the teaching profession, my colleagues and I have been studying ways to design a national board assessment for teaching, parallel in several ways to the National Board of Medical Examiners (Shulman & Sykes, 1986; Sykes, 1986). This challenge renders the questions about the definition and operationalization of knowledge in teaching as far more than academic exercises. If teachers are to be certified on the basis of well-grounded judgments and standards, then those standards on which a national board relies must be legitimized by three factors: they must be closely tied to the findings of scholarship in the academic disciplines that form the curriculum (such as English, physics, and history) as well as those that serve as foundations for the process of education (such as psychology, sociology, or philosophy); they must possess intuitive credibility (or "face validity") in the opinions of the professional community in whose interests they have been designed; and they must relate to the appropriate normative conceptions of teaching and teacher education.

The new reform proposals carry assumptions about the knowledge base for teaching: when advocates of reform suggest that requirements for the education of teachers should be augmented and periods of training lengthened, they assume there must be something substantial to be learned. When they recommend that standards be raised and a system of examinations introduced, they assume there must exist a body of knowledge and skill to examine. Our research and that of others (for example, Berliner, 1986; Leinhardt & Greeno, 1986) have identified the sources and suggested outlines of that knowledge base. Watching veterans such as Nancy teach the same material that poses difficulties for novice teachers helped focus our attention on what kinds of knowledge and skill were needed to teach demanding materials well. By focusing on the teaching of particular topics—*Huck Finn,* quadratic equations, the Indian subcontinent, photosynthesis—we learned how particular kinds of content knowledge and pedagogical strategies necessarily interacted in the minds of teachers.

What follows is a discussion of the sources and outlines of the required knowledge base for teaching. I divide this discussion into two distinct analyses. First, after providing an overview of one framework for a knowledge base for teaching, I examine the *sources* of that knowledge base, that is, the domains of scholarship and experience from which teachers may draw their understanding. Second, I explore the processes of pedagogical reasoning and action within which such teacher knowledge is used.

The Knowledge Base

Begin a discussion on the knowledge base of teaching, and several related questions immediately arise: What knowledge base? Is enough known about teaching to support a knowledge base? Isn't teaching little more than personal style, artful communication, knowing some subject matter, and applying the results of recent research on teaching effectiveness? Only the last of these, the findings of research on effective teaching, is typically deemed a legitimate part of a knowledge base.

The actions of both policymakers and teacher educators in the past have been consistent with the formulation that teaching requires basic skills, content knowledge, and general pedagogical skills. Assessments of teachers in most states consist of some combination of basic-skills tests, an examination of competence in subject matter, and observations in the classroom to ensure that certain kinds of general teaching behavior are present. In this manner, I would argue, teaching is trivialized, its complexities ignored, and its demands diminished. Teachers themselves have difficulty in articulating what they know and how they know it.

Nevertheless, the policy community at present continues to hold that the skills needed for teaching are those identified in the empirical research on teaching effectiveness. This research, summarized by Brophy and Good (1986), Gage (1986), and Rosenshine and Stevens (1986), was conducted within the psychological research tradition. It assumes that complex forms of situation-specific human performance can be understood in terms of the workings of underlying generic processes. In a study of teaching context, the research, therefore, seeks to identify those general forms of teaching behavior that correlate with student performance on standardized tests, whether in descriptive or experimental studies. The investigators who conduct the research realize that important simplifications must be made, but they believe that these are necessary steps for conducting scientific studies. Critical features of teaching, such as the subject matter being taught, the classroom context, the physical and psychological characteristics of the students, or the accomplishment of purposes not readily assessed on standardized tests, are typically ignored in the quest for general principles of effective teaching.

When policymakers have sought "research-based" definitions of good teaching to serve as the basis for teacher tests or systems of classroom observation, the lists of teacher behaviors that had been identified as effective in the empirical research were translated into the desirable competencies for classroom teachers. They became items on tests or on classroom-observation scales. They were accorded legitimacy because they had been "confirmed by research." While the researchers understood the findings to be simplified and incomplete, the policy community accepted them as sufficient for the definitions of standards.

For example, some research had indicated that students achieved more when teachers explicitly informed them of the lesson's objective. This seems like a perfectly reasonable finding. When translated into policy, however, classroom-observation competency-rating scales asked whether the teacher had written the objective on the blackboard and/or directly told the students the objectives at the beginning of class. If the teacher had not, he or she was marked off for failing to demonstrate a desired competency. No effort was made to discover whether the withholding of an objective might have been consistent with the form of the lesson being organized or delivered.

Moreover, those who hold with bifurcating content and teaching processes have once again introduced into policy what had been merely an act of scholarly convenience and simplification in the research. Teaching processes were observed and evaluated without reference to the adequacy or accuracy of the ideas transmitted. In many cases, observers were not expected to have content expertise in the areas being observed, because it did not matter for the rating of teacher performance. Thus, what may have been an acceptable strategy for research became an unacceptable policy for teacher evaluation.

In this paper I argue that the results of research on effective teaching, while valuable, are not the sole source of evidence on which to base a definition of the knowledge base of teaching. Those sources should be understood to be far richer and more extensive. Indeed, properly understood, the actual and potential sources for a knowledge base are so plentiful that our question should not be, Is there really much one needs to know in order to teach? Rather, it should express our wonder at how the extensive knowledge of teaching can be learned at all during the brief period allotted to teacher preparation. Much of the rest of this paper provides the details of the argument that there exists an elaborate knowledge base for teaching.

A View of Teaching

I begin with the formulation that the capacity to teach centers around the following commonplaces of teaching, paraphrased from Fenstermacher

(1986). A teacher knows something not understood by others, presumably the students. The teacher can transform understanding, performance skills, or desired attitudes or values into pedagogical representations and actions. These are ways of talking, showing, enacting, or otherwise representing ideas so that the unknowing can come to know, those without understanding can comprehend and discern, and the unskilled can become adept. Thus, teaching necessarily begins with a teacher's understanding of what is to be learned and how it is to be taught. It proceeds through a series of activities during which the students are provided specific instruction and opportunities for learning,[2] though the learning itself ultimately remains the responsibility of the students. Teaching ends with new comprehension by both the teacher and the student.[3] Although this is certainly a core conception of teaching, it is also an incomplete conception. Teaching must properly be understood to be more than the enhancement of understanding; but if it is not even that, then questions regarding performance of its other functions remain moot. The next step is to outline the categories of knowledge that underlie the teacher understanding needed to promote comprehension among students.

Categories of the Knowledge Base

If teacher knowledge were to be organized into a handbook, an encyclopedia, or some other format for arraying knowledge, what would the category headings look like?[4] At minimum, they would include:

- content knowledge;
- general pedagogical knowledge, with special reference to those broad principles and strategies of classroom management and organization that appear to transcend subject matter;
- curriculum knowledge, with particular grasp of the materials and programs that serve as "tools of the trade" for teachers;
- pedagogical content knowledge, that special amalgam of content and pedagogy that is uniquely the province of teachers, their own special form of professional understanding;
- knowledge of learners and their characteristics;
- knowledge of educational contexts, ranging from the workings of the group or classroom, the governance and financing of school districts, to the character of communities and cultures; and
- knowledge of educational ends, purposes, and values, and their philosophical and historical grounds.

Among those categories, pedagogical content knowledge is of special interest because it identifies the distinctive bodies of knowledge for teaching. It represents the blending of content and pedagogy into an understanding of how particular topics, problems, or issues are organized, represented, and adapted to the diverse interests and abilities of learners, and presented for instruction. Pedagogical content knowledge is the category most likely to distinguish the understanding of the content specialist from that of the pedagogue. While far more can be said regarding the categories of a knowledge base for teaching, elucidation of them is not a central purpose of this paper.

Enumerating the Sources

There are at least four major sources for the teaching knowledge base: (1) scholarship in content disciplines, (2) the materials and settings of the institutionalized educational process (for example, curricula, textbooks, school organizations and finance, and the structure of the teaching profession), (3) research on schooling, social organizations, human learning, teaching and development, and the other social and cultural phenomena that affect what teachers can do, and (4) the wisdom of practice itself. Let me elaborate on each of these.

SCHOLARSHIP IN CONTENT DISCIPLINES. The first source of the knowledge base is content knowledge—the knowledge, understanding, skill, and disposition that are to be learned by school children. This knowledge rests on two foundations: the accumulated literature and studies in the content areas, and the historical and philosophical scholarship on the nature of knowledge in those fields of study. For example, the teacher of English should know English and American prose and poetry, written and spoken language use and comprehension, and grammar. In addition, he or she should be familiar with the critical literature that applies to particular novels or epics that are under discussion in class. Moreover, the teacher should understand alternative theories of interpretation and criticism, and how these might relate to issues of curriculum and of teaching.

Teaching is, essentially, a learned profession. A teacher is a member of a scholarly community. He or she must understand the structures of subject matter, the principles of conceptual organization, and the principles of inquiry that help answer two kinds of questions in each field: What are the important ideas and skills in this domain? and How are new ideas added and deficient ones dropped by those who produce knowledge in this area? That is, what are the rules and procedures of good scholarship or inquiry?

These questions parallel what Schwab (1964) has characterized as knowledge of substantive and syntactic structures, respectively. This view of the sources of content knowledge necessarily implies that the teacher must have not only depth of understanding with respect to the particular subjects taught, but also a broad liberal education that serves as a framework for old learning and as a facilitator for new understanding. The teacher has special responsibilities in relation to content knowledge, serving as the primary source of student understanding of subject matter. The manner in which that understanding is communicated conveys to students what is essential about a subject and what is peripheral. In the face of student diversity, the teacher must have a flexible and multifaceted comprehension, adequate to impart alternative explanations of the same concepts or principles. The teacher also communicates, whether consciously or not, ideas about the ways in which "truth" is determined in a field and a set of attitudes and values that markedly influence student understanding. This responsibility places special demands on the teacher's own depth of understanding of the structures of the subject matter, as well as on the teacher's attitudes toward and enthusiasms for what is being taught and learned. These many aspects of content knowledge, therefore, are properly understood as a central feature of the knowledge base of teaching.

EDUCATIONAL MATERIALS AND STRUCTURES. To advance the aims of organized schooling, materials and structures for teaching and learning are created. These include: curricula with their scopes and sequences; tests and testing materials; institutions with their hierarchies, their explicit and implicit systems of rules and roles; professional teachers' organizations with their functions of negotiation, social change, and mutual protection; government agencies from the district through the state and federal levels; and general mechanisms of governance and finance. Because teachers necessarily function within a matrix created by these elements, using and being used by them, it stands to reason that the principles, policies, and facts of their functioning comprise a major source for the knowledge base. There is no need to claim that a specific literature undergirds this source, although there is certainly abundant research literature in most of these domains. But if a teacher has to "know the territory" of teaching, then it is the landscape of such materials, institutions, organizations, and mechanisms with which he or she must be familiar. These comprise both the tools of the trade and the contextual conditions that will either facilitate or inhibit teaching efforts.

FORMAL EDUCATIONAL SCHOLARSHIP. A third source is the important and growing body of scholarly literature devoted to understanding the processes of schooling, teaching, and learning. This literature includes the findings and methods of empirical research in the areas of teaching, learning, and human development, as well as the normative, philosophical, and ethical foundations of education.

The normative and theoretical aspects of teaching's scholarly knowledge are perhaps most important. Unfortunately, educational policymakers and staff developers tend to treat only the findings of empirical research on teaching and learning as relevant portions of the scholarly knowledge base. But these research findings, while important and worthy of careful study, represent only one facet of the contribution of scholarship. Perhaps the most enduring and powerful scholarly influences on teachers are those that enrich their images of the possible: their visions of what constitutes good education, or what a well-educated youngster might look like if provided with appropriate opportunities and stimulation.

The writings of Plato, Dewey, Neill, and Skinner all communicate their conceptions of what a good educational system should be. In addition, many works written primarily to disseminate empirical research findings also serve as important sources of these concepts. I count among these such works as Bloom's (1976) on mastery learning and Rosenthal and Jacobson's (1968) on teaching expectations. Quite independent of whether the empirical claims of those books can be supported, their impact on teachers' conceptions of the possible and desirable ends of education is undeniable. Thus, the philosophical, critical, and empirical literature which can inform the goals, visions, and dreams of teachers is a major portion of the scholarly knowledge base of teaching.

A more frequently cited kind of scholarly knowledge grows out of the empirical study of teaching effectiveness. This research has been summarized recently by Gage (1978, 1986), Shulman (1986a), Brophy and Good (1986), and Rosenshine and Stevens (1986). The essential goal of this program of research has been to identify those teacher behaviors and strategies most likely to lead to achievement gains among students. Because the search has focused on generic relationships—teacher behaviors associated with student academic gains irrespective of subject matter or grade level—the findings have been much more closely connected with the management of classrooms than with the subtleties of content pedagogy. That is, the effective-teaching principles deal with making classrooms places where pupils can attend to instructional tasks, orient themselves toward learning with a minimum of disruption and distraction, and receive a fair and adequate opportunity to learn. Moreover, the educational purposes for which these research results are most relevant are the teaching of skills. Rosenshine

(1986) has observed that effective teaching research has much less to offer to the teaching of understanding, especially of complex written material; thus, the research applies more to teaching a skill like multiplication than to teaching critical interpretations of, say, the *Federalist Papers*.

There are a growing number of such generic principles of effective teaching, and they have already found their way into examinations such as the National Teachers Examination and into state-level assessments of teaching performance during the first teaching year. Their weakness, that they essentially ignore the content-specific character of most teaching, is also their strength. Discovering, explicating, and codifying general teaching principles simplify the otherwise outrageously complex activity of teaching. The great danger occurs, however, when a general teaching principle is distorted into prescription, when maxim becomes mandate. Those states that have taken working principles of teaching, based solely on empirical studies of generic teaching effectiveness, and have tendered them as hard, independent criteria for judging a teacher's worth, are engaged in a political process likely to injure the teaching profession rather than improve it.

The results of research on learning and development also fall within the area of empirical research findings. This research differs from research on teaching by the unit of investigation. Studies of teaching typically take place in conventional classrooms. Learning and development are ordinarily studied in individuals. Hence, teaching studies give accounts of how teachers cope with the inescapable character of schools as places where groups of students work and learn in concert. By comparison, learning and development studies produce principles of individual thought or behavior that must often be generalized to groups with caution if they are to be useful for schoolteaching.

The research in these domains can be both generic and content-specific. For example, cognitive psychological research contributes to the development of understanding of how the mind works to store, process, and retrieve information. Such general understanding can certainly be a source of knowledge for teachers, just as the work of Piaget, Maslow, Erikson, or Bloom has been and continues to be. We also find work on specific subject matter and student developmental levels that is enormously useful; for example, we learn about student misconceptions in the learning of arithmetic by elementary school youngsters (Erlwanger, 1975) or difficulties in grasping principles of physics by university and secondary school students (for example, Clement, 1982). Both these sorts of research contribute to a knowledge base for teaching.

WISDOM OF PRACTICE. The final source of the knowledge base is the least codified of all. It is the wisdom of practice itself, the maxims that guide (or provide reflective rationalization for) the practices of able teachers. One of the more important tasks for the research community is to work with practitioners to develop codified representations of the practical pedagogical wisdom of able teachers. As indicated above, much of the conception of teaching embodied in this paper is derived from collecting, examining, and beginning to codify the emerging wisdom of practice among both inexperienced and experienced teachers.

The portrait of Nancy with which this paper began is only one of the many descriptions and analyses of excellent teaching we have been collecting over the past few years. As we organize and interpret such data, we attempt to infer principles of good practice that can serve as useful guidelines for efforts of educational reform. We attempt to keep the accounts highly contextualized, especially with respect to the content-specificity of the pedagogical strategies employed. In this manner we contribute to the documentation of good practice as a significant source for teaching standards. We also attempt to lay a foundation for a scholarly literature that records the details and rationales for specific pedagogical practice.

One of the frustrations of teaching as an occupation and profession is its extensive individual and collective amnesia, the consistency with which the best creations of its practitioners are lost to both contemporary and future peers. Unlike fields such as architecture (which preserves its creations in both plans and edifices), law (which builds a case literature of opinions and interpretations), medicine (with its records and case studies), and even unlike chess, bridge, or ballet (with their traditions of preserving both memorable games and choreographed performances through inventive forms of notation and recording), teaching is conducted without an audience of peers. It is devoid of a history of practice.

Without such a system of notation and memory, the next steps of analysis, interpretation, and codification of principles of practice are hard to pursue. We have concluded from our research with teachers at all levels of experience that the potentially codifiable knowledge that can be gleaned from the wisdom of practice is extensive. Practitioners simply know a great deal that they have never even tried to articulate. A major portion of the research agenda for the next decade will be to collect, collate, and interpret the practical knowledge of teachers for the purpose of establishing a case literature and codifying its principles, precedents, and parables (Shulman, 1986b). A significant portion of the research agenda associated with the Carnegie program to develop new assessments for teachers involves the conducting of "wisdom-of-practice" studies. These studies record and organize the reasoning and actions of gifted teachers into cases to establish standards of practice for particular areas of teaching.[5]

A knowledge base for teaching is not fixed and final. Although teaching is among the world's oldest professions, educational research, especially the systematic study of teaching, is a relatively new enterprise. We may be able to offer a compelling argument for the broad outlines and categories of the knowledge base for teaching. It will, however, become abundantly clear that much, if not most, of the proposed knowledge base remains to be discovered, invented, and refined. As more is learned about teaching, we will come to recognize new categories of performance and understanding that are characteristic of good teachers, and will have to reconsider and redefine other domains. Our current "blueprint" for the knowledge base of teaching has many cells or categories with only the most rudimentary place-holders, much like the chemist's periodic table of a century ago. As we proceed, we will know that something can be known in principle about a particular aspect of teaching, but we will not yet know what that principle or practice entails. At base, however, we believe that scholars and expert teachers are able to define, describe, and reproduce good teaching.

The Processes of Pedagogical Reasoning and Action

The conception of teaching I shall discuss has emerged from a number of sources, both philosophical and empirical. A key source has been the several dozen teachers whom we have been studying in our research during the past three years. Through interviews, observations, structured tasks, and examination of materials, we have attempted to understand how they commute from the status of learner to that of teacher,[6] from being able to comprehend subject matter for themselves, to becoming able to elucidate subject matter in new ways, reorganize and partition it, clothe it in activities and emotions, in metaphors and exercises, and in examples and demonstrations, so that it can be grasped by students.

As we have come to view teaching, it begins with an act of reason, continues with a process of reasoning, culminates in performances of imparting, eliciting, involving, or enticing, and is then thought about some more until the process can begin again. In the discussion of teaching that follows, we will emphasize teaching as comprehension and reasoning, as transformation and reflection. This emphasis is justified by the resoluteness with which research and policy have so blatantly ignored those aspects of teaching in the past.

Fenstermacher (1978, 1986) provides a useful framework for analysis. The goal of teacher education, he argues, is not to indoctrinate or train teachers to behave in prescribed ways, but to educate teachers to reason soundly about their teaching as well as to perform skillfully. Sound reasoning requires both a process of thinking about what they are doing and an adequate base of facts, principles, and experiences from which to reason. Teachers must learn to use their knowledge base to provide the grounds for choices and actions. Therefore, teacher education must work with the beliefs that guide teacher actions, with the principles and evidence that underlie the choices teachers make. Such reasons (called "premises of the practical argument" in the analysis of Green, 1971, on which Fenstermacher bases his argument) can be predominantly arbitrary or idiosyncratic ("It sure seemed like the right idea at the time!" "I don't know much about teaching, but I know what I like"), or they can rest on ethical, empirical, theoretical, or practical principles that have substantial support among members of the professional community of teachers. Fenstermacher argues that good teaching not only is effective behaviorally, but must rest on a foundation of adequately grounded premises.

When we examine the quality of teaching, the idea of influencing the grounds or reasons for teachers' decisions places the emphasis precisely where it belongs: on the features of pedagogical reasoning that lead to or can be invoked to explain pedagogical actions. We must be cautious, however, lest we place undue emphasis upon the ways teachers reason to achieve particular ends, at the expense of attention to the grounds they present for selecting the ends themselves. Teaching is both effective and normative; it is concerned with both means and ends. Processes of reasoning underlie both. The knowledge base must therefore deal with the purposes of education as well as the methods and strategies of educating.

This image of teaching involves the exchange of ideas. The idea is grasped, probed, and comprehended by a teacher, who then must turn it about in his or her mind, seeing many sides of it. Then the idea is shaped or tailored until it can in turn be grasped by students. This grasping, however, is not a passive act. Just as the teacher's comprehension requires a vigorous interaction with the ideas, so students will be expected to encounter ideas actively as well. Indeed, our exemplary teachers present ideas in order to provoke the constructive processes of their students and not to incur student dependence on teachers or to stimulate the flatteries of imitation.[7]

Comprehension alone is not sufficient. The usefulness of such knowledge lies in its value for judgment and action. Thus, in response to my aphorism, "those who can, do; those who understand, teach" (Shulman,

1986b, p. 14), Petrie (1986) correctly observed that I had not gone far enough. Understanding, he argued, must be linked to judgment and action, to the proper uses of understanding in the forging of wise pedagogical decisions.

Aspects of Pedagogical Reasoning

I begin with the assumption that most teaching is initiated by some form of "text": a textbook, a syllabus, or an actual piece of material the teacher or student wishes to have understood. The text may be a vehicle for the accomplishment of other educational purposes, but some sort of teaching material is almost always involved. The following conception of pedagogical reasoning and action is taken from the point of view of the teacher, who is presented with the challenge of taking what he or she already understands and making it ready for effective instruction. The model of pedagogical reasoning and action is summarized in Table 1.

Given a text, educational purposes, and/or a set of ideas, pedagogical reasoning and action involve a cycle through the activities of comprehension, transformation, instruction, evaluation, and reflection.[8] The starting point and terminus for the process is an act of comprehension.

COMPREHENSION. To teach is first to understand. We ask that the teacher comprehend critically a set of ideas to be taught.[9] We expect teachers to understand what they teach and, when possible, to understand it in several ways. They should understand how a given idea relates to other ideas within the same subject area and to ideas in other subjects as well.

Comprehension of purposes is also central here. We engage in teaching to achieve educational purposes, to accomplish ends having to do with student literacy, student freedom to use and enjoy, student responsibility to care and care for, to believe and respect, to inquire and discover, to develop understandings, skills, and values needed to function in a free and just society. As teachers, we also strive to balance our goals of fostering individual excellence with more general ends involving equality of opportunity and equity among students of different backgrounds and cultures. Although most teaching begins with some sort of text, and the learning of that text can be a worthy end in itself, we should not lose sight of the fact that the text is often a vehicle for achieving other educational purposes. The goals of education transcend the comprehension of particular texts, but may be unachievable without it.

Saying that a teacher must first comprehend both content and purposes, however, does not particularly distinguish a teacher from non-teaching

Table 7.1. A Model of Pedagogical Reasoning and Action.

Comprehension

Of purposes, subject matter structures, ideas within and outside the discipline

Transformation

Preparation: critical interpretation and analysis of texts, structuring and segmenting, development of a curricular repertoire, and clarification of purposes

Representation: use of a representational repertoire which includes analogies, metaphors, examples, demonstrations, explanations, and so forth

Selection: choice from among an instructional repertoire which includes modes of teaching, organizing, managing, and arranging

Adaptation and Tailoring to Student Characteristics: consideration of conceptions, preconceptions, misconceptions, and difficulties, language, culture, and motivations, social class, gender, age, ability, aptitude, interests, self concepts, and attention

Instruction

Management, presentations, interactions, group work, discipline, humor, questioning, and other aspects of active teaching, discovery or inquiry instruction, and the observable forms of classroom teaching

Evaluation

Checking for student understanding during interactive teaching

Testing student understanding at the end of lessons or units

Evaluating one's own performance, and adjusting for experiences

Reflection

Reviewing, reconstructing, reenacting and critically analyzing one's own and the class's performance, and grounding explanations in evidence

New Comprehension

Of purposes, subject matter, students, teaching, and self

Consolidation of new understandings, and learnings from experience peers. We expect a math major to understand mathematics or a history specialist to comprehend history. But the key to distinguishing the knowledge base of teaching lies at the intersection of content and pedagogy, in the capacity of a teacher to transform the content knowledge he or she possesses into forms that are pedagogically powerful and yet adaptive to the variations in ability and background presented by the students. We now turn to a discussion of transformation and its components.

TRANSFORMATION. Comprehended ideas must be transformed in some manner if they are to be taught. To reason one's way through an act of teaching is to think one's way from the subject matter as understood by the teacher into the minds and motivations of learners. Transformations, therefore, require some combination or ordering of the following processes, each of which employs a kind of repertoire: (1) preparation (of the given text materials) including the process of critical interpretation, (2) representation of the ideas in the form of new analogies, metaphors, and so forth, (3) instructional selections from among an array of teaching methods and models, and (4) adaptation of these representations to the general characteristics of the children to be taught, as well as (5) tailoring the adaptations to the specific youngsters in the classroom. These forms of transformation, these aspects of the process wherein one moves from personal comprehension to preparing for the comprehension of others, are the essence of the act of pedagogical reasoning, of teaching as thinking, and of planning—whether explicitly or implicitly—the performance of teaching.

Preparation involves examining and critically interpreting the materials of instruction in terms of the teacher's own understanding of the subject matter (Ben-Peretz, 1975). That is, one scrutinizes the teaching material in light of one's own comprehension and asks whether it is "fit to be taught." This process of preparation will usually include (1) detecting and correcting errors of omission and commission in the text, and (2) the crucial processes of structuring and segmenting the material into forms better adapted to the teacher's understanding and, in prospect, more suitable for teaching. One also scrutinizes educational purposes or goals. We find examples of this preparation process in a number of our studies. Preparation certainly draws upon the availability of a curricular repertoire, a grasp of the full array of extant instructional materials, programs, and conceptions.

Representation involves thinking through the key ideas in the text or lesson and identifying the alternative ways of representing them to students. What analogies, metaphors, examples, demonstrations, simulations, and the like can help to build a bridge between the teacher's comprehension and that desired for the students? Multiple forms of representation are desirable. We speak of the importance of a representational repertoire in this activity.[10]

Instructional selections occur when the teacher must move from the reformulation of content through representations to the embodiment of representations in instructional forms or methods. Here the teacher draws upon an instructional repertoire of approaches or strategies of teaching. This repertoire can be quite rich, including not only the more conventional alternatives such as lecture, demonstration, recitation, or seatwork, but also a variety of forms of cooperative learning, reciprocal teaching, Socratic dialogue, discovery learning, project methods, and learning outside the classroom setting.

Adaptation is the process of fitting the represented material to the characteristics of the students. What are the relevant aspects of student ability, gender, language, culture, motivations, or prior knowledge and skills that will affect their responses to different forms of representation and presentation? What student conceptions, misconceptions, expectations, motives, difficulties, or strategies might influence the ways in which they approach, interpret, understand, or misunderstand the material? Related to adaptation is tailoring, which refers to the fitting of the material to the specific students in one's classrooms rather than to students in general. When a teacher thinks through the teaching of something, the activity is a bit like the manufacture of a suit of clothing. Adaptation is like preparing a suit of a particular style, color, and size that can be hung on a rack. Once it is prepared for purchase by a particular customer, however, it must be tailored to fit perfectly.

Moreover, the activity of teaching is rarely engaged with a single student at a time. This is a process for which the special term "tutoring" is needed. When we speak of teaching under typical school circumstances, we describe an activity which brings instruction to groups of at least fifteen—or more typically, twenty-five to thirty-five—students. Thus, the tailoring of instruction entails fitting representations not only to particular students, but also to a group of a particular size, disposition, receptivity, and interpersonal "chemistry."

All these processes of transformation result in a plan, or set of strategies, to present a lesson, unit, or course. Up to this point, of course, it is all a rehearsal for the performances of teaching which have not yet occurred. Pedagogical reasoning is as much a part of teaching as is the actual performance itself. Reasoning does not end when instruction begins. The activities of comprehension, transformation, evaluation, and reflection continue to occur during active teaching. Teaching itself becomes a stimulus for thoughtfulness as well as for action. We therefore turn next to the performance that consummates all this reasoning in the act of instruction.

INSTRUCTION. This activity involves the observable performance of the variety of teaching acts. It includes many of the most crucial aspects of pedagogy: organizing and managing the classroom; presenting clear explanations and vivid descriptions; assigning and checking work; and interacting effectively with students through questions and probes, answers and reactions, and praise and criticism. It thus includes management, explanation, discussion, and all the observable features of effective direct and heuristic instruction already well-documented in the research literature on effective teaching.

We have compelling reasons to believe that there are powerful relationships between the comprehension of a new teacher and the styles of teaching employed. An example, based on the research of Grossman (1985), will illustrate this point.

Colleen had completed a master's degree in English before entering a teacher education program. She expressed confidence in her command of the subject matter and began her internship with energy and enthusiasm. Her view of literature and its teaching was highly interpretive and interactive. She saw fine literature as layered communication, capable of many diverse readings and interpretations. Moreover, she felt that these various readings should be provided by her students through their own careful reading of the texts.

Colleen was so committed to helping students learn to read texts carefully, a habit of mind not often found among the young or old, that she constructed one assignment in which each student was asked to bring to school the lyrics of a favorite rock song. (She may have realized that some of these song lyrics were of questionable taste, but preferred to maximize motivation rather than discretion in this particular unit.) She then asked them to rewrite each line of the song, using synonyms or paraphrases to replace every original word. For many, it was the first time they had looked at any piece of text with such care.

When teaching a piece of literature, Colleen performed in a highly interactive manner, drawing out student ideas about a phrase or line, accepting multiple competing interpretations as long as the student could offer a defense of the construction by reference to the text itself. Student participation was active and hearty in these sessions. Based on these observations, one would have characterized Colleen's teaching style with descriptors such as student-centered, discussion-based, occasionally Socratic, or otherwise highly interactive.

Several weeks later, however, we observed Colleen teaching a unit on grammar. Although she had completed two university degrees in English, Colleen had received almost no preparation in prescriptive grammar. However, since a typical high school English class includes some grammar in addition to the literature and writing, it was impossible to avoid teaching the subject. She expressed some anxiety about it during a pre-observational interview.

Colleen looked like a different teacher during that lesson. Her interactive style evaporated. In its place was a highly didactic, teacher-directed, swiftly paced combination of lecture and tightly-controlled recitation: Socrates replaced by DISTAR. I sometimes refer to such teaching as the Admiral Farragut style, "Damn the questions, full speed ahead." Students were not given opportunities to raise questions or offer alternative views. After the session, she confessed to the observer that she had actively avoided making eye contact with one particular student in the front row because that youngster always had good questions or ideas and in this particular lesson Colleen really didn't want to encourage either, because she wasn't sure of the answers. She was uncertain about the content and adapted her instructional style to allay her anxiety.[11]

○

Colleen's case illustrates the ways in which teaching behavior is bound up with comprehension and transformation of understanding. The flexible and interactive teaching techniques that she uses are simply not available to her when she does not understand the topic to be taught. Having examined the processes of pedagogical reasoning and performance that are prospective and enactive in nature, we now move to those that are retrospective.

EVALUATION. This process includes the on-line checking for understanding and misunderstanding that a teacher must employ while teaching interactively, as well as the more formal testing and evaluation that teachers do to provide feedback and grades. Clearly, checking for such understanding requires all the forms of teacher comprehension and transformation described above. To understand what a pupil understands will require a deep grasp of both the material to be taught and the processes of learning. This understanding must be specific to particular school subjects and to individual topics within the subject. This represents another way in which what we call pedagogical content knowledge is used. Evaluation is also directed at one's own teaching and at the lessons and materials employed in those activities. In that sense it leads directly to reflection.

REFLECTION. This is what a teacher does when he or she looks back at the teaching and learning that has occurred, and reconstructs, reenacts, and/or recaptures the events, the emotions, and the accomplishments. It is that set of processes through which a professional learns from experience. It can be done alone or in concert, with the help of recording devices or solely through memory. Here again, it is likely that reflection is not merely a disposition (as in, "she's such a reflective person!") or a set of strategies, but also the use of particular kinds of analytic knowledge brought to bear on one's work (Richert, in preparation). Central to this process will be a review of the teaching in comparison to the ends that were sought.

NEW COMPREHENSION. Thus we arrive at the new beginning, the expectation that through acts of teaching that are "reasoned" and "reasonable" the teacher achieves new comprehension, both of the purposes and of the subjects to be taught, and also of the students and of the processes of pedagogy themselves. There is a good deal of transient experiential learning among teachers, characterized by the "aha" of a moment that is never consolidated and made part of a new understanding or a reconstituted repertoire (Brodkey, 1986). New comprehension does not automatically occur, even after evaluation and reflection. Specific strategies for documentation, analysis, and discussion are needed.

Although the processes in this model are presented in sequence, they are not meant to represent a set of fixed stages, phases, or steps. Many of the processes can occur in different order. Some may not occur at all during some acts of teaching. Some may be truncated, others elaborated. In elementary teaching, for example, some processes may occur that are ignored or given short shrift in this model. But a teacher should demonstrate the capacity to engage in these processes when called upon, and teacher education should provide students with the understandings and performance abilities they will need to reason their ways through and to enact a complete act of pedagogy, as represented here.

Knowledge, Teaching Policy, and Educational Reform

The investigations, deliberations, and debates regarding what teachers should know and know how to do have never been more active. Reform efforts are underway: they range from raising standards for admission into teacher education programs, to establishing state and national examinations for teachers; from insisting that teacher preparation require at least five years of higher education (because there is so much to learn), to organizing elaborate programs of new-teacher induction and mentoring (because the most important learning and socialization can occur only in the workplace).

Most of the current reforms rest on the call for greater professionalization in teaching, with higher standards for entry, greater emphasis on the scholarly bases for practice, more rigorous programs of theoretical and practical preparation, better strategies for certification and licensure, and changes in the workplace that permit greater autonomy and teacher leadership. In large measure, they call for teaching to follow the model of other professions that define their knowledge bases in systematic terms, require extended periods of preparation, socialize neophytes into practice with extended periods of internship or residency, and employ demanding national and state certification procedures.

Implicit in all these reforms are conceptions of teacher competence. Standards for teacher education and assessment are necessarily predicated on images of teaching and its demands. The conception of the knowledge base of teaching presented in this paper differs in significant ways from many of those currently existing in the policy community. The emphasis on the integral relationships between teaching and the scholarly domains of the liberal arts makes clear that teacher education is the responsibility of the entire university, not the schools or departments of education alone. Moreover, teachers cannot be adequately assessed by observing their teaching performance without reference to the content being taught.

The conception of pedagogical reasoning places emphasis upon the intellectual basis for teaching performance rather than on behavior alone. If this conception is to be taken seriously, both the organization and content of teacher education programs and the definition of the scholarly foundations of education will require revision. Teacher education programs would no longer be able to confine their activity to the content-free domains of pedagogy and supervision. An emphasis on pedagogical content knowledge would permeate the teacher preparation curriculum. A national board examination for teachers would focus upon the teacher's ability to reason about teaching and to teach specific topics, and to base his or her actions on premises that can bear the scrutiny of the professional community.

We have an obligation to raise standards in the interests of improvement and reform, but we must avoid the creation of rigid orthodoxies. We must achieve standards without standardization. We must be careful that the knowledge-base approach does not produce an overly technical image of teaching, a scientific enterprise that has lost its soul. The serious problems in medicine and other health professions arise when doctors treat the disease rather than the person, or when the professional or personal needs of the practitioner are permitted to take precedence over the responsibilities to those being served.

Needed change cannot occur without risk, however. The currently incomplete and trivial definitions of teaching held by the policy community comprise a far greater danger to good education than does a more serious attempt to formulate the knowledge base. Nancy represents a model of pedagogical excellence that should become the basis for the new reforms. A proper understanding of the knowledge base of teaching, the sources for that knowledge, and the complexities of the pedagogical process will make the emergence of such teachers more likely.

NOTES

1. Most of the empirical work on which this essay rests has been conducted with secondary school teachers, both new and experienced. While I firmly believe that much of the emphasis to be found here on the centrality of content knowledge in pedagogy holds reasonably well for the elementary level as well, I am reluctant to make that claim too boldly. Work currently underway at the elementary level, both by Leinhardt (1983) and her colleagues (for example, Leinhardt & Greeno, 1986; Leinhardt & Smith, 1985) and by our own research group, may help clarify this matter.
2. There are several aspects of this formulation that are unfortunate, if only for the impression they may leave. The rhetoric of the analysis, for example, is not meant to suggest that education is reduced to knowledge transmission, the conveying of information from an active teacher to a passive learner, and that this information is viewed as product rather than process. My conception of teaching is not limited to direct instruction. Indeed, my affinity for discovery learning and inquiry teaching is both enthusiastic and ancient (for example, Shulman & Keislar, 1966). Yet even in those most student-centered forms of education, where much of the initiative is in the hands of the students, there is little room for teacher ignorance. Indeed, we

have reason to believe that teacher comprehension is even more critical for the inquiry-oriented classroom than for its more didactic alternative.

Central to my concept of teaching are the objectives of students learning how to understand and solve problems, learning to think critically and creatively as well as learning facts, principles, and rules of procedure. Finally, I understand that the learning of subject matter is often not an end in itself, but rather a vehicle employed in the service of other goals. Nevertheless, at least at the secondary level, subject matter is a nearly universal vehicle for instruction, whatever the ultimate goal.

3. This formulation is drawn from the teacher's perspective and, hence, may be viewed by some readers as overly teacher-centered. I do not mean to diminish the centrality of student learning for the process of education, nor the priority that must be given to student learning over teacher comprehension. But our analyses of effective teaching must recognize that outcomes *for teachers* as well as pupils must be considered in any adequate treatment of educational outcomes.

4. I have attempted this list in other publications, though, admittedly, not with great cross-article consistency (for example, Shulman, 1986b; Shulman & Sykes, 1986; Wilson, Shulman, & Richert, in press).

5. It might be argued that the sources of skilled performances are typically tacit, and unavailable to the practitioner. But teaching requires a special kind of expertise or artistry, for which explaining and showing are the central features. Tacit knowledge among teachers is of limited value if the teachers are held responsible for explaining what they do and why they do it, to their students, their communities, and their peers.

6. The metaphor of commuting is not used idly. The journey between learner and teacher is not one-way. In the best teachers, as well as in the more marginal, new learning is constantly required for teaching.

7. The direction and sequence of instruction can be quite different as well. Students can literally initiate the process, proceeding by discovering, inventing, or inquiring, to prepare their own representations and transformations. Then it is the role of the teacher to respond actively and creatively to those student initiatives. In each case the teacher needs to possess both the comprehension and the capacities for transformation. In the student-initiated case, the flexibility to respond, judge, nurture, and provoke student creativity will depend on the teacher's own capacities for sympathetic transformation and interpretation.

8. Under some conditions, teaching may begin with "Given a group of students." It is likely that at the early elementary grades, or in special educa-

tion classes or other settings where children have been brought together for particular reasons, the starting point for reasoning about instruction may well be at the characteristics of the group itself. There are probably some days when a teacher necessarily uses the youngsters as a starting point.

9. Other views of teaching will also begin with comprehension, but of something other than the ideas or text to be taught and learned. They may focus on comprehension of a particular set of values, of the characteristics, needs, interests, or propensities of a particular individual or group of learners. But some sort of comprehension (or self-conscious confusion, wonder, or ignorance) will always initiate teaching.
10. The centrality of representation to our conception of pedagogical reasoning is important for relating our model of teaching to more general approaches to the study of human thinking and problem solving. Cognitive psychologists (for example, Gardner, 1986; Marton, 1986; Norman, 1980) argue that processes of internal representation are key elements in any cognitive psychology. "To my mind, the major accomplishment of cognitive science has been the clear demonstration of the validity of positing a level of mental representation: a set of constructs that can be invoked for the explanation of cognitive phenomena, ranging from visual perception to story comprehension" (Gardner, 1986, p. 383). Such a linkage between models of pedagogy and models of more general cognitive functioning can serve as an important impetus for the needed study of teacher thinking.
11. In no way do I wish to imply that effective lectures are out of place in a high school classroom. On the contrary, good lecturing is an indispensable teaching technique. In this case I am more interested in the relationship between knowledge and teaching. It might be suggested that this teaching style is more suited to grammar than to literature because there is little to discuss or interpret in a grammar lesson. I do not agree, but will not pursue the matter here. In Colleen's case, the rationale for a linear lecture was not grounded in such an argument, but quite clearly in her concern for limiting the range of possible deviations from the path she had designed.

REFERENCES

Baxter, J. (in preparation). *Teacher explanations in computer programming: A study of knowledge transformation.* Unpublished doctoral dissertation in progress, Stanford University.

Ben-Peretz, M. (1975). The concept of curriculum potential. *Curriculum Theory Network, 5,* 151–159.

Berliner, D. (1986). In pursuit of the expert pedagogue. *Educational Researcher, 15*(7), 5–13.

Bloom, B. S. (1976). *Human characteristics and school learning.* New York: McGraw-Hill.

Brodkey, J. J. (1986). *Learning while teaching: Self-assessment in the classroom.* Unpublished doctoral dissertation, Stanford University.

Brophy, J. J., & Good, T. (1986). Teacher behavior and student achievement. In M. C. Wittrock (Ed.), *Handbook of research on teaching* (3rd ed., pp. 328–375). New York: Macmillan.

Carnegie Task Force on Teaching as a Profession. (1986). *A nation prepared: Teachers for the 21st century.* Washington, DC: Carnegie Forum on Education and the Economy.

Clement, J. (1982). Students' preconceptions in introductory mechanics. *American Journal of Physics, 50,* 67–71.

Dewey, J. (1904). The relation of theory to practice in education. In C. A. McMurry (Ed.), *The relation of theory to practice in the education of teachers* (Third Yearbook of the National Society for the Scientific Study of Education, Part I). Bloomington, IL: Public School Publishing.

Erlwanger, S. H. (1975). Case studies of children's conceptions of mathematics, Part I. *Journal of Children's Mathematical Behavior, 1,* 157–283.

Fenstermacher, G. (1978). A philosophical consideration of recent research on teacher effectiveness. In L. S. Shulman (Ed.), *Review of research in education* (Vol. 6, pp. 157–185). Itasca, IL: Peacock.

Fenstermacher, G. (1986). Philosophy of research on teaching: Three aspects. In M. C. Wittrock (Ed.), *Handbook of research on teaching* (3rd ed., pp. 37–49). New York: Macmillan.

Gage, N. L. (1978). *The scientific basis of the art of teaching.* New York: Teachers College Press.

Gage, N. L. (1986). *Hard gains in the soft sciences: The case of pedagogy.* Bloomington, IN: Phi Delta Kappa.

Gardner, H. (1986). *The mind's new science: A history of cognitive revolution.* New York: Basic Books.

Green, T. F. (1971). *The activities of teaching.* New York: McGraw-Hill.

Grossman, P. (1985). *A passion for language: From text to teaching* (Knowledge Growth in Teaching Publications Series). Stanford: Stanford University, School of Education.

Gudmundsdottir, S. (in preparation). *Knowledge use among experienced teachers: Four case studies of high school teaching.* Unpublished doctoral dissertation in progress, Stanford University.

Hashweh, M. Z. (1985). *An exploratory study of teacher knowledge and teaching: The effects of science teachers' knowledge of subject-matter and their conceptions of learning on their teaching.* Unpublished doctoral dissertation, Stanford University.

The Holmes Group (1986). *Tomorrow's teachers: A report of the Holmes Group.* East Lansing, MI: Author.

Leinhardt, G. (1983). Novice and expert knowledge of individual student's achievement. *Educational Psychologist, 18,* 165–179.

Leinhardt, G., & Greeno, J. G. (1986). The cognitive skill of teaching. *Journal of Educational Psychology, 78,* 75–95.

Leinhardt, G., & Smith, D. A. (1985). Expertise in mathematics instruction: Subject matter knowledge. *Journal of Educational Psychology, 77,* 247–271.

Marton, F. (1986). *Towards a pedagogy of content.* Unpublished manuscript, University of Gothenburg, Sweden.

Norman, D. A. (1980). What goes on in the mind of the learner? In W. J. McKeachie (Ed.), *New directions for teaching and learning: Learning, cognition, and college teaching* (Vol. 2). San Francisco: Jossey-Bass.

Petrie, H. (1986, May). *The liberal arts and sciences in the teacher education curriculum.* Paper presented at the Conference on Excellence in Teacher Preparation through the Liberal Arts, Muhlenberg College, Allentown, PA.

Richert, A. (in preparation). *Reflex to reflection: Facilitating reflection in novice teachers.* Unpublished doctoral dissertation in progress, Stanford University.

Rosenshine, B. (1986, April). *Unsolved issues in teaching content: A critique of a lesson on Federalist Paper No. 10.* Paper presented at the meeting of the American Educational Research Association, San Francisco, CA.

Rosenshine, B., & Stevens, R. S. (1986). Teaching functions. In M. C. Wittrock (Ed.), *Handbook of research on teaching* (3rd ed., pp. 376–391). New York: Macmillan.

Rosenthal, R., & Jacobson, L. (1968). *Pygmalion in the classroom.* New York: Holt, Rinehart & Winston.

Scheffler, I. (1965). *Conditions of knowledge: An introduction to epistemology and education.* Chicago: University of Chicago Press.

Schwab, J. J. (1964). The structure of the disciplines: Meanings and significances. In G. W. Ford & L. Pugno (Eds.), *The structure of knowledge and the curriculum.* Chicago: Rand McNally.

Schwab, J. J. (1983). The practical four: Something for curriculum professors to do. *Curriculum Inquiry, 13,* 239–265.

Shulman, L. S. (1986a). Paradigms and research programs for the study of teaching. In M. C. Wittrock (Ed.), *Handbook of research on teaching* (3rd ed., pp. 3–36). New York: Macmillan.

Shulman, L. S. (1986b). Those who understand: Knowledge growth in teaching. *Educational Researcher, 15*(2), 4–14.

Shulman, L. S., & Keislar, E. R. (Eds.). (1966). *Learning by discovery: A critical appraisal.* Chicago: Rand McNally.

Shulman, L. S., & Sykes, G. (1986, March). *A national board for teaching?: In search of a bold standard* (Paper commissioned for the Task Force on Teaching as a Profession, Carnegie Forum on Education and the Economy).

Smith, B. O. (1980). *A design for a school of pedagogy.* Washington, DC: U.S. Department of Education.

Sykes, G. (1986). *The social consequences of standard-setting in the professions* (Paper commissioned for the Task Force on Teaching as a Profession, Carnegie Forum on Education and the Economy).

Wilson, S. M., Shulman, L. S., & Richert, A. (in press). "150 different ways" of knowing: Representations of knowledge in teaching. In J. Calderhead (Ed.), *Exploring teacher thinking.* Sussex, UK: Holt, Rinehart & Winston.

ACKNOWLEDGMENTS

Preparation of this paper was made possible, in part, by grants to Stanford University from the Spencer Foundation for the project, Knowledge Growth in a Profession, and from the Carnegie Corporation of New York for research on the development of new modes of assessment for teachers, Lee S. Shulman, principal investigator. Suzanne Wilson, Pamela Grossman, and Judy Shulman provided criticism and counsel when it was most needed. A longer version of this paper will be available from the Carnegie Forum on Education and the Economy. The views expressed are the author's and are not necessarily shared by these organizations or individuals.

INTRODUCTION

THE WISDOM OF PRACTICE: MANAGING COMPLEXITY IN MEDICINE AND TEACHING (1987)

THIS ESSAY IS THE FINAL CHAPTER of the Festschrift for N. L. Gage, a Stanford University colleague and well-known researcher of teaching. Gage had spent much of his career reflecting on the nature of teaching—is teaching a science or art?—and he and Shulman had been engaged in many discussions about the relative importance of understanding appropriate teaching behaviors and/or understanding teacher thinking. In this essay, Shulman explicitly links his research on medical problem solving to his research on teaching, using the notion of the "wisdom of practice" as the conceptual and methodological theme. He discusses the lessons he and his collaborators learned from their studies of physicians and how physicians' practice at times ran counter to traditional medical belief and the results of psychological research, as well as to the lessons researchers have learned from studying the practice of experienced teachers. While a wisdom of practice is important, Shulman warns us that it, too, has its limitations. He concludes by arguing for a dialectic between different kinds of research (controlled experiments and case studies of wise practice) and between research, theory, and model building.

Two of Shulman's favorite lines are in this chapter, both buried in notes. The first is his long-delayed retort to Gage's accusation, echoing Guthrie's criticism of Tolman, that Shulman's research leaves teachers "lost in thought." Shulman responded, "Better to be lost in thought than missing in action!" The other was Shulman's only citation of his mother in any of his writing. While writing about the research on turn taking and wait-time in the study of teaching, Shulman remembered his mother, Sonia Shulman's, refusal to have customers take numbers at the door to the family's tiny Chicago delicatessen. Instead, she depended on the honesty of her patrons, controlling the order in which they were served by asking in her heavily accented English "Whose *next* is it?" As Shulman wrote then, "by transforming an adjective of subsequence into a noun of consequence, Sonia Shulman made her own contributions to the wisdom of practice."

8

THE WISDOM OF PRACTICE

MANAGING COMPLEXITY IN MEDICINE AND TEACHING

Art is the solving of problems that cannot
be expressed until they are solved.

—Piet Hein

THE STORY IS TOLD of a young man who approached his rabbi for advice on the building of a *sukkah,* the ritual hut that is erected by religious Jews in celebration of the Feast of Tabernacles, Sukkot, the autumn festival that follows less than a week after Yom Kippur. Rather than simply telling his congregant how to build the *sukkah,* the rabbi urged that he read the appropriate sections of the Talmud, which includes an entire tractate dedicated to the laws pertaining to this holiday. The young man agreed and proceeded to spend several months in careful study of the designated volume.

When autumn arrived and Yom Kippur had passed, the small shelter was built precisely as the Talmudic text advised. Several days later, the visibly upset young man appeared once again at the rabbi's door. A moderate rainstorm had occurred the evening before and much to his dismay the sukkah had been blown flat. "How is it possible," implored the youthful builder, "that I could follow the instructions of the Talmud so religiously and yet have the structure blow over so easily?" The rabbi gazed at his visitor as he silently stroked his long beard. He sighed, "You know, many of the commentaries ask exactly the same question!"

The movement from theory to practice is frequently accompanied by embarrassments. The sukkah falls, the economy totters, a bridge collapses, crops wither, patients falter, pupils flounder. All too frequently we who conduct and interpret educational research are asked similar questions by the teachers whose work our scholarship is intended to inform. How can our theories, so carefully crafted and empirically grounded, frequently fail to hold up against even the most gentle winds of practical exigency? What is the contribution of scholarly theory to the enhancement of practice?

A traditional stance for psychologists who wished to influence practice was to conduct research in their laboratories, to formulate theories or principles based upon the findings of their well-controlled studies, and then to prescribe those principles as the proper bases for grounded practice. An alternative research strategy is to study accomplished practice as it actually occurs and to ask how it has been achieved.

This focus on expert practice is a major strategy of contemporary cognitive psychological research in the information-processing tradition. This stream of inquiry, especially as exemplified by the "expert-novice" research programs, begins with the recognition that, in principle, the human animal is a very limited information processor. That is, given the modest limits within which the human short-term memory operates (the magic number seven plus or minus two was George Miller's estimate, apparently an overly optimistic one by more recent accounts), it is quite amazing what feats of intelligence we *Homo sapiens* are capable of performing. From Godel's Proof to the Sistine Chapel ceiling, the accomplishments of the human mind are quite substantial.

Regarding these achievements, the information-processing psychologist asks, "How can the human mind, a mechanism with so many limitations, produce works of art, intellect, and practice that are so complex and subtle?" Thus, the psychologist asks how the "expert" human thinker and problem solver manages to simplify the complexities of the world around him so they can fit through the bottlenecks of human memory and information processing. Such psychologists are typically interested in developing a theory *of* practice, a theoretical formulation adequate to explain the miracle of cognition in the expert thinker.

Articulating the relationships of theory to practice, of science to art, has been the prevailing theme in N. L. Gage's distinguished career. It is a problem that besets both scholarly practitioners and practical theorists. It is a central theme of this chapter.

I have had the opportunity during the past 20 years to engage in research on the professional activities of members of two professions: medicine and teaching. I have been particularly interested in the question of what makes the intellectual work of each occupation difficult. That is, as both physicians and teachers think their ways through the complex and demanding tasks that their respective clients and professional obligations place upon them, how do they manage? More specifically, since the hallmark of a profession is the presence of enormously complex and indeterminate problem situations, and the exercise of professional judgment characterizes such practice, how is complexity managed in the doing of both medicine and teaching?[1]

Studying the Wisdom of Practice in Medicine

I shall begin with a description of a program of research on the ways in which experienced physicians go about their diagnostic work. This was research I conducted in collaboration with Arthur Elstein and Sarah Sprafka during an eight-year period in the late 1960s and the 1970s (Shulman & Elstein, 1976; Elstein, Shulman, & Sprafka, 1978).[2]

We wished to understand how expert diagnosticians solved the complex clinical cases they encountered. We recognized that diagnosis represented only a limited portion of the physician's work. It left out the processes of medical management and follow-up as well as the all-important affective and interpersonal aspects of the doctor-patient relationship. Nevertheless, the intellectual processes of diagnosis were of great interest psychologically and were quite central to the education of physicians. Moreover, there could be connections between diagnosis in medicine and the kinds of strategies employed by teachers in the diagnosis of educational difficulties.

We had clear expectations regarding the strategies that expert physicians would use. First, through reading the standard medical textbooks and consulting with medical educators we found a clear consensus regarding how physicians ought to proceed in their diagnostic work-ups. Harrison's (1973) textbook of medicine, the most widely used among medical students, asserted "the clinical method is an orderly intellectual activity which proceeds from symptom to sign to syndrome to disease. "We thus expected to observe a highly inductive process in which the physicians would first collect a large body of data, following the injunction to "keep an open mind," and only after gathering a rich data base would then begin to organize the data into larger units and move toward a diagnosis.

This expectation was also consistent with the then-current psychological understandings regarding the management of cognitive strain during information processing. Bruner, Goodnow, and Austin (1956), in their classic *A Study of Thinking,* had investigated the strategies employed by individuals attempting to learn a new concept from examination of positive and negative examples of that concept. For example, they could provide participants in their studies with examples of dogs (collie, scottie, doberman, spaniel) and examples of non-dogs (cat, parakeet, mule, college professor) with the task of finding the general category or rule that could organize all the positive examples, and exclude the negative ones. However, rather than use commonplace categories like dogs, tools, or "countries with seaports on the Indian Ocean with populations of less than 10,000,000" (the concepts can get very complicated), they used geometrical figures or similarly unfamiliar stimulus objects. What resulted was a Twenty-Questions-like game.

They concluded from their studies that the most frequently employed strategy in such instances was "conservative focusing," an inductive, step-by-step process in which the problem solver systematically reduced the field by ruling out alternatives. The alternative strategy, guessing particular hypotheses and testing them directly, was untenable. It simply placed too much strain on the fragile vessel of human memory. As soon as one tried to keep the result for more than one or two hypotheses in mind simultaneously, errors of memory increased rapidly. Thus, the findings of psychology and the principles of traditional medical lore concurred. We should expect to observe physicians employing a conservative, inductive strategy in diagnosis.

Through a survey of practicing internists in three geographical areas, we identified a small number of internists who were viewed by their peers as particularly gifted diagnosticians, physicians to whom you would turn for help with a particularly difficult case. For comparison purposes we also identified a group of similarly experienced and certified specialists who, while apparently competent, had not been so nominated by their colleagues. We expected to find that there would be differences in problem-solving strategies or abilities that distinguished the consistently more effective diagnosticians from their less wily colleagues.

Each physician came to our laboratory, which housed a simulated examination room with remote-controlled television cameras for taping the encounters between physician and patient. The patients were carefully trained actors and actresses who had been prepared to provide the medical histories that corresponded to the actual clinical cases we had selected for our simulations. For two of the cases—a hematology problem and a gastrointestinal disorder—the actors provided the history, a "resident" who had ostensibly conducted a comprehensive physical examination provided all requested physical information, and all possible laboratory tests could be ordered as they would normally. Unlike the real world, however, the results of lab tests were made available almost immediately.

For the third case, the actor was encountered in an "emergency room" setting, lying on an examining table complaining of inability to move or feel anything in her legs. The participating actors had been trained to simulate the sensory and motor losses associated with a neurological disorder—in this case the acute onset of multiple sclerosis—and a full physical examination could be conducted by the physician since all nonneurological symptoms were expected to be normal in any event.

I remember well the first pilot study we conducted using these procedures. The distinguished chief of medicine of a regional diagnostic and treatment center had agreed to come to our laboratory for two days and work on all three of the simulated cases. He sat in the simulated examination room/office, interviewing the "patient" as our television cameras silently tilted and panned, sending their signals to the videotape recorders. He alternated between asking sequences of questions and ruminating out loud about what he was thinking and what alternatives he was considering. An advantage to using the actors and refraining from any deception was that the physicians could think aloud without fear of traumatizing the patients. To our amazement, within 30 seconds of the patient's first descriptions of her ailment ("college student in a dorm . . . headache . . . fatigue . . . bad sore throat . . . some fever . . ."), he had already generated his first diagnostic hypothesis (infectious mononucleosis) to be followed less than a minute later by two others (infectious hepatitis; some kind of flu). And so did he proceed, working directly with specific diagnostic alternatives, at times three or four at a time, and organizing much of his questioning using the working hypotheses as a framework. He was apparently violating all the rules, whether they were those of medicine or cognitive psychology.

He continued to operate in that manner during his full two days in our lab, with all the cases we presented to him. When we did stimulated recall showing him his own videotapes for review, he confirmed his use of the strategy we had identified. We assumed he was an anomaly until, as the pilot studies continued and we proceeded into the full investigation, we came to realize that every physician we studied performed in the same manner. Inductive processing where early judgments were withheld, where one first gathered all the information one would need and only then began to diagnose, was by and large a myth. The wisdom of practice proceeded otherwise.

Moreover, the physicians characteristically generated *multiple competing hypotheses,* that is, pairs or triplets of diagnostic alternatives arrayed such that evidence that was positive for one was likely to be negative for the others. This in turn was related to another feature of their diagnostic work. Although constantly talking of the strategy of "rule-outs" in their approach, they in fact favored modes of inference in which they gathered evidence to confirm a particular hypothesis rather than to disconfirm it. Finally, we failed to find evidence of the general competence in medical diagnosis whose existence was an underlying assumption of our work. (Why else ask medical peers to nominate experts in diagnosis in general?) Indeed, as far as we could tell, medical diagnostic expertise was case- or domain-specific. Knowing that a physician was excellent in diagnosing diseases of the gastrointestinal tract was no help in predicting his or her competence with hematological or neurological complaints. Basic problem-solving strategies and procedures were remarkably similar across all physicians (a finding strikingly parallel to that of de Groot (1965) regarding different levels of chess expertise). The appropriate question was not "Who is a good physician?" but "When is a physician good?"

What, then, did we conclude from our studies of the wisdom of practice in medicine? Both traditional medical belief and the ostensible lessons of psychological research were misleading. In general, the clinician's competence in problem formulation and hypothesis generation was the key to diagnostic success. Both of these processes are closely related to the physician's substantive knowledge base and specific experiences in a particular domain. Strategies are employed to reduce the complexity of the problem-solving process and to reduce cognitive strain, just as Bruner and his colleagues asserted. However, unlike their laboratory studies with tasks for which the research participants had no relevant prior knowledge or experience, inductive processing is not most adaptive in situations where substantial prior knowledge, much of it well organized, already exists. Diagnostic hypotheses form the schema, the intellectual scaffolding, on which the rest of the medical inquiry is suspended.

By respecting the wisdom of practice we had discovered the rules that governed medical diagnostic work. What's more, the rules were a real surprise to us because they appeared to break the rules, to violate the commonly held assumptions about the proper ways to do medical diagnostic problem solving. An important reason for understanding this was the likelihood that medical educators were teaching students a set of strategies that were in fact maladaptive in practice. The beliefs regarding how diagnosis ought to be conducted were the most significant determiners of how diagnosis was taught to medical students. Better empirical data on how expert physicians perform served to guide medical teaching in important new ways.[3] The key to understanding why physicians thought through medical problems as they did lay in the complexity they had to manage and the most powerful strategies available for controlling the intricacies of medical work.

Wisdom of the Practitioner

In 1966 I coedited a book called *Learning by Discovery* in which David Hawkins, eminent mathematics and science educator and distinguished philosopher, wrote:

> Our efforts are being made, I believe, in an historical situation where the best practice excels the best theory in quite essential ways; this fact defines a strategy we ought to follow.
>
> There have often been times in the history of science when the personal knowledge of practitioners was significantly deeper than anything embedded in the beliefs and writings of the academically learned. Indeed, science has never started in a social vacuum, but has grown typically out of the interplay of Theorizein and those practically achieved mappings of nature embodied in the working arts. (Hawkins, 1966, p. 3)

Hawkins' observations were the first to alert me to the importance of the wisdom of practice as a source for understanding the complexities of skilled performance. The challenge is to get inside the heads of practitioners, to see the world as they see it, then to understand the manner in which experts construct their problem spaces, their definitions of the situation, thus permitting them to act as they do.

This notion of getting inside the head of the practitioner whose skills you wish to understand is reflected in a very different context in the writings of Thomas Kuhn. Kuhn has long been interested in how a historian of science can make sense of the writings of scientists who lived centuries or even millennia before. He especially reports his frustrations in attempting to understand the concept of mechanics found in Aristotle's *Physics*.

He was especially troubled by all the serious inaccuracies in the philosopher's reported observations of natural phenomena. He concluded that the only way to understand Aristotle was to avoid reading him within the framework of contemporary physics. When he came to understand Aristotle's physics in the light of the more general Greek worldview, the incongruities in the work of that ancient philosopher dissolved.

> Trying to transmit such lessons to students, I offer them a maxim: When reading the works of an important thinker, look first for the apparent absurdities in the text and ask yourself how a sensible person could have written them. When you find an answer, I continue, when those passages make sense, then you may find the more central passages, ones you previously thought you understood, have changed their meaning. (Kuhn, 1977, p. xii)

We thus treat the actions of the practitioner as, in principle, adaptive. That is, when practitioners are observed to behave in a manner that appears irrational, silly, maladaptive, or just plain foolish, we ask what would make their choice of behavior sensible.

Now, it may be that the observed behavior is just plain silly and we would be unwise to accept any observed performance of a veteran practitioner (or the rules we infer from detecting regularities in some particular individual's thoughts and actions) as adequate reason to stipulate that such rules ought to serve as grounds for the actions of others. Other decision rules are needed.[4] Strategies for avoiding this version of the naturalistic fallacy will be discussed at the conclusion of this chapter.

Wisdom of Practice in Teaching

The practice of teaching involves a far more complex task environment than does that of medicine. The teacher is confronted, not with a single patient, but with a classroom filled with 25 to 35 youngsters. The teacher's goals are multiple; the school's obligations far from unitary. Even in the ubiquitous primary reading group, the teacher must simultaneously be concerned with the learning of decoding skills as well as comprehension, with motivation and love of reading as well as word-attack, and must both monitor the performances of the six or eight students in front of her while not losing touch with the other two dozen in the room. Moreover, individual differences among pupils are a fact of life, exacerbated even further by the worthwhile policies of mainstreaming and school integration. The only time a physician could possibly encounter a situation of comparable complexity would be in the emergency room of a hospital during or after a natural disaster. Thus the question How do teachers manage the complexity of classroom life? is not only as legitimate to raise regarding teachers as it is for physicians; it is far more germane.

I shall illustrate this way of looking at the management of complexity in classrooms by focusing on a set of studies that are linked together by a common interest in the way teachers use *time*. As Gage (1978) has pointed out in a critique of the work of Berliner and his colleagues, time is an empty vessel, and simply looking at the amount of time used by either teachers or students is in itself not particularly illuminating. But for Berliner, time is a proxy, a variable of interest because of what it hides, because of what it represents in the minds and motives of those whose lives center on classrooms. What fills the empty vessel of time are inferences about what teachers and students who use more or less time, or use the time in particular ways, are thinking, feeling, attending to, or withdrawing from as they confront the tasks of schoolrooms.

From a teacher's perspective, time is a precious resource, a commodity to be invested in both children and activities, a valuable resource that must be used carefully because it is available in such limited amounts.[5] One of the reasons classroom teaching is so complex is that a limited amount of time and energy must somehow be allocated among individuals and groups while promoting equity and achieving excellence. When a teacher provides time—in the form of a question addressed to a pupil, a chance to ask a question, to present an idea, to do a problem at the board with the teacher's assistance—the teacher is providing an opportunity to learn, an occasion for the student to respond, construct, and test a thought. Trade-offs are always necessary; some children inevitably remain untaught while others are receiving special attention. Cooperative learning and peer tutoring can help, but in the final analysis teachers must teach.

I shall give a couple of brief examples of how teachers manage the complexities of allocating opportunities to learn, the triage of turn taking. Time does not float through classrooms unpackaged. Indeed, most of classroom time, especially during recitations, discussions, and the monitoring of seatwork, is incorporated within that ubiquitous vessel of social interaction, the *turn*. One of the most important accomplishments of any child's development is learning how to take turns, whether waiting to bat in a softball game or waiting to buy a ticket in a movie line. Much of the commerce of classroom life is the management of a turn-taking economy.[6] Let's talk first about some studies of how teachers allocate turns and then move on to an examination of the internal anatomy of a turn, what a turn is made of.

Anderson, Evertson, and Brophy (1979), in a study I am quite fond of citing, examined the behaviors of first-grade reading teachers that correlated significantly with pupil end-of-year achievement gains. Among the many questions they asked was one that relates directly to this question of turn allocation. How should turns be allocated within a primary-grade reading group? Every teacher who deals with groups of any size readily understands the dilemma of turn allocation. Basically three strategies are available: ordered turns, random turns, and volunteered turns. In an ordered strategy, youngsters are called upon in a predetermined order, usually the order in which they are seated. In a random approach, the teacher employs the weapon of surprise, calling on students guerrilla-style to maintain attention and an optimal level of adaptive anxiety. When the teacher permits volunteering, the children themselves take the initiative by either raising their hands or calling.

Which of these strategies will, in general, yield the largest achievement gains over a year of work in first-grade reading groups? When this question is posed before experienced teachers in talks like this one, the general consensus is clear. Teachers assert that random turns will be best. Student attention has a tendency to wander; fear of a sneak attack will keep students on their toes. At times, Kounin's (1970) management principle of "group alerting" is also cited in support of the virtues of random turns.

Most often educational research is said to confirm the intuitively obvious, though Gage (1986) has argued persuasively that the "obvious" is not always readily apparent. In fact, it can be demonstrated that the same individuals will claim that both a particular assertion *and its opposite* are both true and obviously so! Nevertheless, what is particularly attractive about the Anderson, Evertson, and Brophy findings regarding turn taking is that the findings are counterintuitive. Contrary to expectations, those children who had the highest achievement gains in reading were members of reading groups whose teachers used *ordered turns*.

What would account for those surprising findings? First, keep in mind that the preferred alternative—random turns—probably does not exist. That is, most studies of classroom interaction reveal that it is nearly impossible for any teacher, however well motivated, to assign turns in a truly random (and, over the long haul, thus equitable) manner. Indeed, a relatively small group of students inevitably garners the bulk of opportunities to respond when a nonstructured turn-taking protocol is employed. This should not surprise us. Those who know the right answers will be more likely to volunteer and will also be called on more frequently by the teacher. Let's face it. Teachers need reinforcement too. After teaching your heart out all morning, you will tend to call on someone whose response will suggest that your teaching produced some learning. As Bruno Bettelheim once observed, teachers need to replenish their own narcissistic reserves too, and student performance is our major source of pride.

Thus, since random turns rarely occur, the *un*ordered turn strategy will usually yield patterns of participation in which many children do not have a chance to perform, to demonstrate their understanding and receive praise or to demonstrate their misconceptions and receive remediation—both necessary features of effective teaching. When a large portion of a classroom's participants is not called upon, it should not surprise that achievement is lower.

But is it not certainly the case that students pay more attention when they do not know who will be called on next? Here we must ask where attention is directed rather than merely whether students are attending. Interviews with students suggest that much of the time during classroom discussions is spent with students thinking about who the teacher is going to call on, more precisely, whether and when the teacher will call on them. Thus, while there may be an increase in attention associated with unordered turns, that attentional increment may not be devoted to the texts, ideas, or materials of instruction, but to the subtle cues from teachers regarding their next pedagogical moves. Instead of focusing on the texts, the students may be working at "psyching out" the teacher. Such patterns of attention are unlikely to lead to increased student achievement. The reasons for the apparent superiority of ordered turns, therefore, may be that the ordering strategy disciplines the teacher's allocation patterns thereby assuring a more equitable distribution of learning opportunities, as well as removing a source of ambiguity for the students, hence permitting them to dedicate more of their energy to concentrating on the academic tasks rather than the teacher's management strategy.[7]

I have discussed this particular study of turn allocation in great detail because it so beautifully exhibits how much can be learned about classroom teaching from careful examination of the character of turns. Some practitioners had already understood intuitively that ordered turns work best and were using them. But the bulk of teachers continue to believe that unstructured turns are best. At times the wisdom of practice is neither obvious nor universal.

Now I would like to discuss a series of studies that explore turns in a very different way. What is the anatomy of a turn? If you dissect a turn, take it apart to examine its constituent parts and their interrelationships, what do you find?

A turn can be defined as a teacher's question, a pupil's response, and a subsequent teacher response. This is one particular kind of turn, a recitation turn; but since recitation remains the most frequently identified mode of group instruction, it is fairly typical of classroom life. Occupying the interstices that separate these three anatomical pieces of a turn is *time*. The teacher asks a question after which we find some time. A student responds and again we find some length of time. The teacher responds to the student and again we observe a passage of time. The pace of classrooms is largely determined by the amount of time that occupies those interstices. In rapidly paced classrooms, question, answer, and response follow on one another's heels with the speed of a machine gun. In more slowly paced arenas, the time dividing these acts is longer, the general pace of recitation is slower, less hectic. What is the significance of this temporal aspect of the anatomy of a turn?

Mary Budd Rowe (1974a; 1974b), a distinguished science educator, became interested in an aspect of the anatomy of a turn she called "wait-time." She designated as wait-times the amount of time between teacher's question and student response (or a teacher repeating, restating, or redirecting the question) and the subsequent amount of time between a student response and a teacher's reaction. She proceeded to ask how the length of wait-times, which appears to be very much under the control of the teacher, relates to student performance and achievement.[8]

The findings of her research, carried out over a decade ago, are by now well known in the educational community. Overall, longer wait-times were associated with higher-order responses on the parts of students. That is, the longer teachers waited after asking questions or following student answers, the more complex, analytic, or creative were the statements made by their students.[9] The importance of wait-time has by now made its way into many staff development programs for teachers.

When staff development programs are designed for the purpose of teaching teachers to increase their wait-times, the results are provocative. During the course of the workshops, teachers seem perfectly capable of increasing their wait-times from the general average (about one second) to a veritable pedagogical eternity (about four seconds). Yet when they are observed upon returning to their own classrooms, the wait-times rapidly return to their earlier values. What accounts for this backsliding? Are teachers simply lazy and shiftless? Or are there good reasons why longer wait-times may look more attractive to researchers than to wise practitioners?

To understand the probable price teachers pay when extending their wait-times, think for a moment about where wait-times occur: in the interstices of turns. As we noted earlier, longer wait-times necessarily entail the slowing of a classroom's instructional pace and the punctuation of its flow with eddies of silence. Periods of reflection (for that is in fact what those wait-times represent) provide opportunities for analysis and deliberation, for cognition and metacognition, but are also likely to present, in their very emptiness, occasions for disruption and misbehavior. Students, like nature, abhor a vacuum. The slowed pace of classroom interaction is likely to exact a toll from the teacher in the form of more frequent classroom disruptions and interruptions. One reason why the wise practitioner may find wait-times unattractive is that they bring with them an increase in the problems of classroom management.

Let us imagine for a moment, however, that the jointly produced drama of the classroom can survive the slower pace through a well-designed classroom rule system, a well-wrought social contract among teacher and students, and the adoption of a more deliberate learning style in the group. What unintended consequences of increased wait-times might motivate teachers to consider reducing them once more? Consider the possibility that the improvements in learning produced through the longer wait-times might themselves be two-edged swords, blessings dipped in acid for teachers. Yet what could possibly be problematic about higher-level and more creative student responses?

I find it easier to think about that question in relation to another study, a dissertation conducted several years ago by Janet Shroyer (1981) at Michigan State University. She asked, "What makes mathematics teaching difficult?" What are those kinds of classroom interaction that place particular stress on the teacher—from a substantive point of view rather than from a management perspective? Shroyer concentrated on a category of event we called a critical moment.[10] The critical moments all involved the consequences of questions asked by teachers and were therefore structurally related to the same kinds of events in which we spoke of wait-times.

We will consider three categories of critical moment. The first occurs when a teacher asks the class a question he or she knows everyone can answer—and no one can! The second occurs when the teacher asks the class a question he or she is confident no one can answer—and many do! In each case, the planned lesson or lesson segment has been disrupted because the expected understanding (or ignorance) has not been demonstrated.

The third kind of critical moment is the most discomfiting of all. Here the teacher asks a question with a range of expectable answers, or at least a sense of the "ball park" within which the possible responses will fall. Instead, someone produces a response that falls beyond the pale, an idea or invention that simply does not fit with the teacher's expectations and is not immediately discernable as right or wrong. This kind of unpredictability produced some of the most painful critical moments of all. It placed the greatest strain on the subject-matter competence of the teacher, who now had to delve into his or her understanding of mathematics to think of a way of coping with this strange, or at least unexpected, response.

I hope it is now clear why I am reminded of Shroyer's study of critical moments in thinking about why prolonged wait-times are not always seen as producing positive outcomes by teachers. Classroom life is characterized by unpredictability. The uncertainties inherent in any simple act of tutoring are multiplied enormously as one attempts to teach a room filled with 30 mindful bodies. A teacher must attempt to keep this unpredictability within an acceptable range at all times. The cognitive strains of teaching become intolerable when the uncertainty of classroom life exceeds a certain threshold, which certainly must vary from teacher to teacher. If the great virtue of wait-time is that it yields more inventive or creative responses from students, then its great liability is that by the same token it necessarily increases the unpredictability of classroom discourse. Most likely, increases in wait-time are accompanied by increases in the frequency and intensity of critical moments. Wait-times may not only make teaching better; they may make teaching more difficult and strainful.

This is not to say that just because increased wait-times may make teaching difficult they ought to be avoided. Indeed, the solution to the problem is not likely to be forgoing both the goals of higher-order thinking and the wait-times needed to foster it. Teachers and students can probably learn to engage in more complex forms of discourse involving longer wait-times and more complex and unpredictable student responses. But more careful preparation of teachers and of their classes may be needed to support such an effort. For one, a teacher may well have to develop deeper content knowledge and pedagogical content knowledge to respond adequately to higher frequencies of less predictable student contributions.

I have invoked these examples to emphasize that the wisdom of practice must be considered even when we are confronted with what appear to be examples of teachers' resistance to change and misunderstandings of the usefulness of new ideas. In the spirit of Kuhn's interpretations of Aristotle, we must always treat teachers and their activities with respect. We must try to understand teachers' actions and reactions from *their* perspective in the classroom, because what may look like foolishness to an observer in the back of the room may look like the only route to survival from behind the teacher's desk.

Embarrassments of Practice

A cautionary tale. Practitioners are not always wise. Not only theory can err. There will be times when despite efforts to find a rationale that supports or explains practitioners' work, they will turn out to be dead wrong. I have two examples, one from medicine, the other from education. Beginning some 30 years ago, a series of studies was conducted to investigate how experienced radiologists interpreted chest x-rays (Garland, 1959; Yerushalmy, 1969). To the dismay of the researchers, they discovered that when the same films were placed in a pile of x-rays to check for reliability of judgment, the experienced radiologists were found to be unacceptably unreliable. They would provide quite different interpretations for the same chest x-ray when looking at it a second time.

More recently, a group of investigators at the Institute for Research on Teaching (Weinshank, 1982; Vinsonhaler, Weinshank, Wagner, & Polin, 1983) conducted a comparable series of studies with reading diagnosticians who were presented with alternate versions of the same case, with a few surface changes to make detection more difficult, within a couple of weeks of one another. The reliability of their diagnoses of the same cases hovered around zero. Could practice be considered wise when it changed radically over a short time? I doubt it. The lesson is thus to treat the wisdom of practice with respect, with deference, albeit with careful skepticism.

In our research, moreover, we do not fall into the trap of simply treating anything practitioners are observed to do as worthy of emulation. Treating what *is* as grounds for what ought to be has long been designated as the "naturalistic fallacy" in philosophy, and its dangers extend with equal validity to the world of practice. There are several ways in which we manage to avoid the excesses of overly celebrating the status quo. First, we do not find, in studying the wisdom of practice, that some uniform, monolithic image of "good practice" or "current practice" emerges. Indeed, we are particularly interested in detecting and documenting the variations among individual examples of practice. Wise practitioners vary. Those variations are responses to the diversity of youngsters whom they teach, the range of subject matters they instruct, the variety of grounded philosophies of education they espouse, or the styles of teaching they adopt. It would be foolish to seek to calculate some grand mean of wise practice, somehow aggregating across these variations to estimate one "best" system of teaching. Instead, we choose to examine those variations carefully and to attempt to understand the grounds on which they rest.[11]

Observed variations are then related to contextual or environmental constraints and opportunities (class size, availability of materials, pupil and community characteristics, prescribed curriculum, and so on), teachers' goals, plans, and strategies, and other conditions—both internal and external—that would help us understand why the actions taken were selected. Such research can only be undertaken through a combination of observation and interview, monitoring both performance and cognition. The behavior of teachers remains inscrutable unless it is understood as a function of the minds and motives of those who behave.[12]

My studies of practice in medicine and teaching have led inevitably to questions of comparison. How are teaching and medicine alike? How are they different? Which places the greater cognitive strain on the problem solver? In which case—teaching or medicine—is the management of complexity a greater challenge?

I have already suggested my response earlier in this chapter. There is little doubt that, from the perspective of complexity management, teaching is a far more demanding occupation than is medicine. Naturally there are many variations in the practice of each. But overall, the diagnosis and treatment of a single patient under circumstances that the physician controls are far easier than the management and teaching of 30 students under constraints of time, materials, and multiple sources of unpredictability. If there is any kind of medicine that resembles teaching, it may be emergency medicine on the battlefield. For an analogy to teaching in medicine, therefore, look to MASH rather than to St. Elsewhere.

Streams of Inquiry

Two streams of research flow in education, two strategies of inquiry to inform practice and policy. In one stream we strive to develop better theory through carefully conducted investigations and controlled conditions. In the second stream we study the variations of practice to discern the underlying causes and reasons for action. A dialectic must ensue between these two streams of inquiry—the theory driven and the practice driven—because through this alternation we begin to grasp both the potential for positive educational change as well as the limits of reform.

At this time the study of teaching and of schools is a rich research site in which the efforts of many disciplines—social sciences, natural sciences, humanities—can be and are fruitfully employed. Our call for continued inquiry may disappoint those who wish simple answers to the pressing problems of education, but one of our responsibilities is to inhibit glib prescriptions of simple solutions to complex dilemmas. One way to ensure that caution is through continued studies of the worlds of professional practice. Thus may the wisdom of practice enrich and inform us all.

NOTES

1. This emphasis is particularly appropriate for the present volume. Nate Gage has maintained a lifelong commitment to the improvement of teaching practice through the study of effective practitioners. Both through his correlational and his experimental work, he has contended that research on teaching is generalizable to practice precisely because it comprises the study of practice. One need not speculate whether a real teacher is capable of en-

gaging in the kinds of practice described in process-product research. The very fact that the behavior described is captured in the research program is evidence that real teachers engage in it. While I have quibbled with Gage regarding how closely his *composite* characterizations of effective teachers necessarily correspond to what any particular teacher might have done, I consider his work well within the traditions of wisdom-of-practice research programs. With Gage, it represents the twin efforts of the applied behavioral scientist and educator—whose goal is to better understand the processes of skilled professionals in order to educate those professionals more responsibly in the future.

2. These studies of medical problem solving were conducted under grant support from the U.S. Public Health Service to the Office of Medical Education Research and Development (OMERAD) at Michigan State University.

3. Several additional comments are in order. Professor Roy Maffly of Stanford University School of Medicine was sufficiently convinced of the validity of our findings to base a new instructional system upon them. He received a grant from the National Fund for Medical Education to support the development of a computer-based learning system to help medical students learn to generate early diagnostic hypotheses most effectively and how to evaluate them critically.

   Interesting things occurred when Elstein and I began to report these findings to members of the medical community. We anticipated strong resistance to the claim that medical work was being pursued in one way while being taught and written about in an utterly different manner. Instead, we were pleased to hear that our account of medical problem solving squared quite well with how individual practitioners intuitively recognized they were working. Somehow, each seemed to believe that he or she was alone in practicing in such an illegitimate manner. In general, physicians were quick to agree that what we described was precisely how they performed.

   A final note. One physician who heard our report acknowledged that we had accurately described how he practiced but voiced disappointment that he did not proceed inductively because he had always wanted to feel that doing medicine was like doing science. We then informed him that most recent work in the philosophy of science (e.g., Peter Medawar) had argued that the typical working strategy of science was in fact hypothetico-deductive, not inductive in a Baconian manner. So our physician friend was thinking like a scientist after all.

4. The process-product researcher has fairly clear-cut decision rules for determining whether an observed behavior is worth emulating. The behavior should correlate significantly with a desired outcome in students. Preferably,

it should be demonstrated that experimental manipulation of the behavior yields the desired outcome under controlled experimental conditions. Fenstermacher (1978), among others, has raised questions regarding the adequacy of these conditions for justifying the stipulation of the behaviors as desirable. Nevertheless, some decision rules are needed and process-product researchers are prepared to state them.

5. I was first led to think about time in this manner by two economist colleagues at the Institute for Research on Teaching, Byron Brown and the late Dan Saks. Their suggestion that microeconomic metaphors be applied to classrooms, seeing them as firms, as oil refineries, as automobile job shops, each of which suggested a different principle for organizing work and allocating resources, had great heuristic value for their colleagues—both teachers and researchers—as they studied classrooms. They subsequently conducted reanalyses of the Beginning Teacher Evaluation Study data employing some of these ideas.
6. I first learned of the importance of turn taking and its rules while working as a preadolescent in my parents' Chicago delicatessen. My late mother, an immigrant from Lithuania, disliked the formalities of queuing systems where customers were told to take a number at the door. She preferred an honor system in which turns were allocated by responses to her repeated question, "Whose *next* is it?" A "next" was a turn in the Logan Delicatessen, and a precious one at that. By transforming an adjective of subsequence into a noun of consequence, Sonia Shulman made her own contributions to the wisdom of practice.
7. Of course, the results of this particular study do not dictate that ordered turns be employed by all teachers under all conditions. Indeed, the reasons behind these findings ought to be analyzed and used as principles to guide practice rather than the specific behaviors themselves. Teaching in ways that distribute opportunities to learn and to perform more equitably and in ways that produce student cognitions that focus on task-relevant characteristics of the teaching rather than on task-irrelevant, these are the proper principles to be learned from this research. Process-product research, like all research on teaching, is valuable for the principles it teaches us to employ as we think about our teaching, not because of the specific behavior that it prescribes for teachers to employ. The failure to understand this important precept regarding the proper relationship between research and practice, a relationship that Gage emphasized repeatedly in his discussions of art and science, has led to the misuse of the results of research in some policy settings.

8. Rowe's interest in wait-time goes well beyond concern for the proper pacing of classroom questions. She is particularly interested in the attitudes that develop among students as a consequence of the ways in which classrooms are run. She has termed one of those attitudes "late control."
9. Naturally, the teachers' questions needed to be appropriately higher order to elicit such responses. Asking in what year Columbus discovered America is not going to elicit higher-order thinking even if wait-time approaches eternity. Increased wait-time only yields higher-order responses when the questions permit (or encourage) such thinking.
10. The idea of a critical moment emerged from a set of seminars that Professor Joseph Schwab was then conducting with the research staff of the Institute for Research on Teaching. Schwab suggested that teaching could be characterized as proceeding in a flow of interactions periodically punctuated by interruptions. We could call these "occurrences" or "occasions." Each word means an interruption (an *occlusion*) in the flow *(current)* of any set of events. An occasion such as a holiday, a wedding, a special visit acts as an occlusion in the flow or current of everyday life. That special category of classroom occurrences with which we were interested were dubbed *critical moments.*
11. This strategy characterizes research my colleagues and I are currently conducting to develop better means for assessing teaching competencies in a National Board for Professional Teaching Standards. We have dubbed these "wisdom of practice" studies.
12. In a lovely critique of my work on teacher decision making, Gage argued correctly that I had placed such great emphasis on teacher decision making and cognition that I had ignored the importance of teacher behavior entirely. He was reminded of a similar disagreement between two learning theorists, Guthrie (the behaviorist) and Tolman (the cognitivist), both of whom studied learning in rats. Guthrie had said of Tolman, "He leaves his rats lost in thought." Similarly, Gage admonished, "Shulman leaves teachers lost in thought." I finally have an opportunity to reply. "Professor Gage, I would rather leave teachers lost in thought than missing in action!"

REFERENCES

Anderson, L., Evertson, C., & Brophy, J. (1979). An experimental study of effective teaching in first-grade reading groups. *Elementary School Journal, 79* (4), 193–223.

Berliner, D. C. (1979). Tempus educare. In P. L. Peterson & H. L. Walberg (Eds.), *Research on teaching*. Berkeley, CA: McCutchan.

Bruner, J. S., Goodnow, J. J., & Austin, G. A. (1956). *A study of thinking*. New York: Wiley.

de Groot, A. D. (1965). *Thought and choice in chess*. The Hague: Mouton.

Elstein, A. S., Shulman, L. S., & Sprafka, S. A. (1978). *Medical problem solving: An analysis of clinical reasoning*. Chicago: University of Chicago Press.

Fenstermacher, G. D. (1978). A philosophical consideration of recent research on teacher effectiveness. In L. S. Shulman (Ed.), *Review of research in education*. Itasca, IL: Peacock.

Gage, N. L. (1978). *The scientific basis of the art of teaching*. New York: Teachers College Press.

———. (1986). Hard gains in the soft sciences: The case of pedagogy. *Phi Delta Kappa Monographs*.

Garland, L. H. (1959). Studies on the accuracy of diagnostic procedures. *American Journal of Roentgenology, 82*, 25–38.

Harrison, T. R. (1973). *Harrison's principles of internal medicine*, 7th ed. New York: McGraw-Hill.

Hawkins, D. (1966). Learning the unteachable. In L. S. Shulman & E. R. Keislar (Eds.), *Learning by discovery: A critical appraisal*. Chicago: Rand McNally.

Kounin, J. (1970). *Discipline and group management in classrooms*. New York: Holt, Rinehart & Winston.

Kuhn, T. S. (1977). *The essential tension*. Chicago: University of Chicago Press.

Rowe, M. B. (1974a). Wait-time and rewards as instructional variables, their influence on language, logic, and fate control: Part I—Wait-time. *Journal of Research in Science Teaching, 11* (1), 81–94.

———. (1974b). Relation of wait-time and rewards to the development of language, logic, and fate control: Part II—Rewards. *Journal of Research in Science Teaching, 11* (4), 291–308.

Shroyer, J. (1981). *Critical moments in the teaching of mathematics: What makes teaching difficult?* Doctoral dissertation, Michigan State University, East Lansing, MI.

Shulman, L. S., & Elstein, A. S. (1976). Studies of problem solving, judgment, and decision making: Implications for educational research. In F. N. Kerlinger (Ed.), *Review of research in education* (Vol. 3). Itasca, IL: Peacock.

Vinsonhaler, J. S., Weinshank, A. B., Wagner, C. C., & Polin, R. M. (1983). Diagnosing children with educational problems: Characteristics of reading and learning disabilities specialists and classroom teachers. *Reading Research Quarterly, 18* (2), 134–164.

Weinshank, A. B. (1982). The reliability of diagnostic and remedial decisions of reading specialists. *Journal of Reading Behavior, 14* (1), 33–50.
Yerushalmy, J. (1969). The statistical assessment of the variability in observer perception and description of roentgenographic pulmonary shadows. *Radiologic Clinics of North America, 7,* 381–391.

ACKNOWLEDGMENT

Preparation of this chapter was made possible, in part, by support from the Spencer Foundation and the Carnegie Corporation of New York. The views expressed are the author's and not necessarily those of Stanford University or the funding agencies.

INTRODUCTION

DISCIPLINES OF INQUIRY IN EDUCATION: A NEW OVERVIEW (1997)

IN 1980, Richard Jaeger told Shulman that the American Educational Research Association (AERA) was preparing an audiotape series to introduce both graduate students and more experienced scholars to the growing diversity of research methods being employed in educational research. Since Shulman had already begun to develop a reputation for advocating methodological eclecticism, AERA invited him to prepare the first tape in the series, presenting an overview of the field of research methodology. The script for the audiotape was subsequently published as an article in *Educational Researcher,* and the full set of tapes was later published as a book, *Complementary Methods for Research in Education* (edited by Richard M. Jaeger and published by the American Educational Research Association), first in 1987, and then republished with new versions of the essays in 1997. In the final version, more recent ideas that derived from Shulman's growing interest in a scholarship of teaching and learning in higher education help shape the final section. (The essay published here is an edited version of the chapter from the second edition, with a reordered beginning that more closely follows the original.)

Since the 1970s, Shulman had been arguing for a broad, eclectic array of research methods to be used to inform both educational practice and policy. This continuing call for methodological eclecticism, which surely characterizes much of Shulman's work, was most skillfully satirized by Fred Erickson in a symposium at AERA. They were presenting their chapters from the *Handbook of Research on Teaching* (third edition); Shulman was speaking about his "Paradigms" chapter, and Erickson about his "Qualitative Research Methods" chapter. After Shulman's presentation, Erickson—who is an ordained Episcopal deacon—commented that Shulman was a closet Episcopalian: "You know what an Episcopalian is, don't you?" he observed. "He's someone who wants to be Catholic and Protestant at the same time!"

In the chapter, Shulman introduces a framework for examining contemporary research in education; its dimensions include: problems, settings, investigators, methods, and purposes. Although one can focus on research methods (as the volume did), any analysis of method is difficult to separate from the problem the method is used to address, the disciplinary perspective of the investigator, the settings in which the research takes place, and the purposes of the investigation.

Shulman goes on to explore the question, What are the distinguishing characteristics of research from other forms of human activity that inquire into the world? How is research, that is, different from journalism? He argues that what makes research different is that it is "disciplined inquiry," with carefully examined arguments and consistent attempts to eliminate or control for error. The products of such inquiries can withstand intensive examination by other researchers. Such inquiries are also shaped by the disciplinary heritage on which they draw—anthropology, psychology, philosophy, sociology, linguistics, aesthetics, history, and the like—and in so doing, are informed by the "well-developed canons of discovery and verification" that characterize those disciplines.

Shulman then explores issues of generalizability, as well as the differences and disagreements about experimental and correlational, quantitative and qualitative methods. He describes several new lines of research, including teacher research and design experiments. Invoking the work of both Robert Merton and Joseph Schwab, he argues for a disciplined eclectic in research programs that draws widely from the vast array of available methods. He concludes by reminding readers that method is not used solely in the realm of research, for method, too, is used to refer to one's pedagogy. Method is used both to discover new knowledge and to make that knowledge public. Researchers belong to communities, and research, Shulman avers, is "community property." Here one sees Shulman's early ideas of a disciplined eclectic in education research begin to merge with his then current work on the scholarship of teaching, which was inspired by Ernest

Boyer and which emphasized that teaching—as well as research—ought to be considered both socially constructed and owned, community property if you will.

9

DISCIPLINES OF INQUIRY IN EDUCATION

A NEW OVERVIEW

On Method

Few works in the English language are as rich as Shakespeare's *Hamlet*. One phrase is of particular interest. Hamlet is in deep grief and despair over the recent death of his father, the king of Denmark. In his melancholy, he has been acting rather strangely, and many have called him mad. Yet, Polonius observes of Hamlet, "Though this be madness, yet there is method in it." What does Shakespeare wish to convey with this phrase? How can the apparent lack of coherence or sanity of Hamlet's behavior be characterized by method? To assert that something has method is to claim that there is an order, a regularity, obscure though it may be, that underlies an apparent disorder, thus rendering it meaningful. Method is the attribute that distinguishes research activity from mere observation and speculation.

When adversaries argue about the nature of the world or the best approach to some particular human endeavor, we typically find ourselves evaluating their respective claims by examining the methods they used to reach their conclusions. There are few subjects that generate as much passion among scientists as arguments over method. This is not surprising, since scholars who agree on matters of method can pursue research questions in a parallel fashion and then argue over the results of their respective investigations. However, if they do not agree even on some matters of research method, then their findings are likely to be incommensurable.

There will be no way to properly compare one inquiry with the other. It is for this reason that major controversies in educational research so frequently focus on problems of research method. What is the role of research methodology in educational research? How can we tell proper from improper uses of research methods? To answer these questions, we must turn to a central concept in educational research methodology: disciplined inquiry.

Method and Disciplined Inquiry

Educational researchers typically are eager to distinguish their work from other forms of discourse that, for them, cannot lay claim to being research. Take, for example, the following statement from the preface of Lawrence Cremin's (1961) prize-winning history of American progressive education, *The Transformation of the School:*

> There is currently afoot a simple story of the rise of progressive education, one that has fed mercilessly on the fears of anxious parents and the hostilities of suspicious conservatives. In it John Dewey, somewhat in the fashion of Abou Ben Adhem, awakes one night with a new vision of the American school: the vision is progressive education. Over the years, with the help of a dedicated group of crafty professional lieutenants at Teachers College, Columbia University, he is able to foist the vision on an unsuspecting American people. The story usually ends with a plea for the exorcising of this devil from our midst and a return to the ways of the fathers. This kind of morality play has always been an influential brand of American political rhetoric, used by reformers and conservatives alike. But it should never be confused with history! (p. vii)

Cremin forcefully draws the distinction between doing history and engaging in political rhetoric. Clearly, he claims, the results of the two forms of discourse must be treated with different degrees of respect and credibility. "Real history" should be given far greater credence than mere political rhetoric. How is one to distinguish between the two? I would suggest that, while not entirely a matter of method, historians would distinguish their work from that of rhetoricians by the ways observations are collected, evidence is marshaled, arguments are drawn, and opportunities are afforded for replication, verification, and refutation.

When we speak of research, we speak of a family of methods that share the characteristics of disciplined inquiry. Cronbach and Suppes (1969) attempted to define disciplined inquiry a number of years ago in a monograph prepared with the collaboration of their colleagues in the National

Academy of Education. The following are some of the definitions of disciplined inquiry they suggest:

> Disciplined inquiry has a quality that distinguishes it from other sources of opinion and belief. The disciplined inquiry is conducted and reported in such a way that the argument can be painstakingly examined. The report does not depend for its appeal on the eloquence of the writer or on any surface plausibility (p. 15).
>
> Whatever the character of a study, if it is disciplined the investigator has anticipated the traditional questions that are pertinent. He institutes control at each step of information collection and reasoning to avoid the sources of error to which these questions refer. If the errors cannot be eliminated he takes them into account by discussing the margin for error in his conclusions. Thus, the report of a disciplined inquiry has a texture that displays the raw materials entering the argument and the logical processes by which they were compressed and rearranged to make the conclusion credible (pp. 15–16).

The preceding definition of disciplined inquiry could be misconstrued to imply that the appropriate application of research methods in education always leads to a sterile, ritualized, and narrowly conceived form of investigation. This is not the case. As Cronbach and Suppes observe subsequently:

> Disciplined inquiry does not necessarily follow well-established, formal procedures. Some of the most excellent inquiry is free-ranging and speculative in its initial stages, trying what might seem to be bizarre combinations of ideas and procedures, or restlessly casting about for ideas (p. 16).

What is important about disciplined inquiry is that its data, arguments, and reasoning be capable of withstanding careful scrutiny by another member of the scientific community.

If it is clear what constitutes disciplined inquiry and there is little disagreement regarding the need for research methods to be consistent with the standards of disciplined inquiries, why should this field be so filled with controversy? There are several reasons.

First, scientific inquiries cannot involve mere recitation of the "facts of the case." Indeed, inquiry demands the selection of a particular set of observations or facts from among the nearly infinite universe of conceivable observations. Just as in a court of law, the legal adversaries may disagree profoundly about the relevance of a piece of evidence or the warrant to be given to the conclusions drawn from each other's reasoning; thus, in disciplined inquiry in education, there is often lack of consensus about the grounds, the starting points, for chains of reasoning.

There is another, even more serious source of disagreements about method. Disciplined inquiry not only refers to the ordered, regular, or principled nature of investigation; it also refers to the disciplines themselves, which serve as the sources for the principles of regularity or canons of evidence used by the investigator. What distinguishes disciplines from one another is the manner in which they formulate their questions, how they define the content of their domains and organize that content conceptually, and the principles of discovery and verification that constitute the ground rules for creating and testing knowledge in their fields. These principles are different in the different disciplines.

A major reason why research methodology in education is such an exciting area is that education is not itself a discipline. Indeed, education is a field of study, a locus containing phenomena, events, institutions, problems, persons, and processes that themselves constitute the raw material for inquiries of many kinds. The perspectives and procedures of many disciplines can be brought to bear on the questions arising from and inherent in education as a field of study. As each of these disciplinary perspectives is brought to bear on the field of education, it brings with it its own set of concepts, methods, and procedures, often modifying them to fit the phenomena or problems of education. Such modifications, however, can rarely violate the principles defining those disciplines from which the methods were drawn.

I begin the chapter by offering a set of dimensions along which we can examine the variety of research methods that are part of the repertoire of educational research. Using these dimensions—problems, investigators, methods, settings, and purposes—we will be able to map the ways in which educational inquiries develop. I will then turn to the topic with which this chapter began: How can we distinguish research from other forms of human activity in which we explore or investigate the world around us and then write or speak about our insights to others? How, if at all, is the work of the research scholar distinguishable from that of the journalist or the playwright? What are the unique functions of scholars, and how can we best understand their obligations as members of research communities? After a discussion of the concept of disciplined inquiry, I will examine the variety of ways in which scholars frame their questions in disciplinary terms, illustrating these orientations by drawing examples of a variety of different approaches to research that can be conducted around a single problem area: the topic of reading. From these examples, we will begin to see that good research is a matter not of finding the one best method but of carefully framing that question most important to the investigator and the field and then identifying a disciplined way in which to inquire into it that will enlighten both the scholar and his or her community.

Conducting a good study is certainly essential, but it is not enough. It is a serious accomplishment to become wiser or more discerning about a particular problem or issue. It is another to claim that your work has more general value beyond the immediate circumstances of your particular setting or investigation. Thus, I will address the challenge of generalizability, the degree to which a scholar can claim that his or her work can be used to support more general claims about the nature of learning, teaching, development, school finance, and the like. We will see that generalizability is a central issue for all forms of inquiry, from the case study to the national survey.

Next I will examine the ways in which one's preferred modes of research often reflect political or ideological dispositions. This is not a flaw of research; indeed, it is an essential feature of all scholarship that the research practitioner should learn to recognize and acknowledge if he or she is not to develop an unearned air of objective omnipotence or blind faith in putatively dispassionate inquiry. I will examine this issue by reviewing the history of two opposing styles of psychological research in education: experimental and correlational research.

I will also discuss the continuing distinction between quantitative and qualitative inquiry in education and the bases on which scholars can elect to conduct their research in one or some combination of these ways. Much of the current volume is dedicated to explicating the character of many forms of qualitative and quantitative inquiry. I conclude the chapter by looking back over the ways educational research has changed in recent decades. Whether these changes are part of a long-term trajectory of investigation, with the immediate past serving as a harbinger of the immediate future, or whether we are witnessing a pendulum swing rather than a progressive continuum is quite simply impossible to predict. Let us, then, proceed with our dimensions of analysis.

Dimensions of Analysis

There are at least five dimensions that define the research agenda of education: research purposes, research problems, research settings, research investigators, and research methods. Taken together, they serve as a set of commonplaces for discussing educational research. One can envision the interaction of the dimensions by imagining a general mapping sentence for describing any particular educational investigation. In any study, a scholar or investigator frames a problem or issue to investigate using particular methods or procedures in certain settings in accord with particular purposes. Are the problems theoretical or practical? Are the investigators social scientists or practitioners? Are the settings real schools or psychological research laboratories? Are the methods experimental or anthropological? Are the purposes descriptions of current conditions or an exploration of fundamental theory? As we explore these kinds of questions, we will find ourselves developing contrasting portraits of research in education.

First, there are the *problems, topics,* or *issues* that constitute the subject matter of research. Educational research changes as a function of which kinds of problems are deemed most important to pursue or most legitimate to support. For a long time, many of the core problems and topics were defined by the fundamental psychological processes of learning, such as memory, transfer, and problem solving. The research problems were expected to be general (e.g., How does learning, per se, occur?) rather than focused on the subjects of the school curriculum (e.g., How do students' prior conceptions of conservation affect their learning of physics?). Moreover, even those who opted to study basic general processes looked almost exclusively at the nature of learning, not considering teaching a proper topic of investigation. In more recent years, the problems for educational research have extended broadly into issues of educational practice, as well as expanding rapidly into issues of education policy. Thus, the first question to ask regarding educational research is, What is it about? What questions does it ask? What problems does it address?

Second, a field of study is defined by the *settings* in which the research is conducted. For many years, the settings for much of educational research were psychological laboratories that could be carefully controlled or classrooms that had been made over to resemble laboratories as closely as possible. Other studies were conducted with carefully designed questionnaires, inventories, or interviews susceptible to the same strategies for achieving control that operate in laboratory settings. In contrast, attempting to study the learning of a school subject within the buzzing, blooming confusion of an ordinary classroom with its own teacher might have seemed unbearably daunting to an earlier generation of educational scholars. Indeed, traditional social scientists conducting educational research often argued that if the setting for an investigation were a particular real classroom with its own real teacher, it would be impossible to generalize from its characteristics to those of classrooms in general. However, they reasoned, if the setting for research looked like no classroom in particular (as would a laboratory or simulated setting), then safer generalizations could be proposed. The challenge of selecting research settings has been paramount in the recent history of educational research.

A third element is the background and training of the *investigators* who conduct educational research. Traditionally, these scholars have been exclusively disciplinary specialists such as psychologists, historians, philosophers, or sociologists. In the modern era, investigators increasingly include a wider range of social scientists (including anthropologists, linguists, and economists) in addition to humanists and subject-matter specialists. Their efforts now include aesthetic criticisms as well as econometric models. Moreover, many of these investigators now collaboratively study classroom life in partnership with active classroom teachers. In addition, a growing number of investigations are conducted by teachers who study their own work in their own classrooms. Thus, the practitioner as investigator has become more commonplace in our day.

A fourth element involves the *methods* of research. For many decades, these methods were dictated by psychology and its own two "disciplines," experimental and correlational methods (about which I will have more to say later in this chapter). Increasingly in the modern era, the methods associated with other disciplines have been introduced into educational scholarship. These include the ethnographic methods of anthropology, discourse analysis procedures from linguistics and sociolinguistics, "think-aloud" and other forms of protocol analysis from cognitive science, and many others. Thus, the traditional procedures of educational research have been augmented by a variety of qualitative or field research methods, often reported in the form of case studies. In addition, a new generation of quantitative strategies has been spawned, ranging from powerful techniques for analyzing complexly nested hierarchical systems to flexible procedures for exploratory data analysis.

A fifth and fundamental element is the *purpose* for which an investigation is initiated and pursued. Research may be undertaken for many and varied purposes. One may wish to discover or invent new theoretical understandings of particular educational processes or phenomena. One may seek to develop new methods, techniques, or strategies for solving specific problems. One may wish to acquire a more complete description or accounting of the conditions associated with particular schools, students, or content areas. One may seek to apply previously acquired understandings in the amelioration or improvement of current educational conditions, whether of practice or policy. One may attempt to connect or integrate previously distinct areas of theory, practice, or policy. In some cases, the research is pursued to improve particular forms of practice or to inform specific policies. In other cases, the research seeks to test or extend a theoretical formulation in a related discipline such as psychology or sociolinguistics. Some research is undertaken to evaluate or understand the impact of practice in a particular school or classroom. Other research is directed at the formulation of broad generalizations and principles. And, often, the research is undertaken in the interest of a particular ideology or value system to which the investigators are committed. These examples surely do not exhaust the range of purposes for which educational inquiries are conducted. Different purposes address different priorities and privilege different research strategies.

Nevertheless, whatever their purposes, researchers must be capable of communicating their discoveries to a community of peers in education. Research begins in wonder and curiosity but ends in teaching. The work of the researcher must always lead to a process in which we teach what we have learned to our peers in the education community. Our work is neither meaningful nor consequential until it is understood by others. The process of research is incomplete until the researcher can communicate his or her understandings clearly, persuasively, and effectively.

The forms of educational research are identified by how they address the following five facets of its structure: its core problems and topics, the settings in which investigations are conducted, the backgrounds and experience of the investigators who conducted its studies, the methods of inquiry they used, and the purposes for which the research was pursued. As these combinations have changed over the past century, the study of education has evolved. Most important, the determination of which kinds of questions or methods are legitimate is not under the jurisdiction of a Supreme Court or other formal authority. The loosely defined "community of scholars and practitioners" in education is continuously at work accommodating to some new influences while resisting others. Since the focus of this book is on research methods, I will devote most of my attention in this chapter to that topic. But, as we shall soon see, questions of method are often difficult to disentangle from the web of relationships in which they are embedded. And the elements of that web include the features designated earlier.

Applications of Research Methods: Some Examples

Differences in method are not merely alternative ways of reaching the same end or answering the same questions. What distinguishes methods from one another, usually by virtue of their contrasting disciplinary roots, is not only the procedures they use but the very types of questions they tend to raise. This point might best be understood if I take an area of educational inquiry and describe how questions would be asked and studies conducted from the perspectives of different forms of disciplined inquiry in that field of study. Each of the examples I draw will be credible pieces of research, that is, forms of disciplined inquiry. This exercise will illustrate the variety of forms of research method that can be used in a disciplined manner in the same domain of inquiry.

One of the most important areas of educational research is the study of reading. Millions of dollars and the efforts of many individual investigators are invested in research to help us understand more about the teaching and learning of reading. What do we wish to know? What kinds of questions ought we to ask about language, reading, and learning? What kinds of reading research are possible, and what can we learn from each?

One reasonable question is, "What makes some people successful readers and others unsuccessful?" How can you predict which sorts of people are going to have difficulty learning to read, in order, perhaps, to institute preventive measures before serious damage has been done? In this sort of research, one would collect a variety of measures on individuals, including measures of their performance on a number of tasks, their demographic or personal characteristics, aspects of their backgrounds, and anything else that could conceivably assist in accurate prediction of the likelihood of reading difficulty or success. An investigator would then use the techniques of correlation and regression to investigate the relationships between those predictors and sets of useful outcome measures of reading performance for students of various ages. Correlation as a statistical procedure could be used to determine how two variables are related or how much they are related. The approach would be quantitative and would involve no intervention or manipulation other than that required to administer the instruments needed to collect the necessary data. In general, correlational research attempts to describe the relationships among naturally occurring variables or phenomena without attempting to change them.

Another investigator might now say, "I'm not really interested in predicting reading failure or success. I want to identify the best possible methods for teaching reading to all youngsters, irrespective of their backgrounds or aptitudes." Such an individual is unlikely to be satisfied with research methods that correlate attributes of individuals with concurrent or subsequent reading performance. This individual will be inclined to design experimental studies. Individuals or groups would be assigned systematically to contrasting methods of reading instruction. The effects of these contrasting methods then would be compared by testing the reading performances of those who have been taught. This approach involves experimental methods that contrast strikingly with those of correlational research. Naturally, there are times when the degree of control over the assignment of individuals or groups to treatments is not as great as may be theoretically desirable. We may, for example, wish to contrast two schools that are using very different reading programs. Since pupils were not originally assigned to those schools at random, this cannot be considered a "true" experiment. In such cases, we see researchers use other methods that attempt to identify which treatment was best without the benefits of random assignment. These often are called "quasi-experimental" procedures.

Yet another investigator may say that neither predicting reading performance nor identifying the best methods of teaching reading constitutes the question of interest for her. Instead, she may ask, "What is the general level of reading performance across different age, sex, social, or ethnic groups in the population?" "Where do the most significant areas of reading success and failure occur?" and "What are the reading habits of particular groups in the general population?" This investigation will be conducted best by using a variety of survey techniques measuring reading performance or questioning reading practices. The work of the National Assessment of Educational Progress or of the International Education Association studies of cross-national achievement exemplifies this approach. Once again, different procedures are used to ask different questions and to solve different problems for different purposes.

In the cases I have described thus far, the significant questions concern how well or how much reading ability has been gained or developed. Thus, there are comparisons between alternative methods of teaching reading or among different individuals or cohorts of students learning to read. Quite another sort of question can be asked about reading. There are many times when we wish to know not how many or how well but simply how. How is reading instruction carried out? What are the experiences and perceptions of teachers and students as they engage in the teaching and learning of reading? What is the underlying or explicit system of rules by which this complex activity is accomplished?

Although at first blush this might seem a much less powerful form of question than the quantitative questions preceding it, this is not necessarily the case. Some of the most important and influential investigations in the history of social science have been of that form. Perhaps an example can illustrate that point. When Binet and Simon were asked to develop a better method for identifying the children in the public schools of Paris who could profit from special education programs, they responded by creating the individual intelligence test. The goal of their research and development was to improve the precision with which one could measure differences in intellectual ability among persons.

Nearly 20 years later, a young Swiss associate of Simon, Jean Piaget, became intrigued with a very different sort of question about human intelligence. He asked, "What does intelligence look like, and how does it develop?" He was most concerned with the common elements characterizing the intellectual performance of all individuals at a given stage of development rather than the levels of performance that distinguished among them. He was attempting to answer questions about shared regularities rather than measuring systematic differences.

By way of analogy, one individual interested in investigating the game of golf may decide to focus on differences in performance among golfers. What distinguishes good golfers from poor golfers? The study can be conducted experimentally, by contrasting alternative methods of training golfers. It can be accomplished correlationally by examining the attributes of poor- and well-scoring golfers through use of everything from videotape analyses to measures of age, experience, and social characteristics. But a very different question would be "How does one play the game of golf?" What are the functional rules of the game? In this case, another investigator is interested in understanding the common elements or regularities shared by all golfers, whether they are national champions or weekend duffers.

To continue the examples about reading, there are investigators attempting to understand how reading instruction is accomplished in the classroom in general. They tend to use the methods of case study as they document or portray the everyday experiences of teachers and students in the teaching and learning of reading. In much case-study work, there is a general assumption that American public schools are very similar to one another as institutions. Therefore, individual experiences of learning to read will not differ enormously from one setting to another. In other case-study work, the assumption may be that "average" reading development is irrelevant. These researchers wish to document the dramatic diversity among individuals in the rate, sequence, and character of their development of reading competence.

These studies are likely to focus on only one classroom or school or, at most, a small number. Depending on the orientation of the researcher, the portrayals could emphasize the social character of learning to read in a classroom group, the intellectual and emotional experiences of individual children struggling to master the intricacies of reading, or even the manner in which individual children acquire the implicit rules for turn taking and status attainment in the classroom. Data gathering can include compiling detailed prose descriptions written longhand on yellow legal pads; videotaping classroom episodes and analyzing their contents exhaustively; interviewing teachers and students to discover their reactions, perceptions, or expectations in classrooms; and collecting examples of work produced by teachers and students for careful review and interpretation.

The disciplines from which these methods draw their rules of discovery and verification typically are anthropology, ethology, linguistics, or particular sub-fields of sociology, such as symbolic interaction. More recently, humanistic disciplines like aesthetics and the hermeneutic methods of philosophy fruitfully have been added to the tool kit. These contrast sharply with the disciplinary roots of the more traditional approaches, predominantly psychology, agriculture, genetics, and quantitative sociology, including demography.

A philosopher approaching the problem of research in reading might raise yet another set of questions. He or she might examine the kinds of inquiry just described and observe that the concept of reading has not been adequately defined. What does it mean to be able to read? Do we denote by the term *reading* the ability to recognize the correspondence between visible symbols and sounds in isolation, mere word identification? Do we imply the ability to comprehend written prose, and, if so, at what level of sophistication or subtlety? For example, does someone who knows how to read have the ability to detect the difference between assertion and irony in a prose passage? Analysis of the meaning of the reading process affects the kinds of tests and measurements of reading achievement that are constructed. What we choose to define as reading will be important whether we are pursuing predictive studies of reading failure or success, experimental studies of reading instruction methods, or general surveys of reading performance. A philosopher would conduct inquiries into the nature of the reading process that would entail quite different research procedures from those of other investigators. These analytic procedures would be disciplined by the rules of evidence proper to philosophy.

Similarly, questions of what distinguishes readers from nonreaders can be approached as historical research. As soon as someone attempts to answer the question "What proportion of the U.S. population is illiterate?" the ambiguity of the definition of "literacy" becomes apparent. How well must a person read and write to be considered literate? How has that definition changed for societies with contrasting economic systems, religious orientations, sex-role prescriptions, or social-class hierarchies? A careful historical analysis can help account for both the conditions that foster increased literacy among members of a society and the possible consequences of illiteracy for those members.

I have attempted in the examples just presented to illustrate the variety of ways in which complementary types of research methods can be applied to a topic of inquiry in education: reading instruction. Moreover, I have tried to indicate that the alternative methods not only approach the doing of research differently but, by and large, ask different questions and hence generate quite different answers. This is hardly surprising and surely not disturbing. The need for a multiplicity of methods was recognized centuries ago, perhaps most eloquently by Aristotle, who, in the introduction to his treatise *De Anima* (On the Soul), observes:

> It might be supposed that there was some single method of inquiry applicable to all objects whose essential nature we are endeavoring to ascertain . . . in that case what we should seek for would be this unique method. But if there is no single and general method for solving the question of essence, our task becomes still more difficult; in the case of each different subject we have to determine the appropriate process of investigation (1947a, pp. 145–146).

Generalizability of Research

However different the objects of investigation and the goals of inquiry, there are certain problems shared by all research methods, including the generalizability of findings: the degree to which findings derived from one context or under one set of conditions may be assumed to apply in other settings or under other conditions. Although there may be disclaimers from some research practitioners, all researchers strive for some degree of generalizability for their results. They are rarely content to have the research they have conducted generate understanding that is relevant only to the particular cases that were observed. There are several forms of generalization. The most frequently discussed is generalization from the particular sample of individuals who are tested, taught, or observed in a given study to some larger population of individuals or groups of which they are said to be representative. For example, if we conduct a study of reading comprehension with third graders in Philadelphia, can we generalize our results to third graders all over the country? Or must we limit our generalizations to children of certain social and economic backgrounds, ability levels, and the like?

A second form of generalization is from the particular tasks or settings in which a piece of work is conducted to that population of tasks or settings that the research situation is claimed to represent. For example, one may compare phonics and whole-language approaches with reading instruction using two particular sets of books or methods. If one finds one approach consistently superior, can one generalize these findings to all phonics and whole-language methods? Or must one limit one's generalizations to those particular teaching materials alone?

Although both types of generalizability are important, much more has been written about the first kind, generalizability across people, than about the second, generalizability across situations. We shall see that the two have certain elements in common. In classical statistics, the argument was made that if one samples randomly from a population in making certain measurements or conducting certain experiments, inferences then can be drawn properly to the entire population from which the random sample was taken. Unfortunately, it is rarely the case that investigators truly sample randomly from a total population to which they might ultimately wish to generalize. A truly random sample is one in which each individual in the population has an equal chance of appearing and in which selection of one individual is independent of the selection of any other. In a now-classic article, Cornfield and Tukey (1956) argued that this is never the case. Indeed, we sample as best we can and then make a case for the subsequent claims of generalizability. To use their metaphor, we must then build an inferential bridge between the particular groups of people we studied directly in our research and those other groups to whom we wish to generalize. We do so by documenting as comprehensively as possible the characteristics of the individuals we have studied and the procedures we have used. Then the reader can examine our documentation and critically evaluate whether our claims of generalizability are warranted. More specifically, the reader must judge whether the findings we report for the individuals we have studied should be considered applicable to any other group of individuals regarding whom our reader might be interested.

Cornfield and Tukey's concept of bridge building extends fruitfully to other aspects of generalization as well. When we report on a setting or a task, we must be equally careful to document in detail its characteristics so that readers who are as concerned about the generalizability of our task characteristics as they are about the generalizability of our sample can make the appropriate inferences.

Finally, we can now see that those who perform case studies are confronted with a problem of generalizability that is not different in kind from that confronted by their quantitative colleagues. To claim that one is conducting a case study requires that an answer be provided to the question "What is this a case of?" Not every description is a case study.

It may be a description of a singular individual or event. To claim that something is a case study is to assert that it is a member of a family of situations or events of which it is in some sense representative. In much the same way that the reader of a quantitative study must build his Cornfield-Tukey bridge to evaluate whether the results of that study are relevant to certain other settings, so the critical reader of a case study must examine whether an inferential bridge can be built between this case and other cases of interest to the reader.

Controversy over Method: Experimental Versus Correlational

One of the best-known examples of a controversy over method was explicated by Cronbach (1957) in his now-classic article, "The Two Disciplines of Scientific Psychology." Cronbach observed that the field of psychology had divided early into two major streams: the correlational and the experimental. Both of these streams share what Cronbach calls the "job of science," which is to ask questions of nature. A discipline, he observes, is a method of asking questions and testing answers to determine whether those answers are sound. Correlational psychology is not a form of research that uses only one statistical technique, namely, correlation. Those researchers who are deemed correlationists are interested in studying the natural covariations occurring in nature. They are committed to understanding the functional relationships between variations in one set of events or characteristics and variations in another. Thus, they may ask about the relationship between income and achievement, or between the number of physicians per thousand population and infant mortality, or between phases of the moon and the behavior of tides on earth. They see nature as presenting itself for inspection and the role of the scientist as that of identifying which of the variations that nature presents are associated with other processes or outcomes.

In contrast, experimentalists are interested, as Cronbach observes, only in the variation they themselves create. The experimental method is one in which scientists change conditions in order to observe the consequences of those changes. They are interested in understanding how nature is put together, not by inspecting nature as it is but by introducing modifications or changes in nature in order to better understand the consequences of those changes for subsequent states. They argue that only through the systematic study of planned modifications can we distinguish causal relationships between events or characteristics from mere chance co-occurrences. Thus, for example, foot size and vocabulary are correlated in the general population, but that does not mean that large feet cause larger word knowledge (or vice versa). It merely reflects the larger vocabulary size of older (and, hence, bigger) people relative to children.

All too frequently ignored is the intersection of research methods with the underlying theoretical, political, or social purposes of the research being conducted. As I indicated earlier in this chapter, research methods are not merely different ways of achieving the same end. They carry with them different questions, different ways of asking questions, and often different commitments to educational and social ideologies. We can observe this intersection of ideology and method in considering the historical roots of correlational and experimental approaches.

In the scientific world of late-19th-century England, the work of Charles Darwin on the origin of the species commanded special attention. Central to his evolutionary theory was the principle of natural selection: Nature selects those species or subspecies for ultimate survival that are best adapted to the conditions confronting them. "Survival of the fittest" is a phrase used to describe the process by which individuals and species adapt to variations in environmental conditions in order to survive. The "struggle for life" favors those whose structure and behavior are adaptive to the challenges of their environment and thus are more likely to produce offspring who flourish.

This view of human evolution as a struggle for survival had a substantial impact on prevailing views of society. Buttressed by the centrality of competition and the free market to the economic thinking of 19th-century England, a movement called "social Darwinism" developed. Social Darwinists viewed members of a society as struggling for rewards and undergoing "selection" based on their talents or merits.

Francis Galton, a cousin of Darwin, observed that it was important to study those variations in human abilities and performance contributing most significantly to successful adaptation. He thus began systematically studying those human attributes contributing most to social effectiveness. He assumed that those characteristics were enduring traits unlikely to undergo change. His research was broad indeed, ranging from studies of what he viewed as hereditary genius to investigation of the efficacy of prayer. His research was characteristic of what we now call correlational studies. He developed early forms of the statistical methods that currently underlie correlational research.

Galton's work is historically linked to the brand of social theory that came to be known as conservative Darwinism (Cremin, 1961). Conservative Darwinists attempted to develop better means for identifying those members of the society who were most likely to adapt successfully and to provide opportunities to those individuals, whatever their social class or family background, to receive education and other perquisites from the society. They constituted the forerunners of the modern testing movement, which can be seen as a way of applying correlational psychology to the problem of identifying the fittest in the society and thereby providing them opportunities for social mobility and leadership.

The testing movement thus began as an attempt to divorce the ability of individuals from their social backgrounds by basing economic and social mobility on performance rather than on patrimony. Ironically, those who now oppose the testing movement base their opposition on the argument that tests merely support and amplify existing social class and ethnic differences.

Opposition to this application of Darwinism to social research developed quickly. Scientists and social reformers questioned the assumption that existing individual or group differences were durable or necessary by nature. Indeed, they claimed that such differences were typically historical or social artifacts created by political inequalities. The role of the educator, they asserted, was not merely to develop better ways of identifying the variations already occurring in nature in order to select individuals who are most competent. The responsibility of educators was to identify those interventions in nature that would lead to more successful adaptation and survival for the largest number of human beings. Thus, while survival of the fittest remained the watchword, the responsibility of the educator was to increase the proportion of individuals in the world who are fit, and the responsibility of the educational researcher was to experiment with alternative methods of rendering individuals more fit, more adaptable, than they might otherwise have become. This group was known historically as reform Darwinists, and their political philosophy is implicit in many applications of experimental methods to educational research.

The goal of the correlationist thus became to understand and exploit the natural and, presumably, enduring variations among individuals, while that of the experimentalist was to create conditions to reduce those variations.

This example of how the two major streams in scientific psychology are ultimately rooted in distinctive political or social commitments is not meant to leave the impression that these two alternatives must always remain sharply contrasted and never integrated. Indeed, many researchers have devoted their careers to identifying research methods capable of transcending the contrast between experimental and correlational methods. These investigators may ask, "For which kinds of learners do which kinds of teaching methods, school reforms, or other interventions work best?" That is a topic, however, that goes far beyond the proper subject of this discussion.

Thus, although Hippocrates was correlating and Galileo experimenting centuries before Darwin, these two strategies of research took on distinctly new ideological implications in the hands of competing Darwinists. In our day, the values commitment implicit in the choice of method is often unrecognized, even by the investigators themselves. This makes it even more dangerous to treat methodological issues without an understanding or concern for the specific substantive questions being asked. One of the enduring problems in research methodology has been the tendency to treat selection of method as primarily a technical question not associated with the underlying theoretical or substantive rationale of the research to be conducted.

Selecting the method most appropriate for a particular disciplined inquiry is one of the most important, and difficult, responsibilities of a researcher. The choice requires an act of judgment grounded in knowledge both of methodology and of the substantive area of the investigation.

Quantitative and Qualitative Methods

In looking at the differences between quantitative research methods and those typically dubbed qualitative, such as case study methods or ethnographic methods, we find another type of political or social contrast that is of interest. Quantitative methods, whether correlational or experimental, require relatively large and carefully selected samples of individuals. Quantitative approaches generally include sampling of both individuals and situations in ways that attempt to maximize the generalizability of the findings to the widest possible population. As noted earlier, correlational researchers sample from individuals and settings as they are rather than as they might be. And in much experimental research, choices of treatment sample conditions that tend to be within the realm of common experience.

In contrast, it is intriguing to examine the types of settings frequently studied by qualitative researchers. For example, studies of open classrooms, free schools, or other radical educational innovations are often conducted through case studies or ethnographic methods. In these studies, the researcher is attempting to portray the workings of circumstances that differ dramatically from what typically presents itself in the "natural" functioning of our society and our educational systems. It is as if the researcher is attempting to document, with vivid characterizations, that nature need not be the way it typically is. The researcher is attempting to communicate that we can create settings far different from those we may discover through random sampling. Moreover, disciplined inquiry carries the implicit message that those settings can be both sensible and rule governed.

Often qualitative researchers studying unusual educational settings accuse quantitative researchers attempting to characterize education, more generally, as committed to maintaining the educational status quo. Qualitative researchers, in contrast, often espouse a commitment to demonstrating the viability of truly alternative educational approaches.

I do not want to create these contrasts too starkly. Obviously, many studies of broader educational questions are conducted with qualitative methods, such as some of the more striking investigations of school desegregation or evaluations of special programs. Conversely, many quantitative studies of educational change, such as those conducted in the National Follow-Through experiment, are attempts to introduce significant new approaches to the practices of contemporary education. Here again, however, I have been trying to draw attention to the intricate ways in which the multiplicity of methods we have available in educational research presents us not merely with an enormous technical challenge but with the opportunity to investigate an impressive variety of questions from a rich set of alternative social and political perspectives.

Newer Forms of Inquiry: Dewey's Influence

This volume is filled with examples and discussions of both time-honored and relatively new developments in educational research methodology. I find it particularly interesting to examine more recent developments and their implications for the work of educational scholars. Although I could choose from many alternatives, there are two newer forms of educational inquiry that I will highlight to exemplify the kinds of changes that are under way in educational research. These examples merely are representative and are far from exhaustive. Other chapters in this volume beautifully exemplify additional contemporary approaches, such as those characterized by building on the methods and concepts of the arts and humanities. I will now, however, examine forms of teacher research and the concept of the design experiment. Each of these can be understood as a reflection of educational research returning to the traditions and principles first proposed by John Dewey at the beginning of this century.

To appreciate how much change is being introduced into educational research, we must acknowledge a rebirth of interest in John Dewey's thinking, not only as a philosopher of education but, indeed, as an educational leader with significant views regarding the conduct of educational scholarship. When Dewey pioneered in the creation of the Department of Pedagogy, Philosophy, and Psychology at the then-new University of

Chicago in the late 1890s, he brought with him a radical conception of educational research. He also introduced the concept of a "laboratory school" as part of a research university and contrasted that institution with the "demonstration schools" that were prevalent among the normal schools of that era.

The historian Ellen Lagemann (1988) has provided particularly important insights into Dewey's thinking at that time. She argues that Dewey held several key principles regarding research in education. Dewey's first principle was that educational research is essentially experimental and that these experiments must be carried out within the naturalistic settings of schools qua laboratories. This commitment to experimentation and intervention set him in clear opposition to the conservative Darwinists. The claim that educational research is both experimental and naturalistic subsequently became unpopular with educational researchers during most of this century. Real research occurred in laboratories, they would claim, not in nature. Only when natural processes could be manipulated under strictly controlled conditions could the power of scientific methods be realized. Nevertheless, Dewey claimed that educational research could and should combine both the experimental and the natural.

A second principle was that educational research should serve as a testing ground of the link between scientific and social innovation. Lagemann quotes Dewey's claim that a laboratory school's special function was to "create new standards and ideals and thus to lead to a gradual change in conditions" (1988, p. 197). Thus, the laboratory school does not serve solely as a setting for testing research hypotheses and discovering psychological principles, although that is a significant role. The laboratory school also is a site for "existence proofs." If we can create and sustain a particular instructional innovation in a real school, we have demonstrated the possibility that it can exist. Once its existence has been demonstrated, we can study its characteristics and the conditions that either foster or inhibit its development. Thus, the laboratory qua school and school qua laboratory become settings for creating and documenting visions of the possible.

In these senses, Dewey's vision was of a field of educational research that was inseparable from developmental efforts in curriculum design and school reform. One studied, for example, the learning and teaching of school subjects through the development of innovative curriculum in a radically redesigned school context. The notion that one could achieve understanding of the principles of school learning in settings far removed from schools and their curriculum materials was absurd for Dewey.

Teacher Research

One of the most dramatic examples of this kind of inquiry in our own day is the creation of forms of "teacher research," such as those exemplified by the work of Magdalene Lampert. In these studies, the investigators are themselves teachers who are both subjects and objects of research. The teacher-scholars in question not only investigate teaching; they are the teachers under investigation. Not since the earliest days of modern psychology, when Hermann Ebbinghaus (1883/1913) used himself as a subject in his own laboratory experiments on memory, have scholars made themselves the objects of study. Even then, the conditions of the research were far more controlled and artificial, and the function under investigation—memory of a list of nonsense syllables—was hardly an arena for special expertise. The research on classroom mathematics teaching of Magdalene Lampert serves as a bridge between the psychological study of the learning and teaching of school subjects and the long-neglected tenets of the Dewey school: to study education by designing new practices of teaching and learning school subjects and examining the conditions and consequences of their implementation.

For a number of years, Magdalene Lampert has taught the mathematics curriculum to a fifth-grade class in a Michigan public elementary school. She would assume responsibility for math teaching from the classroom's full-time teacher and would teach the mathematics lessons for each day, collect abundant examples of student work, videotape many of the classroom interactions, maintain detailed journals recounting and reflecting on her own practice, periodically examine the children using both standardized and custom-designed assessments, plan the next day's lessons, and then begin the process anew. Using her own thinking, acting, and reflecting as the database, she analyzed the practice of teaching and learning mathematics. She attempted to document her plans, goals, and strategies; to reconstruct the recurring dilemmas and decisions she faced; and to analyze and classify those dilemmas and decisions in systematic terms. Here was reflective teaching in nearly prototypical form.

In her published papers, Lampert attempted to characterize the routine dilemmas of mathematics teaching, employing extensive case materials from her own practice to support her arguments. She asked what it meant to teach and learn mathematics with understanding and used detailed descriptions of her interactions with students to illustrate her points. Reading Lampert's articles, one begins to develop a clearer sense of the complexities of teachers' thinking, judgments, and decisions, as well as their actions and their consequences, when they actively pursue the goals of higher order mathematical thinking with their students. In this work, Lampert exemplified several aspects of a new approach to research in education. She exemplified most specifically an emphasis on analysis of the nature of mathematical learning and knowing among students and the development of a research methodology for teachers conducting reflective case studies of their own practice.

In Lampert's work, we encounter a research method that substantially erodes the time-honored distinction between subject and object, between the researcher and the researched. Lampert is in fact a university professor who spends part of each day in classrooms, but teacher research is not limited to university-based scholars. We are also witnessing an upsurge in the study of teaching by full-time classroom teachers (Cochran-Smith & Lytle, 1993). I anticipate that this development will grow sufficiently in strength to provide yet another new paradigm for educational research in which teachers organize efforts to investigate their own practice, to document and analyze student learning and motivation, and to pursue other inquiries best undertaken by educators who maintain an ongoing and continuous relationship with life in schools and classrooms because they are full-time inhabitants of those settings rather than episodic visitors.

Let no one be deceived regarding the complexity of such work and the demands it places on its practitioners. Lampert and her like-minded colleagues are quite unusual scholar-practitioners. They are not only experienced classroom teachers with the skills and dispositions to conduct disciplined inquiries into their own practice; they are also deeply knowledgeable about their subject matter and the principles of its pedagogy. The admonition that researchers must be well versed in the substance of the subject matters whose pedagogy they study is not limited to university personnel. If teacher researchers wish to pursue investigations of the psychology and/or pedagogy of particular school subjects, they will need the kind of substantive sophistication displayed by Lampert. Equally important, Lampert and her colleagues have solid grounding in the canons of disciplined inquiry and its documentation. The legitimacy of being "insiders" and speaking with the "teacher's voice" does not, in itself, establish a warrant for the claims of teacher research.

Teachers as Collaborators and Investigators

The work of Lampert and her colleagues is likely to signal the entry of many more teachers into the world of school-based research. Once we privilege the natural classroom and school site as a proper setting for research on the psychology of school subjects and proceed to relax our methodological orthodoxies and offer legitimacy to such forms of inquiry as case studies and investigations of one's own practice, we invite classroom teachers to join us as investigators. Interestingly, John Dewey argued that the teachers in the Laboratory School should be co-investigators with the professors and graduate students. When Lagemann (1988) characterized the relationship that Dewey and his close colleague George Herbert Mead had with the remarkable Jane Addams, she observed that Addams's "most characteristic medium was the anecdote and . . . [Dewey and Mead's] was the theoretical hypothesis" (p. 195). Narrative may be a much more natural form of discourse for schoolteachers than are the more paradigmatic forms favored by social scientists. The new language of a collaborative form of inquiry may well evolve into a kind of narrative-paradigmatic pidgin.

However, there is always a danger that any study undertaken by a practitioner is treated with deference and any investigation pursued by an outside investigator is greeted with suspicion. The "worry over warrant" should never wane (Phillips, 1987). The identity, role, experience, and skill of the investigator is an important aspect of a work's validity, especially in those research methods (such as ethnography) in which separation of the method from the investigator is difficult. Nevertheless, judgments of validity can never be reduced to reading the resumé of the investigator, whether in teacher research or in any other form of inquiry.

If teacher research represents one new strategy of educational inquiry, another is the development of "design experiments." These strategies can be seen as attempts to wed the systematic design and intervention impulses of the classical experiment with the natural classroom-based adaptiveness of real teachers teaching real children.

Design Experiments

Alan Collins (1992) and Ann Brown (1992) have begun to advocate a new form of theory-oriented action research in classrooms that they call "design experiments." These are curriculum-specific interventions in classrooms that are theoretically driven, collaboratively designed, and progressively adapted with classroom teachers, and documented and assessed via combinations of quantitative and qualitative methods (conjunctions of ethnography and measurement); such interventions willfully confound multiple independent variables in ways that would make most traditional methodologists blanch. Consistent with Dewey's principles, they are both experimental and naturalistic. If it is necessary to work within a natural classroom learning environment to study real school learning in a generalizable manner, then we may have no choice but to pursue much of educational research in such settings. Brown insists that there remain good reasons to explore some psychological processes under more pristine and controlled laboratory conditions, and I certainly have no cause to disagree. The alternation between natural sites and highly controlled settings may characterize the future dance steps of educational research. And the other needed form of flexibility may well be a methodological versatility that will include much more vigorous uses of field research methods and case studies in the pursuit of understanding. Along with their design characteristics, another feature of these approaches is the frequency with which the investigators either do their own teaching or, more frequently, collaborate actively and interactively with classroom teachers, who participate as partners in both the design and adaptation of the interventions studied.

Design experiments in natural settings conducted collaboratively with practitioners produce a set of research methods unimagined by the educational researcher of the 1940s and 1950s, not to mention a set of approaches that makes many contemporary educational researchers profoundly uncomfortable. Pretest and posttest measures are regularly used (along with midcourse monitoring) to establish the direction and degree of changes in students' knowledge, understandings, and attitudes. These measures include multiple-choice examinations, essays, project reports, and analyses of discourse during lessons. Ethnographers, videographers, and discourse analysts collect data in many forms to document the patterns of interaction and engagement, of self-regulation and conversation, characteristic of teachers and students in the classroom under different circumstances. Teacher journals are compared with the participant observer's notes, and student portfolios provide evidence of how the students made sense of the instruction. The control group, that most ubiquitous of signs that the "scientific method" is in use, typically disappears in a design experiment. Since this is not an experiment in which a single variable is manipulated while all else remains constant, it is unclear what one would control. An entire program or curriculum is the treatment, and that treatment is redesigned and adapted as needed. The logic of the classic control group thus becomes moot. Control must be introduced, needless to say, but through systematic documentation and frequent, precise measurement.

In addition to serving as a manifestation of Dewey's conception of educational research that is both experimental and naturalistic, the design experiment also represents an attempt to bridge the gap between new versions of the "two disciplines" of educational scholarship. If, in Cronbach's day, the tension was between the interventionism of experimentation and the naturalism of correlation, both of which are quantitative forms of psychological inquiry usually carried out under laboratory or carefully instrumented conditions, the contemporary tension might be characterized as one between the classroom-based experimental program and the naturalistic documentation and analysis of classroom life. That is, the two disciplines of today could be viewed as broad-scale, systematic, classroom-based experimentation on the one hand and rich, ethnographic descriptions and analyses of classroom life on the other hand. A design experiment is typically a marriage of experiment and ethnography, of adaptive experimentation and thick ethnographic description.

Choosing Among Methods

For many years, the most frequently used educational research methods, and therefore those with the greatest legitimacy, have been the quantitative methods of experimental, correlational, quasi-experimental, and survey research. Their disciplinary roots are in agriculture, genetics, and other studies of heredity, psychology, and actuarial studies of life expectancies conducted two centuries ago in the service of insurance companies. They not only share fairly long traditions in education but also carry with them the prestige of quantifiable precision. Through the application of modern statistical methods, researchers can more precisely estimate the likelihood and size of errors in estimates of the state of nature than is usually possible in approaches deriving from anthropology, history, the arts, or philosophy. Should we tend to use the more traditional methods because we understand them better and they have a longer track record? John Stuart Mill argued:

> If there are some subjects on which the results obtained have finally received the unanimous assent of all who have attended to the proof, and others which . . . have never succeeded in establishing any considerable body of truths, so as to be beyond denial or doubt; it is by generalizing the methods successfully followed by the former enquiries and adapting them to the latter, that we may hope to remove this blot on the face of science.

Yet, an equally brilliant British philosopher of the next century, Alfred North Whitehead, was far less certain that well-developed and understood methods were always likely to be superior. He observed: "Some of the major disasters of mankind have been produced by the narrowness of men with a good methodology . . . to set limits to speculation is treason to the future."

If we are not always well advised to choose the methods that have been used the longest and that we understand best, what of choosing methods on the grounds of precision, on the grounds that some methods provide us a much better base for knowing exactly how much we know and how much is likely to be error? Here again, we are advised to focus first on our problem and its characteristics before we rush to select the appropriate method. We can again hark back to Aristotle, who made this famous point about precision in *Ethics:*

> Our discussion will be adequate if it has as much clearness as the subject matter admits of, for precision is not to be sought for alike in all discussions, any more than in all the products of crafts. . . . For it is the mark of an educated man to look for precision in each class of things just so far as the nature of the subject admits; it is evidently equally foolish to accept probable reasoning from a mathematician and to demand from a rhetorician scientific proofs (1947b, pp. 309–310).

We must avoid becoming educational researchers slavishly committed to a particular method. The image of the little boy who has just received a hammer for a birthday present and suddenly finds that the entire world looks to him like a variety of nails is too painfully familiar to be tolerated. We must first understand our problem and decide what questions we are asking, and then we must select the mode of disciplined inquiry most appropriate to those questions. If the proper methods are highly quantitative and objective, fine. If they are more subjective or qualitative, we can use them responsibly as well.

The anthropologist Geertz (1973) probably put it best:

> I have never been impressed by the argument that, as complete objectivity is impossible in these matters (as, of course, it is) one might as well let one's sentiments run loose. As Robert Solow has remarked, that is like saying that as a perfectly aseptic environment is impossible, one might as well conduct surgery in a sewer (p. 30).

Geertz also observed, as cited in Wolcott's discussion of ethnographic research method, "You don't have to know everything to understand something."

Summary

I shall now summarize the important points I have tried to make in this introductory discussion of research methodology. What distinguishes research from other forms of human discourse is the application of research methods. When we conduct educational research, we make the claim that there is method to our madness. Educational research methods are forms of disciplined inquiry. They are disciplined in that they follow sets of rules and principles for pursuing investigations. They are also disciplined in another sense. They have emerged from underlying social or natural science disciplines that have well-developed canons of discovery and verification for making and testing truth claims in their fields. Education itself is not a single discipline but, rather, a field of study on which we bring to bear the various forms of disciplined inquiry discussed here.

Each of these forms of inquiry asks different questions. I have tried to illustrate some of the questions characteristic of several forms of educational research methodology. I also have tried to indicate the ways in which the selection of research method is frequently related to theoretical or ideological commitments of the investigator (for a particularly instructive example of this principle in the history of education, see Tyack, 1976). (Parenthetically, the possibilities of doing certain kinds of social research change as the political and social mood of a society evolves. For example, the notion of randomly assigning individuals to contrasting experimental treatment groups may seem far less acceptable a research strategy in these days of legislation requiring informed consent and protection of human subjects. Can we continue to practice experimental social and educational research and still abide by the law of the land that requires informed consent of all participants in research?)

Finally, each of the examples of research methodology discussed must in some fashion deal with questions of precision and generalizability, although the standards and criteria will vary from one form of disciplined inquiry to another.

The neophyte educational researcher, when confronted with this imposing array of alternative research methodologies, may be tempted to throw up his or her hands in despair and say, "What can I possibly do to become competent in this field?" I can suggest several answers. First, attempt to become skilled and experienced in at least two forms of research methodology. Facility in only one strikes me as somewhat dangerous, the equivalent of a methodological "Johnny One-Note." Second, be fully aware of the full, rich variety of methods that constitute the family of disciplined inquiry in educational research. Recognize that the most effective programs of educational research are likely to be characterized by what Merton (1975), the distinguished sociologist, and Schwab (1969), the eminent philosopher of education, have called applications of "disciplined eclectic." The best research programs will reflect intelligent deployment of a diversity of research methods applied to their appropriate research questions. Finally, do not limit your education to methodology alone; only by combining substantive knowledge and methodological competence will you become a well-rounded, effective educational researcher. Here, once again, an insight of Aristotle's is relevant.

> Now each man judges well the things he knows, and of these he is a good judge. And so the man who has been educated in a subject is a good judge of that subject, and the man who has received an all-round education is a good judge in general (1947b, p. 310).

Selection of appropriate methods is an act of judgment that may be undertaken privately but must be justified and explained publicly.

Epilogue: Method Revisited

Ernest Boyer made a simple claim in his influential monograph *Scholarship Reconsidered.* He stated that the work of the scholar "becomes consequential only as it is understood by others" (p. 23). While Boyer placed that sentence thoughtfully and strategically in his introduction to the notion of the scholarship of teaching, clearly the claim applies equally well to all forms of scholarship. That is, scholarship in all of its forms becomes consequential only as it is understood by others—others who are engaged in related processes of discovery, invention, and investigation—and thus it becomes consequential as it stimulates, builds upon, critiques, or otherwise contributes to any community of scholars who depend on one another's discoveries, critical reviews, and inventive applications to move the work of the field ahead.

In that connection, it may be useful to recall that the root meaning of the word *method* did not originally refer to a technique for collecting or analyzing data. The "method" used by scholars was traditionally the form of argument, the chain of reasoning in which they organized their premises, their evidence, and their logical moves to create a cogent, persuasive argument that would enlighten their students and peers. Thus, a scholar's method referred to the manner in which he or she organized and taught what was discovered to others. Even today, although we ordinarily distinguish clearly between methods of teaching and methods of research, both are based on the same underlying notion: the organization and application of a coherent, well-reasoned, and persuasive argument that can enlighten and shape the understandings of others. One's method combines the ways one organizes one's ideas, the cogency with which one presents them in a reasoned argument, and the routines one uses to conduct one's disciplined inquiries. To understand research methods properly, therefore, we must understand the function of method within the larger operation of scholarly work and scholarly communities. In the final analysis, a shared sense of research method holds a scholarly community together and permits it to operate communally and collaboratively.

The Community of Scholars and Scholarship as Community Property

To engage in the processes of inquiry, to become a scholar of and in education, is not only to take on the mantle of method and the rigor of discipline. It entails becoming an active member of a community of scholars and a community of educators. We must pursue and publish our research in ways that reflect the moral obligations of community membership. These obligations are entailed when we recognize that this is a community whose members are interdependent; each of us depends on the trust we can place in the work of other members of the community, because an intellectual and scholarly community rests on the assumption that its members can build on each other's work. We offer our findings, our new knowledge, to one another as community property. (Think of the trust we place in the purity of the food we eat, the preparation and training of the pilots in whose planes we fly, or the physicians in whose hands we entrust our bodies.)

It is no accident that the most grievous sins that a scholar can commit are not the sins of intellectual error. That is, if you do a piece of research and report your findings honestly in a manner consistent with the technical and ethical standards of "method," and subsequently other scholars conclude that your argument was flawed or your data do not hold up, you remain an honorable and respected member of the scholarly community. You are like the judge on a lower court whose decision is reversed by a higher one. All good scholars can point to examples of their own published papers whose claims did not hold up over time because of the critical scrutiny of their research community. Indeed, that is the way the system is designed to work.

The unforgivable sins, however, are plagiarism, appropriating the work of others without attribution, and fraud, the willful misrepresentation of one's data and methods. That is, if a researcher uses the words and work of another scholar (especially taking his or her very words verbatim) without acknowledgment of the source, he or she has committed an act of plagiary. So important is the trust we place in the care with which other scholars have conducted their studies and the accuracy with which they have reported their work that we have developed a system of citations, references, and bibliographic acknowledgments to document our use of their ideas and the extent to which we are building on their findings. Thus, if a scholar makes a claim and cites another scholar's work in conjunction with that claim, the presence of the reference is judged to strengthen the warrant of the claim.

If an investigator knowingly misrepresents findings or procedures of analysis, he or she is guilty of fraud. If a researcher reports having conducted an analysis following certain rules or principles, and it turns out that he or she did not, that scholar has violated so fundamental a tenet of the scholarly community that he or she risks severe public censure or even expulsion by its members. Simply put, no individual scholar working alone can possibly discover or integrate the knowledge he or she needs. We depend on the trust we can place on the methodological integrity of our peers to support and advance one another's work.

How is knowledge as community property different from other forms of property? For scholars, research is community property because it can be used again and again in the building and rebuilding of knowledge. The same findings, the same cases, the same criticisms and analyses can be used in the construction of many arguments and chains of narrative. A work of research does not get used up. It is not like a brick, a board, or any other piece of normal building material. If anything, a piece of research becomes more robust and sturdy the more often it is used by its author and by others to support new arguments and to undergird new claims.

So, what is the most fundamental obligation of the disciplined inquirer, the responsibility from which all of the canons of method derive? I will never forget a conversation I had with my former teacher, Benjamin Bloom of the University of Chicago, while serving as his research assistant. He had just conducted an unconventional (to my youthful eyes) statistical analysis on a set of data we had discovered in a 60-year-old archival source. "Are you permitted to do that?" I asked suspiciously. Bloom smiled at me indulgently and replied, "You are permitted to do anything you please as long as you honestly and completely report what you did, how you did it, and your reasons for doing it so that your colleagues are fully informed. They are then in a position to judge whether or not they are prepared to accept the warrant for your claims and to be persuaded by your findings." As the physicist Percy Bridgeman once asserted (doubtless having heard these lines from his own teachers), "Scientific method is doing one's damnedest with one's mind, no holds barred." As long, I would add, as you fully reveal to your readers exactly which "holds" you employed.

Every researcher must ask of his or her investigation, "What is this a case of?" whether the study is a design experiment, a school-reform ethnography, a classical regression analysis, or a singular piece of teacher research. The claim to generalizability for any study, whether to a population of persons or of situations, must be established through exhaustive reporting of one's settings, data, and methods, along with a carefully reasoned argument. Most often, the argument must be rooted in a combination of theory and careful documentation of conditions. Technique alone can never warrant generalizability.

The well-known adage "publish or perish" is typically understood as a commentary on the academic profession and its vicissitudes. It has a deeper meaning, however. Scholars must recognize that their obligation is not only to learn but to teach. If scholars do not publish important discoveries, integrations, or applications for their peers, their ideas will perish, their insights will wither and die.

Research Methods and Their Disciplines

Taken together, the observations I have made lead to the conclusion that the research methods of education have undergone a radical change in recent years. There has been a decided qualitative turn reflecting the influence of cognitive science, anthropology, the arts, and linguistics. Interpretive, aesthetic, and hermeneutic approaches have become more widespread. This turn has been further amplified by an interest in everyday school and classroom life as a basis for both disciplinary and interdisciplinary investigation. Nevertheless, formal experiments and the increasingly inventive methods of inferential statistics remain quite central to our enterprise, and appropriately so. In fact, the norm for educational research has become an eclectic combining of approaches that were once considered noncommensurable. Design experiments are a lovely example of that combination.

A variety of methods comprise educational research: historical, philosophical, case studies, ethnographic field studies, hermeneutics, experiments, quasi-experiments, aesthetic criticisms, surveys. Each is demanding and rigorous and follows disciplined rules or procedures. Taken together, these approaches build a methodological mosaic that is the most exciting current field of applied social research: the study of education.

REFERENCES

Aristotle. (1947a). De anima [On the soul]. In R. McKeon (Ed.), *Introduction to Aristotle* (pp. 135–245). New York: Modern Library.

Aristotle. (1947b). Nicomachean ethics. In R. McKeon (Ed.), *Introduction to Aristotle* (pp. 308–543). New York: Modern Library.

Boyer, E. L. (1990). *Scholarship reconsidered: Priorities of the professoriate.* Princeton, NJ: The Carnegie Foundation for the Advancement of Teaching.

Brown, A. L. (1992). Design experiments: Theoretical and methodological challenges in creating complex interventions in classroom settings. *Journal of the Learning Sciences, 2*(2), 141–178.

Cochran-Smith, M., & Lytle, S. L. (1993). *Inside-outside: Teacher research and knowledge.* New York: Teachers College Press.

Collins, A. (1992). Toward a design science of education. In E. Scanlon & T. O'Shea (Eds.), *New directions in educational technology.* New York: Springer.

Cornfield, J., & Tukey, J. W. (1956). Average values of mean squares in factorials. *Annals of Mathematical Statistics, 27,* 907–959.

Cremin, L. A. (1961). *The transformation of the school.* New York: Vintage Books.

Cronbach, L. J. (1957). The two disciplines of scientific psychology. *American Psychologist, 12,* 671–684.

Cronbach, L. J., & Suppes, P. (Eds.). (1969). *Research for tomorrow's schools: Disciplined inquiry for education.* New York: Macmillan.

Ebbinghaus, H. (1913). *Memory: A contribution to experimental psychology.* New York: Teachers College Press. (Original work published 1883).

Geertz, C. (1973). Thick description. In C. Geertz (Ed.), *The interpretation of cultures* (pp. 3–30). New York: Basic Books.

Lagemann, E. (1988). The plural worlds of educational research. *History of Education Quarterly, 29*(2), 184–214.

Merton, R. K. (1975). Structural analysis in sociology. In P. Blau (Ed.), *Approaches to the study of social structure.* New York: Free Press.

Phillips, D. C. (1987). Validity in qualitative research: Why the worry about warrant will not wane. *Education and Urban Society, 20*(1), 9–24.

Schwab, J. J. (1969). The practical: A language for curriculum. *School Review, 78,* 1–23.

Tyack, D. (1976). Ways of seeing: An essay on the history of compulsory schooling. *Harvard Educational Review, 46,* 355–389.

INTRODUCTION

TEACHING ALONE, LEARNING TOGETHER: NEEDED AGENDAS FOR THE NEW REFORMS (1988)

IN AN ARTICLE not included in this anthology, Shulman and a Stanford graduate student, Neil Carey, had explored the idea of bounded and collective rationality and the importance of community for learning (Shulman and Carey, 1987). In this essay, Shulman begins to work out the connections between his interests in teacher knowledge and collective rationality, especially with regard to the role of case knowledge in teaching and the functions of such a literature in a professional community. He begins by arguing that, if teachers are to learn and change, they need both collegiality and community. The professionalization of teaching will require an empowerment of teachers' minds, for accomplished teaching requires considerable knowledge and judgment.

REFERENCE

Shulman, L. S., and Carey, N. B. "Psychology and the Limitations of Individual Rationality: Implications for the Study of Reasoning and Civility." *Review of Educational Research,* 1984, *54*(4), 501–524.

10

TEACHING ALONE, LEARNING TOGETHER

NEEDED AGENDAS FOR THE NEW REFORMS

A SKEPTIC APPROACHED the great rabbi Hillel and asked that sage to teach him the full message of the Torah in a single proposition. Hillel responded, "Do not do unto your fellow man what you would not have him do unto you. That is the essence; the rest is commentary." There is a parallel proposition I now suggest as the essential principle of educational reform. Do not do unto teachers what you would not have teachers do unto students. This is the essence; the rest (which I shall not, alas, spare you) is commentary.[1]

The theme of this volume, directing reforms to issues that count, echoes the recurrent calls for reform of the nation's schools and of the preparation of its teachers. Those reform agendas have many authors and many locations, but they are remarkably similar in many of their visions, if often mixed in their motives.

Tracing back the discussion of quality education to first principles, one is bound to examine, not issues of schooling or even teaching, but of learning. The argument of this chapter is that twenty-first century conceptions of learning now coexist with nineteenth-century conceptions of teaching. What is held to be true of learning in students must, of necessity, hold true for teaching and teachers. Most reform agendas rest on the assumption that teachers are capable of learning, both in programs of formal preservice preparation and in the course of an extended professional career, and that teachers can improve with experience. Changes are needed in classrooms to render them more powerful environments for student learning, and similar changes are needed in classrooms and schools to make them suitable settings for teacher learning. Teacher collegiality and collaboration are not important merely for the improvement of morale and teacher satisfaction (which always sounds like a lame argument in favor of satisfied teachers, regardless of whether they succeed in teaching kids); they are absolutely necessary if teaching is to be of the highest order and thus compatible with the standards of excellence demanded by the recent reforms. Collegiality and collaboration are also needed to ensure that teachers benefit from their experiences and continue to grow during their careers. However, few accomplishments are as hellishly difficult as learning from experience. Both teaching and learning to teach are remarkably challenging tasks.

The Reforms and Their Assumptions

In looking at the new reforms, one must examine the assumptions that undergird them and the assertions they share. The reforms that have been proposed since 1982, whether by the Excellence Commission, the Carnegie Task Force on the Teaching Profession, the Holmes Group, or the many state advisory groups, generally share certain key assumptions and characteristics. These can be organized under three headings: assumptions about learners, about teachers, and about schools and schooling.

Learners

The "first wave" of reform called for much greater emphasis on the achievement of excellence for all students, and "excellence" increasingly took on a more "classical" character. The generally improving results of the National Assessment of Educational Progress (NAEP) testing around the country and the apparent reversal of the decline in SAT scores have quieted the call to go back to basics, at least basics as defined by the fairly simple fundamentals of reading, computation, and writing. However, the NAEP results also reported that the American learner is incapable of employing higher-order thinking, that his or her problem-solving abilities are stunted and critical thinking skills untapped. Moreover, this learner is ignorant of the most basic ideas of Western civilization and is unenlightened by the culture's most central texts. These texts include works of the great philosophers, works of great writers from Homer and the Bard to Sinclair Lewis and Ralph Ellison, and fundamental tracts on the formation of U.S. government, such as the Federalist Papers and the Constitution.

In a tone reminiscent of earlier calls for reform (such as that of Joseph Mayer Rice in the 1890s), reformers urge a reduction of rote learning and uninspired teaching in the schools and a quest for the higher-order thinking and reasoning that ought to characterize American classrooms. Dumbed-down curricula are to be shunned; dumbed-down teachers are to be unemployed. Moreover, in recent critical reviews of the research on Title I programs for disadvantaged students, it was concluded that principles of excellence are not limited in their application to the most advantaged learners. The children of the poor have been frequently mistaught in programs that overemphasized remedial and basic-skills orientations, thus depriving them of the stimulation of needed schoolwork on problem solving and reasoning. Thus, emphasis on higher-order goals is the strategy of choice for the achievement of equity as well as for the promotion of excellence.

This conception of learning as higher order, constructive, and inventive is not all that new, yet for the first time it has a substantial body of psychological and anthropological research to support it. The view of the learner as someone who can discover new principles through active involvement with the materials and media of instruction is predicated on fairly recent concepts of how meanings are constructed in the learning process. Those views will be examined shortly, after first focusing on the reform assumptions associated with that other indispensable partner in the educational process, the teacher.

Teachers

Without question, teachers and the professionalization of teaching are at the heart of the recent "second wave" of reform initiatives. The first assumption is that teaching is difficult. It requires substantial content preparation, so a minimum standard of a bachelor's degree in a discipline is called for—even for elementary school teachers, who have not traditionally been viewed as content specialists. Teaching requires additional preparation in pedagogy, perhaps including a master's degree as a minimum standard. Teaching requires a serious period of supervised internship or residency. Most of all, teaching requires the definition and application of rigorous standards for entry into the occupation and progress through it. The current standards (or lack thereof) will simply not do.[2]

These reform documents link the vision of a profession peopled by more talented and better prepared practitioners to a new image of schools as organizations and of a teaching career. The schools, reformers say, should be organized to provide far greater opportunities for leadership and differentiation of role for the gifted veteran teachers. The career of a teacher should develop alternative trajectories that would permit the able pedagogue to remain in the classroom for substantial periods, yet also perform other roles as teacher educator, mentor, curriculum developer, university faculty member, and the like. A greater variety of teaching roles should be defined, as befits the variations in both degrees of preparation and advanced specialization that could become commonplace.

These reform recommendations are rooted in several fundamental assumptions. Teachers can learn to teach. Moreover, they can become better teachers as they learn from experience. They are capable of reflecting on their own practice (both in action and in reenactment), thereby discerning the proper ways to adapt their thoughts and actions to future challenges. Yet the vision of learning to teach, of improving with experience through the employment of strategies of reflection and review, is predicated on the availability of that most precious and rare commodity for a teacher—time. This includes both time for individual reflection and for collective deliberation, for thinking alone and for being thoughtful with others. Thus, there is a need to reorganize schools to become places where the opportunities for thought, the organizational characteristics that promote thinking, and an institutional reward system can work jointly to make learning from experience (and teaching by the experienced) commonplace.

EMPOWERMENT AND RESPONSIBILITY. The word that is bandied about most frequently in discussing the needed reforms of teaching is "empowerment." It is an unfortunate choice of terms, because it conjures up visions of a struggle for control over the schools. Empowerment in my terms is not expressed in collective bargaining victories or in wrestling authority from principals and distributing it among juntas of teachers. The empowerment needed in the current reforms is a complex phenomenon that would enable teachers to exercise the talents and capacities that the new conceptions of teaching require.

Teacher empowerment in this sense is an empowerment of *mind,* of *spirit,* of *status,* and of *role.* The teacher is enabled by a knowledge base—the knowledge and skill needed to be effective in teaching; by commitment—the passion, motivation, and ethical norms necessary to persevere responsibly in the face of discouragement and difficulty; by the status of a professional—the standing associated with a trusted and respected individual whose functions are viewed by the society as absolutely essential for its survival; and by his or her formal institutional roles—ascribed functions within organizations that permit the fruits of mind, spirit, and status to be exercised productively in the education of students.

Without such elaborations, the concept of empowerment is empty and even dangerous. Societies should not grant power to those who do not have the intellectual commitments and moral capacities to wield it justly. Teacher empowerment is justified when it affords teachers the autonomy needed to perform their tasks effectively and the freedom required to engage students productively.

The Schools

With this new image of a setting and a career path for teachers, new images of schools emerge. These tend to take on two competing forms. Those that derive from the first wave of reform emphasize the model of "effective schools." They identify leadership with charismatic and powerful administrators, who help create a climate of shared high academic expectations for all students and a collective commitment to academic values and activities. However, in the most recent teacher-centered reform conceptions of groups such as Holmes and Carnegie, quite a different view emerges. Teachers are now seen as exercising substantial leadership at the building level. Schools are asked to become more like our best corporations, employing modern methods of management to decentralize authority, to make important decisions where the street-level bureaucrats reside. Leadership is not monopolized by administrators but is shared with teachers.

I began with the argument that we should guide the reform of teaching and schooling with a variation on the principle of Hillel. We should not treat teachers in a manner inconsistent with the ways in which we treat students. Teaching must be viewed as resting on a case of learning, thinking, and reasoning quite similar to the standards of student learning, thinking, and reasoning that have inspired the first wave of reform.

In the next section, I describe the current conceptions of learning and teaching that underlie efforts to reform the conditions for student learning. These efforts rest on ideas about human rationality and its enhancement that emphasize the centrality of higher-order reasoning and its fostering in the real world. The next section examines the extent to which these notions of rationality and deliberation also characterize valued conceptions of schooling in a democratic society, as reflected in the writings of John Dewey. Then follows a discussion of the ways in which the requirements for student learning are also requirements for teacher development, as the parallels between the conditions for learning and the conditions for teaching are reviewed.

Varieties of Rationality: Conceptions of Learning and Teaching

Several years ago I published a paper with Neil Carey,[3] in which we explored the ways in which human learning had been represented by philosophers and psychologists. We argued that there were at least four ways in which philosophers and psychologists had attempted to explain why human beings reason and act as they do. They are all responses to Aristotle's claim that man is a rational animal. These accounts can be summarized in the following assertions:

- Humans are rational; they think and act in a manner consistent with their goals, their self interest, and their reinforcement histories. To induce them to behave in a given way, make the desired behavior clear to them and make it worth their while to engage in it.
- Humans are irrational; they are driven by motives and needs of which they are generally unconscious and over which they exercise little control. To induce them to change, help them grasp and come to terms with their underlying motives and fears, so that they can exercise more direct control over their intentions and actions.
- Humans are limited in their rationality; they can make sense of only a small piece of the world at a time, and they strive to act reasonably with respect to their limited grasp of facts and alternatives. They must therefore construct conceptions or definitions of situations rather than passively accept what is presented to them. To induce them to change, engage them in active problem solving and judgment; don't just tell them what to do.
- Humans are rational only when acting together; since individual reason is so limited, men and women find opportunities to work jointly on important problems, achieving through joint effort what individual reason and capacity could never accomplish. To induce them to change, develop ways in which they can engage in the change process jointly with peers.

The first principle (man as rational) was consistent with claims that individuals learned to do those things for which they were rewarded, learned best through imitation, drill, and practice, and generally learned to act in ways consistent with their self-interest as they understood it. Thus, schools were defined as places where the contents of a culture were arranged and transmitted, where pupils were evaluated on the basis of their mastery of the contents of that culture, and where teachers were most likely to improve when they could receive rewards based on their merit—which was defined as their success in transmitting the cultural capital to their students.

According to the second principle (man as an irrational animal), the human being's sources of inconsistency and anxieties were of greatest moment. Why did people so often appear to act against their own self-interest? Why did they fail to feel motivated toward activities that they sincerely felt were desirable? Why did they misunderstand the "plain meaning" of a communication and distort their interpretation in such outlandish ways? Applied to schools, these principles called upon educators to engage the emotional and affective commitments of teachers and students—to influence their unconscious motives as they responded to the goals and processes of schools as sites for human interaction and passions.

The third principle (man as boundedly rational) held that human beings were always constructing meanings because they had no other way to keep track of everything that was going on around them. Individuals had no choice but to simplify the world around them in terms of some principles, the most powerful of which was that new learnings must be rendered consistent with older knowledge and belief. Thus, children sitting in classrooms always reinterpreted whatever teachers said to them, the better to coordinate what they were learning with what they had learned earlier. Teachers were also forced to simplify their perceptions and understandings of students; it was simply impossible to be accurate in thinking about all 160 or more students that an average high school teacher saw in a day. Simplifications should not be read as distortions, but as unavoidable adaptations.

Thus, young children learning new methods of calculation in primary arithmetic classes regularly adapt the method they are taught by the teacher and invent new algorithms of their own. High school students learning about natural selection in a biology course often manage to leave the course continuing to believe that evolution involves the transmission of acquired characteristics, even though teachers never teach them that. Teachers adopt modes of instruction that reduce the complexity and unpredictability of classroom life, especially when they feel relatively unfamiliar with the content being taught.[4]

The fourth principle, called *collective rationality,* argues that the solution to the limitations of individual rationality does not lie exclusively in the construction or invention of individual solutions. On the contrary, human beings regularly accomplish tasks whose complexity exceeds the limitations of individual information processing, by collaborating on the different aspects of an otherwise overwhelming task. For an individual, piloting a Boeing 747 is impossible; for a three-person crew, it is straightforward. However, the crew does not work in isolation; they are dependent on large numbers of mechanics and other service personnel, cabin attendants, air traffic controllers, pilot educators who keep crewmembers abreast of the latest developments and sharp in their responses to problem situations, and many others. From the prosaic demands of repairing a flat tire on a dark highway ("If you'll just hold that flashlight while I . . .") to the complex requirements of flying a modern passenger jet, collective rationality is the most frequent human response to the challenges of coping with otherwise impossible tasks.

The four conceptions of rationality, while posed as alternatives, are not necessarily incompatible. There are aspects of each that can be invoked appropriately to characterize different facets of human activity, or different settings in which human beings employ reason and emotion in the pursuit of their goals. Nevertheless, I write this chapter from a particular point of view. The demands being made on teachers call for them to act critically, decisively, and self-correctively under conditions that do not promote or support those processes. The solution to the dilemma is inherent in the principles of collective rationality.

It is now understood that teaching is, in many ways, an impossible job in which to succeed as an individual. The demands are too great, the range of talents required is too broad and varied, the requirements for learning from experience exceed the capacities of an individual learner. Nevertheless, the jobs of both students and of teachers are defined in ways that treat collectivization as odd or sinful. When students work together on an assignment or test, they are often accused of cheating. Teachers who seek to collaborate are provided with few facilitating structures (scheduling changes to encourage joint planning, or team teaching arrangements) and even fewer incentives.

Ironically, the lessons of recent research attest to the virtues of collective learning and teaching. They testify to the ways in which both students and teachers can come to achieve more and learn more effectively when the artificial barriers that limit collaboration are removed. It is no accident that the "real world" of work and play treats collaboration as a norm. Professionals as diverse as nurses, lawyers, newspaper reporters, and football players meet together daily in working groups to review their responsibilities, check their progress, solicit ideas for next steps, and design ways to work together on tough problems. Their workplaces are built around the recognition of the necessity of such meetings. Neither hospital nurses' stations nor newspaper staff meeting rooms are organizational accidents. However, schools are not organized like the world outside them; the individual student and the individual teacher are the units around which the structures of classrooms and schools are built. Opportunities for collective work are afterthoughts.

In her presidential address to the American Educational Research Association, Lauren Resnick summarized the ways in which school learning and learning in the real world are different.[5] Since learning in schools appears to be far less successful than its out-of-school counterpart, this contrast can be useful for understanding how to make schools more effective places. Resnick argues that there are four general characteristics that distinguish in-school from out-of-school learning.

1. Learning in the world is cooperative; learning in schools is pursued alone.
2. Learning in schools uses "pure mentation." Learning in the outside world uses tools—the efforts needed to complete a task are shared with others who have invented cognitive tools such as "ready reckoners," statistical tables, or computer simulations. Using tools devised by others is not cheating; it is acting intelligently.
3. In schools, the learners reason about and with symbols; outside of school they reason about real things. In the real world, therefore, you rarely see people make the kinds of really stupid mistakes regularly made by youngsters learning arithmetic, who will often, in manipulating symbols, make errors that are orders of magnitude off target.
4. Learning in school is directed at generalization; outside of school, learning is usually situation-specific.

Resnick concludes that school itself should perhaps become more like life. In itself this is no great innovation—Dewey argued for a compatibility between life and school nearly a century ago, as did educational thinkers both before and after him—but Resnick can bring new evidence in support of her recommendations. She reviewed dozens of programs that claim to teach youngsters to think critically or engage in better problem solving. The few such programs that could present evidence of success tended to share five characteristics. Successful critical thinking programs:

1. Involve socially shared intellectual work.
2. Are organized around mutual accomplishment of tasks, so that

elements of the skills to be learned take on meaning in the context of the whole.

3. Make usually hidden processes overt and thus subject to explicit observation and commentary by participants and teacher.
4. Permit skills to be built up bit by bit, yet allow participatory roles even for the relatively unskilled. They thus enable learning by social sharing.
5. Are organized around particular bodies of knowledge and interpretation rather than general abilities.

Thus, contemporary thinking about learning borrows from two recent traditions: humans as boundedly rational and humans as collectively rational. The more complex and higher-order the learning, the more it depends on reflection—looking back—and collaboration—working with others. For example, studies of expertise in the solving of physics problems indicated that the most able problem solvers did not learn by doing; they did not learn from simply practicing the solving of physics problems. They learned from looking back on the problems they had solved (or, less frequently, had failed to solve) and learned by reflecting on what they had done to solve them. They learned, not by doing, but by thinking about what they were doing.[6]

Resnick[7] has commented on the scenario that opens a major section of the Carnegie Task Force's *A Nation Prepared,* describing a school in which students are working together in small groups on quite difficult problems, with the assistance of teachers. She observed that, in the light of her review of critical thinking programs, the Carnegie description could be characterized as that of a "critical thinking school."

The real world is regularly organized to provide opportunities for such planning, reflection, and review in the company of others. The schools are not. Thus, Tamir[8] has reported that a most frequent error of laboratory teaching in biology, chemistry, and physics is to provide sufficient time for students to conduct the assigned experiment but insufficient opportunity for discussion of the meaning of the experiment and the observations it made possible. Learning in a science laboratory occurs when a group is looking back on the experiments and discussing what they mean, why not all results yielded the same values, and how the experiment related to other topics that had gone before.

If learning to learn requires the establishment of such conditions, then learning to teach will also demand them. Learning to teach is enormously complex, a clear example of learning the highest-order forms of knowledge, skill, and problem solving. If the conditions described above are needed for student learning to occur, they are certainly needed to foster learning and development among teachers. The preconditions for school reform, therefore, are to create circumstances in schools that permit and support teacher learning, and it is likely that teacher learning will require conditions quite similar to those needed for student learning.

Before proceeding to a discussion of the needed circumstances for learning from experience within the teaching profession, I wish to consider one other aspect of the current emphasis on the importance of higher-order thinking, problem solving, and critical reasoning. Resnick points out in her address that a democratic society must place particular emphasis on students learning to reason, to consider alternative views. This is a perspective on the relationship between learning in schools and living in a democratic society that was strongly emphasized by John Dewey in his writings on teaching and schooling.

The Search for Understanding: A Deweyan Perspective

In the preface to his masterful *Experience and Education,*[9] Dewey presents his analysis of the tyranny of dualisms, the "either/or" arguments against which he railed for so many years. I do not wish to focus on the dualisms themselves, or any particular dualism, in this chapter. Instead, I will look more closely at the underlying psychology and philosophy that led Dewey to his dialectical style of analysis.

Dewey presented an idea of education that rooted the pursuit of truth in the creation of dialogue. His argument against "either/or" thinking was also, somewhat ironically, an assertion about its inevitability. Powerful ideas always generate refutations; theses breed antitheses; stipulations bring about their contradictions. People state their positions by uttering straightforward propositions. Politics is not unique in its dependence on the slogan; the simple claim guides us all.

Because such claims are intrinsically incomplete relative to the complexities of the world whose actors they purport to guide, they will inevitably stimulate counterclaims rooted in recognition of the missing ideas. Thus, calls for greater freedom and self-direction in learning predictably elicit pleas for teaching the young the eternal verities of our culture.

Dewey argued that the reason why human discourse is characterized by controversy is that we are intrinsically incapable of uttering the whole truth and nothing but the truth. Claimed truth is inherently incomplete. Assertions can never do justice to the full complexity of the world, any more than perceptions and cognitions can grasp the full richness of any setting.

For this reason, controversies are both inevitable and desirable. Individuals or groups will sense the incompleteness of any argument and oppose it with an alternative that builds on what was left out of the original position, thus advancing the overall deliberation and deepening the analysis.

Thus, arguments for more content in teaching predictably elicit calls for more critical processes. Arguments for excellence breed counterarguments for equity. A case for basic skills is refuted with a case for higher-order reasoning. "Either/or" thinking is at the very heart of social and intellectual discourse, because all arguments are intrinsically incomplete.

What, then, is knowledge? Since what is held to be true by any individual or group is intrinsically incomplete, knowledge is a process of continuous debate, dialogue, deliberation, and reasoning. Reason is a process of constantly comparing incomplete, insufficient views. "Either/or" thinking is therefore always the starting point for deliberation. If the achievement of knowledge is a good thing, then a good society is one that permits (even fosters) the competition between different views. The more different a view, the more likely it is to contain a seed of truth absent in prevailing notions. Freedom of speech and the encouragement of open dialogue and debate are therefore not only political virtues; they are epistemological ones. If the survival and flourishing of a society is dependent, in large measure, on its capacity to seek out what is warranted, then its openness to new and different ideas is essential.

What must schools look like in such a society? They should be microcosms for the kinds of debate and deliberation needed by the society more generally. They must be organized to permit and encourage competition among ideas. They must discourage doctrine and dogma. Both the selection of content and the organization of interactions within the classroom should reflect the collaborative/competitive conception of the search for knowledge.

For Dewey, this image of an inquiring society defined the character of learning, of teaching, of classroom organization, and of schooling. As Larry Cuban,[10] among others, has repeatedly stated, the image has more often been fulfilled in dreams than in reality, and there are probably understandable reasons for that. However, the Deweyan quest must proceed if reformers are serious about these "higher-order" educational goals. Yet it is unlikely to be accomplished without creating conditions in which teachers can learn as readily as do their students.[11] Teacher learning in schools does not occur in formal classes and through a formal curriculum, as does student learning. Teacher learning depends on the possibility of learning from experience. What is needed to foster such learning? An examination of the conditions for experiential learning is a prerequisite for addressing that question adequately.

Learning from Experience

The great challenge for teaching and teacher education is the demand that teachers learn from their teaching experiences. How does teaching become learning for the teacher? Teaching, like learning, is an act of construction, simplification, and invention, but often without an adequate opportunity to learn from the experience.

What is required for someone to learn from experience? The general paradigm for such learning is simple. An individual or group engages in a particular action for the sake of achieving a desired end. A pitcher throws a particular pitch to strike out a given batter. A woman invests in a given stock to increase her net worth. A doctor prescribes a specific treatment to alleviate a patient's pain. A teacher changes a child's seat to reduce the frequency of classroom disruption. When the desired end is achieved, people learn to use the action again under similar circumstances. When the end is not achieved, or a less desirable condition arises, people learn to avoid that action or class of actions.

The general paradigm of experiential learning is thus a fairly simple and quite rational one. Unfortunately, both the limits of human rationality and the complexities of the real world render that apparently simple model badly flawed in practice. There have been substantial programs of research demonstrating why human beings are such abysmal experiential learners.[12] I shall spare my readers yet another review of the literature and instead tell two stories that illustrate why learning from teaching experience is so difficult. They demonstrate respectively that the two most obvious requirements—knowing what you did and accurately identifying the consequences of what you did—can be hard to achieve.

Cases of Socratic Teaching

During the past summer my research group ran a two-week field test of new exercises for the assessment of teaching, designed in conjunction with the development of a National Board for Professional Teaching Standards.[13] Forty teachers, twenty elementary and twenty secondary level, came to Stanford for four days each to participate in the field test. A local elementary school was transformed into an assessment center, and each teacher participated in ten different exercises, ranging in length from forty-five minutes to three hours.

One of the exercises was "Teaching a Familiar Lesson," in which a candidate was to send ahead to the center a lesson plan from which he or she had already taught. The candidate was first interviewed for about thirty minutes over the lesson plan. The interviewer asked the teacher to provide a rationale for the selection of the lesson, to discuss how this particular lesson fit into a larger unit, and how that unit related to a larger curriculum. The teacher was asked to describe how the lesson would be taught, what assumptions were being made about the students, and how he or she would know if the lesson were going well.

After completing the interview, six youngsters were brought into the classroom to serve as pupils. They were instructed to act naturally, to avoid creating discipline problems, but otherwise to participate in the class as they normally would. Each teacher was given about fifteen minutes to become acquainted with the pupils in any way he or she desired, and then the balance of an hour to teach the lesson. The full lesson was videotaped for later analysis. At the conclusion of the lesson, the pupils were debriefed by one of the observers, while the original interviewer conducted a "reflection interview" with the candidate to discuss how things had gone, what had been learned about each of the individual pupils, and what he or she would do differently if given an opportunity to teach this lesson again under similar conditions. The videotape was not reviewed with the teacher.

I remember quite vividly one candidate whom I interviewed. He described a lesson he would be teaching on an aspect of the U.S. Constitution. When asked how he would conduct the lesson, he replied that he would teach Socratically, asking the students questions and following up their answers with more penetrating follow-up questions. Knowing how hard it is to teach Socratically, I awaited the lesson expectantly. The candidate opened the lesson with a question for the students. The students remained silent. After waiting no more than a couple of seconds, the teacher proceeded to answer his own question. He then asked another question. Student silence was again interrupted by the teacher's answer to his own question, and so it proceeded for nearly thirty minutes, with hardly a variation. The Socratic dialogue had become a Socratic monologue! The students had realized quite early that a little patience on their parts—an exhibition of student wait-time, if you will—would relieve them of any obligation to respond.

When we sat down together for the reflection interview, I asked the candidate to describe the lesson he had just taught. Without hesitation, he reported that he had conducted the lesson Socratically; he appeared to have no idea that the students had deferred to him to provide both questions and answers. He apparently had no idea that there was a discrepancy between his intention to teach in a particular manner and the reality of his performance.

I had had a similar experience nearly twenty years earlier while teaching a seminar on teaching to the members of a medical school faculty. A young pediatrician had volunteered to videotape his bedside teaching to a group of four medical students. He too had characterized his plan as Socratic teaching, but he had conducted a series of Socratic monologues at the bedsides of the youthful patients, responding energetically to the encouraging yet silent nods of his medical students. When we viewed the videotape in the faculty seminar a week later, he had truly been in a state of shock as it slowly dawned upon him that the students themselves had almost never contributed to the discussion.

I offer these brief "cases" to illustrate a basic principle of teaching performance. The act of teaching itself demands so much attention and energy that it is difficult for any teacher, especially when under some pressure, to monitor his or her own performance with great accuracy. Distortions of perception occur, especially in the direction of consistency with prior expectations. Yet if it is difficult to depend on one's own perceptions or recollections of what was actually done, then the first precondition for learning from experience becomes problematic. We may not be able to discern what we have actually done without the assistance of colleagues who can help us observe or monitor our own teaching behavior or a system of recordkeeping or reporting that transcends the limitations of our own subjective recollections. Since a teacher cannot be observed by someone else all the time, he or she must learn to use the feedback of colleagues, videotaping with supervised review, and reports from students, among other direct and vicarious strategies, to improve the calibration of his or her own observations and recollections.

The Case of the Unanticipated Vectors

If having a clear grasp of what one has actually done can be a problem, so can discerning the *consequences* of one's actions. In the next vignette, it becomes clear that establishing what students have learned from one's teaching—that is, knowing the consequences of one's actions—is not always particularly easy.

My teacher education course has designed an assignment in which students engage in reciprocal observation and interviewing. Teacher education candidates pair off and interview one another about a lesson that will be conducted in the immediate future. In each interview they are expected to describe the goal of the lesson—the concepts, facts, skills, and/or attitudes they intend their high school students to learn—and how the lesson will be conducted. The students of teaching then observe one another teaching the respective lessons that have been planned, taking detailed notes on the classroom events. After the lesson is completed, two high school students are selected for interviewing. Each is asked independently what the lesson was about and what the main ideas were. They are asked probing questions designed to tap the depth of their understanding. The observer then provides feedback to the teacher, who subsequently reciprocates when roles are reversed.

Bob was a fine physics graduate who was learning to be a physics teacher. As part of his year-long internship, he taught an honors physics class, which was the setting for the reciprocal observation exercise. His colleague Alice interviewed him regarding the lesson on conceptions of force he planned to introduce the unit on mechanics in the physics course. During the lesson he conducted an animated lecture-discussion on the various kinds of force. Alice thought it was one of the most effective lessons she had ever observed. She interviewed the students and opened each interview with the question: "What was this lesson about?" Both students answered, "This was a lesson about vectors."

She was shocked. Bob had devoted no more than ten minutes of a forty-five minute period to a blackboard demonstration of how to represent the direction and magnitude of forces using arrows with lines of varying length called vectors. How had they concluded that this brief presentation, at best a kind of subordinate clause in the main exposition, was the key point of the lesson? When Bob was informed of the student responses, he was also surprised. If there had not been an interview immediately after the class, there was no way in which he could have guessed that there was such a substantial gap between what he had taught and what the students had learned. Given that information, he was able to generate some hypotheses with his observer and other science teaching candidates to account for the anomalous finding. Their best guess was that the students were fooled by the fact that Bob had used the blackboard only one time in the period—during the ten-minute discussion of vectors—and they associated blackboard work with what was "really important." Whatever the cause, this story illustrates how very difficult it can be for a teacher working alone to know what his teaching has accomplished unless he is trained to do so and gets assistance in learning from experience.

Learning from experience requires that a teacher be able to look back on his or her own teaching and its consequences. The ordinary school setting does not lend itself to such reflection. It is characterized by speed, solitude, and amnesia. Too much is occurring too rapidly. One is alone attempting to make sense of the buzzing, blooming confusion of classroom life. The students are unlikely to help the teacher to pin down either causes or consequences unless he or she has learned how to elicit and exploit such feedback. Sadly, there is evidence from other sources that even when learning does occur in a classroom setting, it is often forgotten from year to year. All too often, a teacher laments, "I was halfway through the lesson before I remembered that I was making the same mistake I had made the year before while teaching the same unit." Even when learning has occurred, the speed and solitude often combine to produce pedagogical amnesia. Are there any possible cures for these problems of learning from experience or for the amnesia that so often attends the learning that does occur?

The difficulties of learning from experience are characteristic of the limitations of any individual trying to make critical sense of a complex world while working alone. A strategy of solution must transform individual work to collective activity. In the next section, collegiality in schools will be considered as a strategy for fostering experiential learning among teachers.

The Concept of Collegium

One of the terms most frequently associated with the necessary reform of teaching and of schools is collegiality. A collegium is a setting in which individuals come together with a shared mission. One of the central features of that shared mission now becomes clear. Collegiality is needed to overcome the limitations of individual rationality. If any individual actor's capacity to learn is bounded, if human reasoning of all kinds—theoretical, practical or moral—remains restricted when pursued alone or without access to a competing point of view, then the collegium is indispensable as a vehicle for educational reform.

Yet it is necessary to be realistic. It is surely impossible logistically and fiscally for most teaching to be accompanied by peer observation and feedback. The reasons for the solitary classroom teaching experience relate to economic and social factors that are not readily ignored. How then can the principle of the collegium be achieved within reasonable bounds?

If collegiality is defined as that set of strategies needed to overcome the limitations of individual rationality and to make learning from experience possible, I suggest that those strategies be divided into two classes: the visible college and the invisible college. The visible college is the forum for direct, face-to-face interactions and deliberations among colleagues in the same building. The "invisible college" refers to the communication among colleagues who do not work in physical proximity but share knowledge of one another's work through the exchange of publications, correspondence, and occasional scholarly meetings. If the problems of affording teachers opportunities to communicate within the same building get in the way of the functioning of visible colleges, collegiality via invisible colleges is even less likely in a teaching community with few forums for joint deliberation and even fewer for recording and analyzing experiences in a scholarly manner. I now propose a number of strategies for promoting the development of both visible and invisible colleges among the nation's school teachers.

Visible Colleges

What might foster greater face-to-face collegiality within existing school buildings? The growing number of mentor teacher programs nationally, especially in conjunction with beginning teacher induction and support initiatives, promises to increase the role of collegiality between more and less experienced teachers (or among teaching peers whose respective experiences are simply different). If the mentoring relationship is accompanied by some expectations for systematic observation, coaching, and eventually some forms of documentation and evaluation, this should go a long way toward creating a new climate of collaboration within schools. Some of the newer conceptions of teacher evaluation for purposes of certification[14] include the design of portfolios that would document the accomplishments of candidates during the course of their teaching. These portfolios would require the attestations and commentaries of mentors or lead teachers who work with the candidate and guide his or her efforts at improvement through modeling and coaching. The visible college would thus include examples of one-to-one teaching within the professional teaching community itself.

Other structures that can foster the creation of visible colleges include the establishment of weekly or biweekly case conferences in schools. These would be conducted in the spirit of the teaching hospital's weekly grand rounds or clinical conferences, in which interesting or problematic cases from the hospital's own recent experience are presented and discussed for the educational benefit of the entire staff. Case conferences in schools, however, should not focus on case studies of youngsters who are "tough to teach." These conferences should be presentations by teachers, individually or in teams, on exciting new teaching units they have implemented (complete with videotapes of their operation and discussions of student work), new forms of classroom organization, approaches to the mentoring of new teachers (co-presented by mentor and novice), as well as experiences with particular students or groups. Case conferences would be one strategy for preserving the experiences of individual teachers and making those experiences and their analysis available to colleagues for review and discussion. Videotapes of these conferences or written versions of the case presentations (perhaps prepared as part of collaborations with local colleges or universities) would be accumulated in school archives creating the beginnings of an institutional memory.

Invisible Colleges

An invisible college is created when the boundaries of a collegium are stretched beyond the walls of a shared building or department. A serious problem for teaching as a profession has been the absence of opportunities to communicate what has been learned from experience through literature that can be shared with colleagues at remote sites. To achieve this form of communication, I would propose the fostering of the written version of school-based case conferences, the writing of cases, and casebooks of teaching.

Teachers are capable of writing about their work in ways that can stimulate and enlighten other teachers. The writing of cases serves as an occasion for reflection and deliberation on teaching by the case authors themselves. The cases, when written and distributed, can elicit commentaries by other teachers as well as by education scholars and teacher educators. These case-based exchanges can well create an entirely new form of educational discourse that centers on the experiences, reflections, and lessons learned by teachers. They may constitute the long-sought antidote for pedagogical amnesia.

This new literature of case and commentary has been pioneered in the casebooks created by Judith Shulman of the Far West Laboratory.[15] Shulman first wrote a series of case studies of mentor teacher programs in California during their initial year of implementation. She then presented these cases to a group of new mentors who had come together to learn about and from each other's experiences. Highly stimulated by Shulman's case studies of mentors, the participants began to write their own short cases, brief vignettes capturing their experiences as mentors and the ways they had coped with them. Shulman and her school-based colleague, Joel Colbert, edited and organized the cases from the perspective of the recurrent problems of learning to mentor. They also solicited commentaries from the mentors on one another's cases, thereby simulating the ways in which physicians comment on one another's case presentations during a clinical case conference. The edited volume of cases and commentaries is now used in the invisible college, by other mentors and trainers in school districts and teacher education programs around the country. Others, including policymakers planning new mentor programs, can now reflect on and learn from the experiences of their invisible peers.

In the most recent casebook,[16] the teaching interns with whom the mentors are responsible for working write their own cases—perspectives on learning to teach written from the vantage point of the learners. These new cases are somewhat longer than the mentor vignettes, but the real innovation in the second casebook is in the treatment of the commentaries. Shulman has solicited and organized *layers of commentary,* in which other novices, mentors, teacher educators, and educational scholars add their interpretive comments to the original cases and to one another's comments. The invisible college that is represented in this casebook now extends the boundaries of collegium from the teaching community to include the world of higher education. For example, a set of cases describing the classroom management dilemmas confronted by interns teaching in the inner city elicits commentaries from experienced inner-city mentors, from teacher educators, and from Professor Jere Brophy, who is perhaps the leading research authority on classroom management. Brophy's comments, while remaining focused on the intern teacher-authored cases, connects them to the research literature on classroom control and discipline, thereby linking the invisible college of teachers with the invisible college of educational scholars on teaching.

If the limits of learning from experience derive from the speed with which experiences occur and the impossibility of deliberation on those fleeting events, then all strategies that help to freeze experience for subsequent analysis and review are promising. There is a need for antidotes (or at least palliatives) in response to the epidemics of pedagogical amnesia and teaching aphasia, of forgetting what has been learned and of being incapable of communicating even what has been remembered. The strategy of creating a case literature of teaching to preserve teacher experiences and to prepare them as a vehicle for teacher learning may well be one of the most important ways available to create and enhance the collegium.

For the Future

What is the desired image of the future? At this point in the history of contemporary educational reform, the position is paradoxical. The first wave has reached the beach and brought with it higher standards for pupils and more demanding expectations for teachers. The second wave is cresting, with its emphasis on the professionalization of teaching and its stress on the importance of teachers learning from teacher education and from their own experiences. However, the force of the second wave is being diminished by the undertow created by the first wave. One reform is caught in the other's backwash.

One of the demons of the current reform movement, a force that will bedevil most of the attempts to improve the qualities of teaching as a profession and a career, is the absence of time. Time tyrannizes teaching. The quest for excellence has been captured by the twin terrors of time on task and the tasks of covering enormous amounts of material. If one play by Shakespeare is good, five are splendid. If one Federalist Paper is desirable, five are dandy. Teachers have no time to think, either alone or with others. Students have no time to think, because they are too busy covering their assignments. Group work takes time; individual worksheets promote efficiency. Accelerated schools should improve by raising expectations for the achievement of all students and then by slowing down so that learning can become deeper, more collaborative, and more critical—not merely more extensive in its coverage.

There is reason to believe that many of today's youngsters are failing to learn what they are now covering. Advanced Placement courses move even more quickly than honors courses, which in turn zoom along faster than ordinary ones. The long lists of E. D. Hirsch[17] notwithstanding, a critical thinking curriculum will entail the study of fewer topics with greater care and collaborative deliberation than is currently the case. The problems of both student learning and teacher learning will require that we recapture control of both pace and time.

One of the most popular research programs of the past fifteen years has been Mary Budd Rowe's work on wait-time. I received a letter from a teacher educator who had been working on teaching teachers to wait longer in the interests of eliciting higher student levels of thinking. I had suggested in my paper "The Wisdom of Practice"[18] that the impediments to increased wait-time were an increase in discipline problems and the greater unpredictability of classroom life that were likely to accompany longer silences on the part of teachers. My correspondent suggested yet a third reason why teachers would not increase their wait-times, even after being convinced of the research grounds for the tactic. The teachers who would not increase their wait-times explained that the tactic slowed teaching down to the point where they could not have covered all the material they were expected to teach in their state or district curriculum standards. The state tests were linked to the pace dictated by the curriculum. The twin demons of time and pace strike again!

Yet, in the final analysis, much of the burden of the proposed reforms rests on assumptions about teachers learning from experience. What, then, is experience? It is reading and studying the teaching materials and the disciplinary sources from which they often derive. It is learning from students. It is watching videotapes, hearing audiotapes, observing peers, mentors, and protégés. It is studying research, reading and writing cases, preparing for and participating in case conferences, planning and teaching in collaboration with fellow professionals. Are these fostered or rewarded in the present structures?

Learning from experience in teaching is more than honing or tuning a skill so that it becomes automatic. It is raising the skill to thinking, giving reason to action and value to goals. It is the transformation of showing and telling into pedagogy. This will require that teachers work in structures that permit such interactions, be prepared in programs and institutions that both teach and model such processes, and be themselves individuals who can engage in the effort.

All the talk of reforming schooling must never lose sight of the ultimate goal: to create institutions where students can learn through interactions with teachers who are themselves always learning. The effective school must become an educative setting for its teachers if it aspires to become an educational environment for its students.

NOTES

1. This chapter was written, in part, with support from the Spencer Foundation and the Carnegie Corporation of New York. The opinions expressed are the author's.
2. There is a curious ambivalence with regard to the emphasis on higher *preparation* standards as against higher *entitlement* standards. Thus, the Carnegie Task Force, in the same text that advocates higher standards of preparation, also recommends strongly in favor of encouraging alternative routes into teaching for those without professional preparation as long as they can pass the individual hurdles of licensure and certification standards.
3. Lee S. Shulman and Neil B. Carey, "Psychology and the Limitations of Individual Rationality: Implications for the Study of Reasoning and Civility," *Review of Educational Research 54,* Winter 1984, pp. 501–524.
4. See my discussion of the phenomenon in Lee S. Shulman, "Knowledge and Teaching: Foundations of the New Reform," *Harvard Educational Review 57,* February 1987, pp. 1–22, especially the discussion of Colleen on pp. 17–18; Pam Grossman, *A Passion for Language: From Text to Teaching* (Stanford, Calif.: Knowledge Growth in Teaching Publications Series, Stanford University School of Education, 1985); and Lee S. Shulman,

"Sounding an Alarm: A Reply to Sockett," *Harvard Educational Review 57,* November 1987, pp. 473–482. See also my discussion of teaching as the management of complexity in Lee S. Shulman, "The Wisdom of Practice: Managing Complexity in Medicine and Teaching," in David C. Berliner and Barak V. Rosenshine, eds., *Talks to Teachers: A Festschrift for N. L. Gage* (New York: Random House, 1987).

5. Lauren Resnick, "Learning in School and Out," *Educational Researcher 16,* 1987, pp. 13–20.
6. J. Larkin, J. McDermott, D. Simon, and H. A. Simon, "Expert and Novice Performance in Solving Physics Problems," *Science 208,* 1980, pp. 1335–1342.
7. Lauren Resnick, Comments during a symposium on the implications of the Carnegie Task Force report made at AERA meetings, April 1987.
8. Pinchas Tamir, personal communication.
9. John Dewey, *Experience and Education* (New York: Macmillan, 1938).
10. Larry Cuban, *How Teachers Taught: Constancy and Change in American Classrooms: 1890–1980* (New York: Longman, 1984).
11. The writings of Joseph Schwab further reflect this Deweyan emphasis on the centrality of deliberation, dialogue, and dialectic in the fostering of critical educational thinking among teachers and students. His papers on "the practical," which emphasize the role of practical deliberation and the eclectic, as well as his writings on the "learning community," eloquently discuss these principles. See Joseph J. Schwab, "The Practical: A Language for Curriculum," *School Review 78,* 1969, pp. 1–29; Joseph J. Schwab, "Learning Community," *The Center Magazine 8,* May–June 1975, pp. 30–44; Schwab's collected papers in Joseph J. Schwab, *Science, Curriculum and Liberal Education: Selected Essays* (Chicago: University of Chicago Press, 1978).
12. See Hillel J. Einhorn and Robin M. Jogarth, "Confidence in Judgment: Persistence of the Illusion of Validity," *Psychological Review 85,* 1978, pp. 395–416; Amos Tversky and Daniel Kahneman, "Judgment Under Uncertainty: Heuristics and Biases," *Science 185,* 1974, pp. 1124–1131.
13. For a full description of that research, see Lee S. Shulman, "Assessment for Teaching: An Initiative for the Profession," *Phi Delta Kappan,* September 1987, pp. 38–44.
14. Ibid.
15. Judith H. Shulman and Joel A. Colbert, eds., *The Mentor-Teacher Casebook* (San Francisco: Far West Laboratory for Educational Research and

Development, and Eugene, Ore.: ERIC Clearinghouse on Educational Management, 1987).

16. Judith H. Shulman, ed., *The Intern Teacher Casebook: Cases and Commentaries* (San Francisco: Far West Laboratory, in press).

17. E. D. Hirsch, *Cultural Literacy* (Boston: Houghton-Mifflin, 1987).

18. Lee S. Shulman, "The Wisdom of Practice: Managing Complexity in Medicine and Teaching," in David C. Berliner and Barak V. Rosenshine, eds., *Talks to Teachers: A Festschrift for N. L. Gage* (New York: Random House, 1987).

INTRODUCTION

THE PARADOX OF TEACHER ASSESSMENT (1988)

WHILE ENGAGED in the Teacher Assessment Project (which informed the developed of the National Board for Professional Teaching Standards), Shulman's work was often conceptualized as a threat to the traditional forms of teacher testing, perhaps most notably the National Teachers Examination (NTE) created by the Educational Testing Service (ETS). When he was invited into "enemy territory," Shulman could hardly refuse the invitation to speak at an ETS conference on teaching testing.

In this invited address, Shulman presents his ideas concerning performance assessments for teachers. He begins by noting that tests are only proxies of teaching competence, yet paradoxically, we live in an age where the tests are treated not as proxies but as conclusive evidence. To correct this trend, Shulman argues for a process of teacher assessment, one that would take place over time and would include a wide range of assessment settings and formats in and out of classrooms, portfolios, performance assessments, and written examinations among them. In particular, he enumerates the considerable advantages of using portfolios, which allow one to track progress over time and can be used to change the culture of teaching by institutionalizing norms of collaboration, coaching, and peer observations. The influence of his previous thinking on the importance of a disciplined eclecticism in curriculum and in research is, thus, extended here into the realm of assessment.

11

THE PARADOX OF TEACHER ASSESSMENT

IN TEACHER ASSESSMENT, WE confront a fundamental paradox, a confusion between what is real and what is proxy. We have turned assessment upside-down in thinking about the relationships between tests and the accomplishments they claim to represent. We should strive to set that world upright before we are done.

Any system of quality control calls for a balance between trust and suspicion. We trust the judgments of educational institutions that provide transcripts and degrees to attest to the accomplishments of their graduates. The state and profession set limits on that trust, however, through programs of licensure and certification that protect the public interest. In that spirit, they establish external examinations to evaluate graduates of educational institutions.

Because attestations and examinations are imperfect, most systems of certification attempt to employ both institutional and external sources of evidence. Those educators who know a candidate best may not always be the most dispassionate judges of his or her competence. The most objective external tests and observations may not always yield the most comprehensive or sensitive assessments.

What, then, is the paradox? Tests are at best *proxies* for the direct experience of teaching, interacting with and verifying a candidate's qualifications over longer periods of time and varying conditions. Yet exams are now seen as the ultimate reality, conclusive tests of candidate competence. Individuals who have completed accredited programs of professional teacher preparation are treated in some states as if they have something fundamental to prove. Professional preparation is seen as indirect proof that candidates lack intelligence or proper training—why else would they have "wasted their time in teacher education"? The individual with a liberal arts degree who can pass a relatively brief test or test battery is afforded the same or greater credibility than one who has responsibly pursued a professional preparation program.

Most professional fields—including medicine and architecture—have internship and residency requirements. During the course of these requirements, supervision ensures the candidate's development of important capacities and evaluates the candidate's accomplishment of the desired ends. The licensing and certification examinations in these fields are not perceived as capable of measuring everything of importance. The training programs are expected to teach and to assess in some measure; the external examinations complement the more substantial system of training and induction.

Even in the earliest examinations for teachers, policy leaders recognized that the test scores were not the final word on a candidate's capacities. Note the following instructions given to examiners by the State Superintendent of Instruction in an early Colorado teachers' test (Cornell, 1988, pp. 23–24):

> A high degree of practical success in teaching should be accepted as sufficient reason for issuing a certificate of a higher grade than is warranted by the percentage upon the examination, and inexperience or want of success should lower the grade of the certificate given, while failure as a teacher might be so marked to make it your [the examining county superintendent's] duty to refuse a certificate, whatever the percentage obtained.
>
> I earnestly recommend that certificates of the first grade be given only to teachers who have earned it by success in the schoolroom as well as the examination. I also recommend the addition of ten [points] to the grade earned on Theory and Practice, for the regular reading of some good educational periodicals, or of one or more reliable books on the subject.
>
> Refuse certificates to applicants of whose moral character you have reasonable doubt.

Even 100 years ago, policymakers charged with maintaining teaching standards at the state and county level were admonished to supplement test results with documentation of actual performance in the field. And when a candidate's test scores were inconsistent with his or her experience, greater weight was given to the latter, to what tests could not and cannot measure.

This paper examines the assessment of teachers, the approaches and strategies likely to be useful for evaluating those critically important individuals to whom we entrust the care and instruction of our nation's children. Discussion of this issue, however, should not begin with an inquiry into assessment methods. Method is a second-order question in these deliberations. We must begin instead with a discussion of good teaching, the construct we wish to measure. If the construct is not defined appropriately, there are no measurement methods fancy enough to provide valid assessments.

A Conception of Teaching

Any discussion of teacher assessment requires an adequate theoretical conception of teaching. Teaching always involves both acting and thinking. It typically occurs in connection with specific content and in a particular context. It is interaction with children in classrooms; it is also sitting alone planning at the kitchen table, or talking with parents on the phone. In many systems of staff development and teacher evaluation, the general skills and understandings used to organize and manage classrooms serve as a complete and sufficient definition of expertise. Although these skills are certainly of critical importance, this view of teaching effectiveness is simply inadequate. Any view of teaching effectiveness that fosters a limited view of teaching distorts teacher assessment.

I think of teaching as classroom management and organization—and more. Teaching is not only teacher behavior; it is thought and action with regard to children, purposes, and content in particular contexts. Teacher assessment must measure what, how, and why teachers think about their actions in teaching particular ideas, attitudes, and skills to youngsters in both institutional and community settings.

In turn, this more elaborate concept of teaching demands modes of assessment that go well beyond conventional methods and their underlying assumptions. It requires approaches that present open-ended problems to candidates in a variety of ways. Assessments must confront candidates with problems that require judgments, decisions, choices, and actions that cannot be constrained by the limitations of a multiple-choice test. Those who share a conception of good teaching that emphasizes the importance of varieties of content and context will not be satisfied by a classroom observation instrument that is so general it can be used to observe a second-grade reading group or an eleventh-grade trigonometry class.

The kinds of understanding and skill that underlie a teacher's expertise distinguish it from the expertise of the subject-matter authority. The teacher deeply understands the content to be learned. The teacher distinguishes between aspects of the content that are absolutely crucial for future understanding and aspects that are more peripheral and less likely to impede future learning if not fully grasped. The teacher recognizes aspects of the content that will be likely to pose the greatest difficulties for pupils.

Teachers also understand that active, constructive, and collaborative student *learning* is the essence of good teaching, not inspired description or energetic demonstration alone. They anticipate persistent preconceptions, misconceptions, or difficulties that are likely to inhibit learning. To form a bridge between students' prior knowledge and key aspects of the concepts to be learned, the teacher invents, borrows, or spontaneously creates powerful representations of the ideas to be learned in the form of examples, analogies, metaphors, or demonstrations. Further, the teacher understands that when students generate such representations themselves, they learn even more successfully. The teacher must therefore be able to distinguish between an inventive contribution from a student that reflects a nonstandard but productive insight into a key idea and another response that communicates confusion and disarray.

The teacher understands how to establish a pedagogically meaningful relationship with youngsters. The exemplary teacher creates a relationship around the subject matter to be learned; he or she does not ignore the curriculum and does not establish relationships around social or personal attributes alone. The fine teacher uses his or her understanding to establish relationships with students of diverse cultural backgrounds. Finally, the teacher exhibits and exemplifies a moral or ethical commitment to teach on the basis of the premise that students are capable of learning. Such teachers maintain high expectations for their students without regard to students' prior successes or failures as individuals or as members of a group.

Our conception of teaching attempts to identify the understandings and skills that distinguish an exemplary teacher from an educated pedestrian (defined as a nonteacher who has comparable subject-matter background but no preparation or experience in teaching). It should also distinguish the teacher of a particular content area from excellent teachers in general. Thus, an outstanding teacher of mathematics would look far more capable when teaching algebra than when teaching *Moby Dick*.

These attributes and accomplishments certainly do not exhaust the types of knowledge and activities that define an excellent teacher. The general pedagogical skills emphasized by Berliner are absolutely essential for effective teaching. Yet any system of teacher assessment must focus substantial attention on these content-specific and context-dependent understandings and skills. My colleagues and I began our work with studies aimed at achieving a coherent conception of teaching (Shulman, 1986a, 1987b; Wilson, Shulman, and Richert, 1987). Only after such work was well under way (and much other work by colleagues in the field had been reviewed and analyzed; e.g., Shulman, 1986b) did we ask which approaches to assessment would be adequate to measure teaching competence. Measurement choices must be controlled by pedagogical principles, rather than vice versa. Even though we sensed that we were moving toward kinds of assessment for which little adequate theory or technology existed, the need for teaching to hold the controlling position could not be contradicted. Any system of teacher assessment, however reliable, economic, or efficient, must first and foremost be faithful to teaching.

Toward a Judicious Blend of Assessment Methods

Teaching is such a complex and contextualized phenomenon that any single mode of measurement will fail to assess its practitioners validly. I have proposed that we develop a broad strategy of teacher assessment in the spirit of a marriage of insufficiencies, a complement of imperfections (Shulman, 1987a; 1988). Each method we can imagine for such assessments—the widely used multiple-choice tests, the frequently employed brief classroom visits, my own work on performance assessments and documentation through portfolios—is marred in some fundamental way. The solution does not lie in perfecting the imperfectible, but rather in deploying complementary modes of evaluation that compensate for the most serious deficiencies of their brothers and sisters in measurement.

Indeed, I envision a process that unfolds and extends over time, a strategy of teacher assessment that will combine nearly all of the following elements: written examinations of knowledge and reasoning, both multiple-choice and open-ended; performance assessments in the form of simulation exercises, computer-based problems, and structured interviews; observations of teaching, both direct and via videotape; documentation through reflective portfolios that include samples or exhibitions of student work (captioned and discussed), teachers' plans, student evaluations, recordings of classes, and other artifacts produced in the course of classroom life; and combinations of the above methods. In particular, linking portfolios to subsequent assessment-center evaluations may be useful. What are the strengths of each approach? Where are its insufficiencies?

Written Examinations

Tests are used regularly to measure basic skills, knowledge of content, and understanding of professional practice. They permit broad sampling of domains and are relatively economical to use. Because they were originally invented to bring greater objectivity to evaluation, they enjoy high reliability in scoring. Newer forms of essay examinations and experimental methods of employing computers to administer and manage objective tests hold promise for the future. The insufficiencies of written exams lie in their remoteness from the complexities and contexts of practice. Tests currently excel at measuring relatively isolated pieces of knowledge (hence their capacity to sample across wide domains) but fail to tap more integrated processes of judgment, decision making, and problem solving in real-life contexts. Taking a written test is quite different from teaching a class, preparing a lesson, or most other activities in which a teacher is engaged.

Assessment-Center Exercises

Performance assessment has been used for years in assessment centers for the foreign service, in several medical boards, in the architecture exams, in the California bar exam, and in principals' assessment centers (see Byham, 1986; Aburto and Haertel, 1986). Assessment-center exercises for teaching simulate the real problems and processes of the profession. In my research, we have created twenty exercises in which, for example, teachers are observed as they lay out the plan for a lesson, teach that lesson to a group of new students, and then reflect on the episode and review it critically. Another exercise asks a teacher to analyze a textbook and plan to adapt it for use in the classroom. Our exercises present teachers with a videotape of teaching to observe and critique. They then recommend what they would do under the same circumstances. Another type of exercise presents examples of student work and asks the teacher to respond to the students' errors and insights (Shulman, Bird, and Haertel, 1988).

In general, performance-assessment exercises can reflect the complexities of teaching more faithfully than a test item does. But they too are insufficient. They are relatively expensive to create, administer, and evaluate. They cannot possibly sample subject-matter content or teaching situations as widely as do conventional written tests. Even though far more realistic than tests, they still cut the teacher off from the actual context of teaching—the school, the students, and the history of teaching and learning they share. How do we design assessments that reflect the actual settings in which teachers do their work?

Classroom Observation

Direct observation of teaching is widely employed, especially in the Southeastern states, in evaluation of teachers for permanent licensure. In principle, classroom observations can reflect the full complexity of teaching, but they rarely achieve their potential in practice. The problem of sampling is staggering. Many more classroom visits than have ever been used for evaluation are needed to establish "typical teaching performance" (Stodolsky, 1988). In addition, most methods of direct observation employ the most generic of rating scales, applying the same categories of analysis to primary-grade and to senior-high-school teaching, to a spelling lesson and to a discussion of the quadratic formula. This grows in part out of the emphasis on generic teaching skills that has dominated thinking about teaching in both the research and policy communities. It also justifies the employment of principals or other observers who are not specifically trained in the relevant content areas, grade levels, or contexts to evaluate the teaching they observe.

Observation is an attractive strategy because there seems to be so much potential in watching real teaching in real classrooms directly. But such methods have been disappointing thus far because they fail to tap many of teaching's critical dimensions. Too often, the typical observation method for evaluating teaching has been like photographing the "Mona Lisa" with a black-and-white Polaroid camera, or like tape-recording the most sumptuous performance of *Carmen* with an office dictaphone. There is so much potential in direct observation, but typically so limited a harvest.

Documentation Through Portfolios

To introduce a connection with the contexts and personal histories that characterize real teaching, portfolios of various kinds have been employed, with limited success. In licensure and career-ladder programs in Tennessee and Florida, among other states, teachers have been asked to submit lesson plans, attendance records, and other indications of their effectiveness. The resulting portfolios were often too large, too well laminated, and of uncertain connection to the efforts of the individuals whose work they were supposed to reflect. The initial idea seemed a worthy one: collect artifacts that reveal how teachers actually teach. But with insufficient time to design specifications for portfolio contents and inadequate opportunities to create conditions that would promote accurate and relevant documentation procedures, states were unable to carry out the experiment successfully. My research group continues to believe that the underlying notion of documentation is sound and, as I shall discuss next, that the insufficiencies can be overcome or compensated for.

Combining Portfolios and Performance Exercises

We have studied the use of performance assessments for several years and feel that we have made substantial progress in the design and scoring of this new facet of teaching assessment. Yet we remain dissatisfied with some of its limitations, especially with regard to those aspects of teaching in which context and time play a central role. In that regard, we are now investigating the use of carefully structured and well-reviewed portfolios whose specifications are carefully defined. Collaboration in the process at the local level is encouraged. Although there have been problems in the past with portfolios as reliable evidence of teacher competence, they retain almost uniquely the potential to document the unfolding of both teaching and learning over time and combine that documentation with opportunities for teachers to analyze what they and their students have done (see the pioneering contribution by Bird, in press).

We are currently field-testing a program of assessment that combines portfolio development and subsequent assessment of performance. Candidates first spend the better part of a year developing a teaching portfolio. In most cases, each required portfolio entry must include evidence of the teacher's plans and activities (including videotapes of teaching when appropriate), as well as examples of student work. When possible, these required entries extend over time, so that changes in teaching and learning and evidence of the relationships between them can also be observed.

Through a portfolio, a teacher can record his or her work with an at-risk child over the course of a semester, or document the different kinds of tests and assignments used to assess student progress. A teaching portfolio is ideal for documenting the teaching of writing, complete with the repeated iterations of instruction and feedback so crucial to learning in that area. Individual entries or groups of entries can include (or be followed by) teachers' reflections on their own work and their students' accomplishments.

But a recurrent anxiety has been expressed in regard to portfolios. How do we know that a given set of documents truly represents the work of the candidate? Isn't a portfolio an invitation to fraud, because teachers might borrow the work of others and present it as their own, or purchase "off-the-shelf" portfolios from catalogues? Such concerns have beset the use of portfolios in the recent past.

I begin with a radical premise. A portfolio *should* represent coached performance; portfolio development *should* be an occasion for interaction and mentoring among peers. In our research, we expect every portfolio entry to be cosigned or commented on by a mentor or peer who has participated, helped, reviewed, or critiqued the effort. Much like a doctoral dissertation or a studio project in architecture, the performance represented by the portfolio reflects both the efforts of the candidate and the advice of the instructor. The solution to the nightmare of coaching as a problem is to treat collaboration as a virtue. In medicine, for example, we justifiably assume that the accomplishments of an obstetric resident have been carefully supervised and mentored by more experienced teachers and peers. Documentation of the residency is not discounted for that reason. Why should teachers be treated differently in the documentation of their performances during periods of internship or induction into teaching?

We are currently investigating how to use the assessment center as a follow-up to the portfolio. Anything placed in the portfolio is subject to review in the assessment center, just as a doctoral dissertation is reviewed in an oral examination, or an architect's drawings or scale models are juried in a subsequent design competition. A candidate could be asked to present what has been documented in the portfolio and explain it to examiners. Such presentations by candidates, accompanied by examples of student work, video- or audiotapes of their teaching, and commentaries by mentors or colleagues, could then become the starting point for about half the assessments that would be conducted. The rest of the assessment-center activity would remain individual exercises, independent of particular experiences unique to any candidate.

Images of Documentation Through Portfolios

In general, the ideal portfolio reflects the accomplishments of teaching. The best portfolio provides evidence of teaching through the documentation of learning—both student learning and teacher learning. It provides not only a description of what the teacher did in particular episodes and over time, but also plentiful examples of student work as that unfolded over time, with as many examples of the teacher's instruction, intervention, coaching, modeling, encouragement, evaluations, corrections, and exhortations as are feasible. In the best sense, a teacher's portfolio should be made up of samples from student portfolios. In addition to examples of student learning that go well beyond the usual end-of-year multiple-choice test results, a good portfolio should include evidence of teacher learning and development over time. Portfolios should become both records and means of support for teacher development.

In considering a special role for documentation through portfolios in the repertoire of approaches to teacher assessment, the following characteristics, attributes, and aspects of the approach are noteworthy:

- It permits the tracking of an extended period of teaching and learning without requiring that an observer be physically present. Stodolsky (1988) points out that stable estimates of teacher behavior require more than a dozen visits to a classroom and sampling across topics and content areas.

- It shifts the focus of teacher evaluation, and thus the unit of pedagogical analysis, from the lesson and lesson fragment to the longer teaching unit, the curriculum, and/or the pupils. Present methods treat an individual lesson as the natural category within which teaching excellence can be assessed. How well are objectives set for *this lesson*? Is an anticipatory set created for *this lesson?* But the most serious embarrassments of contemporary education are not simply the result of poor lesson teaching. The lack of continuity and cumulative learning across days and weeks of lessons is among the most serious failures of our educational system.
- It permits inclusion of data on student outcomes, such as student performances, attitudes, dispositions, and evaluations of teaching, in closer connection to the actual teaching that preceded and accompanied those outcomes.
- It is, of necessity, content- and context-specific. Documentation is always a record of teaching something in particular to students in some specific setting.
- It can institutionalize norms of collaboration and coaching. Development of approaches to teacher assessment that call for collaboration among teachers to produce the necessary records will lead to greater emphasis on reflection and the evolution of professional ethics regarding good practice.
- It can lead to portfolios that can become the basis for subsequent assessments. These assessments, instead of being based solely on hypothetical examples, can be based on the actual context in which the candidate has worked. Thus, by linking portfolios with performance assessment, we increase the credibility of the former, the validity of the latter, and the utility of both.
- It need not be limited to any particular time period in the teacher's career. The development of a portfolio can begin during the early stages of teacher education and extend through the residency and beyond. Some teachers may take only a year to complete a required set of portfolio entries; others may need (or prefer to take) several years. As in mastery learning, no stigma is attached to the amount of time or number of iterations required.
- Participants in stronger teacher-education programs or more structured induction experiences would have an advantage in portfolio preparation. But it would be a legitimate advantage, tied to the

likelihood that they were being better prepared. Similarly, graduates of excellent teacher-preparation programs would emerge with half-full portfolios. They would have an advantage over those who were entering teaching through alternate routes that did not include professional preparation. But this would be a legitimate advantage rather than an artificial, politically legislated one. The ways in which a portfolio is accumulated, reviewed, and reflected on alone and with others could thus serve as a model for teacher education and professional development.

- A portfolio is not part of a teacher's personnel file. A teacher owns and controls his or her portfolio and can add to it and rearrange it regularly, sorting and crafting it into new forms for new purposes, including personal reflection, professional advancement, district evaluation, and job hunting.
- Documentation may reduce the adverse impact of teacher testing on some minority candidates, because the approach emphasizes actual accomplishments. I base this prediction on my belief that many minority candidates can teach better than they currently test. Documentation may also help to identify another problematic group of teaching candidates to which we devote far too little attention—those who test far better than they teach.

In summary, the virtue of documentation approaches is that the structured portfolio can become a *portable residency,* a set of standards and activities to guide both candidates and institutions during the period of teacher education and induction. Within that framework, teacher preparation and teacher assessment can interact during the critical early years of a teaching career. Assessment using portfolios can thus become more than a new technology for quality assurance; it can become a significant opportunity for the reform of teaching.

The Aims of New Approaches to Teacher Assessment

This paper began with a discussion of paradox. How can we raise teaching standards without emphasizing more stringent forms of external assessment that further erode the credibility of teacher-education programs as sources of attestation? We seek a model of teacher assessment that will ultimately make the institutions of teacher education and teacher induction less dependent on external assessment, less prone to suspicion, and more deserving of trust from the policy community and the society at large.

Sadly, teacher-preparation programs and, in particular, the undergraduate or graduate liberal arts programs with which they are associated, appear to have earned a fair amount of the suspicion they now evoke. Passing grades in content courses cannot be taken as evidence that a future teacher adequately understands the facts and principles of the school subjects in the curriculum. Positive evaluations during student teaching rarely inspire confidence that the novice teacher has demonstrated readiness to teach. One of the implicit messages of this paper is that newer forms of assessment, especially the development of documentation through portfolios, can help restore trust in preparation programs by providing visible evidence of what students accomplish.

Ironically, the externalization of assessment could result in less-responsible professional education. Education improves as instruction and assessment are integrated; this was the message of last year's ETS conference, and it is as true for professional education as it is for grades K–12. The emphasis on high-stakes mandatory external assessment for all teacher-education graduates tends to relieve instructional programs of their obligation to evaluate candidates during the course of instruction. Approaches to teacher assessment that would include systematic documentation of the developing capacities and accomplishments of new teachers during their period of preparation could help to convince policymakers that teacher-preparation institutions can be trusted to evaluate their students appropriately.

Assessment can become a powerful tool for reform when it is used to coordinate otherwise disparate, insular efforts for change. Assessment will lead to the enablement and empowerment of teachers when it withers away, when its standards and procedures become integral parts of professional preparation and not external appendages to instruction.

The criteria of validity in such an assessment program extend beyond the usual concerns with reliability and conventional forms of validity. An assessment program must be validated against the degree to which its implementation moves the entire enterprise of which it is a part closer to accomplishment of its social purposes (Cronbach, 1987). We must ask whether a given form of assessment will lead to actions on the parts of teachers and candidates that will make them better teachers, benefit their students and schools, and help move the profession in desired directions.

We cannot afford to be blinded by any particular research program's limited view of the teaching enterprise. Teaching is more than classroom management and organization; more than knowledge of subject matter; more than can be observed solely in a laboratory, or an hour's classroom visit, or an assessment center, or an interview, or surely in a three-hour test battery. Any approach to teacher assessment that lures us into believing that its method alone captures the essence of teaching should be subject to the most skeptical scrutiny.

Members of the educational policy community have been seduced by their own reckless demand for a quick fix in the matter of teacher standards. And we in the research and measurement communities have meekly acquiesced to their plans, providing them with the instruments they ordered rather than the responsible criticisms they deserve. The time has come to close ranks as a responsible professional community and communicate to our policy colleagues that important and complex problems will not be solved through simple-minded strategies that can be implemented on a large scale overnight.

The National Board of Medical Examiners (NBME) presents a telling example of how modestly the most powerful and influential of professional-standards boards began its work. The first NBME examination was held in Washington, D.C., on October 16–21, 1916. Thirty-two physicians applied for the examination, and only sixteen were deemed eligible, perhaps through the equivalent of some sort of portfolio review. Ten candidates, who had earned their medical degrees between 1907 and 1916, appeared for the examination, which consisted of written, oral, laboratory, and clinical tests. Five passed (Hubbard and Levit, 1985, p. 163).

What, then, is my dream for an ideal strategy of teacher assessment? Let us arrange a marriage of insufficiencies. Join together both portfolios and direct observation as sources of information about how teachers teach, sources that are specific to the particular context in which a teacher works. And context is important, because the sharing of a history of experiences with a group of children provides the basis for much of any teacher's decisions. Then add a well-crafted set of performance assessments, complete with exercises that follow up on the contents of the portfolios, as well as other exercises that can stand alone. Finally, to ensure broad coverage of the many areas of teacher subject-matter competence and knowledge of student characteristics, supplement these approaches with a new generation of written examinations that are less fragmented and discontinuous than the current crop.

If we can achieve such a program of assessment, in which most of the methods are far more faithful to the practice of teaching than current approaches are, we may be on the threshold of both better teacher assessment and, far more important, better teaching and learning in our schools.

REFERENCES

Aburto, S., & Haertel, E. (1986). *Study group on alternative assessment methods.* Summary of working seminar. Stanford, CA: Teacher Assessment Project, Stanford University School of Education.

Bird, T. (in press). The schoolteacher's portfolio. In L. Darling-Hammond & J. Millman (Eds.), *Handbook on the evaluation of elementary and secondary school teachers.* Newbury Park, CA: Sage Publications.

Byham, W. C. (1986). *Use of the assessment center method to evaluate teacher competencies.* Commissioned paper. Stanford, CA: Teacher Assessment Project, Stanford University School of Education.

Cornell, L. S. (1988). *Colorado state superintendent's biennial report.* Denver, CO: State Department of Education.

Cronbach, L. J. (1987). Five perspectives on test validation. In H. Wainer & H. Braun (Eds.), *Test validity.* Hillsdale, NJ: Erlbaum.

Hubbard, J. P., & Levit, E. J. (1985). *The National Board of Medical Examiners: The first seventy years.* Philadelphia, PA: National Board of Medical Examiners.

Shulman, L. S. (1986a). Those who understand: Knowledge growth in teaching. *Educational Researcher, 15*(2), 4–14.

Shulman, L. S. (1986b). Paradigms and research programs for the study of teaching. In M. C. Wittrock (Ed.), *Handbook of research on teaching* (3rd Ed.). New York, NY: Macmillan.

Shulman, L. S. (September 1987a). Assessment for teaching: An initiative for the profession. *Phi Delta Kappan,* 38–44.

Shulman, L. S. (1987b). Knowledge and teaching: Foundations of the new reform. *Harvard Educational Review, 57*(1), 1–22.

Shulman, L. S. (November 1988). A union of insufficiencies: Strategies of teacher assessment in a period of educational reform. *Educational Leadership,* 36–46.

Shulman, L. S., Bird, T., & Haertel, E. (April 1988). *Toward alternative assessments of teaching: A report of work in progress.* Stanford, CA: Teacher Assessment Project, Stanford University School of Education.

Stodolsky, S. (1988). *The subject matters.* Chicago, IL: University of Chicago Press.

Wilson, S., Shulman, L. S., & Richert, A. (1987). 150 different ways of knowing: Representations of knowledge in teaching. In J. Calderhead (Ed.), *Exploring teacher thinking.* London, UK: Cassell.

INTRODUCTION

A UNION OF INSUFFICIENCIES: STRATEGIES FOR TEACHER ASSESSMENT IN A PERIOD OF EDUCATIONAL REFORM (1988)

IN THIS ESSAY, which began as an address to the American Association of Colleges of Teacher Education, Shulman explains both the conception of teacher knowledge that emerged from the Knowledge Growth in a Profession Project and the eclectic approach to teacher assessment that was emerging in the Teacher Assessment Project. While this essay shares much in common with "The Paradox of Teacher Assessment," Shulman here is attempting to communicate the ideas that drove his assessment work in a nontechnical way to a wide readership (consisting primarily of teachers and administrators, not researchers).

Using pedagogical content knowledge as an example, Shulman explains and illustrates how teachers must find powerful ways to represent ideas to their students. He then describes the array of assessment techniques that ought to be used in an unfolding process of teacher assessment, including written examinations, assessment center activities, documentation through portfolios, and classroom observations.

12

A UNION OF INSUFFICIENCIES

STRATEGIES FOR TEACHER ASSESSMENT IN A PERIOD OF EDUCATIONAL REFORM

TWO YEARS AGO, my colleagues at Stanford and I were invited to initiate a program of research in the assessment of teachers. The National Board for Professional Teaching Standards was more than a year away from formation (Shulman and Sykes, 1986). But a new generation of ways to assess the capacities required for teaching was needed. There was widespread dissatisfaction with the quality and character of existing tests and observation instruments for evaluating teachers. Given the nature of the existing approaches, which comprised primarily multiple-choice tests and generic observation scales, the challenge was to find a starting point for our effort.

Our work on a new set of approaches to teacher assessment did not emerge from an interest in measurement or testing per se. For over three years, with the support of a grant from the Spencer Foundation, my colleagues and I had already been conducting in-depth longitudinal studies of how new high school teachers learn to teach. More specifically, in the context of several teacher education programs in California, we were investigating the ways in which individuals who possessed differing levels of expertise in particular subject matters—mathematics, social studies, English, and biology—learned to teach what they knew to young people.

Begin with the Activities of Teaching

By starting our research with an interest in the teacher's content knowledge, we arrived at conceptions of teaching quite different from the conclusions of the teaching effectiveness studies. Our research led us to develop a theoretical formulation around the centrality of content-specific pedagogy and the kind of teacher understanding that appeared to lie behind such teaching, which we dubbed *pedagogical content knowledge.* Our contention was that there existed (and was continually being developed in the minds of teachers) a kind of knowledge unique to able teachers of particular content domains, including elementary teachers of reading, mathematics, and other subjects. The existing conception of teacher knowledge, with its preoccupation with generic principles of classroom management and organization, was only a partial picture. Pedagogical content knowledge transcended mere knowledge of subject matter as well as generic understanding of pedagogy alone (Leinhardt and Smith, 1985; Shulman, 1987b; Wilson et al., 1987).

This kind of knowledge can best be depicted with reference to a recent movie about teaching, *Stand and Deliver.* There is a memorable scene in which the high school mathematics teacher, Jaime Escalante, is attempting to teach his class a fundamental concept in mathematics, negative numbers. His class of general mathematics students in the barrio of East Los Angeles is convinced that it cannot learn real mathematics, much less algebra. Escalante persists. I paraphrase:

"Negative numbers . . . very important. You dig a hole in the sand and put the sand next to the hole. The hole, minus two. The sand, plus two. You see that?" He is gesturing and acting out the digging to these students who have spent a great deal of their young lives at the beach. "The hole is minus two. The pile of sand is plus two. What do you get if you add them back together?" Finally, a hostile gang member to whom Escalante has addressed this question can no longer resist: he mutters almost inaudibly "zero." Escalante smiles. He begins to talk about the wonders of both negative numbers and of zero, and of how *their* ancestors, the Mayans, invented *zero,* when even the Greeks had no such concept.

This brief scene illuminates the several kinds of understanding and skill that underlie a teacher's expertise and distinguish it from that of the mere subject matter expert. The teacher not only understands the content to be learned and understands it deeply, but comprehends which aspects of the content are crucial for *future* understanding of the subject and which are more peripheral and are less likely to impede future learning if not fully grasped. The teacher comprehends which aspects of the content will be likely to pose the greatest difficulties for the pupils' understanding. The most crucial to learn is not always the most difficult; the most difficult is not always the most crucial.

The teacher also understands when persistent preconceptions, misconceptions, or difficulties are likely to inhibit student learning. The teacher has invented or borrowed or can spontaneously create powerful representations of the ideas to be learned in the form of examples, analogies, metaphors, or demonstrations. These will serve to bridge the students' knowledge (digging holes in the sands of L.A.'s beaches) and a critical concept to be learned (positive and negative numbers). Further, the teacher can distinguish between an inventive contribution that reflects a nonstandard but productive insight into a key idea and another response that communicates the confusion and disarray in a student's mind.

The teacher understands how to establish a *pedagogically* meaningful relationship with youngsters. Notice that Escalante created a relationship around the subject matter to be learned; he did not ignore the curriculum and establish relationships around social or personal attributes alone. He used his cultural understanding to establish credibility and trust. Finally, Escalante exhibited a moral or ethical commitment to teach as if his students were capable of learning what was important. He sustained high expectations for them without regard for their prior successes or failures as individual students or as members of a group.

Our conception of teaching attempts to identify the understandings and skills that distinguish an exemplary teacher from an educated pedestrian (defined as the proverbial man-on-the-street, a nonteacher who has comparable subject matter background, but no preparation or experience in teaching). It should also distinguish the teacher of a particular content area from excellent teachers in general. Thus, even Escalante, were he to teach *Moby Dick* instead of calculus, might not measure up to the stature of a very fine English teacher.

These attributes and accomplishments certainly do not exhaust the list of knowings and doings that define an excellent teacher. Yet any system of teacher assessment must attempt to measure these content-specific understandings and skills. In our work we first came up with a coherent conception of teaching. Only then did we ask which approaches to assessment would be adequate to measure the accomplishment of such teaching competence. We insisted that the measurement choices be controlled by pedagogical principles, rather than vice versa. Even though we sensed that we were moving toward kinds of assessment for which little adequate theory or technology yet existed, the need for teaching itself to hold the upper position could not be violated. Any system of teacher assessment, however reliable, must first and foremost be faithful to teaching.

A Union of Insufficiencies

Social scientists have long recognized that characterizing a human being or a social group is exceedingly complex. It is akin to getting a "fix" on a remote, moving, and not clearly perceived target. Such scholars typically urge their peers to engage in some form of "triangulation," posing and combining evidence from several alternative perspectives to compose a coordinated, coherent, and more valid image of whatever is studied. In fact, even in the field of educational testing, validity is no longer viewed as an attribute of a test that can be summarized in a single coefficient, a number representing the relationship between test performance and a particular criterion. Instead, argues Lee Cronbach (1987), validity is an argument. One conducts a set of observations, inquiries, and deliberations regarding the instruments under review and the variety of conditions and purposes for which they have been designed. In light of their full range of purposes and associated consequences, both intended and not, users make inferences regarding the value and utility of an assessment. One establishes the validity of a test through crafting such an argument rather than through calculation of a mathematical term. And central to that argument is concern with the effects or consequences of that test and its use, for those who are examined with it, and for the society in which they function.

For this reason, I no longer think of the assessment of teachers as an activity involving a single test or even a battery of tests. I instead envision a process that unfolds and extends over time, in which written tests of knowledge, systematic documentation of accomplishments, formal attestations by colleagues and supervisors, and analyses of performance in assessment centers and in the workplace are combined and integrated in a variety of ways to achieve a representation of a candidate's pedagogical capacities (Shulman, 1987a). Each of these several approaches to the assessment of teachers is, in itself, as fundamentally flawed as it is reasonably suitable, as perilously insufficient as it is peculiarly fitting. What we need, therefore, is a union of insufficiencies, a marriage of complements, in which the flaws of individual approaches to assessment are offset by the virtues of their fellows.

Consider again these alternative approaches to teacher assessment: written examinations including multiple-choice, computer-controlled, and essay formats; exercises in assessment centers that simulate problems of planning, teaching, evaluating, critically observing teaching, and the like; documentation and attestation of accomplishments as in a structured, prescribed portfolio; and direct observation of teaching by a dispassionate observer. What are the strengths of each approach? Where are its insufficiencies?

Written Examinations

Tests are regularly used to measure basic skills, knowledge of teaching content, and understanding of professional practice. They permit broad sampling of domains and are relatively economical to use. They enjoy high reliability in scoring, having been originally invented to bring greater objectivity to examinations. Newer forms of essay examination, and experimental methods to employ computers to administer and manage objective tests, promise further improvement. Their insufficiencies lie in their remoteness from the complexities and contexts of practice. They excel at measuring relatively isolated pieces of knowledge (hence their capacity to sample across wide domains), but they fail to tap more integrated processes of judgment, decision making, and problem solving in more realistic contexts. The experience of taking a written test is quite different from that of teaching a class, preparing a lesson, or most other aspects of the teacher's craft.

Assessment Center Exercises

Performance assessment has been used for years in assessment centers for the foreign service, in several medical boards, in the architecture exams, in the California Bar Exam, and in principals' assessment centers (Byham, 1986; Aburto and Haertel, 1986). Assessment center exercises for teaching simulate the real problems and processes of teaching. In my research, we have created exercises in which teachers are observed as they lay out the plan for a lesson, teach that lesson to a group of new students, and then reflect on the episode and review it critically. Another exercise asks the teacher to analyze a textbook and plan to adapt it for use in his or her own classroom. Our exercises present teachers with a videotape of teaching to observe, critique, and then recommend what they might do under the same circumstances. Another exercise presents examples of student work and asks the teacher to respond to the students' errors and insights (Shulman et al., 1988). Thus far, we have experimented with nearly 20 assessment exercises.

In general, performance assessment exercises can reflect the complexities of teaching more faithfully than do test items. But they too are insufficient. They are relatively expensive to create, administer, and evaluate. They cannot possibly sample areas of content as widely as do conventional written tests. Even though far more realistic than tests, they still cut off the teacher from the actual contexts of his or her teaching—the school, the students, and the history of teaching and learning they share. How do we begin to bridge between assessments that introduce realism of performance and the need to reflect the actual settings in which teachers do their work?

Documentation Through Portfolios

To introduce a connection with the contexts and personal histories that characterize real teaching, portfolios of various kinds have been tried, with limited success, in teacher assessment. In licensure and career ladder programs in Tennessee and Florida, among other states, teachers were asked to submit lesson plans, attendance records, and other indications of their effectiveness. The resulting portfolios were often too large, too nonselective, and of uncertain connection to the efforts of the individuals whose work they were supposed to reflect. The initial idea seemed a worthy one: collect artifacts that would reveal how teachers actually teach in their classrooms. But with insufficient time to design specifications for portfolio contents and inadequate opportunities to create local conditions that would promote accurate and relevant documentation procedures, the states were unable to pull off the experiment successfully. My research group continues to believe that the underlying notion of documentation is sound; and, as I shall discuss later, we believe that the insufficiencies can be overcome or compensated for (Bird, in press).

Classroom Observation

If indirect monitoring of classroom activity through some form of documentation or portfolio has failed, why not observe the teacher directly? Direct observation of teaching is widely employed, especially in the Southeastern states, for permanent licensure. While the full complexity of teaching can, in principle, be reflected in observations, in practice they rarely achieve their potential. The problem of sampling is staggering. Many more classroom visits are needed to establish "typical teaching performance" than have ever been used for evaluation (see Stodolsky, 1988). In addition, most methods of direct observation employ the most generic of rating scales, applying the same categories of analysis to the 2nd grade teaching of reading and the 11th grade teaching of trigonometry. This problem grows in part out of the emphasis on generic teaching skills that dominates current thinking. It also explains how authorities justify the employment of principals or other observers who are not content specialists to evaluate any teaching they observe.

Observation is tempting because there seems so much potential in watching real teaching in real classrooms directly. But such methods are ultimately disappointing, because they fail to tap many of teaching's critical dimensions. Too often, the typical observation method for evaluating teaching is like photographing the *Mona Lisa* with a black-and-white Polaroid camera, or like tape-recording the most sumptuous *Carmen* with an office dictaphone. So much potential, so limited a harvest.

Teacher Assessment in the Service of Reform

The proposed reforms of teaching call for reductions of the educational bureaucracy because critical decisions and policies ought not to be set at a level remote from the instruction of children. In this context, *teacher empowerment* is a misleading phrase. Teachers require *enablement* as much as empowerment. They deserve conditions that would enable them to develop their talents and capacities and to exercise them in the interests of children.

Reform through restructuring presents teachers with the opportunity to decide and to act. Greater competence, however, can *enable* a teacher with the understanding, the skill, and the commitment to act wisely and sensitively. Both empowerment through restructuring and enablement through improved standards, preparation, and support must occur if the desired improvements are to be achieved. Power will flow more easily to those who are viewed and trusted as able. Enablement will develop more readily in institutions where autonomy, flexibility, and discretion have been granted.

If the locus of decision making shifts to the school and the classroom, standards for teacher competence must necessarily rise and become more explicit. As expectations for teachers expand, the obligation of teacher education and induction programs grows as well. At present, states have instituted a web of tests and classroom visits to assure themselves of their teachers' competence, examining everything from basic intellectual skills to general pedagogical skills. But these approaches too often reflect the limits of conventional instruments rather than clear conceptions of the complexity and richness of all that must be appraised if we envision a faithful assessment of pedagogy.

Members of the teaching community can no longer tolerate this kind of blindness to the essential character of their work. Schoolteachers and their colleagues in supervision, administration, and teacher education must establish that conventional conceptions of testing simply will not suffice for the assessment of teaching. Twenty-first-century conceptions of school reform and the professionalization of teaching cannot co-exist with early twentieth-century models of testing and evaluation, especially when these yield unacceptably simplistic definitions of teaching. We who engage in the practice and theory of education need to become more proactive in asserting the purposes and conditions for teacher assessment. The time for reaction has passed; the time for initiative has come.

○

Coping with Insufficiency

Our research group has been studying the use of performance assessments over the past year and a half. We have made substantial progress in the design and scoring of this new kind of teaching assessment. Yet we remain uncomfortable with its limitations, especially with regard to those aspects of teaching in which context and time play a central role. In that regard, we are now investigating the use of carefully crafted and well-reviewed portfolios, where specifications for the contents are very carefully defined, and where monitoring of the process at the local level is encouraged. Although there have been problems in the past with several aspects of portfolios as reliable sources of evidence on teacher competence, they retain almost uniquely the potential for documenting the unfolding of both teaching and learning over time and combining that documentation with opportunities for teachers to engage in the analysis of what they and their students have done.

In our current research we are preparing to field-test a program of assessment in which portfolio development and subsequent assessment of performance are combined. "Candidates" will first spend a year developing their entries for a portfolio. In most cases, the specifications for each required portfolio entry[1] will be clearly defined to include evidence of the teacher's plans and activities (including videotapes of teaching when possible) as well as examples of student work. When possible, these defined entries will extend over time so that changes in teaching and learning and evidence of the relationships between them can also be included.

How else but through a portfolio can we examine a teacher's work with an at-risk child over the course of a semester? How else can we evaluate the different kinds of tests and assignments teachers use to assess their own students' progress? How else can we examine the teaching of writing, complete with the repeated iterations of instruction and feedback so crucial in learning that skill?

But how do we know that a portfolio truly represents the work of the candidate? This is one of the problems that has beset the use of portfolios in the past.

I advocate a radical premise. A portfolio should represent "coached" performance; portfolio development should be an occasion for interaction and mentoring among peers. Far from avoiding the admission that the portfolio contents have profited from the assistance of others, we might well require that every portfolio entry be cosigned or commented upon by a mentor or peer who has participated, helped, reviewed, or critiqued the effort. Much like a doctoral dissertation or a studio project in architecture, the performance in the portfolio reflects both the efforts of the candidate and the advice of the instructor. The solution to coaching as a problem is to treat it as a virtue.

That is why we are currently investigating how to use the assessment center as a follow-up to the portfolio. Anything that is placed in the portfolio is "at risk" for subsequent review in the assessment center just as a doctoral dissertation is reviewed in an oral examination, or an architect's drawings or scale model are "juried" in a subsequent design competition. What has been documented in the portfolio can then be presented at the assessment center as "a case of teaching and learning." Such presentations by the candidate, accompanied by examples of student work, video- or audiotapes of his or her teaching, and commentaries by mentors or colleagues, then become the starting point for about half of the assessments that are conducted. The rest of the assessment center activity would remain individual exercises, independent of any particular experiences unique to any candidate.

A True Portrait of Teaching

What, then, is my dream for a marriage of insufficiencies? Combine the virtues of portfolios and direct observation as sources of information about how teachers teach with their own children. These sources are limited by the particular context in which a teacher works. But context is important, as is the sharing of a history of experiences with a group of children, to provide the basis for looking at much of teaching. Then add a well-crafted assessment center, complete with exercises that follow up on the contents of the portfolios as well as others that are capable of standing alone. Finally, to ensure that broad coverage of the many areas of teacher subject matter competence is adequately achieved, supplement these with a new generation of written examinations less fragmented and discontinuous than the current crop. If we can achieve such a program of assessment, in which most of the methods are far more faithful to the practice of teaching than are the current approaches, we may be on the threshold of both better teacher assessment and, far more important, better teaching and learning in our schools.

NOTE

1. In addition to the pre-specified portfolio entries, there may well be optional sections selected by candidates to represent areas of individual accomplishment.

REFERENCES

Aburto, S., and E. Haertel. (1986). *Study Group on Alternative Assessment Methods.* Summary of Working Seminar, Teacher Assessment Project, Stanford University School of Education.

Bird, T. (In press). "The Schoolteacher's Portfolio." In *Handbook on the Evaluation of Elementary and Secondary Schoolteachers,* edited by L. Darling-Hammond and J. Millman. Newbury Park, Calif.: Sage.

Byham, W. C. (1986). "Use of the Assessment Center Method to Evaluate Teacher Competencies." Commissioned paper, Teacher Assessment Project, Stanford University School of Education.

Cronbach, L. J. (1987). "Five Perspectives on Test Validation." In *Test Validity,* edited by H. Wainer and H. Raun. Hillsdale, N.J.: Erlbaum.

Leinhardt, G., and D. A. Smith. (1985). "Expertise in Mathematics Instruction: Subject-Matter Knowledge." *Journal of Educational Psychology* 77: 247–271.

Shulman, L. S. (September 1987a). "Assessment for Teaching: An Initiative for the Profession." *Phi Delta Kappan:* 38–44.

Shulman, L. S. (1987b). "Knowledge and Teaching: Foundations of the New Reform." *Harvard Educational Review* 57, 1: 1–22.

Shulman, L. S., and G. Sykes. (March 1986). *A National Board for Teaching? In Search of a Bold Standard.* Paper commissioned for the Carnegie Forum on Education and the Economy, available through the Teacher Assessment Project, Stanford University School of Education.

Shulman, L. S., T. Bird, and E. Haertel. (April 1988). *Toward Alternative Assessments of Teaching: A Report of Work in Progress.* Teacher Assessment Project, Stanford University School of Education.

Stodolsky, S. (1988). *The Subject Matters.* Chicago: University of Chicago Press.

Wilson, S., L. S. Shulman, and A. Richert. (1987). "150 Different Ways of Knowing: Representations of Knowledge in Teaching." In *Exploring Teacher Thinking,* edited by J. Calderhead. London: Cassell.

AUTHOR'S NOTE

The research reported here was supported by grants from the Carnegie Corporation of New York and the Spencer Foundation. The opinions expressed are those of the author, and in no way reflect positions taken by either of those foundations. Moreover, although much of the work undertaken has been in the interests of the National Board for Professional Teaching Standards, the author is neither a member of nor staff to that organization, and in no way speaks on its behalf.

INTRODUCTION

RESEARCH ON TEACHING: A HISTORICAL AND PERSONAL PERSPECTIVE (1992)

ON THE OCCASION of the centennial of the University of Fribourg in Switzerland, a weeklong conference was held that brought together two groups of education scholars who did not typically convene jointly—researchers on teaching and scholars of moral development and education. The theme of the conference—the study of effective and responsible teaching—set the terms for Lee Shulman's keynote address that opened the week's exchanges. When "Knowledge and Teaching" was published nearly five years earlier, Shulman had been criticized for proposing a conception of teaching that was far too cognitive and rational, leaving little room for the moral dimensions of teaching. In this paper, he reviews the field of research on teaching, drawing heavily from "Paradigms and Programs," his opening chapter in the third *Handbook of Research on Teaching* (not included in this volume). He discusses how the cognitive, behavioral, and moral perspectives on teaching can be understood as fully compatible and mutually reinforcing. But he also cannot resist the temptation to begin the discussion with some stories about Père Girard, patron educational saint of Fribourg, whose integration of the intellectual and the moral ends of teaching set a fine example.

13

RESEARCH ON TEACHING

A HISTORICAL AND PERSONAL PERSPECTIVE

I expected something much greater—an instructor of the young, training the mind in order to train the heart.

—Père Girard (quoted in Compayre, 1894)

THIS BOOK CHAPTER WAS inspired by a conference to celebrate the centennial of the University of Fribourg. It is appropriate that we celebrate the birthday of a university with a conference on the study of teaching, for deliberations on teaching and learning lie at the heart of the educational enterprise. In this chapter, I develop five central assertions about this enterprise:

- Teaching is and has always been at the center of all education and educational reform.
- Theory underlies research on teaching, even when that research is assertively practical and self-consciously atheoretical; much of current policy and practice in education reform rests on research and theory.
- A major failing of both practice and policy is that they typically rest on incomplete, partial views of teaching. The most widespread view emphasizes observable performance of teachers—a perfectly legitimate feature to address—but ignores other critical aspects of

teaching, such as cognition, content, context, culture, character, and collaboration.

- All approaches to the study of teaching entail both epistemic and moral commitments. These two facets of thought are intertwined in fundamental ways.
- The contemporary movement in the study of teaching to reclaim a more complete view of pedagogy and pedagogical inquiry is consistent with concurrent developments in the social sciences and with dramatic changes in the condition and organization of the teaching profession itself.

Beginnings

The concept of teaching as a profession, which implies a field of knowledge that can be systematized and thus imparted to others, began long ago. However, I shall begin my story at the turn of the nineteenth century in Switzerland.

The Ideas of Père Girard

I devote special attention to the work of the eminent Swiss educator Père Girard for several reasons. First, he was the great educational pioneer of Fribourg, site of the university whose centennial the conference leading to this volume celebrated. Second, although far less famous than his contemporary Johann Heinrich Pestalozzi, his ideas carry a wisdom and value that deserve the attention of the modern reader. Finally, his conjoining of skill and understanding, especially of the intellective and the moral, foreshadowed the work of his compatriot Fritz Oser and the subject of the present book, effective and responsible teaching.

Père Gregoire Girard was born in Fribourg in 1765. He was a marvelously patient man, waiting until he had reached the age of seventy-nine to publish his masterwork (Girard, 1844). Girard believed strongly in the primacy of ideas over skills and in the necessary fusion of intellectual with moral work in the schools. For example, Girard argued that the purposes of elementary instruction, even in a subject such as grammar, should include development of the mind and of the judgment—grammar should not be taught for cultivation of the memory alone. He is quoted as asserting "This [grammar] instruction becomes a pure affair of memory, and the child becomes accustomed to pronounce sounds to which he attaches no meaning. The child needs a *grammar of ideas. . . .* Our *grammars of words* are the plague of education" (Compayre, 1894, pp. 470–471). Perhaps anticipating somewhat the contributions of his future compatriot Jean Piaget, Girard argued that grammar should be an exercise in thinking, a movement toward "the logic of childhood."

As for the links between mind and morality, Girard argued that all subject matters could be learned in ways that improve the moral fiber of the students as well. He wrote of both moral arithmetic and moral geography. The following is an example of Girard's arithmetic: "A father had the habit of going every evening to the dramshop, and often left his family at home without bread. During the five years that he led this life, he spent, the first year, 197 francs, the second, 204 francs, the third, 212 francs, and the fourth, 129 francs. How many francs would this unfortunate father have saved if he had not had a taste for drink?" (Compayre, 1894, pp. 471–472).

I am not eager to claim that contemporary theorists, even his successors in Fribourg, would find Girard's particular strategies of intellectual and moral education compelling. However, when we read the work of educational thinkers of the nineteenth century such as Girard, we encounter images of teaching that are broad and inclusive. They see no problems in joining the intellectual and the moral elements of education. For further evidence of this comprehensiveness of view, let us cross the Atlantic to a contemporary of Girard, the American educator David Page.

David Page

One of the most widely used textbooks of pedagogy in nineteenth-century United States was that of David Page, founder of the first normal school in the state of New York, a disciple of Horace Mann, and particularly inspired by Pestalozzi's work. One grasps a sense of his broad, inclusive view of teaching from the chapter titles of his textbook, *Theory and Practice of Teaching or the Motives and Methods of Good School Keeping* (Page, 1885):

1. "The Spirit of the Teacher"
2. "Responsibility of the Teacher"
3. "Habits of the Teacher"
4. "Literary Qualifications"
5. "Right Views of Education"
6. "Right Modes of Teaching"

7. "Conducting Recitations"
8. "Exciting Interest"
9. "School Government"
10. "School Arrangements"
11. "Relating to Parents"
12. "Teacher's Care of His Health"
13. "Teacher's Relations to His Profession"
14. "Rewards of Teaching"

Unfortunately, the rewards of teaching for Page included an early demise at the age of thirty-seven, brought on, we are told by his biographer, by his overwork to establish the state normal school. The biographer describes Page the pedagogue thus: "As a teacher, he exhibited two valuable qualifications: the ability to turn the attention of his pupils to the principles which explain facts, and in such a way that they could clearly see the connection; and the talent for reading the character of his scholars so accurately that he could at once discern what were their governing passions and tendencies, what in them needed encouragement and what repression" (from the biographical essay in Page, 1885).

A concern for both principles and character permeated David Page's thought and writing as an educator. He equally values both effective and responsible teaching.

John Dewey

Another thirty-seven-year-old educationist, John Dewey, was invited to the University of Chicago in 1896 (when the university itself was barely five years old) by its president, William Rainey Harper, to become professor of philosophy, psychology, and pedagogy. Dewey addressed the questions of why a research university (in itself a new conception in American higher education) should include a school of pedagogy and how such a school should differ from the already existing normal schools. Dewey too employed a broad and comprehensive vision of pedagogy. He argued for the conjunction of interest and intelligence, of the needs of the child as well as the progressive organization of the subject matter. He did not hold a narrow view of education.

Dewey argued that a school of pedagogy within a research university was to have a special role. It would not only prepare practitioners, both teachers and administrators; it would also be expected to contribute to the development of "science of education," the systematic investigation of the processes and institutions of educating that would place education on a par with physics and the other sciences. The disciplinary key to a science of education was likely to be the emerging science of psychology, through Dewey, and the laboratory for its investigations would be the schools themselves. In that spirit, Dewey established the Laboratory School of the University of Chicago. It was not a demonstration school, like those found in the many existing normal schools, whose purpose was solely the training of teachers. It was intended to serve as a site for the scientific study of learning, teaching, and child development, as well as the systematic investigation of school curriculum and organization.

Although Dewey was caught up in the creation of the Laboratory School, his spirit of educational experimentation and investigation captured the imagination of several presidents of the university as well. Both President Ernest D. Burton and President Robert M. Hutchins asserted that the University of Chicago's undergraduate college was itself an educational experiment. Just as the Laboratory School was to be a site for experimentation from kindergarten through secondary school, the college would be a site for research on an evaluation of higher education. It was no accident that many of the leading educationists of the University of Chicago emerged from the University Examiner's Office, where the evaluation functions for the college were placed. Among its leading figures were university examiners Ralph Tyler and Benjamin Bloom.

In spite of the genius of his vision, Dewey made two fundamental errors. The first was his undue optimism regarding the adequacy of psychology for providing a comprehensive scientific base for education and even the likelihood that psychology could ever achieve the status of a science such as physics. The second was his failure to recognize the costs of treating education—a complex field of practice—as a science, the most profound consequence of which was a tragic narrowing of its investigations as we entered the modern era.

The Modern Era: The Implicit Roles of Theory and Moral Stance

When we come to the modern era, we encounter a paradoxical narrowing of the conception of teaching found in the writing of scholars. Ironically, this narrowing came about in the interest of developing the very *science* of education that Dewey envisioned, and the effects of this quest were particularly visible in the study of teaching. To achieve such a science, scholars were required to do what any science quite properly requires of its savants:

observation of and experimentation with the phenomena of interest. To do science, we seek objectivization, abstraction, and generalization. These all demand a simplification and narrowing of the field of view so that lawlike statements can be made. The goals of scientific inquiry also demanded a degree of contextualization, with "all other things being equal" standing as the implicit credo for generalizations emerging from the research. Thus, though Dewey held a highly complex and contextualized conception of education, his call for a science of education undermined precisely the view of the enterprise that he most valued.

For scholars (or policy makers), a theory, however implicit and unacknowledged, determines the questions that they ask; their data will be answers to their questions, and they really cannot ask about everything at once. The theories that underlie such research both sharpen and narrow their efforts. I shall show how each successive paradigm for research on teaching typically begins with a criticism of the blindness of its predecessor, only to blinker its own eyes in a somewhat different manner. These problems of theoretical myopia (or, more precisely, tunnel vision) become particularly acute when research findings and methods are translated into educational policies by bureaucrats and political leaders. As the economist John Maynard Keynes once observed, "Practical men, who believe themselves to be quite exempt from any intellectual influences, are usually the slaves of some defunct economist. . . . [I]t is ideas, not vested interests, which are dangerous for good or evil" (Keynes, 1844/1936, pp. 383–384).

Policies act comprehensively even when they employ narrowly formulated theories. Policy makers are almost never conscious of the pervasively theoretical cast of their educational mandates. I have been involved in such activity over the past four years as I have worked with colleagues to develop new approaches to the evaluation of teachers. Approaches to teacher assessment and evaluation constitute the ultimate policy statement; they enshrine in standards and instrumentation the tastes and theoretical preferences of political leaders. That does not make them evil; on the contrary, political leaders are often more sensitive to the interests of disenfranchised or underrepresented groups than are the cloistered scholars of the academy.

What of morality? Is there any connection between the epistemic and methodological conceptions carried by alternate theories and any moral visions that they embody? If competing paradigms for the study of teaching have been myopic with regard to their implicit theories, they have been positively blind in failing to grasp the moral philosophy underlying their work. I can attest to that blindness from personal experience. In my own work over the past twenty-five years, much influenced by my teacher

Joseph Schwab, I have constantly sought to identify those critical aspects of the process of education that have been ignored by other scholars and then to design a program of research to repair the gap. I have typically failed to recognize that my critiques of other paradigms, as well as those criticisms skillfully leveled at my own work, reflect both epistemic and moral values.

A Succession of Paradigms

In the balance of this chapter, I shall have two interwoven stories to tell. First, I shall recount the succession of approaches to the study of teaching with which I have been personally associated since the 1960s. These will be limited primarily to work in the United States, and for this I apologize. As I summarize each approach, I shall emphasize its critique of prior work, its own theoretical approach, and the often implicit moral theme that permeates its concepts and methods.

Process-Product Research

In the modern era, research on teaching began as an attempt to answer a straightforward question: How are the behaviors and actions of teachers related to variations in student achievement? This research was dubbed "process-product" research because its goal was to discern the links between teaching processes and the kinds of student achievement that constituted the sought-after products of formal education. The research usually proceeded by having observers use categorical observation scales to record classroom teacher behavior and student responses. Observations might be made as few as three or as many as fifteen times during the school year. At the end of the year, children in each observed class were tested through the use of standardized achievement examinations. The teachers' behavior was correlated with student performance, and those forms of teacher behavior found to be positively correlated with student achievement were hypothesized to be part of "teaching effectiveness." Whenever possible, those correlations were replicated in further studies or tested more rigorously in experimental studies.

Much was gained from this research. Careful, systematic observation of practice occupied the center of the research program. The arena of inquiry shifted from the laboratory or the questionnaire to the classroom itself, with the actions of the teachers and students at its heart. (For an analysis of the different paradigms and programs in the study of teaching, see the *Third Handbook of Research on Teaching* [Shulman, 1986], which reviews these programs more formally and with numerous references. In this chapter, I wish to examine the progression of alternate research programs in a more personal and autobiographical mode.)

Although the proponents of this research program claim it to be atheoretical (perhaps motivated by the bloody and unproductive wars between learning theorists that characterized the 1930s and 1940s in the United States), it was far from that. While its goal was not to create and test formal theory, it rested undeniably on a host of implicit theoretical and ideological claims. Thus, research in the process-product tradition rests on the assumption that teaching can be divided into molecular acts, which in turn can be counted, combined, and analyzed. It assumes that teaching is, by and large, a singular phenomenon, about which much can be learned without worrying too much about context. It also assumes that teaching is an activity in which the representatives of the society, in this case teachers, learn to act on their students to bring them the educational benefits that the greater society has deemed best for them. We therefore learn which teacher behaviors are most effective so that we can encourage all teachers to engage in them for the benefit of their pupils.

Process-product research dominated the study of teaching for about fifteen years (1960–1975), reaching its peak in the late 1960s and early 1970s. It was especially effective in providing a response to critics who claimed that teaching was incapable of making a difference in the learning of children, because school achievement was overwhelmingly determined by social class and other characteristics of students' home background. Whether one agreed with the conceptual framework of process-product research or not, the enterprise certainly demonstrated that teacher behavior could be related to student achievement.

Another important feature of process-product research was its moral component. While it did not particularly emphasize moral behavior on the part of teachers or moral outcomes as its student products, it unambiguously rested on a moral claim: teaching ought to be understood and valued primarily through its effects on student learning. The purpose of teaching is the amelioration of ignorance, and studies of teaching that make claims of excellence for some kinds of pedagogy must buttress those claims with evidence of impact of the teaching on the lives and capacities of students. Thus, although some critics (including this writer) have been rather harsh judges of process-product research on epistemic and methodological grounds, we must acknowledge the importance of its clear moral stance.

Nevertheless, the image of teaching found in the process-product literature was quite narrow. The teacher *behaved*. Those behaviors were observed, counted, and combined without reference to teachers' intentions or cognitions, oblivious to their contexts and constraints. Of all those omissions, that most striking to me in 1975 was the ignoring of thought as a central element of teaching. By the mid-1970s, the cognitive revolution was well under way. Every human being was acknowledged to engage in thinking, reasoning, judgment, decision making, and problem solving; everyone, that is, except teachers, who were still described exclusively in terms of their behavior. It was time to introduce a new research paradigm. (Nathaniel Gage humorously criticized my cognitive approach during a debate between us at an annual meeting of the American Educational Research Association. Paraphrasing the learning theorist Edwin R. Guthrie's critique of his contemporary Edward Tolman, Gage opined that "Shulman leaves teachers lost in thought." A number of years later, in a paper prepared for Gage's own *festschrift,* I finally found the proper response. "Better to be lost in thought than missing in action." Neither fate is desirable.)

Teacher Thinking

When my colleagues and I established the Institute for Research on Teaching (IRT) at Michigan State University in 1975, we formulated its mission in reaction to the dominant process-product paradigm and its emphasis on behavior rather than cognition. As consistent with the growing cognitive revolution in psychology, we designed a research program built around the "mental life" of the teacher. Research on teacher planning, decision making, diagnosis, reflection, and problem solving dominated our research agenda. We pursued one of the earliest studies examining the ways in which teachers' decisions mediated the effects of administrative policies and mandated textbooks. Our critiques of process-product research were successful in pointing out the overly narrow focus of its efforts, especially its blindness to the centrality of thinking in the work of teachers.

The orientation of our work on teacher thinking, however, remained as dominated by psychology as the process-product tradition had been; it simply took a cognitive rather than a behaviorist slant. Like Dewey, we continued to "psychologize" teaching. Nevertheless, once again a moral perspective could be discerned in this work. Teachers were not merely automatons, machines that emitted behavior that could be measured. They were intelligent, thoughtful, sentient beings characterized by intentions, strategies, decisions, and reflections. Thus, their work could not be studied in the old-fashioned ways, as if they were mere "subjects" to be examined like rats in mazes or first-year psychology students in required laboratory courses. We could not merely do research *on* teachers; we were obligated to work collaboratively *with* teachers in our research.

Collaboration in Research on Teaching

A parallel movement, which began during our IRT days and has continued to grow in strength in the past few years, has been the emergence of collaboration, the design and pursuit of research on teaching with teachers themselves playing an increasingly collaborative role in the enterprise. In the IRT, we had "teacher collaborators," active classroom practitioners who spent half the day teaching and the other half at the university participating as researchers. We were not alone. Classroom ethnographers had begun to work with classroom teachers as coethnographers, full partners in the endeavor. The action research movement in the United Kingdom was taking shape, and this group too emphasized the importance of their partnership with teachers.

The emphasis on the need for more active collaboration between teachers and researchers carried both a moral and an epistemic quality. The moral perspective reflected a recognition that if research were to be used to influence the ways in which teachers worked, then they were entitled to be full partners in any efforts destined to affect their lives. The epistemic perspective was somewhat more subtle. If teachers' thoughts and judgments were indeed so central to understanding teaching, then how could any reasonable insights into teaching be accomplished without their active participation? Ironically, in this argument, the perspectives of morality and validity joined together. Not only were teachers entitled to be treated as full collaborators in research; the validity of the investigations might well be suspect without evidence of their collaboration.

In conjunction with these research developments, the occupation of teaching began to take a new turn toward greater professionalization. Teachers began to speak of autonomy and empowerment, of moving control of school policies to the building and classroom levels, and of the need for more research that documented teaching from the perspective of the classroom teacher. They began to call for research that would carry the "teacher's voice," rather than the "outsider" perspective of the ostensibly objective observer. Slowly but surely, collaboration has evolved from a courtesy practiced by a few scholars to an emerging norm for the relationship between researchers and teachers.

And Then We Discovered Context and Culture

During the second year of the IRT, we began to bring anthropologists into the picture. They addressed a totally new set of issues, methodologically, conceptually, and ideologically. Far more was changed than merely a shift from quantitative to qualitative methods. They formulated different questions, conceptualized utterly distinctive programs, and conducted research in the interests of other parties. With the coming of the ethnographers, we added context and culture to a picture that had previously included only cognition and behavior.

The contexts were both cultural and political. While some of our researchers—predominantly the anthropologists—were especially taken with the cultural mismatches between the school and the home, others, taking a perspective from political science, looked at the school and the teacher's cognitions in the classroom within a policy context of federal, state, local, and building-level organizations. Here again, a methodological paradigm carried both epistemic and moral weight. The anthropologists argued that prior research had emphasized an "*etic*" perspective, seeing the world—however acutely—from the point of view of the research observer, an outsider. The ethnographer's interest was in an "*emic*" view, reconstructing how the participants in a situation made their own sense of their worlds.

How did this methodological stance carry moral views as well? Ethnographers have in recent years been particularly interested in capturing the perspectives of those individuals and classes in society least likely to be able to speak for themselves. These politically weakest members of society often include teachers but more frequently include pupils, their parents, and especially the poor and disenfranchised elements of the society. Moreover, ethnographers tend to believe that the most critical aspects of classrooms are their social arrangements, the ways in which power relationships are distributed, the affinities between students afforded by systems of grouping or tracking, and the ways in which groups function interactively. The anthropologists therefore focus our attention on aspects of classroom life, those involving culture and context, that other methods tend to ignore. On the other hand, this emphasis is not accomplished without paying some price.

Teacher behavior had been augmented by teacher cognition, though at some expense, because the more attention we paid to thought, the less we were likely to attend to action. Then we added collaboration, culture, and context, putting more ingredients on the plate but undoubtedly leaving room for smaller amounts of each. Nevertheless, I was soon to discover that there were quite important ingredients still missing from our diet, an insight I failed to achieve until I had physically moved from one university to another.

The Missing Paradigm: Teacher Knowledge

In 1983, after moving from Michigan State University to Stanford, I observed that there still remained a significant "missing paradigm" in the study of teaching: the *content,* or substance, of the curriculum being taught and learned. The subject matter was missing. Whether conducted in traditions of behavioral study, cognitive research, or ethnography, most investigations treated teaching as a generic activity rather than as one that changed significantly as a function of what was being taught, to whom, and at what level. I initiated a research program in the interests of recovering the missing paradigm.

We began to ask a new question: How do people who already know something learn to teach what they know to others? That is, how does someone who learned Shakespeare's *Hamlet* learn to teach that play to others? How does one learn to teach the principles of human evolution, or the concept of democracy, or the equivalence of fractions, or the past perfect conjugation of French? We conducted longitudinal studies of men and women becoming secondary school teachers and negotiating the transition from "expert learners" to "novice teachers" with special reference to the subjects they taught. We also studied experienced teachers in a variety of content areas.

As we conducted that research, we realized that our question was not quite right. Teachers did not either know something or not know it. They knew their subjects in different ways and with different areas of specialization or familiarity. The teacher of social studies or science, for example, was sometimes teaching topics that he or she knew very well and at other times teaching topics with which he or she had only superficial acquaintance. In addition, teachers had different explicit or implicit theories of their disciplines and how they are learned. So we began to ask: How do teachers who know their subjects in different ways and at different levels teach their subjects to others? And as we proceeded further into our studies, these questions became further differentiated and deepened to accommodate variations in contexts and in the backgrounds of students.

As I have come to examine the ways in which these perspectives on the processes of teaching have emerged in response to one another, I have become especially conscious of the ways in which syntax of the research questions determined the shape of the investigation that followed. "What do good teachers do that distinguishes them from ordinary teachers?" yields very different studies than the question "What do good teachers of history do that distinguished them from ordinary ones?" or "that distinguishes them from good teachers of mathematics?" Similarly, what effective teachers *do* is a different question from what effective teachers *know.* And "What do good teachers of biology for urban minority children do and think?" yields yet another challenge for scholars.

With the defining of the "missing paradigm," I began to feel that we had finally arrived at a comprehensive view of teaching. Content had now joined the mix, and the picture was complete—or so I had deluded myself into thinking. No sooner had our work on the "pedagogy of substance" begun to flourish than a cogent critique appeared in response to a paper I had published in the *Harvard Educational Review*, "Knowledge and Teaching" (Shulman, 1987). Hugh Sockett (1987) asserted that I had missed the point completely. The essence of teaching was no more content that it had been behavior, cognition, or culture. Teaching was essentially a moral activity; I had missed the centrality of *character*, or what my friend Fenstermacher would call *manner*.

I will not presume to characterize the research program proposed by those who would place character or manner at the center of their problem definition. To some extent, much of this volume examines this idea as it explores the notions of responsible teaching. In other ways, Sockett, Fenstermacher, and other members of the moral wing of teacher education are more comfortable playing the role of astute critic than they are at conducting their own empirical research. But I am confident that the research will come, and I am equally optimistic that this research will also add significant new facets to our understanding of teaching.

Quests for the Grand Strategy

The question remains whether it is possible to ask research questions that simultaneously include all the important perspectives—behavior, cognition, culture, context, collaboration, character—and still preserve the precision and reproducibility associated with classical social scientific models, or whether we need quite different research models that approach the study of teaching in quite new ways.

I have expressed in several other publications my admiration for the research in mathematics teaching pioneered by Magdalene Lampert of Michigan State University. Other colleagues at Michigan State—Lampert's collaborator Deborah Ball in math, Suzanne Wilson in history and social studies, Katherine J. Roth in science—have pursued similar investigatory styles. I present this approach to you as a case in point of research that manages to blend in an uncanny way the full gamut of perspectives that I have identified.

Lampert's approach to research on the teaching of mathematics exemplifies a new conception of the teacher as investigator, a new way of thinking about the university professor as a classroom-based researcher, and a broad, comprehensive perspective on the teaching of school subjects. Her approach to the study of math teaching is best exemplified in a recent paper (Lampert, 1990). She conducts her research by assuming full responsibility for all the mathematics teaching in a fifth-grade classroom during an entire school year. She documents her teaching and her students' learning meticulously, through a combination of classroom videotapes, daily journal keeping, clinical interviews with students, observations by research assistants, and active commentaries solicited from outside experts.

In her 1990 paper, Lampert begins her exposition with several pages on the nature of mathematics, drawing heavily from the writings of the eminent mathematicians Georg Polya and Imre Lakatos. She emphasizes the intellectual aspects of mathematical learning as explicated by such mathematicians. She also gives surprising and enlightening attention to the moral and social aspects of the mathematical discourse community, as discussed by those same mathematicians. After laying out the intellectual, moral, and social parameters of mathematics as a knowledge-finding and knowledge-testing collegium, she proceeds to provide a detailed analytical account of her own teaching of a unit on exponentiation. In this elaborated case study, we can vividly see the ways in which she incorporates and instantiates her understanding of mathematics as a way of knowing and of socially engaging in the everyday workings of her classroom.

At the end of her paper, Lampert deftly relates her case to broad national concerns for the learning of mathematics with understanding and to the practical issues of how to accomplish such an extraordinary, difficult agenda in the setting of real classrooms. Lampert's work is both teacher's work and mathematics educator's work; it is both practice and theory. It informs and inspires practitioners while enlightening and stimulating researchers.

But is this social science? When the focus of the research is a single teacher, and that teacher is also the investigator, what forms of generalization and theoretical knowledge are possible? And even if Lampert's work does succeed in addressing behavior, cognition, context, character, and collaboration, is it not inevitable that there yet remain one, two, and more theoretical or practical perspectives that even she has not included?

I conclude that our quest for the full picture, the complete pedagogue, is a fruitless one if we insist on maintaining a traditional conception of social science. We are, as human thinkers, actors, and believers, unable to achieve completeness, destined to be partial from a disciplinary, an ideological, and policy perspective. To be properly comprehensive, we will instead move toward a more local, case-based, narrative field of study, as exemplified in Lampert's research.

Meanwhile, unfortunately and dangerously, education policy makers remain most heavily influenced by the older work on teacher behavior. In part, the influence of process-product research is stronger because its findings are older and more easily translated into prescriptions for policy. Unlike most other research on teaching, it ties the acts of teaching directly to socially valued student outcomes. Perhaps most significantly, this work is also most readily compatible with a top-down view of educational reform and policy making, in which the best approaches are determined at the top and teachers are then trained, advised, and mandated to behave accordingly.

Effective and Responsible Teaching

This volume addresses the interacting topics of effective and responsible teaching. They are most typically addressed independently, as if educators trade off intellectual against moral ends, in a zero-sum game in which an emphasis on effectiveness must entail a sacrifice of responsibility or vice versa. Alternately, they are viewed hierarchically, as in Sockett's (1987) assertion that all aspects of teaching must be subordinated to the moral, for all teaching is fundamentally, to use Alan Tom's (1984) lovely phrase, a moral craft.

I too assert that all teaching represents a confluence of the intellectual and the moral, but in ways that are not normally addressed in these discussions. I treat as my text the most famous sentence ever written about education by the eminent American psychologist Jerome Bruner (1960). In paraphrase, he claimed that any child could learn any subject at any stage of his development in an intellectually honest way. Most of the discussions of his claim have focused on its developmentally ambitious manifesto that any learning is attainable by any child. But for the pedagogy of substance, the most significant phrase is contained in the words "in an intellectually honest way." (I was most recently reminded of this connection in a paper by Deborah Ball [forthcoming].) In those four words, we recognize the essential conjunction of the moral and the intellectual, of the responsible and the substantive, in all pedagogy.

All teaching entails a fundamental tension between ideas as they are understood by mature scholars of a discipline and as they might be grasped by schoolchildren. Teachers explain complex ideas to children by offering examples, analogies, or metaphors, by telling stories or providing demonstrations, by building bridges between the mind of the child and the more developed understanding in the mind of the teacher. These bridges carry two-way traffic, as children offer their own representations to the teacher and to one another as well. Teachers not only represent the content of their disciplines; they model the processes of inquiry and analysis, the attitudes and dispositions of scholarship and criticism, and they purposively create communities of interaction and discourse within which ideas are created, exchanged, and evaluated.

How can these experiences of the mind be accomplished "in an intellectually honest way"? What are the teacher's responsibilities to both the student and the subject matter, to the child and the curriculum? This tension captures an inherently moral aspect of all teaching, a tension central to any definition of effective *and* responsible pedagogy. The implicit social contract between teacher and students implies that the mathematics that the teacher offers will be real mathematics and the history, honest history. To the extent that teachers themselves can grasp the complexities and uncertainties of a field, these subtleties will be shared with the student, not obscured or camouflaged. But the pedagogical contract presumes that the teacher is capable of gauging the likely compatibility between mind and idea in much the way that a physician is responsible for discerning the physical compatibility of body and medication. In these situations, the moral and substantively pedagogical fuse.

Dewey's conception of education, to which I enthusiastically subscribe, rests on the unity of his epistemology and his political philosophy. Dewey's theory of knowledge rests on a never-consummated neo-Hegelian spiral of alternating, competing, and inherently incomplete knowledge claims. Anticipating, perhaps, the modern information processing psychologist's view that human cognition is severely limited in its capacities to grasp the richness of the world in its full complexity, Dewey argued that no knowledge claim, however well grounded and soundly argued, can ever be immune to critical attack. In principle, any thesis will have left some part of the argument inadequately covered. There is always room for another opinion. Indeed, another opinion is mandatory. Knowledge is socially constructed because it is always emerging anew from the dialogues and disagreements of its inventors.

Similarly, the ideal classroom must be a setting where opposing views collide, where every thesis is subjected to critical scrutiny and communally sanctioned doubt. Recognize that this is not only a conception of knowing and teaching. It is a moral argument as well. To permit knowledge claims to be offered that appear immune to critical examination, that appear to be warranted in *principle* without the negotiated warrant of learning community, is to violate both the intellectual and the moral code of Dewey's conception of education. Moreover, it is nearly impossible to discern where the intellectual ends and the moral begins in this formulation.

Conclusions

What, then is the future for research on teaching? First, because we are both educators and scholars, women and men of action as well as students of human behavior we are fated to be frustratedly schizophrenic. We must be both impassioned and dispassionate, deeply committed and objectively accurate.

Second, our work will grow increasingly cognitive, substantive, contextual, and—in several senses—local. We will tell stories more often than we conduct true experiments, we will modify situations more often than we manipulate variables, we will construct allusions to history as often as we rely on psychology, and disciplinary boundaries will fade and blur.

Third, we will take ever more seriously the wisdom of practice, both in the definition of what we study and in our design of collaborative, interactive studies. Teachers will become research agents as well as research subjects. We will watch as the profession of teaching and the community of scholarship intersect and interpenetrate.

Fourth, in this sense, the activity of research and the practice of teaching will become purposefully and mutually *reactive*. In spite of decades of preaching in manuals of research design that warn against reactivity as a threat to validity, we will come to see educator reactivity as one of the signs of its vitality and validity. Research on teaching will contribute to the increased professionalization of teaching by rendering teachers full partners in the making of research. We will resist the deskilling of teachers through the uses of research as a source of elite expertise. We will begin to judge the validity of research by its consequences for the improvement of teaching and learning.

We will not forgo entirely our search for generalizations about human learning, teaching, and classrooms, for generalization and simplification are essential to the understanding of our work. But the teachers and scholars who are at the center of our field, I am confident, will be prepared to exchange the quest for a science of education for a much higher goal—a search for meaning and worthwhile improvement in the practice and profession of education.

REFERENCES

Ball, D. L. "With an Eye on the Mathematical Horizon: Dilemmas of Teaching Elementary School Mathematics." *Elementary School Journal,* forthcoming.

Bruner, J. *The Process of Education.* Cambridge, Mass.: Harvard University Press, 1960.

Compayre, G. *The History of Pedagogy.* (2nd ed.). (W. H. Payne, trans.). Lexington, Mass.: Heath, 1894.

Girard, G. *De l'enseignement réguli de la langue naturelle dans les écoles et les familles* (On the systematic teaching of the mother tongue in schools and families). Paris: Dezobry, 1844.

Keynes, J. M. *The General Theory of Employment, Interest and Money.* New York: Harcourt Brace Jovanovich, 1844.

Lampert, M. "When the Problem Is Not the Question and the Solution Is Not the Answer." *American Educational Research Journal,* 1990, *27,* 29–63.

Page, D. P. *Theory and Practice of Teaching or the Motives and Methods of Good School Keeping.* New York: Barnes and Noble, 1885.

Schwab, J. J. "The Practical: A Language for Curriculum." *School Review,* 1969, *78*(5), 1–23.

Shulman, L. S. "Paradigms and Research Programs in the Study of Teaching: A Contemporary Perspective." In M. C. Wittrock (ed.), *Handbook of Research on Teaching.* (3rd ed.). New York: Macmillan, 1986.

Shulman, L. S. "Knowledge and Teaching: Foundations of the New Reform." *Harvard Educational Review,* 1987, *57*(1), 1–22.

Sockett, H. "Has Shulman Got the Strategy Right?" *Harvard Educational Review,* 1987, *57*(2), 208–219.

Tom, A. *Teaching as a Moral Craft.* White Plains, N.Y.: Longman, 1984.

INTRODUCTION

TEACHER PORTFOLIOS: A THEORETICAL ACTIVITY (1998)

IN THIS ESSAY, Shulman describes the work of the Teacher Assessment Project (TAP), both its earlier attempts at developing performance assessments and the later work in developing portfolios. He begins by asserting that a portfolio is a theoretical act; that is, by creating a framework with which to both document and assess teaching, we are making a theoretical claim about the nature of teaching practice. He then explores how the TAP staff became interested in the use of portfolios as an answer to the problem of the decontextualized nature of most teacher testing, even performance assessments. Shulman emphasizes both the dual benefits of portfolios—not only can they be used to assess teacher knowledge and practice, they can also create new opportunities for teacher learning, for prospective and practicing K–12 teachers—as well as teachers in higher education. In particular, portfolios allow teachers to make their work public, to be examined and critiqued by their colleagues. One sees in this argument Shulman's growing interest in what would become a scholarship of teaching and learning in higher education, as well as in teacher education and K–12 teaching.

14

TEACHER PORTFOLIOS

A THEORETICAL ACTIVITY

WHEN I THINK ABOUT portfolios and their beginnings, I am reminded of a recent summer visit to a perfectly wonderful place in northern Spain, Santiago de Compestela. Until arriving there, we had not known that Santiago (the reputed burial place of the Apostle St. James) vied with Jerusalem and Rome as one of the three great pilgrimage destinations of the Middle Ages. As we toured the area, we began to realize that when you talk about a pilgrimage, you are not talking about a single path. Finding ourselves on an obscure road, we would be told, "Oh, yes, this is part of the pilgrimage to Santiago." When we said we thought the pilgrimage followed a nearby freeway, we were assured: "No, no, some of the pilgrims made this side trip to this little convent and then they went on to Santiago." Apparently pilgrims from Hamburg even took side trips to Paris.

Somehow, even though engaged in some shared purpose, individual pilgrims and groups of pilgrims took very different paths—at times quite parallel, at other times simply intersecting. This feature of pilgrimages seems like a reasonable metaphor for some of the things I want to discuss about portfolios.

Key aspects of the trip that some colleagues and I have taken with portfolios can be captured in three stories. The first story recounts the work on teacher assessment that we began doing in 1985 with the Teacher Assessment Project (TAP) and how that work drove us to the development and use of portfolios. That story continues in its own way today in the portfolio work of the National Board for Professional Teaching Standards (NBPTS). A second story is about the experiences that I have had and continue to have in the course that I teach at Stanford in the teacher education program, which uses portfolios as a central feature. The third is the Larry

Cuban story, which I think is a very important instance of what happens when we take the portfolio notion and move it not only from students to teachers, but from teachers to teacher educators. After a few words of caution about some clear and present dangers in the use of portfolios, I conclude with my views on what I see as some of the virtues of the use of portfolios in teacher education.

The Portfolio as a Theoretical Act

A key point I want to stress at the beginning—and it is a theme that I will return to regularly—is that a portfolio is a theoretical act. By this I mean that every time you design, organize, or create in your teacher education program a template, a framework, or a model for a teaching portfolio, you are engaged in an act of theory. Your theory of teaching will determine a reasonable portfolio entry. What is declared worth documenting, worth reflecting on, what is deemed to be portfolio-worthy, is a theoretical act.

Let me elaborate. I am increasingly aware of the fact that the work we did in the TAP and the ways in which the teaching portfolio evolved there are really part of a continuing critique of theories of teaching. For me this critique first found concrete formulation in the creation of the Institute for Research on Teaching at Michigan State University. In 1975, when we created the Institute, we designed it as a powerful argument against the prevailing views of teaching as skilled behavior—the process-product conception of teaching that clearly reigned at that time. We argued then that teaching was a form of thought and judgment, that it was an act of an autonomous agent engaged in creating opportunities for students and adapting all kinds of goals and materials to the conditions of the moment and the students being taught. Therefore, we contended, an utterly new paradigm of research was needed for studying teaching, one that was much more cognitive and much more focused on the idiographic components of teaching, the uniquely local. That is why ethnographers—with their emphasis on concrete situations—became so important in our work. Rather than simply looking at what all teachers held in common, or considering effective teaching generically, we believed we had to talk about it in its contexts and intricate complexity.

What has become clearer to me is that this kind of theoretical and, if you will, ideological act—stipulating, "No, teaching is not really like that; it's more like this"—is also what we're doing when we design and conceptualize teaching portfolios. In all these discussions, it is important to keep in mind that the portfolio is a broad metaphor that comes alive as you begin to formulate the theoretical orientation to teaching that is most valuable to you. This became apparent with the work of the TAP and the emergence of the teaching portfolio.

New Assessments for a National Board for Professional Teaching Standards: The Emergence of the Portfolio

The TAP, begun in 1985, was part of a continuing critique of the prevalent notions of teaching, which viewed teaching much too behaviorally, much too generically, and much too context-free. (A very important part of the missing context was what was being taught—the subject matter content.) At that time, two forms of teacher assessment were widely used, the National Teachers Examination and classroom observations. Neither had context or much thought associated with them. Classroom observations used exactly the same instrument, irrespective of whether one was looking at an eleventh-grade teacher teaching trigonometry or a second-grade teacher working with a reading group.

Dissatisfaction with these approaches produced this impossible dream: creating a National Board for Professional Teaching Standards. Toward that goal, we tried to invent a generation of assessments that would capture teaching in a much broader sense. I am not going to go into any of the details of those assessments. But what we created was an "assessment center" concept where we simulated various situations that teachers actually engage in. Some assessments required participants to look at textbook materials, critique them, and talk about how they would adapt them for use with particular groups of students. Videotapes of other teachers' teaching presented opportunities for participants to offer constructive, critical feedback. The champion simulation of all we called "Teaching a Familiar Lesson." In that situation, a teacher brought to the assessment center a lesson that he or she really enjoyed and was skilled at teaching. We first interviewed the teacher about the lesson: how it connected to the broader curriculum of which it was a part, what the teacher intended to do, and what kind of difficulties might be anticipated. Then we videotaped the teacher presenting the hour-long lesson to a group of students. Afterwards we interviewed the students about the lesson. We asked them deep, difficult questions such as, "What was that lesson about?" This turned out to be a very important question. In a separate interview, the teacher "candidate" had an opportunity to reflect on, critique, and analyze the lesson just taught, responding to questions such as, "What can you tell me about some of the individual kids you just taught?" Little questions like that.

This experience yielded good news and bad news. The good news was that as far as we could tell, compared with existing forms of teacher assessment, this was a winner. Both those doing the observation as well as those being assessed agreed that this was much more faithful to teaching than anything any of them had ever experienced before. One teacher examiner said at the end of 4 days, "I have watched more teaching and thought more about teaching in the last 4 days than I have in the previous 25 years." That was the good news.

The bad news was that the activity was still highly decontextualized. We kept asking ourselves, "But what are these folks like back in their classrooms?" Granted, we were putting them in situations that bore a much closer resemblance to the kinds of things they did in classrooms than a set of multiple choice test items did. And granted, there were virtues in basing our observations on a very systematic sampling of the work they did, not only in classroom-like settings, but in what I call kitchen table settings—where planning, analyzing, critiquing, and evaluating took place. But these assessments totally omitted classroom observation in a curriculum-specific way. With all those virtues, there was still this sense that something was missing.

At that time it was becoming clear that for the next generation of our assessments, we wanted to put more emphasis on some form of documentation, some way for teachers systematically to document what they were doing in their classrooms. We wanted that to become the core of the assessment. I don't remember when we began talking about such documentation as portfolios; it just sort of happened.

At some point I do remember my colleague Tom Bird engaged in what I would call a "thought experiment." He phoned some architects from the Yellow Pages, asking: "Do you have a portfolio?" and, if so, "Why?" We were just kind of mucking around trying to figure out how other professions document their work. Tom then wrote the first paper in our project on the teaching portfolio. It became a chapter in the Millman and Darling-Hammond volume on new approaches to the assessment of teaching. What is interesting is that Tom wrote that chapter before we had ever done a teaching portfolio. It was simply his attempt to describe what a portfolio would be like—if we did one.

And then we did. We tried to design portfolios with carefully specified entries that teacher candidates for National Board assessment would complete over the course of a year, a large part of a year. These entries would become the heart of their National Board review. In thinking of that sort of portfolio, we asked: "What would happen if you could embody an assessment center concept in different kinds of exercises?" Our mental image was the assessment center as a sort of rug that you rolled up. You put it under your arm and you took it to a school and into somebody's classroom and you unrolled it. What had been exercises in an assessment center now became, in some sense, entries in a portfolio. So the conceptual structure remained, but now it was sited in the real world and it was being done in real time, which meant weeks instead of hours, perhaps months in some cases.

At that time one of our closest and most helpful advisors was the Stanford University's already emeritus professor Lee Cronbach, the psychometrician. Lee's job in our project was to give us permission to violate yet another rule that he had written. We would come up with some notion of a portfolio entry and we'd say, "Lee, can we do that?" He would respond: "Don't worry. You create reasonable assessments and let the psychometricians figure out how you can do it." That's very important advice. We have let the tail of psychometrics wag our work for far too long.

Portfolio Entries: A Coached, Collaborative Activity

So we moved to this second generation of work on assessment in which the portfolio, rather than the assessment center, became the heart of the assessment. I recall vividly that the year we started our work, I was approached by someone at the American Educational Research Association (AERA) annual meeting who took me aside and said, "Lee, I want to save you a lot of trouble. We've tried portfolios in my state; they don't work." I said, "Well, why don't they work?" And then in that wonderful way in which people tell little secrets they don't want everybody to know, he just leaned over and said, "Teachers cheat." I said, "Oh, oh. What do they do?" He continued: "They help each other out on their portfolios. That invalidates it. It's like students copying from each other's test papers."

The underlying notion here is that what we were doing is testing and, in testing, the individual working alone is the unit of analysis. It is really quite a powerful orientation. In response, I suggested that the reason we had undertaken the National Board assessment project in the first place was to help create the conditions under which teachers could live lives that were more truly professional in the best sense of the word. One of the things that members of the professions did was work together and collaborate and talk to one another and advise one another and mentor one another, and isn't this what we have in mind? He shook his head, "That's cheating. It's cheating."

This conversation came to be repeated so many times that I composed a mini-interview. I came to say to these people: "Do you have a Ph.D.? Where did you get it? Did you have a committee? Who was your chair? Anybody else on the committee? They didn't give you any guidance, did they?" When each person recounted a story of interactions with dissertation committee members, I countered: "Then I can't take your dissertation very seriously as any kind of evidence of your competence, can I? You cheated!" The typical response claimed: "Well, that's different."

It isn't different: So many of the accomplishments we value are not accomplishments that we achieved in some kind of monastic solitude. Rather, they are the outcome of often extended periods of mentoring and coaching and deliberation and exchange. In the end, we feel pride in the achievement. Why, then, when teachers do it, even in a context of assessment, is this collaboration suddenly invalidated and seen as cheating?

In the assessment project, we literally turned necessity into virtue. (But again, I think it was ideologically driven.) In our design of portfolios, we mandated that every portfolio entry had to be coached. There had to be some evidence that some other person—teacher, mentor, whomever—had some chance to review, discuss, or coach an entry. Now it didn't always work. Some teachers never got that kind of help, so there was a source of variation that we were worried about. But the notion that teamwork ought to be commonplace, rather than be seen as some sort of idiosyncratic act of cheating, is really terribly important and it was important to us.

In 1994, with 1,500 portfolios being sent to teachers, the National Board had to confront the issue of teamwork again. They commissioned Sam Wineburg at the University of Washington to prepare a position paper on collaboration in teaching portfolios. I would like to share with you just the first page of Sam's position paper, called "Collaboration in Teacher Assessment."

> Ezra Pound called it a masterpiece, one of the most important 19 pages in English. Conrad Aiken heralded it as "one of the most moving and original poems of our times." Even the trenchant I. A. Richards said that it expressed "the plight of a whole generation."
>
> *The Wasteland,* T. S. Eliot's brilliant and infuriating critique of modernity, is known by anyone who has ever taken a college literature course. It is a jarring juxtaposition of classic and modern. Its magisterial allusions and disquieting meter have occupied and mystified literary critics for nearly a century, not to mention the untold hours spent by baffled freshmen trying to decipher its meaning. Published in 1922, the poem immediately thrust Eliot into the limelight. But the story behind his poem remained shrouded in mystery until 1968. In that year the original manuscript of *The Wasteland* was discovered and a facsimile edition appeared three years later. This edition showed a typewritten version of *The Wasteland* with whole stanzas crossed out with

> marginal comments such as, "Too loose, inversions not warranted by any real exigents of meter, dogmatic deduction and wobbly as well." When Eliot wrote "the cautious critics" in the section called "The Fire Sermon," the marginal note focused on the word cautious, pointing out that, when speaking of London, this "adjective is tautological." In a handwritten section the critic drew a large X across the whole page and in a marginal squib issued this judgment: "Bad, but I can't attack it until I get the typescript."

The man behind the big X was none other than Ezra Pound. Ezra Pound, as Sam goes on to describe, had critiqued, suggested revisions, rewritten, and commented on all of *The Wasteland* in successive drafts. Sam raises the interesting question: So whose poem is it? Is it still Eliot's? Should *The Wasteland* be considered by Eliot and Pound? By Eliot with the assistance of Pound? Or is it still fundamentally Eliot's work because whatever your critics say, it is still your job to put it all together and take responsibility for the whole?

Sam Wineburg goes on to offer a whole series of analyses and suggestions for the role of coaching in teaching portfolios for National Board assessment. But he points out, again in the spirit of my previous argument, that all this work is theory. Since the mid-1980s, new psychological and anthropological theories have emerged to inform our work as educators—and these are not the same theories that we were using in the 1960s and 1970s. A Russian psychologist named Vygotsky is suddenly on the lips of almost every educator in the country. His sociocultural perspectives, and the idea of "distributed expertise" among learners, are studied by teachers across the nation. As the theoretical models that undergird our work change, activities such as portfolios will change in response. Both of those things have been going on with our work on portfolios.

One important point that drives all of our work in the TAP and continues to drive the National Board is a source of enormous tension: If you are going to introduce new forms of assessment, or argue for the continuation of older ones, you no longer can make arguments that are limited to the four great forms of validity—concurrent validity, predictive validity, content validity, and construct validity. The four kinds of validity have been the basis for determining whether a test either is or is not valid. But, in the past four or five years, even the psychometricians have changed their perspective. From Sam Messick to Lee Cronbach, to Ed Haertel, psychometricians write about the fifth form of validity. Some call it *consequential validity;* some call it systemic validity. The notion is rather simple: The claim that some form of assessment is valid requires that you offer evidence that when you deploy it, it has positive consequences for the entire system of which it is a part. The assessment cannot merely discriminate reliably, or correlate with some other indicator. In terms of teacher assessment, this new requirement means that any form of teacher assessment has to meet a new standard: that the manner in which it is deployed improves the quality of teaching and opportunities for becoming a better teacher. That's consequential validity for teacher assessment.

Again and again on the TAP, we kept asking what we called the "Stanley Kaplan question": Have we designed either a portfolio entry—or a form of assessment—that could be passed by somebody who had become test-wise, but who had not become a better teacher? Could you be trained to pass the test without having to become a better practitioner in order to do so? And if the answer was, "Probably," then we wanted to toss that one into the dustbin. If portfolios represented ways in which teachers had improved themselves, and if portfolios were having a positive impact on teachers' work in classrooms, then portfolios were beginning to meet the standard of consequential validity.

One other response to the critics who charged that teachers cheat was, in fact, a spin-off of the notion of the doctoral dissertation. Just as a doctoral dissertation ultimately is defended in an oral examination, so too do teacher assessments need a similar defense. The point is that somebody ought to be able not only to display their work, but to discuss it, to defend it, to engage in discourse about it. Therefore, the eventual design of the assessments that we handed over to the National Board in 1989 was a three-part assessment. The first part was a portfolio prepared by candidates in their own classrooms. These portfolios then were sent to the Stanford TAP project for review and the candidates came to Stanford for 2 days of interviews, discussions, and questioning. Through these interactions, candidates had a chance to elaborate, critique, and defend their portfolios—much in the spirit of a dissertation review.

So that was the story of the experience of the TAP.

Portfolios for Teacher Education: The Stanford Teacher Education Program Story

In doing this assessment work, we came to understand more clearly that, whatever its effectiveness as an assessment form, the portfolio approach provided dynamite educational experiences. The teachers who have worked with us over the years continue to comment enthusiastically on their experiences. Their responses helped us to realize how rarely teachers have an opportunity to engage with somebody else in any piece of teaching or teaching-like activity and then to talk about it, think about it collaboratively. It was at this point that Grace Grant, then Director of Stanford's Teacher Education Program, and I began talking about introducing portfolios into the Stanford Teacher Education Program (STEP).

My teaching in this program reveals another connection to students' portfolios. Again, the theory-driven nature of portfolios becomes clear. Those who know me, know my obsession is with the intersection of pedagogy and content. Inevitably that is what the portfolio for this course is about: teaching particular ideas in one's field to particular students in one's classroom and how that plays itself out. So student teacher portfolios for this course include, for example, carefully written and rewritten cases of their own teaching. You might ask: "What do cases have to do with portfolios?" A case written by a teacher is, for me, a supreme act of reflection, an attempt to capture an extended piece of one's own teaching, and of student learning, which then is transformed narratively so that it can be examined, looked at, and thought about.

The student cases, much inspired by the research of Judy Shulman at the Far West Lab, include an account of not only what the students did, but their interpretation and attempt to explain what they did, and to think about how it might be otherwise, what they might do the next time, and so on. They include, as appendices, artifacts that indicate what the materials looked like and what the students did. Every case is accompanied by two commentaries: one from a fellow student in the class and one from somebody who had nothing to do with the class, such as another teacher in the school or one of the children in the classroom. The case and the commentaries all become part of a portfolio entry. The entry also includes commentaries on cases presented by other students because these too are indicators of how a person is learning to think, act, and reflect as a teacher. Similarly, records of observations of one another's teaching—notes or interviews with the apprentice teacher and students—offer insight into student reflections on the teaching efforts of their peers. Again, the point is that this is a theory-driven portfolio. It is a reflective essay in which student teachers look back on the contents of the portfolio and analyze it from one of several perspectives.

As I reflect on this use of the portfolio, my most pointed critique is something that I intend to do something about. In some ways, the weakest part of our portfolio approach is the strongest part of an approach described by Nona Lyons. Nona's portfolios are much less structured than mine, but they end with an extraordinary, in-depth debriefing interview—almost therapeutic in some cases. I am now beginning to realize that those portfolios only begin to scratch the surface of their potential if the only reflection that's done is by the student *in* his or her own portfolio. Somehow the portfolio needs to become the basis for what is now called supervision. Too often supervision is focused on classroom interactions and therefore becomes a form of crisis intervention and often true psychotherapy. Portfolios that include written cases and go beyond an individual episode offer extraordinary potential for critical reflection and for creative use as a central tool of supervision. That is the STEP story.

Portfolios for Teachers of Teachers: The Larry Cuban Story

Larry Cuban, my colleague at Stanford, is a very unusual historian of education. After 8 years as superintendent of schools in Arlington County, Virginia, like all great administrators, he was, as Clark Kerr put it, fired with enthusiasm. Larry Cuban constructed a teaching portfolio in unusual circumstances.

At the time of his promotion to full professor at Stanford, Larry asked if he could refuse tenure. This, of course, created a crisis in the provost's office. The prompt reply was, "No." Larry argued: "I don't want tenure because as soon as you give me tenure you give up your obligation to provide me with an intelligent review of my work. I refuse to work in an organization that does not take responsibility for reviewing the quality of my work regularly and providing me feedback on it." After an exchange of letters, Larry accepted tenure and, in turn, had a letter put in his file signed by the dean and the provost, saying that every 5 years, as a full professor, he would receive a careful review of his work by his colleagues.

At the first 5-year mark, Larry was president of AERA. His post-tenure review committee included Mike Smith, the Dean of Stanford at the time, John Baugh, a psycholinguist new to the faculty, Mike Atkin, chair of the committee, and me. At our first meeting, Larry proposed putting together a portfolio of his work, including scholarship, teaching, and service, and asked for a discussion of what ought to be included. Three months after that discussion we received a rather large box of materials: annotated copies of syllabi of courses he had designed and was teaching; a videotape of one or two sessions of courses he taught; and commentaries on how that videotape represented both the best things he did as a teacher and some of the enduring dilemmas he confronted as a teacher—ones he was still working on. The box also included copies of student evaluations of Larry's work and copies of student work that he thought particularly exemplified some of the best things that happened in his class. In addition, it held copies of essays that he had written, memoranda to himself about his teaching, and research documents. After reviewing the portfolio materials, we met with

Larry for an hour and a half, talking about stuff that was in the portfolio, raising questions, challenging him. After that, Larry said, "Well, I clearly have to think about this some more and do some more writing." In a subsequent memo, he tried to respond to our questions and the process continued. We met three times in all. At the end, I made a brief report to the faculty, at a regular faculty meeting, about the whole process.

What was clear, was that it was not only Larry Cuban who profited from the experience; each of us benefited. John Baugh reported that he learned more quickly about teaching at Stanford than he ever would have learned in the normal ways in which new faculty could possibly learn. When do we get a chance to peer into the window of our colleagues' teaching?

My insights were somewhat different. I realized that as colleagues in the teacher education program, Larry and I both taught the same students. I came to see some aspects of my students through Larry's eyes and through Larry's course, and in ways I never saw them before because we were doing different things. The students were performing in different contexts and, suddenly, a two-dimensional view of students became three dimensional. I became much more sensitive to Larry's teaching and he to mine, and that is also very important. One of the reasons that my own portfolio has remained incomplete, although I've got all the parts around, is that I am not part of an ad hoc community organized to discuss my portfolio. It was Larry who was thoughtful enough to make sure that we provided such a community, created a group to discuss his portfolio. I am left with the question: What would happen if we as teacher educators organized ourselves to review each other's work in this way? If we supported each other in this way, what would that do for us and our students?

When we began this work on teaching portfolios for assessment purposes, we did not have a glimmer of an idea that it might have consequences for teacher development quite independent of assessment. I don't think any of us anticipated how rapidly this perspective would blossom in higher education. In both state and private universities there are efforts to find better ways of evaluating the quality of teaching than current reliance on student evaluation forms. The American Association of Higher Education is encouraging the development of teaching portfolios as the basis both for pre-tenure and tenure reviews. In the long run, however, portfolios may be more important as a professional development activity through peer review—another kind of Larry Cuban story.

The consequences of these initiatives are very hard to predict. But, in a nutshell, my argument for the importance of peer review of teaching at universities goes like this: I don't accept the complaint that teaching is valued less than research in universities. In principle, I don't think that's true.

I think what universities and colleges value are those things that become community property. Research becomes community property. The word *publish* and the word *public* come from the same root. They become part of the community's discourse. While research becomes part of the community's discourse, teaching has remained for most of us a private act. Of course, it is not strictly private if our students come to class. But teaching is still seen as private in the same way that doing medicine is private—as long as the only people who see you do it are your patients. The argument for peer review and portfolios in teaching is that they contribute to making teaching community property in colleges and universities and, therefore, put teaching and research into the same orbit. We will see whether that argument or hypothesis works.

Portfolios: Some Dangers, Some Virtues

Because all promising practices can be misused or abused, I would like to mention five dangers quickly. The first danger, one that Tom Bird many years ago dubbed "lamination," is that a portfolio becomes a mere exhibition. If the notion of exhibition dominates, then style or how glossy it is begins to take control rather than substance. This potential for mere "showmanship" explains some of the resistance to teaching portfolios that I find from university faculty and I suspect exists among K–12 teachers as well. People are uncomfortable—and justifiably so—if they are simply asked to do some sort of advertisements for themselves, to show off.

The second danger is what I call "heavy lifting." Portfolios done seriously take a long time. They are hard to do. Teaching is a job that occupies every waking and some nonwaking moments of good teachers. (Some of those nonwaking moments are at night, some while teaching.) Given such demands, the question is: Is that much work worth it? And, if it's worth it, is there any chance in the world of reorganizing the life of teachers so that they can do this hard work without killing themselves? Heavy lifting.

The third danger is trivialization. As we learned with multiple choice tests, once you've got a mode of assessment, you start asking the kinds of questions that best fit that mode. Then follows a shift to lines of least resistance and to the increased trivialization of what gets documented. If this happens with portfolios, people will start documenting stuff that isn't even worth reflecting on.

A fourth danger is perversion. If portfolios are going to be used, whether at the state level in Vermont or California, or the national level by the National Board, as a form of high stakes assessment, why will portfolios be more resistant to perversion than all other forms of assessment have been? And if one of the requirements in these cases is that you develop a sufficiently objective scoring system so you can fairly compare people with one another, will your scoring system end up objectifying what's in a portfolio to the point where the portfolio will be nothing but a very, very cumbersome multiple choice test?

A final danger of portfolios is misrepresentation. With such a heavy emphasis on portfolios as samples of a teacher's best work, at what point do we confront the danger that these isolated samples of best work may be so remote from the teacher's typical work that they no longer serve the purpose—any of the purposes—that we have in mind?

But this litany of dangers needs to be balanced by a listing of the virtues of teaching portfolios. First, portfolios permit the tracking and documentation of longer episodes of teaching and learning than happens in supervisory observation. Too, much of our work as teacher educators is organized around the lessons or lesson fragments that we can observe when we make school site visits. Yet, most of the embarrassments of pedagogy that I encounter are not the inability of teachers to teach well for an hour or even a day. Rather they flow from an inability to sustain episodes of teaching and learning over time that unfold, accumulate, into meaningful understanding in students. This becomes especially pertinent with the current renewed emphases on higher standards, higher-order thinking, and so forth. You don't get higher-order thinking in an hour. If portfolios have the virtue of permitting students to display, think about, and engage in the kind of intellectual work that takes time to unfold, then certainly we need something parallel in teaching. That is one of the virtues of a portfolio.

Second, portfolios encourage the reconnection between process and product. I am a great critic of process-product approaches to teaching, except for one thing: They are fundamentally moral in their perspective. They affirm that the end of the teaching is learning. Yet, often in our work we so focus on the practice of teaching, that we don't ask, "But what do the students learn?" Portfolios of the best kind include not only the documentation of teaching, but the documentation of student learning. In the ultimate nirvana, the very best teaching portfolios will consist predominantly of student portfolios. If you want to see my teaching portfolio, I will quickly produce my students' dissertations. And if you're smart, you'll say, "How about the ones that never got finished?" We can structure portfolios that way: to document not only the successes, but the failures, and talk about why that happened and what role you might have played.

Third, portfolios institutionalize norms of collaboration, reflection, and discussion. A research group for the National Board discovered that teachers preparing portfolios were forming video clubs. They began regularly discussing videos of their own teaching for the purpose of eventually putting them in their portfolios. The video became almost epiphenomenal; it was discussion and collaboration that became the core.

Fourth, a portfolio can be seen as a portable residency. The typical student teaching or internship experience that we all value so much has a great Achilles heel. Once you send interns out there, you don't have a clue about what they're doing. Once interns are in classrooms, they become part of whatever happens to be going on in that teacher's classroom or in that school, with that particular group of students. A portfolio introduces structure to the field experience. The candidate, the supervising teacher, and the faculty supervisor share some joint sense of what the student is supposed to learn during that period and what's supposed to be documented and reflected on. I see this as a possible virtue.

Fifth, and really most important, the portfolio shifts the agency from an observer back to the teacher interns. This is a sharp contrast to classroom observations, student evaluations, and most other forms of assessment. Portfolios are owned and operated by teachers; they organize the portfolios; they decide what goes into them. It was Tom Bird who asked us to think about the distinction between the teachers' filing cabinet and the teachers' portfolios. As teachers, we accumulate a great deal of documentation of our work. But depending on the case we have to make, we draw from the filing cabinet and create a particular portfolio. I suspect that that is true of artists and architects as well. In taking charge of their portfolios, teachers select materials to illuminate concepts of teaching and learning that undergird their work.

The three stories I have recounted traced different paths I have followed or observed for constructing and using portfolios. In subsequent chapters, other authors present similar journeys and outline the paths they followed. Although my rubrics for a portfolio change over time, I would like to conclude with my current working definition of a portfolio: A teaching portfolio is the structured, documentary history of a set of coached or mentored acts of teaching, substantiated by samples of student portfolios, and fully realized only through reflective writing, deliberation, and conversation. I think all of those parts are necessary—but I may be wrong.

INTRODUCTION

ARISTOTLE HAD IT RIGHT: ON KNOWLEDGE AND PEDAGOGY (1990)

THIS ESSAY was the keynote address at the annual meeting of the Holmes Group—an organization dedicated to the improvement of teacher preparation—in 1989. In it, Shulman reminisces about his own liberal learning, as well as on his studies of new teachers learning to teach and the wisdom of practice of experienced teachers. Shulman's growing interest in understanding the qualities of subject matter knowledge that afford teachers opportunities to create flexible and adaptable pedagogies subsequently led him to an involvement in Project 30, an effort to enhance the links between teacher education, liberal education, and general education.

As president of The Carnegie Foundation for the Advancement of Teaching, Shulman would spend considerable time working in the area of liberal education. In this piece, which foreshadows that later work, Shulman argues that a liberally educated person understands contemporary ideas, as well as their historical roots. Such a person also understands how to reason and critically evaluate those ideas, or, as he puts is, a liberal education is a combination of "reverence and respect . . . skepticism and doubt." Shulman draws heavily on his own experiences as a student at the University of Chicago to illuminate this image of learning.

15

ARISTOTLE HAD IT RIGHT

ON KNOWLEDGE AND PEDAGOGY

I FEEL ABOUT LIBERAL education what our teacher Joe Schwab felt about science in particular and knowledge in general. He said, "When you really understand it you know that it's fundamentally contingent, dubitable, and hard to come by." And so what I'd like to do this morning is not what I thought I'd do: give a clear, highly organized, well crafted, almost syllogistic exposition about the liberal arts, what they are, what teaching is, and therefore what their relationship should be. Instead, I find the remarks I've prepared are a little less like that and a little more Proustian, if you will; and maybe even Shandean—a combination of reminiscence, of footnotes on footnotes, of flashbacks, and of deliberations.

To protect you against those wanderings, I thought it was only fair to begin with what I think are my conclusions. Which is not to say that everything I'm going to say is going to lead inexorably to them. It's just where I happen to end up. Let me read you those conclusions. Then I hope you'll join me on this journey.

I see us being here this morning to discuss two aspects of liberal education, which on the face of it appear to be two separate questions, and which I believe will turn out to be but one. When discussing the relationship between liberal education and pedagogy, first, "What is the proper education in the liberal arts for future pedagogues?" and, second, "What is the kind of pedagogy needed for the proper education of future teachers and, for that matter, anyone else in the liberal arts?"

That certainly has been dealt with as two separate questions in most of the literature. I think we'll find they are not two separate questions. Let me proceed with my conclusions.

First: Debates about liberal education, especially recently, have too often been obsessed with defining something called the canon. What are the books, the readings, the topics, the contents, that every educated person or every educated teacher or every educated citizen needs to know? I think we will find that the essence of a liberal education is not discovered in producing any list of books, any list of readings; that the content of the canon must be understood in deliberations about *what* is taught but, equally important, with *how* it is organized, taught, and evaluated. That second half has been remarkably absent in discussions by folks like the former Secretary of Education.

Second: Liberal education is a combination of the passionate embrace and understanding of general simplifications of facts and ideas along with the development of critical, skeptical attitudes. The emphasis of a general liberal education should be on understanding a human activity—achieved through human action and thought at particular times, in particular places, by real people. The twin dangers of the need for simplification are, on the one hand, the argument for a canon of works, and just as dangerous, simplification by rejecting a canon of works and positing instead an equally universal canon of processes. Both forms of simplification are misleading and dangerous.

Third: A pedagogy appropriate to such goals is not, however, a pedagogy of universals. Indeed, the kind of pedagogy needed to achieve that kind of combination of understanding and skepticism is a pedagogy of cases: accounts of the development of human understanding that are rooted in stories of human accomplishment within a historical and cultural context. This contextualization of understanding provides the needed depth, the needed context, the needed humanity.

Fourth: The distinction we all have been taught between liberal education on the one hand, and professional or vocational education on the other—if you will, knowledge for its own sake and knowledge for application—collapses—*collapses*—in thinking about the education of teachers, because, as I think we will come to see, the teacher is the liberal educator of our society, and therefore, the teacher's vocation is itself liberal.

Finally: Aristotle judged that teaching was the highest form of understanding, that no test of human understanding was more demanding than the test of whether you could take something you thought you knew and teach it to someone else. What someone needs to know in order to do that kind of teaching, and how that sort of teaching can be the centerpiece of both liberal and teacher education are the topics that all of us have come here this weekend to wrestle with.

So those are the conclusions. Now the rather circuitous path for getting there.

When I approached this problem, I realized I had two choices of starting points. I could start with the literature of liberal education—the literature of liberal arts going back to the Greeks and the Romans—to Socrates, to Plato, to Aristotle; to Isocrates, the Sophists, the rhetoricians; on to Cicero. I did! I really did. That's one of the things you can do with long plane rides. And it became very clear that there was no "there" there if what you were looking for was a distillate—if what you were looking for in this literature was some grand mean, some underlying consensus about what it meant to be liberally educated. It simply wasn't there.

You have some very recent attempts to argue that there are basically two competing conceptions of liberal education—one by Bruce Kimball, in his book on orators and philosophers. But there too there's an awful lot of noise and mess in the literature. The lovely thing about the literature, however, is that it's beautifully written. The best minds of the generations have devoted enormous attention to the question of what it means to be liberally educated, and thus it is a literature that is rich, as long as you don't approach it with the delusion that there will be this funneling down to *a* conception that is well worth your attention. So that was one possibility.

The other was to begin at the end, as it were, and to think about teaching, and the studies that my colleagues and I have been doing over the past 13 years on what exemplary teaching looks like. And that was the tack I decided to take. And so the journey I'd like you to take with me will begin with the consideration of the nature of exemplary teaching—at least of the sort that we have been looking at in our most recent research programs.

Multiple Perspectives in Expert Teachers of Substance

We began with a fairly simple question: "How does somebody who already knows something figure out how to teach it to somebody else?" That didn't seem like a particularly revolutionary question at the time, until we began to discover that almost no one was asking that question. The question they were asking was, "What makes someone an effective teacher?" And it turned out that effectiveness was coextensive with the management and organization of classrooms, so that they were smoothly running, and kids were "on task," and teachers were asking proper mixes of higher and lower order questions. But what the literature didn't say very much about was what the tasks were that they were supposed to be "on" and what the questions were that they were supposed to be asked—what the substance of the pedagogy should be. And so we began to ask this question: "How does someone take something they know and teach it to somebody else?"

Well, as we watched more and more teachers we began to see that the question needed refinement because it turned out that people knew what they knew at very different depths. Some people knew what they knew deeply, thoroughly, richly. Others knew what they knew much more superficially, more tentatively. And it became an even more interesting question to ask, "How does how *well* you know something relate to how you teach it to someone else?"

As we began to pursue that one, even that question began to crumble. Because it turned out that very few of us simply know our field deeply or don't know our field deeply. Our fields are too complex for that kind of oversimplification. In fact, we know a real lot about some parts of our fields, and damn little about others, even when we are professors thereof. There is no more poignant, more crippling state of anxiety than that experienced by the full professor who, after 15 or 20 years on the faculty, is asked to teach the introductory course. "I don't know that stuff any more! I never knew that stuff in the first place. I haven't known that stuff since my prelims. And I didn't know it well then."

And so what we began to look at was not simply the differences between people but the differences within them. If you will, how does the teaching someone does *vary* as that person moves from teaching what they know very well to teaching things they know less well? And finally—although it isn't final in the sense of our inquiries—we began to realize that even that is an incomplete way to formulate the question, because the notion of an amount, or even depth, of understanding ignores the kind, or character, of understanding. As we began to study teachers of history for example, we found they were not different from one another because of how deeply each understood his or her history but because of the conception of history or historiography each held. And not necessarily the conception of history in general but often a conception of the history of a particular period, or of a particular nation, or of a particular set of themes in history. I am reminded of Will Rogers' great observation that everybody's ignorant, just about different things. We began to see that in the ways teachers moved among the oases of particular kinds of deep knowledge they had and the deserts of areas in which they knew a good deal less.

The work was strictly case study research. From each case we generated hypotheses, and then we tested them against other cases of teaching.

One exemplar can create doctrine; 11 examples can create puzzlement and the beginning of understanding.

Experienced teachers' heads are filled with information about what kids would misunderstand, misperceive, and make mistakes on. What the experienced teachers had was an epidemiology of misconceptions among students. But they couldn't codify it. One of the most important things young teachers learn from experience is what students *don't* understand, what enduring misconceptions they have. Experienced teachers already have made sense of what those are.

A striking difference we noted between two groups of teachers was that physics teachers would explain physics concepts with an extraordinary repertoire of examples, analogies, metaphors; but that biology teachers who were teaching physics had only one example, and then they just died. So we began to understand teachers' representations.

We began to develop a sense of the understanding that characterizes expert teachers of substance. It had to do with the way they understood the content. They could come at it from multiple perspectives. A disciplinarian who knows only one way of knowing something is positively dangerous as a teacher. What is necessary is knowing not just as a hodgepodge but as an understanding of the different points of view in which the different perspectives were grounded.

The heart of teaching is both active and receptive explanation. You create circumstances in which students have to create understandings and you have a repertoire with which to understand what the student knows.

Pedagogical content knowledge distinguishes teachers of particular content areas from the educated layman in that area. The teacher of substance can also be distinguished from the general pedagogue. We are not talking about an additive thing—taking so and so many measures of content and adding to it so many measures of pedagogy. It is the blending of the two.

Case Studies: Revealing the Complexity of Pedagogy

As our research group at Stanford studied those exemplary teachers, what was fascinating was the ways in which particular cases that we studied stuck in memory because they exemplified principles that we were discovering in our work. Sometimes these were and are the first case you study, which three or four years later you begin to understand much more deeply than you did in the first encounter.

I remember one member of our staff—Suzanne Wilson—coming back from an observation early in our research and telling the following story: A young teacher just learning to teach has to teach *Julius Caesar* to a group of high school sophomores. *Julius Caesar*—deadly dull, boring. That's what this young teacher remembered. He hadn't studied *Julius Caesar* since he himself was a sophomore in high school.

Suzanne described this young teacher's struggle to figure out how to teach *Julius Caesar* to this average, recalcitrant group of high school sophomores. He approached the class and said, "Don't open your books. I want you to imagine that we're all members of the crew of the Starship Enterprise. Captain Kirk, your leader, is someone you worship, you venerate. He has been your captain since you became a member of the crew. He has saved your lives repeatedly. There is nothing you would not do for your captain. Except that recently he's begun to act a bit odd, in fact a bit . . . megalomaniacal? and arrogant? . . . and you're beginning to worry that left to his own devices he will take the enormous power of this galactic battleship and use it against the empire instead of in its service. What are you going to do?"

The class rapidly divided between the loyalists and the revolutionaries, between those who would stick with the captain and those who would mutiny. And they began to debate all the issues involved, because, let's face it, unlike *Caesar,* Star Trek is important stuff. The next day they began to study *Caesar,* and this young teacher, 22 years old, said to them, "You're now going to read a play about a group of people who were confronted with very much the same problem that you grappled with yesterday. They too had a terrible moral and personal conflict, and it revolved around many of the issues that we were struggling with together." With that as a frame, with that as a scaffolding, they began to read *Caesar.*

Now it was clear to us, and to the teacher, who of course was an English major, that this was not the only way to read *Julius Caesar.* The very special thing about *Caesar* and about other plays of Shakespeare is the very many ways and levels at which it could be read. But this young teacher had a very important pedagogical understanding, which is that among the many ways he knew for reading *Caesar,* he had to find some ways, some representations, some "transformations"—in the language of our own research—that would connect with the understandings—not the blank slates but the positive, constructed understandings—of a particular group of students. He understood a lot about those students, he understood a lot about how to read a piece of Shakespeare, and he was able to bring those two together in a pedagogical transformation.

There's an interesting contrast to that. Pam Grossman, now at the University of Washington, studied young teachers of Shakespeare, and in a lovely study which she titled "A Tale of Two Hamlets"—pun intended—she studied two teachers—one who had had a thorough preparation in pedagogy and one who had had none at all; both with equally rich backgrounds and degrees in English literature—teaching two groups of high school students *Hamlet*.

In one case *Hamlet* was transformed in a manner analogous to the Star Trek example I've just given you. There are problems with it. The teacher recognized it. In the other case, the young teacher taught *Hamlet* to a group of ninth graders as an instance of linguistic reflexivity, which was the way this teacher had most recently studied *Hamlet*. And so, clearly, this was the way to read *Hamlet*.

"Don't you see, kids? This is what Shakespeare is doing here. This is a play about the uses of language to talk about language. Isn't that *incredible?*"

"Sure. Whatever you say."

The transformation was missing. In place of transformation, you had transmission. In place of examining the multiple ways you might have for reading the text, and the multiple ways you might have for reading the reader, and then finding fits, bridges, connections, what you had was *my* reading of the text: "Here it is baby; go for it."

So we have many, many examples. We've been studying teachers, both veterans and novices, in literature, in history, in mathematics, in science. And you see the same kinds of patterns again and again. You begin to appreciate the complexity of the pedagogical performance, the complexity of the pedagogical understanding that lies behind good teaching. You begin to see how much more there is to teaching than either just managing a classroom or just "knowing your subject." And, as we begin to understand that more clearly, we find ourselves asking, "How does someone come to know those sorts of things?"

How You Learn a Subject in College Affects How You Teach It

We are, after all, all teacher educators. Whether we call ourselves professors of education or professors of mathematics, to the extent that in our classrooms day after day sit men and women who will subsequently go out and teach youngsters, we are teacher educators. To the extent that they are likely to teach both *what* and *as* they have been taught, unlike any other students in your classes, the future teachers are, if you will, carriers. Whatever understandings or misunderstandings you infect them with, both about the content and regarding the pedagogy, they will carry to generations of young people whom they will subsequently teach, and who themselves will eventually appear at your doorstep.

It's clear that ways of reading the texts—be they scientific, mathematical, literary, social-scientific—are not conveyed only in that limited layer of courses formally called teacher education, but are constantly being constructed by students throughout their experience in the university. Therefore, the question for all of us as teacher educators is, "*What is the relationship between how the liberal arts are taught and learned in the university and how those become available for participants in the pedagogical transformations that follow?*"

As I said before, in struggling with these questions of liberal arts, my first impulse was to try to distill a sense of those liberal arts from the literature. I gave up and decided to reflect on my own experiences as someone who had the good fortune to participate as a student in one of the ways in which educators have defined the liberal arts—the College of the University of Chicago. (As my own children have reached college age, they've asked me—with the brochures for all these colleges spread out on the dining room table—"Dad, how did you decide where to go to college?" And I explained that my parents told me I could go to any university in the country as long as I could get there by public transportation and the college would pay most of the tuition. Through no fault of my own the University of Chicago met both of those standards.) Let me first give you the conception of liberal education which I find I carry in my head and then tell you three personal stories that I think are instances of that general conception.

What is a liberal education? I find that liberal education is skeptical, historical, questioning, passionate, revisionary, personal, and reverent. It is disciplined but skeptical about the disciplines. It is mostly and most importantly *rooted.* The liberally educated person does not believe that knowledge is simply created anew in a given generation. The liberally educated person understands that there are roots, there are beginnings, there is a genesis, an evolution to ideas. At the time when I was educated, and I suspect when most of you were educated, we thought those roots were only Greek and Roman, Jewish, Christian, and Western European. We've now come to understand that to appreciate rootedness appropriately we have to understand those roots as African, as Asian, as Latin American as well.

The important concept is the sense of ideas developing, crafted by human minds and human emotions, in places and times, rather than existing as Platonic innate ideas that transcend time and place and purpose. A liberal education permits its participants both to eavesdrop and to participate in the Great Conversation. And some writers have argued that it is in fact an education in conversation. To understand that the topics and perspectives of a liberal education are themselves ongoing and conditioned by what has preceded and prefigured them. Therefore, in a very real sense all liberal education, in the sciences and mathematics as well as in the humanities and the social sciences, is humanistic, because the emphasis is on the creation, the invention, the construction, and the deconstruction of understanding. That, I found, was for me the essential feature of liberal education. Then the questions were, "Where did that kind of view come from, and what good is it?"

Learning Pedagogy: Three Personal Cases

Let me tell you three stories.

The first story goes back to the time when I was professor of medical education, and we had invented a new medical curriculum, in which instead of students spending two full years learning the basic sciences and then going and doing clinical work for two years we got them going doing clinical problem solving the first day of their first year in medical school. I remember sitting around with a group of students—there were three of us team-teaching 10 students (well, we needed it more than they did)—and one of the cases we had given the students was a case of polyuria, which is the way physicians fancily say "frequent urination." In order to understand this case the students had to go out and do library research, and one of the students, who had been trained in engineering before coming to medical school, came and presented to the class an elaborate exposition on the renal system. The transfer of training from his sanitary engineering background was profound and important. He had big diagrams and was showing how these little buggers went through the loop of Henle and came out . . . it was lovely, just lovely.

Although the physiologist and the pediatrician on the team clearly knew more about the renal system than I did, I found myself beginning to question the young medical student. I said to him, "What would happen if this part of the system weren't there?" He thought about it, and the class began to work together with him on it, and they came up with a response. "What would happen if *this* part of the system weren't there?" "Oh, gee! But it's there!" "No. What if it weren't there?" We went on to some other things, but it was clear that his understanding of the renal system was deepening.

After the class was over the three of us who were doing the teaching got together, and the physiologist said to me, "Lee, I didn't know you had that much background in physiology." I said, "I don't know squat about physiology." He said, "You've got to know physiology. What you were doing is exactly the way we physiologists think our way through the relations of structures and functions in systems. In fact that's the way we generate our research problems." At which point I had to make a confession to him. I said, "While I was asking those questions about the renal system, what I was really thinking about was the way that I had learned to look at a painting."

In fact, I was thinking about El Greco's "Assumption of the Virgin" in the Chicago Art Institute, and the way in which Harold Hayden, professor of art in the College, had sat with us for two full weeks studying that one magnificent work of art: looking at it from different perspectives, looking at it in slides, looking at details, going to the Institute and studying it some more, and among other things asking us, "What functions are being played by the different portions of this painting? How do the parts relate to the whole?" And more questions of that sort. And I began to have some insight about some of the consequences of liberal education, and why it made sense for us to spend two weeks on one painting instead of doing what I think is usually the impulse of undergraduate educators—to do six paintings or painters a day, three days a week, so that you can "cover" art history.

Second story: Sitting in a classroom with Joe Schwab reading the first section of Book Two of Aristotle's *Physics*. Mr. Schwab says to 18-year-old Mr. Shulman, "Mr. Shulman, read!"

Mr. Shulman reads, "Of things that exist, some exist by nature, some from other causes."

"Stop! What is the author doing in that line?"

I paraphrased what Aristotle was saying.

"That's not what I asked you, Shulman! Don't tell me what Aristotle said. What did he *do?*"

Sweat. The students around me began to sweat. (In this kind of class there is a kind of concentric circle of perspiration, which is related by, I think, the inverse square law to proximity to the target of the Socratic interaction.) I think the interaction went on for 10 or 15 minutes at the most. It seemed like 45 minutes or an hour. I learned only years later that Schwab did that all the time with that piece of text and with others like it. I understood that piece of text very deeply.

Many, many years later when I read Herbert Simon's *The Sciences of the Artificial,* I understood the distinction between things that exist by nature and those by other causes more deeply than I had when Schwab taught it to me. But we spent three class sessions on a page and a half of Aristotle. We never got to cover *The Metaphysics.* I didn't start reading *The Metaphysics* until a few years ago when I had a reason to do it. And found that I could. Found that I could. Not only because Schwab had taught a set of processes for reading a text but because I really understood what Aristotle was doing. Not philosophy. Aristotle. And philosophers like him. I had a set of ways of reading particular kinds of texts.

And years later, when I read a book by Schwab called *The College Curriculum and Student Protest*—a book written faster than Joe Schwab ever wrote anything he wrote in his life, because of the passion that emerged from the confrontations at the end of the sixties between college students and faculties—he talked about the kinds of things that you learn in those liberally educating interactions. He said that they have four outcomes.

First: "Mastery of the sense and soundness of the work treated: The student 'really' knows it. He knows the facts, or fact-like materials which ground it. He knows the ideas in the shape of terms, distinctions, and premises, which directed the choice of facts covered and the significances assigned to them."

Second: "The student has enjoyed an increment to his command of language in the service of sense." It was always fascinating to me, but I never appreciated it, that none of those questions which so bombarded us in those interactions were questions that required that we generate new information. We were always being asked to reflect on and analyze information that was right in front of all of us. Understanding was reflective and analytic understanding; it was not increments of new information alone.

Third: "The student not only knows something more but knows *what* he knows and *that* he knows." Schwab was very concerned with what he later would call "metalearning"—similar to what we're now calling "metacognitive activity"—that students be enormously aware of the very processes they were using and how they were becoming smarter about what they were studying.

And finally, and very important: "The student has done his work in concert with an instructor who has been part exemplar, part guide, part critic, part source of stimulus, reward, and respect. He has worked with other students . . . assisting and being assisted, receiving and giving criticism, profiting from others' examples, both good and bad." Those students who were perspiring with me were also learning with me; they were contributing ideas, contributing interpretations. There was something collaborative and affective going on because we were working on some damn tough stuff together and coming to see that there were things we could understand jointly that most of us couldn't figure out sitting by ourselves alone with the text.

The third reminiscence is another biological one. I still remember 30 years later a set of readings on embryonic induction, a set of studies that asked a simple question: "How does a cell know that it's supposed to grow up to be what it turns out to be? How does a cell know that it's supposed to be spinal cord and another cell know that it's supposed to be finger nail?" Of course, that's a very anthropomorphic way of saying it, but the question was, "How do cells manage to become what they become as the embryo develops?" Now, again, we did not read a standard textbook of embryology. We read a set of original papers in which we followed a 60-year history of research on this topic and began to see the ways in which human beings struggled with these kinds of problems.

The striking thing about all of these examples—especially the ones in the sciences—was that instead of studying these things propositionally we were studying them at the level of the case. We were studying *cases* of science, cases of history, cases of politics, as reflected in the work of the people who had generated them. By embedding our understanding in those cases, we were unavoidably seeing the human hand, the historical context of those cases.

Pedagogy for Teachers Inheres in Case-Based Liberal Studies

What I find fascinating is that there's a real parallel between this conception of liberal education and a conception of the education of teachers that we began to come to several years ago, for many of the same reasons. We came to see how difficult it was to teach someone to teach—when teaching is so rooted in context, so rooted in the particulars—if you were trying to train the teachers through generalizations and propositions. We began to explore what teacher education would look like if instead of teaching it didactically we began to develop case-based curricula so that the contingencies, the situatedness, the particularities of teaching situations could be understood in relation to the generalizations.

What I was reminded of was that this is a tradition in the liberal arts, not just at the University of Chicago but at a number of other places as well. For example, just after World War II James Conant wrote a remarkable book. He was president of Harvard. He had participated actively in the Manhattan Project, and he was scared to death about what the consequences would be of a scientifically illiterate population in an atomic age. He proposed an approach to the teaching of science within the liberal arts through the method of cases. He gave examples. I strongly urge that you go back to this lovely little book, *On Understanding Science,* where again and again he presents cases of scientific discovery that are enormously illuminating.

I want to give you just one example because I think it helps bring together the sense I now have of the connection between the education for liberal understanding and the education for pedagogy. He described a set of investigations that dealt with understanding air pressure and the work of water pumps. In these studies there is the point in which Galileo has all of the facts he needs in front of him to come to the proper generalization about air pressure. He has done the right experiments, and he comes to the wrong conclusion. And Conant writes, "Concerning this episode Martha Ornstein, a historian writes, 'Galileo was strangely conservative on a few points. For instance, he accepted in Aristotelian fashion the resistance of a vacuum—a modified version of nature abhorring a vacuum—as an explanation of why a pump could raise water only 32 feet.' She goes on to say, 'He never could see what was perfectly obvious!'"

Conant writes: "'Strangely conservative on a few points?' Heaven help us! Does the author of this excellent historical study imagine that scientific pioneers first tear up all former conceptual schemes and then try to put something in their place? This passage implies that here was a case of a great man who had a momentary lapse when he failed to introduce a whole new concept into science as a result of pondering on one set of facts. Something easy but carelessly overlooked. I call attention to the misunderstanding about science that this reflects."

At that point I realized that these cases of discovery, and, more important, the cases of *non*discovery are cases of pedagogy. They are cases of learning and of teaching. Galileo had all the facts. He couldn't come up with the concept. He couldn't do the fundamental transformation. As it turned out, what he didn't have was something that in our research we have found is perhaps the most powerful tool a teacher has. He didn't have the right analogy. He kept on thinking in terms of a *spring* of air, as in a coiled metal spring, and as long as he thought about it as a spring of air, all the facts couldn't get him closer to the conception of air pressure he was looking for.

I came to understand that one of the beauties of a case method, in various versions—not only of original documents but in the form that Schwab called "narratives of inquiry"—was that as we trace the history of actual discoveries we are in fact studying cases of conceptual invention in which the preconceptions held by members of a scientific community are often what precludes "seeing what the facts tell you." As I looked at case after case, I saw them again and again as cases of pedagogy.

If you could teach future teachers the disciplines, the domains of knowledge, through this historical, contextualized way, you would not only be teaching them the content and the processes, you would simultaneously be teaching them the pedagogy—the ways in which student preconceptions and new transformations make what was previously not understandable and not learnable accessible, and the ways in which this is not an exclusively individual process but is in most cases a social and communal process.

I also remembered then why it was that in the late sixties almost all our undergraduate students and most of our graduate students were running around with copies of Thomas Kuhn's book in their pockets. Kuhn's *Structure of Scientific Revolutions* is, though he never expressed it that way, precisely that kind of pedagogical representation of the history of science. In fact, Kuhn in one of his other writings says that if you really want to understand how anybody as smart as Aristotle could say the foolish things he said about falling bodies, you have to get yourself into Aristotle's head, into that time and that place, and then you'll appreciate what an extraordinarily difficult job it would have been not to see falling bodies as he did.

Mathematics educators like Bob Davis and Max Beberman have told their teaching students for years: when a child makes a mistake, don't ask "Why did he do something so stupid?" Get inside that student's head and ask, "What would make that a *reasonable* thing for him and her to say?"

That's why I say that the fundamental and essential character of a liberal education is a combination of, on the one hand, reverence and respect and on the other skepticism and doubt. And that's also the essence of pedagogy. You must respect the intelligence and understanding of your students *especially* when they misunderstand. Because only if you can understand that misunderstanding can you begin to build those transformational bridges between the array of understandings that you might have in your head and the misconceptions, misunderstandings, and difficulties that they have in theirs. The history of ideas is a history of pedagogy.

Cognitive Psychology Endorses Case-Based Studies

The conception of a liberal education through the use of cases or case-like activity has become increasingly consistent with the newest and most exciting kinds of cognitive psychology. When most of us were trained, the benefits that psychology conferred on those of us who educate were few. "Massed versus distributive practice." That was always a good one; it was easily applicable if you could somehow distill mathematics to a list. "Inductive versus deductive sequences." Should you teach examples first and then rules, or rules first and then examples? And stuff like that. A very different psychology is developing now. People are beginning to study the acquisition and understanding of very complex kinds of learning in real schools.

For example, a group of people at the University of Illinois under the direction of Rand Spiro and Paul Feltovich have been studying how medical students come to understand and misunderstand human physiology. And they came up with a set of principles of learning and of teaching that are remarkably consistent with the kinds of principles of liberal learning and exemplary pedagogy that I've been discussing.

If you want students to develop deep, complex knowledge in poorly structured domains, attend to some of their principles.

One: *Avoid oversimplification and overregularization.* One of the most important sources of misunderstanding on the part of students is the early analogies and examples that teachers use to introduce a new topic, which then subsequently never get refined and corrected. A major source of misconceptions is we, the teachers.

Two: *Always use multiple representations, multiple analogies, multiple metaphors; not just one favorite powerful one.*

Three: *Cases are central.* You must work bottom up from cases to principles rather than trying to guide knowledge application from the top down.

Four: *Conceptual knowledge is knowledge in use.* Tie principles to applications whenever you can.

Five: *Don't compartmentalize concepts and cases.* Constantly relate abstract principles and the more concrete narrative to one another.

Six: *Have students participate actively with one another in the construction of the ideas.* Passive learning is particularly ineffective in ill-structured domains.

Let me conclude: I believe that I can make the argument that an education in the content areas—a liberal education that prepares future teachers for their pedagogical and clinical studies—is essentially coextensive with a liberal education and its pedagogy for nearly anyone. The goals of a liberal education are best addressed through the combination of deep learning, carefully selected exemplars, strong emphasis on process, strong emphasis on history and context, and therefore a strong dose of skepticism with regard to how long any particular formulation is likely to be useful, and the conditions under which it will.

These simplifications themselves, however, are not only our most powerful tools, they are also enormously dangerous if not tempered. As Whitehead observed, "Seek simplification, and distrust it." That is the essential message of the liberal arts. The kind of education in the liberal arts that I'm advocating is itself an education in pedagogy, because the problems of creating, testing, and wrestling with ideas historically directly parallel the problems of creating, testing, and wrestling with ideas pedagogically. The one preparation will in fact foster the other.

Benjamin Bloom had a taxonomy of educational objectives, the highest level of which was evaluation. That's no accident, given that he was an evaluator, I might add. I would argue that, properly understood, there is an even higher level of understanding. Beyond analysis and synthesis and evaluation there is a seventh level to the cognitive taxonomy, for which the others are prerequisite. And that is pedagogical understanding. Aristotle was right: the deepest understanding one can have of any field is an understanding of its pedagogy, because pedagogical understanding is predicated on the kind of multiple readings, the kind of contingent understandings that reflect the deep objectives of a liberal education. Deep knowledge is never enough for rich pedagogy. Advanced skill in the processes of teaching will not suffice either. To reach the highest level of competence as an educator—that seventh level—demands a melding of knowledge and process.

INTRODUCTION

JOSEPH JACKSON SCHWAB (1909–1988) (1991)

AS PART OF the centennial celebration of the University of Chicago, one hundred teachers, scientists, and scholars who had worked on the faculty were selected. Shulman wrote the memorial essay for his teacher, Joseph Jackson Schwab, and describes in detail what it was like to be a student of Schwab's teaching. In particular, he describes Schwab's gift for teaching discussions, in which he simultaneously helped students learn to interrogate texts and their authors, while also asking students to reflexively consider their own discussions. All the while, Schwab also made his pedagogical decisions transparent and modeled for his students both good teaching and accomplished pedagogical reasoning. Shulman also describes Schwab's considerable contributions to curriculum, both in the pathbreaking high school science curriculum—the Biological Sciences Curriculum Study—and the Melton curriculum, an inquiry-based Bible curriculum in Jewish education. In both projects, Schwab aimed to bring to life his image of teaching and learning as colloquy and enquiry.

16

JOSEPH JACKSON SCHWAB

1909–1988

JOE SCHWAB TAUGHT. Whatever else he accomplished as educational theorist, philosopher of science and education, and curriculum developer, when graduates of the College of the University of Chicago think about the greatness of the teaching they received at the University, they think of Schwab.

Joseph Schwab died on April 13, 1988, in Lancaster, Pennsylvania. He left behind a legacy of teaching and scholarship that will influence many fields of education. The University of Chicago Press published his volume of collected papers, edited by Ian Westbury and Neil Wilkof, entitled *Science, Curriculum, and Liberal Education.* These three topics certainly cover the domains in which he made his most significant contributions. Yet properly to appreciate both the sources of his wisdom and the fields of his substantial influence, I would have to entitle this reminiscence "Joseph Schwab: Science, Curriculum, Liberal Education . . . and the University of Chicago." In a real sense, the University of Chicago remained a not-so-silent partner in all of his achievements and a continuing beneficiary of his many accomplishments.

Joe Schwab played a central role in my personal and professional life for about thirty years. During that period, as teacher, mentor, colleague, critic, gadfly, and friend, he influenced my ways of thinking and seeing, of teaching and of learning, in a manner I am still discovering. As I continue to meet his former students from Chicago, I find that I am not alone. This extraordinary scholar and pedagogue shaped those he taught in a profound and unforgettable manner.

He was a Southerner who moved North; a biologist turned educator; a Deweyan in the Aristotelian and Thomistic environment which existed in parts of the University of Chicago when Robert Hutchins was president; an eclectic, in a world that valued a unitary theoretical doctrine; and a dedicated teacher in a community that celebrated the pure scholar and scientist. Schwab straddled the chasm between Cobb Hall and Judd Hall, between the Hutchins curriculum he shaped and loved, and the study of curriculum as an object of enquiry in its own right.

Writing about Schwab is a challenge because so much of his impact was personal; it arose in the course of interaction with him. Nevertheless, his writings have left a mark on the teaching of biology, the philosophy of curriculum, and the field of education as a whole. I shall write of Joseph Schwab through a mingling of my personal recollections and my study of his writings, combining reminiscences of his pedagogical and consultative impact with reference to his more formal writings.

I

The following exchange is reported in the proceedings of the Educational Testing Service annual conference on testing in 1950:

> Dr. Schwab: Dr.———illustrates very clearly one of the doctrinaire adhesions to which I made passing reference in my talk. One axis of doctrinaire adhesion consisted of a line of which one extreme consisted of persons who felt they deserved the name "no-nonsense" people. The no-nonsense people turn out to be simply people who have honed a problem down until it looks simple. Their "common-sense" view of reality looks good because it is an unexamined notion of what reality is. . . . What is required is conversation. . . .
>
> Dr.———: I call this conversing you are talking about by teachers who don't know much about the facts of life a pooling of ignorance.
>
> Dr. Schwab: But that is precisely the way in which all research is done, isn't it?
>
> Dr.——: That isn't the way I do it.
>
> Dr. Schwab: Then I really fear for your results, because it seems to me that the first condition of discovery is recognition of ignorance and [of] the delusion of knowledge; believing that one knows, for instance, what deduction or induction is, or that science is certain, firmly padlocks the door to any reinvestigation of the question of what science is.

That dialogue captures the essence of Joseph Schwab—his directness to the point of insult, his commitment to doubt as the source of wisdom, and his devotion to the "other view" as the key to the growth of understanding.

Schwab's connections with the University of Chicago began early. Born on February 2, 1909, in Columbus, Mississippi, to parents who had originally met in Chicago, he ran away from home immediately after his precocious high-school graduation to attend the College of the University of Chicago at the ripe age of fifteen. He graduated with a bachelor's degree in English literature and physics in 1930 and immediately pursued graduate work in biology. He received his Ph.D. in mathematical genetics in 1939. Even before completing his doctoral work, however, he was identified as an outstanding educator. He received a fellowship in science education from Teachers College, Columbia, in 1937, spending the year studying testing and measurement under Irving Lorge. He returned to Chicago in 1938 as an instructor, while working as the examiner in biology under Ralph Tyler and also completing his dissertation.

Schwab remained on the faculty of the University of Chicago, first in the College alone, later jointly in the College and the department of education, from 1938 until his retirement in 1974. He was professor of education and William Rainey Harper professor of biological sciences in the College. He retired to accept an appointment at the Center for the Study of Democratic Institutions in Santa Barbara, which had been created by one of his Chicago mentors, President Robert Maynard Hutchins. He remained in Santa Barbara until the year before his death.

II

Schwab's most powerful influences were as a teacher, and I write this essay as his student. His pedagogical imprint was pervasive, profound, and lasting. No student could ignore his impact; no student could ever forget his pedagogical power. He eschewed the lecture, though he could be a fine lecturer when he wished. His teaching was superbly Socratic in the classical sense. He posed problems for students, often in the text being read. "What is the author doing?" he would ask. The student would attempt a response. Then Schwab would begin his relentless questioning, pressing the student to reflect on his answer, to apply it to examples, to examine the inconsistencies among his responses. Sitting in Joe Schwab's classes fostered clammy hands, damp foreheads, and an ever-attentive demeanor.

I will always remember a morning in one of his classes, probably the first quarter of Natural Sciences 3 or of "OMP," i.e., Organizations, Principles, and Methods, which was the capstone course of the undergraduate curriculum in the mid-1950s. I was sitting near the window in a Judd Hall classroom with a clear view of Rockefeller Chapel. I was nineteen. Schwab asked me to read aloud the opening passage of Book 2 of Aristotle's *Physics*. "Of things that exist, some exist by nature, some from other causes." (Naturally, we used Richard McKeon's edition of Aristotle.) "All right, mister, what is the author doing in that sentence?" I provided a careful paraphrase of what Aristotle had said. "I didn't ask what he was saying. What is he doing?" I remember feeling tense. It took what seemed like half an hour—probably no more than ten minutes in reality—for me to understand the difference between what the author said and what he was doing that made what he said appropriate. Now, more than thirty years later, I have not forgotten the distinction, nor the strategy of critical reading that yielded up its meaning.

Schwab not only taught masterfully, he made his procedures in teaching marvelously transparent. He wanted you to understand what he was doing as a pedagogue, not only what he was saying as biologist, philosopher, and educator. He would say, after posing a question that left his students speechless, "Let's see if I can replace that big fat question with a few long skinny ones." And he would then demonstrate his indispensable teaching capacity for breaking down a complex question into a series of steps or components, pursuing each in turn. Yet cleverness was never sufficient in Schwab's teaching; mere brilliance was not enough. An incredible passion for learning enlivened every moment in his presence, whether in class or in a tutorial. You not only learned from Joe Schwab; you came to love and value what you learned with him. His talent as a teacher was not a secret cherished only by his students. He was the first member of the faculty to be cited as a repeated winner of the Quantrell Prize for teaching excellence awarded to outstanding teachers in the College of the University of Chicago.

In 1969, Schwab published the essential ideas behind the pedagogy of the College as he conceived of it. Although, by then, he had been continuously reinventing and practicing this form of teaching for some thirty years, he was motivated to write *College Curriculum and Student Protest* by his shock at the character of student demonstrations at Chicago against the Vietnam War. It was not the political beliefs of the protesters that upset him; he may well have agreed with their political inclinations. He was taken aback by the unwillingness of the student leaders, many of them outstanding students in the College, to permit the free flow of ideas in the critical examination of the foreign policy of the United States. Once the world of Plato's *Republic* was left behind for the hurly-burly of real political struggle, the values of enquiry and dialogue were disdained. Opposing ideas were refuted through angry shouts and severed microphone connections, not solid evidence and reasoned arguments. This caused Schwab to reevaluate the quality of higher education he had been providing and to reiterate the necessary conditions for effective general education.

For Schwab, good teaching rested on the twin foundations of a well-conceived curriculum, with carefully selected and designed materials, combined with forms of pedagogy appropriate to the goals of the curriculum. The reason that the College rejected textbooks as the medium for instruction was that they simplified and predigested the rich complexity of ideas needed to stimulate young minds. Curriculum materials could not be simplistic and schematic if the goal was to draw students into active learning and critical reasoning. The materials had to be sufficiently complex that multiple alternative interpretations could be offered and defended. In this way, with texts that rewarded close reading and a disposition toward interpretation, a proper atmosphere for discussion and debate could be fostered. A primary virtue of "great books" and other original sources was their hermeneutic potentiality; they had demonstrated over the years that they could yield new insights to novel interpretive approaches. Actual cases, especially medical or legal cases, were also highly useful in this regard. They invited enquiry, deliberation, and debate.

Schwab was just as interested in the conduct of class discussions as with the substance of instructional materials. In *College Curriculum and Student Protest,* published by the University of Chicago Press in 1969, he illustrates the approach to teaching he practiced and advocated. His description of a class session that began with the reading of a medical case of a woman who was brought to the physician in a "cretinoid state" can be summarized as follows:

> Schwab opens the discussion with a broad question: What is going on in this paper? What is the author's purpose?
>
> After some hesitations, misconstruals of the question and false starts, one student offers an answer to the question. The teacher probes for clarification, qualification and purpose. The student revises and refines his proposal.
>
> The teacher then calls for an alternative view. A second student now proposes another reading. After necessary clarification of the second proposal, the teacher turns back to the first student and asks her to consider and comment upon the second reading. He then asks Student 2 to reconsider and criticize the first reading.
>
> At that time, other students begin to participate. What began as a debate between two views is steered into conjoint enquiry regarding several alternative readings.

> Under the teacher's direction, the number and extent of different readings is reduced and simplified. The discussion then begins to consider its own course, with members reflecting on the path taken by their deliberation.
>
> The class concludes with several alternative proposals remaining on the floor, but these have undergone considerable refinement and analysis.

Schwab comments that in a properly conducted discussion of such an original document or a case, there are two distinct layers of discourse. In the first, the text or case itself is the object of enquiry, as the group moves toward the collection and elaboration of multiple alternative readings. In the second layer, the dialogue becomes reflexive. The students begin to work reflectively on their own dialogue and analyses, treating them as a form of second-order text. They thus alternate between cognition and metacognition, between analyzing the text and analyzing their own processes of analysis and review. In that way, the processes of learning come to mirror the processes of teaching, wherein Schwab regularly would reflect aloud about why he was posing a particular question at a particular moment in the course of the discussion. For Schwab, the processes of teaching and learning were easily as fascinating as the subject matter of the discussions. As he taught, he was simultaneously serving as a powerful teaching model. He not only educated future scholars; he educated future teachers and scholars.

What purposes are achieved in the forms of classroom discussion that Schwab conducted so masterfully? Why would anyone choose to engage in such patently difficult and inefficient approaches to teaching instead of employing the far more economical method of the traditional lecture? Schwab posited four virtues that accompanied teaching organized as discussion.

First, students achieve a mastery of the work that has been analyzed and discussed. After such a thoroughgoing analysis, the document in question—whether the case of a woman in a cretinoid state, an excerpt from Galileo's *Two New Sciences*, or the exposition of a particular historical interpretation—has been apprehended in fact and in principle, with attention to its virtues as well as its flaws.

Second, such discussions provide a student with the opportunity to "enjoy an increment to his command of knowledge in the interest of sense." The student now sees the potential complexities inherent in doctrinaire solutions and becomes more alert to the vulgarity of simple systems such as the seven steps of the scientific method.

Third, the student comes to know what he knows and that he knows. He has learned tactics of analysis and reflection and why they are appropriate, and how to identify new situations that will make use of these same tactics. He thus also comes to understand what he does not know, and the sense of accomplishment that ought to accompany the recognition of the areas of one's ignorance.

Fourth, the student has entered into a community of learning embracing both students and teachers, giving and receiving help with neither undue pride nor undeserved shame, and establishing person-to-person relations which attach affective significance to cognitive operations.

These aspects of a proper liberal education were central for Schwab. The processes of discussion were essential to gain the potential profit of reading worthwhile texts. Lectures, however well delivered, always flirted with the danger of doctrine, of presenting knowledge as definitive and settled truth. The kinds of discussions Schwab valued involved students' emotions as well as their intellects. Students could participate jointly in the creation of understanding as well as in the equally important accomplishment of doubt. The joining of cognition and emotion in learning was significant for Schwab. In his "Eros and Education" he portrays the art of discussion as fostering the blending of thought and feeling in educationally significant ways.

He urgently warned against a "rhetoric of conclusions" dominating educational transactions, preferring instead the honesty of "narratives of enquiry." Schwab valued the realism and humility associated with students coming to understand how knowledge truly grows rather than accepting schematic and false notions about its systematic discovery. They would thus learn, in Schwab's words, that knowledge was "contingent, dubitable and hard to come by."

III

Beginning in the late 1950s, Schwab began to work on two quite different curriculum projects. By then Hutchins had left Chicago, and perhaps Schwab's intense involvement in the curriculum of the College had waned. One project, the "Biological Sciences Curriculum Study," flowed directly from his activity as a biologist and science teacher in the College. The other project involved the teaching of the Pentateuch, the first five books of the Hebrew Bible. This project emerged from Schwab's collaboration with a former student, Seymour Fox. Fox, an ordained Conservative rabbi and holder of a Chicago doctorate in education under Schwab, wished to create a Bible curriculum that would combine an emphasis on original sources with a strong Deweyan orientation toward inquiry.

"The Biological Sciences Curriculum Study" was to become the most enduring of the major high school curriculum reforms stimulated by the shock of Sputnik. Schwab was a creator and inspiration for significant aspects of this curriculum. The brilliantly conceived laboratories in that program were built around "invitations to enquiry," which Schwab designed to reflect his conception of discovery and method in science. His *Teacher's Handbook* for the study remains to this day a masterpiece of writing for biology teachers. But his most pervasive contribution lay in the organization of the program itself, especially in the decision by the program's developers to issue the curriculum in three distinctive versions—dubbed the yellow, the blue, and the green—rather than in only one. This was the only one of the "new curricula" of the 1960s to be published as a set of parallel alternative organizations rather than as a single version.

The reason for the three versions is uniquely Schwabian, and reflects his strong predilection toward respecting the pluralism inherent in all disciplines. The alternate versions of the biological sciences curriculum reflect Schwab's concern that we give proper recognition to the variety of organizations or structures in terms of which disciplines can be created and examined. He insisted that students and teachers understand that disciplines are the outcome of human inventions whose structure varies as a consequence of human decisions concerning starting points, units of analysis, and central questions.

The curriculum writings that inspired the post-Sputnik reforms emphasized the importance of new programs reflecting the "structure" of their subject matters rather than merely comprising loosely organized collections of facts and concepts. The biologists and educators working on the biological sciences curriculum discovered in their deliberations that they were having a terrible time agreeing on one proper structure for biology, and thus a single coherent organization for the curriculum. Schwab helped them to see that the root of their difficulty lay in the fact that there were at least three very different ways of knowing biology that coexisted in the community of biologists. The reason most biology texts are such a mishmash is because the authors simply and arbitrarily collapse all of these perspectives together.

What were the three perspectives? One can argue that the natural starting point for biological inquiry and explanation is the individual cell, for it is the building block of all other forms of life or biological structures. To explain any biological phenomenon, therefore, should require that the biologist relate structures and functions to their underlying cellular components. To understand how living systems function is to explain how cells aggregate to form organs, organ systems, and organisms. Thus, biological explanations proceed from below, from the bottom up, from biochemistry, biophysics, and the like. The biological curriculum that flows from that perspective is a molecular or cell biology, which was dubbed the "blue" version of the biological sciences curriculum.

Alternatively, it can be asserted that the organism itself, that entity capable of independent existence and functioning—whether composed of one cell or millions—is the proper unit of analysis. Starting from the organism, one would then seek explanations of how individual organs function to enable the organism's activities, how they are organized into systems and how equilibrium among and within those systems is maintained. Biological explanation would focus on asking how the parts of intact organisms are themselves organized into functioning wholes, and on how different types of organisms compare and contrast with one another as adaptive systems across variations in environment. This organ, organ system, structure-function perspective became the basis of a second biological sciences curriculum, the "yellow" version.

Finally, though by no means exhaustively, one could argue that neither cells nor organisms are adequate as units of enquiry, for each is no more than a part of an even more comprehensive natural whole, which is the community or ecosystem. It is as impossible to understand the workings of any individual organism independent of its ecosystem as it is impossible to define the functions of a cell independent of the organized system of organs to which it contributes. To explain biological functioning, therefore, one must ask about the larger community of which any organism is a part, and reason from the top down, from the largest whole to its constituent parts. The third biological sciences curriculum—the "green" version—took this perspective and stressed the centrality of ecological principles in understanding biology.

These turn out to be extraordinarily important contrasts, and not only for biology. Schwab's message was that in fields where multiple paradigms compete with one another, it is rarely wise to make a forced choice of one over all the others. Consistent with Dewey's warnings regarding the dangers of "either/or" thinking, Schwab argued that each conceptual scheme or structure is probably a way of knowing that yields its own particular types of insights and understandings but is incapable of yielding them all. The way we know is through simplifying, through eliminating, through focusing. Ways of knowing are most importantly ways of *not* knowing. Full understanding is possible only through permitting alternative views to flourish, compete, and interact.

IV

The Jewish Theological Seminary of New York wished to create an enquiry-based form of religious education that treated biblical texts as both holy and yet warranting historical, critical, comparative, and eclectic analysis. The Melton curriculum presented a remarkable challenge for Schwab: advising on the construction of a curriculum around a text of richness and complexity augmented by centuries of layered commentaries and interpretation and a religious tradition which rested on an unspecified balance between revelation and interpretation, between revealed truth and requisite inference and invention. Schwab's contributions to this curriculum are not widely known outside of Jewish education circles, though Ralph Tyler remarked on this work in his comments during the Schwab memorial held at Bond chapel in May 1989. Nevertheless, the activities surrounding the development of an enquiry-based Bible curriculum may well have comprised the fullest expression of Schwab's conceptions of curriculum.

V

There was a consistent pattern to Joseph Schwab's scholarship as well as his teaching. He distrusted single theoretical solutions to the practical problems of education. This disdain for theoretically unitary positions continued as a theme throughout Schwab's career. In the early 1960s he published an essay called "On the Corruption of Education by Psychology" in which he attacked educators who embraced a particular psychological theory—e.g., group dynamics, operant conditioning, Rogersian psychotherapy—and attempted to erect a complete pedagogical edifice upon it. He argued persuasively that any theoretical position necessarily represents a narrowing of the field, a self-conscious exclusion of important elements of the field from its purview. No practical enterprise such as education could afford to be theoretically univocal because practical work could not tolerate that kind of narrowness or tunnel vision.

Similarly, in his Inglis Lectures at Harvard University, Schwab expounded on the four "commonplaces" of education which he and his colleagues, Ralph Tyler and Harold Dunkel, had been discussing for many years. The commonplaces, a concept he drew from the classical rhetorical tradition of "topics" (hence, commonplaces), were (1) the subject matter; (2) the teacher; (3) the learner; and (4) the milieu. Schwab argued that no comprehensive statement about education could be offered that did not treat, in some fashion, each of the four commonplaces. Education always involved the teaching of something by someone to someone else in some context. To ignore any of the four commonplaces was to risk leaving out a critical aspect of an educational problem.

It was typical of educational rhetoric, argued Schwab, to rest an argument primarily on a single commonplace, thus leaving it fatally flawed. The progressive educators who distorted Dewey were obsessively concerned with the learner, but paid far too little attention to the subject matter or the teacher. The curriculum reformers of the 1960s focused on the subject matter or on the need for our society to compete with the Soviets, but tended to pay little attention to whether their new curricula could be taught or learned by human teachers and their equally human pupils. In the analysis of the commonplaces, Schwab was again concerned with educational arguments that were dangerously incomplete because they placed the narrowness of theoretical perspectives on the broad and multifaceted problems of practice.

Out of this set of ideas emerged the conceptions of curriculum theory and practice that are likely to represent Schwab's most enduring contributions to educational thought. Beginning in 1968, he wrote a series of four papers on "the practical." In those essays he argued that the greatest deficiencies in curriculum deliberations lay in their theoretical character. An eclectic and practical approach was needed to design curriculum.

Schwab was not opposed to training in the theoretical disciplines nor did he disparage their intrinsic value. Any particular discipline can enlighten and improve the capacities of an investigator or curriculum maker. It can also limit the teacher's purview. This becomes particularly problematic in education, since it is a field of study that presents its problems, topics, and issues to its investigators and practitioners in ways that do not readily fold into any one neat disciplinary package.

Schwab argued that the field of curriculum was moribund because relentlessly theoretical solutions were imposed on a fundamentally practical domain. Instead of permitting any single theoretical perspective to dominate the construction of a curriculum, thereby consigning it to an unavoidably narrow and restricted view, he advocated the creation of deliberative forums for curriculum work. In these forums, each of the necessary theoretical and practical points of view would be assured a place at the table and a role in the conversation. Some version of the commonplaces would be useful in defining the minimum variety of viewpoints needed to ensure an adequately comprehensive discussion. Moreover, as he demonstrated in his work on the biological sciences curriculum, even the definition of the subject matter of the curriculum had to be subjected to such an analysis. Whether the subject was the science of biology or the literary analysis of the novel, one had to consider the likelihood that several alternative views of the subject were in competition. His essays on the practical gave a number of examples of how such deliberations might be conducted.

In the late 1970s, Schwab was asked to serve as the final discussant on a distinguished panel of social scientists invited to examine the relationships between the social science disciplines and the theory and practice of education. Nearly all these social scientists stressed the ways in which their investigations in education contributed to the furtherance of their disciplines, as well as the importance that their disciplinary knowledge held for the improvement of education. Schwab would have none of it. He alienated nearly every member of the panel by accusing them of vainly seeking legitimacy under the umbrella of the traditional social science disciplines instead of pursuing educational questions in their own right. He concluded his remarks with the charge that his fellow panelists were simply "whoring after respectability." They were furious, but once again Schwab had made his point. The disciplines were essential to the practice of education, but only if they were ready to relinquish their propriety and become eclectic fodder for the deliberations that were needed.

VI

In 1976, while teaching at Michigan State University, my colleagues and I received a federal grant to establish a national research center for the study of classroom teaching, the Institute for Research on Teaching. The institute brought together scholars from a number of different academic disciplines and curriculum areas to design and conduct research on teaching in elementary and secondary schools. In my role as codirector of the institute, I invited Schwab to come to Michigan State to conduct several weeks of seminars for the members of the research group that would assist them to communicate intelligently across the borders of their respective disciplines. It was one thing to argue for an eclectic, multidisciplinary approach; it would be quite another to accomplish such a collaboration without reinventing the Tower of Babel.

The seminar was quintessential Schwab. About twenty-five scholars and public-school teachers sat around the inner tables. A similar number of graduate students and teachers sat around the outside of the room. On the first afternoon, Schwab distributed the initial reading, the first three chapters of *Genesis*. He said, "Let's read this familiar text together and see if we can figure out what the author had in mind." And so we began.

The seminar met for two hours at the end of the afternoon, three days a week. It was exceedingly rare for anyone to miss a meeting. Using his ubiquitous cigarette as a combination pointer, conducting baton, and general pedagogical prosthesis, Schwab led the seminar through a series of readings designed to lay bare their disciplinary professional premises. We spent three or four sessions after *Genesis* with Faulkner's short story "A Rose for Emily." We read Aristotle's treatment of the elements of biological knowledge, and then studied William Harvey's paper on the circulation of the blood to examine a good example of Aristotelian biology.

Having convinced ourselves of the wisdom of a structure-function biology, rooted in the inherent natures of organisms and their parts, we read a recent article from *Science* on the fascinating topic, "Sex Change in a

Coral Reef Fish." The article described a type of fish that lived in communities composed of a single male and many females. Upon the death of the male, the dominant female metamorphosed into a male. We now had to wonder if even categories like gender could be viewed as permanent and unchanging. Was the influence of community membership even more powerful than the "inherent" characteristics of organisms? Thus did Schwab continue his lifelong quest to cure his students, whatever their ages or stations in life, of the malady that some came to call the "hardening of the categories." As with all students who experienced his Socratic pedagogy, no member of that seminar would ever forget the experience.

In 1977, Schwab returned to Michigan State to offer another seminar for the institute faculty, devoted to the study of thinking. He invited me to teach with him and for the first time I was offered an insider's view of the master-teacher in action. What appeared so spontaneous in the classroom was meticulously planned by Schwab. Before each meeting we would meet for a couple of hours and think through the text to be read and its most important questions. We would then rehearse the likely course or courses the conversation might take, the kinds of questions that could provoke the most serious doubts and the counterexamples we could prepare that might prove problematic in response to the generalizations most likely to be offered by our students. He not only thought through the seminar's probable paths like a chessmaster in midgame, he considered explicitly which participants might be counted on to make which contributions. As we planned together, it was almost as if we were composing an improvisation.

By 1977 he had paid the price for a lifelong smoking habit so inescapably connected to any student's memory of his teaching. To remember Joe Schwab in the classroom was to remember that cigarette in his right hand, gracefully swooping, pointing, and underscoring. But his emphysema had by then advanced to a point where he had to forego smoking entirely. An empty pipe replaced the lighted cigarette as pacifier and prop. But it was never quite the same. After the faculty seminar in the fall of 1977, he never again taught a regularly scheduled course.

VII

Two of the most significant influences on Schwab's thinking were Hutchins and Dewey. At first blush, this might seem paradoxical, since in both popular and academic circles these two men were perceived as occupying opposite ends of most continua. Hutchins stood for the importance of great books and eternal ideas, the primacy of a canon the study of which would benefit all learners. Dewey, in contrast, advocated that educators begin with the background, interests, and understanding of the learner, building instruction on a foundation of that interest and understanding. Schwab was never convinced that the differences between the two positions was so very great. Dewey never neglected the importance of systematic consideration of the subject matter; he argued strongly for the progressive organization of the curriculum.

One common concept that both men held dear, and that Schwab placed at the center of his own thinking about education, was that of the democratic community as both a goal of liberal education and a crucible for the creation and testing of understanding. Both Dewey and Hutchins shared a belief in the centrality of democracy for both the pursuit of knowledge and the conduct of a just society. The two commitments were inextricably linked.

I remember spending at least three hours of class time in our graduate seminar on John Dewey reading the rather brief preface to *Experience and Education.*

> All social movements involve conflicts which are reflected intellectually in controversies . . . the practical conflicts and the controversies that are conducted upon the level of these conflicts only set a problem. It is the business of an intelligent theory of education to ascertain the causes for the conflicts that exist and then, instead of taking one side or the other, to indicate a plan of operations proceeding from a level deeper and more inclusive than is represented by the practices and ideas of the contending parties.

Schwab argued that the essence of Dewey's philosophy of inquiry and of education could be found in that preface and its treatment of "either/or" thinking. I would argue that the same could be said for Schwab himself.

Dewey argued that human discourse is characterized by controversy because we are intrinsically incapable of uttering the whole truth and nothing but the truth. Claimed truth is unavoidably incomplete. Our assertions can never do justice to the full complexity of the world around us any more than our perceptions and cognitions can grasp the full richness of any setting. For this reason controversies are both inevitable and desirable. Individuals or groups will sense the incompleteness of any argument and oppose it with an alternative that builds on what was left out of the original position, thus advancing the original deliberation and advancing the analysis.

If the achievement of knowledge is a good thing, then a good society permits, even fosters the competition between competing views. The more distant a view from the mainstream, the more likely that it contains a seed of truth absent from prevailing views. Freedom of speech and the encouragement of open dialogue and debate are therefore not only political virtues, they are also epistemological virtues. If the survival and flourishing of a society is dependent, in large measure, on its capacity to seek out what is warranted and true, then its openness to new and different ideas is essential.

Schools and classrooms in such a society should be microcosms for the kind of debate and deliberation needed by the society more generally. They must be organized to permit, encourage, and model the competition between ideas. They must discourage dogmatic doctrine. Both the selection of content and the organization of interactions within the classroom should embody the collaborative and competitive conception of the search for knowledge.

This Deweyan understanding of the social and democratic character of education and of society was the theme underlying Schwab's conception of teaching. It permeated his work. After arriving in Santa Barbara, he wrote a lovely essay for the *Encyclopaedia Britannica* on "Education and the State: Learning Community," in which he emphasized the pun of the subtitle.

> First, community can be learned. It is not merely a matter of place, of village or small town, but a body of propensities toward action and feeling, propensities which can be expressed in many social circumstances.
>
> Second, human learning is a communal enterprise. The knowledge we learned has been garnered by a community of which we are only the most recent members and is conveyed by languages of work and gesture devised, preserved, and passed on to us by that community. . . . Even experience as a form of learning *becomes* experience only as it is shared and given meaning by transactions with fellow human beings.

Those of us who were transformed as we learned in the classrooms, lounges, and halls of the University of Chicago, acquired dispositions toward dialogue, questioning, and deliberation that seem to characterize a "Chicago style" of thinking. Joe Schwab exemplified that style in both method and manner. Through Schwab, we came to experience Chicago as a community of scholars, a community whose members conversed regularly about curriculum and about evaluation, a community of teachers who were scholars and scholars who were teachers. He strove to create that sense in his classes and his curricula. His image of deliberation on the curriculum was such an image of colloquy and enquiry. He taught it to generations of students in the College and in the department of education, and they in turn have passed it on to their own students.

INTRODUCTION

CALM SEAS, AUSPICIOUS GALES (1993)

WHEN SHULMAN WAS INVITED to write the final chapter to Margret Buchmann and Robert Floden's volume *Detachment and Concern: Conversations in the Philosophy of Teaching and Teacher Education,* he decided to write in a style not his own but rather adopt the style of Maxine Greene (who wrote the introduction to the book) and Margret Buchmann. Both Greene and Buchmann wrote in a style of philosophy that drew heavily on novels, drama, and poetry. Similarly, in this piece, Shulman begins and ends with Shakespeare and weaves in Virginia Woolf, Robertson Davies, and Cynthia Ozick.

Shulman concludes the essay by recounting that at the end of *The Tempest,* Shakespeare's last play, Prospero blesses Miranda and her princely lover as they return to the mainland and reassume their ruling roles. His blessing to them is for "calm seas, auspicious gales." The good life he wishes them is characterized both by the serenity of calm seas and by unpredictable and nerve-wracking auspicious gales. To live only on calm seas would mean never learning anything. To live only on gales would mean having no time to reflect. These are the conditions for growth, and Shulman argues in this essay that teacher education is too comfortable and consensual for its own good: it needs gales. The philosophers who have written chapters in this book, Shulman claims, have a critical role to play, for as insiders to teacher education, they can both be knowledgeable about the challenges and character of that work while also introducing necessary dissonance and turmoil.

17

CALM SEAS, AUSPICIOUS GALES

If it be true that good wine needs no bush, 'tis true that a good play needs no epilogue. Yet to good wine they do use good bushes; and good plays prove the better by the help of good epilogues.

—Shakespeare, *As You Like It,* Rosalind's Epilogue

A GOOD PLAY NEEDS no epilogue, and by implication, neither does a fine book. Nonetheless, having been invited to essay this final chapter, I shall proceed, hoping that my observations will prove neither redundant nor misguided. I prefer to consider this contribution an epilogue, or even less pretentiously, an afterword. I dare not attempt to draw a simple conclusion, to provide closure or summation to this group of essays. Buchmann and Floden persuasively attack the quest for certainty and consistency in discussions of teaching and teacher education. As a teacher educator, all I can claim with confidence is the last word. It is a position of advantage in both courts of law and books of essays. I accept it gratefully.

What is the role of the last word in this provocative volume of essays, critiques, and responses? My colleague-at-a-distance Maxine Greene has already done all the heavy lifting. In her introduction (which I prefer to view as a prologue or foreword) she has summarized the arguments of all the essays and of the critiques, as well as adding a few well-crafted glosses and elaborations of her own. With all the serious work having been completed, I am left with the envious opportunity to suspend the rules, to reminisce and recount, to explicate and pontificate, as befits the last player to leave the stage. I will indeed offer my observations as if I had been sitting silently at Margret's table during this marvelous set of conversations. Now that the last of the guests has left, and I am helping Margret and Bob clean up, I can offer gratuitous comments on the contributions of their guests, and sage advice to the hosts themselves.

As befits the late hour, my remarks will wander over several topics. I will first offer slight emendation to Maxine Greene's suggestion that Professor Buchmann is reminiscent of Virginia Woolf's Mrs. Ramsay, orchestrating conversations at her dinner table. I will then offer a personal reminiscence of the early years of the Buchmann/Floden careers, proffering an explanation for the unusual focus of their work on teacher education and the particularly Deweyan and Schwabian character of their perspectives.

What is the context in which Buchmann and Floden offer their analyses? Although philosophers may lay claim to timelessness, their work commands even more interest if it is timely. They philosophize in an era where the functions of teaching and teacher education are beset by a particularly excruciating ambiguity. The juxtaposition of national standards and national examinations on the one hand, and the growth of site-based management and local school control on the other, establishes a tricky tension within which teachers must work through their roles and responsibilities. In this setting, philosophers offer their critiques and analyses to lend sober reflection to the enthusiasms of their peers.

Out of this analysis, I will suggest that the policy environment introduces a tension between teacher as policy implementor and teacher as local problem solver. I will suggest an image of teacher as curriculum broker and transformer, using a conception of pedagogical reasoning and action as my model. How does one prepare teachers for such a demanding role? I will suggest the need to develop a dramatically new approach to the pedagogy of teacher education, with the use of cases and case methods at its heart.

Finally, lest we forget that teaching is more than an exquisitely complex form of reasoning and judgment, I will follow Buchmann and Floden's lead and draw from the literary wisdom of several writers for a countervailing image of teaching, one that emphasizes the necessary hope and trust that must undergird the teacher's intellectual capacities. Now, if you will assist me in clearing the cups and saucers, we can proceed from the dining room, where norms of gentility may reign, into the kitchen, where we can speak less formally and more frankly about the evening's conversations.

At Mrs. Ramsay's Dinner Table

What are the contributions of philosophers to the educational conversation? Maxine Greene, in her role as my partner bookend, compares Margret Buchmann with Virginia Woolf's Mrs. Ramsay at her dinner table. "She is the Mrs. Ramsay who strives to create a space of calm consideration in the noisy, banal domains of teaching and teacher education: a space where probing questions can be posed; where the tensions can be lived out between what is and what ought to be." The image of a calming and coherent space among the noisy and banal cacophony of voices in teaching and teacher education is soothing. Many philosophers of education attempt to accomplish as much, to make education's rough places smooth. Nevertheless, in this set of essays, I don't find the team of Buchmann and Floden offering calm and coherence to their brothers and sisters in teacher education. They provoke and challenge received wisdom, providing breeze to the becalmed but blowing them in directions for which they are ill-prepared. They are less like Mrs. Ramsay, I would suggest, than they are like the "tummlers" at a Catskills resort.

In their heyday, I am told, every resort in the "Jewish Alps" of the Catskill Mountains north of New York City had a valued employee known as the "tummler." The etymology of this Yiddish word may derive equally from "tumult" and "tumbler," but his function (and I suspect he was usually a "he") was utterly indispensable. His job was to keep things stirred up. Remarkably like Mrs. Ramsay, he was listed on the books as the "social director." And his responsibility was to create "trouble," but of a socially productive sort. He rousted guests out of their comfortable deck chairs beside the pool and induced them into hotly contested games of shuffleboard. He taught the rhumba and the cha-cha-cha. Amateur night was his responsibility, and he probably did stand-up comedy in the lounge before the handsome young singer (named either Fisher or Damone) sang popular love songs by Irving Berlin or Rodgers and Hammerstein. The tummler's role was to replace calm with cacophony; where quiet reigned, there would tumult be.

Why are Buchmann and Floden more like a Catskills tummler than like Mrs. Ramsay? Or, more likely, why would Virginia Woolf's protagonist have been considered a tummler had she presided over her dining room at Grossinger's rather than Ramsay's? I find the world of teacher education all too comfortable and consensual in its attitudes. Whether advocating the magic of reflective practice, the routine of Madeline Hunter, or the organizational rhetoric of professional development schools, this beleaguered field has circled its wagons and developed the appearance of consensus far too readily. Our philosophers have detected this quiet self-satisfaction and, like good tummlers, have set out to create a disturbed space amid the dull consistencies. They argue that the needed coherence will result only from a struggle with the disarray they must create.

The worlds of teaching and teacher education are not places where most philosophers dwell. While Maxine Greene, Thomas Green, and Gary Fenstermacher have addressed problems in that domain, it remains relatively free of philosophers. Why do we find Buchmann and Floden in the heat of the teacher education kitchen instead of in the safer and more benign places where most philosophers do their work?

What's a Nice Philosopher Like You Doing in a Place Like That?

Most philosophers shy away from the analysis of teaching. Even among philosophers of education, questions of truth, beauty, morality, and virtue are far more attractive topics than that prosaic commonplace, teaching. And if teaching is unpopular, teacher education is toxic. How does it happen, then, that two gifted philosophers devote their attention almost exclusively to the educationally rich but philosophically prosaic problems of teachers and their preparation? In her introductory remarks, Maxine Greene urges our philosophers to devote more attention "to situation, to location . . ." in the analysis of education. I shall address the question of philosophical choices by reference to situation and location, employing biography more than philosophy to suggest an answer. In the spirit of the kitchen counter kibbitzer rather than the dining table sage, I shall reminisce in quite personal terms.

Bob Floden and Margret Buchmann arrived at Michigan State University from Stanford's gentle climate on a Christmas eve when the temperature was barely at zero Fahrenheit and the wind-chill was well below that mark. They came to work in an organization that was a department neither of philosophy nor of educational foundations. Instead, they would begin to teach and to conduct research in a department of teacher education and a newly founded Institute for Research on Teaching. The institute, whose direction I shared with Professor Judith Lanier, was founded on a number of premises. We believed that problems of education were far too complex to be addressed by members of any one discipline or educational specialty. Inspired in part by Joseph Schwab's image of practical deliberation informed by a disciplined eclectic, we had begun to organize an institutional cloak of many disciplines, a place where psychologists, teacher educators, economists, anthropologists, linguists, policy analysts, curriculum specialists, philosophers, and practicing school teachers could work together in the study of teaching. Yes, even philosophers. Hence, Margret and Bob. We also believed that the study of teaching had to be tempered by a continuing taste of reality. We therefore continued strong connections between the institute's work and the continuously reforming teacher education programs at Michigan State. We ensured that each research program included a practicing classroom teacher as a full participant, typically purchasing half the teacher's contract so he or she could spend substantial time with other members of the research teams.

While both were completing Ph.D.s in philosophy of education at Stanford, their backgrounds and orientations were quite different. Margret's dissertation was on Dewey and Hegel, with substantially more of the latter than the former. She brought a background in political and social theory. She came to these philosophical studies from a strong foundation in the classical curriculum of the German *gymnasium*. Bob's earlier studies had been in philosophy and mathematics. At Stanford his work in philosophy sometimes was subordinated to his activity with the Evaluation Consortium directed by Professor Lee J. Cronbach, itself a remarkable interdisciplinary research and deliberation group. Indeed, his dissertation topic reflected this hybrid vigor, as he studied the uses of analysis of covariance in evaluation research from the perspective of philosophical investigations of the logic of reasoning from counterfactuals.

Among the most memorable occasions in the early history of the institute were the transdisciplinary staff seminars taught by visiting University of Chicago philosopher Joseph Schwab. In those seminars he modeled the power of deliberations across disciplines in the examination of educational questions. He certainly influenced the intellectual climate of the institute. I believe he also continued to inspire our growing image of the centrality of philosophical criticism and analysis to the study of educational theory and practice. He also had a profound effect on the thinking of both Buchmann and Floden.

The traditional role of the philosopher vis-à-vis empirical research is of the outsider, the critic, speaker of the last word. We held the view that even philosophers should be insiders, participating actively in all phases of research, thereby lending a critical and normative cast to aspects of a project's activity. Similarly, we appointed practicing teachers as members of each research team, not as "research translators" but as full collaborators. Thus, shortly after their arrival in Michigan, Margret began working on a project studying how teachers integrate across subject matters in teaching the language arts; Bob worked on a long-term study of the impacts of state testing and curriculum policies on teachers' decisions about what topics to teach in elementary school mathematics. Shortly afterward, both added teaching in the teacher education program to their roster of responsibilities.

Why do I bother with such an extended account of the context in which Buchmann and Floden assumed their first (and continuing) academic appointments? With Greene, I believe that situation and location are essential to understanding any enterprise. I also believe in the importance of the kind of philosophical work contained in this book, in which philosophers who are deeply involved in the activities of teacher education and research on teaching write as philosophical insiders about the complexities of those worlds. Therefore, I must try to explain what kinds of locations and situations make such scholarship flourish. Organizations like the Institute for Research on Teaching and its progeny at Michigan State and elsewhere, where philosophers work actively with colleagues from other fields of study on problems of practice and policy, become the locations and settings for this kind of work. The vitality and value of the essays in this book serve as elegant argument against the continued separation of the educational foundations—philosophy, psychology, history—from the practice of teacher education and the empirical study of teaching.

What's a Nice Philosopher Like You Doing in an Educational Policy Environment Like This?

Another aspect of "situation and location" is the policy environment in which considerations of teaching and teacher education occur. Buchmann and Floden's analysis of the teacher's needed capacities and dispositions is particularly relevant to the demands that the current directions of education reform are likely to place on teachers. Through the multitude of educational reform proposals, a few common themes are emerging. They outline a new countenance for education and significantly more demanding conditions for America's teachers. Commitment to these commonplaces, for example, was one of the few areas of agreement between the contending 1992 presidential campaigns of Clinton and Bush.

Higher national standards in the core subject areas and national examinations for all students are the twin foundation stones atop which a national policy for educational reform is being erected. The most enlightened reform proposals reject the curricular impulse derived from those who believe that a fairly fixed body of cultural literacy must be conveyed to all students. They disclaim the view that our students simply do not know enough history, science, mathematics, literature, or geography. They argue with those advocates who propose a coordinated system of national curriculum and standard examinations that will hold educators and students responsible for knowing what they must know. In the more enlightened view, the national goals would not take the form of prescribed syllabi, however, but of detailed curriculum frameworks tied to quite different systems of student assessment. Teachers would be free to select from the options offered by the curriculum frameworks and to fashion programs of study that would prepare their students for the new genres of national examinations.

Alongside this apparent nationalization of educational renewal, however, was a countervailing move. Schools and teachers would become more autonomous and responsible at the local level to fashion programs that would gain student interest and be responsive to local needs, interests, culture, and values. Teachers would still be expected to help students reach the national standards and do well on the national examinations. But the belief was that a lockstep national curriculum tethered to narrowly defined traditional examinations would be harmful for American education. There should be a way to share common goals and standards while permitting, even encouraging, locally responsive variations in methods, emphases, and values. Thus national definitions of educational goals and national examinations could be paired with greater site-based management and local control.

What kinds of national curriculum frameworks and examinations permit the coexistence of such contradictory directions? The proposals are somewhat utopian, perhaps almost quixotic. Here we see curriculum frameworks rather than mandated curricula, eschewing the stereotype of French or German education in which an entire nation of fourth graders is on the same page of every text on the second Tuesday in May. Examinations would be conducted in the spirit of Lauren Resnick and Marc Tucker's *New Standards Project* or of Ted Sizer's *Coalition of Essential Schools,* in which performance assessments, projects, and portfolios worthy of exhibition and display replace the machine-scored answer sheet.

The new view of assessment carries with it striking new images of teaching. The teacher is a coach, much more in the spirit of advanced placement (AP) tests than of standardized tests. In standardized tests the teacher is unprofessional if she teaches to the test; in APs the teacher is unworthy if she doesn't. Indeed, she knows what should be on the test and actively coaches the students to perform well on it. Unlike advanced placement tests, however, the forms of assessment are vigorously local even as the tests are scored in light of national standards, no small challenge for the psychometricians but no small revolution in educational thinking.

"Less Is More" and the Rediscovery of Zipf's Law

A key element in the image of new standards, whether following the model of the mathematics standards of the National Council for Mathematics Education (NCTM) or the science, mathematics, and technology standards of Project 2061 of the prestigious American Association for the Advancement of Science, is Sizer's motto, "Less is more!" (borrowed wisely from the architect Ludwig Mies Van der Rohe, who probably borrowed it in turn from someone else in the spirit of Robert Merton's [or was it Whitehead's] line, "Everything of importance has been said before by someone who did not invent it").

The countervailing impulse of reform through national goals also reflects the belief that national standards may be needed to guide the reform of American education. However, advocates of "less is more" begin by challenging the assumption that our conceptions of needed knowledge are adequate. They deny that we need only develop a "delivery system" to ensure that the intellectual goods get from suppliers to clients. This perspective argues that we must radically reconstruct our conception of what knowledge is of most worth. We must replace the emphasis on coverage and the audit of results with the need for selectivity, depth, and the demonstration and display of accomplishments. The "less is more" principle calls for the curriculum to eschew coverage and to replace that seductively simple virtue with the exploration in depth, variation, and richness of the essential questions and central ideas of the disciplines and interdisciplines. The principle is hardly new, and no less valuable for its age or lineage. In our century, Dewey, Whitehead, Bruner, and Schwab are among the thinkers who argued for the idea. The principle is revolutionary, however, especially as it relates to significant consequences for the work of students and teachers in schools.

When we emphasize the core essential ideas of disciplines or interdisciplines, we do not merely reduce the amount of material to be covered nor do we take a shorter list of ideas and merely address them more deeply. The ideas themselves change character. Indeed, I would argue, the more central and hence essential are ideas to any field, the more likely they are to be ambiguous, elusive, and multidimensional in their complexity.

Thus, not only is less more valuable than more, less is more complex and difficult to learn than more.

Which finally brings us back to Zipf's Law. Who, you may ask, is Zipf, and what is he suddenly doing in our kitchen? George Kingsley Zipf was a Harvard instructor whose passion was comparative philology. Zipf (1935, 1949) verified that, in nearly all languages, word frequency is correlated with word shortness. The more frequently words are used, the shorter and less phonemically complex they are or they become. The process of abbreviation and curtailment that apparently produces this effect, however, also leads to one of the great agonies of second-language learning.

We all remember the ease with which we negotiated the first few months of high school Spanish or French. The regular conjugations were straightforward, and so—regular. Then we discovered that these languages engage in the ultimate *bait-and-switch* operation with respect to the regularities of grammar and syntax. The verbs we really needed to use, the verbs "to go" and "to be" and others like them, turned out to be regularly irregular in their conjugations! That's a manifestation of Zipf's Law, a pattern he attempted to apply to many features of human individual and collective behavior as a manifestation of the "principle of least effort."

Shulman's corollary to Zipf's Law is quite simple. The more central a concept, principle, or skill to any discipline or interdiscipline, the more likely it is to be irregular, ambiguous, elusive, puzzling, and resistant to simple propositional exposition or explanation. Thus, if we are to make less into more, we had better recognize that less is harder than more, less is more complex than more, less is more enigmatic or cryptic than more. It is far easier to remember how a bill becomes a law than to understand *democracy* as a concept.

What will be the role of the teacher in this form of education? Teachers will serve as honest brokers between the ideas, skills, and dispositions contained in national and state curriculum frameworks, and the specific conditions, understandings, and interests of students, schools, and communities. Bruner has used the term "intellectual honesty" to characterize the teacher's pedagogical imperative. Teachers must discern the most significant ideas contained in the curriculum frameworks and examine them critically from their own perspectives, which combine the wisdom of subject-matter experts and pedagogues. They must simultaneously examine the minds and motives of their students, sensing the knowledge and experience they bring to the table, and the kinds of thinking that will help the students make the most sense out of the curriculum's ideas. To teach in an intellectually honest way is to create instructional representations that are faithful simultaneously to the structure of the subject matter, on the one hand, and to the constructive understandings of students, on the other.

The great challenge of teaching these less-is-more essential ideas is that they do not permit clear, clean, direct propositional expositions. You can't just learn the definitions. They require instead a "criss-crossing of the landscape," the active application of multiple representations through metaphors, analogies, narratives, and inventive examples. They require student constructions, iterations, and, most important, dialogues and debates. Policy makers will need to abandon their illusions about the remote control of teaching. Teachers will need to depend even more on their own deep subject-matter understanding and their abilities to transform that knowledge into powerfully adaptive representations that connect with the experiences and preconceptions of students. They must learn to employ groupwork, for example, not as a fashion, but as an indispensable crucible in which ideas are tempered and internalized through collaboration, competition, and exchange. Teachers must then be in a position to monitor and respond to the active, multiple constructions of meaning by their students.

The essential feature of teaching is its uncertainty and unpredictability. Teaching cannot be directed by formal theory, lockstep national syllabi, or centralized procedural policies, yet remain responsive to both student insights and misconceptions. Moreover, as our educational goals increasingly emphasize higher-order thinking and reasoning and student collaborations around real problems, the education of teachers must emphasize their development of flexibly powerful pedagogical understanding and judgment. Therefore, discourse on teaching must go beyond broad principles and propositions as its objects. This set of conditions not only defines the difficult conditions for teaching; it also identifies the reasons why the education of teachers represents a challenge of the first magnitude.

When confronted with so much uncertainty and unpredictability, teachers will find only temporary value in simple admonitions and checklists. Recipes for teaching and prefabricated lesson plans will work only as long as conditions remain within the predicted range. This is the reason I advocate the development of new approaches to the education of teachers, a long-overdue reinvention of the pedagogy of teacher education. Consistent with Buchmann and Floden's critiques, we cannot improve teacher education merely by increasing the amount of firsthand experience. Nor will more theory or more practical maxims suffice. A case-based curriculum strikes the ideal middle ground between the high impact of direct experience and the thoughtful reflection engendered by fine literature, insightful theory, and engaging discussions (Shulman, 1992).

Knowledge of teaching comprises combinations of cases and principles. Future teachers can be guided to develop a repertoire of cases that can help to guide their thinking and reflections on their own teaching. They can then use their experience with cases, their own and those of others, as lenses for thinking about their work in the future. Their development as teachers can be guided through their study of prototype cases written by others, as well as through reflecting on their own teaching and crafting cases of their own.

By reading and discussing such cases, we begin to detoxify the recounting of failures and make the possibilities for learning from such experiences more real. We try to help our students celebrate their failures if they can learn from them, rather than denying them to avoid embarrassment. Bosk (1979) has written about learning in the surgical residency, in a book that carries the wonderful title *Forgive and Remember.* The title communicates the message that internships are occasions in which errors must be made. They will be forgiven only if they can be remembered and reflected upon and become a source of learning. "Forgive and forget" is a motto for good relationships without growth. "Forgive and remember" is a slogan for all practical internships and an inspiration for those who would learn from cases.

Thus far I have been in fundamental agreement with Buchmann and Floden, supporting their more complex and uncertain view of teaching and their eschewal of highly rationalized approaches to teacher preparation. However, there are limits to the degree to which human agents can be asked to tolerate ambiguity and unpredictability. To the outsider, coping with the demands of an inconsistent curriculum may seem like a great humanistic adventure. To the insider who is undergoing the experience, the price may be far too high.

Managing Complexity

For our philosophers, coherence is a rebel angel and the quest for consistency and simplicity is foolish and misguided. They argue that teachers and teacher educators must learn to live with the necessary ambiguities and complexities that are inherent in education. Yet, they ask of educators what may well be unreasonable to ask of anyone—to seek to complicate rather than simplify their lives. The issue may not be a matter of choice or preference. The need to reduce complexity or ambiguity to optimal or tolerable levels may well be wired into our nervous systems.

An example from medicine may illustrate my point. When Arthur Elstein and I were studying how gifted internists arrived at difficult diagnoses (Elstein, Shulman, & Sprafka, 1978), we first read the standard textbooks of medicine. They instructed physicians to gather the patient information they needed from medical histories, physical examinations, and routine laboratory procedures, all the while *maintaining an open mind.* We therefore approached our first direct observations of diagnostic work in internal medicine fully expecting to document inductive search procedures. To our amazement, when we worked with our first physician, he proceeded to generate several diagnostic hypotheses within the first minutes of the patient encounter, long before he had collected much information at all. What, we wondered, had happened to the open mind? He devoted much of the ensuing investigation to pitting his working hypotheses against one another as he continued to collect new information.

As our studies continued, we came to understand that the first physician was not an anomaly or exception. Indeed, all the experienced physicians we studied employed essentially the same heuristic. They sized up the presenting complaint and rapidly moved toward generating one or more diagnostic hypotheses. This early closure did not doom them to frequent error. The method of multiple hypotheses, as we came to call the strategy, was remarkably robust. Yet it appeared to violate both the tenets of the medical textbooks and the principles of open-minded inductive reasoning!

We came to understand our findings in terms of the management of complexity. Examined closely, the admonition to gather all the information needed while maintaining an open mind was a recipe for madness. The modest capacities of human memory were quickly overwhelmed by the burdens of unscaffolded information-gathering. Even though the search could be divided into history, physical, and laboratory phases, and some of those processes could be further organized by anatomical location (proceeding cephalocaudally, from head to toes), the sheer volume of information accumulates much too rapidly to be held in mind efficiently. Simply put, the textbook admonitions were impossible to follow. Inductive, open-minded diagnostic work was an illusion. Physicians regularly generated multiple working hypotheses because without them they couldn't find their place. The intellectual world of medical diagnosis would be unmanageably complex if the inductive imperative were followed.

Why then generate *multiple* working hypotheses if the primary motivation is simplification? A single hypothesis would be quite enough. But the motivation is not solely to avoid complexity. The diagnostician seeks to control complexity within the bounds of real problems that demand solution. The great danger of early hypothesis generation is, indeed, premature closure around a favored hypothesis that has not been adequately challenged. The method of multiple competing hypotheses serves the dual purpose of memory management and safeguarding the reasoning process from inappropriately early narrowing of the field. And in this example, I believe, we find an important moral for our analysis of teaching and teacher education.

The physician addresses diagnostic problems of great complexity against a background of stability and routine. The order and contents of the medical history, the physical examination, and the ordering of laboratory tests is stable and routine. The physician engages with a single patient at a time, both in the examining room and in the operating room. When the task becomes more complex, as in a surgical procedure, the physician works as part of a team, including nurses and other physicians. When a diagnostic problem exceeds her range, the physician readily solicits the consultation of peers. Both the internal structure of medical work and the organizational structure of medical practice combine to control the complexity and unpredictability of the physician's work. This is not so in teaching.

Except for a busy emergency room (always staffed by a team), no medical context approximates the flux of an elementary school classroom. The teacher faces the uncertainties of teaching as a solo practitioner, and with responsibility for two or three dozen lives and minds at any one time. Critics of teaching and teacher education who wish to celebrate complexity and the importance of seeking coherence must be mindful of the potentially overwhelming demands of life in classrooms. The proper education of teachers as well as the needed restructuring of schools must take account of the need to provide a stable and supportive set of conditions within which teachers might then be expected to cope with ambiguity and uncertainty.

Coherence and Experience: Twin Rebel Angels?

As befits the vocation of tummlers, this collection of essays begins and ends with challenges to a conventional wisdom that celebrates two of the pillars of contemporary teacher education programs: firsthand experience and program consistency. Belief in the importance of these two principles has supported attempts to reform the preparation of teachers for nearly a century. How can these be questioned?

We are first urged to be suspicious of the great value ascribed to experience, hands-on direct involvement with life in classrooms through observation, participation, and internship. In the spirit of those who have admonished that we learn not from experience, but from thinking about our experience, our authors warn that too much experience will likely fail to yield the advertised skill and wisdom. Instead, it might well bring about unwarranted confidence, uncritical habits of practice, and limitations to pedagogical imagination and inventiveness.

The book's final chapter praises "coherence, the rebel angel." Needlessly confused with the "guardian angels" of systemic educational reform such as consistency, direction, and program, coherence is of a different species, valuable in quite different ways. Coherence actually presupposes inconsistency, complexity, a modicum of disorder, and contradiction that can be negotiated by future teachers only if they actively transform the inconsistencies into coherence. Consistency can be a characteristic of programs or curricula; coherence must be constructed by the learners themselves.

The image of the rebel angel is telling. Rebel angels are said to have resisted the control and discipline of God and defied his commands. They descended from heaven, mated and matriculated with human beings, taught them the secrets of divine wisdom, and thus robbed humankind of its innocence. Buchmann and Floden argue that program consistency, by oversimplifying the world of classrooms and schools, breeds a form of pedagogical innocence. This innocence must be challenged by the cacophonies of mismatched theories and incompatible principles that make up the useful teacher education program. The rebel angel of coherence teaches mortal pedagogues to cope with the complexities of their responsibilities and to construct the meaning and order needed to guide their work.

This provocative claim by our two tummlers stimulates me to express both assent and dissent. The magical properties of student teaching guided by the invisible hand of systematic teaching models certainly make teaching appear far more orderly and regular than is warranted. Nevertheless, there are lessons to be learned from experience, both one's own and that of others. Coherence is a worthy goal, but one unlikely to be accomplished by students working alone. They will need considerable support from thoughtful and sensitive faculty members who are prepared to create the conditions that make for coherence without falling prey to the temptation to do the work on behalf of the students. (Deborah Ball's conception of mathematics teaching in the elementary grades is a good model for this delicate balance.)

Here again, I see particular value in the potential of case methods in teacher education. Cases are powerful representations of experience, secondhand experience if you will. While "secondhand" is generally a term of derision in the world of clothing or automobiles, secondhand experience may actually have advantages over its firsthand counterpart for some aspects of teacher development. As I discussed earlier, I see value in both the study of cases and the crafting of one's own. When a student studies, discusses, analyzes, and wrestles with the facts, feelings, and issues in a well-crafted case, she re-frames the experiences of the case to make them her own. Thus, learning with cases entails two complementary processes—one studies the secondhand accounts of others' firsthand experiences, transforming them vicariously into one's own. One also writes cases based on firsthand experiences, and this process of case-making renders the merely firsthand experiences into a form of reflective practice. The teacher not only has immediate experience, he constructs it. Constructing one's own teaching, like composing one's life, confronts and captures it in new ways.

The ease with which we attack experience, however, leaves me uneasy. I grant that mere experience is an overrated condition for developing expert pedagogical judgment. Nevertheless, it seems so typical for academics to demean that which *hoi polloi* have in far greater abundance than do professors. Varieties of firsthand experience are the prerequisite for secondhand experience. One cannot think about experiences one has never had, and even cases gain their educative power through their interchange with direct experience.

In yet another sense, experience's value may lie less in how it guides our actions, and more in how it permits us wisely to refrain from action. In her novel *The Cannibal Galaxy* Cynthia Ozick portrays a philosopher named Hester Lilt, who delivers a lecture on the nature of pedagogy. She reads to her audience the following *midrash,* a tale from the Jewish sources:

> There ran the little fox . . . on the Temple Mount, in the place where the Holy of Holies used to be, barren and desolate, returned to the wild, in the generation of the Destruction. And Rabbi Akiva was walking with three colleagues, Rabbi Gamliel, Rabbi Elazar, and Rabbi Joshua, and all four saw the little fox dash out. Three of the four wept, but Akiva laughed. Akiva asked, "Why do you weep?" The three said, "Because the fox goes in and out, and the place of the Temple is now the fox's place." Then the three asked Akiva, "Why do you laugh?" Akiva said, "Because of the prophecy of Uriah and because of the prophecy of Zechariah. Uriah said, 'Zion shall be ploughed as a field, and Jerusalem shall become heaps.' Zechariah said, 'Yet again shall the streets of Jerusalem be filled with boys and girls playing.' So you see," said Rabbi Akiva, "now that Uriah's prophecy has been fulfilled, it is certain that Zechariah's prophecy will also be fulfilled." And *that,*

> said Hester Lilt, "is pedagogy. To predict not from the first text, but from the second. Not from the earliest evidence, but from the latest. To laugh out loud in that very interval which to every reasonable judgment looks to be the most inappropriate—when the first is accomplished and future repair is most chimerical. To expect, to welcome, exactly that which appears most unpredictable. To await the surprise which, when it comes, turns out to be not a surprise after all, but a natural path." Again she lifted her head. "The hoax is when the pedagogue stops too soon. To stop at Uriah without the expectation of Zechariah is to stop too soon. And when the pedagogue stops too soon, he misreads every sign." (Ozick, 1983, pp. 67–68)

The wisdom of Akiva suggests a caution for Buchmann and Floden's elegant critiques of experience. The value of experience may lie less in providing grounds for action than in offering sound reasons for inaction. Strategic action may depend far less on the contributions of experience than most professional educators are wont to believe. But the wisdom of practice is often the wisdom to forbear, to withhold, "to predict not from the first text, but from the second." It is no accident that young parents are always seeking ways to act when confronted with a problem, while more mature parents recognize the prudence of patience and the wisdom of forbearance.

In a novel by Canadian author Robertson Davies, ironically titled *The Rebel Angels,* a character observes that fine teaching often takes on a surprising character.

> Only those who have never tried it for a week or two can suppose that the pursuit of knowledge does not demand a strength and determination, a resolve not to be beaten, that is a special kind of energy, and those who lack it or have it only in small store will never be scholars or teachers, because real teaching demands energy as well. To instruct calls for energy, and to remain almost silent, but watchful and helpful, while students instruct themselves, calls for even greater energy. To see someone fall (which will teach him not to fall again) when a word from you would keep him on his feet but ignorant of important danger, is one of the tasks of the teacher that calls for special energy, because holding in is more demanding than crying out. (Davies, 1981, p. 87)

Thus, teachers need to give heed to that voice of wisdom that courageously yells, "Wait!" when the crowds clamor for the attack, or softly whispers "Listen," when the teacher's every instinct is to tell. Experience, whose teachings can be so misleading and dangerous, may also be a second rebel angel, whose gift is the wisdom to withhold, to permit learning to replace teaching as the essential feature of classroom life. Perhaps the lesson of experience is that two significant nouns are missing in the glib phrase "less is more." Less *teaching* is more *learning*. If we wish students to learn more, teachers may have to teach less. And both groups will discover that they can use the time profitably.

Epilogue

"It is not the fashion to see the lady epilogue; but it is no more unhandsome than to see the lord the prologue." So Rosalind comments on both her person and her position as she concludes Shakespeare's great comedy. It is certainly not the fashion to see the teacher educator the epilogue in a book of philosophical analysis, but perhaps no less worthy than to have given a distinguished philosopher the prologue. It is only civil for the tummlers to give their clients the last word. We are the ones whose serenity is so rudely, albeit fruitfully, disturbed by their analyses.

Since good plays need no epilogue, Shakespeare used this device only once more among his prodigious creations. In his very last play, *The Tempest,* he provides a closing valedictory for his alter ego, Prospero. This wise philosopher-duke recognizes that neither the storm with which the play opens nor its absence, perfect calm, is a suitable setting for human progress. He sagely blesses his children, therefore, with the promise of "calm seas, auspicious gales." Without the combination of both, we can enjoy neither the serenity of peace nor the adventures of progress and growth. The safe setting of a calm ocean can permit sailors to risk raising all their largest sails and thus take advantage of strong winds. In a similar fashion, the field of teacher education will flourish if we can find the proper balance of consistency and coherence, a judicious blend of calm seas and auspicious gales to permit our fields to accomplish their needed reforms. The competing images of a calming Mrs. Ramsay and an abrasive tummler suggest that our philosophers may play both roles in turn as they help guide the educational conversation.

REFERENCES

Bosk, C. L. (1979). *Forgive and remember: Managing medical failure.* Chicago: University of Chicago Press.

Davies, R. (1981). *The rebel angels*. New York: Viking.

Elstein, A. S., Shulman, L. S., & Sprafka, S. (1978). *Medical problem solving: An analysis of clinical reasoning*. Cambridge, MA: Harvard University Press.

Ozick, C. (1983). *The cannibal galaxy*. New York: Knopf.

Shulman, J. H. (Ed.). (1992). *Case methods in teacher education*. New York: Teachers College Press.

Zipf, G. K. (1935). *The psycho-biology of language*. Boston: Houghton Mifflin.

Zipf, G. K. (1949). *Human behavior and the principle of least effort*. New York: Addison-Wesley.

INTRODUCTION

TEACHING AS COMMUNITY PROPERTY (1993)

THIS PIECE (also reprinted in the companion volume, *Teaching as Community Property*) officially begins Shulman's writing in higher education and his evolving argument that teaching is a legitimate form of scholarly work. By 1993, Shulman was in the midst of working on the Peer Review of Teaching Project with the American Association for Higher Education. As an initial step in building his argument, Shulman posits that we need to make teaching "community property" (echoing the argument he makes for research being community property in "Disciplines of Inquiry"), and in so doing, we open our work as teachers in higher education to public discussion and scrutiny. He suggests three strategies for making teaching public: making the evaluation of teaching part of the responsibility of the relevant disciplinary communities, making it visible through artifacts that capture the complexity of teaching, and creating processes of peer review. These strategies, he notes, will require considerable cultural change in higher education, and he recommends one modest step toward that change: pedagogical colloquia. If we expected prospective colleagues to speak both about their research and their teaching when they interviewed for jobs, we might begin to change the ways that we think about a scholarly career. Doctoral students would need to be prepared to give such talks when they interviewed for jobs upon graduation, as would their more senior colleagues, and higher education in general would need to develop new norms for talking about teaching—as well as research—as part of its ordinary work.

18

TEACHING AS COMMUNITY PROPERTY

PUTTING AN END TO PEDAGOGICAL SOLITUDE

AT THE END OF the June commencement at which I received my graduate degree, George Beadle, then president of the University of Chicago, turned to those of us baking in our robes in Rockefeller Chapel and proclaimed, "Welcome to the community of scholars." Perspiring though I was, a chill went through me because this was something I had aspired to—membership in a community of scholars.

As the years have gone by, I've come to appreciate how naïve was my anticipation of what it would mean to be a member of a scholarly community. My anticipation contained two visions. One was the vision of the solitary individual laboring quietly, perhaps even obscurely, somewhere in the library stacks, or in a laboratory, or at an archaeological site; someone who pursued his or her scholarship in splendid solitude. My second vision was of this solitary scholar entering the social order—becoming a member of the community—interacting with others, in the classroom and elsewhere, as a teacher.

What I didn't understand as a new Ph.D. was that I had it backwards! We experience isolation not in the stacks but in the classroom. We close the classroom door and experience pedagogical solitude, whereas in our life as scholars, we are members of active communities: communities of conversation, communities of evaluation, communities in which we gather with others in our invisible colleges to exchange our findings, our methods, and our excuses.

I now believe that the reason teaching is not more valued in the academy is because the way we treat teaching removes it from the community of scholars. It is not that universities diminish the importance of teaching because they devalue the act itself; it is not that research is seen as having more intrinsic value than teaching. Rather, we celebrate those aspects of our lives and work that can become, as we say in California, "community property." And if we wish to see greater recognition and reward attached to teaching, we must change the status of teaching from private to community property. I would suggest three strategies that can guide us in this transformation.

First, we need to reconnect teaching to the disciplines. Although the disciplines are easy to bash because of the many problems they create for us, they are, nevertheless, the basis for our intellectual communities. Like it or not, the forms of scholarship that are seen as intellectual work in the disciplines are going to be valued more than forms of scholarship (such as teaching) that are seen as non-disciplinary.

Notice that I say non-disciplinary, not inter-disciplinary. (I would argue that most modern disciplines are in fact inter-disciplines.) The distinction is not between disciplinary and *inter*-disciplinary but disciplinary and *non*-disciplinary. Look, for instance, at the way the improvement of teaching is *treated* in most of our schools. Institutional support for teaching and its improvement tends to reside in a universitywide center for teaching and learning where many of the TAs are trained, and where faculty—regardless of department—can go for assistance in improving their practice. That's a perfectly reasonable idea. But notice the message it conveys—that teaching is generic, technical, and a matter of performance; that it's not part of the community that means so much to most faculty, the disciplinary, interdisciplinary, or professional community. It's something general you lay on top of what you *really* do as a scholar in a discipline.

Similarly, in most of our institutions, the student evaluation forms are identical across the disciplines, as if teaching civil engineering and teaching Chaucer were the same. But of course they're not. We would never dream of sending out examples of someone's research for peer review to people at another university who were on that other university's faculty *in general*. The medievalists evaluate the research of other medievalists; research by civil engineers is reviewed by other civil engineers. Not so with teaching.

The first strategy I would argue for, then, in attempting to make teaching community—and therefore *valued*—property, is that we recognize that the communities that matter most are strongly identified with the disciplines of our scholarship. "Discipline" is in fact a powerful pun because it not only denotes a domain but also suggests a process: a community that disciplines is one that exercises quality, control, judgment, evaluation, and paradigmatic definition. We need to make the review, examination, and support of teaching part of the responsibility of the disciplinary community.

The second strategy I would propose is that if teaching is going to be community property it must be made visible through artifacts that capture its richness and complexity. In the absence of such artifacts teaching is a bit like dry ice; it disappears at room temperature. You may protest, "But that's so much work!" Notice that we don't question this need to document when it comes to more traditional forms of scholarship. We don't judge each other's research on the basis of casual conversations in the hall; we say to our colleagues, "That's a lovely idea! You really must write it up." It may, in fact, take two years to write it up. But we accept this because it's clear that scholarship entails an artifact, a product, some form of community property that can be shared, discussed, critiqued, exchanged, built upon. So, if pedagogy is to become an important part of scholarship, we have to provide it with this same kind of documentation and transformation.

The third strategy is that if something is community property in the academy, and is thus deemed valuable, this means we deem it something whose value we have an obligation to judge. We assume, moreover, that our judgments will be enacted within the disciplinary community, which means, I'm afraid, that the terrifying phrase "peer review" must be applied to teaching. Think what this would mean: if your institution is like mine, the principle of peer review is best expressed not as an inverse-square law but as a direct-square law. The influence of any evaluation of someone's scholarship is directly related to the square of the distance from the campus where the evaluator works. So for Stanford faculty, a Berkeley review is pretty good, but Oxford is *much* better. (I haven't checked to see whether the curve continues as you go to Australia or if there's a plateau, but this is the sort of thing higher education researchers would probably enjoy studying.) My point is that the artifacts of teaching must be created and preserved so that they can be judged by communities of peers beyond the office next door.

This kind of peer review may seem far-fetched on many campuses; it is far from the norm. But one of the sources of pleasure I have had at Stanford is serving on the universitywide Appointments and Promotions Committee and thus reviewing promotion and appointment folders for the business school. In our business school, and I suspect in a number across the country, the promotion folders look very different from those in, say, history or biology. The portfolios of business school faculty are often just as thick in the domain of teaching as they are in the area of traditional social science and business scholarship. Included in them are samples of instructional materials developed by the teachers, cases they have written, and detailed essays in which candidates gloss and interpret the course syllabi that are included in their portfolios. Most impressive of all, one finds reviews by colleagues who visit their classes and critique their case-based teaching, and reports by faculty at other business schools who examine their teaching materials and their cases. What a contrast to the promotion dossier that provides three sets of student ratings and two letters that say, "She must be a good teacher, she sure gives a good talk!"

There's an important corollary point to mention here too. We should evaluate each other as teachers not only with an eye to deriving accurate measurements of our teaching effectiveness—though of course we must have precision. Our evaluations should also have positive consequences for the processes and persons being evaluated. We are obliged, that is, to organize the evaluation of teaching so that the very procedures we employ raise the likelihood that teaching gets treated seriously, systematically, and as central to the lives of individual faculty and institutions. This means we are obliged to use procedures from which faculty are likely to learn how to teach better. I like the way the chair of the English Department at Stanford put it: "What we're trying to do," he said, "is to create a culture of teaching, one in which the conversations, the priorities [and, I would add, the rituals and kinship systems] of the department have teaching at their center."

No single change will produce this culture, but let me end with one suggestion that would, I think, take us a long way toward it. If we really want a different kind of culture, we ought to change our advertising. By way of example, I've drafted an ad for *The Chronicle* announcing a new position in 20th Century U.S. History at Shulman College. "We seek a new faculty member who is good at both research and teaching"—the ad says the usual things along those lines. But then it goes on to say that candidates who are invited to campus will be asked to offer two colloquia. In one colloquium, they will describe their current research—the usual research colloquium. In the second, which we'll call the *pedagogical colloquium,* they will address the pedagogy of their discipline. They will do so by expounding on the design of a course, showing systematically how this course is an act of scholarship in the discipline, and explaining how the course represents the central issues in the discipline and how in its pedagogy it affords students the opportunity to engage in the intellectual and moral work of the discipline.

Think of the impact on our doctoral programs if we knew that there were colleges and universities out there that had agreed to employ the *pedagogical colloquium* as a regular, central portion of that mating ritual we call recruitment. We could begin to change the ways we think about preparation for a life or career of scholarship. Moreover, the public nature of this *pedagogical colloquium* would change the culture of the institution doing that recruiting. We could begin to look as seriously at evidence of teaching abilities as we do at research productivity. We would no longer have merely to pray that this good young scholar can educate. We would have evidence of his or her abilities as an educator-in-the-discipline.

To change academic culture in this way will not be easy. But colleges and universities have always taken justifiable pride in their commitment to inquiry and criticism in all fields, even those where dogma and habit make real scrutiny uncomfortable. Now we must turn this tough scrutiny on our own practices, traditions, and culture. Only by doing so will we make teaching truly central to higher education.

This essay is excerpted from Lee S. Shulman's presentation at the AAHE National Conference on Faculty Roles and Rewards, held in January, 1992 in San Antonio.

INTRODUCTION

JUST IN CASE: REFLECTIONS ON LEARNING FROM EXPERIENCE (1996)

THIS CHAPTER IS FROM *The Case for Education: Contemporary Approaches for Using Case Methods,* a volume that its editors dedicated to Judith Shulman for her extensive work in the creation of cases and the development of a case method for professional development. Lee Shulman had been wrestling with the idea of cases as both a form of teacher knowledge and a medium for teacher learning since the early 1980s. Implicit in his thinking up to this point was the notion that cases can play a critical role in learning from experience, and he addresses this issue explicitly in this chapter.

Shulman launches the essay by arguing the many benefits of cases: they situate instruction in place and time, they afford teachers the opportunity to reflect on their own experiences; they capture the uncertainties of teaching, and they help teachers "chunk" their experience into units that lend themselves to reflection and analysis. He then describes his own use of case methods as a teacher educator and explains how he has the prospective teachers in his class read and discuss cases, as well as write their own, comment on those of their colleagues, and hold conversations and conferences about cases generated by the class.

Shulman goes on to delineate a theoretical conception of cases and case methods. The essence of any case, he argues, is chance, and a case becomes educative when it combines four functions or components: intention, chance, judgment, and reflection. Similarly, there are four psychological processes at play when a teacher is learning from a case, from the initial experience to the retelling and subsequent theorizing about the event: activity or agency, reflection, collaboration, and community or culture. In this way, Shulman was beginning to bring together his past work on cases and learning from experience with the work he was then doing on communities of learners.

One also sees Shulman moving away from a conception of teaching as managing complexity to teaching as involving judgment under uncertainty. Although there is much in common between these two perspectives, the shift to an emphasis on judgment foreshadows Shulman's future work in the professions at The Carnegie Foundation for the Advancement of Teaching.

19

JUST IN CASE

REFLECTIONS ON LEARNING FROM EXPERIENCE[1]

THIS BOOK IS FILLED with contributions from leading educators who both use cases and think about them. I also fall into that category. I use cases regularly in my teaching of both new and veteran teachers. I also think about them obsessively, wondering why they work so well at some times, and so marginally at others. This chapter represents my attempt to subject my own case methods to a reflective analysis, and to connect the use of cases to a broader arena of educational and psychological theory.

I begin with a reconsideration of the functions of cases in the education of teachers and the pedagogical and professional challenges that cases are intended to address. I will describe in some considerable detail the ways in which I have been using cases—both reading cases and writing them—in my own pedagogy of teacher education. This account will itself serve as a kind of case-in-point, an instantiation of a particular strategy of case method in teacher education which can then serve as a touchstone for the analyses that follow. I will then examine the example from two perspectives: the structure of case (or what makes a story function as a case); and the theoretical principles of learning and teaching needed to explain why cases can function in powerful ways pedagogically. I will conclude with reflections on the role of cases in the creation of teacher communities.

Working with Cases

I work with case methods in teacher education for a number of reasons. First, I believe that the admonition that practitioners should reflect on their own practice is both absolutely correct and painfully demanding.

Discerning the object of reflection—which kind of experience is "caseworthy"—is a nontrivial challenge. Should I reflect on the problems of a particular child, on the complexities of a lesson, on the subtleties of an interaction, or the unfolding of a teaching episode? How can I keep an event in focus long enough to engage in reflection with respect to it? Using cases as the unit of reflective analysis may aid in organizing the process of reflection as a firm component of teacher education programs.

Second, too much of teacher education is unbearably generic, offering vague general principles and maxims that purport to apply broadly to a vast range of situations. A case of instruction is—by definition—*situated* in place, time *and* subject matter. If the case is faithful in its particularities, it cannot ignore the subject- and situation-specificity of teaching, because we are always teaching some *subject matter* to some *student(s)* in some *context*.

Third, the essential feature of teaching is its uncertainty and unpredictability. Teaching cannot be directed by formal theory and lockstep national syllabi, yet remain responsive to both student insights and misconceptions. Moreover, as our educational goals increasingly emphasize higher-order thinking and reasoning and student collaborations around real problems, the education of teachers must emphasize their development of flexibly powerful pedagogical understanding and judgment. Therefore, discourse on teaching must go beyond broad principles and propositions as its objects. Knowledge of teaching is comprised of combinations of cases and principles. We intend for our students to develop a repertoire of cases which can help to guide their thinking and reflections on their own teaching. They can then use their experience with cases, their own and those of others, as lenses for thinking about their work in the future.

Most other professions already structure much of their clinical knowledge in terms of some sort of case format for both the documentation of practice and the organization of instruction. Professions that divide their work into case-like segments include law, medicine, nursing, social work, architecture, even business. These cases then serve as the building blocks for professional reasoning, professional discourse, and professional memory. Cases may have many advantages over arrangements of expository rules, standards, or maxims. For example, they take advantage of the natural power of narrative ways of knowing, a topic that has been addressed with considerable vigor by psychologists such as Jerome Bruner (1986). They also appear to fit well with the intuitions of practitioners.

The great challenge for professionals who wish to learn from experience is the difficulty of holding experiences in memory in forms that can become the objects of disciplined analysis and reflection. Consider the possibility that cases are ways of parsing experience so that practitioners can examine and learn from it. But teachers are typically confronted with a seamless continuum of experience from which they can think about individual kids as cases, or lessons as cases, but rarely coordinate the different dimensions into meaningful experiential chunks. Case methods thus become strategies for helping teachers to "chunk" their experience into units that can become the focus for reflective practice. They therefore can become the basis for individual teacher learning as well as a form within which communities of teachers, both local and extended, as members of visible and invisible colleges, can store, exchange and organize their experiences.

In this chapter, I offer one model of case method in teacher education. It does not depict *the* case method, for no such enterprise exists, in spite of the claims of some educators. Instead, I shall present a particular example of how cases are used in teacher education, an example that combines: 1) the study of cases written by others, 2) the crafting of one's own written cases, 3) the process of commenting upon and discussing the cases written by other members of one's teaching community, and 4) the beginnings of a case literature for teacher education.

I will follow this account with three exercises in theory development. First, I will ask what counts as a case. What are the elements of those narrative accounts that are more than stories and can function educatively as teaching cases? Second, I examine the much-misunderstood connections between cases and theory, attempting once again to explain how cases can draw their pedagogical power *from* theory without cases being *about* theory. Third, I will address the question of learning from cases. If cases—as forms of narrative—have a certain structure and form, what are the principles that describe how and why they can serve as an educative medium for professional learning? I conclude with a discussion of the connections between conceptions of case method and an emerging image of teachers as members of learning communities. I begin with a description of one type of case method for teacher education: the Analysis-Construction-Commentary-Community Cycle.

An Example of Case Methods

Case Reading and Discussion

I begin my course on "Foundations of Learning for Teaching" each year by having my students read a case written by Vickie White (1988), describing her experiences as a first-year intern teacher in Los Angeles. The case, taken from Judy Shulman and Joel Colbert's (1988) *Intern Teacher*

Casebook, is titled "One Struggle After Another" and describes Ms. White's experience in attempting to teach Shakespeare's *Romeo and Juliet* to a class of inner-city African-American adolescents, in a secondary school located in the same general area of south east Los Angeles in which Vickie herself grew up.

Vickie describes in poignant detail her increasingly frustrating attempts to engage her students in the complexities of language and plot of Shakespeare's masterpiece. Her students challenge Vickie at every step. "Why do we have to read this?" "This is too hard to read." She assigns scenes for homework, and very few students complete the assignment. She works with a group of university friends to make a tape recording of the play for the students to hear the power of the Shakespearean language. Her students complain that one character's voice is too nasal and that her friends sound like they are white (they are; Vickie is not). The narrative is a tale of trial and error, of difficulty and repair. In the end, Vickie seeks assistance from more experienced teachers, who suggest alternative ways for her to teach *Romeo and Juliet* to her class.

When my own students, themselves first-year intern teachers of English (including literature and drama), mathematics, science, foreign language or social studies at the secondary level, have finished reading the case, I ask them how they would characterize Vickie's situation. They begin to analyze her circumstances ("She's never really thought about why she is teaching Shakespeare. Telling the students they must learn it because it is in the California state curriculum won't satisfy them." "Her situation is typical. I teach social studies and I have problems like that regularly"). Soon they begin to connect Vickie's experiences to their own. As dialogue among the students develops, two kinds of response are typically offered: the analysis of Vickie's case leads students to invoke more theoretical principles ("She has forgotten that you must begin where the kids are." "She has not diagnosed the students' prior knowledge, abilities or interests adequately." "She should have thought through her goals and rationale more thoroughly, and she should have asked for help from her mentors in a more timely manner"); and students use the occasion of Vickie's story to begin telling stories of their own about their own experiences in teaching.

At this point in the analysis, we begin to introduce a theme that becomes a recurrent refrain in all our work with cases. "What is this a case of?" we ask incessantly. How would you characterize this account in relation to other accounts, to your own experiences and to conceptual or theoretical categories with which you are familiar? "What is this a case of?" is a locution whose purpose is to stimulate students to initiate the intellectual work that makes cases powerful tools for professional learning.

They must learn to move up and down, back and forth, between the memorable particularities of cases and the powerful generalizations and simplifications of principles and theories. Principles are powerful but cases are memorable. Only in the continued interaction between principles and cases can practitioners and their mentors avoid the inherent limitations of theory-without-practice or the equally serious restrictions of vivid practice without the mirror of principle.

The answer to "what is this a case of?" is rarely singular. That is, rarely if ever is a particular account related to only one theoretical, conceptual or descriptive category. Indeed, part of the power of cases rests in a given case's capacity to be related to multiple categories and to numerous other instances. Because of their complexity, contextuality and richness, cases provide excellent opportunities for learners to "criss-cross the landscape" of theory and practice (Spiro, Coulson, Feltovich and Anderson, 1988) linking experiences to ideas in a network of associations. Were it grammatically correct, I would prefer asking the question "what are this a case of?" Later in this chapter, I shall return to "what is this a case of?" in a discussion of the connections between cases and theory.

Vickie's case is but the first of a series of cases that we read and discuss during the first few weeks of the course. Some cases are written by intern teachers like themselves. These cases may be taken from casebooks, but increasingly I draw from cases that have been written by their predecessors in this same program. Other cases have been written by veteran teachers. Still others have been written by researchers like Deborah Ball (1993), Magdalene Lampert (1990) or Suzanne Wilson (1992) who conduct research on their own school teaching. Although the students are not aware of it at the time, I select those first few cases carefully, with special attention to their organization, their focus and their tone.

Case Organization

For my purposes, I try to ensure that each case has roughly the same focus and plot. Each case must be a narrative about *the teaching of subject matter.* It must dwell on a teacher's attempts to teach some particular body of knowledge, skill, understanding or appreciation to a group of students, whether directly, by discovery or through some project or simulation. It is not a case of a troubled child, nor primarily a case of classroom management problems, nor of a confrontation with parents, principals or fellow teachers. Though each of these is a worthwhile topic, in principle, I am interested in engaging my own students in the careful contemplation of the complexities of substantive pedagogy, in which a teacher is attempting to teach something he or she understands reasonably well to a group of students. This is a nontrivial specification since if you ask a teacher to tell a story about teaching, it is not typical that you are told about the teaching of subject matter. I believe that cases can be classified into genres, much like types of writing or literature. This particular genre can be called "instructional cases of subject matter."

The plot of each case[2] must revolve around a plan that goes awry, an intention unfulfilled or some surprise that disrupts the expected scenarios and requires that the teacher re-examine, re-plan, revise or otherwise reflect on her original plans and modify them in some way. Thinking in dramaturgical terms, *Act I* of each case sets the scene by laying out the context of the classroom and students, describing the intentions, the dreams, the hopes and plans for the unit or course of instruction, and exploring the content to be learned fully and critically. *Act I* ends on a note of hope and high expectations as the goals of instruction and the expected scenario of teaching and learning are portrayed.

Act II of the case provides an account of what actually happened, complete with unanticipated problems and difficulties. It should be rich in the detail of classroom dialogue and interaction. This act ends in a state of tension, uncertainty and unresolved conflict.

Act III resolves the tension in some fashion, either by describing the actions that were taken to relieve the difficulties, or by sifting through emerging insights about why the problems occurred as they did. *Act III* is the resolution, the recapitulation and the reflection, through which we begin to discern the teacher's current grasp of the issues and how the resolution (or the resignation to the absence of any resolution) has left the teacher with a different level of understanding than she had before. Each of the cases they read, whether written by a teaching novice or by a veteran expert, more or less follows that set of guidelines: a focus on the teaching of substance and a similar narrative plot of plans, disruption of the intended and resolution or reflection on the outcomes and consequences for the students and for the self.

As I observed earlier, a case of subject matter pedagogy is a particular genre of case, not the only legitimate type of case. I am convinced, however, that if teachers are to learn from experience—whether their own or vicariously through the case-based experiences of others—they must learn to parse the flow of experience into the structure of cases. They must learn a syntax, a grammar of cases, which provides a set of terms within which they can organize and analyze their understanding of experience. If they can see the structure in cases they read, they can begin to see the structure of cases in their own lived experiences. For this reason I begin with the analysis of instructional cases, all of which share the same overall plot or structure.

There is another feature to the cases our students read. They are largely "self-disclosing." That is, the case is a first-person account of an episode of teaching, an episode that may well have extended over several days or weeks, in which the narrator has experienced some form of surprise, difficulty or clear failure. The essence of the case is in the problem, the surprise or the failure. The case writer presents his account of the difficulties without embarrassment, much as physicians learn to present difficult cases for clinical-pathological conferences. The case is educative precisely because it is built around some form of failure or surprise, requiring a comparison of intentions and outcomes and demanding either improvisational or deliberative responses to the problems.

As we have come to see, by reading and discussing such cases, we begin to "detoxify" the recounting of failures and make the possibilities for learning from such experiences more real. We try to help our students celebrate their failures if they can learn from them, rather than denying them to avoid embarrassment. There is a research monograph written about learning in the surgical residency, that carries the wonderful title, *Forgive and Remember* (Bosk, 1979). The title communicates the message that internships are occasions in which errors must be made. They will be forgiven only if they can be remembered, reflected upon and become a source of learning. "Forgive and forget" is a motto for good relationships without growth. "Forgive and remember" is a slogan for all practical internships and an inspiration for those who would learn from cases.[3]

Case Writing

Following the model of Judy Shulman (1991) and her extensive research on teachers as *case writers*, I next ask my students to examine their own teaching experiences to find personal instructional cases they can write. If the discussions stimulated by the case reading have been successful, the students should now be able to locate cases within the remembered flow of their own teaching experiences. They are asked to write subject matter instructional cases that follow the plot structure of the cases they have been reading. All of them write such cases over the period of about a month, usually in early February. They have been teaching two classes each day since September and continue teaching for two hours each morning. They almost always have enough experiences from which to write their own case.[4]

One example of such a case is Mark Ellis's case of teaching the mathematical concept of "pi," which he wrote during the Winter of 1992, while serving as a teaching intern. Mark was teaching 10th grade geometry and understood that all his students had already encountered "pi" in their earlier mathematical learning. But he was convinced that they viewed pi as an arbitrary constant, which held the value 3.14159 . . . for no particular reason other than that some Greek mathematician had defined it that way. Mark wanted his students to understand that pi was a ratio, that it was a rational number and that its identity rested on the universal relationships that held among the circumference, the diameter and the area of a circle.

As Mark wrote his case, he lays out his analysis of the instructional challenge, and of his recognition that an understanding of ratio necessarily rested on understanding the concept of proportion, and proportion rested on notions of scale. As he began to draw examples of representing scale in a proportional way, he designed demonstrations and discussions of scale models, architectural drawings, maps and other artifacts in which the idea of scale is central. Mark's analysis of the complexity of both the concepts of the subject matter and the strategies of instruction are compelling. So ends *Act I*.

Mark then describes how the actual instruction unfolded and proceeded. At some points students failed to know things that he had thought elementary. At other points, his examples and exercises seemed to work almost too well. Did the students really understand, or were they operating with a delusion of comprehension? As *Act II* ends, Mark has concluded his teaching of the unit on pi and has given the students an essay final examination, which includes an open-ended question on the meaning of pi. As he reads the answers, his heart sinks. Only two of the students' responses reflect anything but the most superficial understanding of pi. His heart sinks as the "curtain" falls.

The final section of the case does not resolve the problem in a simple way. Mark does not re-teach pi and achieve his goals in some miraculous manner. But he analyzes the student responses carefully, reflects on his assumptions and anticipations, and develops a theory that accounts for his experience and suggests a strategy to employ the next time, an approach based on his inferences regarding the persistence of the students' prior knowledge of pi in the face of his attempts to modify or even eradicate their earlier ideas. His reflective analysis brings together his technical and theoretical understanding of the power of prior knowledge and preconceptions on student understanding, and his personal reflections on his own and his students' intentions and actions.

Case Commentary

The students write cases of this sort based on their own teaching experiences. They have now applied the syntax of the cases they have read to telling the stories of cases they have themselves lived. They have moved from reading and discussing the cases of others' experiences to the writing of their own cases. They are now ready to move to the next level of exchange, case discussion and commentary. Once a narrative has been completed, the initial stage of reflection has been initiated.[5] The reflective processes undertaken to capture the features of one's own practice for case writing are essentially intrapersonal (even though they have probably been stimulated by some pre-case conversations with peers or supervisors). We now have the students exchange the first draft of their cases and prepare written commentaries on each other's case. We thus move from individual reflection to socially mediated reflection, from introspection to conversation.

Case Conversations

Cases with commentaries can now be circulated for broader conversations within the community of those learning to teach. At this point, the direct experiences of some members of the group can be shared with others who experience them vicariously as cases. We now create contexts for small-group conversations among students regarding cases they have written and read. There is no question that such conversations are experienced as stimulating and enlightening by the participating students. Based on these conversations and commentaries, each case-writer now re-drafts the case into a new and improved version. We have barely begun to explore why certain types of conversation are particularly fruitful and stimulating while others stimulate yawns and worse.

Case Conferences and Case Literatures

Once teacher-written cases have emerged from the private property of their authors, have been enriched by commentaries and become the foci of conversations, they become candidates for inclusion in the discourse of the larger pedagogical community. In our course, we employ two related approaches to creating a community around teacher-written cases. We have experimented with small teacher conferences or congresses where we bring together participants in teacher education programs from different institutions who make presentations on their own cases and then discuss them jointly. This is a provocative experience for young teachers, who begin to see their work as a form of scholarship that can be shared with other members of the profession.

We also collect the cases that have been written and publish an annual *casebook* from the teacher education program, organized by subject-specific categories. These casebooks can be read by all members of the graduating class of teachers, and a copy is placed on permanent deposit in the library of the program. A number of the cases are selected for inclusion in the reading materials for future generations of teacher education candidates. In this way, each group of teacher education students leaves a legacy of cases for those who follow.

As we continue to collect instructional cases written by teachers as well as by others, we can begin to discern the outlines of a case literature for subject-specific teaching. We have several cases on the teaching of "democracy" or "feudalism" in history and social studies; several cases on the teaching of logical argument or proof in geometry, or of zero in arithmetic. I envision the eventual development of large bodies of subject-specific cases with commentaries, organized perhaps the way chessbooks present the variety of ways in which particular openings can be pursued, or particular endgames can be contemplated. By collecting and organizing a multiplicity of subject matter cases, with analyses and commentaries, we will provide rich food for thought to both inexperienced and experienced teachers. Moreover, as new teachers become more experienced at seeing their own teaching and that of others in terms of cases, I suspect that they will also become more adept at making analytic sense of different genres of case, written in different ways and from different perspectives. The purpose of scaffolding is to provide support for structures that are incomplete or immature. As they continue to develop as teachers, they will depend less and less on the particular structures they employ earlier in their educations.

Having described in some detail the manner in which I work with cases, I can now turn to three related questions. First, what are the attributes of a narrative that make it worthy of the designation "case"? That is, what story do cases tell that distinguish them from mere anecdotes? Second, what are the connections between cases and theory? Third, what are the theoretical reasons why cases "work"? Can we relate our emerging theory of case methods to more general principles of teaching and learning?

Conceptions of Cases: Attributes, Theory and Principles

Attributes of a Case

The essence of any case is *chance*. In remarks to one of the annual case conferences organized by Judy Shulman and the Far West Laboratory, Judith Kleinfeld of the University of Alaska recalled Jerome Bruner's (1986) observation that a narrative is an account of the "vicissitudes of human intention" (p. 16). To call something a narrative is to assert that it tells of the encounter between a plan and an accident, between a goal that was pursued and an impediment that delayed or interrupted the quest. In a fundamental way, narratives are the children born of a liaison between design and chance.

Imagine the following account: "Little Red Riding Hood went into the woods to bring lunch to her grandmother . . . and she did." That is hardly a compelling narrative. It's hardly a story at all. But change the account to "Little Red Riding Hood went into the woods to bring lunch to her grandmother . . . and she *happened* to meet the Big Bad Wolf." Enter vicissitudes and you have a narrative. Enter chance and you have the makings of a case. The connection of case and chance is no accident. The Oxford English Dictionary tells us that one of the etymological roots of "case" is the idea of "chance." Thus, we employ locutions like "just in case" to describe situations when we must prepare for the unpredictable. We bring along an umbrella "in case" it rains, that is, on the *chance* that rain might fall.

I would argue, however, that an educative case is more than a good narrative, more than a clever juxtaposition of intention and vicissitude. An educative case is a form of communication that places intention and chance into the context of a lived and reflected experience. A case doesn't just happen; it creates conditions that demand of its narrator (or protagonist) that she both render judgments among alternative tacks and act on those judgments. A case has consequences. One learns from deliberating reflectively on the connections among the elements of a case. Thus, an educative case combines at least four attributes or functions: intention, chance, judgment and reflection. They are the functions that explain or delineate the educative power of cases for learning to engage in any practice:

- *intention:* The existence of a formal or tacit plan, itinerary, or purpose.
- *chance:* The plan is interrupted by a surprise, by a "glitch," by the unexpected.
- *judgment:* In the face of uncertainty and surprise, the actor must exercise judgment, because no simple answer is available.
- *reflection:* Examining the consequences of action taken in light of judgment and learning in a way that produces the basis for a new plan or intention.

First, there has to be an intention, a plan of action. There is no case if there has been no plan, no itinerary, no sense of a path to be taken. A case is a "chance" event, a disruption of the itinerary. So we have a path that has been set out upon, and a chance event or events that disrupts the plan, that occludes the anticipated flow of experience. The blocking of intention provides the foundation for reflection, thought and deliberation.

This sense of a case is quite consistent with Dewey's (1938) concept of inquiry. Dewey argues that thought is a response to the blocking of habit. Only when our habitual or reflexive modes of behavior fail to attain the desired goals, do we then begin to think about what to do. We have educative experiences when we are obligated to reflect on our actions and strategically select new paths because our habitual paths have been blocked. A case, therefore, is an account of an experience in which our intentions have been unexpectedly obstructed, and the surprising event has triggered the need to examine alternative courses of action. Surprise becomes the impetus for thought, and reflection on our responses to the surprise and the consequences that flow from our actions become the basis for new learning.

We do not learn from experience; we learn by thinking about our experience. A case takes the raw material or first-order experience and renders it narratively into a second-order experience. A case is the re-collected, retold, re-experienced and re-flected version of a direct experience. The process of remembering, retelling, reliving and reflecting is the process of learning from experience.

Cases and Theory

To assert that a narrative is a *case* is to engage in an act of theory. When I first made that claim (Shulman, 1986), I created more misunderstanding than was stimulated by nearly any statement I have ever written. I do *not* mean that cases are, in themselves, inherently theoretical. Nor do I mean that the purpose of cases is to teach theory. Instead, I am claiming that any story that can be called a case must be arguably a case *of* something. It must be seen as an exemplar of a class, an instance of a larger category.

For this reason, the key move made in teaching with cases occurs when instructor and students explore the question, "what is this a case of?" As they wrestle with this question, they move the case in two directions simultaneously. They connect this narrative to their remembered (personal) experiences or to vicariously experienced cases written or recounted by others, thus relating this particular case to other specific cases. They also connect this narrative to categories of experience, to theoretical classifications through which they organize and make sense of their world.

First, an encounter with a case invites both the reader and the author to forge connections between this narrative and other narratives. Note that I say we are connecting narratives, not the experiences themselves. The transformation of an experience into a narrative is itself an act of selection and conceptualization. In converting a first-order experience into a second-order experience through narrative, an author has chosen to frame an experience in a particular way, has placed that experience in more general terms. When the reader of a case connects that narrative to his or her own experiences, a second kind of selection has taken place. Like story-swappers who respond to a tale by stating, "That reminds me of when . . . ," one person's narrative connects with other narratives. A story about a classroom simulation that went awry elicits yet another account of a similar problem. An account of a social studies groupwork project in which a hitherto silent ESL student suddenly blossomed and stepped forward in a leadership role generates a second story of group processes, or of blossoming students or of surprises from language-minority students. It appears to be a characteristic of our species that stories explicitly breed yet other stories and, implicitly, the categories of analysis that connect stories to one another conceptually. Even in the concrete act of narrative, underlying theoretical categories emerge and often become explicit.

There are four processes at work in learning from the writing and contemplation of cases. These are *enactment, narration, connection* (or recounting) and *abstraction.* Stories begin in the raw experience itself, are transformed into cases through narration, become part of a network of narratives through connections with other cases and both enrich and are enriched by theory when they are analyzed, interpreted and/or classified in the teachers' conversations.

Principles of Learning from Cases

Most educators who work with cases and case methods do not spend much time worrying about the structure of cases or their development, as I have in the previous two sections. Educators tend to emphasize case *methods* rather than the cases themselves. As we review the variety of approaches to the study, discussion, writing and interpretation of cases described in this volume, we may begin to discern a set of principles that underlie the extended family of case methods, even acknowledging their great diversity. Are there a small set of principles that might explain the efficacy of case methods for stimulating and effecting significant learning among those who work with them? At the risk of sounding as if all my first principles fall into groups of four (in other papers they come out in threes), I shall now offer four constructs that may account for the efficacy of case methods.

I draw these principles from the current research that Judith Shulman and I are conducting on communities of learners and teachers in schools. After observing the workings of several classrooms in which Brown and Campione's "community of learners" (Brown, 1994) concepts have been implemented, and the apparently remarkable levels of student learning that resulted, the remarkable Jerome Bruner (once again!) offered four ideas on which he claimed these approaches appear to rest (Bruner, 1994). I have modified and adapted these principles to serve our current purposes, but they remain quite close to Bruner's original formulation. They are fitting in this context because, I believe, the varieties of effective case methods create conditions of learning that are quite consistent with those achieved in communities of learners.

The four principles that seem to characterize the conditions for effective, substantive and enduring learning are: *activity or agency; reflection or meta-cognition; collaboration;* and the formation of a supportive *community* or a sustaining culture. To elaborate, authentic and enduring learning occurs when:

- learners are *active* agents in the process, not passive, an audience, clients or collectors. This is a modestly constructivist claim, implying both a view of cognition as the active construction of meaning by learners who take responsibility for making sense of their world, as well as a physical construction of understanding through writing, project work, the manipulation of their environment and research-like activities.
- learners not only behave and think, but can "go meta-," that is, can *reflectively* turn around on their own thought and action and analyze how and why their thinking achieved certain ends or failed to achieve others. Metacognition—consciousness of how and why one is learning particular things in particular ways—is the key to deep learning.
- learners engage in *collaboration,* working together in ways that scaffold and support each others' learning, and in ways that supplement each others' knowledge. Collaboration is a marriage of insufficiencies, not exclusively "cooperation" in a particular form of social interaction. Moreover, there are difficult intellectual challenges that are nearly impossible to accomplish alone, but are more readily addressed with others.

- learners are scaffolded—that is, supported, legitimated and nurtured—in the processes of activity, reflection and collaboration within a *community* or *culture* that values such experiences and creates many opportunities for them to occur and to be accomplished with success and pleasure. Such communities create "participant structures" that reduce the labor-intensity of the activities needed to engage in the most daunting practices that lead to teaching and learning.

These principles were originally applied to explaining why students who participated in communities of learners were successful in their work. However, I would claim that these same principles apply to both new and veteran teachers who are learning from cases. First, whether as case analyst or as case writer, the case learner becomes an active agent in his or her own understanding. When a student is wrestling with a case, whether as an occasion for analysis or a stimulus to reflect on his own experience as a prelude to writing, active agency is engaged. Second, cases are inherently reflective. They begin with an act of re-cognition, of turning around on one's own lived experiences and examining them to find events and episodes worthy of transformation into telling cases. Even when the goal of case learning is not case writing, the discussion of cases eventually stimulates reflection on one's own experiences and reactions.

Third, case methods nearly always emphasize the primacy of group discussion, deliberation and debate in the examination of a case. The thought process of cases is dialogic, as members of a group explore different perspectives on the nature of the problem, the available elective actions or the import of the consequences. In the example of case-based teaching I offered above, the interaction of activity, reflection and collaboration is apparent. But what of community or culture?

Teaching and learning with cases is not an easy pedagogy. Active learners are much more outspoken and assertive than are passive learners. They are less predictable than their more passive counterparts, as they investigate their options, explore alternative interpretations and challenge prevailing views. Since cases encourage the connections between personal experiences and those vicariously experienced through the narratives, the directions in which discussions might develop are rather difficult to anticipate, further complicating the pedagogy. Finally, the collaborative mode of instruction once again reduces the authority of the teacher and vests a growing proportion in the initiatives of students. Taken together, the enhancement of agency, reflection and collaboration make teaching more complex and unpredictable, albeit by reducing the authority of the teacher and his ability to plan for contingencies. When uncertainty increases and power is distributed, the need for a supportive culture or community becomes paramount for teachers and students alike. A supportive culture helps manage the risk of contemplating one's failures and reduces the vulnerability created when one candidly discusses a path not taken. A supportive culture engages each member of the community in parallel risks. It celebrates the interdependence of learners who will rely on one another for both insights and reassurance. A learning environment built on activity, reflection and collaboration—which is an apt characterization of a well-functioning case-learning and case-writing community—proceeds smoothly only in the presence of a sustaining culture and community.

Learning from Experience: A Recapitulation on Cases and Communities

I began this chapter with the assertion that case methods were a particularly potent instructional vehicle for accomplishing that most difficult of learnings, that which derives from the inspection of one's own experience (see Figure 1). After a brief discussion of the ways in which cases address the challenge of experiential learning, I offered an extended account of my own method of teaching with cases within a teacher education program. In this approach, which I have called the Analysis-Construction-Commentary-Community Cycle, students progress from reading the cases of others analytically, to drafting their own cases, to commenting on one another's cases in small case discussion groups that lead to new drafts of the same cases, to the presentation and discussion of cases in writing and orally within larger communities.

I then offered three sets of principles for examining the nature of cases and case methods. I first argued that a case was a narrative with a particular formal organization, composed of intentions, chance, judgment and reflective analysis. A case narrative depicts the protagonist's intentions and intended path, portrays the surprises and accidents that impeded direct movement toward the goal, explores the judgments and reasoning that contributed to the choices subsequently made and, then, in the light of the consequences of the elective actions, reflects on the wisdom of the choices and their grounds. All the components are needed for a case. Without intention, there can be no surprise. Without chance, there is no narrative. Without judgment, there is no thinking. And without reflection, there is no analysis of the ebb and flow of the engagement and hence, no learning from experience.

Figure 1. Theoretical Perspectives on Cases and Case Methods.

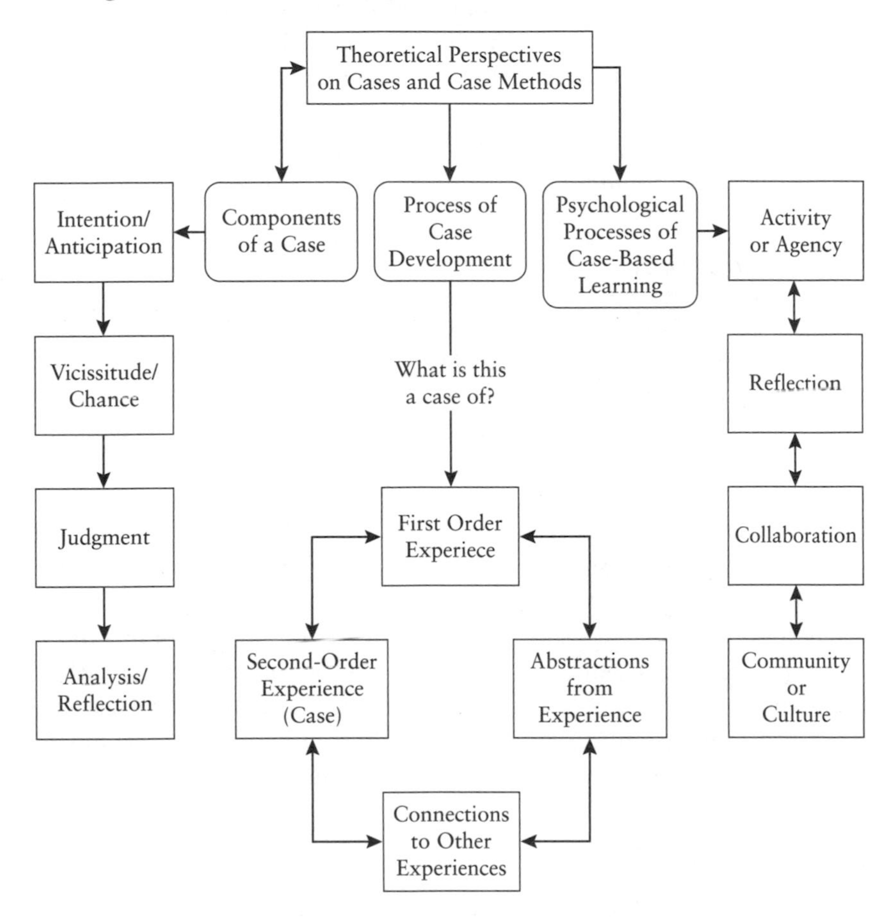

I then explored the mischievous contention that declaring something a "case" was an inherently theoretical claim. In this section I elaborated on the argument that both crafting and learning from cases involved a dialectic between first-order and second-order experience, between the direct undergoing of an event and its reconstruction in narrative. This transformation of experience to case is mediated by the question "what is this a case of?" The answers emerge from connecting one's own case to other cases—relating stories to one another—and from relating cases to larger theoretical categories of which they are instances. Thus every case, in its particularity, derives its "case-ness" from its connections to other cases and to organizing principles or theories.

But the structure of a case is only part of the story. A few pages of prose cannot alone educate. Cases are taught and learned using a small range of methods. I go on to assert that these methods share in common a set of learning principles that account for the effectiveness of all learning within learning communities: activity, reflection, collaboration and culture. The methods of case teaching share an affinity for those principles of learning, as well they should.

Communities of Teachers

Which brings us to the centrality of *community* to the efficacy of the "case idea." Cases become educative for teachers within teaching communities. Learning from experience is nearly impossible without the scaffolding of others, their alternative views, their complementary perspectives, their roles as active listeners and critical friends. If "collaboration" is one of the key inner principles of effective and enduring learning, the "community" is its external scaffolding, which keeps the structure erect in spite of the tensions of the processes that occur within it (Shulman, 1989). When McLaughlin and Talbert (1993) identified the conditions that permitted teachers at the secondary school level to teach with understanding, they identified the critical importance of communities and networks, within and across institutions, for sustaining the difficulties of adventurous teaching. Cases can be a critical element of the glue that holds such communities together and gives their deliberations substance and form.

Just in Case . . .

So much of teacher education emphasizes the importance of playful intention and disciplined improvisation. Lesson planning, unit planning, test design, classroom organization and management all attest to the essential character of planfulness and preparation in the success of teachers. But design is less than half the story. Teachers learn quickly that the heart of teaching is developing the capacity to respond to the unpredictable. Teaching begins in design, but unfolds through chance. And cases—as the narrative manifestations of chance—offer teachers the opportunities to contemplate the variety of ways in which the unpredictable happens. Case-based teacher education offers safe contexts within which teachers can explore their alternatives and judge their consequences.

John Dewey argued, in his classic essay, "The Influence of Darwinism on Philosophy" (Dewey, 1910), that Darwin signaled the emergence of a new era of modern science with his theory of natural selection and evolution, when he demonstrated that it was chance, not design, and variation, not fixedness, that explained why the biological world had evolved as it had. The secret of adaptation is the species' response to and management of chance through the nurturing of variability, flux and change. Similarly, case methods bring the vicissitudes of intended practice front and center, so that teachers might learn to respond and manage pedagogical chance adaptively and successfully. Cases and case methods are surely no panacea for the challenges of teacher education. But in the needed redesign of teacher education programs at all levels, they will occupy a central role.

NOTES

1. Preparation of this chapter was supported by grants from the Mellon Foundation (for the project "Fostering a Community of Teachers and Learners") and the Spencer Foundation (for the project "Toward a Pedagogy of Substance"). I am grateful to both foundations for their support; they bear no responsibility for the chapter's contents or its claims.
2. Readers will discern that this form of case is quite different from the business school model. It presents students with a full narrative accompanied by an analysis and often commentaries, rather than the open-ended problem-solving case preferred by those teacher educators who prefer the business school model.
3. Some colleagues argue that I place too much stress on exclusively asking for cases of surprise or failure. They claim that teachers need to contemplate success and accomplishment in addition to disappointment and the unexpected. They are probably correct. I have not yet had the opportunity to experiment with different kinds of cases and their relative efficacy.
4. Some may argue that imposing a structured genre on teacher case-writing stifles their creativity and is unnecessary. I disagree. Writing to a genre specification is done widely in the field of creative writing, and does not appear to limit the inventiveness of writers.
5. In this analysis, I build upon Judy Shulman's (1991) four-stage model of case-based reflection. She posits the first stage as the direct experience of the event; the second stage as the joint reflection on the event by the actor and a case editor or mentor out of which emerges the written case itself; the third stage as the case with written commentary, which is now a part of a broader education community and in the fourth stage the case is part of the broader case literature, now an element in the community of educators.

REFERENCES

Ball, D. (1993). With an eye on the mathematical horizon: Dilemmas of teaching elementary school mathematics. *Elementary School Journal, 93*(4), 373–397.

Bosk, C. L. (1979). *Forgive and remember.* Chicago: University of Chicago Press.

Brown, A. L. (1994). The advancement of learning. *Educational Researcher, 23*(8), 4–12.

Bruner, J. S. (1986). *Actual minds, possible worlds.* Cambridge, MA: Harvard University Press.

Bruner, J. S. (1994). *The humanly and interpretively possible.* Paper presented at the American Educational Research Association, New Orleans.

Dewey, J. (1910). *The influence of Darwinism on philosophy and other essays.* New York: Henry Holt & Co.

Dewey, J. (1938). *Logic: The theory of inquiry.* New York: Henry Holt & Co.

Lampert, M. (1990). When the problem is not the question and the solution is not the answer. *American Educational Research Journal, 27*(1), 29–63.

McLaughlin, M. W., & Talbert, J. E. (1993). *Contexts that matter for teaching and learning.* Stanford, CA: Center for Research on the Context of Secondary School Teaching, Stanford University.

Shulman, J. H. (1991). Revealing the mysteries of teacher-written cases: Opening the black box. *Journal of Teacher Education, 42*(4), 250–262.

Shulman, J. H., & Colbert, J. A. (1988). *The intern teacher casebook.* San Francisco: Far West Laboratory.

Shulman, L. S. (1986) Those who understand: knowledge growth in teaching. *Educational Researcher,* 15(2), 4–14.

Shulman, L. S. (1989). Teaching alone, learning together: Needed agendas for the new reforms. In T. M. Sergiovanni & J. H. Moore (Eds.), *Schooling for tomorrow* (pp. 166–187). Boston: Allyn and Bacon.

Spiro, R. J., Coulson, R. L., Feltovich, P. J., & Anderson, D. K. (1988). Cognitive flexibility theory: Advanced knowledge acquisition in ill-structured domains. In *Tenth annual conference of the cognitive science society* (pp. 375–383). Hillsdale, NJ: Erlbaum.

White, V. (1988). One struggle after another. In J. H. Shulman & J. A. Colbert (Eds.), *The intern teacher casebook* (pp. 12–13). San Francisco: Far West Laboratory.

Wilson, S. M. (1992). A case concerning content: Using cases to teach about subject matter. In J. H. Shulman (Ed.), *Case methods in teacher education* (pp. 64–89). New York: Teachers College Press.

INTRODUCTION

COMMUNITIES OF LEARNERS AND COMMUNITIES OF TEACHERS (1997)

THE NEXT TWO ESSAYS emerged from the period in the early 1990s when Lee and Judy Shulman were codirecting the project "Fostering Communities of Teachers as Learners." It was the first time that Shulman had tried to directly fashion a school reform effort, working directly with both preservice and veteran teachers to reshape their practice in the direction of a particular vision of reform. In this case, the reform was based on Ann Brown and Joe Campione's model of Fostering Communities of Learners.

At the same time, Judy and Lee Shulman had also been working with the Mandel Foundation's programs in Jerusalem for over a decade, both in the School for Educational Leadership and in the Jerusalem Fellows Program in Jewish Education. In 1995, Shulman was invited by the Mandel Institute in Jerusalem to lecture on the work he was doing in collaboration with Brown, Campione, and Judith Shulman (among others) on communities of learners. In his work on this project, Shulman pursued the teaching question—How can teachers learn to create and teach in communities of learners?—a question that extended his earlier work on teacher learning. In this essay, Shulman begins by describing the activities of a community of learners in Oakland, California, including the use of benchmarks, research groups, investigations, crosstalks, jigsaws, and consequential tasks.

Drawing on the work of Jerome Bruner and Peter Drucker, Shulman nominates six essential characteristics of such communities and their work: generative content, active learning, reflective thinking and practice, collaboration, a shared passion and commitment to the material, and a supportive culture. He concludes by arguing that, just as students learn in communities, so too do teachers. And he suggests that the use of cases and case teaching in those communities might be a powerful form of teacher education and professional development.

20

COMMUNITIES OF LEARNERS AND COMMUNITIES OF TEACHERS

I COME TONIGHT to talk to you about work in progress. This is work in which I am engaged with my colleague Judy Shulman, my students and collaborators across the United States. Our topics are communities of learners and communities of teachers. I shall begin by summarizing the major themes of tonight's lecture. The rest, as Hillel said, is commentary; but as you know, in the Jewish tradition, the commentary always takes far longer than the text.

I will begin by describing a few examples of what I mean by communities of learners. One of the lovely things about being in Israel is that nothing can initiate a longer and more extensive discussion than the simple question, "How would you translate 'community' into Hebrew?" We could spend an entire week, I am sure, with the Hebrew *balshanut* [linguistical study] of the word community. We have tried *kehillah* [congregation]. *Kehiliyah* [a self-governing society] is what ended up in the Hebrew title. *Chevrutah* [society of learners] has certain implications that are interesting. I tried to invent a new word, *chevrutiyah,* but failed to receive approval from knowledgeable Hebrew speakers.

The difficulty of this translation in itself suggests the richness, the ambiguity and the multifaceted character of the concept of community, both in reference to learners and teachers. In a deep sense, I agree with the educator in New York, Deborah Meier, who wrote that the essence of learning is telling, and the essence of teaching is listening.[1] Thus, perhaps communities of learners and communities of teachers are actually the same thing, when you come to understand them fully.

In any event, I will begin with examples of what we might mean by communities of learners. I expect that you will find that the examples do not sound too alien. In fact, you will probably say they sound very familiar and that you are doing these things already. Many of the approaches that I describe here are quite consistent with practices that many of us have tried to employ for many years.

After giving examples of what I mean by communities of learners, I will describe briefly the project in which I am currently engaged. Then I am going to ask the following kinds of questions:

1. What are the underlying principles which explain how these learning communities work as well as they do? What are the fundamental principles?
2. If these principles and practices are the answers then to what questions are they the answers? We are often much more adept at giving the answers than explicating the underlying questions to which they respond.
3. If these principles are such good answers to important questions, then why is it that we so rarely find these principles put into practice? What makes them so very difficult to apply? Here I am reminded of the work of my teacher, the late Joseph Schwab, who wrote, on the 100th anniversary of the birth of John Dewey, a brilliant essay called, "The Impossible Role of the Teacher in Progressive Education."[2] I am going to ask the question, "Is this conception of teaching in a community of learners fundamentally impossible?" And, in a related way, "Is that why, even though the theory is good, and we have good operational models, we so rarely see them put into practice?"
4. If we want this kind of learning to go on, how can the most critical component of the educational system learn to employ these principles? By that I do not mean school administrators, and I certainly do not mean professors. I refer to classroom teachers. What are the conditions under which teachers can learn to engage in this kind of teaching? Under what circumstances can teachers sustain these practices over time? As I see it, this is the key question. Indeed, I will conclude my address with the argument that the very same principles that explain why *students* can learn under these circumstances explain the kinds of conditions we must create if we want *teachers* to learn to engage in this kind of teaching.

What Is a Community of Learners?

What do we mean by a community of learners? This idea, and the very few documented enactments of this idea, were extremely inspiring to me, and to some of the leading experts in the field, such as Jerome Bruner and Marshall Smith, because we were able to observe and to read accounts of classrooms that were operating in ways that we had not encountered before.

The first example was developed in Oakland, California, by the eminent psychologists, Anne Brown and Joseph Campione. Some of you may know their work, especially the work of Brown and Palinscar on reciprocal teaching[3] and the present research on communities of learners.[4] Anne Brown devoted her American Educational Research Association Presidential address to this latter topic.[5]

What would you see if you walked into one of the small number of classrooms in Oakland, California, in which a group of youngsters is learning as a community of learners? Let us imagine that the class is about to begin. They are studying a unit in biology on the topic of endangered species, species that are in danger of becoming extinct. The instruction begins with a series of lessons that Brown and Campione call *benchmark lessons*. These are lessons whose purpose is twofold. The first is to create a foundation, a shared base of knowledge among all the students, so that what they already understand about endangered species can be made explicit and put on the table. Their prior knowledge includes both their correct conceptions and their misconceptions, their prior theories and understandings, so that after the benchmark lessons, everyone starts in more or less a similar place. That is one aspect of a benchmark.

The second purpose of a benchmark is to help the students understand at the very beginning of the unit where they will be 15 weeks later. What is the goal? Where is all this heading? In this case, the teacher explains that at the end of the unit, the class is going to prepare a series of reports to the City Council of Oakland, and in these reports they will recommend new policies to protect endangered species that live in their community. This will not be merely an exercise, but in fact, three members of the City Council have already scheduled a date and the students are going to go to the Council and make a public report that may even be televised so that others can watch it. They thus can prefigure the goal of their activities.

How does the benchmarking begin? Again, nothing here will be a surprise to any of you. The teacher asks questions like, "Does anyone know what an endangered species is?" and "Do you know examples of endangered species?" Students begin to pull out bits and pieces of the information they already have, and the teacher starts to organize it and collate it on the board in front of the students. The teacher offers other concepts and principles to fill in the gaps in the fundamental benchmark understanding of the students. The students are also asked to begin generating the important questions they will need to address if they wish to know enough to complete the final tasks. These student questions, once collected and organized, become the basis for the second phase.

The second phase is *research groups*. At this point, something rather revolutionary happens. That is, the teacher forgoes the dream that all of the students will learn all of the material. Many of us are teachers, and we know the deep sense of guilt that accompanies those rare moments in which we acknowledge that everyone is not going to learn all of the material. Yet, this step is absolutely essential in this particular conception of a community of learners. Instead, the teacher says, "Now is the time for you to break up into smaller groups, and each group is going to become knowledgeable through its own research and its own reading, through its writing and through its communication by computers with other experts. Through watching videos and through doing interviews. Each group is now going to become more proficient in only one aspect of the problem of endangered species."

They can then break up the problem in several different ways. One possibility, which some classes use, is that each group investigates a different species and tries to understand all the different aspects of its status as an endangered species. One group may become specialists on the spotted owl, another group may become specialists on the problem of the peregrine falcon, and another on some kind of whale. Thus, they can become knowledgeable about particular types of endangered species. Or, they can divide the problem differently. One group can look at aspects of habitat with respect to a variety of endangered species. Another group can become more expert in reproduction, while another investigates issues of toxicity and disease.

What matters is that two things happen in the research groups. The first is that students have the opportunity—through active investigation, reading, writing, interviewing and learning—to become more deeply knowledgeable about a piece of the larger problem. This second aspect of their work is the most difficult part for us as educators to design. The parts in which they become expert must fit together like a jigsaw puzzle in the next phase of learning, because they are necessary pieces of what they will need in order to confront a more complicated task later on. Thus, the parts are already seen by the designer, by the teacher and by the curriculum maker (who may all be the same person) as necessary, but not themselves sufficient, parts of a larger task.

For the next month or two, each group does its investigations. They study in depth. They go out on the Internet and gather information. The Internet is increasingly becoming a regular part of many classrooms. The group members make phone calls and interview experts at museums and universities. They read widely. They learn from each other. Periodically, the members of the different groups talk to one another to see what the other groups are doing, so that they are not totally unaware of what is happening in the rest of the community. These are called *crosstalks*. The teacher coaches and monitors the work of the groups and periodically brings all the students together for additional benchmark lessons. These may include lectures, interactive discussions or demonstrations.

At the end of the period of research, each group has essentially prepared a book. They have written a text on their specialty—in some of these classrooms, they actually compose it together on the computer, collate it and print it.

At this point we come to the third phase, when the specialists from each group engage in what we call a *jigsaw*. Here, one or more members of each of the specialist groups comes together in a new group, whose responsibility is to solve a problem that can only be solved by synthesizing and bringing together the knowledge that was previously possessed only by the separate groups. In this phase, the students begin to spend time teaching one another. They take turns literally teaching their ideas to one another, and beginning to address a new problem. This new problem often involves the process of design. The new problem might be something like designing an animal, where the teacher will present them with a new set of conditions, and the challenge for the students is to design a new animal that will succeed in adapting to these conditions and will not be endangered. Or, they might be given an animal that is in the process of becoming extinct and be asked to design a set of conditions under which this animal that is currently endangered will be able to survive and flourish. To do this, they have to draw on the individual expertise that they bring to the problem in order to create the needed design.

Finally, the capstone experience—the *consequential task*—is a public exhibition, demonstration or display, a presentation of what these new design groups have been able to do together. It can be a presentation of new ideas to the Oakland City Council. That is the way this community of learners worked in that Oakland classroom.

Towards a Deeper Understanding of the Community of Learners Model

What was striking, as you looked at community of learners classrooms, is first of all, how much the students were learning. Even though what they were doing did not map very well onto the standard tests that were used to measure student achievement, their test scores went up in reading, in science, in the areas being covered. There was impressive academic and social accomplishment by the students in the classroom. Yet, this kind of learning did not take up the entire day, five days a week; in most cases, it occupied about two hours a day, three days a week.

When care was taken to ensure that students really became expert in their research groups, every student had something important to contribute to the design (jigsaw) groups, because investment had been made in developing their understanding and knowledge in the earlier phase. What you saw was a kind of authentic interdependence. It did not depend on saying, "Ah, Shmulik draws well. Let us make sure that whenever we need something drawn, Shmulik does the drawing." I believe that is a weak basis for building on the strengths of the multiple intelligences which are to be found in any given classroom. In a community of learners under the model I am presenting, you engage students in acquiring precisely the kind of understanding and knowledge that you want the students to be able to contribute to the larger group and to the community.

In such classrooms you also encounter some surprises, because once you turn kids loose, the dangerous thing that happens is that they go where they want to go! I remember Anne Brown's account of one student who was trying to understand the relationship of disease to endangerment and he came up with an hypothesis. The hypothesis was this: "You know, in my community"—this was an African American youngster—"I have relatives who have both AIDS and sickle cell anemia [a very special kind of anemia, a hereditary blood disease that is unique to black Africans and those of black African descent]." The child's hypothesis was consistent with everything he knew up until that point. "I predict that black people have both conditions because you catch AIDS and sickle cell anemia in the same way." Of course he did not know enough science to know that his theory was incorrect, but his hypothesis initiated a research project to investigate how AIDS and sickle cell anemia were related. Consequently, he learned that he had misformulated the problem and, in turn, others learned from him and he learned from them. This was something unplanned in the original design of the curriculum, yet also clearly something that neither he nor the other students would have learned if they had not been given the latitude to explore.

As I both observed and read about this kind of teaching and learning, I realized that if I was going to understand it better, I would have to try it myself. I therefore organized a graduate seminar on exactly the same basis. It was my annual graduate seminar on research on teacher education. I used the community of learners model in the following manner. We spent the first two weeks with all participants acquiring a common base of knowledge on teacher education, through reading, lectures and discussions. This was our benchmark or anchoring stage. I explained to the students that at the end of the course, they would form groups that would create proposals for the reform of teacher education. In order to do that, they then divided into research groups, in which they spent a number of weeks learning in depth some particular aspect of teacher education, and they then jigsawed as specialists into new groups to design new programs of teacher education. No individual student knew everything, but when does anyone know everything? They were all able to take what they had learned in depth, and then in a community of learners, teach one another and accomplish jointly what no one of them could have done alone.

I was also asked to design a community of learners exercise for teachers in Jewish education, one that could be completed in a single day. I created a brief unit for the study of *Tanach*. We worked with three groups of Jewish educators. One group studied a section from *Sefer Bereishit* dealing with the destruction of Sodom. A second studied a section from *Sefer Shoftim*, the infamous incident of the concubine at Givah, and a third group studied the coronation of Saul, from *Sefer Shmuel Aleph*. The members of each group became specialists, each of them in their own portion of the *Tanach*—specialists as much as one can be in an hour and a half. Then I divided them into new groups, made up of combinations of specialties and gave them textual interpretation problems to solve, that could only be solved if you could look at connections between the different texts. This meant that people would have to teach the others in the group their texts, and would then have to work together on the combinations.

How Do We Investigate Communities of Learners and Teachers?

We now have a national project in the United States, supported by the Mellon Foundation, to try to understand how and why the community of learners model seems to work. What is the character of the project? There are several research teams. One research team, directed by Brown and Campione, is from the University of California at Berkeley. This team continues to conduct more studies in a small number of classrooms to understand how these principles work with pupils, mainly at the elementary school and middle school level.

I am directing the second project at Stanford in collaboration with Judy Shulman of the Far West Laboratory. We are asking the following question: If pupils do learn well under these conditions, how can teachers learn to teach in these ways? We are asking the questions of *teacher-learning* in relation to those of *student-learning.*

Then there is a third question, dealing with the organizational aspects of such reforms. Even if teachers can learn to teach in these ways, what does it take to create the conditions in an organization, whether a school or a network of teachers, to make it possible for teachers who have learned to teach this way to sustain such teaching? How many of us teach as well as we know how? Not a single one of us, I trust. Even though we have learned to teach in certain ways, we work within organizations, contexts and settings that often actively discourage the application of these understandings on our part. Even more important, what does it take to create an organization in which teachers can continue to learn to teach from their own practice? We have a third research team looking at these issues, and it is directed at Stanford by my colleagues Milbrey McLaughlin and Joan Talbert.

The fourth research group concerns itself with assessment. In Israel, people are interested in institutions like the *bagrut* matriculation examinations, because no matter what you want to teach, the students will end up learning what their important tests measure. All the effective influence will be from the tests, not from your good intentions. In the United States we typically create these wonderful school reforms, change the curriculum, modify teacher education and then never get around to changing the assessments. Therefore, very little eventually changes. Some of the most important lessons that we in the United States know about the centrality of assessment is based on work that was done here in Israel by Pinchas Tamir in the biology reform 20 years ago, in which he and his colleagues reformed the biology matriculation exams. So, we have a research team led by my colleague at Stanford, Edward Haertel, who is looking at questions of how we can design new kinds of assessment that will be consistent with the goals of this kind of teaching.

Finally, since it is apparent that technology is going to play a larger part in the instruction of the teacher, we have a team at Peabody College at Vanderbilt University, Tennessee—which has, I think, the best group in the world in educational technology. They are looking at how technologies of different types can contribute to the education of both students and teachers who are attempting to create learning communities.

As you can see, our research teams themselves comprise a community of learners. Each group attempts to become expert in a part of the larger problem through its research work. We then combine our understanding to address the problem jointly.

Principles That Characterize Communities of Learners

As I say, this is a work in progress. We are still trying to understand how and why such teaching and learning work. At least six distinct principles appear to characterize effective and substantive learning in the community of learners model. These are principles which I have found to be useful in trying to explain why this kind of learning seems to work so well.

The six principles which appear to characterize the conditions for authentic and enduring learning in the community of learners model are *generative content; active learning; reflective thinking* and *practice; collaboration; passion;* and *community* or *culture.* These ideas were originally stimulated by an address to the American Educational Research Association by Jerome Bruner in 1994, but have been adapted to the point where Bruner might well neither recognize nor support them. They naturally owe a debt to the work of our collaborators Brown and Campione as well.[6] According to these principles, authentic and enduring learning occurs when:

- The subject-matter content to be learned is *generative,* essential and pivotal to the discipline or interdiscipline under study, and can yield new understandings and/or serve as the basis for future learning of content, processes and dispositions.
- The learner is an *active* agent in the process, not passive, an audience, a client or a collector. Learning becomes more active through experimentation and inquiry, as well as through writing, dialogue and questioning.
- The learner not only behaves and thinks, but can "go meta"—that is, can *reflectively* turn around on his/her own thought and action and analyze how and why their thinking achieved certain ends or failed to achieve others. Metacognition—consciousness of how and why one is learning particular things in particular ways—is the key to deep learning.
- There is *collaboration* among learners. They can work together in ways that scaffold and support each other's learning, and in ways that supplement each other's knowledge. Collaboration is

a marriage of insufficiencies, not exclusively cooperation in a particular form of social interaction. Moreover, there are difficult intellectual challenges that are nearly impossible to accomplish alone, but are more readily addressed in the company of others.

- Teachers and students share a *passion* for the material, are emotionally committed to the ideas, processes and activities and see the work as connected to present and future goals.
- The process of activity, reflection and collaboration are supported, legitimated and nurtured within a *community* or *culture* that values such experiences and creates many opportunities for them to occur and be accomplished with success and pleasure. Such communities create participant structures which reduce the labor-intensity of the activities needed to engage in the most daunting practices that lead to teaching and learning. Classrooms and schools that are characterized by activity, reflection and collaboration in learning communities are inherently uncertain, complex and demanding. Both learning and teaching in such settings entail high levels of risk and unpredictability for the participants. Both students and teachers require a school and community culture that supports, scaffolds and rewards those levels of risk-taking and invention characteristic of these new ways of learning for understanding and commitment.

The Question of Curricular Scope

Naturally, there are many kinds of questions which arise from the principles enumerated above. A particularly glaring problem is the eternal universal question of curriculum, namely, "How can we possibly teach everything we know when we have so little time?" Even if we have the time, the students do not. Even if we had three times as much time, there would not be enough. How do we solve the problem of creating a curriculum that is intellectually honest, to use Bruner's phrase, with respect to the knowledge that our communities have acquired?

There are different kinds of solutions to this dilemma. One is the solution of coverage. It is the one most of us practice in our national curricula, even though we know it is doomed to fail. There is a simple reason why we continue to cover everything, even though we know it fails, and that is because if we, as teachers, try to teach everything, we need no longer feel guilty. The student's problem is to learn all we have taught, and if she or he fails, it is not our fault.

There is also a political reason why we opt for coverage. The different stakeholders value different kinds of knowledge. If we really engaged in the kind of deliberations that Schwab argued for, and taught only those topics related to the deeper underlying principles, it would permit us, in an intellectually honest way, to make the curriculum more authentically learnable.[7] The curriculum would be shorter and more meaningful. However, we would have to have discussions that would be very painful and very difficult. Some favorite topics, books or heroes would not be covered. The politically easy solution is always to add three more chapters, to let everybody get a place at the bigger table by making the curriculum more extensive. The Advanced Placement biology text book in the United States is a symbol of this strategy. This book is so heavy that teachers now advise students not to carry it back and forth to their homes, because they might injure themselves. Every new edition grows larger. Why? It is because the system has surrendered to the principle of coverage.

A second approach attempts to identify the structures of the subject matter, the essential questions of disciplines and their applications. This is a very promising approach, but it has a fatal flaw. The fatal flaw is that the structures turn out to be incredibly complex, difficult, ambiguous and multifaceted themselves. So that when you say with Ted Sizer that less is more, and that you must teach the structures,[8] no one faces the fact that less is *more complex,* less is *more ambiguous,* less is *more difficult to learn,* less is *more difficult to teach.* Consequently, attempting to reduce the curriculum to its essence may not actually solve the problem, as long as all students are expected to learn the same essence.

The community of learners model suggests a third approach. The third approach argues that while it is worthwhile to look for the structures, to look for the essential questions, and for the generative topics, we must not believe for a moment that everyone can learn even these. We must be prepared to live in a world where different people have come to know different things in depth, and where they develop the capacity to collaborate with one another when there are problems to solve, problems that transcend what any individual can do alone.

One of the people who has most beautifully expressed this sense of the way the world is becoming, not just in schools, but in the world of work and play, is not a philosopher of education, but if you will, a philosopher of management, Peter Drucker. Drucker lately has been claiming that the world of work is increasingly becoming a place where the *individual* is no longer the unit; he or she has been supplanted by the *team.* A team is defined as a group of people who have individually specialized in particular bodies of understanding and skills, who have developed a capacity to learn how to learn, because what may be an understanding today, becomes obsolete next week. A manager is someone who has learned to bring together groups to optimize the contributions of each member.

Let me read you one quote from Drucker, which I shall modify in a particular way. Every place in this excerpt where Drucker uses a form of the word manage, I am going to replace it with a form of the word teach. I think you will understand the point:

> Teaching is the distinctive organ of all organizations. All of them require teaching whether they use the term or not. All teachers do the same things, whatever the purpose of their organization. All of them have to bring people, each possessing different knowledge, together for joint performance. All of them have to make human strengths productive in human performance, and human weaknesses irrelevant. The essence of teaching is to make knowledge productive. Teaching, in other words, is a social function, and in its practice, teaching is truly a liberal art.[9]

Now, Drucker was saying all that about management, not teaching. What he has not yet quite understood is that, in its essential character, management is a form of pedagogy, a kind of teaching. Teaching is the highest and most complex of the liberal arts.

Why Is This Approach So Rare?

Another question is: "If these practices and these principles are so good, and if both our theory and the wisdom of our experience support these ideas, then why do we not engage in this kind of practice on a regular basis? Why, indeed, do we see it so rarely?" I have two related answers to that question. The first is that if you take those principles seriously, and you imagine what a classroom would look like, in which activity, reflection, collaboration, passion, generativity and community were all going on at the same time, you would likely have what you call in Hebrew a *balagan,* a chaotic mess. It would not be a quiet or an orderly place. In fact, it would violate the first rule of teachers' survival, that teachers create classroom organizations in order to reduce the amount of uncertainty and unpredictability in their environment.

The principles that characterize communities of learners, if taken seriously, say to teachers, "In spite of every instinct in your body and in your mind to design a classroom environment that will be under control, that will be predictable, where you can predict what is going to happen, design a classroom environment where the students will engage in the kind of reflective, collaborative, intellectual and emotional activities which, if successful, will lead them to construct understandings and to ask questions that were not in your lesson plans or in your unit designs. Design for uncertainty, not certainty. Design to maximize chance." This may be an exciting prospect for some teachers, but hardly a comforting one. Uncertainty is very uncomfortable.

This leads me to the second and related answer. We have prepared generations of teachers who are very uncomfortable with uncertainty, and who are intolerant of uncertainty. I would contend that the major reason why the kind of teaching we have been discussing, even though it is productive, is rarely put into practice, is because we have not yet created the conditions in schools, in institutions or in teacher education that not only will tolerate the creation of uncertainty and unpredictability, but will in effect develop values that will support teachers and learners in those communities to engage in such activities. Even though we may pay lip service to the work of John Dewey, Joseph Schwab or others who advocate this kind of progressive education, in fact most of what we do, both to prepare teachers and to support them in schools, works directly contrary to those principles.

Communities of Teachers and the Case Method of Learning

This leads me to the last section of this evening's lecture: Conceptions of teacher learning that might reverse the emphasis on seeking certainty and predictably, and might help create a cadre of teachers who are much more tolerant of, even engaged with, uncertainty and unpredictability.

Judy Shulman and I have been working on the use of *cases* and *case methods* in the preparation of teachers.[10] Most of the work we have traditionally done in the preparation of teachers has focused on design—planning lessons, planning units, coming up with systems for classroom organization and management. We are very invested in the design functions of a teacher, and this is certainly appropriate, because teachers require planning, design, organization. However, teachers also understand that the realities of classrooms are that no one can fully design the world. Once the teaching and learning begin to unfold, uncertainty never disappears. That is even more the case if you engage in the kind of teaching we have been talking about in this lecture, the kind of teaching that occurs in communities of learning. Such teaching may begin with design, but in the end it is shaped by uncertainty and it becomes a case.

What is a case? A case is a special kind of story; it is a narrative. My colleague and friend Jerome Bruner has a lovely definition of a narrative, of a story. Bruner says that a story is an account of the vicissitudes of intention.[11] These are the accidents of planning. A story happens when intention collides with reality. What do we mean? If I tell you the following story, "Little Red Riding Hood took a walk into the forest to bring her grandmother lunch. And that is what she did," you sit there waiting for the story. You ask yourself, what is the story? But if I say to you, "Little Red Riding Hood went into the forest to bring her grandmother lunch and she happened to meet the big bad wolf," now we have got a story! It became a narrative because the plan collided with chance, an accident, something that was not intended.

If you look in the *Oxford English Dictionary,* you will find that the root of the word case means chance. So, if I say to you, "Let us meet at such and such a corner, but just in case we miss each other, I will see you at the restaurant," I am changing what was a plan into a story which includes chance. Thus, a case is a story, because it involves chance.

Being accounts of what happens when intention and chance meet, cases are useful for the training of professionals. They are already used in the training of business and military people. In the field of education, they are badly needed for teacher preparation. Teachers understand that it is not enough just to study the theories, the intentions, the plans, the designs. We need to create strategies of teacher education that permit both intention and chance to be represented in their collision as well as in their separateness. The most important source of such cases is the experiences of the teachers themselves. That is why we must shape institutions of teacher education and of teaching that create opportunities for teachers to actively reflect on their own practice by collaboratively investigating their own experiences through the use of cases.

If you attend to my language carefully, you will understand how we have come full circle in this lecture. The very same principles that explain why students learn in communities of learners explain how teachers can learn in communities of teachers. Teachers must be in communities where they can actively and passionately investigate their own teaching, where they can consistently reflect on their own practice and its consequences, where they can engage collaboratively with one another, to investigate, discuss, explore and learn from one another about what happens when chance occurs in their teaching and thereby, where they can, as members of the community, generate a base of knowledge that goes beyond what any one of them could learn in the isolation which now characterizes their classrooms.

That is the principle of a community of teachers. It is so bound up with the principle of a community of learners that if you ask me what is my definition of an effective school, I will say: An effective school is an institution that is as educative for its teachers as it is for its students. It creates the same kinds of conditions for both.

I have come to the end of this journey. It was a long journey, but the problem is a hard one. It cannot be solved by good intentions alone. It can be solved only through courage in both policy investment and practice. And lest you think that I place too much emphasis on the issue of chance and learning from experience, keep in mind what John Donne, the poet, said about love, because in this sense good love is like good teaching. He said, "Though it is got by chance, it is kept by art." That is, many fruitful activities begin with a fortuitous accident, but it requires serious and persistent effort (art in the language of the poet) to sustain the fruits of chance and make them endure. In the case of improved teaching, enduring improvement will be accomplished through disciplined reflection, through active experimentation, and through the collaborations that we pursue together in a learning community of teachers.

NOTES

1. Deborah Meier, *The Power of Their Ideas* (Boston: Beacon Press, 1995), p. xi.
2. Joseph Schwab, "The Impossible Role of the Teacher in Progressive Education." This essay appeared originally in *School Review* 67 (1959), pp. 139–159 and was reprinted in an anthology of Schwab's essays entitled *Science, Curriculum, and Liberal Education: Selected Essays,* edited by Ian Westbury and Neil J. Wilkof (Chicago: University of Chicago Press, 1978), pp. 167–183.
3. See A. S. Palinscar and A. L. Brown, "Reciprocal Teaching of Comprehension-Fostering and Monitoring Activities," in *Cognition and Instruction* 1(2), (1984), pp. 117–175.
4. See A. L. Brown and J. C. Campione, "Communities of Learning and Thinking, or a Context by Any Other Name," in *Human Development* 21 (1990), pp. 108–125. See also, Joan I. Heller and Anne Gordon, "Lifelong Learning: A Unique School-University Collaboration Is Preparing Students for the Future," in *Educator* (Spring 1992), vol. 6, no. 1, pp. 4–19.
5. Anne Brown's Presidential address to the American Educational Research Association was published as A. L. Brown, "The Advancement of Learning," in *Educational Researcher* 23(8), 1994, pp. 4–12.
6. Jerome Bruner's address to the American Educational Research Association in 1994 was published in J. S. Bruner, "Teaching the Present, Past and Possible," in *The Culture of Education* (Cambridge, MA: Harvard

University Press, 1996), pp. 86–99. On the work of Campione and Brown, see above note 4.

7. See Schwab's suggestions in "The Practical: A Language for Curriculum," in *Science, Curriculum, and Liberal Education,* op. cit., pp. 287–321.
8. See Sizer's suggestions in *Horace's Compromise: The Dilemma of the American High School* (Boston: Houghton Mifflin Company, 1985), pp. 225, 230.
9. Peter Drucker, "The Age of Social Transformation" in *The Atlantic,* November 1994, vol. 274, n5, p. 53(18).
10. See *Case Methods in Teacher Education,* edited by Judith H. Shulman (New York: Teachers College Press, 1992), and my paper "Toward a Pedagogy of Cases," on pages 1–32 therein. See also *The Intern Teacher Casebook,* edited by Judith H. Shulman and Joel A. Colbert (Far West Laboratory and ERIC Clearinghouse; vol. 1: 1987 and vol. 2: 1988), and *Diversity in the Classroom,* edited by Judith H. Shulman and Amalia Mesa-Bains (New Jersey: Research for Better Schools and Lawrence Erlbaum Associates; *Casebook for Teachers and Teacher Educators:* 1993, and *Facilitators Guide:* 1994).
11. J. S. Bruner, *Actual Minds, Possible Worlds* (Cambridge, MA: Harvard University Press, 1986), p. 16.

INTRODUCTION

PROFESSIONAL DEVELOPMENT: LEARNING FROM EXPERIENCE (1997)

THIS ESSAY was originally delivered as a speech at a national conference at Hebrew Union College in Cincinnati on school reform and its necessary conditions. In it, Shulman explores three questions: What makes teaching complex work? How do teachers learn to manage that complexity? What forms of school reform can create productive settings for teacher learning? Using examples from the research of both Mary Budd Rowe and Deborah Loewenberg Ball, he portrays the complexities of teaching, especially reform-minded teaching, which asks teachers to use far more participatory structures in their classrooms. "Under what conditions can teachers learn to teach in this way?" Shulman asks. His answer: There are five principles of effective and enduring learning—for students and for their teachers. These include: meaningful activity, metacognitive awareness and processing of those activities, collaboration with others, passion and commitment, and a supportive and nurturing community. These principles characterize any learning community. One challenge for teachers is that as a community of learners, they must also become a community of practice, moving from deliberation and reflection to action.

Shulman concludes by arguing that we cannot rely simply on reforms that focus exclusively on student learning, for teachers too must learn and change if reforms are to flourish. This requires asking schools to become environments that are designed to be educative for teachers, as well as for their students.

21

PROFESSIONAL DEVELOPMENT

LEARNING FROM EXPERIENCE

THE STORY IS TOLD about a schoolteacher, a *melamed* as we call him in the Jewish tradition, who sat late one evening next to the fire, ruminating with an unopened book in his lap. Suddenly he observed to his wife of many years, "You know, Yentl, I was just thinking. If I were the czar, I would be richer than the czar." Now his wife, after 25 years of marriage, had learned that many things come out of this fellow's mouth—not all of which are particularly profound—but she humored him and said, "I really don't understand; if you were the czar (that's a wonderful thought), you would be as rich as the czar." He replied, "No, no, no! I've been thinking. If I were the czar, I would indeed be richer than the czar." "How could that be?" she queried. "Because," he responded, "if I were the czar, I could still do a little teaching on the side!"

Why that story? In some ways, that wonderful story also reflects a deeper and more disturbing set of premises that many of us carry, including those of us whose lives are bound up as teachers and with teaching, with regard to the activity and profession of teaching. It is that teaching is something that one does "on the side." It is not particularly complicated. It is not particularly demanding. Anyone could do it, if they didn't already have something more important to do.

I have spent most of my scholarly career trying to understand teaching. I interrupted this effort for a period of about 10 years when I tried to ask similar questions about the practice of medicine. The question in both cases has been a very straightforward and simple one: How is this apparently simple, straightforward activity conducted? What are people really doing when they teach? Or when they meet a patient and make a diagnosis and prescribe a treatment? What I have found in years of studying the women and men engaged in these professions is that, of the two, teaching is by far the more complex and demanding. The more time I spend in classrooms with teachers—talking with them, observing, watching videotapes, talking some more, reflecting on my own teaching—the more I peel off layer upon layer of incredible complexity. After some 30 years of doing such work, I have concluded that classroom teaching—particularly at the elementary and secondary levels—is perhaps the most complex, most challenging, and most demanding, subtle, nuanced, and frightening activity that our species has ever invented. In fact, when I compared the complexity of teaching with that much more highly rewarded profession, "doing medicine," I concluded that the only time medicine even approaches the complexity of an average day of classroom teaching is in an emergency room during a natural disaster (Shulman, 1987, 369–397). When 30 patients want your attention at the same time, only then do you approach the complexity of the average classroom on an average day.

For every strategy of reform, I believe that the engine of reform—its regulator and ultimately its bottleneck—is the classroom teacher. In Larry Cuban's terms, this makes me a pedagogical rather than a systemic reformer, and I think he has me correctly pegged. I would argue that whatever your conception of reform—whether the classroom door is open or closed, whether the curriculum is mandated or invented—its success ultimately rests on the quality of the pedagogical interaction between teacher and students. And I say "students" rather than "student" because we do not teach in situations where we and an individual student are sitting on opposite ends of a tutorial log and thus can work clinically, one-on-one in the educational process. We are always working with groups of students, often several groups each day, and nearly always in larger numbers than we think is prudent.

I now offer this chapter's sole argument: Efforts at school reform must give as much attention to creating the conditions for teacher learning as for student learning. Any effort at school reform will ultimately fail if it does not ask itself: "As I design this grand plan for improving the quality of learning in students, have I designed with equal care and concern a plan for teacher learning in this setting?" The effective school must be educative for its teachers. The proposals for reform reported—the Coalition of Essential Schools, Central Park East Secondary School, Comer Project schools—share in common the commitment to creating the conditions for teacher learning.

You may ask, "What are the conditions for teacher learning?" I invite you to examine Jerome Bruner's propositions regarding the conditions that make student learning flourish: He suggests that these are agency or activity, reflection, collaboration or interaction, and culture or community. We teachers are just older members of the same species as our students. We do not suddenly change the necessary conditions for learning when we pass our 21st birthday and earn teaching credentials. Those principles, along with several more that I shall add, define the conditions for teacher learning as well.

To paraphrase the famous Rabbi Hillel in an analogous situation roughly 2,000 years ago, "That is the essence; the rest is commentary." That commentary now follows.

Three Questions

I have three questions: What makes teaching so difficult? How can teachers learn to manage, cope with, and eventually master those difficulties? What forms of school reform can contribute to creating the conditions for teacher learning? These are difficult questions, so permit me to describe my approach to answering them. I stand correctly accused, as a university academician, of being a theoretician. I believe that theory is indispensable. However, my approach to theory is somewhat different from that of many of my colleagues.

Our usual sense of theory is that we invent theories and then we apply them to practice. I, on the other hand, am the kind of person who finds things that work in practice, and then I try to make them work in theory. I am thus utterly dependent on learning from what David Hawkins once dubbed "the wisdom of practice." Nearly 30 years ago, I edited a book entitled *Learning by Discovery,* to which Jerome Bruner and I were both contributors (Shulman and Keislar, 1966). David Hawkins wrote a paper in that volume called "Learning the Unteachable," in which he argued that there are times in human history when there is much more wisdom in practice than in the academy, when gamblers know more about probability than statisticians, and when sailors know more about the heavens than astronomers (Hawkins, 1966, 3–12). He claimed, and I think correctly, that we are probably at a time in the history of education when there is more, and indeed even a distinctive, wisdom about teaching among practicing teachers than there is among academic educators. But the wisdom of teachers is isolated and unvoiced. We as teachers indeed can become smarter about what we do, but we work in lonely circumstances that make it difficult for us to articulate what we know and to share what we have learned with others. The nature of our work habits and conditions is so unreflective that we even forget some of the understandings that we have achieved in the course of our practice.

How many times do we find ourselves teaching something that we have taught before, only to realize that we are making the same mistakes that we made the last time we taught the same topic? Because of the pedagogical isolation of teaching, even at universities, and because of our own lack of adequate discipline in documenting and reflecting on our own practice, we fail to incorporate what we have learned into our new practices. We continue to repeat the same mistakes. We suffer from chronic pedagogical amnesia.

We all know the old saw that there are two kinds of teachers: One has 20 years of experience; the other has 1 year of experience 20 times. There is a large difference between learning from experience and simply having experience. Many teachers have experience. It takes special teachers working under special circumstances to learn from that experience. Yet learning from experience is one of the requirements of any school reform. Most of our school reform efforts encourage teachers to create conditions in which students will be creative and inventive, both problem solvers and innovators. Teachers are asked to create conditions for learning that they themselves may never have encountered before. Under those conditions, teachers must learn to anticipate the unexpected, because they have created circumstances in which successful students have been given the freedom and encouragement to come up with surprises.

If such reforms are to flourish and grow, the teachers must be capable of apprehending those surprises, analyzing the extent to which they are educative for their students, and adapting their future teaching either to enhance or discourage such student performances. Teachers must therefore learn from the experiences they create with their students. In cases of school reform, the classroom becomes the educator's laboratory, a setting in which new forms of teaching and learning are painstakingly grown in a fertile culture of exploration. The teacher manages that laboratory and is responsible for detecting and reporting its lessons for improved educational practice.

When I study or conduct research on practice, I strive to mine the "wisdom of practice" that grows in the minds of those experimenting teachers. In mining that wisdom, I attempt to develop more powerful theories of practice, which I can then share with my fellow educator-academicians and classroom teachers—who in turn correct those theories and comment on them as we continue to refine them together.

In doing this kind of work, I often find that the theories developed independent of practice are either wrong or dangerously incomplete. I now invite you into that most intriguing of places, the valley where theory and practice intersect.

Theory into Practice . . . Almost

Let us take an example of an excellent theory, rooted in superb research, and how that theory must be adapted in the context of practice. I have a colleague at Stanford who I think is one of the most gifted practitioners and theorists in the field of science education during this past half-century. Her name is Mary Budd Rowe. She is a former president of the National Science Teachers Association and was an experienced classroom teacher for many years before she became a professor. She shares membership on the National Board for Professional Teaching Standards with Albert Shanker, Deborah Meier, and a host of classroom teachers around the country. She is widely known all over the world for her research on a phenomenon that is now part of the standard vocabulary of all teachers: wait-time (Rowe, 1974a and 1974b). Rowe discovered in her classroom research that when teachers question students, the longer they wait for answers without either shifting to another student or saying something else themselves, the greater the likelihood that the answers the students eventually give will be of a higher order intellectually. The less time they offer students, the more probable it is that student responses will be at a "lower" level of rote or procedural understanding. Rowe and her students demonstrated repeatedly that longer wait-times promote higher-order and more creative responses in students. Since all school reform advocates prefer students to display deeper understanding, Rowe's findings have broad significance.

There is an important corollary to that finding. Not every question deserves long wait-time. If I ask you to tell me your phone number, wait-time is unlikely to enhance the depth of the answer. There has to be a proper fit between the depth or complexity of the question and whether it demands an answer worth waiting for.

Soon after the research became well known, entrepreneurs all over the country began developing wait-time workshops based on Rowe's excellent studies. Evaluators began doing studies to see whether, under training, teachers would subsequently lengthen their wait-times during interactions with students. They also asked whether teachers would learn to distinguish between higher-order and lower-order questions so that they would know when the longer wait-times would be appropriate. During the workshops, teacher wait-times and question discriminations developed nicely in the desired directions. However, when teachers returned to their classrooms, within a short time, their wait-times were back to the usual fraction of a second. Evaluators often interpreted that finding as evidence of teachers' resistance to change.

Those of us who are respectful of the wisdom of practice would not readily accept that interpretation. When I see a teacher who rejects the behavior of a recommended reform, my first question is: What is it about what teachers have elected to do, instead of using the strategies the reform says they should, that makes their choice more sensible? Again, I'm following the dictum that we treat teachers with as much respect as we do students. In mathematics education, we learned years ago to ask, when a pupil makes a mathematical error, what could be going on inside the learner's head that would make that mathematical response sensible? We need to ask the same thing about teachers.

As we began to research why teachers would not extend their wait-time, we found ourselves converging on two different but mutually consistent responses. The first was: Can classroom life afford silence? If nature abhors a vacuum, classrooms abhor silence with a vengeance. As classroom silences are created, students (and teachers) get very uncomfortable with them and fill them not only with responses to questions but with other "creative" activity as well. Indeed, one reason why we teachers find ourselves so often engaging in machine-gun recitation is that if we keep the pace of classroom interactions really fast, it serves as a powerful form of classroom management and control. Similarly, long wait-times may become irresistible invitations to disruption and loss of control.

Nevertheless, there is another, deeper reason why longer wait-times may be difficult to accomplish. Mary Budd Rowe was absolutely right: The longer teachers wait, the higher the probability that the student will come up with a higher-order response. What are higher-order responses? They are, in principle, more unpredictable, more inventive, and more likely to fall outside the range of responses that teachers expect students to make. Therefore the longer we wait, the greater the likelihood that the students will introduce into the classroom discourse ideas, concepts, conjectures, hypotheses, and proposals that we teachers have not anticipated and for which we have no ready response. At one level, that is exactly what we want! At another level, it creates enormous cognitive strain, especially on the substantive understanding that teachers bring to their teaching. Moreover, through no fault of teachers themselves, they often enter classrooms without some of the deep disciplinary knowledge that is increasingly expected of teachers by the new standards in such areas as math, history, literature, and science. In large measure, these disciplinary gaps may be attributed to poor undergraduate liberal education in universities. So when we are asking teachers to increase their wait-time, we may well be asking them to employ a strategy that is guaranteed to turn their safe classroom into an intellectual minefield. And they sensibly say that they cannot risk it. Classroom teaching is hard enough under current conditions.

This small example may be a metaphor for many of the dilemmas that accompany our preferred forms of school improvement and reform. Nearly all of these reforms call for more attention to deepened disciplinary and interdisciplinary understanding among students. They ask teachers to employ forms of instruction in which students are less passive, more collaborative in their interactions with one another, and given more opportunities for creative projects. These kind of experiences, in turn, require teachers to create far more complex participant structures in their classrooms. An unintended consequence of these proposed innovations is that there will be much more significant challenges to teachers' understandings, organizational skills, and capacities to learn and adapt from their experiences. Traditional forms of teaching help teachers maintain some modicum of control over the unpredictable quality of classroom life (Cuban, 1993). The new reforms threaten that stability and create unusual challenges for teachers. A modest "reform," such as increasing wait-time, can produce significant elevations in the quality, and unpredictability, of student contributions. These changes are good for learning, but they add strain to the already heavy burden of teaching.

If the simple proposal that teachers extend their wait-times can render teaching far more difficult, what might the complexity of a full-blown classroom and curricular reform entail? One of the areas in which such reforms are most advanced is the teaching of mathematics. Deborah Ball of Michigan State University has been one of the nation's leaders in implementing and investigating the classroom teaching-learning processes associated with such changes. We can examine the work of Deborah Ball to see how classroom life might change if even more pervasive reforms were introduced. Many of the features of Ball's classroom are congruent with more general attributes of the new pedagogy.

Ball spent 10 years as an elementary school teacher with a special interest in mathematics. She then completed a Ph.D. but decided not to leave the classroom and mathematics teaching behind. Instead, she has spent much of the past few years of her career teaching mathematics in elementary school classrooms and conducting research on her own teaching (Ball, 1993). She uses her own teaching experiences in a third-grade classroom as a way of trying to understand the complexities of mathematical teaching and learning. I have had the pleasure of sitting and watching Ball's classroom because she videotapes her teaching, analyzes it thoroughly, keeps her own journals, and gathers the mathematics portfolios in which her youngsters write daily. She can track how the pupils are thinking about the mathematics they are learning all during the process. Ball creates a mathematical community in her classroom where pupils work collaboratively to solve the problems they are presented with and the problems that they themselves create. They learn never to be satisfied with merely understanding procedures but to expect instead to understand the conceptual reasons behind mathematical processes. Ball steadfastly avoids saying "right" or "wrong" to the pupils when they offer a mathematical conjecture because she insists that the rules of mathematics be used to determine an idea's validity; students cannot depend on the teacher as an ultimate authority. Once they learn to turn mindlessly to authority, they forget that mathematics is essentially a way of thinking and reasoning, a language of analysis and representation, not an arbitrary system of rules in which only people with special talents or authority are permitted to have the answers.

The following episode reflects the type of teaching that Ball routinely pursues (Ball, 1993). Ball had been teaching about the concepts of odd and even numbers for several weeks. The students had already passed a test on odd and even numbers. Just as Ball was preparing to make a transition to a new topic, she asked whether anyone had any other ideas they wanted to express about even and odd numbers before they continued with the next topic. Shea raised his hand. Shea was a pupil who had not been participating very much during the odd and even unit. He observed, "Some numbers can be both even and odd. Like six. Six could be odd and even." Most of us would now say, "No, that's not true; you remember the rule that distinguishes odd from even numbers. If a number can be divided by two and having nothing left over, it is even. Six is therefore even. Understand? Good. Let's move along to our next topic." Others of us might temporize and say, "That's a very interesting idea, Shea. Would you come and talk to me about it after class?" Ball was concerned about Shea; she wanted to make sure that he was included in the mathematics-making process. She also was curious about what he had in mind and always tried to show respect for student conjectures.

Ball's students had learned an idea that lies at the heart of mathematics, an idea we call factoring—which is that any number can be taken apart and put back together again in all kinds of ways. It is fundamental because it lies at the heart of everything that we do mathematically later; it is essential to dealing with equalities and inequalities, and in algebra, it seems that all we do is take things apart and put them back together in different ways. It is critical to learn this disposition and strategy early on. Shea proceeded to explain that six must be both odd and even because six is made up of three groups of two. He knows that an even number is defined as a number that can be divided into groups of two with nothing left over, but the definition says nothing about how many groups there should be. Shea thought that should be important. He observed that six has three groups of two, and while there is no remainder, there are three groups, so six is both an odd and even number. Ball recognized that Shea was engaged in authentic mathematical reasoning. Learning to reason and think mathematically was the most important goal of her mathematics instruction. He was certainly wrong about six being both an odd and even number, but he was working on the problem deeply and mathematically.

This incident occurred because Ball had created a classroom in which that kind of mathematical invention was both possible and encouraged. It was modeled and rewarded. The other pupils immediately engaged with Shea. Lin ran up to the board and said, "Shea, if you say six is odd and even, if I use your logic, then so is ten!" Shea thought about her claim for a moment and responded, "Thank you very much; I hadn't thought of that. Yes, you're right. Ten is odd and even, too." Lin became more exasperated, as befits a bright and tenacious third grader. "If ten is odd, then so's fourteen." After a moment's thought, Shea again agreed. Lin finally declared, "But before you're done, every number is going to be both odd and even, and then if that's the case, why have we been having this discussion of even and odd numbers for the last three weeks?"

One of the things that happened in the classroom was that Shea's conjecture was posted on the wall with other student propositions that were under active consideration and debate in the classroom community. In the days that followed, some students began exploring the properties of "Shea numbers," as they called them. After a while, everyone was quite clear on which numbers were odd and which were even. But they arrived at those conclusions mathematically, rather than passively accepting them from an authority.

There are at least two interesting things to examine in connection with this account. First, notice the unpredictability inherent in classrooms where pupils actually have an opportunity to think and to display their reasoning. Educationally speaking, it is simultaneously a gold mine and a minefield! Ball and her counterparts have to be the kind of teachers who understand mathematics well enough to be able to handle that level of complexity, who are sufficiently skilled mathematical pedagogues to create the classroom conditions that produce and nurture such complexity, and who will not panic when their pupils produce surprising conjectures. Equally important, however, is the second feature of this account. It occurred in a classroom where Ball was able to take time to reflect on what had happened, not only to learn for her own benefit, but ultimately in ways that made her experiences and reflections accessible to countless educators who could thereby learn vicariously from her experience. Her private intellectual property thereby became community property when she analyzed this case, wrote it up, and published it. She has produced many other cases like this one, and they result not only in a growing case literature of mathematics teaching but also in an evolving theory of mathematical pedagogy.

All of us who teach encounter similar cases regularly. But, as I suggested earlier, we suffer from persistent pedagogical amnesia. And amnesiacs are incapable of learning from experiences because they just cannot hold their experiences in memory long enough to reflect on them. What can we learn from Ball's experience? One thing that we learn from this case is that we cannot trust "the test" as the basis for ensuring what pupils know. These pupils had all passed "the test" on odd and even numbers. Tests have limits as indicators of student knowledge for several reasons. It is not only because pupils forget tomorrow what they knew today. It is also because understanding something deeply means you can understand it when challenged by new situations to which it has to apply, in different representations, and under different circumstances. Learning is highly contextualized and situated. Any traditional test, however, selects a single "neutral" way to frame a question that it puts to students. The test results cannot tell us how flexibly the knowledge is held. Because of the emphasis on multiple ways of learning and representing important ideas, it is important for all learners who wish to learn something deeply to continue to revisit it again and again.

There is a lovely Hebrew proverb that asserts, when studying holy texts, "Turn it over repeatedly, because there is so much within it." Almost anything worth teaching in classrooms should be worthy of being turned over repeatedly, because there is so much to it. The reason why we should be seeking to evaluate student learning through projects, performance assessments, and portfolios is because these approaches afford more opportunities to tap into learners' flexibility of understanding, representations, and applications. This insight also lies behind the repeated claim that, in curriculum reform, "less is more." Bruner's conception of the spiral curriculum also implies that some ideas are sufficiently pivotal that they deserve regular revisiting by students as they traverse the grades of the school.

I related the Deborah Ball example in such detail in order to support the claim that all teaching—even the ostensibly simple teaching of arithmetic—is incredibly complex and enormously demanding. It does not require the threat of violence in schools to make teaching complicated. It is not only the multiplicity of roles that we, as teachers, have to play—at times social workers, nurses, counselors, parents, and, yes, pedagogues—that makes teaching complicated. The pedagogy of subject matter for understanding is both a handful and a mind-full all by itself. We thus encounter two sources of complexity: the intellectual demands of deep disciplinary understanding paired with the social demands of coping with the unpredictability that accompanies such teaching. The examples from Mary Budd Rowe and Deborah Ball, taken together, help us to see that complexity more clearly. They also underscore the need for teachers to be continuous learners if they are to become capable of coping with the manifold challenges of these new, widespread classroom reforms.

Teachers as Learners

Under what conditions can teachers learn to teach in the manner of a Deborah Ball or consistent with other models of school reform? Are there a set of principles that can guide our efforts to support teachers to learn this kind of teaching? I believe that the conditions for teacher learning are directly parallel to those needed for pupil learning. Jerome Bruner has proposed a set of principles that account for why those reforms we call the "community of learners" work as well as they do. I will review my reading of Bruner's principles for student learning in a community of learners as my starting point for discussing the conditions of teacher learning. Although Bruner proposed four principles, I have elaborated them into five because as I work with teachers on these principles, they continue to teach me new ways of looking at what student and teacher learning are, and they have insisted that we add at least one more. What are the principles that account for why this kind of learning seems to be so effective? I will argue that there are at least these five: activity, reflection, collaboration, passion, and community or culture. I shall discuss them first in conjunction with pupils as learners and then extend them to teachers.

Five Principles of Effective and Enduring Learning for Students and Their Teachers

The first principle is the principle of activity. The students who are the learners in these settings are remarkably active most of the time. They are active in that they are writing, they are investigating, and they are at the computer getting information. They are talking to one another, sharing information, and challenging one another's ideas. At every opportunity, the level of activity of the students is higher than in the average classroom.

This might not surprise anyone. We all know it from our practice as well as from theory—active learning results in more enduring learning than passive learning. It is one of the key principles of all human learning, equally relevant for adults as well as children.

Similarly, in the lives of teachers, authentic and enduring learning occurs when the teacher is an active agent in the process—not passive, not an audience, not a client or a collector. Teacher learning becomes more active through experimentation and inquiry, as well as through writing, dialogue, and questioning. Thus the school settings in which teachers work must provide them with the opportunities and support for becoming active investigators of their own teaching.

The second thing that we have seen in these classrooms is that they are not merely active, because activity alone is insufficient for learning. As Dewey observed many years ago, we do not learn just by doing; we learn by thinking about what we are doing. Successful students in these settings spend considerable time, as Bruner calls it, "going meta," that is, engaging in metacognition. They are thinking about what they are doing and why. Their teachers give them plenty of opportunities to talk about how they are learning, why they are learning in these ways, and why they are getting things wrong when they get them wrong and why they are right when they get them right. A very high level of carefully guided reflection is blended with activity in the work of the students.

As with students, reflection is needed in the lives of teachers. They cannot become better teachers through activity and experimentation alone. Schools must create occasions for teachers to become reflective about their work, whether through journal writing, case conferences, video clubs, or support for teaching portfolios. Such work requires both scheduled time and substantial support.

Activity and reflection are hard work. If you are a typical learner, you often find yourself working alone, intending to read an article or a book. You sit down after dinner with a good reading light on, with good music playing softly in the background, and with no distractions in the room. Ten minutes later, you find yourself in the middle of a chapter, with absolutely no recollection of what you have read up to that point. It can be very hard to engage in active and reflective learning all by yourself. For students, it is even harder. This is one of the reasons why one of the most important inventions of Ann Brown, with Annemarie Palinscar, is called "reciprocal teaching" (Palinscar and Brown, 1984). Reciprocal teaching is a process of enhancing students' reading comprehension through working with one another, scaffolding each other's learning, and helping each other focus, attend, and question actively, critically, and reflectively as they jointly read complicated text. Thus active, reflective learning proceeds best in the presence of a third principle, which is collaboration.

With teachers, authentic and enduring learning also requires collaboration. When teachers collaborate, they can work together in ways that scaffold and support each other's learning, and in ways that supplement each other's knowledge. Collaboration is a marriage of insufficiencies, not exclusively "cooperation" in a particular form of social interaction. There are difficult intellectual and professional challenges that are nearly impossible to accomplish alone but are readily addressed in the company of others.

This kind of learning is not exclusively cognitive or intellectual in nature. Indeed, there is a significant emotional and affective component that inheres in such work. Authentic and enduring learning occurs when teachers and students share a passion for the material, are emotionally committed to the ideas, processes, and activities, and see the work as connected to present and future goals. Although the language of the reforms is heavily intellectual, the importance of emotion, enthusiasm, and passion is central to these efforts, both for students and for teachers. And there is a special quality to those affective responses that develop within individuals who have become interdependent members of well-functioning, cohesive groups. Simply observe the spirit that develops among the members of an athletic team, or the cast of a play, or members of a cabin at camp, and you can begin to discern the special emotional qualities associated with working collaboratives.

In that same vein, authentic and enduring learning works best when the processes of activity, reflection, emotion, and collaboration are supported, legitimated, and nurtured in a community or culture that values such experiences and creates many opportunities for them to occur and to be accomplished with success and pleasure. Such communities create "participant structures" that reduce the labor-intensity of the activities needed to engage in the most daunting practices that lead to teaching and learning. Classrooms and schools that are characterized by activity, reflection, and collaboration in learning communities are inherently uncertain, complex, and demanding. Both learning and teaching in such settings entail high levels of risk and unpredictability for the participants. Students and teachers both require a school and community culture that supports and rewards those levels of risk taking and invention characteristic of these new ways of learning for understanding and commitment.

What are the hallmarks of learning communities? It is one thing to declare the importance of community. It is quite another matter to accomplish one. Many teachers and teacher educators who wish to employ the power of learning communities in which the five principles of active learning can be learned, rewarded, and nurtured have found that creating such communities is a daunting task. Brown, Ash, Rutherford, Nakagawa, Gordon, and Campione (1993) have suggested that effective learning communities share certain salient features. First, the members must have something significant to offer one another; the basis for interdependence within a community is that its members represent an array of different talents, understandings, skills, and dispositions. This feature of "distributed expertise" is needed within such communities. It is present either because the community is formed through bringing together a diverse group of individuals, or because the community encourages a division of labor in which different members invest in developing their individual expertise for the sake of the larger group. Thus group members are characterized by "individuality"—in which members develop their individual talents for the sake of the community—rather than "individualism"—in which members develop their particular talents for the sake of maintaining their own competitive edge.

Individual talent once developed must be shared. A working community of learners, therefore, is not only constituted of diversely capable members, but its members engage in the kinds of dialogue, peer instruction, conversations, and collaborative work that permit knowledge to be transmitted and shared among the group members. Thus a second attribute of a learning community is a commitment to the sharing of expertise among its diverse members.

As learning communities begin to engage in such processes of discussion, dialogue, and sharing, another critical feature of their functioning becomes apparent. Members must hold one another in sufficient respect to trust the value of their respective contributions. They must be prepared to engage their peers with civility, patience, and regard if the trust that makes for authentic interdependence can be achieved. Thus trust and respect are additional attributes of the community.

Finally, I suspect that effective learning communities must be capable of moving from talk to action, and from deliberation to the joint pursuit of tasks that are publicly visible and whose outcomes hold real consequences for all of the group members. This is the feature that has been called developing a "community of practice." If members of a group are to work together effectively to perform a consequential task more complex and difficult than any of them could have accomplished alone, they will have to form a learning community in which distributed expertise is nurtured, the sharing of that expertise is actively pursued, and the respect needed to fuel that sharing is developed.

I am prepared to assert that the same principles that explain learning among students can also be used to explain learning among teachers. That is, if we are to design teacher education and professional development activities that will assist teachers to learn to teach in these reform-oriented ways, then we must employ teacher education approaches in which teachers will be active, reflective, collaborative, impassioned, and communal. The communities in which such processes can flourish will be characterized by diversity, dialogue, respect, and mutually valued practices. We can use these principles to design our interventions and to construct the instruments that we use to evaluate our efforts. We can use the results of those evaluations to critique and revise our approaches.

Organizational Contexts and Communities for Teacher Learning

What are the necessary organizational contexts and conditions for all teachers to learn to teach in these new ways? One never learns to teach once and for all. It is a continuous, ongoing, constantly deepening process. We would not want to depend on teachers who would, for the rest of their careers, only continue to implement what they had learned even in the best preservice program we can imagine. Similarly, we would not want to teach in a university whose library was constituted of all the books ever published up to the day the university was opened but that had never acquired another book or journal for the rest of the history of the institution. Thus any school that wishes its teachers to teach well had better provide the conditions for them to be learning continually.

My colleagues, Milbrey McLaughlin and Joan Talbert (1993), whose work is frequently cited, have studied the conditions that are associated with teachers who regularly teach for deep understanding in secondary schools. Their findings confirm our claim that teaching of the sort we are discussing is not only complicated but also risky. It leaves teachers open to uncertainty and, quite frankly, to failure. A classroom in which the kind of complexity we have just described is commonplace is one where teachers are taking worthwhile risks. What kind of organizational and institutional conditions permit that kind of risk taking?

Teachers who were found to teach for understanding had been members of high school departments in which faculty members were collaborative and supportive of one another in trying out new ideas. They were truly participants in teacher learning communities. This is a finding of the greatest importance, because it points to the critical nature of school-based opportunities for teachers to work together on matters of curriculum, teaching, evaluation, and mutual support. In addition, most of the teachers who were systematically and consistently displaying teaching for understanding were also part of out-of-school networks. Whether it was the National Writing Project or a local affiliate of that project, a math collaborative, or a union-centered teacher research effort, they were not solely dependent on the persistence of a powerful learning community within their own school. Our educational institutions can change dramatically and rapidly when the principal or a department chair moves, a critical partner/teacher retires or takes a leave, or a school district shifts its policies for political reasons. Under such circumstances, the functioning of an outside teacher network can sustain the commitment to reform. Teachers can have other people to talk to, to inspire them, to share a vision, to share a dream, to boost their spirits, and to offer constructive suggestions. As I contemplate the reforms discussed in this book, reforms that were created to sustain student learning of a high order, many of them reflect the organizational conditions of groups of collaborating teachers who talk to one another about their work, support one another's efforts, and are affiliated with a broader network of institutions and of teachers that interconnect to provide a scaffolding for their common efforts. The functioning of faculty and administrators in Deborah Meier's Central Park East Secondary School, and their networked connections to the Coalition of Essential Schools and other collaborative efforts, provides a vivid illustration of these principles.

Summing Up

I will sum up with a series of assertions. We cannot be satisfied with school reform efforts that focus exclusively on student learning, even though all the rhetoric claims that student learning is the bottom line of every reform effort. I think of school reform as an ellipse, not as a circle. An ellipse has two foci that define its orbit, not just one. For me, the two foci that define the orbit of school reform are student learning and teacher learning. If you do not have both of them as real foci, the orbit will be askew and off-course. I do not argue for the priority of teacher learning over student learning because that is equally untenable. The two purposes mutually define the orbit.

We also must recognize how much risk is entailed in doing the kind of teaching we are advocating, and why we must create structures within our schools that permit teachers to take those risks and then celebrate them, not bury them. One of the lessons we can learn from the medical community is the character of a ritual called the clinical pathological conference. A clinical pathological conference (CPC) is a weekly conference in which a member of the medical staff or the medical faculty presents a case that did not go well. The CPC is not built around a story such as: "I did an ideal appendectomy last week." Instead, the CPC will attest: "I did an appendectomy last week and some things happened that I didn't think were going to happen. We ought to discuss these unanticipated findings and see what we can learn from them." Within the culture of that community, there is a value placed on examining what happens when mistakes are made, when problems arise, and when surprises occur. These become occasions for learning, not opportunities for shame.

We all know that the more we teach well, the more surprises we will encounter. Those are special moments for learning. I have never learned much from planning a lesson that runs smoothly. I learn when I have to confront the discomfort of a lesson that did not go quite the way I had intended, whether because it was poorly designed or because someone like Shea came up with a surprise conjecture. Under these conditions, if I have achieved the conditions of deliberation, reflection, and collaboration, my colleagues and I can learn from one another. Where are the CPC-like case conferences in our public schools? One of the most important books written on medical education was Charles Bosk's *Forgive and Remember* (Bosk, 1979). Writing about the surgical residency, his point was that if the principle was "forgive and forget," it would be a recipe for safety and stasis, not for learning from experience. If you want to learn from experience, you must both forgive and remember. The entire organization and the organization of the profession have to be organized so that learning from your reflective memories becomes the essence of the community's commitment to teacher development and teacher learning.

I return to my central theme. If we wish to create schools where reform will be enduring and not evanescent, we need to ask: Is this a school where teachers can learn? Unless we create the conditions for teacher learning, every single reform that we initiate, even if it looks like it is working at the beginning, will eventually erode and disappear. An effectively reformed school is a setting that is educative for its teachers. That is the essence; the rest has been commentary.

REFERENCES

Ball, D. 1993. With an eye on the mathematical horizon: Dilemmas of teaching elementary school mathematics. *Elementary School Journal,* 93(4): 373–397.

Bosk, C. L. 1979. *Forgive and remember: Managing medical failure.* Chicago: University of Chicago Press.

Brown, A. L., D. Ash, M. Rutherford, K. Nakagawa, A. Gordon, and J. C. Campione. 1993. Distributed expertise in the classroom. In *Cognitions:*

Psychological and educational considerations, ed. G. Solomon. New York: Cambridge University Press.

Cuban, L. 1993. *How teachers taught: Constancy and change in American classrooms, 1880–1990.* New York: Teachers College Press.

Hawkins, D. 1966. Learning the unteachable. In *Learning by discovery: A critical appraisal,* ed. L. S. Shulman and E. R. Keislar. Chicago: Rand McNally.

McLaughlin, M. W., and J. E. Talbert. 1993. *Contexts that matter for teaching and learning: Strategic opportunities for meeting the nation's education goals.* Stanford, CA: Center for Research on the Context of Secondary School Teaching, Stanford University.

Palinscar, A. S., and A. L. Brown. 1984. Reciprocal teaching of comprehension-fostering and monitoring activities. *Cognition and Instruction* 1(2): 117–175.

Rowe, M. B. 1974b. Wait-time and rewards as instructional variables, their influence on language, logic, and fate control: Part I—Wait-time. *Journal of Research in Science Teaching* 11(2): 81–94.

Rowe, M. B. 1974a. Relation of wait-time and rewards to the development of language, logic, and fate control: Part II—Rewards. *Journal of Research in Science Teaching* 11(4): 291–308.

Shulman, L. S. 1987. The wisdom of practice: Managing complexity in medicine and teaching. In *Talks to teachers: A Festschrift for N. L. Gage,* ed. D. C. Berliner and B. V. Rosenshine. New York: Random House.

Shulman, L. S., and E. R. Keislar. 1966. *Learning by discovery: A critical appraisal.* Chicago: Rand McNally.

INTRODUCTION

THEORY, PRACTICE, AND THE EDUCATION OF PROFESSIONALS (1998)

IN CELEBRATION of the one-hundredth anniversary of Dewey's ten years at the University of Chicago, noted educational scholars were asked to read and respond to an article or book written by Dewey. Shulman chose Dewey's "The Relation of Theory to Practice in Education," an article that was originally published in the third *National Society for the Study of Education Yearbook,* an issue that focused entirely on the relationship of theory and practice in teacher education. Two critical aspects of Dewey's argument were that (1) theory must drive teacher education, for practice can be a conservative force, and (2) that we ought to look at other professions—in this case, law or medicine—to resolve the issues of how to immerse new teachers in practice in ways that are educative.

In this essay, Shulman makes professional education problematic. He first proposes six commonplaces that are characteristic of professional work: the obligation of service to others ("a calling"), scholarly or theoretical understanding, skilled performance or a practice, the exercise of judgment under uncertainty, the need to learn from experience, and a professional community that both monitors the performance of individuals and aggregates and disseminates new knowledge. He then offers a critique of Dewey's argument through the lens of these characteristics and wonders why Dewey, himself such a supporter of attending to the student's perspective in K–12 teaching, was not more attentive to the teachers' perspective in teacher education. Shulman concludes the essay by describing a new vision of professional education, one that attends much more systematically to issues of the moral obligation of professionals and that uses pedagogies well suited to bridging the divide between theory and practice, including the use of case methods.

22

THEORY, PRACTICE, AND THE EDUCATION OF PROFESSIONALS

THE NATIONAL SOCIETY FOR THE SCIENTIFIC STUDY OF EDUCATION was only a year old when it devoted large portions of both its second *Yearbook* (1903) and its third (1904) to the topic "The Relation of Theory to Practice in the Education of Teachers." John Dewey's contribution, "The Relation of Theory to Practice in Education," led off the 1904 volume (Dewey, 1904, pp. 9–30). These two volumes were identified in a preface as addressing "the normal school problem." They aimed to address the research university problem as well, at least with regard to the connections between its research missions and its role in the education of teachers.

The society had changed its name in 1902 from its previous identity as the National Herbart Society. The leadership had apparently concluded that an association with *science* was likely to be more propitious than with the work of a German philosopher whose influence on American education had, in Harold Dunkel's wry phrase, gone "up like a rocket and down like a stone" (Dunkel, 1970, p. 1). The University of Chicago Press was the society's publisher, and the University of Chicago was home to its headquarters. At the time of the 1904 publication, its elected officers represented the cross section of the several worlds the society was intended to bridge. The officers were drawn from the University of Chicago, Columbia, Cornell, University of Indiana-Bloomington, and the State Normal University in Normal, Illinois, and included the state superintendent of schools in Wisconsin. With representation from the research universities, normal schools, and public schools, the theory-practice problem was quite real for the society.

Dewey was nearing the end of his decade at the University of Chicago when he wrote this essay. He had established the Department of Education, which he chaired while also leading the Department of Philosophy (including the field of psychology). He established the Laboratory School in 1896. But his disagreements with the university president William Rainey Harper had festered, and in 1904 he accepted an offer from Columbia's president Nicholas Murray Butler, who had chaired the board of the National Society for the Scientific Study of Education until 1903, to join the philosophy department at Columbia, a position he would take up in 1905. Thus, while the present essay is one of Dewey's oldest statements on the topic of theory and practice, it may stand as a valedictory to his extraordinary decade at Chicago.

I have organized this article in the tripartite manner. I will first summarize Dewey's argument, with special attention to his perspectives on the professions and professional education as models for teacher education. I shall then offer my own perspective on education for the professions, emphasizing a conception of the enduring challenges of all professional learning and practice. I shall conclude with a critical examination of Dewey's views and offer an outline of a contemporary variation.

Dewey's Argument

Dewey's Perspectives

Dewey opens his essay by stating "without argument" his assumption that "adequate professional instruction of teachers is not exclusively theoretical, but involves a certain amount of practical work as well. The primary question as to the latter is the aim with which it shall be conducted" (Dewey, 1904, p. 9). What an interesting reversal! The author takes for granted that theoretical preparation is needed for future teachers. The central issue is whether practical work is needed, and if so, of what kind.

Dewey then asserts that there are basically two positions regarding the goals of practical preparation. We can seek to develop those practical skills needed to do the job smoothly and capably on a daily basis. This he calls the *apprenticeship* approach. Alternately, we can design practical experiences to inform and "make real and vital" the two components of theoretical work—subject matter knowledge and knowledge of educational principles and theory. This second perspective he identifies as the *laboratory* view. Clearly the two perspectives are not exclusive and will interact. Nevertheless, they are clearly different, and the view that is preferred will dictate overall strategy considerably.

The apprenticeship looks backward; the laboratory looks forward. The apprentice learns from the demonstration of and exercise of "best practice." The laboratory is a setting for experimenting with new practices and essaying yet-untested proposals. The apprenticeship is tradition; the laboratory is science. The concept of apprenticeship rests on modeling after and imitating the wisdom of experience and practice, seeking to consolidate the hard-won gains of past traditions of practice. Apprenticeships are local, particular, situated. Laboratories produce more general knowledge that is portable, cosmopolitan, and broadly transferable.

After considering both sides of the distinction, Dewey favors the scientific orientation of the laboratory over the practical and traditional perspectives of the apprenticeship. This view is consistent with the preferred orientation of the research university and its commitment to skepticism, scientific experimentation, invention, discovery, and progress. He uses the rest of the essay to articulate the grounds for preferring the laboratory approach and to describe in detail the ways in which that approach would unfold in the creation of professional teacher education in research universities and in the needed reform of normal schools. The heart of his argument is drawing an analogy between teacher education and other forms of education in the professions (especially medicine). He views these more mature forms of professional education as offering support to his preference for the laboratory perspective.

The Model of Education in the Professions

In 1904, as continues to be the case in our own day, the model of education in the more prestigious professions carried considerable allure for teacher educators. So it was that, when confronted with the challenge of confronting the relation of theory to practice in education, Dewey was attracted to education in other professions as the source of a model:

> I doubt whether we, as educators, keep in mind with sufficient constancy the fact that the problem of training teachers is one species of a more generic affair—that of training for the professions. Our problem is akin to that of training architects, engineers, doctors, lawyers, etc. Moreover, since (shameful and incredible as it seems) the vocation of teaching is practically the last to recognize the need of specific professional preparation, there is all the more reason for teachers to try to find what they may learn from the more extensive and matured experience of other callings. (Dewey, 1904, p. 10)

Dewey finds three "marked tendencies" that characterize education for the more matured professions and ostensibly distinguish them from preparation for teaching:

> 1. The demand for an increased amount of scholastic attainments as a prerequisite for entering upon professional work.
> 2. Development of certain lines of work in the applied sciences and arts, as centers of professional work.
> 3. Arrangement of the practical and quasi-professional work upon the assumption that . . . the professional school does its best for its students when it gives them typical and intensive, rather than extensive and detailed, practical work. . . . This arrangement necessarily involves considerable postponement of skill in the routine and technique of the profession, until the student, after graduation, enters upon the pursuit of his calling. (Dewey, 1904, pp. 10–11)

Dewey thus focuses our attention on three program elements he imputes to more mature forms of professional education. These include increased academic prerequisites for initial entry into both the professional school and professional practice, ensuring that the future professional is a well-educated adult in his or her own right. In addition, he supports a more significant role for the relevant applied sciences in the professional curriculum itself, much as chemistry and physiology have become central to medical education. Finally, and most relevant to my analysis, he calls for greater emphasis in the practical work of the professional school on the "intellectual methods" of the profession rather than on "turning out at once masters of the craft" (Dewey, 1904, p. 11).

In this essay on theory and practice, Dewey chooses to focus on the last aspect, the deferral of extensive practical work for the sake of deeper, more scientifically oriented theoretical understanding. He offers several arguments in support of his view. The professional school has a limited amount of time to invest in its students, and it ought to use this time for those kinds of learning that it can do best. Moreover, practical skills are best learned in a true apprenticeship, when someone is indeed on the job, authentically responsible for the classroom and not simply observing or role playing. Indeed, Dewey avers, to place the emphasis on securing proficiency in the techniques of pedagogy and discipline—that is, on schoolkeeping—puts the attention in the wrong place and tends to fix it in the wrong direction.

Teachers face two central problems, claims Dewey, each of which demands the absorbed and undivided attention of the novice. One challenge is the mastery of the subject matter from the standpoint of its educational value, which to Dewey is the same thing as the mastery of educational principles and their application. Mastery of the subject matter for teaching, and of the principles of education, properly understood, is at once both the material of instruction and *the basis for* discipline and control. In contrast, novice teachers also face the challenge of *mastering the techniques* of classroom management and discipline. The mind of the student teacher cannot offer equal attention to both problems, he asserts. When the two goals compete, the attention to technical mastery is almost certain to win out over the development of an understanding of the "inner attention" of the learner, and a deeper grasp of the principles of education.

Dewey believes that prematurely plunging the student teacher into the complexities of responsibility for classroom control and management will preclude achievement of the most important objective of teacher education. Teachers must be educated and socialized to develop dispositions toward inquiry, reflection (what we might now call "metacognition"), and an orientation to direct their attention at the underlying intellectual and motivational processes of the child. When using practical experience to master classroom discipline and control, they are likely to be focused on the external behavior of the children rather than their internal, less visible processes. The teacher needs to become a classroom psychologist, to "psychologize" the subject matter and to interpret the inner mental life of the learner. Such an orientation is likely to emerge from the laboratory model of practice, not from the apprenticeship model.

The argument goes even further. Dewey worries that an apprenticeship experience would build bad pedagogical habits. Consistent with the earlier analysis, Dewey wants teachers to base their teaching on scientific principles rather than empirical ones. He wants them to distrust their own wisdom of practice, based on personal experience and that of their teaching peers, and instead to trust in the findings of scholars. He worries that teachers are far too susceptible to passing fads and lofty rhetoric. "Such persons seem to know how to teach, but are not students of teaching" (Dewey, 1904, p. 15).

Dewey's essay continues in this vein, with additional discussions of how both educational theory and subject matter should be taught to prospective teachers. He makes the persuasive (certainly to this writer) claim that, unless the teacher has learned a subject deeply and flexibly, it will be near impossible to lead students to learn it deeply themselves.

To summarize, Dewey mounts a vigorous attack on the technically oriented design of an apprenticeship model of teacher education. He associates this approach with the typical and traditional normal school, intent on producing skilled classroom managers and disciplinarians who will uncritically continue traditional practices. He instead advocates a period of at least two full postsecondary school years of deep subject matter preparation in the school subjects followed by intensive study of educational theory and its related disciplines (especially psychology). This theoretical work would be accompanied by extensive practical work, the goal of which would be to enhance and enrich the theoretical understandings. The goal of practical work in the academy would be the immediate preparation not of skilled practitioners but of reflective professionals disposed to examine their teaching and their students' learning critically. The well-trained professional, for Dewey, will mistrust learning from his own and colleagues' experience and will instead look to the scientific inquiries of the academy for guidance. The proper flow of knowledge is primarily from the academy to the field.

A Contemporary Perspective on Education in the Professions

I first introduce my own analysis of education for professional work, for I agree with Dewey that the lessons learned from the other professions can be useful ones for those of us who educate teachers. But I do not find the analysis of professional education in Dewey's 1904 essay adequate to the task.

The Argument

I begin with a discussion of both the philosophy and reality of the concepts "profession" and "professional." Given some sense of these, I will then explore what makes the education of professionals so challenging, and how the turn-of-the-century reforms of professional education were fashioned. These reforms were "in the air" during the early years of the American research university, whose founders hoped to exercise control over education in the professions. This quest would eventually be reflected in the 1910 Bulletin No. 4 of The Carnegie Foundation for the Advancement of Teaching, known more generally as the "Flexner Report" on medical education (Flexner, 1910). These perspectives already influenced John Dewey in 1904 when he wrote about the connections between theory and practice in education. (Indeed, since Dewey characterizes the pedagogical choices created by the "new professional education" as the choice between "the apprenticeship" and "the laboratory," it is noteworthy that six years later, Abraham Flexner begins his critique of American medical education with the observation that the American medical school "began soundly as a supplement to the apprenticeship system still in vogue during the seventeenth and eighteenth centuries" [Flexner, 1910, p. 1].)

I then explore the kinds of philosophies and pedagogies that have developed to respond to the challenges of professional learning and how these ideas might look if we were to employ them to address the problems of teacher education. I focus most particularly on the respective functions of theory, practice, and their connections; to conceptions of "science" and its relevance to the improvement of practice; to the relative roles of the academy and the field; to the prevailing theory of how new knowledge and wisdom develop in a profession; and to the resulting image of the ideal forms of education for the professions generally and for teaching in particular.

Features of a Profession

The idea of a "profession" describes a special set of circumstances for deep understanding, complex practice, ethical conduct, and higher-order learning, circumstances that define the complexity of the enterprise and explain the difficulties of prescribing both policies and curriculum in this area. What do we mean by a profession, and what is so hard about preparing people for professions? Let us begin with a recent discussion of the "ideology" of "profession":

> As an ideology, professionalism had both a technical and a moral aspect. Technically, it promised competent performance of skilled work involving the application of broad and complex knowledge, the acquisition of which required formal academic study. Morally, it promised to be guided by an appreciation of the important social ends it served. In demanding high levels of self-governance, professionals claimed not only that others were not technically *equipped* to judge them, but that they also could not be *trusted* to judge them. The idea was expressed in classic form by R. H. Tawney: "[Professionals] may, as in the case of the successful doctor, grow rich; but the meaning of their profession, both for themselves and for the public, is not that they make money, but that they make health or safety or knowledge or good government or good law. . . . [Professions uphold] as the criterion of success the end for which the profession, whatever it may be, is carried on, and [subordinate] the inclination, appetites, and ambition of individuals to the rules of an organization which has as its object to promote performance of function." These functions for Tawney and for many other advocates of the professions, were activities that embodied and expressed the idea of larger social purposes. (Brint, 1994, p. 7)

This account bears family resemblance to many other characterizations of the ideal concept of a "profession." There are, in principle and at the very least, six characteristics of a profession that set the terms for the challenge of educating professionals. I believe that these are universal features that are traditionally associated with the idea of a profession and that define the unavoidable dilemmas of professional education.

All professions are characterized by the following attributes:

- the obligations of *service* to others, as in a "calling";
- *understanding* of a scholarly or theoretical kind;
- a domain of skilled performance or *practice;*
- the exercise of *judgment* under conditions of unavoidable uncertainty;
- the need for *learning from experience* as theory and practice interact; and
- a professional *community* to monitor quality and aggregate knowledge.

These attributes are as relevant to designing the pedagogies of the professions as they are to understanding their organization and functions. I shall now discuss each of these attributes in turn.

Service: The Moral and Ethical Ideal

First, the goal of a profession is *service:* the pursuit of important social ends. Professionals are those who are educated to serve others using bodies of knowledge and skill not readily available to the man or woman in the street. This means that practitioners of professions must develop *moral understanding* to aim and guide their practice. The ultimate rationale for their work is, in Tawney's words, "that they make health or safety or knowledge or good government or good law" (Brint, 1994, p. 7). They are obliged to employ their technical skills and theoretical knowledge in a matrix of moral understanding. The starting point for professional preparation is the premise that the aims of professionalism involve social purposes and responsibilities that are both technically and morally grounded. The core meaning of a profession is the organized practice of complex knowledge and skills in the service of others. The professional educator's challenge is to help future professionals develop and shape a robust moral vision that will guide their practice and provide a prism of justice, responsibility, and virtue through which to reflect on their actions. Medicine's Hippocratic Oath, therefore, is a central manifestation of the moral foundations of a profession.

In most professions, however, with the possible exception of the preparation of clergy, the moral dimension remains in the background. The demands of learning the necessary research and theories, as well as becoming technically adept in the many skills and practices, tend to subordinate the service dimensions. It is noteworthy that when business schools, law schools, or medical schools receive grants to initiate or strengthen programs in professional ethics, the event is so remarkable that it becomes front-page news.

Theory: The Functions of Research and the Role of the Academy

A profession is always a form of highly complex and skilled practice. But what makes it a profession is not the complexity of skills alone. A profession is a practice whose agents claim is rooted in bodies of knowledge that are created, tested, elaborated, refuted, transformed, and reconstituted in colleges, universities, laboratories, and libraries. To call something a profession is to claim that it has a knowledge base in the academy broadly construed. Professions legitimate their work by reference to research and *theories*. Therefore, professions change their practices not only because rules of practice, circumstances, or policies change but because the process of knowledge growth, criticism, and development in the academy leads to the achievement of new understandings, new perspectives, or new ways of interpreting the world.

The notion that formal professional knowledge is rooted in an academic knowledge base creates the conditions for the essential pedagogical problem of professional education. This problem is the relation between theory and practice. The recurrent challenge of all professional learning is negotiating the inescapable tension between theory and practice. That is, in nearly every form of professional education, students perceive the practicum experiences as truly valuable, while barely tolerating the academic experiences. It is perfectly clear to both the students and laypersons how a clinical internship, a student-teaching experience, or a student pulpit are relevant to preparing the new physician, teacher, or minister. It is the more theoretical preparation in cell biology, developmental psychology, or the interpretation of Augustine's writings that often appear of dubious value.

The role of theory is problematic for at least two reasons. Theory achieves its power through simplification and narrowing of a field of study. In that sense, theories deal with the world in general, for the most part treating variations as error and randomness as noise. Similarly, the research that informs theory is often conducted under controlled or otherwise artificial conditions, whose connections to the everyday world of practice are tenuous. A second characteristic of theories is that they generally operate within discrete disciplines, in contrast to practical problems, which typically cross disciplinary boundaries. Theories are extraordinarily powerful, which is why they are the treasure of the academy and should be valued by the professions; they are also frequently so remote from the particular conditions of professional practice that the novice professional-in-training rarely appreciates their contributions.

Any reader who has been educated for one of the professions—say, in the two with which I am most familiar, medical education or teacher preparation—will immediately recognize the theory-practice problem. My University of Chicago teacher Joseph Schwab devoted most of the last 20 years of his career to the problems of practical knowledge and its relations to theory. One need only try to connect the Krebs cycle with the intricacies of a particular clinical diagnosis, or the loop of Henle with some specific aspect of kidney failure, to appreciate the problem. As a teacher educator, I have tried to help students see how one traverses the gap between Piaget's developmental theory and what to teach on Monday morning or between Vygotsky's zones of proximal development and the pedagogical potential of groundwork. We who have tried to educate future professionals understand the challenge that is created when one's starting point for an education in a learned profession is immersion in vast bodies of academic knowledge. We prepare professionals in universities because we make the strong claim that these are *learned* professions and that academic knowledge is absolutely essential to their performance.

Now, this may be, in spite of Dewey's assumptions and argument, a false claim. It may well be that academic knowledge is essential only as an *entitlement* to practice and is not functionally necessary for practice. My point is that the claim of rootedness in a theoretical, empirical, and/or normative knowledge base is central to all of the professions. The view (shared by both Dewey and Flexner) that a liberal education of some sort is a prerequisite for the study of medicine, law, teaching, and other professions sets an interesting problem for professional education: How does one define the foundational basic sciences for understanding and practicing a profession? What are the liberal arts and sciences per se whose grasp would identify an individual as "educated" or "learned" and therefore entitled to pursue a learned profession?

Practice: The Skills and Strategies of the Profession

Although a significant portion of the knowledge base of a profession is grown by scholars in the academy, it is not *professional* knowledge unless and until it is enacted in the crucible of the "field." Professions are ultimately about *practice.* The field of practice is the place where professions do their work, and claims for knowledge must pass the ultimate test of value in practice. While the theoretical is the foundation for the entitlement to practice, professional practice itself is the end to which all the knowledge is directed. This is why in all professional preparation we find some conception of a supervised clinical experience. Student teaching, medical residencies, architects' apprenticeships, student nursing, all are examples of carefully designed pedagogies to afford eased entry into practice accompanied by intensive supervision, to ensure the acquisition of needed skills and the demonstration of appropriate behavior, manner, and values. In medicine, the periods of internship, residency, and fellowship typically extend for many years after completion of formal professional preparation in the medical school. By contrast, student teaching internships rarely last more than six to nine months. In further contrast, one of the features of preparation in the law is that legal educators have somehow managed to avoid the responsibility to introduce a serious clinical component into legal education, expecting the employing law firm to assume that burden.

The apprenticeship, the practice, and the application that goes on in the field not only is a nearly universal element of professional learning, but typically once the professionals reach the field of practice, they look back on the theoretical preparation and begin to devalue it. We thus see the universal features of professional education—a strong emphasis on service but without much classroom work, substantial theoretical preparation with uncertain connections to everyday practice, and formal practicum experiences through varieties of supervised field experience, whether directly under the supervision of the university-based educators or in some loose connection to the academy. As observed above, the tensions between the theoretical and practical elements of the education are nearly always palpable.

One of the sources of those tensions is the conflict between standards and conceptions of practice affirmed in the academy and those typically manifested in the field. Theoretical preparation, in spite of the legendary conservatism of higher education, tends to be more radical and reform oriented than is the general tenor of practice itself. Indeed, academicians often see themselves as the critical conscience of professional practice, taking on themselves the responsibility for criticizing current practice and developing a vision for the future. It is not at all unusual for university-based professional educators to hold quite different conceptions of good practice than do field-based professionals. And it is, again, almost universally the case in professional preparation that the students arrive at their clinical experiences only to hear the nursing supervisor, or the veteran teacher in the fifth grade where they are student teaching, or the chief of clinical services in the hospital admonish them to forget all the nonsense they were taught at the university because now they will learn the way it is really done. Thus, counterintuitively, the ostensibly conservative academy is the source of radical ideas. The field is where you encounter the elastic cord that pulls matters back to the conservation of extant habits of practice. This kind of tension is endemic in all forms of professional education.

Judgment Under Uncertainty

In spite of the importance of both theory and practice, professions are not simply conduits for taking knowledge from the academy and applying it to the field. The process of judgment intervenes between knowledge and application. Human judgment creates bridges between the universal terms of theory and the gritty particularities of situated practice. And human judgment always incorporates both technical and moral elements, negotiating between the general and the specific, as well as between the ideal and the feasible.

To the extent that the academy addresses problems of practice at all, it necessarily presents them as *prototypes,* simplified and schematized theoretical representations of the much messier and variable particulars of everyday life. When student professionals move out to the fields of practice, they find inevitably that nothing in the real world precisely fits the prototypes. The responsibility of the developing professional is not simply to apply what he or she has learned to practice but to transform, adapt, merge and synthesize, criticize, and invent in order to move from the theoretical and research-based knowledge of the academy to the kind of practical clinical knowledge needed to engage in professional work.

As I observed earlier, one of the reasons that judgment is such an essential component of clinical work is because theoretical knowledge is generally knowledge of what is true universally. It is true in general and for the most part. It is knowledge of regularities and of patterns. It is an invaluable simplification of a world whose many variations would be far too burdensome to store in memory with all its detail and individuality. Yet the world of practice is beset by just those particularities, born of the workings of chance. To put it in Aristotelian terms, theories are about *essence,* practice is about *accident,* and the only way to get from there to here is via the exercise of *judgment.*

Learning from Experience

Up to this point, my analysis has treated primarily the movement of knowledge from the academy to the field, whether directly or as mediated via professional judgment. However, the most formidable challenge for anyone in a profession is not applying new theoretical knowledge but learning from experience. While an academic knowledge base may be necessary for professional work, it is far from sufficient. Therefore, members of professions have to develop the capacity to learn from the experience and contemplation of their own practice. This is not only true for individual professionals; it is equally true for the entire professional community of practice. Lessons of practice learned from experience must have a way of getting back to the broad community of practitioners so all can profit from one another's experiences. Lessons of practice must also find their ways back to the academy to inform, as well as to problematize, knowledge development in the academy itself.

Dewey (1910/1951) subsequently observed in his classic essay on the influence of Darwinism on philosophy that chance, error, and accidents present both the sciences and the fields of practice with their most fascinating puzzles. The great challenge for professional learning is that *experience* occurs where design and intention collide with chance. Without the violation of expectations, it is impossible to learn from experience. Learning from experience, therefore, requires both the systematic, prototype-centered, theoretical knowledge characteristic of the academy and the more fluid, reactive, prudential reasoning characteristic of practice. The professional must learn how to cope with those unpredictable matters and how to reflect on her own actions. Professionals incorporate the consequences of those actions into their own growing knowledge base, which ultimately includes unique combinations of theoretical and moral principles, practical maxims, and a growing collection of narratives of experience.

In comparing John Dewey and George Herbert Mead with Jane Addams, all of whom were good friends in Chicago in the first five years of this century, Ellen Lagemann (1988) observed that, for Dewey and Mead, the tools of their trade were the scientific hypothesis and the investigation; for Addams, it was the anecdote and the biography. In professional practice, hypothesis rapidly gives way to narrative. Jane Addams's Hull House was the setting in which the academic perspectives of Dewey and Mead were brought into collaborative contact with the truly professional practice embodied by Addams and the settlement house movement. The ideals of service clearly dominated the thinking of those who were inventing the professions of social work and community development, but the desire to ground those practices in the academic disciplines of social philosophy, sociology, and a professional school of social service administration were already a serious challenge.

In Bruner's (1986) terms, in these situations the paradigmatic way of knowing, characteristic of science, shares space with the narrative modes, more characteristic of the wisdom of practice. When we seek a pedagogy that can reside between the universal principles of theory and the narratives of lived practice, we invent approaches—such as the varieties of case methods—capable of capturing experience for subsequent analysis and review. We render individual experiential learning into "community property" when we transform those lessons from personal experience into a literature of shared narratives. Such connections between theoretical principles and practical narratives, between the universal and the accidental, forge professional knowledge. Such knowledge cannot be developed and sustained adequately by individuals experiencing and reflecting in isolation, however. No professional can function well in isolation. Professionals require membership in a community.

Professions as Learning and Monitoring Communities

Finally, professions are inherently public and communal. We speak of someone not only *being a professional,* but being a *member of a profession.* Professional knowledge is somehow held by a community of professionals who not only know collectively more than any individual member of the community but also maintain certain public responsibilities and accountabilities with respect to individual practice. Thus professionals operate within their particular communities under privileges granted by the broader society. Such autonomy and privilege is granted when the profession is viewed as holding specialized knowledge whose warrant only its own members can evaluate and when its members are *trusted* to take ethical responsibility for such evaluation.

Although individual professionals carry the responsibility for practice, the assumption is that they are members of a community that defines and regulates the standards for that practice and that as a community, knows more than any individual practitioner. The public can turn to the professional community when questions of the quality of practice are at stake. From the perspective of professional pedagogy, however, the community of practice plays a critical role. The academic discipline serves the academy as a learning community whose invisible college ensures that knowledge gained is vetted for its warrant through peer review and then distributed among members of the community through journals and other forms of scholarly communication. The community of practice for a profession plays a similar role with regard to learning from experience, accumulating and critiquing the lessons gained and subsequently codified, and in general helping practitioners overcome the limitations of individual practice and individual experience. Without a community of practice, individual professionals would be trapped in a solipsistic universe in which only their own experiences were potentially educative. By creating and fostering the work of communities of practice, individual experience becomes communal, distributed expertise can be shared, and standards of practice can evolve.

I have argued in this section that a comprehensive view of the concept of "profession" must take account of six universal features of professions: service, theory, practice, judgment, learning from experience, and community. I have further argued that each of these attributes sets a challenge for the pedagogies of the professions (e.g., How does one instill personal values of service and altruism? How is an understanding of theory best acquired? What kinds of experiences and supervision are most likely to sharpen the capacity for reasoned practical judgment in the face of uncertainty?). Moreover, I have also suggested that some of these attributes compete for attention and emphasis within the curriculum of the professions. Thus, theory competes with practice, and an emphasis on values often is at odds with the acquisition of technical proficiency. Dewey's essay is an early attempt to formulate some of these issues and to offer a resolution, with particular reference to the education of teachers. I shall now turn to a brief concluding section that reflects on Dewey's views, in the light of his own era and from the perspective of our own.

Theory, Practice, and Professional Education

Dewey's Era

The central feature of all professional education is indeed the tense relationship between theory and practice. It is an essential tension, as unavoidable as the tensions found within families whose members have become highly dependent on one another. It is a painful tension because theory and practice are not only competing conceptions. Different stakeholders in the social and political worlds exercise control over these domains, and any preferences given to theory over practice, or to conceptual mastery over technical proficiency, for example, will have serious consequences for the future of institutions, the allocation of scarce resources, and the conferral of valued prestige.

In the context of this tension, Dewey argued that theory and intellectual mastery must take a certain precedence in the preparation of professionals. Not only must theory be taught directly, vigorously, and extensively. It must serve as the rationale for the teaching of practice. Therefore, those responsible for theory and its development should also control the conditions of practice. Dewey was writing in the first decade of the twentieth century, a time when the struggle over control of education in the professions was becoming particularly hot. The traditional normal schools represented a segment of the world of postsecondary education—free-standing schools of professional preparation similar to proprietary medical schools, law schools, schools of nursing, and so on—that was in serious conflict with the universities over just such issues.

Dewey's writings reflect his times and anticipate the subsequent writings of the famous critic and reformer of medical education, Abraham Flexner. When in 1908 Henry Pritchett, the first president of The Carnegie Foundation for the Advancement of Teaching, commissioned the retired schoolmaster Abraham Flexner to conduct a study of American medical education, the Foundation was hardly dispassionate about the likely consequences of the report. The Foundation was quite new, having been established in 1905, but its board represented *the* establishment in American higher education. Pritchett himself had been president of the Massachusetts Institute of Technology. Other board members included Woodrow Wilson of Princeton, Charles W. Eliot of Harvard, William Rainey Harper of Chicago, David Starr Jordan of Stanford, and the same Nicholas Murray Butler of Columbia who had chaired the National Society for the Scientific Study of Education board and lured Dewey to his institution. These were institutions that saw the creation and preservation of research and of theoretical knowledge as their special preserve. Science was emerging as the dominant force in the universe of knowledge, and science was housed in institutions like theirs. If the professions were to be appropriately grounded in the most solid firmament of knowledge and its discovery, then the education of professionals ought necessarily to be the province of the universities (see Lagemann, 1983).

When he began the design and implementation of his study of the medical schools of the United States and Canada, Flexner encountered a distributed system of medical education dominated by apprenticeships, relatively unenlightened in its practice or its professional education by the powers of science, and often unconnected to the traditional institutions of postsecondary education, colleges and universities. Small, independent medical schools flourished. These included not only local proprietary schools but also independent institutions designed to prepare women and

African Americans for medical careers. Flexner strongly believed that the emerging research universities, where science was flourishing, needed to be given greater control over medical education, both by increasing the academic prerequisites to practice and by requiring that medical judgment be justified by science rather than by practical precedent. For Flexner, Johns Hopkins was the prototype of the university-based, research university home for a medical school. Its curriculum, resting solidly on courses in the basic natural sciences, exemplified these principles. This was a conception of professional preparation that harmonized beautifully with the views expressed by Dewey in his essay in teacher education.

Within a decade of the Flexner Report's publication in 1910, nearly half of America's extant medical schools had closed (including, alas, all but one of those dedicated to the education of women and all but two of those educating African Americans). The "Flexner Curriculum" had taken shape and would continue to dominate American medical education until the present day: an undergraduate degree in the sciences, followed by four years of "undergraduate medical education" consisting of two more years of basic science and then two years of clinical medical rotations, followed by one or more years of supervised internship and residency. Premedical education and undergraduate medical education were always under the aegis of a university. Most of the particularly prestigious approved internships and residencies were also undertaken at university-based or university-affiliated "teaching hospitals." Consistent with Dewey's views of professional education, though not necessarily influenced directly by them, medical education was heavy on an initial immersion in theory and in science, with practical work deferred until after the science had been learned. Becoming a skilled practitioner was a goal of the clerkships and internships, not a priority of the earlier years of study.

Although Dewey writes of this approach in 1904 as if it were already canonical for professional education, the organization, structure, and institutional locations for professional education would remain contested terrain for many years. Ironically, the "revolutionary" Flexner curriculum would ultimately be perceived as a conservative barrier to later proposed reforms in medical education, which often cited John Dewey as their inspiration for more problem-based, field-centered, and practice-intensive approaches to the education of physicians.

This leads to another important observation. Dewey understood that, although theory had a certain priority for the education of teachers, it would be deadly if the theory were taught absent immersion in contexts and conditions of practice. He therefore advocated a special kind of professional education, in which a curriculum of theory-in-practice dedicated to the understanding of theory-for-practice was at its heart. Theory was paramount, he asserted, yet it could not be understood in a purely academic setting. This insight was important, not only for Dewey's conception of education for the professions, but ultimately for his pragmatic conception of theory and its relations to practice in general.

Thus, Joseph Schwab observes in his 1959 essay, "The 'Impossible' Role of the Teacher in Progressive Education" (coincidentally written for another Chicago publication, *School Review*, in a volume commemorating the centennial of Dewey's birth):

> For Dewey, any theory of practice, including his, finds its full meaning only as it is put into practice and gains its verification only as it is tested there. A theory includes a body of logical forms, conceptions designed to embrace and relate to one another all the facts in a problematic situation which are seen as relevant to its resolution. These logical forms take part of their meaning from the facts they are designed to hold, and another part from what they do to the facts by way of making them signify actions to be taken. Hence, the theory cannot be understood until the facts are experienced in the form given them by the organizing conceptions of the theory; and experienced means that they must be seen and felt and that the actions they signify must be undertaken.
>
> Further, the theory is verified only by such an undertaking, for a theory is good to the extent that it does take account of all the pregnant facts and leads to actions which resolve the problem to the satisfaction of those who are caught up in it. . . . Now, it must be remembered that this view of knowledge plays two roles. In part it is the conception of education which Dewey hopes to convey. At the same time, it represents to him the way it must be conveyed. Remember too, that it is a wholly novel view of meaning and of truth. To this day, it remains far from being generally understood. . . . Dewey seeks to persuade men to teach a mode of learning and knowing which they themselves do not know and which they cannot grasp by their habitual ways of learning. (Schwab, 1959, pp. 168–170)

Practice serves as a major vehicle for testing the validity and efficacy of theory, both for learning a profession and for developing theories more generally. Practice is a significant source of the evidence on which new theory development can be based. Learning from practical experiences is the major contributor to creating and testing theories of practice, which are the defining constructs of professional knowledge and learning.

There is an impressive, if somewhat ironic, confluence between these Deweyan ideas and major developments in the theories of learning and cognition that have emerged in the field of cognitive science. Cognitive scientists have become increasingly interested in the very idea that Dewey dismissed in his 1904 analysis, the idea of *apprenticeship*. They have shown a renewed interest and respect for the apparent educational potency of traditional apprenticeships. In these apprenticeships, "unschooled" children and adults can apparently learn complex forms of reasoning, understanding, and practice that are very difficult for formal educational institutions to teach. What kinds of learning do apprenticeships foster? How are they different from those typically pursued in formal education, both in schools and colleges?

Reflecting Dewey's basic ideas, if not his language, the notion of a "cognitive apprenticeship" has taken hold. This view of learning asserts that in academic settings theoretical knowledge is separated from practical applications and complex processes are taught far from the situations in which they can be used. An effective apprenticeship, whether for a midwife or a gambler, teaches the practical, judgmental, and situated intellectual work that characterizes traditional crafts and occupations with the reflective and elaborative mechanisms that characterize higher-order thinking. It achieves these daunting goals by embedding the learning in the social context of practice, permitting the apprentice to move from observation to limited participation to full responsibility slowly and with serious modeling and supervision. Thus, ironically, the most significant corroboration of Dewey's conception of education has taken place through respectful contemplation of a form of learning that he denigrated. He had preferred the laboratory to the apprenticeship.

Nevertheless, Dewey had espoused an intermediate position: he argued that only theoretical learning *situated in practice* would be rich and meaningful, even though he continued to privilege the theory side of the distinction. He was far less clear on the indispensable role of practice as a source for new theory and on the importance of learning from experience as the key element in practitioners' capacities to increase the wisdom of their practice. That is, Dewey appears to believe that the most important source for new practical knowledge would remain research and theory conducted in the academy. He anticipated that in teaching, as in medicine, the flow of new ideas would be from university laboratories (or laboratory schools) and their professional schools to the communities of practice.

Why would Dewey, the great champion of experience as a source for *student* learning, be so blind to the experiences of school teachers as the sources for teacher learning and, indeed, for learning on the part of academic scholars of education? I suspect that there are several explanations. First, Dewey's entire philosophy rested on a belief that the methods of science could be brought to bear fruitfully on the workings of society. Science flourished, was nurtured, and grew in the halls of the academy. With special laboratory schools in which educational and psychological scientists could pursue their inquiries, a science of education would do for teaching what the biological sciences were doing for medicine.

Second, in spite of his admiration for Jane Addams, Dewey may have tacitly shared with many of his generation a sense that the women in the classroom needed to be directed by the men in the principal's office and the male scientists in the university. Although probably an "anticipatory feminist" in many ways, the prevailing views of gender roles would have the technical functions of classroom teaching carried out primarily by normal-school educated women while the scientific activity remained in the hands of university men. Granted, Dewey argued that the theoretical preparation of teachers was intended to render them more critical, skeptical, and watchful of those groundless fads and fashions that sweep over the schools. He wanted teachers to understand the principles of educational science and to apply them critically to their work with curriculum and with their youngsters. But they were to *apply* science, they were not to do science (see Lagemann, 1988).

We now would place much greater emphasis on the importance of the communities of practice creating new networks, institutions, and capacities to learn from individual and collective experience. In teaching, we are observing the growth of groups like the National Writing Project, the National Board for Professional Teaching Standards, and a variety of collaboratives that encourage teachers to conduct inquiries in their classrooms and share their findings and insights with one another. Professional development schools have been designed as sites for collaborative inquiry into teaching and learning, as well as new versions of the old "practice schools" of the normal school era. Much more academic research is conducted in classrooms with teachers as active partners and even authors. Teacher-written cases of practice have become legitimate components of educational research. Taken together, these practice-centered sources of wisdom are becoming at least as important as the investigations of psychological science in guiding the work of educators.

Finally, Dewey was apparently far more impressed by the apparent success of the "more matured" professional schools than was warranted. He was appropriately impressed with their heavy emphasis on the prerequisites of the liberal arts and on their commitment to theory and research as the scientific basis for their practice. He failed to see the extent to which much of that emphasis had little to do with the improvement of professional practice and far more with buttressing the control of the prestigious and powerful world of professional education by the newly emerging research universities. While he was certainly justified in valuing a more rigorous, skeptical, and investigation-based foundation for the professions, he gave inadequate attention to the need to nurture such activities and perspectives within the communities of professionals themselves.

A New Era for Professional Education

We may now be seeing an emergent new view of education in the professions, and of teacher education. These emergent ideas connect to each of the commonplaces of professional learning: moral vision, theoretical understanding, practical skills, the centrality of judgment, learning from experience, and the development of responsible professional communities.

We see renewed interest in the moral and character aspects of the professions. Although the moral foundations for professionalism had been acknowledged for generations, the achievement of moral ends was rarely seen as a focus of the professional curriculum. Skepticism regarding the Flexner curriculum has led to experiments with new models of professional education, which take the acquisition of practical skills and immersion in practical situations as necessary conditions for theoretical understanding. Early clinical experiences are now commonplace.

There is increased emphasis on the importance of those pedagogies that foster the combining of theory and practice in local, situated judgments. The continued and growing interest in case methods in business, law, education, and medicine reflects that emphasis. A case resides in the territory between theory and practice, between idea and experience, between the normative ideal and achievable real. Cases capture pieces of experience that initially existed solely within the life of a single individual, and they transform that solitary experience into text. Members of a larger group, all of whom are trying to make sense of the practice that the text documents and preserves, can share cases as texts. As pedagogical devices, cases confront novice professionals with highly situated problems that draw together theory and practice in the moral sea of decisions to be made, actions to be taken. Options are rarely clean; judgments must be rendered.

Cases are ways of parsing experience so practitioners can examine and learn from it. Case methods thus become strategies for helping professionals to "chunk" their experience into units that can become the focus for reflective practice. Cases therefore can become the basis for individual professional learning as well as a forum within which communities of professionals, both local and extended, as members of visible and invisible colleges, can store, exchange, and organize their experiences. They may well become, for teacher education, the lingua franca of teacher learning communities.

In his 1904 essay, John Dewey explored a set of problems that continue to beset professional education to this day. Science has flourished beyond the wildest dreams of anyone living a century ago. But the problems of education remain as challenging as ever. Dewey recognized that the solutions to these problems might lie in novel ways to think about the connections between theory and practice. Many of his insights were remarkably prescient. Yet we continue to struggle with the problems he formulated.

REFERENCES

Brint, S. (1994). *In an age of experts: The changing role of professionals in politics and public life.* Chicago: University of Chicago Press.

Bruner, J. S. (1986). *Actual minds, possible worlds.* Cambridge, MA: Harvard University Press.

Dewey, J. (1904). The relation of theory to practice in education. In *The third yearbook of the National Society for the Scientific Study of Education: Part I: The relation of theory to practice in the education of teachers* (pp. 9–30). Chicago: University of Chicago Press.

Dewey, J. (1951). The influence of Darwin on philosophy, and other essays in contemporary thought. New York: P. Smith. (Original work published 1910).

Dunkel, H. (1970). *Herbart and Herbartianism.* Chicago: University of Chicago Press.

Flexner, A. (1910). *Medical education in the United States and Canada.* Carnegie Foundation for the Advancement of Teaching (Bulletin No. 4). Menlo Park, CA: Carnegie Foundation.

Lagemann, E. C. (1983). *Private power for the public good.* Middletown, CT: Wesleyan University Press.

Lagemann, E. C. (1988). The plural worlds of educational research. *History of Education Quarterly,* 29, 184–214.

Schwab, J. J. (1959). The "impossible" role of the teacher in progressive education. *School Review,* 67, 139–159.

INTRODUCTION

PROFESSING THE LIBERAL ARTS (1997)

THE CAMPUS COMPACT, a consortium (headquartered at Brown University) of about 600 colleges and universities across the country, which have a strong commitment to service learning, invited Shulman to give a talk at a conference that was held at Stanford University. The title of the original talk was "Service Learning: The Missing Clinical Component in Liberal Education," and in it, Shulman began working out his argument that liberal education needed a clinical component similar to internships in the professions. Service learning could be conceptualized as that clinical component, and as such, a critical component in the liberal education of a citizen in a democracy.

The Campus Compact circulated the talk among its constituents, and when The College Board decided to host a conference in memory of Dewey's contributions to education, someone remembered the talk and suggested that Shulman give it again in that context. Reviewing the manuscript, Shulman decided to strengthen his argument, using the models of the professions to indict the liberal arts.

He begins the essay by making the radical claim that liberal education is not endangered by a push toward vocationalism and professionalism; rather, liberal education is not professional enough. He argues that, in order to sustain liberal education, we must "profess" the liberal arts. In order to make this argument, Shulman first lays out a set of features that characterize professions, building upon the work of Steven Brint. These include an obligation to serve, deep knowledge and understanding, a practice, professional judgment, learning from experience, and community membership. He elaborates on these by laying out a set of challenges inherent in professional education given these characteristics.

Shulman then posits that there are three central challenges faced in liberal learning: the loss of learning, illusory learning, and the uselessness of learning that comes of ideas being inert. "What pedagogical strategies might we use in liberal education to confront these challenges?" Shulman asks. Drawing on the lessons he learned while working on the Communities of Learners Project, Shulman suggests that students need to be actively engaged in their own learning, they need to collaborate with others in that learning, they need to reflect on what they are learning, and they need to have a passion for what they are learning. Service learning is a pedagogy that serves these ends. He then goes on to argue that if undergraduates were engaged in service learning projects that they then had to write cases about, we might begin to both achieve the "moral ends of service" and "overcome the challenges of liberal learning": "Through service, through application, through rendering their learning far more active, reflective, and collaborative, students would actually learn more liberally, understand what they have learned more deeply, and develop the capacity to use what they have learned in the service of their communities."

23

PROFESSING THE LIBERAL ARTS

ONE OF THE PREVAILING THEMES of this volume is the presumed tension between the *liberal* and the *pragmatic.* These strains are often associated with a distrust of "the vocational" or "the professional" among liberal arts faculty and administrators, who view these orientations as slippery slopes down which unsuspecting educators might slide into a horrific purgatory. Liberal learning, we are warned, is pursued for its own sake, and cannot be subordinated to the aims of application or vocation. I come to offer a shocking alternative view. I wish to argue that the problem with the liberal arts is not that they are endangered by the corruption of professionalism. Indeed, their problem is that they are not professional enough. If we are to preserve and sustain liberal education, we must make it more professional; we must learn to *profess the liberal arts.*

I offer this heresy as a peculiar hybrid of two ostensibly incompatible traditions. I am a graduate of the College of the University of Chicago which ought to identify me as a devotee of the purest form of liberal education, the Hutchins orientation toward the great books, the traditional canon itself. And I view my education in the Hutchins College as the most precious gift I have ever received. However, I am also a student of Joseph Schwab, the Chicago biologist and philosopher who was one of John Dewey's strongest advocates and spokespersons in higher education, even though he was also seen as a protégé of Hutchins. Many educators whom I respect deeply, such as Tom Ehrlich, point out that the Hutchins and Dewey views of liberal education are inherently incompatible. Yet I would claim, without embarrassment, that I define myself as a legitimate offspring of that liaison between Dewey and Hutchins and I feel unusually blessed to be progeny of that unlikely coupling.

I am reminded of David Hume's clever characterization of abstract ideas such as "cause" or "external existence," which he claimed were illegitimate logical constructs because they lacked direct empirical sources. How was it possible that the human knower could be so confident that he could use concepts such as "cause" even though they were not adequately connected to experience? Hume dubbed such concepts "bastards of imagination impregnated by experience." These abstract ideas were the illegitimate offspring of a liaison between imagination and experience, but could claim no legitimate epistemological standing. In that spirit, I come to you as a bastard of Deweyan progressivism impregnated by the Hutchins College. I am the illegitimate issue of an illicit liaison between two incompatible philosophies. As with most other bastards, I not only insist that I can live my life without being crippled by an ancestry, I claim that this merger of perspectives offers an unusually fruitful perspective.

I am also, I must confess, someone who does not spend most of his time engaged with the liberal education of undergraduates. I've actually spent most of my career of more than 30 years actively engaged in the education of two distinct groups of professionals called school teachers and physicians. I have designed new programs for the education of these professionals. I have taught in these programs. I have conducted empirical research on the processes and outcomes of such professional education. I have attempted to develop theories of learning and of action that explain how such professionals learn and how they organize and use their knowledge and skill. I am, in both senses of that ambiguous phrase, a "professional educator." Education is my profession and the education of professionals is my area of inquiry.

I come to challenge you, therefore, with these questions. What if all those who fear the corruption of liberal education by professionalism and vocationalization have got it wrong? What if the problem of liberal education is that it isn't professional or vocational enough? If, indeed, we were to professionalize liberal education, might we not only give it an end, a purpose in practice, and in application and in human service, and instead of thereby diluting and corrupting it, might we even make it more liberal? I hope you will find that a provocative conjecture.

The Challenges of Professional Learning

Features of a Profession

I am prepared to argue that the idea of a "profession" describes a special and unique set of circumstances for deep understanding, complex practice, ethical conduct, and higher-order learning, circumstances that define the complexity of the enterprise and explain the difficulties of prescribing both policies and curriculum in this area. What do we mean by a *profession* and what is so hard about preparing people for professions? Let us begin with a recent definition:

> As an ideology, professionalism had both a technical and a moral aspect. Technically, it promised competent performance of skilled work involving the application of broad and complex knowledge, the acquisition of which required formal academic study. Morally, it promised to be guided by an appreciation of the important social ends it served. In demanding high levels of self-governance, professionals claimed not only that others were not technically *equipped* to judge them, but that they also could not be *trusted* to judge them. The idea was expressed in classic form by R. H. Tawney: "[Professionals] may, as in the case of the successful doctor, grow rich; but the meaning of their profession, both for themselves and for the public, is not that they make money, but that they make health or safety or knowledge or good government or good law. . . . [Professions uphold] as the criterion of success the end for which the profession, whatever it may be, is carried on, and [subordinate] the inclination, appetites, and ambition of individuals to the rules of an organization which has as its object to promote performance of function." These functions for Tawney and for many other advocates of the professions, were activities that embodied and expressed the idea of larger social purposes.[1]

Steven Brint's characterization of professions is consistent with many others. From this account, I will claim that there are, at the very least, six characteristics of professional learning that set the terms for the challenge of preparing people to "profess." These characteristics are 1) service, 2) understanding, 3) practice, 4) judgment, 5) learning, and 6) community.

- First, the goal of a profession is *service;* the pursuit of important social ends. Professionals are those who are educated to serve others using bodies of knowledge and skill not readily available to the man or woman in the street. This means that, fundamentally, a mature professional or someone learning a profession must develop *moral understanding* to aim and guide their practice. The ultimate rationale for their work is, in Tawney's words, "that they make health or safety or knowledge or good government or good law." They must develop both technical and moral understanding.
- Second, a profession is a practice rooted in bodies of knowledge that are created, tested, elaborated, refuted, transformed, and reconstituted in colleges, universities, laboratories, libraries, and

museums. To call something a profession is to claim that it has a knowledge base in the academy broadly construed. It has research and *theories*. Therefore, professions change not only because rules of practice change, or circumstances change, or policies change, but because the process of knowledge growth, criticism, and development in the academy leads to the achievement of new understandings, new perspectives, or new ways of interpreting the world.

- Third, although a significant portion of the knowledge base of a profession is generated by scholars in the academy, it is not professional knowledge unless and until it is enacted in the crucible of "the field." The field of *practice* is the place where professions do their work, and claims for knowledge must pass the ultimate test of value in practice. Thus, the arenas for theory and practice in a profession are quite disparate, and this constitutes one of the defining problems for professional education. There is always a wide and troublesome gap between theory and practice.
- Fourth, professions are nevertheless not simply conduits for taking knowledge from the academy and applying it to the field. If that were all that were necessary, professions would not be as complex, interesting, and respected as they are. What intervenes between knowledge and application is the process of *judgment*. The challenge of understanding the complexities of judgment defines another of the essential puzzles of professional education. Human judgment bridges the universal terms of theory and the gritty particularities of situated practice. And human judgment always incorporates both technical and moral elements.
- Fifth, up to this point my analysis has implied that all of the movement of knowledge is, as it were, from left to right, from the academy to the field. But the most formidable challenge for anyone in a profession is *learning from experience*. While an academic knowledge base is necessary for professional work, it is far from sufficient. Therefore, members of professions have to develop the capacity to learn not only from the academy but, even more importantly, from the experience and contemplation of their own practice. This is true not only for individual professionals, but equally for the entire community of practice. Lessons of practice must have a way of getting back to inform and to render problematic knowledge development in the academy itself.
- Sixth and finally, professions are inherently public and communal. We speak of someone not only *being a professional*, but also being

a *member of a profession*. Professional knowledge is somehow held by a community of professionals who not only know collectively more than any individual member of the community ("distributed expertise" is a distinctive feature of a professional community, even though each member is thought to possess a substantial common core of skill and knowledge), but also have certain public responsibilities and accountabilities with respect to individual practice. Thus, professionals operate within their particular communities under privileges granted by virtue of their recognition by the broader society. Such autonomy and privilege is granted when the profession is viewed as holding specialized knowledge whose warrant only its own members can evaluate, and when its members are trusted to take responsibility for such evaluation.

Elaborating on the Principles: Educating for Profession

What can we say about the challenges of professional education in light of these six principles?

Profession as Service

As Brint observed, the starting point for professional preparation is that the aims of professionalism involve social purposes and responsibilities that are grounded both technically and morally. The core meaning of a profession is the organized practice of complex knowledge and skills in the service of others. The professional educator's challenge is to help future professors develop and shape a robust moral vision that will guide their practice and provide a prism of justice and virtue through which to reflect on their actions.

Theory for Practice

Second, the notion that formal professional knowledge is rooted in academic knowledge bases creates the essential pedagogical problem of professional education. That is, the recurrent challenge of all professional learning is the unavoidable gap between theory and practice. There are at least two versions of the problem. Theory achieves its power through simplification and narrowing of the field of study. In that sense, theories deal with the world in general and for the most part, making rough places smooth and messy settings neat. A second characteristic of theories is that they generally operate within identifiable disciplines while practical problems cross disciplinary boundaries with the abandon of rum-runners and meandering streams. Theories are extraordinarily powerful, which is why they are the treasure of the academy and valued by the professions; they are also frequently so remote from the particular conditions of professional practice that the novice professional-in-training rarely appreciates their contributions.

Any reader who has been educated for one of the professions, say in the two with which I am most familiar, medical education or teacher preparation, will immediately recognize the problem. My teacher, Joseph Schwab, devoted most of the last 20 years of his life and career to the problems of practical knowledge and its relations to theory. One need only try to connect the Krebs cycle with the intricacies of a particular clinical diagnosis, or the Loop of Henley with some specific aspect of kidney failure, to appreciate the problem. As a teacher educator, I have tried to help students see how one traverses the gap between Piaget's developmental theory and what to teach on Monday morning, or between Vygotsky's zones of proximal development and the pedagogical potential of group work. We who have tried to educate future professionals understand the challenge that is created when your starting point for a learned profession is bodies of academic knowledge. We prepare professionals in universities because we make the strong claim that these are *learned* professions and that academic knowledge is absolutely essential to their performance.

Now, this may be a false claim. It may well be that academic knowledge is essential only as an *entitlement* to practice and is not functionally necessary for practice. My point is that the claim of rootedness in a theoretical, empirical, and/or normative knowledge base is central to all of the professions. This is a crucial issue for the liberal arts, both conceptually and fiscally. The uniquely American view that a liberal education of some sort is a prerequisite for the study of medicine, law, teaching (foundations), and the like sets an interesting problem for the liberal arts at two levels: defining the foundation for understanding and practicing a profession on the one hand, and stipulating the liberal arts and sciences per se whose grasp would identify an individual as "educated" or "learned" and therefore entitled to pursue a learned profession. Only the second of these concerns is uniquely American, because the United States is nearly unique in treating most professions as graduate rather than undergraduate domains.

Third, while the theoretical is the foundation, practice is the end to which all the knowledge is directed. Student teaching, medical residencies, architects' apprenticeships, student nursing, all are examples of carefully designed pedagogies to afford eased entry into practice accompanied by intensive supervision. This is why in all professional preparation we find some conception of a supervised clinical experience. In medicine it seems to go on forever. One of the things that makes law so interesting is that legal educators have somehow managed to avoid the responsibility for introducing a serious clinical component into legal education, expecting the employing law firm to assume that burden.

The apprenticeship, the practice, the application that goes on in the field is not only a nearly universal element of professional learning, but typically, once a professional reaches the field of practice, he or she looks back on the theoretical preparation and begins to devalue it. There are always interesting tensions between the clinical and the theoretical.[2]

One of the sources of those tensions is that theoretical preparation, in spite of the conservatism of the academy, tends to be more radical and reform-oriented than is practice itself. Indeed, academicians often see themselves as the critical conscience of professional practice, taking upon themselves the responsibility for criticizing current practice and developing a vision for the future. And it is, again, almost universally the case in professional preparation that the students arrive at their clinical experiences only to hear the nursing supervisor, or the veteran teacher in the fifth grade where they're student teaching, or the chief of clinical services in the hospital admonish them to forget all the b.s. they were taught at the university because now they will learn the way it is really done. So, interestingly, the academy is the source of radical ideas. The field is where you encounter the bungee cord that pulls things back to the conservation of habits of practice. This kind of tension is, as I say, generally characteristic of professional education.

The Role of Judgment

Another complication of professional learning is that the academy, to the extent that it addresses problems of practice at all, presents them as *prototypes*—simplified and schematized theoretical representations of the much messier and variable particularities of everyday life. When student-professionals move out to the fields of practice, they find inevitably that nothing quite fits the prototypes. The responsibility of the developing professional is not simply to apply what he or she has learned to practice, but to transform, to adapt, to merge and synthesize, to criticize, and to invent in order to move from the theoretical knowledge of the academy to the kind of practical clinical knowledge needed to engage in the professional work. One of the reasons judgment is such an essential component of clinical work is that theoretical knowledge is generally knowledge of what is true universally. It is true in general and for the most part. It is knowledge of regularities and of patterns. It is an invaluable simplification of a world whose many variations would be far too burdensome to store in memory with all their detail and individuality. Yet the world of practice is beset by just those particularities, born of the workings of chance. To put it in Aristotelian terms, theories are about *essence,* practice is about *accident,* and the only way to get from there to here is via the exercise of *judgment.*

Experience

As Dewey observed in his classic essay on the influence of Darwinism on philosophy, chance, error, and accidents present both the sciences and the fields of practice with their most fascinating puzzles.[3] The great challenge for professional learning is that *experience* occurs where design and intention collide with chance. Without the violation of expectations, it is impossible to learn from experience. Learning from experience, therefore, requires both the systematic prototype-centered, theoretical knowledge characteristic of the academy and the more fluid, reactive, prudential reasoning characteristic of practice. The professional must learn how to cope with those unpredictable matters, and how to reflect on his or her own actions. Professionals incorporate the consequences of those actions into their own growing knowledge base, which ultimately includes unique combinations of theoretical and moral principles, practical maxims, and a growing collection of narratives of experience.

In comparing John Dewey and George Herbert Mead with Jane Addams, all of whom were good friends in Chicago in the first five years of this century, Ellen Lagemann observed that for Dewey and Mead, the tools of their trade were the scientific hypothesis and the investigation; for Jane Addams it was the anecdote and the biography. In professional practice, the hypothesis rapidly gives way to the narrative. Jane Addams's Hull House was the setting in which the academic perspectives of Dewey and Mead were brought into collaborative contact with the truly professional practice embodied by Addams and the settlement movement.[4] The ideals of service clearly dominated the thinking of those who were inventing the professions of social work and community development, but the desire to ground those practices in the academic disciplines of social philosophy, sociology, and a professional school of social service administration were already a serious challenge.[5]

In Jerome Bruner's terms, in these situations the paradigmatic way of knowing shares space with the narrative. To foreshadow the concluding section of this essay, when we seek a pedagogy that can reside between the universal principles of theory and the narratives of lived practice, we invent something called a *case method* that employs cases as ways of capturing experience for subsequent analysis and review, and then creating a pedagogy of theoretically grounded experience. We render individual experiential learning into community property when we transform those lessons from personal experience into a literature of shared narratives. Connections between theoretical principles and case narratives are established when we not only ask, "what's the case?" but more critically, "what is this a case of?" In developing those connections between the universal and the particular, between the universal and the accidental, we forge professional knowledge. Such knowledge cannot be developed and sustained adequately by individuals experiencing and reflecting in isolation.

Community

The sixth and final term is the notion of a community of practice. Although individual professionals carry the responsibility for practice, the assumption is that they are members of a community that defines and regulates the standards for that practice and that, as a community, knows more than does any individual practitioner. The public can turn to the professional community when questions of the quality of practice are at stake. From the perspective of professional pedagogy, the community of practice plays a critical role. The academic discipline serves the academy as a learning community whose invisible colleges ensure that knowledge gained is vetted for its warrant through peer review and then distributed among members of the community through journals and other forms of scholarly communication. The community of practice for a profession plays a similar role with regard to learning from experience, accumulating and critiquing the lessons gained and subsequently codified, and, in general, helping practitioners overcome the limitations of individual practice and individual experience. Without a community of practice, individual professionals would be trapped in a solipsistic universe in which only their own experiences were potentially educative. When the work of communities of practice is created and fostered, individual experience becomes communal, distributed expertise can be shared, and standards of practice can evolve.[6]

Professing and Liberal Learning

I began by asking what liberal learning would look like if we treated it as a profession. If we said, that is, that liberal learning has as its end professional practice, doing something of service to the community in a manner that is both technically defensible and morally desirable. If we, therefore, saw the theory/practice problem as an inherent problem, as an inherent challenge in all liberal learning. If we recognized that taking theory and moving it into practice may not only be the challenge for theoretical understanding, but also the crucible in which merely theoretical understanding becomes meaningful, memorable, and internalizable. Indeed, what if we argued that theoretical understanding is inherently incomplete, even unrequited, until it is "practiced"? To address those questions I will begin by asking what are the major impediments in liberal learning now? That is, what challenges do liberal educators currently confront that define some of the perennial problems of that endeavor?

The Challenges of Liberal Learning

What are the challenges of liberal learning? I will rather dogmatically suggest that liberal learning, as all learning for understanding (that endangered species of cognition), confronts three central challenges: the loss of learning, or *amnesia;* the illusion of learning, or *illusory understanding;* and the uselessness of learning, or *inert ideas.* These states can be exemplified by three student exclamations: "I forgot it," "I thought I understood it," and "I understand it but I can't use it." If we were ever to conduct proper evaluations of the long-term benefits of liberal education, I suspect we would encounter all three of these with painful frequency.

The first challenge of liberal learning is the problem of *amnesia.* It is a problem exemplified by the fact that, after having participated in a wide variety of courses and programs in colleges and universities, it is very sobering to discover that students rapidly forget much of what we have taught them or that they have ostensibly learned. Let me suggest a depressing exercise: conduct an exit interview with students at the end of their senior year (or a couple of years beyond) in which you sit them down with the transcript of the four years they have spent with you in the institution and say: "Treat the transcript as a kind of itinerary that you have followed for the last four or five years. Why don't you simply go course by course and just tell me what you remember doing and learning." This is not a test of deep understanding, but if students don't even remember the experience, it's quite hard for them to learn from it. This is one of the reasons that nearly every one of the professions, with the stunning exception of teaching, spends an incredible amount of time and energy teaching future professionals to develop habits of documentation and recording their practice. In medicine, in law, in nursing, in social work, in architecture, there are incredible archives of practice because amnesia is the great enemy of learning from experience. Yet in liberal learning, one of the ubiquitous problems we face is the fragility of what is learned. It's like dry ice. It just evaporates at room temperature and is gone. Students seldom remember much of what they've read or heard beyond their last high-stakes exam on the material. The first problem, therefore, is how do we address the problem of amnesia?

A second enemy of liberal learning is *illusory understanding*. It's far more dangerous and insidious than amnesia, because it is the kind of understanding where you think you do remember and understand, but you don't. A great problem of liberal learning is the confidence with which our graduates imagine that they understand many things with which they have only superficial acquaintance and glib verbal familiarity. They thus can throw around phrases like "supply and demand" or "survival of the fittest" with marvelous agility, albeit without substantial comprehension. There is a wonderful video that begins with graduating students at a Harvard commencement being asked two questions by faculty: Why do we have seasons and what accounts for the phases of the moon? In every case the respondent replied with great confidence. With little hesitation, and very few exceptions, respondents offered a similar theory of the seasons. They explained that we had summer when the elliptical orbit of the earth brought it closer to the sun, and winter when we were further away. When asked to explain the phases of the moon, similarly mistaken accounts were put forward. Here were well-educated students, many of whom had taken courses in the sciences, including astronomy and astrophysics, who were confidently expounding quite misconceived theories of how the solar system functioned. The illusion of understanding is as frequently encountered as it is infrequently detected by educators. The study and documentation of these kinds of misconceptions before and after formal education has become one of the most fascinating aspects of research in science and mathematics learning.

Some of the most interesting work in the history of philosophy deals with the philosophers' concern with illusory understanding. Nearly every one of the Socratic dialogues is an example. The Socratic dialogue is a form of pedagogy designed to confront the knower with what he was sure he knew but indeed doesn't understand. Socratic wisdom is said, therefore, to begin with the unveiling of Socratic ignorance. The whole metaphor of the cave in Plato's *Republic* is a metaphor about illusory understanding. And it is no accident that the way Socrates attempts to diagnose and treat illusory understanding is through an active, interactive process of dialogue in a social setting. Similarly, one of Francis Bacon's most memorable essays is about "the idols of the mind," all the ways in which we, as human intelligences, come to believe we know things that, in fact, we just don't understand.

Alfred North Whitehead warned us that "above all we must beware" of "*inert ideas,*" thus punning on Plato's reverence for the innate variety. Such ideas, he said, "are merely received into the mind without being utilized, or tested, or thrown into fresh combinations." Ideas escape inertness by being used, tested, or thrown into fresh combinations. Application is not only the ultimate test, it is the crucible within which ideas come alive and grow. Whitehead observes, "Pedants sneer at an education which is useful. But if education is not useful, what is it? Is it a talent, to be hidden away in a napkin?"[7]

Principles of Professional Learning

If the three horsemen of the liberal learning apocalypse are amnesia, illusion, and inertness, what kinds of pedagogical strategies can we invoke to fend them off? The salvation of understanding is in our grasp. *The key to preserving the liberal arts is to profess the liberal arts.*

The principles through which we overcome amnesia, illusory understanding, and inertness are the same as those that enumerate the conditions of profession: activity, reflection, collaboration, passion, and community. These principles not only derive from current research in cognitive science and social learning, they also map very nicely onto the wisdom of practice in professional education. At the risk that an overly dogmatic rhetoric may give the lie to the very points I am making, I shall briefly explain these principles.

The first is *activity.* Students who are learning in professional settings are remarkably active most of the time in that they are engaged in clinical or practical work. They are designing, diagnosing, and arguing. They are writing; they are investigating; they are in the library or at the computer getting information. The are talking to one another, sharing information, and challenging one another's ideas. At every opportunity, the level of activity of the students is higher than in the average college classroom. The outcome should not surprise anyone. We all know from our practice as well as from theory that active learning results in more enduring learning than does passive learning. It is one of the key principles of all human learning, equally relevant for young adults as for children.

As a first principle, authentic and enduring learning occurs when the learner is an *active* agent in the process. Student learning becomes more active through experimentation and inquiry, as well as through writing, dialogue, and questioning. Thus, the college settings in which the students work must provide them with the opportunities and support for becoming active agents in the process of their own learning.

The second thing we know about effective learners is that they are not merely active, because activity alone is insufficient for learning. As Dewey observed many years ago, we do not learn by doing; we learn by thinking about what we are doing. Successful students spend considerable time, as Bruner calls it, "going meta," that is, thinking about what they are doing and why. Their teachers give them plenty of opportunities to talk about how they are learning, why they are learning in these ways, why they are getting things wrong when they get them wrong and right when they get them right. A very high level of carefully guided *reflection* is blended with activity.

Activity and reflection are hard work. If you are a typical learner, you often find yourself working alone, intending to read an article or a book. You sit down after dinner with a good reading light on, with good music playing softly in the background, and with no distractions in the room. Ten minutes later, you find yourself in the middle of a chapter with absolutely no recollection of what you have read up to that point. It can be very hard for anyone to engage in active and reflective learning alone. For college students, it is even harder.

One of the most important inventions of Ann Brown (with Annemarie Palinscar) was called "reciprocal teaching"—a process of enhancing young students' reading comprehension as they work with one another, scaffolding each others' learning; helping each other focus, attend, and question, actively, critically, and reflectively as they jointly read complicated text.[8] Active, reflective learning thus proceeds best in the presence of a third principle, which is *collaboration.*

College students can work together in ways that scaffold and support each other's learning, and in ways that supplement each other's knowledge. Collaboration is a *marriage of insufficiencies,* not exclusively "cooperation" in a particular form of social interaction. There are difficult intellectual and professional challenges that are nearly impossible to accomplish alone, but are readily addressed in the company of others.

Sandy Astin discusses the educative functions of collaboration—the educational advantages enjoyed through the juxtaposition and confrontation of perspectives for people to rethink, to reflect on what they thought they already knew, and through collaborative exchange *eventually to deepen their understanding of an idea.* So when we say that reflection is important, that collaboration is important, these aren't just pieties. These are essential elements of a pedagogical theory, a theory of learning and teaching that explains why it is that even if your goal is liberal learning, per se, and if what you want is people to learn ideas and concepts and principles that will be robust, that will be deep, that will be not merely inert ideas, shadows on the wall of the cave—the way you temper those ideas is through reflection and through interaction and collaboration. Otherwise it may well be just the illusion of understanding. These are some of the things we're learning about liberal learning.

This kind of learning is not exclusively cognitive or intellectual. Indeed, there is a significant emotional and affective component that inheres in such work. Authentic and enduring learning occurs when students share a *passion* for the material, are emotionally committed to the ideas, processes, and activities, and see the work as connected to present and future goals. Although the language of liberal learning is heavily intellectual, the importance of emotion, enthusiasm, and passion is central to these efforts, for both students and for their teachers. And there is a special quality to those affective responses that develop within individuals who have become interdependent members of well-functioning, cohesive groups. Simply observe the spirit that develops among the members of an athletic team, or the cast of a play, or residents of a cabin at camp, and you can begin to discern the special emotional qualities associated with working collaboratives that function as learning communities.

In that same vein, authentic and enduring learning works best when the processes of activity, reflection, emotion, and collaboration are supported, legitimated, and nurtured within a *community* or *culture* that values such experiences and creates many opportunities for them to occur and to be accomplished with success and pleasure. Such communities create "participant structures" that reduce the labor intensity of the activities needed to engage in the most daunting practices that lead to teaching and learning. Put another way, this kind of learning can rarely succeed one course at a time. The entire institution must be oriented toward these principles, and the principles must be consistently and regularly employed throughout each course and experience in a program. One of the "secrets" of the remarkable impact of the Hutchins College was probably the persistent and all-encompassing effect—course after course—of critical dialogue within small seminars as *the* pedagogical practice of the college.

Consistent with the centrality of teaching and learning, professional education programs that are characterized by activity, reflection, and collaboration in learning communities are inherently uncertain, complex, and demanding places. Both learning and teaching in such settings entail high levels of risk and unpredictability for the participants. Students and faculty both require a school and a community that support and reward those levels of risk taking and invention characteristic of such approaches to learning for understanding and commitment.

If we take these principles seriously as instruments for overcoming the major challenges to liberal learning, then, with Whitehead, I would assert that the kind of pedagogy that we associate with, say, service learning, is not simply a cocurricular extravagance. It may actually be central to the kind of pedagogy that would make a liberal education more professional, in the case of service learning, a pedagogy that would give the liberal arts a clinical component or the equivalent of an internship experience. Moreover, it may well be one of the ways in which we overcome the triple pathologies of amnesia, illusory understanding, and inert ideas. How might that sort of thing go on?

A Pedagogy for Professing

Cases as Conduits Between Theory and Practice

I shall now discuss a pedagogy of cases as an example of the kind of teaching and learning that begins to address the central problems of academic learning, in general, and professional learning, in particular. I am *not* arguing that all liberal and professional learning should immediately become case based!

For me, what is so alluring about a case is that it resides in that never-never land between theory and practice, between idea and experience, between the normative ideal and achievable real. One of the interesting things about cases is that they capture pieces of experience that initially existed solely within the life of a single individual and transform that solitary experience into text. You can do all kinds of things when you've rendered something into a text that can be shared by members of a group, all of whom are trying to make sense of the text. The function of the case as a means for preserving and communicating experience is clear given the persistent problems of amnesia.[9]

The great challenge for professionals who wish to learn from experience is the difficulty of holding experiences in memory in forms that can become the objects of disciplined analysis and reflection. Consider the possibility that cases are ways of parsing experience so that practitioners can examine and learn from it. Professionals are typically confronted with a seamless continuum of experience from which they can think about individual episodes or readings as cases, but rarely coordinate the different dimensions into meaningful experiential chunks. Case methods thus become strategies for helping professionals to "chunk" their experience into units that can become the focus for reflective practice. They therefore can become the basis for individual professional learning as well as a forum within which communities of professionals, both local and extended, as members of visible and invisible colleges, can store, exchange, and organize their experiences. How is case learning related to the principles we reviewed above? I will describe a situation—not infrequent in professional education—where the learners not only study and discuss cases written by others, but are actively participating in some sort of field experience around which they also write cases that document and analyze their own practice.

First, whether as case analyst or as case writer, the case learner becomes an active agent in his or her own understanding. When a student is wrestling with a case, whether as an occasion for analysis or a stimulus to reflect on his or her own experience as a prelude to writing, active agency is engaged. Second, cases are inherently reflective. They begin with an act of cognition, of turning around one's own lived experiences and examining them to find events and episodes worthy of transformation into telling cases. Even when the goal of case learning is not case writing, the discussion of cases eventually stimulates reflection on one's own experiences and reactions. Third, case methods nearly always emphasize the primacy of group discussion, deliberation, and debate. The thought process of cases is dialogic, as members of a group explore different perspectives, the available elective actions, or the import of the consequences. In case-based teaching, the interaction of activity, reflection, and collaboration is apparent. But what of community or culture?

Teaching and learning with cases is not an easy pedagogy. Active learners are much more outspoken and assertive than are passive learners. They are less predictable than their more passive counterparts, as they investigate their options, explore alternative interpretations, and challenge prevailing views. Because cases encourage connections between personal experiences and those vicariously experienced through narratives, the directions in which discussions might develop are rather difficult to anticipate, further complicating the pedagogy. Finally, the collaborative mode of instruction once again reduces the authority of the teacher and vests a growing proportion in the initiatives of students. Taken together, the enhancement of agency, reflection, and collaboration makes teaching more complex and unpredictable, albeit by reducing the authority of teachers and their ability to plan for contingencies. When uncertainty increases and power is distributed, the need for a supportive culture or community becomes paramount for teachers and students alike. A supportive culture helps manage the risk of contemplating one's failures and reduces the vulnerability created when one candidly discusses a path not taken. A supportive culture engages each member of the community in parallel risks. It celebrates the interdependence of learners who rely on one another for both insights and reassurance. A learning environment built on activity, reflection, and collaboration—which is an apt characterization of a well-functioning case-learning and case-writing community—proceeds smoothly only in the presence of a sustaining culture and community.

An Example

How might we envision a clinical component to a liberal education? Consider the possibility that there are forms of service learning that could perform the function. One of the most frequently encountered forms of service learning is tutoring. Although only one among many activities that are quite appropriately classified as legitimate service learning, I want to offer the hypothesis that the tutoring of young children, of adults, or of peers has some uniquely powerful characteristics with regard both to the objectives of offering service and the objectives of making liberal learning more meaningful, more memorable, and more useful, that is, less inert.

In this regard I share the values of the medieval university, which viewed the ability to teach something to someone else as the highest, most rigorous, and final test of whether a scholar understood his discipline or profession deeply. It based this view on Aristotle's observation in the *Metaphysics* that it is the distinctive sign of a man who knows deeply that he can teach what he knows to another. Aristotle recognized that, in order to teach something to someone else, you have to engage in an act of reflection on and transformation of what you know, and then connect those insights to the mind, experience, and motives of somebody else. Teaching is a dual act of intelligence and empathy. It entails both technical and moral reason. By the same token, in order to make your own learning more meaningful and memorable, you have to somehow interconnect the many things you know in an intrapersonal network of associations and implications. Each time you can make a connection, whether in your own mind or with the minds of others, amnesia becomes less likely. Each connection serves as both anchor and springboard. Every time you can figure out a new way to take what you know and apply it, connect it, teach it to someone else, you've not only rendered a service, but you have deepened and enriched your own understanding.

I propose that one of the ways in which we can combine the notion of service and the notion of liberal learning is with the expectation that every one of our undergraduates who is engaged in liberal learning undertake the service of teaching something they know to somebody else. They also undertake writing about the experience as a case, describing both teaching and student learning. For me this isn't hypothetical. It's the way I prepare people to teach. They write cases of their own practice. But they don't write them for me. They write them for the other members of their community, because our argument is that experience is too precious to be limited in its benefits solely to the person who experienced it. We need to move from individual experiential learning to a scholarly community of practice.

Then we form small case conferences where groups of students come together and exchange their cases. Case discussions are very interesting. When the discussions are well managed, participants can move the case discussion in two directions. One is exploring the facts of the case. Here, participants are pressed to describe the context more richly and in greater detail. They are urged to elaborate on their accounts of what actually happened, what was said and done, how all that occurred made them feel. They are pressed to dig deeply into the particularity of the context, because it is in the devilish details that practice dramatically differs from theory.

Yet, at the same time that the participants are being sucked into depths of the particular, the skillful pedagogue (and eventually the students themselves) begins to build in a second-order genre of question which is, "what is the case an exemplar of?" What are some other principles, concepts, or ideas that link these two or three cases together or that make you think about your case in relation to some more general principle?[10]

Sitting astride theory and practice, the case both enriches the grasp of practice and at the same time links back to the world of theory and the world of principle. I already do that kind of work with prospective and veteran teachers, and can readily imagine being able to do something similar with undergraduates. Such a strategy would be an example of professing the liberal arts, in having students teach others what they know, in providing service in conjunction with our academic learning which was then captured in written cases. Those cases would then become the curriculum for seminars whose purpose was to link the experiences of application back to the theoretical understanding.

There is a powerful strategic value in writing and analyzing cases that have been written by the members of a case forum, and in systematically exploring the tough question "what is this a case of?" When I write a case describing my own practice, I am the protagonist in the plot. This means that I'm writing not only *what* I did, but I am writing about *why* I did it. I am writing not just about my strategies and actions, but about my intentions, goals, and values. I write, in Martin Buber's terms, not only about "I" and "thou," but reflexively about "I." In that sense, by injecting the self as protagonist into the deliberations around one's academic learning, we bring the moral dimensions of liberal learning back to center stage. This is only proper; the ultimate rationale for treating liberal learning as a worthy end in itself is a moral argument, not an instrumental one.

If we were to professionalize in these terms, if we were actively to connect learning with service, with practice, with application, and were further to capture that practice in a kind of pedagogy that uses cases and case methods in ways analogous to some of the ways we use them for professional preparation, we would not only achieve the moral ends of service, we would very likely do better at overcoming the challenges to liberal understanding. Through service, through application, through rendering their learning far more active, reflective, and collaborative, students would actually learn more liberally, understand what they have learned more deeply, and develop the capacity to use what they have learned in the service of their communities.

NOTES

1. Steven Brint, *In an Age of Experts: The Changing Role of Professionals in Politics and Public Life* (Princeton, NJ: Princeton University Press, 1994), 7.
2. It is also quite interesting when the supervised clinical experience affords such opportunities in only part of a future role, as when the future university professor is heavily mentored in the scholarship of discovery but receives little or no supervised clinical experience in the scholarship of teaching.
3. John Dewey, "The Influence of Darwinism on Philosophy," in Martin Gardner, editor, *Great Essays in Science* (Buffalo: Prometheus, 1994).
4. Ellen Condliffe Lagemann, "The Plural Worlds of Educational Research," *History of Education Quarterly* 29 (1988), 184–214.
5. William Rainey Harper, first president of the University of Chicago, wrestled with questions of how the professional school could fit into the new research university. Chicago had schools of theology, pedagogy, and social service. Dewey wrote a short paper on the topic of how the university-based school of pedagogy must be distinct from the traditional normal school, most particularly in its relationships with academic disciplines and research.
6. At least that's the theory. Professions are not equally successful in creating communities of practice that effectively play this role. Thus, medicine and engineering probably do it rather well. Law does it well for court cases but badly for the daily practice of law. Teaching, both K–12 and postsecondary, has barely scratched the surface of transforming the experiences of pedagogy into scholarship and community property.

7. Alfred North Whitehead, *The Aims of Education and Other Essays* (New York: Macmillan, 1929).
8. A. S. Palinscar and A. L. Brown, "Reciprocal Teaching of Comprehension-Fostering and Monitoring Activities," *Cognition and Instruction* 1 (1984), 117–75.
9. Sibling to amnesia is the challenge of *nostalgia,* in which forgetting is replaced by mis-remembering, usually in the service of reinforcing the mnemonist's interests, needs, or preferences. Nostalgia is not identical to illusory understanding, but it is likely to be a significant contributing condition.
10. Although I am using the example of tutoring, it should be apparent that this strategy for case-based liberal learning could be applied to a variety of other clinical experiences as well, both those that entail service and others that are more traditional—applied research and the like.

INDEX

D

E

F

G

H

M

N

O

P